Ford Mondeo
Owners Workshop Manual
John S. Mead & Euan Doig

Models covered

Hatchback, Saloon & Estate

Petrol: 2.0 litre (1998cc) Duratec

Turbo-Diesel: 1.8 litre (1753cc) & 2.0 litre (1998cc) Duratorq TDCi

Does NOT cover models with 1.6 litre, 2.0 litre 'Ecoboost', 2.3 litre or 2.5 litre petrol engines,
or 1.6 litre or 2.2 litre diesel engines
Does NOT cover flex fuel models or Powershift transmission, or new Mondeo range introduced January 2015

(5548 - 3AY2 - 368)

© Haynes Publishing 2019

ABCDE
FGH

A book in the **Haynes Owners Workshop Manual Series**

ISBN **978 1 78521 442 4**

British Library Cataloguing in Publication Data
A catalogue record for this book is available from the British Library.

Printed in Malaysia

Haynes Publishing
Sparkford, Yeovil, Somerset BA22 7JJ, England

Haynes North America, Inc
859 Lawrence Drive, Newbury Park, California 91320, USA

Printed using NORBRITE BOOK 48.8gsm (CODE: 40N6533) from NORPAC; procurement system certified under Sustainable Forestry Initiative standard. Paper produced is certified to the SFI Certified Fiber Sourcing Standard (CERT - 0094271)

Contents

Contents

REPAIRS AND OVERHAUL

Originally introduced in October 2000, the latest Ford Mondeo is available in four-door Saloon, five-door Hatchback and five-door Estate configurations. This manual covers the revised range introduced in February 2007. The range was simplified and underwent a cosmetic facelift in the autumn of 2010.

An extensive range of petrol and diesel engines are available in the Mondeo range. This manual covers the most popular variants – the 2.0 litre Duratec-HE petrol engines, and the 1.8 and 2.0 litre Duratorq diesel engines.

The 2.0 litre Duratec-HE 16-valve DOHC (double overhead camshaft) four-cylinder petrol engines are based on the familiar Ford range of engines. The engines are controlled by a sophisticated engine management system, which combines multipoint sequential fuel injection and distributorless ignition systems with evaporative emissions control, exhaust gas recirculation, variable intake geometry and a three-way regulated catalytic converter to ensure compliance with increasingly stringent emissions control standards, while providing the expected levels of performance and fuel economy.

The 2.0 litre Duratorq diesel engine is used by Ford, Citroën and Peugeot – a result of joint projects between Ford and PSA (Citroën/Peugeot's parent company), whilst the 1.8 litre unit is of Ford's own design, used in numerous Ford vehicles. All of the engines are four- cylinder turbo-diesel units, with the 2.0 litre engines being of a 16-valve DOHC design. They incorporate the latest design of direct injection common rail fuel system, with a variable geometry turbocharger, intercooler, catalytic converter and exhaust particulate filter (2.0 litre engines only).

The transversely-mounted engines drive the front roadwheels through either a five- or six-speed manual transmission with a hydraulically-operated clutch. 2.0 litre diesel engines are also available with a six-speed, electronically-controlled automatic transmission.

The fully-independent suspension is by MacPherson struts and transverse lower arms at the front, with multilink independent suspension at the rear; anti-roll bars are fitted at front and rear.

The braking system has discs all round, with ABS, Electronic Stability Program (ESP), Emergency Brake Assist (EBA) and Electronic Brakeforce Distribution (EBD) for extra safety when braking in emergency situations.

Hydraulic power-assisted steering is standard on all models. Air conditioning is available, and all models have an ergonomically-designed passenger cabin with high levels of safety and comfort for all passengers.

Provided that regular servicing is carried out in accordance with the manufacturer's recommendations, the Mondeo should prove a reliable and economical car. The engine compartment is well-designed, and most of the items needing frequent attention are easily accessible.

Your Ford Mondeo Manual

The aim of this manual is to help you get the best value from your car. It can do so in several ways. It can help you decide what work must be done (even should you choose to get it done by a garage). It will also provide information on routine maintenance and servicing, and give a logical course of action and diagnosis when random faults occur. However, it is hoped that you will use the manual by tackling the work yourself. On simpler jobs it may even be quicker than booking the car into a garage and going there twice, to leave and collect it. Perhaps most important, a lot of money can be saved by avoiding the costs a garage must charge to cover its labour and overheads.

The manual has drawings and descriptions to show the function of the various components so that their layout can be understood. Tasks are described and photographed in a clear step-by-step sequence.

References to the 'left' and 'right' of the car are in the sense of a person in the driver's seat facing forward.

Project vehicles

The main vehicle used in the preparation of this manual, and which appears in many of the photographic sequences, was a Ford Mondeo 5-door Hatchback with a 2.0 litre diesel engine. Additional work was carried out on a Mondeo 5-door Estate with a 1.8 litre diesel engine and a Mondeo 5-door Hatchback with a 2.0 litre petrol engine.

Acknowledgements

Thanks are due to Draper Tools Limited, who provided some of the workshop tools, and to all those people at Sparkford who helped in the production of this manual. **We take great pride in the accuracy of information given in this manual, but vehicle manufacturers make alterations and design changes during the production run of a particular vehicle of which they do not inform us. No liability can be accepted by the authors or publishers for loss, damage or injury caused by any errors in, or omissions from, the information given.**

Working on your car can be dangerous. This page shows just some of the potential risks and hazards, with the aim of creating a safety-conscious attitude.

General hazards

Scalding

• Don't remove the radiator or expansion tank cap while the engine is hot.
• Engine oil, transmission fluid or power steering fluid may also be dangerously hot if the engine has recently been running.

Burning

• Beware of burns from the exhaust system and from any part of the engine. Brake discs and drums can also be extremely hot immediately after use.

Crushing

• When working under or near a raised vehicle, always supplement the jack with axle stands, or use drive-on ramps.
Never venture under a car which is only supported by a jack.
• Take care if loosening   or tightening high-torque nuts when the vehicle is on stands. Initial loosening and final tightening should be done with the wheels on the ground.

Fire

• Fuel is highly flammable; fuel vapour is explosive.
• Don't let fuel spill onto a hot engine.
• Do not smoke or allow naked lights (including pilot lights) anywhere near a vehicle being worked on. Also beware of creating sparks (electrically or by use of tools).
• Fuel vapour is heavier than air, so don't work on the fuel system with the vehicle over an inspection pit.
• Another cause of fire is an electrical overload or short-circuit. Take care when repairing or modifying the vehicle wiring.
• Keep a fire extinguisher handy, of a type suitable for use on fuel and electrical fires.

Electric shock

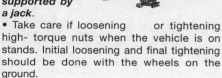

• Ignition HT and Xenon headlight voltages can be dangerous, especially to people with heart problems or a pacemaker. Don't work on or near these systems with the engine running or the ignition switched on.

• Mains voltage is also dangerous. Make sure that any mains-operated equipment is correctly earthed. Mains power points should be protected by a residual current device (RCD) circuit breaker.

Fume or gas intoxication

• Exhaust fumes are poisonous; they can contain carbon monoxide, which is rapidly fatal if inhaled. Never run the engine in a confined space such as a garage with the doors shut.
• Fuel vapour is also poisonous, as are the vapours from some cleaning solvents and paint thinners.

Poisonous or irritant substances

• Avoid skin contact with battery acid and with any fuel, fluid or lubricant, especially antifreeze, brake hydraulic fluid and Diesel fuel. Don't syphon them by mouth. If such a substance is swallowed or gets into the eyes, seek medical advice.
• Prolonged contact with used engine oil can cause skin cancer. Wear gloves or use a barrier cream if necessary. Change out of oil-soaked clothes and do not keep oily rags in your pocket.
• Air conditioning refrigerant forms a poisonous gas if exposed to a naked flame (including a cigarette). It can also cause skin burns on contact.

Asbestos

• Asbestos dust can cause cancer if inhaled or swallowed. Asbestos may be found in gaskets and in brake and clutch linings. When dealing with such components it is safest to assume that they contain asbestos.

Special hazards

Hydrofluoric acid

• This extremely corrosive acid is formed when certain types of synthetic rubber, found in some O-rings, oil seals, fuel hoses etc, are exposed to temperatures above 4000C. The rubber changes into a charred or sticky substance containing the acid. *Once formed, the acid remains dangerous for years. If it gets onto the skin, it may be necessary to amputate the limb concerned.*
• When dealing with a vehicle which has suffered a fire, or with components salvaged from such a vehicle, wear protective gloves and discard them after use.

The battery

• Batteries contain sulphuric acid, which attacks clothing, eyes and skin. Take care when topping-up or carrying the battery.
• The hydrogen gas given off by the battery is highly explosive. Never cause a spark or allow a naked light nearby. Be careful when connecting and disconnecting battery chargers or jump leads.

Air bags

• Air bags can cause injury if they go off accidentally. Take care when removing the steering wheel and trim panels. Special storage instructions may apply.

Diesel injection equipment

• Diesel injection pumps supply fuel at very high pressure. Take care when working on the fuel injectors and fuel pipes.

⚠ *Warning: Never expose the hands, face or any other part of the body to injector spray; the fuel can penetrate the skin with potentially fatal results.*

Remember...

DO

• Do use eye protection when using power tools, and when working under the vehicle.

• Do wear gloves or use barrier cream to protect your hands when necessary.

• Do get someone to check periodically that all is well when working alone on the vehicle.

• Do keep loose clothing and long hair well out of the way of moving mechanical parts.

• Do remove rings, wristwatch etc, before working on the vehicle – especially the electrical system.

• Do ensure that any lifting or jacking equipment has a safe working load rating adequate for the job.

DON'T

• Don't attempt to lift a heavy component which may be beyond your capability – get assistance.

• Don't rush to finish a job, or take unverified short cuts.

• Don't use ill-fitting tools which may slip and cause injury.

• Don't leave tools or parts lying around where someone can trip over them. Mop up oil and fuel spills at once.

• Don't allow children or pets to play in or near a vehicle being worked on.

The following pages are intended to help in dealing with common roadside emergencies and breakdowns. You will find more detailed fault finding information at the back of the manual, and repair information in the main chapters.

If your car won't start and the starter motor doesn't turn

- ☐ If it's a model with manual transmission, make sure that the clutch pedal is fully depressed. On models with automatic transmission, make sure the selector is in P or N and the brake pedal is fully depressed.
- ☐ Open the bonnet and make sure that the battery terminals are clean and tight.
- ☐ Switch on the headlights and try to start the engine. If the headlights go very dim when you're trying to start, the battery is probably flat. Get out of trouble by jump starting (see next page) using a friend's car.

If your car won't start even though the starter motor turns as normal

- ☐ Is there fuel in the tank?
- ☐ Is there moisture on electrical components under the bonnet? Switch off the ignition, then wipe off any obvious dampness with a dry cloth. Spray a water-dispersant aerosol product (WD-40 or equivalent) on engine and fuel system electrical connectors like those shown in the photos.

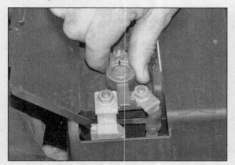

A Check the security and condition of the battery connections.

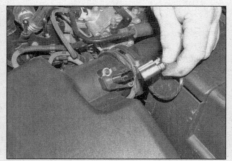

B With the ignition off, check that all accessible wiring connectors are securely connected.

C Check that all fuses are still in good condition and none have blown.

Check that electrical connections are secure (with the ignition switched off) and spray them with a water-dispersant spray like WD-40 if you suspect a problem due to damp.

Jump starting

When jump-starting a car using a booster battery, observe the following precautions:

✔ Before connecting the booster battery, make sure that the ignition is switched off.

Caution: Remove the key in case the central locking engages when the jump leads are connected

✔ Ensure that all electrical equipment (lights, heater, wipers, etc) is switched off.

✔ Take note of any special precautions printed on the battery case.

✔ Make sure that the booster battery is the same voltage as the discharged one in the vehicle.

✔ If the battery is being jump-started from the battery in another vehicle, the two vehicles MUST NOT TOUCH each other.

✔ Make sure that the transmission is in neutral (or PARK, in the case of automatic transmission).

 Jump starting will get you out of trouble, but you must correct whatever made the battery go flat in the first place. There are three possibilities:

1 *The battery has been drained by repeated attempts to start, or by leaving the lights on.*

2 *The charging system is not working properly (alternator drivebelt slack or broken, alternator wiring fault or alternator itself faulty).*

3 *The battery itself is at fault (electrolyte low, or battery worn out).*

1 Unclip the plastic cover and connect the red jump lead to the positive (+) battery terminal.

2 Connect the other end of the red jump lead to the positive (+) terminal of the booster battery.

3 Connect one end of the black jump lead to the negative (-) terminal of the booster battery.

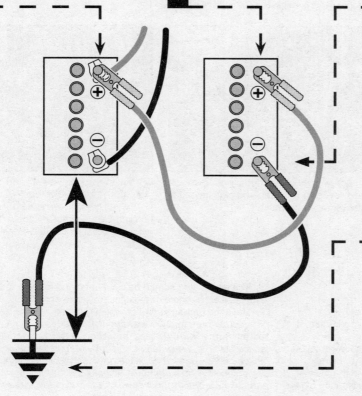

4 Connect the other end of the black jump lead negative (-) terminal to the metal casting bracket on the front of the cylinder head.

5 Make sure that the jump leads will not come into contact with the fan, drivebelts or other moving parts of the engine.

6 Start the engine, then with the engine running at fast idle speed disconnect the jump leads in the reverse order of connection.

Wheel changing

Note: *Certain Mondeo models are equipped with a puncture repair kit and do not have a spare wheel and jack. If your car has a puncture repair kit, refer to the information contained in the Owner's handbook.*

 Warning: Do not change a wheel in a situation where you risk being hit by other traffic. On busy roads, try to stop in a lay-by or a gateway. Be wary of passing traffic while changing the wheel – it is easy to become distracted by the job in hand.

Preparation

☐ When a puncture occurs, stop as soon as it is safe to do so.

☐ Park on firm level ground, if possible, and well out of the way of other traffic.

☐ Use hazard warning lights if necessary.

☐ If you have one, use a warning triangle to alert other drivers of your presence.

☐ Apply the handbrake and engage first or reverse gear (or Park on models with automatic transmission).

☐ Chock the wheel diagonally opposite the one being removed – a couple of large stones will do for this.

☐ If the ground is soft, use a flat piece of wood to spread the load under the jack.

Changing the wheel

1 The spare wheel and tools are stored under the floor in the luggage compartment. Lift up the cover panel. Unscrew the retaining bolt, and lift the spare wheel out. The jack and wheel brace are located beneath the spare wheel. The screw-in towing eye is located alongside the spare wheel.

2 Where applicable, using the flat end of the wheel brace, prise off the wheel trim or centre cover for access to the wheel nuts. Models with alloy wheels may have special locking nuts – these are removed with a special tool, which should be provided with the wheel brace (or it may be in the glovebox).

3 Slacken each wheel nut by a half turn, using the wheel brace. If the nuts are too tight, DON'T stand on the wheel brace to undo them – call for assistance from one of the motoring organisations.

4 Two jacking points are provided on each side – use the one nearest the punctured wheel. Locate the jack head in the groove at the jacking point in the lower sill flange (don't jack the vehicle at any other point of the sill, nor on a plastic panel). Turn the jack handle clockwise until the wheel is raised clear of the ground.

5 Unscrew the wheel nuts, noting which way round they fit (tapered side inwards), and remove the wheel.

6 Fit the spare wheel, and screw on the nuts. Lightly tighten the nuts with the wheel brace, then lower the vehicle to the ground. Securely tighten the wheel nuts then, where applicable, refit the wheel trim or centre cover.

Finally . . .

☐ Remove the wheel chocks. Stow the punctured wheel and tools back in the luggage compartment, and secure them in position.

☐ Check the tyre pressure on the tyre just fitted. If it is low, or if you don't have a pressure gauge with you, drive slowly to the next garage and inflate the tyre to the correct pressure. In the case of the narrow 'space-saver' spare wheel this pressure is much higher than for a normal tyre.

☐ The wheel nuts should be slackened and retightened to the specified torque at the earliest possible opportunity.

☐ Have the damaged tyre or wheel repaired as soon as possible, or another puncture will leave you stranded.

Note: *Some models are supplied with a special lightweight 'space-saver' spare wheel, the tyre being narrower than standard. The 'space-saver' spare wheel is intended only for temporary use, and must be replaced with a standard wheel as soon as possible. Drive with particular care with this wheel fitted, especially through corners and when braking; do not exceed 50 mph.*

Identifying leaks

Puddles on the garage floor or drive, or obvious wetness under the bonnet or underneath the car, suggest a leak that needs investigating. It can sometimes be difficult to decide where the leak is coming from, especially if an engine undershield is fitted. Leaking oil or fluid can also be blown rearwards by the passage of air under the car, giving a false impression of where the problem lies.

 Warning: Most automotive oils and fluids are poisonous. Wash them off skin, and change out of contaminated clothing, without delay.

 The smell of a fluid leaking from the car may provide a clue to what's leaking. Some fluids are distinctively coloured. It may help to remove the engine undershield, clean the car carefully and to park it over some clean paper overnight as an aid to locating the source of the leak. Remember that some leaks may only occur while the engine is running.

Sump oil

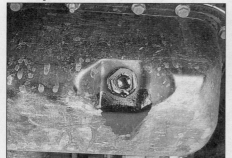

Sump oil – Engine oil may leak from the drain plug…

Oil from filter

Oil from filter -…or from the base of the oil filter.

Gearbox oil

Gearbox oil – Gearbox oil can leak from the seals at the inboard ends of the driveshafts.

Antifreeze

Leaking antifreeze often leaves a crystalline deposit like this.

Brake fluid

A leak occurring at a wheel is almost certainly brake fluid.

Power steering fluid

Power steering fluid may leak from the pipe connectors on the steering rack.

Towing

When all else fails, you may find yourself having to get a tow home – or of course you may be helping somebody else. Long-distance recovery should only be done by a garage or breakdown service. For shorter distances, DIY towing using another car is easy enough, but observe the following points:

☐ Use a proper tow-rope – they are not expensive. The vehicle being towed must display an ON TOW sign in its rear window.

☐ Always turn the ignition key to the 'On' position (or press the 'Power' button once) when the vehicle is being towed, so that the steering lock is released, and the direction indicator and brake lights work.

☐ The towing eye is of the screw-in type, and is found in the spare wheel well. The towing eye screws into a threaded hole, accessible after prising out a circular cover on the right-hand side of the front or rear bumper. **Note:** *The towing eye has a left-hand thread – rotate it anti-clockwise to install it.*

☐ Before being towed, release the handbrake and make sure the transmission is in neutral. On models with automatic transmission, special precautions apply: do not exceed 30 mph or travel further than 30 miles, and the wheels must always roll forwards.

☐ Note that greater-than-usual pedal pressure will be required to operate the brakes, since the vacuum servo unit is only operational with the engine running.

☐ Greater-than-usual steering effort will also be required.

☐ The driver of the car being towed must keep the tow-rope taut at all times to avoid snatching.

☐ Make sure that both drivers know the route before setting off.

☐ Only drive at moderate speeds and keep the distance towed to a minimum. Drive smoothly and allow plenty of time for slowing down at junctions.

Introduction

There are some very simple checks which need only take a few minutes to carry out, but which could save you a lot of inconvenience and expense.

These checks require no great skill or special tools, and the small amount of time they take to perform could prove to be very well spent, for example:

☐ Keeping an eye on tyre condition and pressures, will not only help to stop them wearing out prematurely, but could also save your life.

☐ Many breakdowns are caused by electrical problems. Battery-related faults are particularly common, and a quick check on a regular basis will often prevent the majority of these.

☐ If your car develops a brake fluid leak, the first time you might know about it is when your brakes don't work properly. Checking the level regularly will give advance warning of this kind of problem.

☐ If the oil or coolant levels run low, the cost of repairing any engine damage will be far greater than fixing the leak.

Underbonnet check points

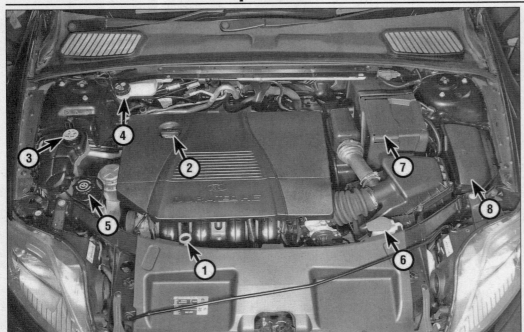

◀ **Petrol engine models**

1 *Engine oil level dipstick*

2 *Engine oil filler cap*

3 *Coolant reservoir (expansion tank)*

4 *Brake and clutch fluid reservoir*

5 *Power steering fluid reservoir*

6 *Washer fluid reservoir*

7 *Battery*

8 *Engine compartment fuse/ relay box*

◀ **1.8 litre diesel engine models**

1 *Engine oil level dipstick*

2 *Engine oil filler cap*

3 *Coolant reservoir (expansion tank)*

4 *Brake and clutch fluid reservoir*

5 *Power steering fluid reservoir*

6 *Washer fluid reservoir*

7 *Battery*

8 *Engine compartment fuse/ relay box*

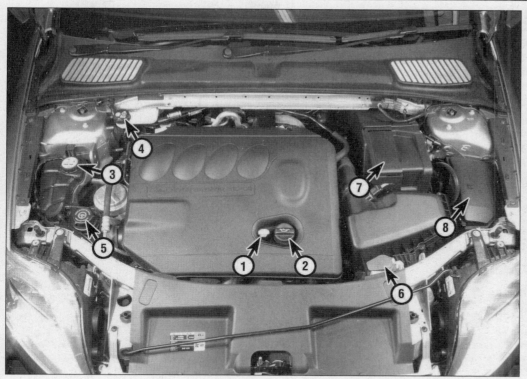

◀ **2.0 litre diesel engine models (emission level Stage III/IV)**

1 *Engine oil level dipstick*
2 *Engine oil filler cap*
3 *Coolant reservoir (expansion tank)*
4 *Brake and clutch fluid reservoir*
5 *Power steering fluid reservoir*
6 *Washer fluid reservoir*
7 *Battery*
8 *Engine compartment fuse/ relay box*

◀ **2.0 litre diesel engine models (emission level Stage V)**

1 *Engine oil level dipstick*
2 *Engine oil filler cap*
3 *Coolant reservoir (expansion tank)*
4 *Brake and clutch fluid reservoir*
5 *Power steering fluid reservoir*
6 *Washer fluid reservoir*
7 *Battery*
8 *Engine compartment fuse/ relay box*

Engine oil level

Before you start
✔ Make sure that the car is on level ground.
✔ The oil level must be checked with the engine at normal operating temperature, however, wait at least 5 minutes after the engine has been switched off.
Caution: If the oil is checked immediately after driving the car, some of the oil will remain in the upper engine components, resulting in an inaccurate reading on the dipstick.

The correct oil
Modern engines place great demands on their oil. It is very important that the correct oil for your car is used (see Section 6).

Car care
● If you have to add oil frequently, you should check whether you have any oil leaks. Place some clean paper under the car overnight, and check for stains in the morning. If there are no leaks, the engine may be burning oil, or the oil may only be leaking when the engine is running.
● Always maintain the level between the upper and lower dipstick marks (see photo 3, 4 or 5). If the level is too low, severe engine damage may occur. Oil seal failure may result if the engine is overfilled by adding too much oil.

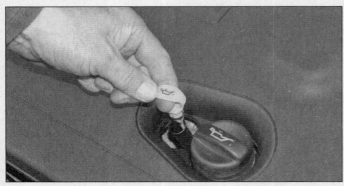

1 The dipstick is brightly-coloured for easy identification (see Underbonnet check points for exact location). Withdraw the dipstick.

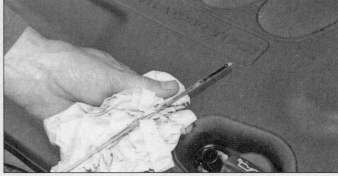

2 Using a clean rag or paper towel remove all oil from the dipstick. Insert the clean dipstick into the tube as far as it will go, then withdraw it again.

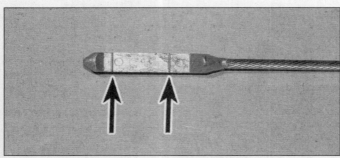

3 Note the level on the end of the dipstick, which should be between the upper (MAX) mark and lower (MIN) mark. Approximately 1.0 litre of oil will raise the level from the lower mark to the upper mark. On petrol engines the MAX and MIN marks are indicated by two lines on the dipstick.

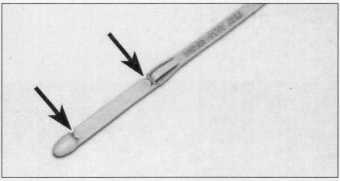

4 On 1.8 litre diesel engines and 2.0 litre diesel engines to emission level Stage III/IV, the MAX and MIN marks are indicated by two notches on the dipstick.

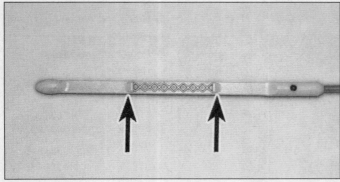

5 On 2.0 litre diesel engines to emission level Stage V, the MAX and MIN marks are above and below the hatched area on the dipstick.

6 Oil is added through the filler cap. Unscrew the cap and top-up the level. A funnel may help to reduce spillage. Add the oil slowly, checking the level on the dipstick frequently. Avoid overfilling (*see Car care*).

Coolant level

Warning: *Do not attempt to remove the expansion tank pressure cap when the engine is hot, as there is a very great risk of scalding. Do not leave open containers of coolant about, as it is poisonous.*

Car care

● Adding coolant should not be necessary on a regular basis. If frequent topping-up is required, it is likely there is a leak. Check the radiator, all hoses and joint faces for signs of staining or wetness, and rectify as necessary.

● It is important that antifreeze is used in the cooling system all year round, not just during the winter months. Don't top-up with water alone, as the antifreeze will become too diluted.

1 The coolant level varies with the temperature of the engine, and is visible through the expansion tank. When the engine is cold, the coolant level should be between the MAX and MIN marks on the front of the reservoir. When the engine is hot, the level may rise slightly above the MAX mark.

2 If topping-up is necessary, wait until the engine is cold. Slowly unscrew the expansion tank cap, to release any pressure present in the cooling system, and remove it.

3 Add a mixture of water and antifreeze to the expansion tank until the coolant level is halfway between the level marks. Use only the specified antifreeze – if using Ford antifreeze, make sure it is the same type and colour as that already in the system. Refit the cap and tighten it securely.

Brake and clutch fluid level

Note: *All manual transmission models have a hydraulically-operated clutch, which uses the same fluid as the braking system.*

Warning:
• *Brake fluid can harm your eyes and damage painted surfaces, so use extreme caution when handling and pouring it.*
Warning: • *Do not use fluid that has been standing open for some time, as it absorbs moisture from the air, which can cause a dangerous loss of braking effectiveness.*

HAYNES HiNT

• *Make sure that your car is on level ground.*

• *The fluid level in the reservoir will drop slightly as the brake pads wear down, but the fluid level must never be allowed to drop below the MIN mark.*

Safety first!

● If the reservoir requires repeated topping-up this is an indication of a fluid leak somewhere in the system, which should be investigated immediately.

● If a leak is suspected, the car should not be driven until the braking system has been checked. Never take any risks where brakes are concerned

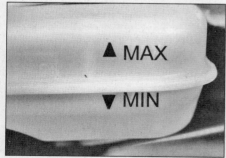

1 The MAX and MIN marks are indicated on the side of the reservoir. The fluid level must be kept between the marks at all times.

2 If topping-up is necessary, first wipe clean the area around the filler cap to prevent dirt entering the hydraulic system. Unscrew the reservoir cap.

3 Carefully add fluid, taking care not to spill it onto the surrounding components. Use only the specified fluid; mixing different types can cause damage to the system. After topping-up to the correct level, securely refit the cap and wipe off any spilt fluid.

Tyre condition and pressure

It is very important that tyres are in good condition, and at the correct pressure – having a tyre failure at any speed is highly dangerous.

Tyre wear is influenced by driving style – harsh braking and acceleration, or fast cornering, will all produce more rapid tyre wear. As a general rule, the front tyres wear out faster than the rears. Interchanging the tyres from front to rear ("rotating" the tyres) may result in more even wear. However, if this is completely effective, you may have the expense of replacing all four tyres at once!

Remove any nails or stones embedded in the tread before they penetrate the tyre to cause deflation. If removal of a nail does reveal that the tyre has been punctured, refit the nail so that its point of penetration is marked. Then immediately change the wheel, and have the tyre repaired by a tyre dealer.

Regularly check the tyres for damage in the form of cuts or bulges, especially in the sidewalls. Periodically remove the wheels, and clean any dirt or mud from the inside and outside surfaces. Examine the wheel rims for signs of rusting, corrosion or other damage. Light alloy wheels are easily damaged by "kerbing" whilst parking; steel wheels may also become dented or buckled. A new wheel is very often the only way to overcome severe damage.

New tyres should be balanced when they are fitted, but it may become necessary to re-balance them as they wear, or if the balance weights fitted to the wheel rim should fall off. Unbalanced tyres will wear more quickly, as will the steering and suspension components. Wheel imbalance is normally signified by vibration, particularly at a certain speed (typically around 50 mph). If this vibration is felt only through the steering, then it is likely that just the front wheels need balancing. If, however, the vibration is felt through the whole car, the rear wheels could be out of balance. Wheel balancing should be carried out by a tyre dealer or garage.

1 Tread Depth - visual check
The original tyres have tread wear safety bands (B), which will appear when the tread depth reaches approximately 1.6 mm. The band positions are indicated by a triangular mark on the tyre sidewall (A).

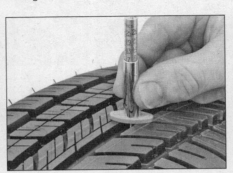

2 Tread Depth - manual check
Alternatively, tread wear can be monitored with a simple, inexpensive device known as a tread depth indicator gauge.

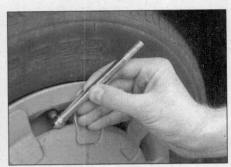

3 Tyre Pressure Check
Check the tyre pressures regularly with the tyres cold. Do not adjust the tyre pressures immediately after the vehicle has been used, or an inaccurate setting will result.

Tyre tread wear patterns

Shoulder Wear

Underinflation (wear on both sides)
Under-inflation will cause overheating of the tyre, because the tyre will flex too much, and the tread will not sit correctly on the road surface. This will cause a loss of grip and excessive wear, not to mention the danger of sudden tyre failure due to heat build-up.
Check and adjust pressures
Incorrect wheel camber (wear on one side)
Repair or renew suspension parts
Hard cornering
Reduce speed!

Centre Wear

Overinflation
Over-inflation will cause rapid wear of the centre part of the tyre tread, coupled with reduced grip, harsher ride, and the danger of shock damage occurring in the tyre casing.
Check and adjust pressures

If you sometimes have to inflate your car's tyres to the higher pressures specified for maximum load or sustained high speed, don't forget to reduce the pressures to normal afterwards.

Uneven Wear

Front tyres may wear unevenly as a result of wheel misalignment. Most tyre dealers and garages can check and adjust the wheel alignment (or "tracking") for a modest charge.
Incorrect camber or castor
Repair or renew suspension parts
Malfunctioning suspension
Repair or renew suspension parts
Unbalanced wheel
Balance tyres
Incorrect toe setting
Adjust front wheel alignment
Note: *The feathered edge of the tread which typifies toe wear is best checked by feel.*

Power steering fluid level

✔ Park the vehicle on level ground.
✔ Set the steering wheel straight-ahead.
✔ The engine should be turned off.

✔ For the check to be accurate, the steering must not be turned once the engine has been stopped.

Safety first!

● The need for frequent topping-up indicates a leak, which should be investigated immediately.

1 The reservoir is mounted at the front right-hand side of the engine compartment. The fluid level can be viewed through the reservoir body and should be between the MIN and MAX marks when the engine is cold. If the level is checked when the engine is running or hot, the level may rise slightly above the MAX mark.

2 If topping-up is necessary, first wipe clean the area around the filler cap to prevent dirt entering the system. Unscrew the reservoir cap.

3 When topping-up, use the specified type of fluid and do not overfill the reservoir. When the level is correct, securely refit the cap.

Screen washer fluid level

Note: *The underbonnet reservoir also serves the tailgate washer, and the headlight washers, where fitted.*

● Screenwash additives not only keep the windscreen clean during bad weather, they also prevent the washer system freezing in cold weather – which is when you are likely to need it most. Don't top-up using plain water, as the screenwash will become diluted, and will freeze in cold weather.

● Don't top-up using plain water as the screenwash will become too diluted, and will freeze during cold weather.

 Warning: Warning: On no account use engine coolant antifreeze in the screen washer system – this may damage the paintwork.

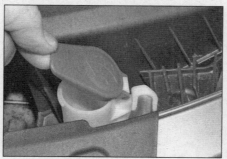

1 The reservoir for the washer systems is located on the left-hand side of the engine compartment. If topping-up is necessary, open the filler cap.

2 When topping-up the reservoir a screenwash additive should be added in the quantities recommended on the bottle.

Battery

Caution: Before carrying out any work on the vehicle battery, read the precautions given in 'Safety first!' at the start of this manual. If the battery is to be disconnected, refer to ' Disconnecting the battery' in the Reference Chapter, before proceeding.

✔ Make sure that the battery tray is in good condition, and that the clamp is tight. Corrosion on the tray, retaining clamp and the battery itself can be removed with a solution of water and baking soda. Thoroughly rinse all cleaned areas with water. Any metal parts damaged by corrosion should be covered with a zinc-based primer, then painted.

✔ Periodically (approximately every three months), check the charge condition of the battery as described in Chapter 5A.

✔ If the battery is flat, and you need to jump start your vehicle, see *Roadside Repairs*.

Battery corrosion can be kept to a minimum by applying a layer of petroleum jelly to the clamps and terminals after they are reconnected.

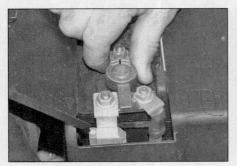

1 Check the tightness of battery clamps to ensure good electrical connections. Also check each cable for cracks and frayed conductors. Note that with the battery fitted it is only possible to check the positive cable clamp and the negative cable connection on the body. To check the negative cable and clamp, and the battery itself, the battery will have to be partially removed as described in Chapter 5A.

2 If corrosion (white, fluffy deposits) is evident, remove the cables from the battery terminals, clean them with a small wire brush, then refit them. Automotive stores sell a tool for cleaning the battery post…

3 … as well as the battery cable clamps.

Electrical systems

✔ Check all external lights and the horn. Refer to the appropriate Sections of Chapter 12 for details if any of the circuits are found to be inoperative.

✔ Visually check all accessible wiring connectors, harnesses and retaining clips for security, and for signs of chafing or damage.

✔ There are three separate fuse/relay boxes on Mondeo models. One is located on the left-hand side of the engine compartment, another is located inside the car below the glovebox (also known as the generic electronics module) and the third is located on the left-hand side of the luggage compartment, behind a cover. Refer to Chapter 12 for detailed information.

If you need to check your brake lights and indicators unaided, back up to a wall or garage door and operate the lights. The reflected light should show if they are working properly.

1 If a single indicator light, brake light or headlight has failed, it is likely that a bulb has blown and will need to be renewed. Refer to Chapter 12 for details. If both brake lights have failed, it is possible that the switch has failed (see Chapter 9).

2 If more than one indicator light or headlight has failed, it is likely that either a fuse has blown or that there is a fault in the circuit (see Chapter 12). To gain access to the engine compartment fuse/relay box, unclip and remove the cover. Refer to the wiring diagrams at the end of Chapter 12 for details of the fuse locations and circuits protected.

3 To renew a blown fuse, remove it, where applicable, using the plastic tool provided or needle-nosed pliers. Fit a new fuse of the same rating, available from car accessory shops. It is important that you find the reason that the fuse blew (see *Electrical fault finding* in Chapter 12).

Wiper blades

✔ Only fit good-quality wiper blades.

✔ When removing an old wiper blade, note how it is fitted. Fitting new blades can be a tricky exercise, and noting how the old blade came off can save time.

✔ While the wiper blade is removed, take care not to knock the wiper arm from its locked position, or it could strike the glass.

✔ Offer the new blade into position the same way round as the old one. Ensure that it clicks home securely, otherwise it may come off in use, damaging the glass.

Note: *Fitting details for wiper blades vary according to model, and according to whether genuine Ford wiper blades have been fitted. Use the procedures and illustrations shown as a guide for your car.*

 HAYNES HiNT *If smearing is still a problem despite fitting new wiper blades, try cleaning the glass with neat screenwash additive or methylated spirit.*

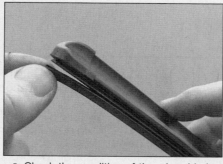

1 Check the condition of the wiper blades; if they are cracked or show any signs of deterioration, or if the glass swept area is smeared, renew them. Wiper blades should be renewed annually.

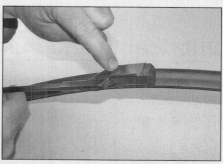

2 To remove a windscreen wiper blade, pull the arm fully away from the screen until it locks. Depress the tab on the side of the wiper arm.

3 Disengage the blade from the end of the arm and lift away the blade.

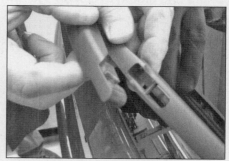

4 Don't forget to check the tailgate wiper blade as well. On Hatchback models the blade is removed in the same way as described for the windscreen wiper blade. On Estate models, simply disengage the blade pivot pin from the end of the arm.

Lubricants and fluids

Engine . . . . Multigrade engine oil, viscosity SAE 5W/30 to
Ford specification WSS-M2C913-C

Cooling system . . . . Motorcraft SuperPlus antifreeze to
Ford specification WSS-M97B44-D

Manual transmission . . . . Gear oil to Ford specification WSS-M2C200-D2

Automatic transmission . . . . Automatic transmission fluid to
Ford specification WSS-M2C924-A

Brake and clutch hydraulic system . . . . Super DOT 4 hydraulic fluid to
Ford specification WSS-M6C57-A2

Power steering . . . . Hydraulic fluid to Ford specification WSS-M2C204-A2

Tyre pressures

Details of the tyre pressures applicable to your vehicle are given on a sticker attached to the driver's side door pillar.

Chapter 1 Part A
Routine maintenance and servicing – petrol models

Contents

Degrees of difficulty

| Easy, suitable for novice with little experience | | Fairly easy, suitable for beginner with some experience | | Fairly difficult, suitable for competent DIY mechanic | | Difficult, suitable for experienced DIY mechanic | | Very difficult, suitable for expert DIY or professional | |

1 Servicing specifications – petrol models

Lubricants and fluids

Refer to Lubricants, fluids and tyre pressures

Capacities

Engine oil (including oil filter)	4.3 litres
Cooling system	6.2 litres
Manual transmission	1.9 litres
Washer fluid reservoir	3.8 litres
Fuel tank	70.0 litres

Cooling system

Antifreeze mixture:

   50% antifreeze .... Protection down to -37°C

Note: *Refer to antifreeze manufacturer for latest recommendations.*

Ignition system

Spark plugs	Refer to Ford dealer or parts specialist
Firing order	1-3-4-2
No 1 cylinder position	Timing chain end of engine

Brakes

Friction material minimum thickness:

Front brake pads	2.0 mm
Rear brake pads	1.5 mm

Remote control battery

Type	CR2032, 3.0 volt

Torque wrench settings

	Nm	lbf ft
Engine oil drain plug	25	18
Ignition coil retaining bolts	10	7
Manual transmission filler/level plug	35	26
Roadwheel nuts	140	103
Spark plugs	12	9

2   Maintenance schedule – petrol models

1 The maintenance intervals in this manual are provided with the assumption that you, not the dealer, will be carrying out the work. These are the minimum maintenance intervals based on the standard service schedule recommended by the manufacturer for vehicles driven daily. If you wish to keep your vehicle in peak condition at all times, you may wish to perform some of these procedures more often. We encourage frequent maintenance, because it enhances the efficiency, performance and resale value of your vehicle.

2 If the vehicle is driven in dusty areas, used to tow a trailer, or driven frequently at slow speeds (idling in traffic) or on short journeys, more frequent maintenance intervals are recommended.

3 When the vehicle is new, it should be serviced by a dealer service department (or other workshop recognised by the vehicle manufacturer as providing the same standard of service) in order to preserve the warranty. The vehicle manufacturer may reject warranty claims if you are unable to prove that servicing has been carried out as and when specified, using only original equipment parts or parts certified to be of equivalent quality.

Every 250 miles or weekly
- [ ] Refer to 'Weekly checks'.

Every 6000 miles or 6 months, whichever comes first
- [ ] Reset the service interval indicator (Section 4)
- [ ] Renew the engine oil and filter (Section 6)

Note: *Ford recommend that the engine oil and filter are changed every 12 500 miles or 12 months. However, oil and filter changes are good for the engine, and we recommend that the oil and filter are renewed more frequently, especially if the car is used on a lot of short journeys.*

Every 12 500 miles or 12 months, whichever comes first
In addition to the items listed above, carry out the following:
- [ ] Renew the pollen filter (Section 7)
- [ ] Check all components, pipes and hoses for fluid leaks (Section 8)
- [ ] Check the condition of the auxiliary drivebelt (Section 9)
- [ ] Check the antifreeze/inhibitor strength (Section 25)
- [ ] Check the condition and operation of the seat belts (Section 10)

Every 12 500 miles or 12 months, whichever comes first (continued)
- [ ] Check the braking system (Section 11)
- [ ] Check the condition of the driveshaft gaiters (Section 12)
- [ ] Check the steering and suspension components for condition and security (Section 13)
- [ ] Check the condition of the exhaust system components (Section 14)
- [ ] Check the roadwheel nuts are tightened to the specified torque (Section 15)
- [ ] Lubricate all door, bonnet, boot lid and tailgate hinges and locks (Section 16)
- [ ] Check the operation of the horn, all lights, and the wipers and washers (Section 17)
- [ ] Carry out a road test (Section 18)

Every 37 500 miles or 3 years, whichever comes first
In addition to the items listed above, carry out the following:
- [ ] Renew the spark plugs (Section 19)
- [ ] Renew the air filter (Section 20)

Every 125 000 miles or 10 years, whichever comes first
- [ ] Renew the auxiliary drivebelt (Section 21)

Every 2 years, regardless of mileage
- [ ] Renew the brake fluid (Section 22)
- [ ] Check the manual transmission oil level (Section 23)
- [ ] Renew the remote control battery (Section 24)
- [ ] Renew the coolant (Section 25)*

Note: *Ford state that, if their SuperPlus antifreeze is in the system, the coolant need only be changed every 10 years. If there is any doubt as to the type or quality of the antifreeze which has been used, we recommend this shorter interval be observed.*

3   Component location – petrol models

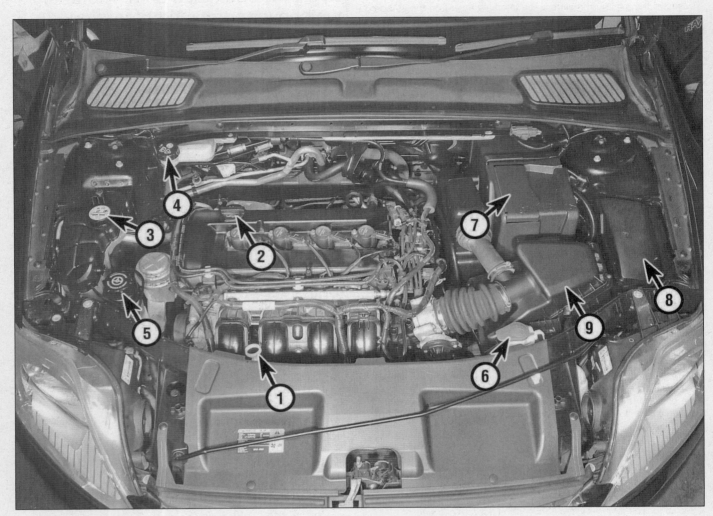

Underbonnet view

1 Engine oil level dipstick
2 Engine oil filler cap
3 Coolant reservoir (expansion tank)

4 Brake and clutch fluid reservoir
5 Power steering fluid reservoir
6 Washer fluid reservoir

7 Battery cover
8 Engine compartment fuse/relay box
9 Air cleaner

Front underbody view

1 Brake caliper
2 Brake hose
3 Air conditioning compressor
4 Oil filter
5 Engine oil drain plug
6 Suspension lower arm
7 Engine rear mounting
8 Exhaust front mounting
9 Driveshaft
10 Subframe
11 Subframe cross-brace
12 Track rod end

Rear underbody view

1 Anti-roll bar
2 Carbon canister
3 Fuel tank
4 Silencer
5 Shock absorber
6 Lateral link
7 Lower control arm
8 Tie rod
9 Subframe

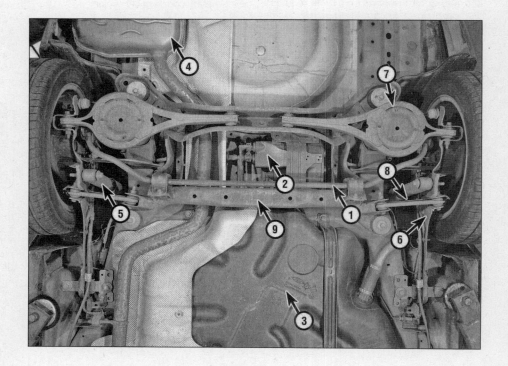

4 General Information

1 This Chapter is designed to help the home mechanic maintain his/her car for safety, economy, long life and peak performance.
2 The Chapter contains a master maintenance schedule, followed by Sections dealing specifically with each task in the schedule. Visual checks, adjustments, component renewal and other helpful items are included. Refer to the accompanying illustrations of the engine compartment and the underside of the car for the locations of the various components.
3 Servicing your car in accordance with the mileage/time maintenance schedule and the following Sections will provide a planned maintenance programme, which should result in a long and reliable service life. This is a comprehensive plan, so maintaining some items but not others at the specified service intervals will not produce the same results.
4 As you service your car, you will discover that many of the procedures can – and should – be grouped together, because of the particular procedure being performed, or because of the proximity of two otherwise-unrelated components to one another. For example, if the car is raised for any reason, the exhaust can be inspected at the same time as the suspension and steering components.
5 The first step in this maintenance programme is to prepare yourself before the actual work begins. Read through all the Sections relevant to the work to be carried out, then make a list and gather all the parts and tools required. If a problem is encountered, seek advice from a parts specialist, or a dealer service department.

Service interval indicator

6 The service interval indicator is a 'change oil' warning lamp or 'service oil' message that must be reset every time the engine oil is changed. The reset procedure is as follows:
a) Ensure that all doors are closed.
b) Switch the ignition on and fully depress both the brake and accelerator pedals for at least 15 seconds.

c) With both pedals still depressed, press the OK button on the steering wheel.
d) Release the pedals and switch off the ignition.

5 Regular maintenance

1 If, from the time the car is new, the routine maintenance schedule is followed closely, and frequent checks are made of fluid levels and high-wear items, as suggested throughout this manual, the engine will be kept in relatively good running condition, and the need for additional work will be minimised.
2 It is possible that there will be times when the engine is running poorly due to the lack of regular maintenance. This is even more likely if a used car, which has not received regular and frequent maintenance checks, is purchased. In such cases, additional work may need to be carried out, outside of the regular maintenance intervals.
3 If engine wear is suspected, a compression test (refer to Chapter 2A Section 2) will provide valuable information regarding the overall performance of the main internal components. Such a test can be used as a basis to decide on the extent of the work to be carried out. If, for example, a compression test indicates serious internal engine wear, conventional maintenance as described in this Chapter will not greatly improve the performance of the engine, and may prove a waste of time and money, unless extensive overhaul work is carried out first.
4 The following series of operations are those most often required to improve the performance of a generally poor-running engine:

Primary operations

a) Clean, inspect and test the battery (refer to Weekly checks).
b) Check all the engine-related fluids (refer to Weekly checks).
c) Check the condition of all hoses, and check for fluid leaks (Section 10).
d) Check the condition of the auxiliary drivebelt (Section 11).
e) Renew the spark plugs (Section 22).
f) Check the condition of the air filter, and renew if necessary (Section 23).

5 If the above operations do not prove fully effective, carry out the following secondary operations:

Secondary operations

6 All items listed under Primary operations, plus the following:
a) Check the charging system (Chapter 5A Section 5).
b) Check the ignition system (Chapter 5B Section 2).
c) Check the fuel system (Chapter 4A).

6 Engine oil and filter renewal - petrol models

1 Frequent oil and filter changes are the most important preventive maintenance procedures which can be undertaken by the DIY owner. As engine oil ages, it becomes diluted and contaminated, which leads to premature engine wear.
2 Before starting this procedure, gather together all the necessary tools and materials. Also make sure that you have plenty of clean rags and newspapers handy, to mop-up any spills. Ideally, the engine oil should be warm, as it will drain more easily, and more built-up sludge will be removed with it. Take care not to touch the exhaust or any other hot parts of the engine when working under the car. To avoid any possibility of scalding, and to protect yourself from possible skin irritants and other harmful contaminants in used engine oils, it is advisable to wear gloves when carrying out this work.
3 Firmly apply the handbrake, then jack up the front of the car and support it on axle stands (see 'Jacking and vehicle support').
4 Remove the oil filler cap.
5 Using a spanner, or preferably a socket and bar, slacken the drain plug about half a turn (see illustration). Position the draining container under the drain plug, then remove the plug completely.

> **HAYNES HINT**
> As the drain plug threads release, move it sharply away so the stream of oil issuing from the sump runs into the container, not up your sleeve.

6 Allow some time for the oil to drain, noting that it may be necessary to reposition the container as the oil flow slows to a trickle.
7 After all the oil has drained, wipe the drain plug with a clean rag. Examine the condition of the sealing O-ring, and renew it if it shows signs of damage which may prevent an oil-tight seal. Clean the area around the drain plug opening, then refit the plug complete with O-ring and tighten it securely.
8 Move the container into position under the oil filter, which is located on the front of the cylinder block (see illustration).

6.5 Engine oil drain plug (arrowed)

6.8 Engine oil filter location on the front of the engine

9 Use an oil filter removal tool to slacken the filter initially, then unscrew it by hand the rest of the way **(see illustration)**. Empty the oil from the old filter into the container.

10 Use a clean rag to remove all oil, dirt and sludge from the filter sealing area on the engine.

11 Apply a light coating of clean engine oil to the sealing ring on the new filter, then screw the filter into position on the engine **(see illustration)** Tighten the filter firmly by hand only – do not use any tools.

12 Remove the old oil and all tools from under the car, then lower the car to the ground.

13 Fill the engine through the filler hole, using the correct grade and type of oil (refer to *Weekly checks* for details of topping-up). Pour in half the specified quantity of oil first, then wait a few minutes for the oil to drain into the sump. Continue to add oil, a small quantity at a time, until the level is up to the lower mark on the dipstick. Adding approximately a further 0.5 to 1.0 litre will bring the level up to the upper mark on the dipstick.

14 Start the engine and run it for a few minutes, while checking for leaks around the oil filter seal and the sump drain plug. Note that there may be a delay of a few seconds before the oil pressure warning light goes out when the engine is first started, as the oil circulates through the new oil filter and the engine oil galleries before the pressure builds-up.

15 Stop the engine, and wait a few minutes for the oil to settle in the sump once more. With the new oil circulated and the filter now completely full, recheck the level on the dipstick, and add more oil as necessary.

16 Dispose of the used engine oil and filter safely, with reference to General repair procedures in the Reference Chapter of this manual. Do not discard the old filter with domestic household waste. The facility for waste oil disposal provided by many local council refuse tips and/or recycling centres generally has a filter receptacle alongside.

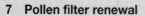

7   Pollen filter renewal

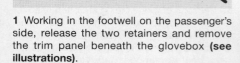

1 Working in the footwell on the passenger's side, release the two retainers and remove the trim panel beneath the glovebox **(see illustrations)**.

2 Turn the locking catch through 90° and lower the generic electronics module (GEM) from its location. Lift the module from the two lower pivots and place it to one side**(see illustrations)**.

3 Undo the three screws and remove the pollen filter housing cover **(see illustrations)**. Note that access is limited in this area but can be improved if the glovebox is removed as described in Chapter 11Section 27.

4 Slide out the pollen filter, into the

6.9 Using a strap wrench to slacken the oil filter

6.11 Apply a light coating of clean engine oil to the filter sealing ring

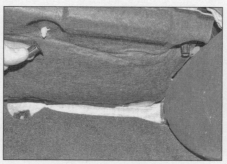

7.1a Release the two retainers...

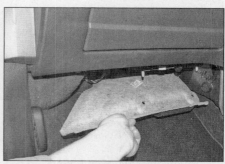

7.1b... and remove the trim panel beneath the glovebox

7.2a Turn the locking catch through 90° and lower the generic electronics module...

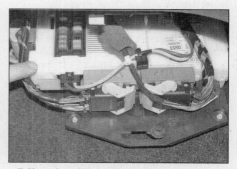

7.2b... then lift the module from the two lower pivots and place it to one side

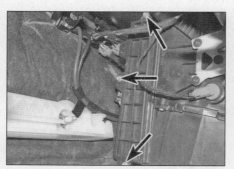

7.3a Undo the three screws (arrowed)...

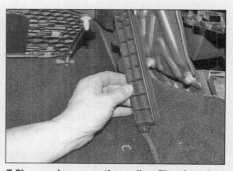

7.3b... and remove the pollen filter housing cover

7.4 Slide out the pollen filter, into the passenger's footwell, and remove it

passenger's footwell, and remove it **(see illustration)**.

5 When fitting the new filter, note the direction-of-airflow arrow marked on its top edge – the arrow should point into the car.

6 Slide the filter fully into position, refit the filter housing cover and secure the cover with the three retaining screws.

7 Where applicable, refit the glovebox as described in Chapter 11 Section 27.

8 Refit the generic electronics module and the trim panel beneath the glovebox.

8 Hose and fluid leak check

Note: *Also refer to Sections 11 and 25.*

General

1 Visually inspect the engine joint faces, gaskets and seals for any signs of water or oil leaks. Pay particular attention to the areas around the cylinder head cover, cylinder head, oil filter and sump joint faces. Bear in mind that, over a period of time, some very slight seepage from these areas is to be expected – what you are really looking for is any indication of a serious leak. Should a leak be found, renew the offending gasket or oil seal by referring to the appropriate Chapters in this manual.

2 High temperatures in the engine compartment can cause the deterioration of the rubber and plastic hoses used for engine, accessory and emission systems operation. Periodic inspection should be made for cracks, loose clamps, material hardening and leaks.

3 When checking the hoses, ensure that all the cable-ties or clips used to retain the hoses are in place, and in good condition. Clips which are broken or missing can lead to chafing of the hoses, pipes or wiring, which could cause more serious problems in the future.

4 Carefully check the large top and bottom radiator hoses, along with the other smaller-diameter cooling system hoses and metal pipes; do not forget the heater hoses/pipes which run from the engine to the bulkhead. Inspect each hose along its entire length, renewing any that is cracked, swollen

or shows signs of deterioration. Cracks may become more apparent if the hose is squeezed, and may often be apparent at the hose ends.

5 Make sure that all hose connections are tight. If the large-diameter air hoses from the air cleaner are loose, they will leak air, and upset the engine idle quality. If the spring clamps that are used to secure some of the hoses appear to be slackening, they should be updated with worm-drive clips to prevent the possibility of leaks.

6 Some other hoses are secured to their fittings with clamps. Where clamps are used, check to be sure they haven't lost their tension, allowing the hose to leak. If clamps aren't used, make sure the hose has not expanded and/or hardened where it slips over the fitting, allowing it to leak.

7 Check all fluid reservoirs, filler caps, drain plugs and fittings, etc, looking for any signs of leakage of oil, transmission and/or brake hydraulic fluid and coolant. Also check the clutch hydraulic fluid lines which lead from the fluid reservoir, master cylinder, and the slave cylinder (on the transmission).

8 If the vehicle is regularly parked in the same place, close inspection of the ground underneath it will soon show any leaks; ignore the puddle of water which may be left if the air conditioning system is in use. Place a clean piece of cardboard below the engine, and examine it for signs of contamination after the vehicle has been parked over it overnight – be aware, however, of the fire risk inherent in placing combustible material below the catalytic converter.

9 Remember that some leaks will only occur with the engine running, or when the engine is hot or cold. With the handbrake firmly applied, start the engine from cold, and let the engine idle while you examine the underside of the engine compartment for signs of leakage.

10 If an unusual smell is noticed inside or around the car, especially when the engine is thoroughly hot, this may point to the presence of a leak.

11 As soon as a leak is detected, its source must be traced and rectified. Where oil has been leaking for some time, it is usually necessary to use a steam cleaner, pressure washer or similar, to clean away the accumulated dirt, so that the exact source of the leak can be identified.

Vacuum hoses

12 It's quite common for vacuum hoses, especially those in the emissions system, to be colour-coded, or to be identified by coloured stripes moulded into them. Various systems require hoses with different wall thicknesses, collapse resistance and temperature resistance. When renewing hoses, be sure the new ones are made of the same material.

13 Often the only effective way to check a hose is to remove it completely from the

vehicle. If more than one hose is removed, be sure to label the hoses and fittings to ensure correct installation.

14 When checking vacuum hoses, be sure to include any plastic T-fittings in the check. Inspect the fittings for cracks, and check the hose where it fits over the fitting for distortion, which could cause leakage.

15 A small piece of vacuum hose (approximately 6 mm inside diameter) can be used as a stethoscope to detect vacuum leaks. Hold one end of the hose new your ear, and probe around vacuum hoses and fittings, listening for the 'hissing' sound characteristic of a vacuum leak.

⚠️ *Warning: When probing with the vacuum hose stethoscope, be very careful not to come into contact with moving engine components such as the auxiliary drivebelt, radiator electric cooling fan, etc.*

Fuel hoses

⚠️ *Warning: There are certain precautions which must be taken when inspecting or servicing fuel system components. Work in a well-ventilated area, and do not allow open flames (cigarettes, appliance pilot lights, etc) or bare light bulbs near the work area. Mop-up any spills immediately, and do not store fuel-soaked rags where they could ignite.*

16 Check all fuel hoses for deterioration and chafing. Check especially for cracks in areas where the hose bends, and also just before fittings, such as where a hose attaches to the fuel rail.

17 High-quality fuel line, usually identified by the word 'Fluoroelastomer' printed on the hose, should be used for fuel line renewal. Never, under any circumstances, use non-reinforced vacuum line, clear plastic tubing or water hose as a substitute for fuel lines.

18 Spring-type clamps may be used on fuel lines. These clamps often lose their tension over a period of time, and can be 'sprung' during removal. Renew all spring-type clamps with proper petrol pipe clips whenever a hose is renewed.

Metal pipes

19 Sections of metal piping are often used for fuel line between the fuel tank and the engine, and for most air conditioning applications. Check carefully to be sure the piping has not been bent or crimped, and that cracks have not started in the line; also check for signs of excessive corrosion.

20 If a section of metal fuel line must be renewed, only seamless steel piping should be used, since copper and aluminium piping don't have the strength necessary to withstand normal engine vibration.

21 Check the metal lines where they enter the brake master cylinder, ABS hydraulic unit or clutch master/slave cylinders (as applicable) for cracks in the lines or loose fittings.

Any sign of brake fluid leakage calls for an immediate and thorough inspection.

Air conditioning refrigerant

 Warning: Refer to the safety information given in Safety First! and Chapter 3 Section 1, regarding the dangers of disturbing any of the air conditioning system components.

22 The air conditioning system is filled with a liquid refrigerant, which is retained under high pressure. If the air conditioning system is opened and depressurised without the aid of specialised equipment, the refrigerant will immediately turn into gas and escape into the atmosphere. If the liquid comes into contact with your skin, it can cause severe frostbite. In addition, the refrigerant contains substances which are environmentally damaging; for this reason, it should not be allowed to escape into the atmosphere.

23 Any suspected air conditioning system leaks should be immediately referred to a Ford dealer or air conditioning specialist. Leakage will be shown up as a steady drop in the level of refrigerant in the system.

24 Note that water may drip from the condenser drain pipe, underneath the car, immediately after the air conditioning system has been in use. This is normal, and should not be cause for concern.

9   Auxiliary drivebelt check

General

1 The auxiliary drivebelt is of flat, multi-ribbed type, and is located on the right-hand end of the engine. It drives the alternator, coolant pump, power steering pump and the air conditioning compressor from the engine's crankshaft pulley.

2 The good condition and proper tension of the auxiliary drivebelt is critical to the operation of the engine. Because of their composition and the high stresses to which they are subjected, drivebelts stretch and deteriorate as they get older. They must, therefore, be regularly inspected.

Check

3 With the engine switched off, open and support the bonnet. For improved access to the right-hand end of the engine, first loosen the right-hand front wheel nuts, then jack up the front right-hand side of the car and support it securely on an axle stand (see 'Jacking and vehicle support'). Remove the roadwheel, then remove the wheel arch liner from inside the wheel arch.

4 Using an inspection light or a small electric torch, and rotating the engine with a spanner applied to the crankshaft pulley bolt, check

11.2 With the wheel removed, the pad thickness can be seen through the front of the caliper

the whole length of the drivebelt for cracks, separation of the rubber, and torn or worn ribs. Also check for fraying and glazing, which gives the drivebelt a shiny appearance.

5 Both sides of the drivebelt should be inspected, which means you will have to twist the drivebelt to check the underside. Use your fingers to feel the drivebelt where you can't see it. If you are in any doubt as to the condition of the drivebelt, renew it as described in Section 25.

Drivebelt tension

6 The auxiliary drivebelt is tensioned by an automatic tensioner – regular checks are not required, and manual 'adjustment' is not possible.

7 If you suspect that the drivebelt is slipping and/or running slack, or that the tensioner is otherwise faulty, it must be renewed.

Drivebelt renewal

8 Refer to Section 25.

10   Seat belt check

1 Check the seat belts for satisfactory operation and condition. Pull sharply on the belt to check that the locking mechanism engages correctly. Inspect the webbing for fraying and cuts. Check that they retract smoothly and without binding into their reels.

2 Check the accessible seat belt mountings, ensuring that all bolts are securely tightened.

11   Braking system check

Front disc brakes

1 Apply the handbrake, then jack up the front of the car and support it on axle stands (see 'Jacking and vehicle support'). For better

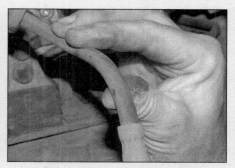

11.7 Check the condition of the flexible brake hoses by bending them slightly and looking for cracks

access to the brake calipers, remove the roadwheels.

2 Look through the inspection window in the caliper, and check that the thickness of the friction lining material on each of the pads is not less than the recommended minimum thickness given in the Specifications **(see illustration)**.

3 If it is difficult to determine the exact thickness of the pad linings, or if you are at all concerned about the condition of the pads, then remove them from the calipers for further inspection (refer to Chapter 9 Section 4).

4 Check the caliper on the other side in the same way.

5 If any one of the brake pads has worn down to, or below, the specified limit, all four pads at that end of the car must be renewed as a set.

6 Check both front brake discs with reference to Chapter 9 Section 6.

7 Before refitting the roadwheels, check all brake lines and flexible hoses with reference to Chapter 9 Section 3. In particular, check the flexible hoses in the vicinity of the calipers, where they are subjected to most movement. Bend them between the fingers and check that this does not reveal previously-hidden cracks, cuts or splits **(see illustration)**.

8 On completion, refit the roadwheels and lower the car to the ground. Tighten the wheel nuts to the specified torque.

Rear disc brakes

9 Chock the front wheels, then jack up the rear of the car and support on axle stands (see 'Jacking and vehicle support'). Remove the rear wheels.

10 The procedure for checking the rear brakes is much the same as described in paragraphs 1 to 8 above.

Handbrake

11 With the car on a slight slope, firmly apply the handbrake lever, and check that it holds the car stationary, then release the lever and check that there is no resistance to movement of the car. If necessary, the handbrake should be adjusted as described in Chapter 9 Section 14.

12 Driveshaft gaiter check

1 With the car raised and securely supported on stands, turn the steering onto full lock, then slowly rotate the roadwheel. Inspect the condition of the outer constant velocity (CV) joint rubber gaiters while squeezing the gaiters to open out the folds. Check for signs of cracking, splits or deterioration of the rubber which may allow the grease to escape, and lead to water and grit entry into the joint. Also check the security and condition of the retaining clips. Repeat these checks on the inner CV joints **(see illustrations)**. If any damage or deterioration is found, the gaiters should be renewed as described in Chapter 8.
2 At the same time, check the general condition of the CV joints themselves by first holding the driveshaft and attempting to rotate the wheel. Repeat this check by holding the inner joint and attempting to rotate the driveshaft. Any appreciable movement indicates wear in the joints, wear in the driveshaft splines, or a loose driveshaft retaining bolt.

13 Steering and suspension check

Front suspension and steering

1 Raise the front of the car, and securely support it on axle stands (see *'Jacking and vehicle support'*).
2 Visually inspect the balljoint dust covers and the steering rack-and-pinion gaiters for splits, chafing or deterioration **(see illustration)**. Any wear of these components will cause loss of lubricant, together with dirt and water entry, resulting in rapid deterioration of the balljoints or steering gear.
3 Grasp the roadwheel at the 12 o'clock and 6 o'clock positions, and try to rock it **(see illustration)**. Very slight free play may be felt, but if the movement is appreciable, further investigation is necessary to determine the source. Continue rocking the wheel while

12.1a Check the outer constant velocity (CV) joint gaiters…

an assistant depresses the footbrake. If the movement is now eliminated or significantly reduced, it is likely that the hub bearings are at fault. If the free play is still evident with the footbrake depressed, then there is wear in the suspension joints or mountings.
4 Now grasp the wheel at the 9 o'clock and 3 o'clock positions, and try to rock it as before. Any movement felt now may again be caused by wear in the hub bearings or the steering track rod end balljoints. If the outer balljoint is worn, the visual movement will be obvious. If the inner joint is suspect, it can be felt by placing a hand over the rack-and-pinion rubber gaiter and gripping the track rod. If the wheel is now rocked, movement will be felt at the inner joint if wear has taken place.
5 Using a large screwdriver or flat bar, check for wear in the suspension mounting bushes by levering between the relevant suspension component and its attachment point. Some movement is to be expected, as the mountings are made of rubber, but excessive wear should be obvious. Also check the condition of any visible rubber bushes, looking for splits, cracks or contamination of the rubber.
6 With the car standing on its wheels, have an assistant turn the steering wheel back-and-forth, about an eighth of a turn each way. There should be very little, if any, lost movement between the steering wheel and roadwheels. If this is not the case, closely observe the joints and mountings previously described. In addition, check the steering column universal joints for wear, and also check the rack-and-pinion steering gear itself.

12.1b… and, though less prone to wear, check the inner gaiters, too

Rear suspension

7 Chock the front wheels, then jack up the rear of the car and support securely on axle stands (see *'Jacking and vehicle support'*).
8 Working as described previously for the front suspension, check the rear hub bearings, the suspension bushes and the shock absorber mountings for wear.

Shock absorber

9 Check for any signs of fluid leakage around the shock absorber body, or from the rubber gaiter around the piston rod **(see illustration)**. Should any fluid be noticed, the shock absorber is defective internally, and should be renewed. **Note:** *Shock absorbers should always be renewed in pairs on the same axle.*
10 The efficiency of the shock absorber may be checked by bouncing the car at each corner. Generally speaking, the body will return to its normal position and stop after being depressed. If it rises and returns on a rebound, the shock absorber is probably suspect. Also examine the shock absorber upper and lower mountings for any signs of wear.

14 Exhaust system check

1 With the engine cold (at least three hours after the vehicle has been driven), check the complete exhaust system, from its starting point at the engine to the end of the tailpipe.

13.2 Check the steering gaiters for signs of splitting

13.3 Check for wear in the front suspension and hub bearings

13.9 Check for signs of fluid leakage from the shock absorbers

Ideally, this should be done on a hoist, where unrestricted access is available; if a hoist is not available, raise and support the vehicle on axle stands (see 'Jacking and vehicle support').

2 Make sure that all brackets and rubber mountings are in good condition, and tight; if any of the mountings are to be renewed, ensure that the new ones are of the correct type – in the case of the rubber mountings, their colour is a good guide. Those nearest to the catalytic converter are more heat-resistant than the others **(see illustration)**.

3 Check the pipes and connections for evidence of leaks, severe corrosion, or damage. One of the most common points for a leak to develop is around the welded joints between the pipes and silencers. Leakage at any of the joints or in other parts of the system will usually show up as a black sooty stain in the vicinity of the leak. **Note:** *Exhaust sealants should not be used on any part of the exhaust system upstream of the catalytic converter (between the converter and engine) – even if the sealant does not contain additives harmful to the converter, pieces of it may break off and foul the element, causing local overheating.*

4 At the same time, inspect the underside of the body for holes, corrosion, open seams, etc, which may allow exhaust gases to enter the passenger compartment. Seal all body openings with silicone or body putty.

5 Rattles and other noises can often be traced to the exhaust system, especially the rubber mountings. Try to move the system, silencer(s), heat shields and catalytic converter. If any components can touch the body or suspension parts, secure the exhaust system with new mountings.

6 Check the running condition of the engine by inspecting inside the end of the tailpipe; the exhaust deposits here are an indication of the engine's state of tune. The inside of the tailpipe should be dry, and should vary in colour from dark grey to light grey/brown; if it is black and sooty, or coated with white deposits, this may indicate the need for a full fuel system inspection.

15 Roadwheel nut tightness check

1 Remove the wheel trims or alloy wheel centre covers, and slacken the roadwheel nuts slightly.

2 Tighten the nuts to the specified torque, using a torque wrench.

16 Hinge and lock lubrication

1 Work around the car and lubricate the hinges of the bonnet, doors and boot lid or tailgate with light oil.

14.2 Check the condition of the exhaust rubber mountings (arrowed)

2 Lightly lubricate the bonnet release mechanism with a smear of grease.

3 Check carefully the security and operation of all hinges, latches and locks, adjusting them where required. Check the operation of the central locking system.

4 Check the condition and operation of the tailgate struts, renewing them both if either is leaking or no longer able to support the tailgate securely when raised.

17 Electrical systems check

1 Check the operation of all instruments and electrical equipment, ie, lights, direction indicators, horn, etc. Refer to the appropriate sections of Chapter 12 for details if any of the circuits are found to be inoperative.

2 Note that the brake light switch is described in Chapter 9 Section 17.

3 Check all accessible wiring connectors, harnesses and retaining clips for security, and for signs of chafing or damage. Rectify any faults found.

18 Road test

Steering and suspension

1 Check for any abnormalities in the steering, suspension, handling or road 'feel'.

2 Drive the car, and check that there are no unusual vibrations or noises.

3 Check that the steering feels positive, with no excessive 'sloppiness', or roughness, and check for any suspension noises when cornering and driving over bumps.

Drivetrain

4 Check the performance of the engine, clutch, transmission and driveshafts.

5 Listen for any unusual noises from the engine, clutch and transmission.

6 Make sure that the engine runs smoothly when idling, and that there is no hesitation when accelerating.

7 Check that the clutch action is smooth and progressive, that the drive is taken up smoothly, and that the pedal travel is not excessive. Also listen for any noises when the clutch pedal is depressed.

8 Check that all gears can be engaged smoothly without noise, and that the gear lever action is smooth and not abnormally vague or 'notchy'.

9 Listen for a metallic clicking sound from the front of the car, as the car is driven slowly in a circle with the steering on full lock. Carry out this check in both directions. If a clicking noise is heard, this indicates wear in a driveshaft joint (see Chapter 8).

Braking system

10 Make sure that the car does not pull to one side when braking, and that the wheels do not lock when braking hard.

11 Check that there is no vibration through the steering when braking.

12 Check that the handbrake operates correctly, without excessive movement of the lever, and that it holds the car stationary on a slope.

13 Test the operation of the brake servo unit as follows. Depress the footbrake four or five times to exhaust the vacuum, then start the engine. As the engine starts, there should be a noticeable 'give' in the brake pedal as vacuum builds-up. Allow the engine to run for at least two minutes, and then switch it off. If the brake pedal is now depressed again, it should be possible to detect a hiss from the servo as the pedal is depressed. After about four or five applications, no further hissing should be heard, and the pedal should feel considerably harder.

19 Spark plug renewal

1 The correct functioning of the spark plugs is vital for the correct running and efficiency of the engine. It is essential that the plugs fitted are appropriate for the engine.

2 If the correct type is used and the engine is in good condition, the spark plugs should not need attention between scheduled intervals. Spark plug cleaning is rarely necessary, and should not be attempted unless specialised equipment is available, as damage can easily be caused to the firing ends.

3 Spark plug removal and refitting requires a spark plug socket, with an extension which can be turned by a ratchet handle or similar. This socket is lined with a rubber sleeve, to protect the porcelain insulator of the spark plug, and to hold the plug while you insert it into the spark plug hole. You will also need feeler blades and/or a spark plug gap checking gauge to check and adjust the spark plug electrode gap, and (ideally) a torque wrench to tighten the new plugs to the specified torque.

19.4 Pull the engine cover upwards

19.5a Undo the coil retaining bolt…

19.5b… and lift each coil from the top of the spark plug

4 To remove the spark plugs, first open the bonnet; the plugs are easily reached at the top of the engine. Pull the plastic cover on the top of the engine straight up to release its mountings **(see illustration)**.

5 The ignition coils are fitted one per plug, on the top of each spark plug. To aid refitment, use paint (or similar) to identify the ignition coils so they are refitted to their original positions. Undo the retaining bolts and lift each coil from the top of the spark plug **(see illustrations)**.

6 It is advisable to soak up any water in the spark plug recesses with a rag, and to remove any dirt from them using a clean brush, vacuum cleaner or compressed air before removing the plugs, to prevent any dirt or water from dropping into the cylinders.

⚠️ **Warning: Wear eye protection when using compressed air.**

7 Unscrew the spark plugs, ensuring that the socket is kept in alignment with each plug – if the socket is forcibly moved to either side, the porcelain top of the plug may be broken off. Remove the plug from the engine.

8 If any undue difficulty is encountered when unscrewing any of the spark plugs, carefully check the cylinder head threads and sealing surfaces for signs of wear, excessive corrosion or damage; if any of these conditions is found, seek the advice of a Ford dealer as to the best method of repair.

9 As each plug is removed, examine it as follows – this will give a good indication of the condition of the engine:

a) *If the insulator nose of the spark plug is clean and white, with no deposits, this is indicative of a weak mixture.*
b) *If the tip and insulator nose are covered with hard black-looking deposits, then this is indicative that the mixture is too rich.*
c) *Should the plug be black and oily, then it is likely that the engine is fairly worn, as well as the mixture being too rich.*
d) *If the insulator nose is covered with light tan to greyish-brown deposits, then the mixture is correct, and it is likely that the engine is in good condition.*

10 If you are renewing the spark plugs, purchase the new plugs, then check each of them first for faults such as cracked insulators or damaged threads.

11 The spark plug electrode gap is of considerable importance as, if it is too large or too small, the size of the spark and its efficiency will be seriously impaired. However, certain models covered by this manual may use spark plugs with multiple earth electrodes – unless there is clear information to the contrary, no attempt should be made to adjust the plug gap on a spark plug with more than one earth electrode.

12 To set the electrode gap on plugs with one earth electrode, measure the gap with a feeler gauge or gap checking/adjusting tool, and then bend open, or closed, the outer plug electrode until the correct gap is achieved **(see illustrations)**. The centre electrode should never be bent, as this may crack the insulation and cause plug failure, if nothing

worse. If the outer electrode is not exactly over the centre electrode, bend it gently to align them.

13 Before fitting the spark plugs, check that the threaded connector sleeves at the top of the plugs are tight (where fitted), and that the plug exterior surfaces and threads are clean. Brown staining on the porcelain, immediately above the metal body, is quite normal, and does not necessarily indicate a leak between the body and insulator.

14 On installing the spark plugs, first check that the cylinder head thread and sealing surface are as clean as possible; use a clean rag wrapped around a paintbrush to wipe clean the sealing surface. Apply a smear of copper-based grease or anti-seize compound to the threads of each plug, and screw them in by hand where possible. Take extra care to enter the plug threads correctly, as the cylinder head is made of aluminium alloy – it's often difficult to insert spark plugs into their holes without cross-threading them (see **Haynes Hint**).

15 When each spark plug is started correctly on its threads, screw it down until it just seats lightly, then tighten it to the specified torque wrench setting. If a torque wrench is not available – and this is one case where the use of a torque wrench is strongly recommended – tighten each spark plug through no more than 1/16th of a turn. Do not exceed the specified torque setting, and NEVER overtighten spark plugs.

16 Align the coil with the mounting bolt hole, then push it down firmly onto the spark plug.

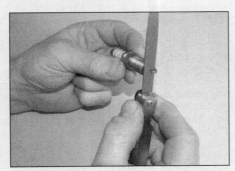

19.12a Measure the spark plug gap with a feeler blade…

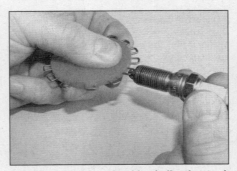

19.12b… or with a checking/adjusting tool

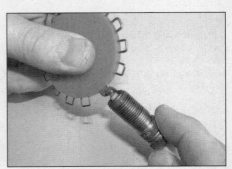

19.12c To change the gap, bend the outer electrode only

HAYNES HINT

It's often difficult to insert spark plugs into their holes without cross-threading them. To avoid this possibility, fit a short length of rubber or plastic hose over the end of the spark plug. The flexible hose acts as a universal joint, to help align the plug with the plug hole. Should the plug begin to cross thread, the hose will slip on the spark plug, preventing thread damage to the aluminium cylinder head.

Tighten the retaining bolt to the specified torque.

17 The remainder of refitting is a reversal of removal.

20 Air filter element renewal - petrol models

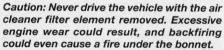

Caution: Never drive the vehicle with the air cleaner filter element removed. Excessive engine wear could result, and backfiring could even cause a fire under the bonnet.

1 The air filter element is located in the air cleaner assembly on the left-hand side of the engine compartment.

20.4 Lift the cover and pull out the filter element

2 Pull the plastic cover upwards from the top of the engine.

3 Undo the bolts securing the cover to the air cleaner housing.

4 The left-hand end of the cover can now be lifted, and the filter element removed **(see illustration)**. If preferred, the cover can be removed completely – this will allow a more thorough cleaning of the filter housing.

5 Loosen the clips and disconnect the air inlet duct and resonator air duct from the air cleaner cover.

6 Withdraw the cover and remove the filter element, noting its direction of fitting.

7 If carrying out a routine service, the element must be renewed regardless of its apparent condition.

8 If you are checking the element for any other reason, inspect its lower surface; if it is oily or very dirty, renew the element. If it is only moderately dusty, it can be re-used by blowing it clean from the upper to the lower surface with compressed air. Because it is a pleated-paper type filter, it cannot be washed or re-oiled. If it cannot be cleaned satisfactorily with compressed air, discard and renew it.

 Warning: Wear eye protection when using compressed air.

9 Where the air cleaner cover was removed, wipe out the inside of the housing. Check that no foreign matter is visible, either in the air inlet or in the air mass meter.

10 Refitting is the reverse of the removal procedure, noting the following points:

a) *Make sure that the filter is fitted the correct way up (observe any direction-of-fitting markings).*

b) *Ensure that the element and cover are securely seated, so that unfiltered air cannot enter the engine.*

c) *Where removed, secure the cover with the bolts, and ensure that the air inlet duct and resonator air duct securing clips are fully tightened.*

21 Auxiliary drivebelt renewal - petrol models

1 With the engine switched off, open and support the bonnet. For improved access to the right-hand end of the engine, first loosen the right-hand front wheel nuts, then jack up the front right-hand side of the car and support it securely on an axle stand (see *'Jacking and vehicle support'*). Remove the roadwheel, then remove the wheel arch liner from inside the wheel arch.

2 If the existing drivebelt is to be refitted, mark it, or note the maker's markings on its flat surface, so that it can be installed the same way round.

3 Using a socket or spanner on the drivebelt tensioner pulley centre bolt, rotate the pulley clockwise to release its pressure on the drivebelt.

4 Slip the drivebelt off the tensioner pulley, and release the tensioner again. Working from below or from the engine compartment as necessary, and noting its routing, slip the drivebelt off the remaining pulleys and withdraw it.

5 Check all the pulleys, ensuring that their grooves are clean, and removing all traces of oil and grease. Check that the tensioner works properly, with strong spring pressure being felt when its pulley is rotated clockwise, and a smooth return to the limit of its travel when released.

6 If the original drivebelt is being refitted, use the marks or notes made on removal, to ensure that it is installed to run in the same direction as it was previously. To fit the drivebelt, arrange it on the grooved pulleys so that it is centred in their grooves, and not overlapping their raised sides (note that the flat surface of the drivebelt is engaged on one or more pulleys) and routed correctly **(see illustration)**. Start at the top, and work down to finish at the bottom pulley; rotate the tensioner pulley clockwise, slip the drivebelt onto the bottom pulley, then release the tensioner again.

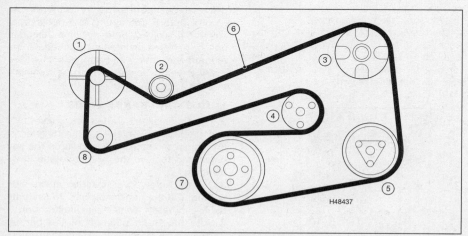

21.6 Auxiliary drivebelt routing

1 Alternator	5 Air conditioning compressor pulley
2 Idler pulley	6 Auxiliary drivebelt
3 Power steering pump pulley	7 Crankshaft pulley
4 Coolant pump pulley	8 Tensioner pulley

H48437

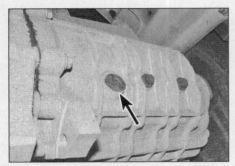

23.2 Manual transmission oil filler/level plug (arrowed)

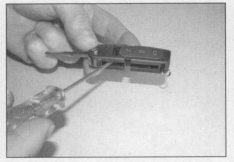

24.2a Insert a small screwdriver into the slot on the side of the transmitter unit...

24.2b... then push the screwdriver towards the key blade and remove the key blade

7 Using a spanner applied to the crankshaft pulley bolt, rotate the crankshaft through at least two full turns clockwise to settle the drivebelt on the pulleys, then check that the drivebelt is properly installed.

8 Refitting components is the reverse of removal, then lower the car to the ground and tighten the wheel nuts to the specified torque.

22 Brake fluid renewal

Warning: Brake hydraulic fluid can harm your eyes and damage painted surfaces, so use extreme caution when handling and pouring it. Do not use fluid that has been standing open for some time, as it absorbs moisture from the air. Excess moisture can cause a dangerous loss of braking effectiveness.

1 The procedure is similar to that for bleeding the hydraulic system as described in Chapter 9 Section 2, except that allowance should be made for the old fluid to be expelled when bleeding each section of the circuit.

2 Working as described in Section 27, open the first bleed screw in the sequence, and pump the brake pedal gently until the level in the reservoir is approaching the MIN mark. Top-up to the MAX level with new fluid, and continue pumping until only new fluid remains

in the reservoir, and new fluid can be seen emerging from the bleed screw. Tighten the screw, and top the reservoir level up to the MAX level line.

3 Work through all the remaining bleed screws in the sequence until new fluid can be seen at all of them. Be careful to keep the master cylinder reservoir topped-up above the MIN level at all times, or air may enter the system. If this happens, further bleeding will be required to remove the air.

4 When the operation is complete, check that all bleed screws are securely tightened, and that their dust caps are refitted. Wash off all traces of spilt fluid, and recheck the master cylinder reservoir fluid level.

5 Check the operation of the brakes before taking the car on the road.

23 Manual transmission oil level check

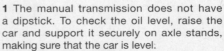

1 The manual transmission does not have a dipstick. To check the oil level, raise the car and support it securely on axle stands, making sure that the car is level.

2 The filler/level plug is located on the lower front side of the transmission housing. Using a suitable Allen key or socket, unscrew and remove it – take care, as it will probably be very tight**(see illustration)**.

3 If the lubricant level is correct, the oil should be up to the lower edge of the hole.

4 If the transmission needs more lubricant (if the oil level is not up to the hole), use a syringe, or a plastic bottle and tube, to add more.

5 Stop filling the transmission when the lubricant begins to run out of the hole, then wait until the flow of oil ceases.

6 Refit the filler/level plug, and tighten it to the specified torque wrench setting. Drive the car a short distance, then check for leaks.

7 A need for regular topping-up can only be due to a leak, which should be found and rectified without delay.

24 Remote control battery renewal

Note: *All the remote control units described below are fitted with a type CR2032, 3 volt battery.*

1 If the door locks repeatedly fail to respond to signals from the remote control at the normal distance, change the battery in the remote control before attempting to troubleshoot any of the vehicle's other systems. Although not in the Ford maintenance schedule, we recommend that the battery is changed every 2 years, regardless of the vehicle's mileage.

With a folding key blade

2 Insert a small flat-bladed screwdriver fully into the slot on the side of the transmitter unit, push the screwdriver towards the key blade and remove the key blade**(see illustrations)**.

3 Use the screwdriver, inserted at the side and front of the transmitter unit, to separate the two halves of the unit **(see illustration)**.

4 Note the fitted position of the battery (positive side down), then prise the battery from its location, and insert the new one**(see illustration)**. Avoid touching the battery or the terminals with bare fingers.

5 Snap the two halves of the transmitter together, and re-attach it to the key blade.

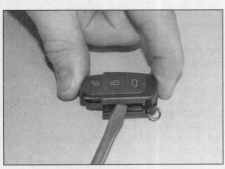

24.3 Insert the screwdriver at the side and front of the transmitter unit to separate the two halves

24.4 Note the fitted position of the battery, then prise it out and insert the new one

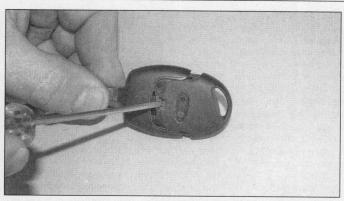

24.6 Insert a small screwdriver into the slot provided and slide the transmitter unit from the key blade

24.7 Release the clip each side and open the transmitter unit

Without a folding key blade

Type 1

6 Insert a small flat-bladed screwdriver into the slot provided and slide the transmitter unit from the key blade **(see illustration)**.

7 Use the screwdriver to release the clip each side and open the transmitter unit **(see illustration)**.

8 Note the fitted position of the battery (positive side up), then prise the battery from its location, and insert the new one **(see illustration)**. Avoid touching the battery or the terminals with bare fingers.

9 Snap the two halves of the transmitter together, and re-attach it to the key blade.

Type 2

10 Slide the release slider at the top of the transmitter sideways and remove the key blade.

11 Insert a small flat-bladed screwdriver into the slot at the top of the transmitter unit, then twist the screwdriver to separate the two halves of the unit.

12 Note the fitted position of the battery (positive side down), then prise the battery from its location, and insert the new one. Avoid touching the battery or the terminals with bare fingers.

13 Snap the two halves of the transmitter together, and refit the key blade.

Type 3

14 Depress the two tabs on the side of the transmitter unit and carefully lift off the cover **(see illustration)**.

15 Remove the key blade from the transmitter unit **(see illustration)**.

16 Insert a small flat-bladed screwdriver into the slot at the top of the transmitter unit, then twist the screwdriver to separate the two halves of the unit **(see illustration)**.

17 Insert the screwdriver into the side of the transmitter to open the unit **(see illustration)**.

18 Note the fitted position of the battery (positive side down), then prise the battery from its location, and insert the new one **(see illustration)**. Avoid touching the battery or the terminals with bare fingers.

19 Snap the two halves of the transmitter together, place the key blade in position and refit the cover.

24.8 Note the fitted position of the battery, then prise it out and insert the new one

24.14 Depress the tabs on the side of the transmitter unit and carefully lift off the cover

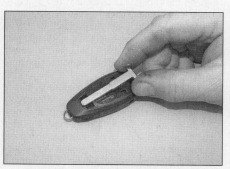

24.15 Remove the key blade from the transmitter unit

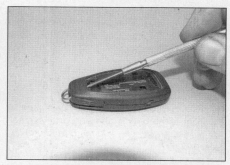

24.16 Insert a small screwdriver into the slot provided, then twist the screwdriver to separate the two halves of theunit

24.17 Insert the screwdriver into the side of the transmitter to open the unit

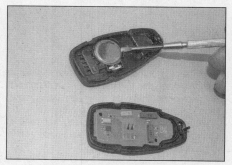

24.18 Note the fitted position of the battery, then prise it out and insert the new one

25 Coolant strength check and renewal

 Warning: Do not allow antifreeze to come in contact with your skin or painted surfaces of the vehicle. Flush contaminated areas immediately with plenty of water. Don't store new coolant, or leave old coolant lying around, where it's accessible to children or pets – they're attracted by its sweet smell. Ingestion of even a small amount of coolant can be fatal. Wipe up garage-floor and drip-pan spills immediately. Keep antifreeze containers covered, and repair cooling system leaks as soon as they're noticed.

Warning: Never remove the expansion tank filler cap when the engine is running, or has just been switched off, as the cooling system will be hot, and the consequent escaping steam and scalding coolant could cause serious injury.

Warning: Wait until the engine is cold before starting these procedures.

Strength check

1 Use a hydrometer to check the strength of the antifreeze. Follow the instructions provided with your hydrometer. The antifreeze strength should be approximately 50%. If it is significantly less than this, drain a little coolant from the radiator (see this Section), add antifreeze to the coolant expansion tank, then recheck the strength.

Coolant draining

2 To drain the system, first remove the expansion tank filler cap.
3 Firmly apply the handbrake, then jack up the front of the vehicle and support it securely on axle stands (see 'Jacking and vehicle support').
4 Place a suitable container beneath the left-hand side of the radiator.
5 Open the radiator drain tap and allow the coolant to drain into the container.
6 Once the coolant has stopped draining from the radiator, close the drain tap.

System flushing

7 With time, the cooling system may gradually lose its efficiency, as the radiator core becomes choked with rust, scale deposits from the water, and other sediment. To minimise this, as well as using only good-quality antifreeze and clean soft water, the system should be flushed as follows whenever any part of it is disturbed, and/or when the coolant is renewed.
8 With the coolant drained and the drain tap closed, refill the system with fresh water. Refit the expansion tank filler cap, start the engine and warm it up to normal operating temperature, then stop it and (after allowing it to cool down completely) drain the system again. Repeat as necessary until only clean water can be seen to emerge, then refill finally with the specified coolant mixture.
9 If only clean, soft water and good-quality antifreeze (even if not to Ford's specification) has been used, and the coolant has been renewed at the suggested intervals, the above procedure will be sufficient to keep the system clean for a considerable length of time. If, however, the system has been neglected, a more thorough operation will be required, as follows.
10 First drain the coolant, then disconnect the radiator top and bottom hoses. Insert a garden hose into the radiator top hose connection, and allow water to circulate through the radiator until it runs clean from the bottom outlet.
11 To flush the engine, insert the garden hose into the radiator bottom hose, wrap a piece of rag around the garden hose to seal the connection, and allow water to circulate until it runs clear.
12 Try the effect of repeating this procedure in the top hose, although this may not be effective, since the thermostat will probably close and prevent the flow of water.
13 In severe cases of contamination, reverse-flushing of the radiator may be necessary. This may be achieved by inserting the garden hose into the bottom outlet, wrapping a piece of rag around the hose to seal the connection, then flushing the radiator until clear water emerges from the top hose outlet.
14 If the radiator is suspected of being severely choked, remove the radiator (Chapter 3 Section 6), turn it upside-down, and repeat the procedure described in paragraph 13.
15 The use of chemical cleaners is not recommended, and should be necessary only as a last resort; the scouring action of some chemical cleaners may lead to other cooling system problems. Normally, regular renewal of the coolant will prevent excessive contamination of the system.

Antifreeze type and mixture

Caution: Do not use engine antifreeze in the windscreen/tailgate washer system, as it will damage the vehicle's paintwork. A screenwash additive should be added to the washer system in its maker's recommended quantities.

16 If the vehicle's history (and therefore the quality of the antifreeze in it) is unknown, owners are advised to drain and thoroughly reverse-flush the system, before refilling with fresh coolant mixture.
17 If the antifreeze used is to Ford's specification, the levels of protection it affords are indicated in the coolant packaging.
18 To give the recommended standard mixture ratio for antifreeze, 50% (by volume) of antifreeze must be mixed with 50% of clean, soft water; if you are using any other type of antifreeze, follow its manufacturer's instructions to achieve the correct ratio.
19 You are unlikely to fully drain the system at any one time (unless the engine is being completely stripped), and the capacities quoted in the Specifications are therefore slightly academic for routine coolant renewal. As a guide, only two-thirds of the system's total capacity is likely to be needed for coolant renewal.
20 As the drained system will be partially filled with flushing water, in order to establish the recommended mixture ratio, measure out 50% of the system capacity in antifreeze and pour it into the hose/expansion tank as described above, then top-up with water. Any topping-up while refilling the system should be done with water – for *Weekly checks* use a suitable mixture.
21 Before adding antifreeze, the cooling system should be drained, preferably flushed, and all hoses checked for condition and security; fresh antifreeze will rapidly find any weaknesses in the system.
22 After filling with antifreeze, a label should be attached to the expansion tank, stating the type and concentration of antifreeze used, and the date installed. Any subsequent topping-up should be made with the same type and concentration of antifreeze.

Coolant filling

23 Before attempting to fill the cooling system, make sure that all hoses and clips are in good condition, and that the clips are tight. Note that an antifreeze mixture must be used all year round, to prevent corrosion of the engine components.
24 As part of the system will already have water in it, initially pour in 50% of the system capacity in antifreeze, then top-up with water.
25 Slowly fill the system until the coolant level reaches the neck of the expansion tank.
26 With the filler cap not fitted, start the engine and run it at 2500 rpm for 1 minute – this will prime the heater circuit.
27 Switch off the engine, then fill the expansion tank to 15 mm over the MAX mark.
28 Refit the filler cap, then start the engine and run it at 2500 rpm for 11 minutes, or until the engine reaches normal operating temperature.
29 Maintain the engine speed at 2500 rpm for a further 3 minutes, then increase the engine speed to 4000 rpm for 5 seconds.
30 Decrease the engine speed to 2500 rpm for 3 minutes and switch off the engine.
31 Check the cooling system for leaks, then allow the engine to cool for at least 30 minutes.
32 Remove the filler cap and top-up the coolant level to the MAX mark on the expansion tank.

General cooling system checks

33 The engine should be cold for the cooling system checks, so perform the following procedure before driving the vehicle, or after it has been shut off for at least three hours.

Routine maintenance and servicing – petrol models

34 Remove the expansion tank filler cap, and clean it thoroughly inside and out with a rag. Also clean the filler neck on the expansion tank. The presence of rust or corrosion in the filler neck indicates that the coolant should be changed. The coolant inside the expansion tank should be relatively clean and transparent. If it is rust-coloured, drain and flush the system, and refill with a fresh coolant mixture.

35 Carefully check the radiator hoses and heater hoses along their entire length; renew any hose which is cracked, swollen or deteriorated.

36 Inspect all other cooling system components (joint faces, etc) for leaks. A leak in the cooling system will usually show up as white- or antifreeze-coloured deposits on the area adjoining the leak. Where any problems of this nature are found on system components, renew the component or gasket with reference to Chapter 3.

Airlocks

37 If, after draining and refilling the system, symptoms of overheating are found which did not occur previously, then the fault is almost certainly due to trapped air at some point in the system, causing an airlock and restricting the flow of coolant; usually, the air is trapped because the system was refilled too quickly.

38 If an airlock is suspected, first try gently squeezing all visible coolant hoses. A coolant hose which is full of air feels quite different to one full of coolant when squeezed. After refilling the system, most airlocks will clear once the system has cooled, and been topped-up.

39 While the engine is running at operating temperature, switch on the heater and heater fan, and check for heat output. Provided there is sufficient coolant in the system, lack of heat output could be due to an airlock in the system.

40 Airlocks can have more serious effects than simply reducing heater output – a severe airlock could reduce coolant flow around the engine. Check that the radiator top hose is hot when the engine is at operating temperature – a top hose which stays cold could be the result of an airlock (or a non-opening thermostat).

41 If the problem persists, stop the engine and allow it to cool down completely, before unscrewing the expansion tank filler cap or loosening the hose clips and squeezing the hoses to bleed out the trapped air. In the worst case, the system will have to be at least partially drained (this time, the coolant can be saved for re-use) and flushed to clear the problem. If all else fails, have the system evacuated and vacuum-filled by a suitably-equipped garage.

Expansion tank cap check

42 Wait until the engine is completely cold – perform this check before the engine is started for the first time in the day.

43 Place a wad of cloth over the expansion tank cap, then unscrew it slowly and remove it.

44 Examine the condition of the rubber seal on the underside of the cap. If the rubber appears to have hardened, or cracks are visible in the seal edges, a new cap should be fitted.

45 If the car is several years old, or has covered a large mileage, consider renewing the cap regardless of its apparent condition – they are not expensive. If the pressure relief valve built into the cap fails, excess pressure in the system will lead to puzzling failures of hoses and other cooling system components.

Chapter 1 Part B
Routine maintenance and servicing – diesel models

Contents

Degrees of difficulty

Easy, suitable for novice with little experience 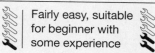 | Fairly easy, suitable for beginner with some experience | Fairly difficult, suitable for competent DIY mechanic | Difficult, suitable for experienced DIY mechanic | Very difficult, suitable for expert DIY or professional

1 Servicing specifications – diesel models

Lubricants and fluids

Refer to Lubricants, fluids and tyre pressures

Capacities

Engine oil (including oil filter)	5.6 litres
Cooling system:	
1.8 litre engines	7.9 litres
2.0 litre engines	8.1 litres
Automatic transmission (total capacity)	7.0 litres
Manual transmission:	
5-speed transmissions....................................	1.9 litres
6-speed transmissions....................................	1.75 litres
Washer fluid reservoir..	3.8 litres
Fuel tank	70.0 litres

Cooling system

Antifreeze mixture:	
50% antifreeze	Protection down to -37°C

Note: *Refer to antifreeze manufacturer for latest recommendations.*

Brakes

Friction material minimum thickness:	
Front brake pads	2.0 mm
Rear brake pads.....................................	1.5 mm

Remote control battery

Type	CR2032, 3.0 volt

Torque wrench settings

	Nm	lbf ft
Automatic transmission fluid drain/filler plugs:		
Drain plug...................................	47	35
Filler plug	40	30
Level checking plug	8	6
Engine oil drain plug:		
1.8 litre engines	36	27
2.0 litre engines	34	25
Manual transmission filler/level plug	35	26
Roadwheel nuts	140	103

2 Maintenance schedule – diesel models

1 The maintenance intervals in this manual are provided with the assumption that you, not the dealer, will be carrying out the work. These are the minimum maintenance intervals based on the standard service schedule recommended by the manufacturer for vehicles driven daily. If you wish to keep your vehicle in peak condition at all times, you may wish to perform some of these procedures more often. We encourage frequent maintenance, because it enhances the efficiency, performance and resale value of your vehicle.
2 If the vehicle is driven in dusty areas, used to tow a trailer, or driven frequently at slow speeds (idling in traffic) or on short journeys, more frequent maintenance intervals are recommended.
3 When the vehicle is new, it should be serviced by a dealer service department (or other workshop recognised by the vehicle manufacturer as providing the same standard of service) in order to preserve the warranty. The vehicle manufacturer may reject warranty claims if you are unable to prove that servicing has been carried out as and when specified, using only original equipment parts or parts certified to be of equivalent quality.

Every 250 miles or weekly
☐ Refer to 'Weekly checks'.

Every 6000 miles or 6 months, whichever comes first
☐ Reset the service interval indicator (Section 4)
☐ Renew the engine oil and filter (Section 6)

Note: *Ford recommend that the engine oil and filter are changed every 12 500 miles or 12 months. However, oil and filter changes are good for the engine, and we recommend that the oil and filter are renewed more frequently, especially if the car is used on a lot of short journeys.*

Every 12 500 miles or 12 months, whichever comes first
In addition to the items listed above, carry out the following:
☐ Renew the pollen filter (Section 7)
☐ Check all components, pipes and hoses for fluid leaks (Section 8)
☐ Check the condition of the auxiliary drivebelt (Section 9)
☐ Check the antifreeze/inhibitor strength (Section 30)
☐ Drain any water from the fuel filter (Section 10)
☐ Check the condition and operation of the seat belts (Section 11)
☐ Check the braking system (Section 12)
☐ Check the condition of the driveshaft gaiters (Section 13)
☐ Check the steering and suspension components for condition and security (Section 14)
☐ Check the condition of the exhaust system components (Section 15)

Every 12 500 miles or 12 months, whichever comes first (continued)
☐ Check the roadwheel nuts are tightened to the specified torque (Section 16)
☐ Lubricate all door, bonnet, boot lid and tailgate hinges and locks (Section 17)
☐ Check the operation of the horn, all lights, and the wipers and washers (Section 18)
☐ Carry out a road test (Section 19)

Every 37 500 miles or 3 years, whichever comes first
In addition to the items listed above, carry out the following:
☐ Check and if necessary adjust the valve clearances – 1.8 litre engines (Section 20)
☐ Renew the fuel filter (Section 21)
☐ Renew the air filter (Section 22)

Every 62 500 miles
☐ Renew the timing belt and tensioner (Section 23)

Note: *On certain 2.0 litre engines, the Ford interval for belt renewal is actually at a much higher mileage than this (125 000 miles or 10 years). It is strongly recommended, however, that the interval is reduced to 62 500 miles, particularly on vehicles which are subjected to intensive use, ie, mainly short journeys or a lot of stop-start driving. The actual belt renewal interval is therefore very much up to the individual owner, but bear in mind that severe engine damage will result if the belt breaks.*

Every 125 000 miles or 10 years, whichever comes first
☐ Renew the auxiliary drivebelt (Section 24)
☐ Renew the fuel pump drive chain or belt – 1.8 litre engines (Section 25)

Every 2 years, regardless of mileage
☐ Renew the brake fluid (Section 26)
☐ Check the automatic transmission fluid level (Section 27)
☐ Check the manual transmission oil level (Section 28)
☐ Renew the remote control battery (Section 29)
☐ Renew the coolant (Section 30)*

Note: ** Ford state that, if their SuperPlus antifreeze is in the system, the coolant need only be changed every 10 years. If there is any doubt as to the type or quality of the antifreeze which has been used, we recommend this shorter interval be observed.*

3 Component location – diesel models

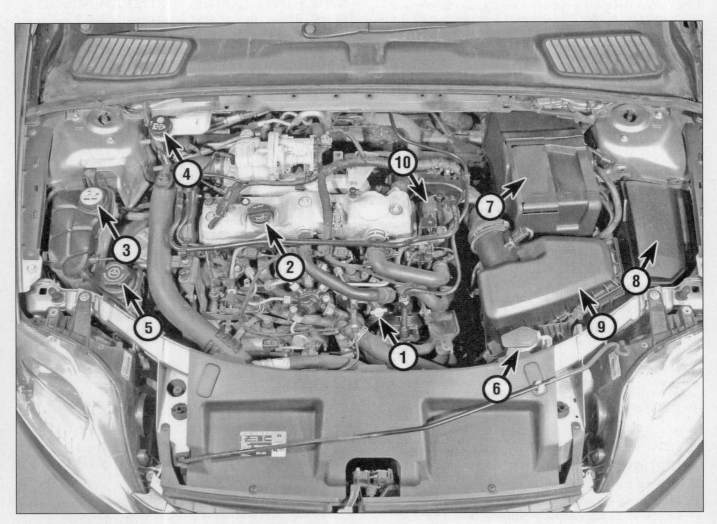

Underbonnet view of a 1.8 litre model

1 Engine oil level dipstick
2 Engine oil filler cap
3 Coolant reservoir (expansion tank)
4 Brake and clutch fluid reservoir

5 Power steering fluid reservoir
6 Washer fluid reservoir
7 Battery cover

8 Engine compartment fuse/relay box
9 Air cleaner
10 Fuel filter

Underbonnet view of a 2.0 litre model (emission level Stage III/IV)

1 Engine oil level dipstick
2 Engine oil filler cap
3 Coolant reservoir (expansion tank)
4 Brake and clutch fluid reservoir
5 Power steering fluid reservoir
6 Washer fluid reservoir
7 Battery cover
8 Engine compartment fuse/relay box
9 Air cleaner

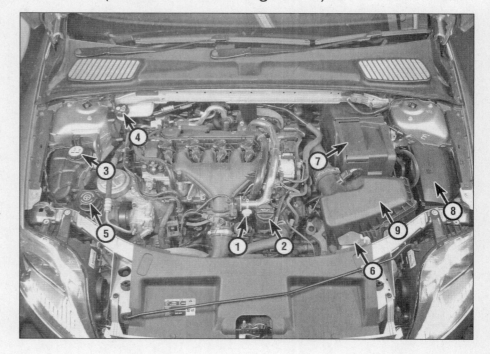

Underbonnet view of a 2.0 litre model (emission level Stage V)

1 Engine oil level dipstick
2 Engine oil filler cap
3 Coolant reservoir (expansion tank)
4 Brake and clutch fluid reservoir
5 Power steering fluid reservoir
6 Washer fluid reservoir
7 Battery cover
8 Engine compartment fuse/relay box
9 Air cleaner

Front underbody view of a 1.8 litre model

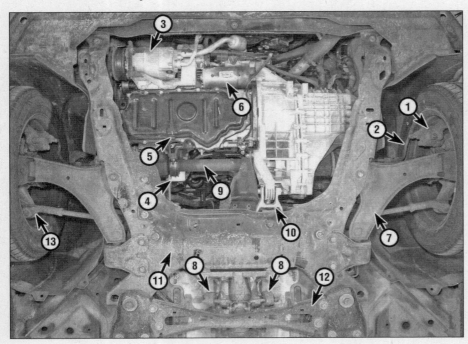

1 Brake caliper
2 Brake hose
3 Air conditioning compressor
4 Oil filter
5 Engine oil drain plug
6 Starter motor
7 Suspension lower arm
8 Exhaust front mounting
9 Driveshaft
10 Engine rear mounting
11 Subframe
12 Subframe cross-brace
13 Track rod end

Front underbody view of a 2.0 litre model (emission level Stage III/IV)

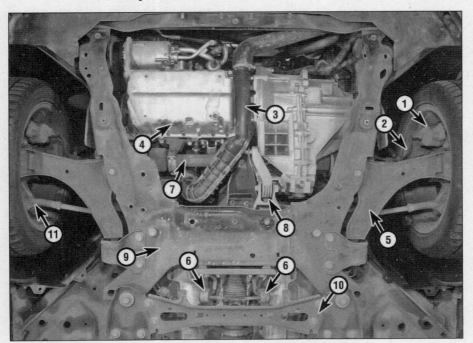

1 Brake caliper
2 Brake hose
3 Intercooler charge air pipe
4 Engine oil drain plug
5 Suspension lower arm
6 Exhaust front mounting
7 Driveshaft
8 Engine rear mounting
9 Subframe
10 Subframe cross-brace
11 Track rod end

Front underbody view of a 2.0 litre model (emission level Stage V)

1 Brake caliper
2 Brake hose
3 Intercooler charge air pipe
4 Engine oil drain plug
5 Suspension lower arm
6 Exhaust front mounting
7 Driveshaft
8 Engine rear mounting
9 Subframe
10 Subframe cross-brace
11 Track rod end

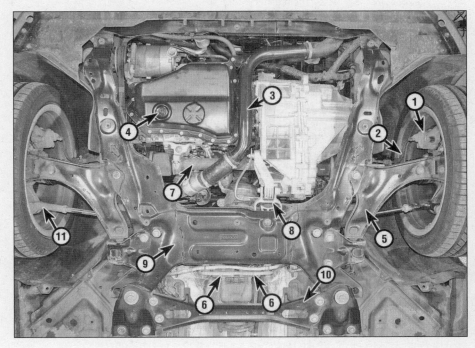

Rear underbody view of a 2.0 litre model

1 Anti-roll bar
2 Fuel filter
3 Fuel tank
4 Silencer
5 Shock absorber
6 Lateral link
7 Lower control arm
8 Tie rod
9 Subframe

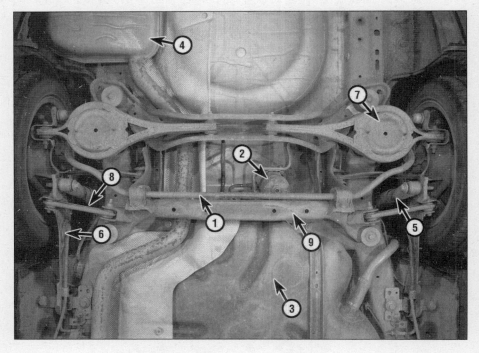

4 General Information

1 This Chapter is designed to help the home mechanic maintain his/her car for safety, economy, long life and peak performance.

2 The Chapter contains a master maintenance schedule, followed by Sections dealing specifically with each task in the schedule. Visual checks, adjustments, component renewal and other helpful items are included. Refer to the accompanying illustrations of the engine compartment and the underside of the car for the locations of the various components.

3 Servicing your car in accordance with the mileage/time maintenance schedule and the following Sections will provide a planned maintenance programme, which should result in a long and reliable service life. This is a comprehensive plan, so maintaining some items but not others at the specified service intervals will not produce the same results.

4 As you service your car, you will discover that many of the procedures can – and should – be grouped together, because of the particular procedure being performed, or because of the proximity of two otherwise-unrelated components to one another. For example, if the car is raised for any reason, the exhaust can be inspected at the same time as the suspension and steering components.

5 The first step in this maintenance programme is to prepare yourself before the actual work begins. Read through all the Sections relevant to the work to be carried out, then make a list and gather all the parts and tools required. If a problem is encountered, seek advice from a parts specialist, or a dealer service department.

Service interval indicator

6 The service interval indicator is a 'change oil' warning lamp or 'service oil' message that must be reset every time the engine oil is changed. The reset procedure is as follows:
a) Ensure that all doors are closed.
b) Switch the ignition on and fully depress both the brake and accelerator pedals for at least 15 seconds.

c) With both pedals still depressed, press the OK button on the steering wheel.
d) Release the pedals and switch off the ignition.

5 Regular maintenance

1 If, from the time the car is new, the routine maintenance schedule is followed closely, and frequent checks are made of fluid levels and high-wear items, as suggested throughout this manual, the engine will be kept in relatively good running condition, and the need for additional work will be minimised.

2 It is possible that there will be times when the engine is running poorly due to the lack of regular maintenance. This is even more likely if a used car, which has not received regular and frequent maintenance checks, is purchased. In such cases, additional work may need to be carried out, outside of the regular maintenance intervals.

3 If engine wear is suspected, a compression test or leakdown test (refer to the relevant Part of Chapter 2A Section 2) will provide valuable information regarding the overall performance of the main internal components. Such a test can be used as a basis to decide on the extent of the work to be carried out. If, for example, a compression test indicates serious internal engine wear, conventional maintenance as described in this Chapter will not greatly improve the performance of the engine, and may prove a waste of time and money, unless extensive overhaul work is carried out first.

4 The following series of operations are those most often required to improve the performance of a generally poor-running engine:

Primary operations

a) Clean, inspect and test the battery (refer to 'Weekly checks').
b) Check all the engine-related fluids (refer to 'Weekly checks').
c) Check the condition of all hoses, and check for fluid leaks (Section 8).
d) Check the condition of the auxiliary drivebelt (Section 9).

e) Renew the fuel filter (Section 21).
f) Check the condition of the air filter, and renew if necessary (Section 22).

5 If the above operations do not prove fully effective, carry out the following secondary operations:

Secondary operations

6 All items listed under Primary operations, plus the following:
a) Check the charging system (Chapter 5A Section 5).
b) Check the preheating system (Chapter 5A Section 11).
c) Check the fuel system (Chapter 4B Section 3).

6 Engine oil and filter renewal – diesel models

1 Frequent oil and filter changes are the most important preventive maintenance procedures which can be undertaken by the DIY owner. As engine oil ages, it becomes diluted and contaminated, which leads to premature engine wear.

2 Before starting this procedure, gather together all the necessary tools and materials. Also make sure that you have plenty of clean rags and newspapers handy, to mop-up any spills. Ideally, the engine oil should be warm, as it will drain more easily, and more built-up sludge will be removed with it. Take care not to touch the exhaust or any other hot parts of the engine when working under the vehicle. To avoid any possibility of scalding, and to protect yourself from possible skin irritants and other harmful contaminants in used engine oils, it is advisable to wear gloves when carrying out this work.

3 Remove the plastic cover on the top of the engine. Pull up the right-hand rear corner and the front edges, then pull the cover forwards to release it (see illustration).

1.8 litre engines

4 The canister-type oil filter is located on the rear of the engine block. Firmly apply the handbrake, then jack up the front of the vehicle and support it on axle stands (see 'Jacking and vehicle support'). Undo the fasteners and remove the engine undertray.

5 Move a container into position under the oil filter, then use an oil filter removal tool if necessary to slacken the filter cartridge initially, then unscrew it by hand the rest of the way (see illustration). Empty the oil from the old filter into the container.

6 Use a clean rag to remove all oil, dirt and sludge from the filter sealing area on the engine.

7 Apply a light coating of clean engine oil to the sealing ring on the new filter, then screw the filter into position on the engine. Tighten the filter firmly by hand only – do not use any tools.

6.3 Remove the plastic cover by pulling it upwards starting at the front edge

6.5 The oil filter (arrowed) is located on the rear of the cylinder block – 1.8 litre engines

6.8 Disengage the retaining tab and lift the engine oil filler pipe from its location – 2.0 litre engines to Stage V emission level

6.9a Undo the oil filter cap (arrowed)...

6.9b... then lift up the cap with the filter element...

2.0 litre engines

8 On engines to emission level Stage V, disengage the retaining tab and lift the engine oil filler pipe from its location (**see illustration**). Move the pipe to one side for access to the oil filter.

9 Using a 27 mm socket on an extension bar, undo the oil filter housing cap. Lift the cap up, with the oil filter inside it. Discard the filter and the O-ring around the circumference of the cap (**see illustrations**).

10 Ensure the oil filter housing and cap are clean, then fit a new O-ring seal to the cap.

11 Fit the new filter element into the cap, then fit the cap to the housing and tighten it securely.

12 Where applicable, refit the oil filler pipe back in position.

All engines

13 If not already done so, firmly apply the handbrake, then jack up the front of the vehicle and support it on axle stands (see '*Jacking and vehicle support*'). Unscrew the fasteners and remove the plastic undertray below the engine.

14 Using a spanner, socket or Allen key as applicable, slacken the drain plug about half a turn. Position the draining container under the drain plug, then remove the plug completely (**see illustrations**).

 As the drain plug threads release, move it sharply away so the stream of oil issuing from the sump runs into the container, not up your sleeve.

15 Allow some time for the oil to drain, noting that it may be necessary to reposition the container as the oil flow slows to a trickle.

16 After all the oil has drained, wipe the drain plug and the sealing washer (where fitted) with a clean rag. Examine the condition of the sealing washer, and renew it if it shows signs of scoring or other damage which may prevent an oil-tight seal (it is generally considered good practice to fit a new washer every time). Clean the area around the drain plug opening, and refit the plug complete with the washer and tighten it to the specified torque (**see illustration**).

6.9c... pull the element from the cap...

6.9d... and discard the O-ring seal – 2.0 litre engines

6.14a Engine oil drain plug (arrowed) – 1.8 litre engines...

6.14b... and 2.0 litre engines (arrowed) to Stage III/IV emission level

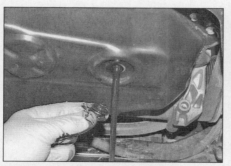

6.14c Unscrew the drain plug and allow the oil to drain – 2.0 litre engines to Stage V emission level shown

6.16 Renew the drain plug sealing washer

17 Remove the old oil and all tools from under the vehicle, refit the undertray, then lower the vehicle to the ground.

18 With the car on level ground, fill the engine, using the correct grade and type of oil (refer to 'Weekly checks' for details of topping-up). An oil can spout or funnel may help to reduce spillage. Pour in half the specified quantity of oil first, then wait a few minutes for the oil to run to the sump.

19 Continue adding oil a small quantity at a time until the level is up to the MIN mark on the dipstick. Adding around 1.0 litre of oil will now bring the level up to the MAX on the dipstick – do not worry if a little too much goes in, as some of the excess will be taken up in filling the oil filter. Refit the dipstick and the filler cap.

20 Start the engine and run it for a few minutes, while checking for leaks around the oil filter seal and the sump drain plug. Note that there may be a delay of a few seconds before the low oil pressure warning light goes out when the engine is first started, as the oil circulates through the new oil filter and the engine oil galleries before the pressure builds-up.

21 Stop the engine, and wait a few minutes for the oil to settle in the sump once more. With the new oil circulated and the filter now completely full, recheck the level on the dipstick, and add more oil as necessary.

22 Dispose of the used engine oil and filter safely, with reference to *General repair procedures* in the Reference Chapter of this manual. Do not discard the old filter with domestic household waste. The facility for waste oil disposal provided by many local council refuse tips and/or recycling centres generally has a filter receptacle alongside.

7 Pollen filter renewal

1 Working in the footwell on the passenger's side, release the two retainers and remove the trim panel beneath the glovebox (**see illustrations**).

2 Turn the locking catch through 90° and lower the generic electronics module (GEM) from its location. Lift the module from the two lower pivots and place it to one side (**see illustrations**).

3 Undo the three screws and remove the pollen filter housing cover (**see illustrations**). Note that access is limited in this area but can be improved if the glovebox is removed as described in Chapter 11 Section 27.

4 Slide out the pollen filter, into the passenger's footwell, and remove it (**see illustration**).

5 When fitting the new filter, note the direction-of-airflow arrow marked on its top edge – the arrow should point into the car.

6 Slide the filter fully into position, refit the filter housing cover and secure the cover with the three retaining screws.

7 Where applicable, refit the glovebox as described in Chapter 11 Section 27.

8 Refit the generic electronics module and the trim panel beneath the glovebox.

8 Hose and fluid leak check

Note: *Also refer to Sections 9 and 26.*

General

1 Visually inspect the engine joint faces, gaskets and seals for any signs of water or oil leaks. Pay particular attention to the areas around the cylinder head cover, cylinder head, oil filter and sump joint faces. Bear in mind that, over a period of time, some very slight seepage from these areas is to be expected – what you are really looking for is any indication of a serious leak. Should a leak be found, renew the offending gasket or oil seal by referring to the appropriate Chapters in this manual.

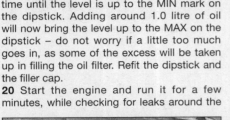

7.1a Release the two retainers…

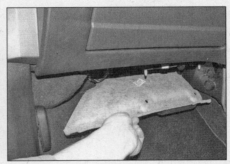

7.1b… and remove the trim panel beneath the glovebox

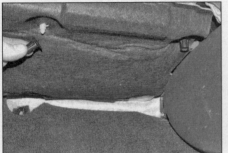

7.2a Turn the locking catch through 90° and lower the generic electronics module…

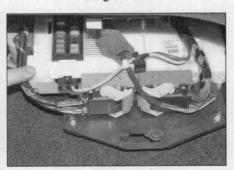

7.2b… then lift the module from the two lower pivots and place it to one side

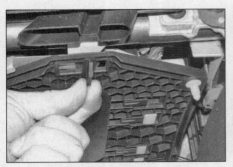

7.3a Undo the three screws (arrowed)…

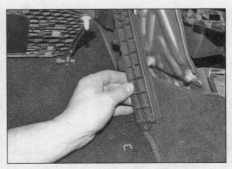

7.3b… and remove the pollen filter housing cover

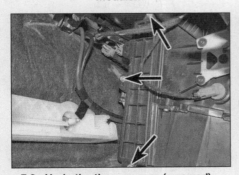

7.4 Slide out the pollen filter, into the passenger's footwell, and remove it

2 High temperatures in the engine compart-ment can cause the deterioration of the rubber and plastic hoses used for engine, accessory and emission systems operation. Periodic inspection should be made for cracks, loose clamps, material hardening and leaks.

3 When checking the hoses, ensure that all the cable-ties or clips used to retain the hoses are in place, and in good condition. Clips which are broken or missing can lead to chafing of the hoses, pipes or wiring, which could cause more serious problems in the future.

4 Carefully check the large top and bottom radiator hoses, along with the other smaller-diameter cooling system hoses and metal pipes; do not forget the heater hoses/pipes which run from the engine to the bulkhead. Inspect each hose along its entire length, renewing any that is cracked, swollen or shows signs of deterioration. Cracks may become more apparent if the hose is squeezed, and may often be apparent at the hose ends.

5 Make sure that all hose connections are tight. If the large-diameter air hoses from the air cleaner are loose, they will leak air, and upset the engine idle quality. If the spring clamps that are used to secure some of the hoses appear to be slackening, they should be updated with worm-drive clips to prevent the possibility of leaks.

6 Some other hoses are secured to their fittings with clamps. Where clamps are used, check to be sure they haven't lost their tension, allowing the hose to leak. If clamps aren't used, make sure the hose has not expanded and/or hardened where it slips over the fitting, allowing it to leak.

7 Check all fluid reservoirs, filler caps, drain plugs and fittings, etc, looking for any signs of leakage of oil, transmission and/or brake hydraulic fluid and coolant. Where applicable, also check the clutch hydraulic fluid lines which lead from the fluid reservoir, master cylinder, and the slave cylinder (on the transmission).

8 If the vehicle is regularly parked in the same place, close inspection of the ground underneath it will soon show any leaks; ignore the puddle of water which may be left if the air conditioning system is in use. Place a clean piece of cardboard below the engine, and examine it for signs of contamination after the vehicle has been parked over it overnight – be aware, however, of the fire risk inherent in placing combustible material below the catalytic converter.

9 Remember that some leaks will only occur with the engine running, or when the engine is hot or cold. With the handbrake firmly applied, start the engine from cold, and let the engine idle while you examine the underside of the engine compartment for signs of leakage.

10 If an unusual smell is noticed inside or around the car, especially when the engine is thoroughly hot, this may point to the presence of a leak.

11 As soon as a leak is detected, its source must be traced and rectified. Where oil has been leaking for some time, it is usually necessary to use a steam cleaner, pressure washer or similar, to clean away the accumulated dirt, so that the exact source of the leak can be identified.

Vacuum hoses

12 It's quite common for vacuum hoses, especially those in the emissions system, to be colour-coded, or to be identified by coloured stripes moulded into them. Various systems require hoses with different wall thicknesses, collapse resistance and temperature resistance. When renewing hoses, be sure the new ones are made of the same material.

13 Often the only effective way to check a hose is to remove it completely from the vehicle. If more than one hose is removed, be sure to label the hoses and fittings to ensure correct installation.

14 When checking vacuum hoses, be sure to include any plastic T-fittings in the check. Inspect the fittings for cracks, and check the hose where it fits over the fitting for distortion, which could cause leakage.

15 A small piece of vacuum hose (approximately 6 mm inside diameter) can be used as a stethoscope to detect vacuum leaks. Hold one end of the hose near your ear, and probe around vacuum hoses and fittings, listening for the 'hissing' sound characteristic of a vacuum leak.

 Warning: When probing with the vacuum hose stethoscope, be very careful not to come into contact with moving engine components such as the auxiliary drivebelt, radiator electric cooling fan, etc.

Fuel hoses

 Warning: There are certain precautions which must be taken when inspecting or servicing fuel system components. Work in a well-ventilated area, and do not allow open flames (cigarettes, appliance pilot lights, etc) or bare light bulbs near the work area. Mop-up any spills immediately, and do not store fuel-soaked rags where they could ignite.

16 Check all fuel hoses for deterioration and chafing. Check especially for cracks in areas where the hose bends, and also just before fittings, such as where a hose attaches to the fuel rail.

17 High-quality fuel line, usually identified by the word 'Fluoroelastomer' printed on the hose, should be used for fuel line renewal. Never, under any circumstances, use non-reinforced vacuum line, clear plastic tubing or water hose as a substitute for fuel lines.

18 Spring-type clamps may be used on fuel lines. These clamps often lose their tension over a period of time, and can be 'sprung' during removal. Renew all spring-type clamps with proper fuel pipe clips whenever a hose is renewed.

Metal pipes

19 Sections of metal piping are often used for fuel line between the fuel tank and the engine, and for most air conditioning applications. Check carefully to be sure the piping has not been bent or crimped, and that cracks have not started in the line; also check for signs of excessive corrosion.

20 If a section of metal fuel line must be renewed, only seamless steel piping should be used, since copper and aluminium piping don't have the strength necessary to withstand normal engine vibration.

21 Check the metal lines where they enter the brake master cylinder, ABS hydraulic unit or clutch master/slave cylinders (as applicable) for cracks in the lines or loose fittings. Any sign of brake fluid leakage calls for an immediate and thorough inspection.

Air conditioning refrigerant

 Warning: Refer to the safety information given in Safety First! and Chapter 3 Section 1, regarding the dangers of disturbing any of the air conditioning system components.

22 The air conditioning system is filled with a liquid refrigerant, which is retained under high pressure. If the air conditioning system is opened and depressurised without the aid of specialised equipment, the refrigerant will immediately turn into gas and escape into the atmosphere. If the liquid comes into contact with your skin, it can cause severe frostbite. In addition, the refrigerant contains substances which are environmentally damaging; for this reason, it should not be allowed to escape into the atmosphere.

23 Any suspected air conditioning system leaks should be immediately referred to a Ford dealer or air conditioning specialist. Leakage will be shown up as a steady drop in the level of refrigerant in the system.

24 Note that water may drip from the condenser drain pipe, underneath the car, immediately after the air conditioning system has been in use. This is normal, and should not be cause for concern.

9 Auxiliary drivebelt check

General

1 The auxiliary drivebelt is of flat, multi-ribbed type, and is located on the right-hand end of the engine. It drives the alternator, coolant pump, power steering pump and the air conditioning compressor from the engine's crankshaft pulley.

2 The good condition and proper tension of the auxiliary drivebelt is critical to the operation of the engine. Because of their composition and the high stresses to which

10.3 Fuel filter water draining nipple (arrowed) – 1.8 litre engines

10.4 Fuel filter bleed screw (arrowed) – 1.8 litre engines

10.8 Fuel filter water draining nipple (arrowed) – 2.0 litre engines

they are subjected, drivebelts stretch and deteriorate as they get older. They must, therefore, be regularly inspected.

Check

3 With the engine switched off, open and support the bonnet. For improved access to the right-hand end of the engine, first loosen the right-hand front wheel nuts, then jack up the front right-hand side of the car and support it securely on an axle stand (see 'Jacking and vehicle support'). Remove the roadwheel, then remove the engine undertray and the wheel arch liner from inside the wheel arch.

4 Using an inspection light or a small electric torch, and rotating the engine with a spanner applied to the crankshaft pulley bolt, check the whole length of the drivebelt for cracks, separation of the rubber, and torn or worn ribs. Also check for fraying and glazing, which gives the drivebelt a shiny appearance.

5 Both sides of the drivebelt should be inspected, which means you will have to twist the drivebelt to check the underside. Use your fingers to feel the drivebelt where you can't see it. If you are in any doubt as to the condition of the drivebelt, renew it as described in Section 24.

Drivebelt tension

6 The auxiliary drivebelt is tensioned by an automatic tensioner – regular checks are not required, and manual 'adjustment' is not possible.

7 If you suspect that the drivebelt is slipping

and/or running slack, or that the tensioner is otherwise faulty, it must be renewed.

Drivebelt renewal

8 Refer to Section 24.

10 Fuel filter water draining – diesel models

Note: It may be necessary to prime and bleed the fuel system after completing this procedure. This entails the use of special tools and can, in some instances, be a difficult operation. Read through the priming and bleeding information contained in Chapter 4B Section 4 before proceeding.

1.8 litre engines

1 The fuel filter is located at the left-hand end of the cylinder head. To gain access, remove the plastic cover on the top of the engine.

2 Undo the two bolts and remove the support bracket above the filter (where fitted).

3 Position a container or cloth beneath the filter, then attach a length of plastic/rubber hose to the drain nipple, with the other end of the hose in a container (see illustration).

4 Slacken the drain nipple and the top bleed screw a few turns, and allow the fuel to drain until it appears clean and free from water droplets. Tighten the bleed screw and drain nipple (see illustration).

5 Remove the hose and, if necessary, bleed

the fuel system as described in Chapter 4B Section 4.

2.0 litre engines

6 The fuel filter is located under the rear of the car, behind the fuel tank.

7 Chock the front wheels, then jack up the rear of the car, and support it securely on axle stands (see 'Jacking and vehicle support').

8 Position a container or cloth beneath the filter, then attach a length of plastic/rubber hose to the drain nipple, with the other end of the hose in a container (see illustration).

9 Slacken the drain nipple a few turns, and allow the fuel to drain until it appears clean and free from water droplets (see illustration). Tighten the drain nipple securely.

10 Remove the hose and lower the car to the ground.

11 If necessary, bleed the fuel system as described in Chapter 4B Section 4.

11 Seat belt check

1 Check the seat belts for satisfactory operation and condition. Pull sharply on the belt to check that the locking mechanism engages correctly. Inspect the webbing for fraying and cuts. Check that they retract smoothly and without binding into their reels.

2 Check the accessible seat belt mountings, ensuring that all bolts are securely tightened.

12 Braking system check

Front disc brakes

1 Apply the handbrake, then jack up the front of the car and support it on axle stands (see 'Jacking and vehicle support'). For better access to the brake calipers, remove the roadwheels.

2 Look through the inspection window in the caliper, and check that the thickness of the friction lining material on each of the pads is not less than the recommended minimum thickness given in the Specifications (see illustration).

10.9 Slacken the drain nipple and allow the fuel to drain until it appears free from water droplets

12.2 With the wheel removed, the pad thickness can be seen through the front of the caliper

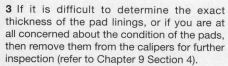

12.7 Check the condition of the flexible brake hoses by bending them slightly and looking for cracks

13.1a Check the outer constant velocity (CV) joint gaiters...

13.1b... and, though less prone to wear, check the inner gaiters, too

3 If it is difficult to determine the exact thickness of the pad linings, or if you are at all concerned about the condition of the pads, then remove them from the calipers for further inspection (refer to Chapter 9 Section 4).

4 Check the caliper on the other side in the same way.

5 If any one of the brake pads has worn down to, or below, the specified limit, all four pads at that end of the car must be renewed as a set.

6 Check both front brake discs with reference to Chapter 9 Section 6.

7 Before refitting the roadwheels, check all brake lines and flexible hoses with reference to Chapter 9 Section 3. In particular, check the flexible hoses in the vicinity of the calipers, where they are subjected to most movement. Bend them between the fingers and check that this does not reveal previously-hidden cracks, cuts or splits **(see illustration)**.

8 On completion, refit the roadwheels and lower the car to the ground. Tighten the wheel nuts to the specified torque.

Rear disc brakes

9 Chock the front wheels, then jack up the rear of the car and support on axle stands (see *'Jacking and vehicle support'*). Remove the rear wheels.

10 The procedure for checking the rear brakes is much the same as described in paragraphs 1 to 8 above.

Handbrake

11 With the car on a slight slope, firmly apply

the handbrake lever, and check that it holds the car stationary, then release the lever and check that there is no resistance to movement of the car. If necessary, the handbrake should be adjusted as described in Chapter 9 Section 14.

13 Driveshaft gaiter check

1 With the car raised and securely supported on stands, turn the steering onto full lock, then slowly rotate the roadwheel. Inspect the condition of the outer constant velocity (CV) joint rubber gaiters while squeezing the gaiters to open out the folds. Check for signs of cracking, splits or deterioration of the rubber which may allow the grease to escape, and lead to water and grit entry into the joint. Also check the security and condition of the retaining clips. Repeat these checks on the inner CV joints **(see illustrations)**. If any damage or deterioration is found, the gaiters should be renewed as described in Chapter 8.

2 At the same time, check the general condition of the CV joints themselves by first holding the driveshaft and attempting to rotate the wheel. Repeat this check by holding the inner joint and attempting to rotate the driveshaft. Any appreciable movement indicates wear in the joints, wear in the driveshaft splines, or a loose driveshaft retaining bolt.

14 Steering and suspension check

Front suspension and steering

1 Raise the front of the car, and securely support it on axle stands (see *'Jacking and vehicle support'*).

2 Visually inspect the balljoint dust covers and the steering rack-and-pinion gaiters for splits, chafing or deterioration **(see illustration)**. Any wear of these components will cause loss of lubricant, together with dirt and water entry, resulting in rapid deterioration of the balljoints or steering gear.

3 Grasp the roadwheel at the 12 o'clock and 6 o'clock positions, and try to rock it **(see illustration)**. Very slight free play may be felt, but if the movement is appreciable, further investigation is necessary to determine the source. Continue rocking the wheel while an assistant depresses the footbrake. If the movement is now eliminated or significantly reduced, it is likely that the hub bearings are at fault. If the free play is still evident with the footbrake depressed, then there is wear in the suspension joints or mountings.

4 Now grasp the wheel at the 9 o'clock and 3 o'clock positions, and try to rock it as before. Any movement felt now may again be caused by wear in the hub bearings or the steering track rod end balljoints. If the outer balljoint is worn, the visual movement will be obvious. If the inner joint is suspect, it can be felt by placing a hand over the rack-and-pinion rubber gaiter and gripping the track rod. If the wheel is now rocked, movement will be felt at the inner joint if wear has taken place.

5 Using a large screwdriver or flat bar, check for wear in the suspension mounting bushes by levering between the relevant suspension component and its attachment point. Some movement is to be expected, as the mountings are made of rubber, but excessive wear should be obvious. Also check the condition of any visible rubber bushes, looking for splits, cracks or contamination of the rubber.

6 With the car standing on its wheels, have

14.2 Check the steering gaiters for signs of splitting

14.3 Check for wear in the front suspension and hub bearings

an assistant turn the steering wheel back-and-forth, about an eighth of a turn each way. There should be very little, if any, lost movement between the steering wheel and roadwheels. If this is not the case, closely observe the joints and mountings previously described. In addition, check the steering column universal joints for wear, and also check the rack-and-pinion steering gear itself.

Rear suspension

7 Chock the front wheels, then jack up the rear of the car and support securely on axle stands (see *'Jacking and vehicle support'*).

8 Working as described previously for the front suspension, check the rear hub bearings, the suspension bushes and the shock absorber mountings for wear.

Shock absorber

9 Check for any signs of fluid leakage around the shock absorber body, or from the rubber gaiter around the piston rod **(see illustration)**. Should any fluid be noticed, the shock absorber is defective internally, and should be renewed. **Note:** *Shock absorbers should always be renewed in pairs on the same axle.*

10 The efficiency of the shock absorber may be checked by bouncing the car at each corner. Generally speaking, the body will return to its normal position and stop after being depressed. If it rises and returns on a rebound, the shock absorber is probably suspect. Also examine the shock absorber upper and lower mountings for any signs of wear.

15 Exhaust system check

1 With the engine cold (at least three hours after the vehicle has been driven), check the complete exhaust system, from its starting point at the engine to the end of the tailpipe. Ideally, this should be done on a hoist, where unrestricted access is available; if a hoist is not available, raise and support the vehicle on axle stands (see *'Jacking and vehicle support'*).

2 Make sure that all brackets and rubber mountings are in good condition, and tight;

if any of the mountings are to be renewed, ensure that the new ones are of the correct type – in the case of the rubber mountings, their colour is a good guide. Those nearest to the catalytic converter are more heat-resistant than the others **(see illustration)**.

3 Check the pipes and connections for evidence of leaks, severe corrosion, or damage. One of the most common points for a leak to develop is around the welded joints between the pipes and silencers. Leakage at any of the joints or in other parts of the system will usually show up as a black sooty stain in the vicinity of the leak. **Note:** *Exhaust sealants should not be used on any part of the exhaust system upstream of the catalytic converter (between the converter and engine) – even if the sealant does not contain additives harmful to the converter, pieces of it may break off and foul the element, causing local overheating.*

4 At the same time, inspect the underside of the body for holes, corrosion, open seams, etc, which may allow exhaust gases to enter the passenger compartment. Seal all body openings with silicone or body putty.

5 Rattles and other noises can often be traced to the exhaust system, especially the rubber mountings. Try to move the system, silencer(s), heat shields and catalytic converter. If any components can touch the body or suspension parts, secure the exhaust system with new mountings.

6 Check the running condition of the engine by inspecting inside the end of the tailpipe; the exhaust deposits here are an indication of the engine's state of tune. The inside of the tailpipe should be dry, and should vary in colour from dark grey to light grey/brown; if it is black and sooty, or coated with white deposits, this may indicate the need for a full fuel system inspection.

16 Roadwheel nut tightness check

1 Remove the wheel trims or alloy wheel centre covers, and slacken the roadwheel nuts slightly.

2 Tighten the nuts to the specified torque, using a torque wrench.

17 Hinge and lock lubrication

1 Work around the car and lubricate the hinges of the bonnet, doors and boot lid or tailgate with light oil.

2 Lightly lubricate the bonnet release mechanism with a smear of grease.

3 Check carefully the security and operation of all hinges, latches and locks, adjusting them where required. Check the operation of the central locking system.

4 Check the condition and operation of the tailgate struts, renewing them both if either is leaking or no longer able to support the tailgate securely when raised.

18 Electrical systems check

1 Check the operation of all instruments and electrical equipment, ie, lights, direction indicators, horn, etc. Refer to the appropriate sections of Chapter 12 for details if any of the circuits are found to be inoperative.

2 Note that the brake light switch is described in Chapter 9 Section 17.

3 Check all accessible wiring connectors, harnesses and retaining clips for security, and for signs of chafing or damage. Rectify any faults found.

19 Road test

Steering and suspension

1 Check for any abnormalities in the steering, suspension, handling or road 'feel'.

2 Drive the car, and check that there are no unusual vibrations or noises.

3 Check that the steering feels positive, with no excessive 'sloppiness', or roughness, and check for any suspension noises when cornering and driving over bumps.

Drivetrain

4 Check the performance of the engine, clutch (where applicable), transmission and driveshafts.

5 Listen for any unusual noises from the engine, clutch and transmission.

6 Make sure that the engine runs smoothly when idling, and that there is no hesitation when accelerating.

7 Where applicable, check that the clutch action is smooth and progressive, that the drive is taken up smoothly, and that the pedal travel is not excessive. Also listen for any noises when the clutch pedal is depressed.

8 Check that all gears can be engaged smoothly without noise, and that the gear

14.9 Check for signs of fluid leakage from the shock absorbers

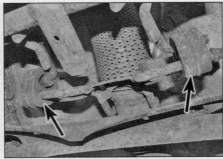

15.2 Check the condition of the exhaust rubber mountings (arrowed)

21.2 Undo the bolts (arrowed) and remove the metal shield – 1.8 litre engines

21.4a Depress the release button and disconnect the fuel supply pipe

21.4b Prise out the locking catch (1), push in or pull out the clip (2), and disconnect the fuel return pipe – 1.8 litre engines

lever action is smooth and not abnormally vague or 'notchy'.

9 Listen for a metallic clicking sound from the front of the car, as the car is driven slowly in a circle with the steering on full-lock. Carry out this check in both directions. If a clicking noise is heard, this indicates wear in a driveshaft joint (see Chapter 8).

Braking system

10 Make sure that the car does not pull to one side when braking, and that the wheels do not lock when braking hard.

11 Check that there is no vibration through the steering when braking.

12 Check that the handbrake operates correctly, without excessive movement of the lever, and that it holds the car stationary on a slope.

13 Test the operation of the brake servo unit as follows. Depress the footbrake four or five times to exhaust the vacuum, then start the engine. As the engine starts, there should be a noticeable 'give' in the brake pedal as vacuum builds-up. Allow the engine to run for at least two minutes, and then switch it off. If the brake pedal is now depressed again, it should be possible to detect a hiss from the servo as the pedal is depressed. After about four or five applications, no further hissing should be heard, and the pedal should feel considerably harder.

20 Valve clearance check and adjustment – 1.8 litre diesel engines

1 Refer to the procedures contained in Chapter 2B Section 5.

21 Fuel filter renewal – diesel models

Note: *It will be necessary to prime and bleed the fuel system after completing this procedure. This entails the use of special tools and can, in some instances, be a difficult operation. Read through the priming and bleeding information contained in Chapter 4B Section 4 before proceeding.*

21.6a Unscrew the collar...

1.8 litre engines

1 The fuel filter is located at the left-hand end of the cylinder head. To gain access, remove the plastic cover on the top of the engine.

2 If fitted, undo the bolts and remove the metal shield over the top of the filter **(see illustration).**

3 Disconnect the wiring plug from the top of the filter housing.

4 Disconnect the fuel supply and return pipes at the quick-release connections on the filter **(see illustrations)**. Plug the disconnected unions to prevent contamination.

5 Slide the filter housing upwards from the mounting bracket.

6 Unscrew the collar and lift the filter cover and element from the housing **(see illustrations)**.

7 Discard the seal **(see illustration)**.

21.7 Renew the seal – 1.8 litre engines

21.6b... then lift the cover and element from the filter housing – 1.8 litre engines

8 Thoroughly clean the filter housing and cover, then position the new seal on the filter housing, and fit the new filter element to the cover.

9 Fit the new element and cover to the housing, ensuring the alignment arrows are aligned correctly **(see illustration)**. Tighten the collar securely.

10 Refit the filter housing to the bracket, and reconnect the pipes/wiring plug.

11 The remainder of refitting is a reversal of removal. Prime and bleed the fuel system as described in Chapter 4B Section 4.

2.0 litre engines

12 The fuel filter is located under the rear of the car, behind the fuel tank.

13 Chock the front wheels, then jack up the rear of the car, and support it securely on axle stands (see *'Jacking and vehicle support'*).

21.9 Ensure the arrows align (arrowed) – 1.8 litre engines

21.14 Attach a length of plastic/rubber hose to the drain nipple and slacken it a few turns – 2.0 litre engines

21.15 Unscrew the filter base a few turns and allow the fuel to drain into the container – 2.0 litre engines

21.16a When the filter has completely drained, fully unscrew and remove the filter base...

21.16b... and withdraw the filter from the housing – 2.0 litre engines

14 Position a container beneath the filter, then attach a length of plastic/rubber hose to the drain nipple, with the other end of the hose in a container. Slacken the drain nipple a few turns **(see illustration)**.

15 Unscrew the filter base a few turns and allow the fuel to drain into the container **(see illustration)**.

16 When the filter has completely drained, fully unscrew and remove the filter base and withdraw the filter from the housing **(see illustrations)**.

17 Remove the O-ring seal from the filter base.

18 Thoroughly clean the filter base and fit the new O-ring seal **(see illustration)**.

19 Locate the new filter in the housing and push it up until it engages with the retainers.

20 Refit the filter base and tighten it securely.

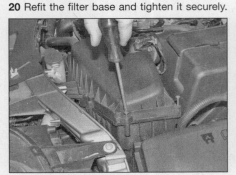

22.2 Undo the screws securing the cover to the air cleaner housing

21.18 Thoroughly clean the filter base and fit the new O-ring seal – 2.0 litre engines

Tighten the drain nipple on the filter base securely.

21 Lower the car to the ground, then prime and bleed the fuel system as described in Chapter 4B Section 4.

22 Air filter element renewal – diesel models

Caution: Never drive the vehicle with the air cleaner filter element removed. Excessive engine wear could result, and backfiring could even cause a fire under the bonnet.

1 The air filter element is located in the air cleaner assembly on the left-hand side of the engine compartment.

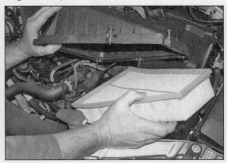

22.3 Lift up the cover and take out the filter element

2 Undo the screws securing the cover to the air cleaner housing **(see illustration)**.

3 The cover can now be lifted, and the filter element removed **(see illustration)**. If preferred, the cover can be removed completely – this will allow a more thorough cleaning of the filter housing.

4 Loosen the clip and disconnect the air inlet duct from the air cleaner cover.

5 Disconnect the wiring connector from the airflow sensor on the air cleaner cover.

6 Withdraw the cover and remove the filter element, noting its direction of fitting.

7 If carrying out a service, the element must be renewed regardless of its apparent condition.

8 If you are checking the element for any other reason, inspect its lower surface; if it is oily or very dirty, renew the element. If it is only moderately dusty, it can be re-used by blowing it clean from the upper to the lower surface with compressed air. Because it is a pleated-paper type filter, it cannot be washed or re-oiled. If it cannot be cleaned satisfactorily with compressed air, discard and renew it.

⚠ *Warning: Wear eye protection when using compressed air.*

23 Timing belt renewal

1 Refer to the procedures contained in Chapter 2B Section 7 or Chapter 2C Section 5.

24 Auxiliary drivebelt renewal – diesel models

1 With the engine switched off, open and support the bonnet. For improved access to the right-hand end of the engine, first loosen the right-hand front wheel nuts, then jack up the front right-hand side of the car and support it securely on an axle stand (see 'Jacking and vehicle support'). Remove the roadwheel, then remove the engine undertray and the wheel arch liner from inside the wheel arch.

24.3 Lift off the fuel hose support clip and undo the air outlet duct retaining nut (arrowed) – 1.8 litre engines

24.4a Disconnect the air temperature sensor wiring connector...

24.4b... then slacken the retaining clips and remove the air outlet duct – 1.8 litre engines

2 Remove the plastic cover over the top of the engine.

1.8 litre engines

3 Lift the fuel hose support clip off the stud at the right-hand end of the engine, then undo the intercooler air outlet duct retaining nut **(see illustration)**.

4 Disconnect the air temperature sensor wiring connector, then slacken the retaining clips and remove the air outlet duct **(see illustrations)**.

5 Engage an open-ended spanner with the lug at the top of the tensioner arm, then rotate the tensioner arm anti-clockwise to release the belt tension. Insert a 4 mm diameter drill bit or rod into the hole on the underside of the tensioner arm, and into the hole in the tensioner body to lock the tensioner in the released position. It is useful to have a small mirror available to enable the alignment of the locking holes to be more easily seen in the limited space available.

6 If the existing drivebelt is to be refitted, mark it, or note the maker's markings on its flat surface, so that it can be installed the same way round.

7 Working from below or from the engine compartment as necessary, and noting its routing, slip the drivebelt off the pulleys and withdraw it.

8 Check all the pulleys, ensuring that their grooves are clean, and removing all traces of oil and grease.

9 If the original drivebelt is being refitted, use the marks or notes made on removal, to ensure that it is installed to run in the same direction as it was previously.

10 Fit the belt around the pulleys, ensuring that the ribs on the belt are correctly engaged with the grooves in the pulleys and the drivebelt is correctly routed **(see illustration)**.

11 Using an open-ended spanner, hold the tensioner arm so that the locking drill bit/rod can be removed, then release the pressure on the spanner so that the automatic tensioner takes up the slack in the drivebelt.

12 Using a socket or spanner applied to the crankshaft pulley bolt, rotate the crankshaft through at least two full turns clockwise to settle the drivebelt on the pulleys, then check that the drivebelt is properly installed.

2.0 litre engines

13 Using a spanner on the tensioner centre bolt, turn the tensioner clockwise to release the drivebelt tension, then insert a 4 mm diameter drill bit or rod through the holes in the arm/body when they align to lock the tensioner in this position. It is useful to have a small mirror available to enable the alignment

of the locking holes to be more easily seen in the limited space available.

14 If the existing drivebelt is to be refitted, mark it, or note the maker's markings on its flat surface, so that it can be installed the same way round.

15 Working from below or from the engine compartment as necessary, and noting its routing, slip the drivebelt off the pulleys and withdraw it.

16 Check all the pulleys, ensuring that their grooves are clean, and removing all traces of oil and grease.

17 If the original drivebelt is being refitted, use the marks or notes made on removal, to ensure that it is installed to run in the same direction as it was previously.

18 Fit the belt around the pulleys, ensuring that the ribs on the belt are correctly engaged with the grooves in the pulleys and the drivebelt is correctly routed **(see illustration)**.

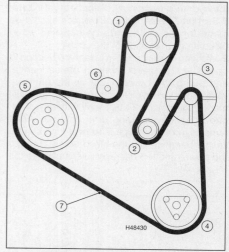

24.18 Auxiliary drivebelt routing – 2.0 litre engines

1 Power steering pump pulley
2 Idler pulley
3 Alternator pulley
4 Air conditioning compressor pulley
5 Crankshaft pulley
6 Tensioner pulley
7 Auxiliary drivebelt

1 Alternator decoupler
  pulley
2 Air conditioning
  compressor
  pulley
3 Idler pulley
4 Crankshaft pulley
5 Tensioner pulley
6 Power steering pump
  pulley
7 Coolant pump pulley
8 Auxiliary drivebelt

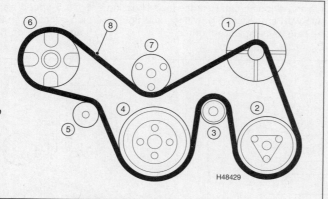

24.10 Auxiliary drivebelt routing – 1.8 litre engines

19 Use a spanner to hold the tensioner arm, then remove the locking drill bit/rod, and allow the tensioner to rotate anti-clockwise and gently tension the belt.

20 Using a socket or spanner applied to the crankshaft pulley bolt, rotate the crankshaft through at least two full turns clockwise to settle the drivebelt on the pulleys, then check that the drivebelt is properly installed.

All engines

21 Refit the wheel arch liner, engine undertray and roadwheel, then lower the car to the ground. Tighten the wheel nuts to the specified torque.

22 Refit the components in the engine compartment removed for access.

25 Fuel pump drive chain/belt renewal

1 Refer to the procedures contained in Chapter 2D Section 10.

26 Brake fluid renewal

> **Warning: Brake hydraulic fluid can harm your eyes and damage painted surfaces, so use extreme caution when handling and pouring it. Do not use fluid that has been standing open for some time, as it absorbs moisture from the air. Excess moisture can cause a dangerous loss of braking effectiveness.**

1 The procedure is similar to that for bleeding the hydraulic system as described in Chapter 9 Section 2, except that allowance should be made for the old fluid to be expelled when bleeding each section of the circuit.

2 Working as described in Chapter 9 Section 2, open the first bleed screw in the sequence, and pump the brake pedal gently until the level in the reservoir is approaching the MIN mark. Top-up to the MAX level with new fluid, and continue pumping until only new fluid remains in the reservoir, and new fluid can be seen emerging from the bleed screw. Tighten the screw, and top the reservoir level up to the MAX level line.

3 Work through all the remaining bleed screws in the sequence until new fluid can be seen at all of them. Be careful to keep the master cylinder reservoir topped-up above the MIN level at all times, or air may enter the system. If this happens, further bleeding will be required to remove the air.

4 When the operation is complete, check that all bleed screws are securely tightened, and that their dust caps are refitted. Wash off all traces of spilt fluid, and recheck the master cylinder reservoir fluid level.

5 Check the operation of the brakes before taking the car on the road.

27 Automatic transmission fluid level check and top-up

Fluid level check

1 The fluid level must be checked with the engine/transmission at operating temperature. This can be achieved by checking the level after a journey of 8 to 10 miles.

2 On your return, position the vehicle over an inspection pit, on vehicle ramps, or jack it up and support it securely on axle stands (see 'Jacking and vehicle support'), but make sure that it is level. Remove the clips and bolts and remove the undertray from beneath the engine.

3 Start the engine and allow it to idle. With the footbrake firmly applied, slowly move the selector lever from position P to position D and back to position P, stopping at each position for at least two seconds. Repeat this procedure twice.

4 Position a container under the combined drain plug/level checking plug at the base of the transmission. Note that the drain plug and level checking plug are incorporated into one unit – the drain plug is the larger of the two plugs, with the level checking plug screwed into the centre of it (see illustration).

5 With the engine still idling, unscrew the fluid level checking plug. Allow the excess fluid to run from the level checking plug aperture until it is only dripping out. Refit the level checking plug with a new sealing washer, and tighten the plug to the specified torque.

> **Warning: The fluid will be hot, take precautions against scalding.**

6 On completion, refit the engine undertray and lower the vehicle to the ground.

Topping-up fluid level

7 If no fluid runs from the level checking plug aperture, switch the engine off and remove the air cleaner assembly as described in Chapter 7B Section 2.

8 Wipe clean the area around the transmission fluid filler plug, located on the top of the transmission housing, adjacent to the selector cable (see illustration). Unscrew and remove the filler plug along with its sealing washer.

9 Slowly fill the transmission with the specified type of fluid, via the filler plug aperture until fluid just starts to drip out of the level checking plug aperture. Use a funnel with a fine mesh gauze, to avoid spillage, and to ensure that no foreign matter enters the transmission.

10 Once the fluid level is correct, refit the filler plug and level checking plug with new sealing washers, and tighten both plugs to the specified torque.

11 Refit the air cleaner assembly as described in Chapter 4B Section 5.

12 If the fluid has cooled to less than operating temperature (under 35°C), recheck the level as described above.

13 On completion, refit the engine undertray and lower the vehicle to the ground.

28 Manual transmission oil level check

1 Slacken the left-hand front roadwheel nuts, then raise the car and support it securely on axle stands (see 'Jacking and vehicle support') making sure that the car is level. Remove the roadwheel.

2 Release the fasteners and remove the engine undertray, then position a suitable container beneath the transmission.

3 On 5-speed transmissions, the filler/level plug is located on the front of the transmission housing, and on 6-speed transmissions it is

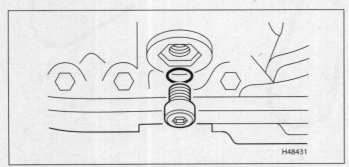

27.4 Automatic transmission fluid level checking plug

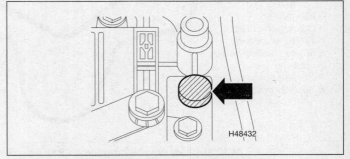

27.8 Automatic transmission fluid filler plug

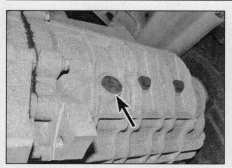

28.3a Manual transmission oil filler/level plug (arrowed) – 5-speed transmission

28.3b Manual transmission oil filler/level plug (arrowed) – 6-speed transmission

located on the left-hand side of the differential casing **(see illustrations)**.

4 Using a suitable Allen key or socket, unscrew and remove the filler/level plug – take care, as it will probably be very tight. Discard the sealing washer (where fitted), a new one must be fitted.

5 If the lubricant level is correct, the oil should be up to the lower edge of the hole.

6 If the transmission needs more lubricant (if the oil level is not up to the hole), use a syringe, or a plastic bottle and tube, to add more.

7 Stop filling the transmission when the lubricant begins to run out of the hole, then wait until the flow of oil ceases.

8 Refit the filler/level plug with a new seal

(where fitted), and tighten it to the specified torque.

9 Refit the undertray and the roadwheel, then lower the vehicle to the ground. Tighten the wheel nuts to the specified torque.

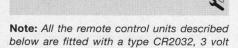

29 Remote control battery renewal

Note: *All the remote control units described below are fitted with a type CR2032, 3 volt battery.*

1 If the door locks repeatedly fail to respond to signals from the remote control at the normal

distance, change the battery in the remote control before attempting to troubleshoot any of the vehicle's other systems. Although not in the Ford maintenance schedule, we recommend that the battery is changed every 2 years, regardless of the vehicle's mileage.

With a folding key blade

2 Insert a small flat-bladed screwdriver fully into the slot on the side of the transmitter unit, push the screwdriver towards the key blade and remove the key blade **(see illustrations)**.

3 Use the screwdriver, inserted at the side and front of the transmitter unit, to separate the two halves of the unit **(see illustration)**.

4 Note the fitted position of the battery (positive side down), then prise the battery from its location, and insert the new one **(see illustration)**. Avoid touching the battery or the terminals with bare fingers.

5 Snap the two halves of the transmitter together, and re-attach it to the key blade.

Without a folding key blade

Type 1

6 Insert a small flat-bladed screwdriver into the slot provided and slide the transmitter unit from the key blade **(see illustration)**.

7 Use the screwdriver to release the clip each side and open the transmitter unit **(see illustration)**.

8 Note the fitted position of the battery

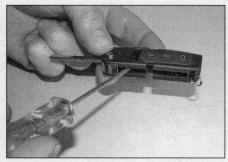

29.2a Insert a small screwdriver into the slot on the side of the transmitter unit...

29.2b... then push the screwdriver towards the key blade and remove the key blade

29.3 Insert the screwdriver at the side and front of the transmitter unit to separate the two halves

29.4 Note the fitted position of the battery, then prise it out and insert the new one

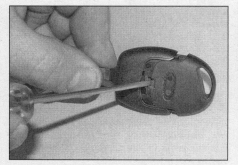

29.6 Insert a small screwdriver into the slot provided and slide the transmitter unit from the key blade

29.7 Release the clip each side and open the transmitter unit

29.8 Note the fitted position of the battery, then prise it out and insert the new one

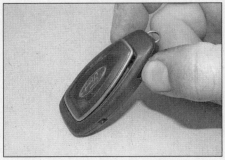

29.14 Depress the tabs on the side of the transmitter unit and carefully lift off the cover

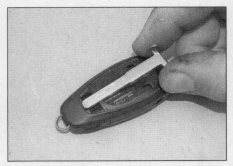

29.15 Remove the key blade from the transmitter unit

29.16 Insert a small screwdriver into the slot provided, then twist the screwdriver to separate the two halves of the unit

29.17 Insert the screwdriver into the side of the transmitter to open the unit

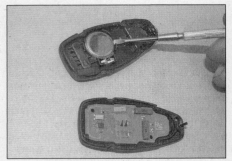

29.18 Note the fitted position of the battery, then prise it out and insert the new one

(positive side up), then prise the battery from its location, and insert the new one **(see illustration)**. Avoid touching the battery or the terminals with bare fingers.

9 Snap the two halves of the transmitter together, and re-attach it to the key blade.

Type 2

10 Slide the release slider at the top of the transmitter sideways and remove the key blade.

11 Insert a small flat-bladed screwdriver into the slot at the top of the transmitter unit, then twist the screwdriver to separate the two halves of the unit.

12 Note the fitted position of the battery (positive side down), then prise the battery from its location, and insert the new one. Avoid touching the battery or the terminals with bare fingers.

13 Snap the two halves of the transmitter together, and refit the key blade.

Type 3

14 Depress the two tabs on the side of the transmitter unit and carefully lift off the cover **(see illustration)**.

15 Remove the key blade from the transmitter unit**(see illustration)**.

16 Insert a small flat-bladed screwdriver into the slot at the top of the transmitter unit, then twist the screwdriver to separate the two halves of the unit**(see illustration)**.

17 Insert the screwdriver into the side of the transmitter to open the unit**(see illustration)**.

18 Note the fitted position of the battery (positive side down), then prise the battery

from its location, and insert the new one **(see illustration)**. Avoid touching the battery or the terminals with bare fingers.

19 Snap the two halves of the transmitter together, place the key blade in position and refit the cover.

30 Coolant strength check and renewal

 Warning: Do not allow antifreeze to come in contact with your skin or painted surfaces of the vehicle. Flush contaminated areas immediately with plenty of water. Don't store new coolant, or leave old coolant lying around, where it's accessible to children or pets – they're attracted by its sweet smell. Ingestion of even a small amount of coolant can be fatal. Wipe up garage-floor and drip-pan spills immediately. Keep antifreeze containers covered, and repair cooling system leaks as soon as they're noticed.

 Warning: Never remove the expansion tank filler cap when the engine is running, or has just been switched off, as the cooling system will be hot, and the consequent escaping steam and scalding coolant could cause serious injury.

Warning: Wait until the engine is cold before starting these procedures.

Strength check

1 Use a hydrometer to check the strength of the antifreeze. Follow the instructions provided with your hydrometer. The antifreeze strength should be approximately 50%. If it is significantly less than this, drain a little coolant from the radiator (see this Section), add antifreeze to the coolant expansion tank, then recheck the strength.

Coolant draining

2 To drain the system, first remove the expansion tank filler cap.

3 Firmly apply the handbrake, then jack up the front of the vehicle and support it securely on axle stands (see 'Jacking and vehicle support'). Remove the engine undertray, followed by the shield under the radiator.

4 Place a suitable container beneath the left-hand side of the radiator.

5 Open the radiator drain tap and allow the coolant to drain into the container.

6 Once the coolant has stopped draining from the radiator, close the drain tap.

System flushing

7 With time, the cooling system may gradually lose its efficiency, as the radiator core becomes choked with rust, scale deposits from the water, and other sediment. To minimise this, as well as using only good-quality antifreeze and clean soft water, the system should be flushed as follows whenever any part of it is disturbed, and/or when the coolant is renewed.

8 With the coolant drained and the drain tap closed, refill the system with fresh water. Refit the expansion tank filler cap, start the

Routine maintenance and servicing – diesel models 1B•21

engine and warm it up to normal operating temperature, then stop it and (after allowing it to cool down completely) drain the system again. Repeat as necessary until only clean water can be seen to emerge, then refill finally with the specified coolant mixture.

9 If only clean, soft water and good-quality antifreeze (even if not to Ford's specification) has been used, and the coolant has been renewed at the suggested intervals, the above procedure will be sufficient to keep the system clean for a considerable length of time. If, however, the system has been neglected, a more thorough operation will be required, as follows.

10 First drain the coolant, then disconnect the radiator top and bottom hoses. Insert a garden hose into the radiator top hose connection, and allow water to circulate through the radiator until it runs clean from the bottom outlet.

11 To flush the engine, insert the garden hose into the radiator bottom hose, wrap a piece of rag around the garden hose to seal the connection, and allow water to circulate until it runs clear.

12 Try the effect of repeating this procedure in the top hose, although this may not be effective, since the thermostat will probably close and prevent the flow of water.

13 In severe cases of contamination, reverse-flushing of the radiator may be necessary. This may be achieved by inserting the garden hose into the bottom outlet, wrapping a piece of rag around the hose to seal the connection, then flushing the radiator until clear water emerges from the top hose outlet.

14 If the radiator is suspected of being severely choked, remove the radiator (Chapter 3 Section 6), turn it upside-down, and repeat the procedure described in paragraph 13.

15 The use of chemical cleaners is not recommended, and should be necessary only as a last resort; the scouring action of some chemical cleaners may lead to other cooling system problems. Normally, regular renewal of the coolant will prevent excessive contamination of the system.

Antifreeze type and mixture

Caution: Do not use engine antifreeze in the windscreen/tailgate washer system, as it will damage the vehicle's paintwork. A screenwash additive should be added to the washer system in its maker's recommended quantities.

16 If the vehicle's history (and therefore the quality of the antifreeze in it) is unknown, owners are advised to drain and thoroughly reverse-flush the system, before refilling with fresh coolant mixture.

17 If the antifreeze used is to Ford's specification, the levels of protection it affords are indicated in the coolant packaging.

18 To give the recommended standard mixture ratio for antifreeze, 50% (by volume) of antifreeze must be mixed with 50% of clean, soft water; if you are using any other type of antifreeze, follow its manufacturer's instructions to achieve the correct ratio.

19 You are unlikely to fully drain the system at any one time (unless the engine is being completely stripped), and the capacities quoted in the Specifications are therefore slightly academic for routine coolant renewal. As a guide, only two-thirds of the system's total capacity is likely to be needed for coolant renewal.

20 As the drained system will be partially filled with flushing water, in order to establish the recommended mixture ratio, measure out 50% of the system capacity in antifreeze and pour it into the hose/expansion tank as described above, then top-up with water. Any topping-up while refilling the system should be done with water – for 'Weekly checks' use a suitable mixture.

21 Before adding antifreeze, the cooling system should be drained, preferably flushed, and all hoses checked for condition and security; fresh antifreeze will rapidly find any weaknesses in the system.

22 After filling with antifreeze, a label should be attached to the expansion tank, stating the type and concentration of antifreeze used, and the date installed. Any subsequent topping-up should be made with the same type and concentration of antifreeze.

Coolant filling

23 Before attempting to fill the cooling system, make sure that all hoses and clips are in good condition, and that the clips are tight. Note that an antifreeze mixture must be used all year round, to prevent corrosion of the engine components.

24 As part of the system will already have water in it, initially pour in 50% of the system capacity in antifreeze, then top-up with water.

25 Slowly fill the system until the coolant level reaches the neck of the expansion tank.

26 Refit the filler cap, then start the engine and run it at 2000 rpm for approximately 13 minutes.

27 Increase the engine speed to 3000 rpm for 5 seconds, then decrease the engine speed to 2000 rpm and run it at this speed for 15 minutes.

28 Check the cooling system for leaks, then allow the engine to cool for at least 30 minutes.

29 If not already done, refit the shield under the radiator, followed by the engine undertray.

30 When the engine has cooled completely, remove the filler cap and top-up the coolant level to the MAX mark on the expansion tank.

General cooling system checks

31 The engine should be cold for the cooling system checks, so perform the following procedure before driving the vehicle, or after it has been shut off for at least three hours.

32 Remove the expansion tank filler cap, and clean it thoroughly inside and out with a rag. Also clean the filler neck on the expansion tank. The presence of rust or corrosion in the filler neck indicates that the coolant should be changed. The coolant inside the expansion tank should be relatively clean and transparent. If it is rust-coloured, drain and flush the system, and refill with a fresh coolant mixture.

33 Carefully check the radiator hoses and heater hoses along their entire length; renew any hose which is cracked, swollen or deteriorated.

34 Inspect all other cooling system components (joint faces, etc) for leaks. A leak in the cooling system will usually show up as white- or antifreeze-coloured deposits on the area adjoining the leak. Where any problems of this nature are found on system components, renew the component or gasket with reference to Chapter 3.

Airlocks

35 If, after draining and refilling the system, symptoms of overheating are found which did not occur previously, then the fault is almost certainly due to trapped air at some point in the system, causing an airlock and restricting the flow of coolant; usually, the air is trapped because the system was refilled too quickly.

36 If an airlock is suspected, first try gently squeezing all visible coolant hoses. A coolant hose which is full of air feels quite different to one full of coolant when squeezed. After refilling the system, most airlocks will clear once the system has cooled, and been topped-up.

37 While the engine is running at operating temperature, switch on the heater and heater fan, and check for heat output. Provided there is sufficient coolant in the system, lack of heat output could be due to an airlock in the system.

38 Airlocks can have more serious effects than simply reducing heater output – a severe airlock could reduce coolant flow around the engine. Check that the radiator top hose is hot when the engine is at operating temperature – a top hose which stays cold could be the result of an airlock (or a non-opening thermostat).

39 If the problem persists, stop the engine and allow it to cool down completely, before unscrewing the expansion tank filler cap or loosening the hose clips and squeezing the hoses to bleed out the trapped air. In the worst case, the system will have to be at least partially drained (this time, the coolant can be saved for re-use) and flushed to clear the problem. If all else fails, have the system evacuated and vacuum-filled by a suitably-equipped garage.

Expansion tank cap check

40 Wait until the engine is completely cold – perform this check before the engine is started for the first time in the day.

41 Place a wad of cloth over the expansion tank cap, then unscrew it slowly and remove it.

42 Examine the condition of the rubber seal on the underside of the cap. If the rubber appears to have hardened, or cracks are visible in the seal edges, a new cap should be fitted.

43 If the car is several years old, or has covered a large mileage, consider renewing the cap regardless of its apparent condition – they are not expensive. If the pressure relief valve built into the cap fails, excess pressure in the system will lead to puzzling failures of hoses and other cooling system components.

Chapter 2 Part A
Petrol engine in-car repair procedures

Contents

Degrees of difficulty

Easy, suitable for novice with little experience	Fairly easy, suitable for beginner with some experience	Fairly difficult, suitable for competent DIY mechanic	Difficult, suitable for experienced DIY mechanic	Very difficult, suitable for expert DIY or professional

Specifications

General

Engine type.	Four-cylinder, in-line, chain-driven double overhead camshafts, aluminium alloy cylinder head and engine block
Designation	Duratec HE
Engine codes*	AOBA and AOBC
Capacity	1998 cc
Bore	87.5 mm
Stroke	83.1 mm
Compression ratio	10.8: 1
Output:	
Power	107 kW (145 PS) @ 6000 rpm
Torque	185 Nm @ 4500 rpm
Firing order.	1-3-4-2 (No 1 cylinder at timing chain end)
Direction of crankshaft rotation	Clockwise (seen from right-hand side of vehicle)

* For details of engine code location, see 'Vehicle identification' in the Reference Chapter.

Camshafts

Camshaft endfloat	0.09 to 0.24 mm
Camshaft bearing journal diameter	24.96 to 24.98 mm

Valves

Valve clearances (cold):	
Inlet valves	0.22 to 0.28 mm
Exhaust valves	0.27 to 0.33 mm

Lubrication

Engine oil type/specification	See *Lubricants and fluids*
Engine oil capacity	See Chapter 1A
Oil pressure (engine at operating temperature):	
At 1500 rpm	1.3 to 2.7 bar
At 3000 rpm	2.3 to 5.2 bar
Oil pressure relief valve opens at	5.0 bar

Torque wrench settings

	Nm	lbf ft
Air conditioning compressor	25	18
Auxiliary drivebelt idler pulley bolt	25	18
Camshaft bearing cap bolts:		
Stage 1	7	5
Stage 2	16	12
Camshaft position sensor	6	4
Camshaft sprocket bolts	72	53
Coolant pump pulley bolts	20	15
Crankshaft oil seal carrier bolts	10	7
Crankshaft pulley bolt: *		
Stage 1	100	74
Stage 2	Angle-tighten a further 90°	
Cylinder block blanking plug	20	15
Cylinder head bolts: *		
Stage 1	5	4
Stage 2	15	11
Stage 3	45	33
Stage 4	Angle-tighten a further 90°	
Stage 5	Angle-tighten a further 90°	
Cylinder head cover bolts	10	7
EGR valve bolts	25	18
Engine mountings:		
Left-hand mounting (transmission):		
Mounting-to-body bolts	25	18
Mounting-to-body nuts	80	59
Mounting-to-transmission bracket centre bolt	133	98
Rear mounting (roll restrictor) bolts	80	59
Right-hand mounting-to-engine nuts	80	59
Right-hand mounting–to-body bolts	90	66
Engine-to-transmission bolts	48	35
Flywheel bolts: *		
Stage 1	50	37
Stage 2	80	59
Stage 3	112	83
Oil pick-up pipe bolts	10	7
Oil pressure switch	15	11
Oil pump chain guide	10	7
Oil pump chain tensioner	10	7
Oil pump sprocket bolt	25	18
Oil pump-to-cylinder block bolts:		
Stage 1	10	7
Stage 2	23	17
Power steering pump bolts	25	18
Roadwheel nuts	140	103
Sump drain plug	25	18
Sump pan to lower crankcase	25	18
Sump pan to transmission	48	35
Timing chain cover:		
M6	10	7
M8	48	35
Timing chain cover lower blanking plug	12	9
Timing chain cover upper blanking plug	10	7
Timing chain guide	10	7
Timing chain tensioner	10	7

* Use new fasteners

1   General Information

How to use this Chapter

1 This Part of Chapter 2 is devoted to in-car repair procedures on the 2.0 litre Duratec HE petrol engines. All procedures concerning engine removal, refitting, and overhaul can be found in Chapter 2D. **Note:** *It is not possible to remove the intermediate/main bearing section or to remove the crankshaft or pistons. No separate parts are available, and replacement/exchange units are supplied with crankshaft, pistons, connecting rods, etc, already fitted. Consult a Ford dealer or parts specialist for further information.*

2 Refer to Vehicle identification13,3 for details of engine code locations.

3 Most of the operations included in this Chapter are based on the assumption that the engine is still installed in the car. Therefore, if this information is being used during a complete engine overhaul, with the engine already removed, many of the steps included here will not apply.

Engine description

4 The engine is of sixteen-valve, double overhead camshaft (DOHC), four-cylinder, in-line type, mounted transversely at the front of the vehicle, with the transmission on its left-hand end.

5 All major engine castings are of aluminium alloy, with cast-iron cylinder liners, and a crankshaft made from forged nodular iron.

6 The crankshaft runs in five main bearings, the centre main bearing's upper half incorporating thrustwashers to control crankshaft endfloat.

7 The connecting rods rotate on horizontally-split bearing shells at their big-ends. The pistons are attached to the connecting rods by gudgeon pins which are an interference fit in the connecting rod small-end eyes. The aluminium alloy pistons are fitted with three piston rings: two compression rings and an oil control ring.

8 The inlet and exhaust valves are each closed by coil springs; they operate in guides which are shrink-fitted into the cylinder head, as are the valve seat inserts.

9 The two camshafts are driven by the same timing chain, each operating eight valves via solid tappets (cam followers). The tappets are graded for thickness, and are renewed in order to adjust the valve clearances. Each camshaft rotates in five bearings that are line-bored directly in the cylinder head and the (bolted-on) bearing caps; this means that the bearing caps are not available separately from the cylinder head, and must not be interchanged with caps from another engine.

10 The coolant pump is bolted to the right-hand end of the cylinder block, and is driven by a multi-ribbed auxiliary drivebelt from the crankshaft pulley.

Lubrication system

11 Lubrication is by means of an eccentric-rotor pump, which is mounted at right-hand end of the cylinder block, and is driven by a chain from a sprocket on the crankshaft, and draws oil through a strainer located in the sump. The pump forces oil through an externally-mounted full-flow cartridge-type filter. From the filter, the oil is pumped into a main gallery in the cylinder block/crankcase, from where it is distributed to the crankshaft (main bearings) and cylinder head.

12 The big-end bearings are supplied with oil via internal drillings in the crankshaft. Each piston crown is cooled by a spray of oil directed at its underside by a jet. These jets are fed by passages off the crankshaft oil supply galleries, with spring-loaded valves to ensure that the jets open only when there is sufficient pressure to guarantee a good oil supply to the rest of the engine components.

13 The cylinder head is provided with two oil galleries, one on the inlet side and one on the exhaust, to ensure constant oil supply to the camshaft bearings and tappets. A retaining valve (inserted into the cylinder head's top surface, in the middle, on the inlet side) prevents these galleries from being drained when the engine is switched off. The valve incorporates a ventilation hole in its upper end, to allow air bubbles to escape from the system when the engine is restarted.

14 While the crankshaft and camshaft bearings receive a pressurised supply, the camshaft lobes and valves are lubricated by splash, as are all other engine components.

Operations with engine in car

15 The following work can be carried out with the engine in the car:
a) *Compression pressure – testing.*
b) *Cylinder head cover – removal and refitting.*
c) *Timing chain cover – removal and refitting.*
d) *Timing chain – renewal.*
e) *Timing chain tensioner and sprockets – removal and refitting.*
f) *Camshaft oil seals – renewal.*
g) *Camshafts and tappets – removal and refitting.*
h) *Cylinder head – removal, overhaul and refitting.*
i) *Cylinder head and pistons – decarbonising.*
j) *Sump – removal and refitting.*
k) *Crankshaft oil seals – renewal.*
l) *Oil pump – removal and refitting.*
m) *Flywheel – removal and refitting.*
n) *Engine/transmission mountings – removal and refitting.*

2   Compression test – description and interpretation

1 When engine performance is down, or if misfiring occurs which cannot be attributed to the ignition or fuel systems, a compression test can provide diagnostic clues as to the engine's condition. If the test is performed regularly, it can give warning of trouble before any other symptoms become apparent.

2 The engine must be fully warmed-up to operating temperature, the oil level must be correct and the battery must be fully-charged. The help of an assistant will also be required.

3 Note that it is necessary to remove the fuse for the fuel pump relay to allow the compression test to be performed. This will log a fault code in the engine management powertrain control module when the engine is turned over on the starter, and the fault code will have to be cleared, using Ford diagnostic equipment or a compatible alternative, on completion of the test. Unless you have access to the necessary diagnostic equipment it may be preferable to have the compression test carried out by a Ford dealer or suitably-equipped garage. Should you wish to proceed, the procedure is as follows.

4 Refer to Chapter 12 Section 3 and remove the fuel pump fuse from the passenger compartment fuse/relay box. Now start the engine and allow it to run until it stalls.

5 Remove all the spark plugs as described in Chapter 1A Section 22.

6 Fit a compression tester to the No 1 cylinder spark plug hole – the type of tester which screws into the spark plug thread is preferable.

7 Arrange for an assistant to hold the accelerator pedal fully depressed to the floor, while at the same time cranking the engine over for several seconds on the starter motor. Observe the compression gauge reading. The compression will build-up fairly quickly in a healthy engine. Low compression on the first stroke, followed by gradually-increasing pressure on successive strokes, indicates worn piston rings. A low compression on the first stroke which does not rise on successive strokes, indicates leaking valves or a blown head gasket (a cracked cylinder head could also be the cause). Deposits on the underside of the valve heads can also cause low compression. Record the highest gauge reading obtained, then repeat the procedure for the remaining cylinders.

8 Due to the variety of testers available, and the fluctuation in starter motor speed when cranking the engine, different readings are often obtained when carrying out the compression test. For this reason, actual compression pressure figures are not quoted by Ford. However, the most important factor is that the compression pressures are uniform in all cylinders, and that is what this test is mainly concerned with.

9 If the pressure in any cylinder is considerably lower than the others, introduce a teaspoonful of clean oil into that cylinder through its spark plug hole and repeat the test.

10 If the compression increases after the oil is added, the piston rings are probably worn. If the compression does not increase significantly, the leakage is occurring at the valves or the head gasket. Leakage past the valves may be caused by burned valve seats and/or faces, or warped, cracked or bent valves.

11 If two adjacent cylinders have equally low compressions, it is most likely that the head gasket has blown between them. The appearance of coolant in the combustion chambers or on the engine oil dipstick would verify this condition.

12 If one cylinder is about 20 percent lower than the other, and the engine has a slightly rough idle, a worn lobe on the camshaft could be the cause.

13 On completion of the checks, refit the spark plugs and refit the fuel pump fuse to the fuse/relay box, then clear the fault code from the powertrain control module.

3 Top Dead Centre (TDC) for No 1 piston – locating

Note: *Only turn the engine in the normal direction of rotation – clockwise from the right-hand side of the vehicle.*

General

1 Top Dead Centre (TDC) is the highest point in its travel up-and-down its cylinder bore that each piston reaches as the crankshaft rotates. While each piston reaches TDC both at the top of the compression stroke and again at the top of the exhaust stroke, for the purpose of timing the engine, TDC refers to the No 1 piston position at the top of its compression stroke.

2 It is useful for several servicing procedures to be able to position the engine at TDC.

3 No 1 piston and cylinder are at the right-hand (timing chain) end of the engine (right- and left-hand are always quoted as seen from the driver's seat).

Locating TDC

4 Remove all the spark plugs as described in Chapter 1A Section 22. This will make it easier to turn the engine.

5 Disconnect the battery negative lead as described in Chapter 5A Section 4.

6 Firmly apply the handbrake, then jack up the front of the vehicle and support it securely on axle stands (see *'Jacking and vehicle support'*). Remove the right-hand front roadwheel.

7 Undo the fasteners, then remove the right-hand front wheel arch liner.

8 There is a timing hole provided on the rear of the cylinder block (behind the crankshaft position sensor) to position the crankshaft at TDC. Using a spanner or socket on the crankshaft pulley bolt, rotate the crankshaft clockwise until it is positioned approximately 45° before TDC **(see illustrations)**. Unscrew the timing hole plug and insert a timing peg

(obtainable from Ford dealers (303-748) – or a tool supplier).

9 Rotate the crankshaft clockwise until it stops against the timing peg.

10 There is a bolt hole in the crankshaft pulley which should align with the threaded hole in the timing chain cover, insert a bolt (M6 x 18 mm) to locate the pulley at TDC **(see illustration)**.

11 Number 1 and 4 pistons are now at TDC, one of them on the compression stroke. To determine which cylinder is on the compression stroke the cylinder head cover will need to be removed as described in Section 4.

12 Obtain Ford service tool 303-376B, or fabricate a substitute from a strip of metal 5 mm thick (while the strip's thickness is critical, its length and width are not, but should be approximately 180 to 230 mm by 20 to 30 mm). If number 1 cylinder is on the compression stroke – rest the tool on the cylinder head mating surface, and slide it into the slot in the left-hand end of both camshafts **(see illustration)**. The tool should slip snugly into both slots while resting on the cylinder head mating surface; if one camshaft is only slightly out of alignment, it is permissible to use an open-ended spanner to rotate the camshaft gently and carefully until the tool will fit.

13 If both camshaft slots (they are machined significantly off-centre) are below the level of the cylinder head mating surface, rotate the crankshaft through one full turn clockwise and fit the tool again; it should now fit as described in the previous paragraph. **Note:** *The timing peg and crankshaft pulley locking bolt will have to be removed before turning the engine.*

14 Do not use the locked camshafts to prevent the crankshaft from rotating – use only the locking methods described in Section 6 for removing the crankshaft pulley.

15 Once No 1 cylinder has been positioned at TDC on the compression stroke, TDC for any of the other cylinders can then be located by rotating the crankshaft clockwise 180° at a time and following the firing order (see Specifications).

16 Before turning the engine again, make sure that the timing peg and crankshaft pulley locating bolt have been removed.

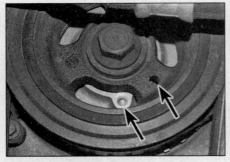

3.8a These 2 holes (arrowed) will align at TDC – so this is about 45° before TDC

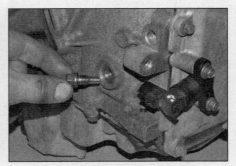

3.8b Remove the timing hole plug...

3.8c... and insert the timing pin

3.10 Insert an M6 bolt though the pulley into the TDC hole in the timing chain cover

3.12 Slide the tool/metal bar into the slots in the end of the camshafts

4.2 Pull the engine cover upwards

4.3 Disconnect the camshaft position sensor wiring plug (arrowed)

4.5 Squeeze together the sides of the collar (arrowed) and disconnect the breather hose

4 Cylinder head cover – removal and refitting

Removal

1 Disconnect the battery negative lead as described in Chapter 5A Section 4.

2 Remove the plastic cover on the top of the engine by pulling it straight up from its mountings **(see illustration)**.

3 On early models, disconnect the wiring connector from the camshaft position sensor **(see illustration)**.

4 Detach the wiring harness from the cylinder head cover.

5 Disconnect the positive crankcase ventilation (PCV) hose from the left-hand rear corner of the cylinder head cover **(see illustration)**.

6 Unscrew the three engine upper plastic cover retaining pegs from the cylinder head cover retaining studs, note the position of the retaining studs.

7 Undo the bolt securing the oxygen sensor wiring plug's bracket **(see illustration)**.

8 Carefully undo the retaining bolts and lift

4.7 Oxygen sensor wiring plug's bracket bolt (arrowed)

out the ignition coils above the spark plugs **(see illustration)**.

9 Working progressively, unscrew the cylinder head cover retaining bolts and withdraw the cover. Note that the bolts are integral with the cover.

10 Check the condition of the cover gasket, and renew if necessary.

Refitting

11 On refitting, clean the cover and cylinder head gasket faces carefully, then fit new

4.8 Undo the bolts and pull out the ignition coils

gaskets to the cover where necessary, ensuring that they locate correctly in the cover grooves.

12 Apply a little silicone sealant (Ford No WSE-M4G323-A4) to the area where the upper edge of the timing chain cover contacts the cylinder head.

13 Refit the cover to the cylinder head. Start all bolts finger-tight, ensuring that the gasket remains seated in its groove.

14 Working in the sequence shown **(see illustration)**, tighten the cover bolts to the specified torque wrench setting. Refit the three engine upper plastic cover retaining pegs to the cover retaining studs noted on removal.

15 The remainder of reassembly is the reverse of the removal procedure.

5 Valve clearances – checking and adjustment

Checking

1 Remove the cylinder head cover as described in Section 4.

2 Set the engine to TDC on cylinder No 1 as described in Section 3. The inlet and exhaust cam lobes of No 1 cylinder will be pointing upwards (though not vertical) and the valve clearances can be checked.

3 Working on each valve, measure the clearance between the base of the cam lobe

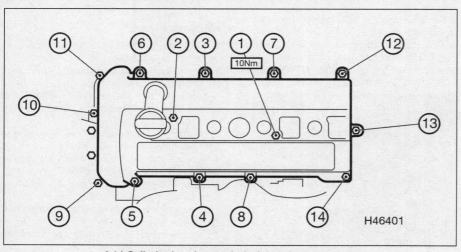

4.14 Cylinder head cover bolt tightening sequence

5.3 Measure the clearance between the base of the cam lobe and the tappet using feeler gauges

5.6 The tappet bucket has a number engraved on the underside

To make a pulley holding tool, obtain two lengths of steel strip about 6 mm thick by about 30 mm wide or similar, one 600 mm long, the other 200 mm long (all dimensions are approximate). Bolt the two strips together to form a forked end, leaving the bolt slack so that the shorter strip can pivot freely. At the other end of each 'prong' of the fork, drill a suitable hole and fit a nut and bolt to allow the tool to engage with the spokes in the pulley.

and the bucket tappet using feeler blades **(see illustration)**. Record the thickness of the blade required to give a firm sliding fit on all the valves of No 1 cylinder. The desired clearances are given in the Specifications. Note that the clearances for inlet and exhaust valves are different. The inlet camshaft is at the front of the engine and the exhaust camshaft at the rear. Record all four clearances.

4 Now turn the crankshaft clockwise through 180° so that the valves of cylinder No 3 are pointing upwards. Check and record the four valve clearances for cylinder No 3. The clearances for cylinders 4 and 2 can be checked after turning the crankshaft through 180° each time.

Adjustment

5 If adjustment is required, the bucket tappets must be changed by removing the camshafts as described in Section 9.

6 If the valve clearance was too small, a thinner bucket tappet must be fitted. If the clearance was too large, a thicker bucket tappet must be fitted. The bucket tappet has a number engraved on the inside **(see illustration)**, if the marking is missing or illegible, a micrometer will be needed to establish bucket tappet thickness.

7 When the bucket tappet thickness and the valve clearance are known, the required thickness of the new bucket tappet can be calculated as follows:

New tappet thickness D
= Existing tappet thickness C
+ Measured clearance B
− Desired clearance A

Sample calculation

Desired clearance (A)	= 0.25 mm
Measured clearance (B)	= 0.20 mm
Existing tappet thickness (C)	= 2.55 mm
Tappet thickness required (D)	= C+B−A
	= 2.5 mm

17 With the correct thickness bucket tappets fitted in the cylinder head, refit the camshafts as described in Section 9.

18 Check the valve clearances are now correct, as described in paragraphs 2 to 4. If any clearances are still not within specification then carry out the adjustment procedure again.

19 It will be helpful for future adjustment if a record is kept of the thickness of bucket fitted at each position. The buckets required can be purchased in advance once the clearances and the existing bucket thicknesses are known.

20 When all the clearances are correct, refit the cylinder head cover as described in Section 4.

6 Crankshaft pulley – removal and refitting

Note: *A new pulley retaining bolt will be required on refitting.*
Caution: The pulley and crankshaft timing gear are not on a keyway, they are held in place by the crankshaft pulley retaining bolt. Make sure the engine is set at TDC (see Section 3) before the pulley is removed.

Removal

1 Remove the auxiliary drivebelt – either remove the drivebelt completely, or just secure it clear of the crankshaft pulley, depending on the work to be carried out (see Chapter 1A Section 25).

2 Set the engine to TDC on cylinder No 1 as described in Section 3.

3 The crankshaft must now be locked to prevent its rotation while the pulley bolt is unscrewed. Ford special tools 205-072 and 205-072-02 are available for this purpose,

7.8 Disconnect the crankshaft position sensor wiring connector

however a home-made tool can easily be fabricated (see **Tool Tip**).

4 Unscrew the pulley bolt and remove the pulley.

Refitting

5 Refitting is the reverse of the removal procedure; making sure the engine has not moved from its setting at TDC (see Section 3).

6 Ensure that a new retaining bolt is used, and tightened to the specified torque then through the specified angle as given in the Specifications.

7 Timing chain cover – removal and refitting

Removal

1 Remove the cylinder head cover as described in Section 4.

2 Firmly apply the handbrake, then jack up the front of the vehicle and support it securely on axle stands (see 'Jacking and vehicle support'). Remove the right-hand front roadwheel.

3 Undo the fasteners, then remove the right-hand front wheel arch liner.

4 Remove the right-hand headlight unit as described in Chapter 12 Section 7.

5 Slacken the coolant pump pulley retaining bolts by approximately three turns.

6 Remove the auxiliary drivebelt as described in Chapter 1A Section 25.

7 Remove the crankshaft pulley as described in Section 6.

8 Disconnect the crankshaft position sensor wiring connector **(see illustration)**.

7.12 Undo the right-hand engine mounting bolts/nuts (arrowed)

9 Undo the three bolts and release the power steering pump from the timing chain cover.
10 Unscrew the retaining bolts and remove the coolant pump pulley and the auxiliary drivebelt idler pulley.
11 Detach the wiring harness from the studs on the lower edge of the timing chain cover.
12 Support the engine using a trolley jack and block of wood beneath the sump, then unscrew the nuts/bolts securing the engine/transmission right-hand mounting bracket and remove the mounting from the engine **(see illustration)**.
13 Undo the retaining nut and release the air conditioning refrigerant pipe support bracket from the front of the timing chain cover.
14 Unscrew the timing chain cover retaining bolts (noting their positions for refitting) and withdraw the cover from the engine.

Refitting

15 Refitting is the reverse of the removal procedure, noting the following points:
a) *Clean the sealant from the timing chain cover, cylinder block and cylinder head mating surfaces. When using a scraper and solvent to remove all traces of old gasket/sealant from the mating surfaces, be careful to ensure that you do not scratch or damage the material of either*

7.15a Apply a 3.0 mm bead of sealant around the timing chain cover, including the inner bolt holes

component – any solvents used must be suitable for this application. If the gasket was leaking, have the mating surfaces checked for warpage at an automotive engineering workshop.
b) *Renew the crankshaft oil seal fitted into the timing chain cover as described in Section 10.*
c) *Provided the relevant mating surfaces are clean and flat, apply a 3.0 mm bead of silicone sealant around the timing chain cover and the inner bolt holes* **(see illustration)**. **Note:** *The cover must be fitted within 10 minutes of applying the sealant.*
d) *Tighten the timing chain cover bolts to the specified torque, following the sequence shown* **(see illustration)**.

8 Timing chain, tensioner and guides – removal, inspection and refitting

Removal

1 Remove the cylinder head cover as described in Section 4.
2 Set the engine to TDC on cylinder No 1 as described in Section 3.

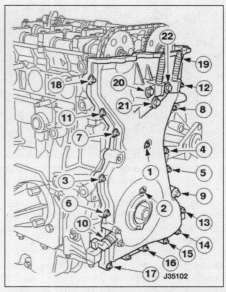

7.15b Timing chain cover bolt tightening sequence

3 Remove the timing chain cover as described in Section 7.
4 Slacken the timing chain tensioner by inserting a small screwdriver into the access hole in the tensioner and releasing the pawl mechanism. Press against the timing chain guide to depress the piston into the tensioner housing. When fully depressed, insert a locking pin (approximately 1.5 mm) to lock the piston in its compressed position **(see illustration)**.
5 Hold the camshafts by the hexagon sections on the shafts to prevent them from turning, using an open-ended spanner.
6 With the camshafts held in position, undo the camshaft sprocket retaining bolts and remove the camshaft sprockets and timing chain. Do not rotate the crankshaft until the timing chain is refitted **(see illustration)**.

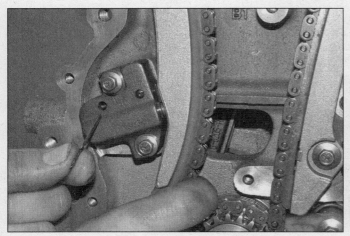

8.4 Press against the timing chain guide and insert a locking pin (approximately 1.5 mm diameter)

8.6 Use a spanner to hold the camshafts whilst undoing the retaining bolts

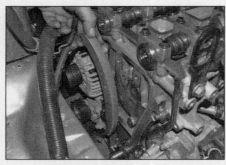

8.7a Withdraw the tensioner guide from the pivot pin...

8.7b... then undo the retaining bolts (arrowed) and remove the fixed guide

8.8 Timing chain tensioner bolts (arrowed)

7 If required, unbolt the fixed timing chain guide and withdraw the tensioner timing chain guide from its pivot pin on the cylinder head **(see illustrations)**.

8 To remove the tensioner, undo the two retaining bolts and remove the timing chain tensioner from the cylinder block, taking care not to remove the locking pin **(see illustration)**.

9 To remove the timing chain sprocket from the crankshaft, the oil pump drive chain will need to be removed as described in Section 13. Note which way round it is fitted and mark the sprocket to ensure it is refitted the same way round.

Inspection

Note: *Keep all components identified for position to ensure correct refitting.*

10 Clean all components thoroughly and wipe dry.

11 Examine the chain tensioner and tensioner guide for excessive wear or other damage. Check the guides for deep grooves made by the timing chain. Renew them both if there is any doubt concerning their condition.

12 Examine the timing chain for excessive wear. Hold it horizontally and check how much movement exists in the chain links. If there is any doubt, compare it to a new chain. Renew as necessary.

13 Examine the teeth of the camshaft and crankshaft sprockets for excessive wear and damage.

14 Before refitting the timing chain tensioner, the piston must be compressed and locked until refitted (if not already done on removal). To do this, insert a small screwdriver into the access hole in the tensioner and release the pawl mechanism. Now lightly clamp the tensioner in a soft-jawed vice and slowly compress the piston. Do not apply excessive

force and make sure that the piston remains aligned with its cylinder. When completely compressed, insert a locking pin/1.5 mm diameter wire rod into the special hole to lock the piston in its compressed position.

Refitting

15 If not already fitted, slide the crankshaft sprocket (and drive shim) onto the crankshaft. Ensure it is refitted the same way round as noted on removal (see Section 13 for further information on refitting the oil pump drive chain).

16 Refit the tensioner to the cylinder block and tighten the retaining bolts to the specified torque setting. Take care not to remove the locking pin **(see illustration)**.

17 Refit the fixed timing chain guide and tighten the two retaining bolts, then slide the tensioner timing chain guide back into place on the upper pivot pin **(see illustration)**.

18 Refit the inlet camshaft sprocket onto the camshaft, DO NOT tighten the retaining bolt at this stage.

19 With the timing chain around the exhaust camshaft sprocket refit the timing chain and sprocket, feeding the timing chain around the crankshaft sprocket and inlet camshaft sprocket **(see illustration)**.

20 With the timing chain in place, press against the tensioner guide and withdraw the tensioner locking pin. This will then tension the timing chain **(see illustration)**.

21 Check that the engine is still set to TDC (as described in Section 3).

22 Tighten the both camshaft sprocket retaining bolts to the specified torque. **Note:** *Use an open-ended spanner on the hexagon on the camshafts to stop them from turning.*

23 Refit the timing chain cover as described in Section 7.

24 Remove the camshaft locking plate and crankshaft timing peg and turn the engine (in the direction of engine rotation) two full turns. Refit the camshaft locking plate and crankshaft timing peg to make sure the engine is still set at TDC (see Section 3 for further information).

25 Refit the cylinder head cover as described in Section 4.

8.16 Refit the timing chain tensioner (still in the locked position)

8.17 Refit the tensioner guides to the engine

8.19 Refit the camshaft sprockets into position, complete with timing chain

8.20 Press against the tensioner guide and withdraw the locking pin (arrowed)

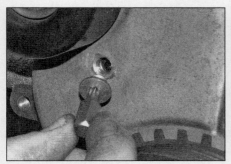

9.3a Remove the timing chain cover lower…

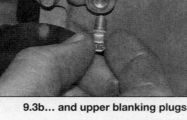

9.3b… and upper blanking plugs

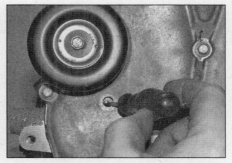

9.4 Insert a small screwdriver into the lower access hole to release the timing chain tensioner

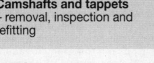

9 Camshafts and tappets
– removal, inspection and refitting

Removal

1 Remove the cylinder head cover as described in Section 4.

2 Set the engine to TDC on No 1 cylinder as described in Section 3.

3 Remove the timing chain cover lower and upper blanking plugs to gain access to the timing chain tensioner and guide **(see illustrations)**.

4 Slacken the timing chain tensioner by inserting a small screwdriver into the lower access hole in the timing chain cover and releasing the pawl mechanism in the tensioner **(see illustration)**.

5 Carefully turn the exhaust camshaft (by using an open-ended spanner on the hexagon on the shaft) in the normal direction of rotation (clockwise), to compress the timing chain tensioner **(see illustration)**.

6 Holding the exhaust camshaft in position, insert a bolt (M6 x 25 mm) into the upper access hole in the timing chain cover to lock the tensioner guide rail in position **(see illustration)**.

7 With the camshafts held in position (by using an open-ended spanner on the hexagon section on the shaft), slacken the camshaft sprocket retaining bolts.

8 Using a cable-tie or similar, fasten the timing chain to the camshaft sprockets.

9 Remove the camshaft sprocket retaining bolts and remove the sprockets, complete with timing chain, away from the camshafts. Using a suitable piece of wire secure the sprockets and timing chain to prevent them dropping into the timing cover.

10 Working in sequence **(see illustration)**, slacken the camshaft bearing cap bolts progressively by half a turn at a time. Work only as described to release gradually and evenly the pressure of the valve springs on the caps.

11 Withdraw the camshaft bearing caps, noting their markings, then remove the camshafts. The inlet camshaft can be identified by the reference lobe for the camshaft position sensor; therefore, there is no need to mark the camshafts **(see illustrations)**.

9.5 Carefully turn the exhaust camshaft in the direction of the arrow

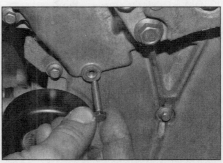

9.6 Whilst holding the exhaust camshaft in position, insert a bolt (M6 x 18 mm) to lock the tensioner guide rail

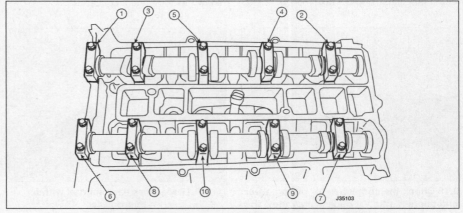

9.10 Sequence for slackening the camshaft bearing caps

9.11a Note the identification markings (arrowed) on the camshaft bearing caps…

9.11b… and the reference lobe (arrowed) on the inlet camshaft for the position sensor

9.12a Remove the tappet bucket with a rubber sucker

9.12b Note the thickness number on the underside of the tappet bucket

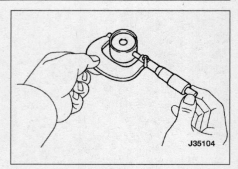

9.14 Use a micrometer to measure the diameter of the tappets

12 Obtain sixteen small, clean containers, and number them 1 to 16. Using a rubber sucker, withdraw each bucket tappet in turn and place them in the containers. Do not interchange the bucket tappets as they are of different sizes; the shim is part of the bucket tappet **(see illustrations)**. Different sizes of bucket tappets are available in the event of wear on the valves or repair on the cylinder head assembly.

Inspection

13 With the camshafts and tappets removed, check each for signs of obvious wear (scoring, pitting, etc) and for ovality, and renew if necessary.

14 Measure the outside diameter of each tappet **(see illustration)** – take measurements at the top and bottom of each tappet, then a second set at right-angles to the first; if any measurement is significantly different from the others, the tappet is tapered or oval (as applicable) and must be renewed. If the necessary equipment is available, measure the inside diameter of the corresponding cylinder head bore. If the tappets or the cylinder head bores are excessively worn, new tappets and/or a new cylinder head will be required.

15 Visually examine the camshaft lobes for score marks, pitting, galling (wear due to rubbing) and evidence of overheating (blue, discoloured areas). Look for flaking away of the hardened surface layer of each lobe **(see illustration)**. If any such signs are evident, renew the component concerned.

16 Examine the camshaft bearing journals and the cylinder head bearing surfaces for signs of obvious wear or pitting. If any such signs are evident, renew the component concerned.

17 Using a micrometer, measure the diameter of each journal at several points **(see illustration)**. If any measurement is significantly different from the others, renew the camshaft.

18 To check camshaft endfloat, remove the tappets, clean the bearing surfaces carefully, and refit the camshafts and bearing caps. Tighten the bearing cap bolts to the specified torque setting, then measure the endfloat using a DTI (Dial Test Indicator, or dial gauge) mounted on the cylinder head so that its tip bears on the camshaft right-hand end.

19 Tap the camshaft fully towards the gauge, zero the gauge, then tap the camshaft fully away from the gauge, and note the gauge reading. If the endfloat measured is found to be at or beyond the specified service limit, fit a new camshaft and repeat the check; if the clearance is still excessive, the cylinder head must be renewed.

Refitting

20 On reassembly, liberally oil the cylinder head tappet bores and the tappets **(see illustration)**. Carefully refit the tappets to the cylinder head, ensuring that each tappet is refitted to its original bore. Some care will be required to enter the tappets squarely into their bores.

21 Turn the engine back approximately 45° so that there are no pistons at the top of the cylinders.

22 Liberally oil the camshaft bearings and lobes **(see illustration)**. Ensuring that each camshaft is in its original location, refit the camshafts, locating each so that the slot in its left-hand end is approximately parallel to, and just above, the cylinder head mating surface.

23 All camshaft bearing caps have an identifying number and letter etched on them. The exhaust camshaft's bearing caps are numbered in sequence E1 to E5 and the inlet camshaft's bearing caps I1 to I5 (see illustration 9.11a).

24 Ensuring that each cap is kept square to the cylinder head as it is tightened down,

9.15 Check the cam lobes for pitting, wear and score marks – if necessary, renew the camshaft

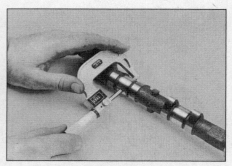

9.17 Measure each journal with a micrometer

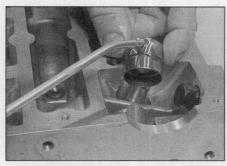

9.20 Liberally oil the tappets when refitting

9.22 Apply clean engine oil to the cam lobes and journals

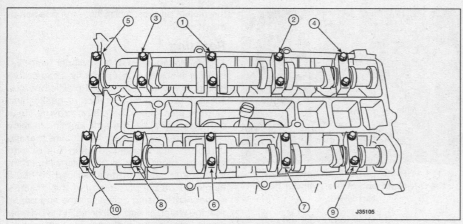

9.24 Camshaft bearing cap bolts tightening sequence

9.25 Fit the camshaft aligning tool to set the TDC position

and working in sequence **(see illustration)**, tighten the camshaft bearing cap bolts slowly and by one turn at a time, until each cap touches the cylinder head. Next, go round again in the same sequence, tightening the bolts to the first stage torque wrench setting specified, then once more, tightening them to the second stage setting. Work only as described to gradually and evenly impose the pressure of the valve springs on the caps.

25 Fit the camshaft aligning tool; it should slip into place as described in Section 3**(see illustration)**.

26 Refit the camshaft sprockets, complete with timing chain to the ends of the camshafts. DO NOT tighten the camshaft sprocket retaining bolts at this stage. Remove the cable-ties from the timing chain and camshaft sprockets.

27 Remove the tensioner guide rail locking bolt from the upper access hole in the timing chain cover. It may be necessary to hold some pressure against the tensioner guide rail to remove the locking bolt.

28 Turn the engine (in the direction of rotation) approximately 45° to TDC. For further information on setting the engine to TDC, see Section 3.

29 With the camshafts held in position (by using an open-ended spanner on the hexagon on the shaft), tighten the camshaft sprocket retaining bolts to the specified torque.

30 Remove the camshaft locking plate and crankshaft timing peg and turn the engine (in the direction of engine rotation) two full

turns. Refit the camshaft locking plate and crankshaft timing peg to make sure the engine is still set at TDC (see Section 3 for further information).

31 Refit the timing chain cover upper and lower blanking plugs, coat the blanking plug threads with a suitable sealant to prevent leaks.

32 Refit the cylinder head cover as described in Section 4.

10 Crankshaft oil seals – renewal

Timing chain end oil seal

1 Remove the crankshaft pulley as described in Section 6.

2 Using a screwdriver, prise the old oil seal from the timing chain cover. Take care not to damage the surface of the timing chain cover and crankshaft. If the oil seal is tight, carefully drill two holes diagonally opposite each other in the oil seal, then insert self-tapping screws and use a pair of pliers to pull out the oil seal.

3 Wipe clean the seating in the timing cover and the nose of the crankshaft.

4 Smear clean engine oil on the outer periphery and sealing lips of the new oil seal, then start it into the timing cover by pressing it in squarely. Using a large socket or metal tubing, drive in the oil seal until flush with the outer surface of the timing cover. Make sure the oil seal remains

square as it is being inserted. Wipe off any excess oil **(see illustrations)**.

5 Refit the crankshaft pulley as described in Section 6.

Transmission end oil seal

Note: *The oil seal can only be renewed as a complete unit with the carrier.*

6 Remove the transmission as described in Chapter 7A Section 7.

7 Remove the clutch assembly as described in Chapter 6 Section 6.

8 Remove the flywheel as described in Section 15.

9 Remove the sump as described in Section 12.

10 Undo the six retaining bolts and remove the oil seal carrier from the cylinder block. Where applicable, remove and discard its gasket.

11 Clean the seal housing and crankshaft, polishing off any burrs or raised edges which may have caused the seal to fail in the first place. Where applicable, clean also the mating surfaces of the cylinder block/crankcase, using a scraper to remove all traces of the old gasket/sealant – be careful not to scratch or damage the material of either – then use a suitable solvent to degrease them.

12 Use the special installation sleeve (supplied with the new oil seal) to slide the seal over the crankshaft.

13 Being careful not to damage the oil seal, move the carrier into the correct position, aligning the guide pins, and tighten its bolts in the correct sequence to the specified torque **(see illustration)**. Remove the installation sleeve once the carrier is installed.

10.4a Ensure the oil seal remains square as it is being fitted

10.4b A socket of the correct size can be used for fitting the new seal

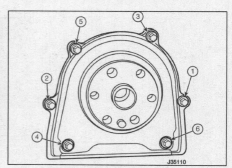

10.13 Oil seal carrier retaining bolts tightening sequence

11.10 Remove the coolant outlet housing (arrowed) from the left-hand end of the cylinder head

11.11 Remove the EGR valve from the left-hand end of the cylinder head (arrowed)

14 Wipe off any surplus oil or grease; the remainder of the reassembly procedure is the reverse of dismantling, referring to the relevant Sections and Chapters indicated.

11 Cylinder head – removal and refitting

Note: *Whenever you disconnect any vacuum lines, coolant and emissions hoses, wiring loom connectors, earth straps and fuel lines as part of the following procedure, always label them clearly so that they can be correctly reassembled.*

Removal

1 Disconnect the battery negative lead as described in Chapter 5A Section 4.
2 Drain the cooling system as described in Chapter 1A Section 30.
3 Remove the air cleaner assembly as described in Chapter 4A Section 5.
4 Remove the alternator as described in Chapter 5A Section 6.
5 Remove the exhaust manifold and heat shields as described in Chapter 4A Section 11.
6 Place rags around the pipes, then depress the locking tab and disconnect the fuel feed pipe from the fuel rail.
7 Undo the two bolts and remove the fuel rail. Plug the openings to prevent dirt ingress. Refer to Chapter 4A Section 10 for more information.
8 Remove the inlet manifold as described in Chapter 4A Section 11.
9 Note their fitted locations, then disconnect the various wiring plugs from the components on the cylinder head, and release any relevant wiring looms from their retaining clips.
10 Undo the four bolts and detach the coolant housing from the left-hand end of the cylinder head **(see illustration)**.
11 Undo the two bolts securing the EGR valve to the cylinder head **(see illustration)**.
12 Remove the cylinder head cover as described in Section 5.
13 Remove the timing chain as described in Section 8.
14 Remove the camshafts and tappets as described in Section 9.
15 Make a final check to ensure that all relevant coolant/vacuum hoses and wiring connectors have been disconnected.
16 Working in sequence **(see illustration)**, slacken the ten cylinder head bolts progressively and by one turn at a time. Remove each bolt in turn, and ensure that new ones are obtained for reassembly; these bolts are subjected to severe stresses and so must be renewed, regardless of their apparent condition, whenever they are disturbed.
17 Lift the cylinder head away; use assistance if possible, as it is a heavy assembly. Remove the gasket and discard it, note the position of the dowels.

Refitting

18 The mating faces of the cylinder head and cylinder block must be perfectly clean before refitting the head. Use a hard plastic or wood scraper to remove all traces of gasket and carbon; also clean the piston crowns. Take particular care, as the soft aluminium alloy is easily damaged. Also, make sure that the carbon is not allowed to enter the oil and water passages – this is particularly important for the lubrication system, as carbon could block the oil supply to any of the engine's components. Using adhesive tape and paper, seal the water, oil and bolt holes in the cylinder block. Clean all the pistons in the same way.
19 Check the mating surfaces of the cylinder block and the cylinder head for nicks, deep scratches and other damage. If excessive, machining may be the only alternative to renewal.
20 If warpage of the cylinder head gasket surface is suspected, use a straight-edge to check it for distortion. Refer to Part D of this Chapter, if necessary.
21 Wipe clean the mating surfaces of the cylinder head and cylinder block. Check that the locating dowels are in position in the cylinder block, and that all cylinder head bolt holes are free from oil.
22 Position a new gasket over the dowels on the cylinder block surface, making sure it is fitted the correct way around.
23 Rotate the crankshaft anti-clockwise so that No 1 cylinder's piston is lowered to approximately 20 mm before TDC, thus avoiding any risk of valve/piston contact and damage during reassembly.
24 Refit the cylinder head, locating it on the dowels. Lubricate the threads, then fit the new cylinder head bolts; carefully enter each into its hole and screw it in, by hand only, until finger-tight.
25 Working progressively and in sequence, use first a torque wrench, then an ordinary socket extension bar and an angle gauge to tighten the cylinder head bolts **(see illustrations)**.

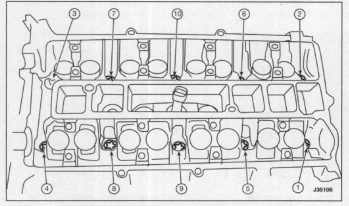

11.16 Cylinder head bolt slackening sequence

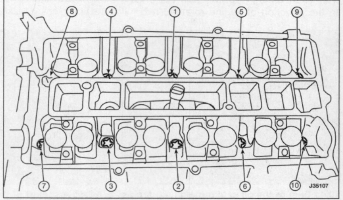

11.25a Cylinder head bolt tightening sequence

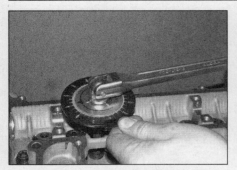

11.25b Use an angle-gauge for the final stages

12.6 Undo the sump-to-transmission bolts (arrowed)

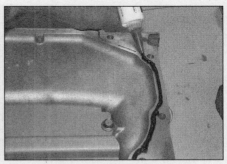

12.9 Apply a 3.0 mm bead of sealant to the sump flange

This is completed in the stages given in the Specifications at the beginning of this Chapter. **Note:** *Once tightened correctly, following this procedure, the cylinder head bolts do not require check-tightening, and must not be retorqued.*

26 Refit the tappets, the camshafts, and the timing chain as described in Sections 9 and 8.

27 The remainder of reassembly is the reverse of the removal procedure, noting the following points:

a) *See the refitting procedures in the relevant Sections and tighten all nuts and bolts to the torque settings specified.*

b) *Refill the cooling system, and top-up the engine oil.*

c) *Check all disturbed joints for signs of oil or coolant leakage, once the engine has been restarted and warmed-up to normal operating temperature.*

12 Sump – removal and refitting

Note: *To carry out this task with the engine/transmission installed in the vehicle requires the assistance of at least one person, plus the equipment necessary to raise and support the front of the vehicle (high enough that the sump can be withdrawn from underneath). It will also require a support bar across the top of the engine bay to hold the complete engine/transmission unit in place while the vehicle is raised. Precise details of the procedure will depend on the equipment available – the following is typical.*

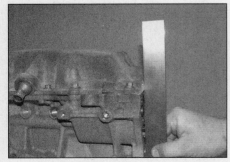

12.11a Use a straight-edge to align the sump to the cylinder block

Removal

1 Firmly apply the handbrake, then jack up the front of the vehicle and support it securely on axle stands (see *'Jacking and vehicle support'*).

2 Drain the engine oil, then clean and refit the engine oil drain plug, tightening it to the specified torque. **Note:** *If the drain plug seal is damaged, a new drain plug will be required. Although not strictly necessary as part of the dismantling procedure, owners are advised to remove and discard the oil filter, so that it can be renewed with the oil (see Chapter 1A Section 7).*

3 Remove the plastic cover from the top of the engine, then support the engine with a cross-beam or hoist.

4 Remove the timing chain cover as described in Section 7.

5 Undo the engine oil level dipstick guide tube retaining bolts, then pull the tube from the sump. Renew the seal at the base of the tube if necessary.

6 Unscrew and remove the sump-to-transmission bolts **(see illustration)**.

7 Progressively unscrew the sump retaining bolts. Use a scraper to break the sealant around the sump, taking care not to damage the mating surfaces of the sump and cylinder block. Lower the

sump and withdraw it from the engine/transmission.

Refitting

8 On reassembly, thoroughly clean and degrease the mating surfaces of the cylinder block/crankcase and sump, then use a clean rag to wipe out the sump.

9 Apply a 3.0 mm bead of sealant (Ford No WSE-M4G323-A4) to the sump flange so that the bead is around the inside edge of the bolt holes **(see illustration)**. **Note:** *The sump must be refitted within 10 minutes of applying the sealant.*

10 Offer up the sump and insert the retaining bolts, do not tighten them at this stage.

11 Using a straight-edge, align the sump to the cylinder block on the timing chain end. With the sump held in position, progressively tighten the retaining bolts to the specified torque in sequence **(see illustrations)**.

12 Refit the sump-to-transmission bolts and tighten them to the specified torque.

13 Refit the timing chain cover as described in Section 7.

14 Lower the car to the ground and refill the engine with oil (and fit a new oil filter) and the cooling system with coolant (see Chapter 1A).

15 Check for signs of oil or coolant leaks once the engine has been restarted and warmed-up to normal operating temperature.

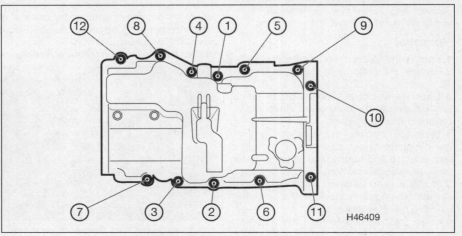

12.11b Sump bolt tightening sequence

13.3 Remove the oil pump pick-up pipe retaining bolts

13.4 Oil pump chain guide and tensioner retaining bolts (arrowed)

13.5 Hold the oil pump sprocket whilst undoing the sprocket bolt

13.7 Undo the 4 retaining bolts (arrowed) and remove the oil pump

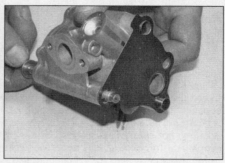

13.11 Use one of the retaining bolts to locate the new gasket in place on the oil pump

13.12 Fit a new O-ring (arrowed) to the oil pump pick-up pipe

13 Oil pump – removal, inspection and refitting

Note: *While this task is theoretically possible when the engine is in place in the vehicle, in practise, it requires so much preliminary dismantling, and is so difficult to carry out due to the restricted access, that owners are advised to remove the engine from the vehicle first. All the illustrations used in this Section are with the engine out of the vehicle and the engine upside down on a work bench.*

Note: *In addition to the new pump gasket and other parts required, read through this Section, and ensure that the necessary tools and facilities are available.*

Removal

1 Remove the timing chain (see Section 8).
2 Remove the sump as described in Section 12.
3 Undo the two bolts securing the oil pump pick-up pipe to the pump **(see illustration)**. Discard the O-ring/gasket.
4 Undo the two retaining bolts and remove the oil pump chain guide, then undo the retaining bolt and remove the oil pump chain tensioner **(see illustration)**.
5 Hold the oil pump drive sprocket to prevent it from turning and slacken the sprocket retaining bolt **(see illustration)**.
6 Undo the bolt and remove the oil pump sprocket complete with the oil pump drive chain.
7 Unbolt the pump from the cylinder block/

crankcase **(see illustration)**. Withdraw and discard the gasket.

Inspection

8 At the time of writing there were no separate parts available for the pump. If there is any doubt about the condition and operation of the oil pump, then the complete pump assembly should be renewed.

Refitting

9 Thoroughly clean and degrease all components, particularly the mating surfaces of the pump, the sump, and the cylinder block/crankcase. When using a scraper and solvent to remove all traces of old gasket/sealant from the mating surfaces, be careful to ensure that you do not scratch or damage the material of either component – any solvents used must be suitable for this application.
10 The oil pump must be primed on installation

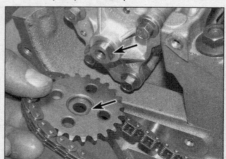

13.13 Align the flats (arrowed) on the oil pump driveshaft and oil pump sprocket when refitting

by pouring clean engine oil into it and rotating its inner rotor a few turns.
11 Fit the new gasket in place on the oil pump using one of the retaining bolts to locate it, refit the pump to the cylinder block/crankcase and insert the retaining bolts, tightening them to the specified torque wrench setting **(see illustration)**.
12 Fit the new O-ring/gasket in place and refit the pump pick-up pipe to the pump, tightening its retaining bolts securely **(see illustration)**.
13 Refit the oil pump drive chain complete with oil pump sprocket **(see illustration)** and tighten the retaining bolt to the specified torque. Hold the oil pump drive sprocket (using the same method as removal) to prevent it from turning when tightening the sprocket retaining bolt.
14 Refit the oil pump chain tensioner to the cylinder block, making sure the spring is located correctly **(see illustration)**. Tighten

13.14 Ensure the spring on the tensioner is hooked behind the bolt (arrowed) to tension the chain

the retaining bolt to its specified torque setting.

15 Refit the oil pump chain guide to the cylinder block, tightening the two retaining bolts to their specified torque setting.

16 Refit the timing chain as described in Section 8.

17 Refit the sump as described in Section 12.

14 Oil pressure warning light switch – removal and refitting

14.1 Oil pressure warning light switch (arrowed)

15.4 Lock the flywheel whilst the bolts (arrowed) are removed

Removal

1 The switch is screwed into the oil filter housing on the front of the cylinder block **(see illustration)**.

2 Disconnect the battery negative lead as described in Chapter 5A Section 4.

3 If required, raise the front of the vehicle, and support it securely on axle stands, this will give better access to the switch. Where fitted, undo the bolts and remove the engine undertray.

4 Disconnect the wiring connector from the switch, and unscrew it; be prepared for some oil loss.

Refitting

5 Refitting is the reverse of the removal procedure; apply a thin smear of suitable sealant to the switch threads, and tighten it to the specified torque wrench setting. Check the engine oil level, and top-up as necessary (see 'Weekly checks'). Check for signs of oil leaks once the engine has been restarted and warmed-up to normal operating temperature.

15 Flywheel – removal, inspection and refitting

Removal

1 Remove the transmission as described in Chapter 7A Section 7.

2 Remove the clutch assembly as described in Chapter 6 Section 6.

3 Use a centre-punch or paint to make alignment marks on the flywheel and crankshaft, to ensure correct alignment during refitting.

4 Prevent the flywheel from turning by locking the ring gear teeth, or by bolting a strap between the flywheel and the cylinder block/crankcase **(see illustration)**. Slacken the bolts evenly until all are free.

5 Remove each bolt in turn, and ensure that new ones are obtained for reassembly; these bolts are subjected to severe stresses, and so must be renewed, regardless of their apparent condition, whenever they are disturbed.

6 Withdraw the flywheel from the end of the crankshaft. **Note:** *Take care when removing the flywheel as it is a very heavy component.*

Inspection

7 Clean the flywheel to remove grease and oil. Inspect the surface for cracks, rivet grooves, burned areas and score marks. Light scoring can be removed with emery cloth. Check for cracked and broken ring gear teeth. Lay the flywheel on a flat surface, and use a straight-edge to check for warpage.

8 Clean and inspect the mating surfaces of the flywheel and the crankshaft. If the crankshaft left-hand oil seal is leaking, renew it (see Section 10) before refitting the flywheel.

9 Thoroughly clean the threaded bolt holes in the crankshaft – this is important, since if old sealer remains in the threads, the bolts will settle over a period and will not retain their correct torque settings.

Refitting

10 On refitting, fit the flywheel to the crankshaft so that all bolt holes align – it will fit only one way – check this using the marks made on removal. If the new bolts are not already pre-coated, apply thread-locking compound to their threads and insert them **(see illustration)**.

11 Lock the flywheel by the method used on dismantling. Working in a diagonal sequence to tighten them evenly, and increasing to the final amount in stages, tighten the new bolts to the specified torque setting **(see illustration)**.

12 The remainder of reassembly is the reverse of the removal procedure, referring to the relevant text for details where required.

15.10 If not already pre-coated, apply suitable locking fluid to the threads of the new bolts on fitting

16 Engine/transmission mountings – inspection and renewal

General

1 The engine/transmission mountings seldom require attention, but broken or deteriorated mountings should be renewed immediately, or the added strain placed on the driveline components may cause damage or wear.

2 While separate mountings may be removed and refitted individually, if more than one is disturbed at a time – such as if the engine/transmission unit is removed from its mountings – they must be reassembled and their fasteners tightened in the position marked on removal.

3 On reassembly, the complete weight of the engine/transmission unit must not be taken by the mountings until all are correctly aligned with the marks made on removal. Tighten the engine/transmission mounting fasteners to their specified torque wrench settings.

Inspection

4 During the check, the engine/transmission unit must be raised slightly, to remove its weight from the mountings.

5 Firmly apply the handbrake, then jack up the front of the vehicle and support it securely on axle stands (see *'Jacking and vehicle*

15.11 Tighten the new bolts, using method used on dismantling for locking the flywheel

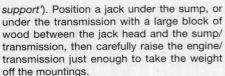

16.11 Right-hand mounting retaining bolts and nuts (arrowed)

16.15 Left-hand mounting retaining bolts and nuts (arrowed)

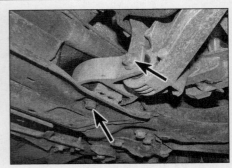

16.19 Rear mounting/roll restrictor bolts (arrowed)

support'). Position a jack under the sump, or under the transmission with a large block of wood between the jack head and the sump/ transmission, then carefully raise the engine/ transmission just enough to take the weight off the mountings.

6 Check the mountings to see if the rubber is cracked, hardened or separated from the metal components. Sometimes the rubber will split right down the centre.

7 Check for relative movement between each mounting's brackets and the engine/ transmission or body (use a large screwdriver or lever to attempt to move the mountings). If movement is noted, lower the engine and check-tighten the mounting fasteners.

Renewal

Note: *The following paragraphs assume the engine is supported beneath the sump or transmission as described earlier.*

Right-hand mounting

8 Pull the plastic cover on the top of the engine upwards from its mountings.

9 Unclip the wiring harness running over the top of the mounting for access to the mounting retaining nuts.

10 Mark the position of the mounting on the vehicle, right-hand inner wing panel, and on the engine bracket.

11 With the engine/transmission supported, unscrew the two locking nuts securing the mounting to the engine bracket, then undo the two bolts securing the mounting to the inner wing panel **(see illustration)**. Withdraw the mounting from the vehicle.

12 On refitting, tighten all fasteners to the torque wrench settings specified. Tighten the two locking nuts to the engine bracket first, then release the hoist or jack to allow the mounting bracket to rest on the vehicle inner wing panel. Re-align the marks made on removal, then tighten the two mounting bracket-to-inner wing retaining bolts.

Left-hand mounting

13 Remove the air cleaner assembly as described in Chapter 4A Section 5.

14 Remove the battery and battery tray as described in Chapter 5A Section 4.

15 With the transmission supported, note the position of the mounting then unscrew the centre retaining nut to release the mounting from the transmission **(see illustration)**.

16 Unscrew the 4 outer retaining nuts, and 2 bolts, then lift the mounting from the stud on the transmission bracket.

17 On refitting, re-align the mounting in the position noted on removal, then tighten all fasteners to the specified torque wrench settings.

18 Refit the battery tray and battery as described in Chapter 5A Section 4, and the air cleaner assembly as described in Chapter 4A Section 5.

Rear mounting (roll restrictor)

19 Unbolt the mounting from the subframe and the transmission by unscrewing the mounting's centre bolts **(see illustration)**.

20 On refitting, ensure that the bolts are securely tightened to the specified torque wrench setting.

Chapter 2 Part B
1.8 litre diesel engine in-car repair procedures

Contents

Degrees of difficulty

Easy, suitable for novice with little experience	Fairly easy, suitable for beginner with some experience	Fairly difficult, suitable for competent DIY mechanic	Difficult, suitable for experienced DIY mechanic	Very difficult, suitable for expert DIY or professional

Specifications

General

Engine type.	Four-cylinder, in-line, single overhead camshaft, cast-iron cylinder head and engine block
Designation	Duratorq TDCi
Engine codes*	FFBA, KHBA and QYBA
Output:	
Power:	
Engine code FFBA	74 kW (100 PS) @ 4000 rpm
Engine codes KHBA and QYBA	92 kW (125 PS) @ 4000 rpm
Torque	250 Nm @ 2000 rpm
Capacity	1753 cc
Bore	82.5 mm
Stroke	82.0 mm
Compression ratio	19.4: 1
Firing order.	1-3-4-2 (No 1 cylinder at timing belt end)
Direction of crankshaft rotation	Clockwise (seen from right-hand side of vehicle)

* For details of engine code location, see 'Vehicle identification' in the Reference Chapter.

Camshaft

Camshaft bearing journal diameter	27.96 to 27.98 mm
Camshaft endfloat	0.100 to 0.240 mm

Valves

Valve clearances (cold):	
Inlet	0.30 to 0.40 mm
Exhaust.	0.45 to 0.55 mm

Cylinder head

Piston protrusion:	Thickness of cylinder head gasket
0.550 to 0.600 mm	1.27 mm (2 notches)
0.601 to 0.650 mm	1.32 mm (3 notches)
0.651 to 0.700 mm	1.37 mm (4 notches)
0.701 to 0.750 mm	1.42 mm (5 notches)
0.751 to 0.800 mm	1.47 mm (6 notches)
0.801 to 0.850 mm	1.52 mm (7 notches)
Camshaft bearing diameter (nominal)	30.500 to 30.525 mm
Maximum permissible gasket surface distortion	0.60 mm

Lubrication

Engine oil type/specification	See Lubricants and fluids on page 0•18
Engine oil capacity	See Chapter 1B
Oil pressure – minimum (engine at operating temperature):	
At idle	0.54 bars
At 2000 rpm	1.39 bars
Oil pump clearance (inner-to-outer rotors)	0.23 mm

Torque wrench settings

	Nm	lbf ft
Air conditioning compressor	25	18
Alternator bracket to block:		
M10 bolts	23	17
M8 bolts	15	11
Nuts	15	11
Auxiliary drivebelt idler pulley bolt	48	35
Big-end bearing cap bolts: *		
Stage 1	27	20
Stage 2	Angle-tighten a further 60°	
Stage 3	Angle-tighten a further 20°	
Camshaft bearing cap	20	15
Camshaft oil baffle plate	20	15
Camshaft sprocket bolt	50	37
Coolant pump pulley bolts	23	17
Crankcase ventilation oil separator	23	17
Crankshaft oil seal carrier	20	15
Crankshaft position sensor bracket	10	7
Crankshaft pulley bolt: *		
Stage 1	100	74
Stage 2	Angle-tighten a further 180°	
Cylinder head bolts: *		
Stage 1	20	15
Stage 2	54	40
Stage 3	Angle-tighten a further 90°	
Stage 4:		
Short bolts	Angle-tighten a further 70°	
Long bolts	Angle-tighten a further 90°	
Cylinder head cover bolts	5	4
Engine mountings:		
Left-hand mounting (transmission):		
Mounting-to-body bolts	25	18
Mounting-to-body nuts	80	59
Mounting-to-transmission bracket centre bolt	133	98
Rear mounting (roll restrictor) bolts	80	59
Right-hand monting bracket-to-engine bolts	28	21
Right-hand mounting-to-engine bracket nuts	80	59
Right-hand mounting–to-body bolts	90	66
Engine-to-transmission bolts	48	35
Flywheel bolts: *		
Stage 1	35	26
Stage 2	Angle-tighten a further 45°	
Fuel pump drive chain guide bolts	23	17
Fuel pump drive chain tensioner	65	48
Lower crankcase to cylinder block	11	8
Main bearing cap bolts: *		
Stage 1	45	33
Stage 2	70	52
Stage 2	Angle-tighten a further 60°	
Oil inlet pipe bracket to block	10	7
Oil pressure switch	20	15
Oil pump bolts/studs:		
M6	10	7
M8	23	17
Power steering pump bolts	23	17
Roadwheel nuts	140	103
Sump bolts:		
Stage 1	7	5
Stage 2	14	10
Sump drain plug	36	27

Torque wrench settings (continued)

	Nm	lbf ft
TDC setting plug cover	24	18
Timing belt inner cover bolts:		
M6	10	7
M8	23	17
Timing belt outer cover	7	5
Timing belt tensioner bolt	50	37
Timing belt tensioner to cylinder head	50	37
Timing chain guide retaining bolts	23	17
Timing chain housing:		
M6	10	7
M8	23	17
Timing chain tensioner	65	48

* Use new fasteners

1 General Information

How to use this Chapter

1 This Part of Chapter 2 is devoted to in-car repair procedures on the 1.8 litre Duratorq TDCi diesel engines. All procedures concerning engine removal, refitting, and overhaul can be found in Chapter 2D.

2 Refer to Vehicle identification13,3 for details of engine code locations.

3 Most of the operations included in this Chapter are based on the assumption that the engine is still installed in the car. Therefore, if this information is being used during a complete engine overhaul, with the engine already removed, many of the steps included here will not apply.

Engine description

4 The engine is an eight-valve, single overhead camshaft (SOHC), four-cylinder, in-line type, mounted transversely at the front of the vehicle, with the transmission on its left-hand end.

5 All major engine castings are of cast-iron; the engine has a lower crankcase which is bolted to the underside of the cylinder block/crankcase, with a sump bolted under that. This arrangement offers greater rigidity than the normal sump arrangement, and helps to reduce engine vibration.

6 The crankshaft runs in five main bearings, the centre main bearing's upper half incorporating thrustwashers to control crankshaft endfloat. The connecting rods rotate on horizontally-split bearing shells at their big-ends. The pistons are attached to the connecting rods by gudgeon pins which are a floating fit in the connecting rod small-end eyes, secured by circlips. The aluminium alloy pistons are fitted with three piston rings: two compression rings and an oil control ring. After manufacture, the cylinder bores and piston skirts are measured and classified into two grades, which must be carefully matched together to ensure the correct piston/cylinder clearance; no oversizes are available to permit reboring.

7 The inlet and exhaust valves are each closed by coil springs; they operate in guides which are shrink-fitted into the cylinder head, as are the valve seat inserts.

8 These engines are unusual in that the fuel injection high-pressure pump is driven by an offset double-row ('gemini') chain (early models) or by a 'wet' rubber composite drive belt (later models) from a sprocket on the crankshaft, with the camshaft being driven from the injection pump sprocket by a conventional toothed timing belt.

9 The camshaft operates the eight valves via conventional cam followers with shims. The camshaft rotates in five bearings that are line-bored directly in the cylinder head and the (bolted-on) bearing caps; this means that the bearing caps are not available separately from the cylinder head, and must not be interchanged with caps from another head.

10 The vacuum pump (used for the brake servo and other vacuum actuators) is driven by a pushrod operated directly by a special lobe on the camshaft.

11 The coolant pump is bolted to the right-hand end of the cylinder block, and is driven by a multi-ribbed auxiliary drivebelt from the crankshaft pulley.

Lubrication system

12 Lubrication is by means of a G-rotor pump, which is mounted on the crankshaft right-hand end, and draws oil through a strainer located in the sump. The pump forces oil through an externally-mounted full-flow cartridge-type filter. From the filter, the oil is pumped into a main gallery in the cylinder block/crankcase, from where it is distributed to the crankshaft (main bearings) and cylinder head. An oil cooler is fitted next to the oil filter, at the rear of the block. The cooler is supplied with coolant from the engine cooling system.

13 While the crankshaft and camshaft bearings receive a pressurised supply, the camshaft lobes and valves are lubricated by splash, as are all other engine components. The undersides of the pistons are cooled by oil, sprayed from nozzles fitted above the upper main bearing shells. The turbocharger receives its own pressurised oil supply.

Operations with engine in car

14 The following major repair operations can be accomplished without removing the engine from the vehicle. However, owners should note that any operation involving the removal of the sump requires careful forethought, depending on the level of skill and the tools and facilities available; refer to the relevant text for details.

a) Compression pressure – testing.

b) Cylinder head cover – removal and refitting.

c) Timing belt cover – removal and refitting.

d) Timing belt – renewal.

e) Timing belt tensioner and sprockets – removal and refitting.

f) Camshaft oil seals – renewal.

g) Camshaft and cam followers – removal and refitting.

h) Cylinder head – removal, overhaul and refitting.

i) Cylinder head and pistons – decarbonising.

j) Sump – removal and refitting.

k) Crankshaft oil seals – renewal.

l) Oil pump – removal and refitting.

m) Piston/connecting rod assemblies – removal and refitting (but see note below).

n) Flywheel – removal and refitting.

o) Engine/transmission mountings – removal and refitting.

Note: It is possible to remove the pistons and connecting rods (after removing the cylinder head and sump) without removing the engine, however, this is not recommended. Work of this nature is more easily and thoroughly completed with the engine on the bench, as described in Chapter 2D.

2 Compression and leakdown tests – description and interpretation

Compression test

Note: A compression tester suitable for use with diesel engines will be required for this test.

1 When engine performance is down, or if misfiring occurs which cannot be attributed to the fuel system, a compression test can provide diagnostic clues as to the engine's condition. If the test is performed regularly, it can give warning of trouble before any other symptoms become apparent.

2.4 Glow plug relay (arrowed)

2 The engine must be fully warmed-up to normal operating temperature, the battery must be fully-charged and the glow plugs must be removed. The aid of an assistant will be required.

3 Note that it is necessary to remove the glow plug relay to allow the compression test to be performed. This will log a fault code in the engine management powertrain control module when the engine is turned over on the starter, and the fault code will have to be cleared, using Ford diagnostic equipment or a compatible alternative, on completion of the test. Unless you have access to the necessary diagnostic equipment it may be preferable to have the compression test carried out by a Ford dealer or suitably-equipped garage. Should you wish to proceed, the procedure is as follows.

4 Remove the glow plug relay from the engine compartment fuse/relay box**(see illustration)**.

5 Pull the plastic cover on the top of the engine upwards to release it from its mountings.

6 Disconnect the wiring plugs from the injectors.

7 Remove the glow plugs as described in Chapter 5ASection 12.

8 Fit a compression tester to the No 1 cylinder glow plug hole. The type of tester which screws into the plug thread is preferred.

9 Crank the engine for several seconds on the starter motor. After one or two revolutions, the compression pressure should build-up to a maximum figure and then stabilise. Record the highest reading obtained.

10 Repeat the test on the remaining cylinders, recording the pressure in each.

11 The cause of poor compression is less easy to establish on a diesel engine than on a petrol one. The effect of introducing oil into the cylinders ('wet' testing) is not conclusive, because there is a risk that the oil will sit in the recess on the piston crown instead of passing to the rings. However, the following can be used as a rough guide to diagnosis.

12 All cylinders should produce very similar pressures; any difference greater than that specified indicates the existence of a fault. Note that the compression should build-up quickly in a healthy engine; low compression on the first stroke, followed by gradually-increasing pressure on successive strokes, indicates worn piston rings. A low compression reading on the first stroke, which does not build-up during successive strokes, indicates leaking valves or a blown head gasket (a cracked head could also be the cause). Deposits on the undersides of the valve heads can also cause low compression.

13 A low reading from two adjacent cylinders is almost certainly due to the head gasket having blown between them; the presence of coolant in the engine oil will confirm this.

14 If the compression reading is unusually high, the cylinder head surfaces, valves and pistons are probably coated with carbon deposits. If this is the case, the cylinder head should be removed and decarbonised (see Part D).

15 On completion, remove the compression tester, and refit the glow plugs.

16 Reconnect the injector wiring plugs, refit the glow plug relay and refit the plastic cover over the top of the engine.

17 Clear the fault code from the powertrain control module.

Leakdown test

18 A leakdown test measures the rate at which compressed air fed into the cylinder is lost. It is an alternative to a compression test, and in many ways it is better, since the escaping air provides easy identification of where pressure loss is occurring (piston rings, valves or head gasket).

19 The equipment needed for leakdown testing is unlikely to be available to the home mechanic. If poor compression is suspected, have the test performed by a Ford dealer or suitably-equipped garage.

3 Top Dead Centre (TDC) for No 1 piston – locating

General

1 TDC is the highest point in the cylinder that each piston reaches as it travels up and down when the crankshaft turns. Each piston reaches TDC at the end of the compression stroke and again at the end of the exhaust stroke, but TDC generally refers to piston position on the compression stroke. No 1 piston is at the timing belt end of the engine.

2 Positioning No 1 piston at TDC is an essential part of many procedures, such as timing belt removal and camshaft removal.

3 The design of the engines covered in this Chapter is such that piston-to-valve contact may occur if the camshaft or crankshaft is turned with the timing belt removed. For this reason, it is important to ensure that the camshaft and crankshaft do not move in relation to each other once the timing belt has been removed from the engine.

Locating TDC

Note: *Suitable tools will be required to lock the crankshaft and camshaft in position during this procedure – see text.*

4 Disconnect the battery negative lead as described in Chapter 5A Section 4.

5 Remove the cylinder head cover as described in Section 4.

6 Remove the fuel filter as described in Chapter 1B Section 21, then undo the bolts and remove the fuel filter mounting bracket **(see illustration)**.

7 Firmly apply the handbrake, then jack up the front of the vehicle and support it securely on axle stands (see *'Jacking and vehicle support'*). Remove the right-hand front wheel.

8 Undo the fasteners and remove the engine undertray.

9 When No 1 cylinder is set to TDC on compression, an offset slot in the left-hand end of the camshaft (left as seen from the driver's seat) should align with the top surface of the cylinder head, to allow a special tool (Ford No 303-376B) to be fitted. This tool can be substituted by a suitable piece of flat

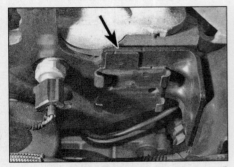

3.6 Remove the fuel filter bracket (arrowed)

3.9a Offset slot in the camshaft aligned with the cylinder head

3.9b Flat bar engaged with the slot in the camshaft

bar **(see illustrations)**. There is no need to fit this tool at this stage, but check that the slot comes into the required alignment while setting TDC – if the slot is above the level of the head, No 1 cylinder could be on the exhaust stroke.

10 If required, further confirmation that No 1 cylinder is on the compression stroke can be inferred from the positions of the camshaft lobes for No 1 cylinder. When the cylinder is on compression, the inlet and exhaust lobes should be pointing upwards (ie, not depressing the cam followers). The camshaft lobes are only visible once the oil baffle plate is removed; the securing nuts also retain two of the camshaft bearing caps – for more information, refer to Section 9.

11 A TDC timing hole is provided on the front of the cylinder block, to permit the crankshaft to be located more accurately at TDC. A timing pin (Ford service tool 303-193, obtainable from Ford dealers or a tool supplier) screws into the hole, and the crankshaft is then turned so that it contacts the end of the tool. A tool can be fabricated to set the timing at TDC, using a piece of threaded rod**(see illustrations)**. The fabricated tool has the following dimensions:
Thread diameter = 10 mm.
Length from 1st nut face to the point = 47 mm
Point ground down to 8 mm.

12 To gain access to the blanking plug fitted over the timing pin hole, remove the auxiliary drivebelt as described in Chapter 1B Section 24, then unbolt and remove the alternator decoupler, as described in the alternator removal procedure in Chapter 5A Section 6.

13 Remove the camshaft setting tool from the slot, and turn the engine back slightly from the TDC position. Unscrew the timing pin blanking plug (which is located in a deeply-recessed hole), and screw in the timing pin **(see illustrations)**. Now carefully turn the crankshaft forwards until it contacts the timing pin (it should be possible to feel this point – the crankshaft cannot then be turned any further forward).

14 Once No 1 cylinder has been positioned at TDC on the compression stroke, TDC for any of the other cylinders can then be located by rotating the crankshaft clockwise 180° at a time and following the firing order (see Specifications).

15 Before rotating the crankshaft again, make sure that the timing pin and camshaft setting bar are removed. When operations are complete, do not forget to refit the timing pin blanking plug.

4 Cylinder head cover –
removal and refitting

Removal

1 Pull the plastic cover on the top of the engine upwards to release the retaining clips**(see illustration)**.

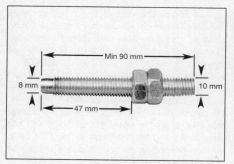

3.11a Tool fabricated to locate the crankshaft at TDC...

3.11b... screw the tool into the cylinder block to locate with the crankshaft

3.13a Unscrew the blanking plug...

3.13b... and insert the timing pin

2 Undo the 2 bolts and detach the manifold absolute pressure (MAP) sensor from the cylinder head cover. Move the sensor to one side **(see illustration)**.

3 Noting their positions carefully for refitting, release the hose clips and detach the crankcase ventilation hoses from the cylinder head cover **(see illustrations)**. There are two hoses at the front, and one at the rear. Move the hoses aside as far as possible.

4.1 Pull the engine cover upwards

4.2 Undo the bolts and move the MAP sensor to one side (arrowed)

4.3a Disconnect the ventilation hoses (1), and the camshaft position sensor (2)...

4.3b... then disconnect the ventilation hose at the rear (arrowed)

4.5 Unscrew the 3 bolts and lift away the cylinder head cover

4 Disconnect the camshaft position sensor wiring plug **(see illustration 4.3a)**.

5 Unscrew the three securing bolts, and lift the cylinder head cover off the engine**(see illustration)**. Inspect the cylinder head cover gasket and renew it if there is any doubt about its condition.

6 If required, the baffle plate fitted below the cover can be removed by unscrewing the nuts and taking off the spacer plates and sleeves – note, however, that these nuts also secure Nos 2 and 4 camshaft bearing caps. Note the positions of all components carefully for refitting.

Refitting

7 Clean the sealing surfaces of the cover and the head, and check the condition of the rubber seals fitted to the cover bolts.

8 Before refitting the cover, check that the crankcase ventilation holes are clear. The

5.2a Unscrew the 4 nuts (arrowed)...

5.2c... then refit the camshaft bearing cap nuts temporarily

connection at the rear of the cover leads to the ventilation valve – if this appears to be blocked, use a suitable degreaser to wash out the valve (it is not advisable to use petrol, as this may damage the valve itself).

9 Lightly lubricate the surfaces of the gasket with fresh oil, then fit the gasket to the cover, making sure it is correctly located.

10 Lower the cover into position, ensuring that the gasket is not disturbed, then fit the three bolts and tighten them a little at a time, so that the cover is drawn down evenly to make a good seal.

11 Further refitting is a reversal of removal. Ensure that the pipes are routed as noted on removal, and that the ventilation hoses are correctly and securely reconnected.

12 When the engine has been run for some time, check for signs of oil leakage from the gasket joint.

5 Valve clearances – checking and adjustment

Checking

1 Remove the cylinder head cover as described in Section 4.

2 Remove the baffle plate fitted below the cover by unscrewing the four nuts and taking off the spacer plates and sleeves. Note, however, that these nuts also secure Nos 2 and 4 camshaft bearing caps – refit the nuts temporarily, once the baffle plate has been removed **(see illustrations)**. Note

5.2b... and lift off the baffle plate...

5.7 Use feeler gauges to measure the exact clearance

the positions of all components carefully for refitting.

3 During the following procedure, the crankshaft must be turned in order to position the peaks of the camshaft lobes away from the valves. To do this, either turn the crankshaft on the pulley bolt or alternatively raise the front right-hand corner of the vehicle, engage 5th gear, and turn the front roadwheel. For improved access to the right-hand end of the engine, first loosen the right-hand front wheel nuts, then jack up the front right-hand side of the car and support it securely on an axle stand (see 'Jacking and vehicle support'). Remove the roadwheel, then remove the engine undertray and the wheel arch liner from inside the wheel arch.

4 If desired, to enable the crankshaft to be turned more easily, remove the glow plugs as described in Chapter 5A Section 12.

5 Draw the valve positions on a piece of paper, numbering them 1 to 8 from the timing belt end of the engine. Identify them as inlet or exhaust (ie, 1I, 2E, 3I, 4E, 5I, 6E, 7I, 8E).

6 Turn the crankshaft until the valves of No 4 cylinder (flywheel end) are 'rocking' – the exhaust valve will be closing and the inlet valve will be opening. The piston of No 1 cylinder will be at the top of its compression stroke, with both valves fully closed. The clearances for both valves of No 1 cylinder may be checked at the same time.

7 Use feeler blade(s) to measure the exact clearance between the heel of the camshaft lobe and the shim on the cam follower; the feeler blades should be a firm sliding fit **(see illustration)**. Record the measured clearance on the drawing. From this clearance it will be possible to calculate the thickness of the new shim to be fitted, where necessary. Note that the inlet and exhaust valve clearances are different, so it is important that you know which valve clearance you are checking.

8 With No 1 cylinder valve clearances checked, turn the engine through half a turn so that No 2 valves are 'rocking', then measure the valve clearances of No 3 cylinder in the same way. Similarly check the valve clearances of No 4 cylinder with No 1 valves 'rocking' and No 2 cylinder with No 3 valves 'rocking'. Compare the measured clearances with the values give in the Specifications – any which fall within the range do not require adjustment.

Adjustment

9 If adjustment is required, turn the engine in the normal direction of rotation through approximately 90°, to bring the pistons to mid-stroke. If this is not done, the pistons at TDC will prevent the cam followers being depressed, and valve damage may result. Depress the cam followers and then either shim can be withdrawn if the peak of the cam does not prevent access. The Ford tools for this operation are Nos 303-195 and 303-196, but with care and patience a C-spanner or screwdriver can be used to depress the cam follower and the shim can be flicked out with a small screwdriver.

10 If the valve clearance was too small, a thinner shim must be fitted. If the clearance was too large, a thicker shim must be fitted. The thickness of the shim (in mm) is engraved on the side facing away from the camshaft. If the marking is missing or illegible, a micrometer will be needed to establish shim thickness.

11 When the shim thickness and the valve clearance are known, the required thickness of the new shim can be calculated as follows:

Sample calculation

Desired clearance (A)	= 0.50 mm
Measured clearance (B)	= 0.35 mm
Shim thickness found (C)	= 3.95 mm
Shim thickness required (D)	= C+B-A
	= 3.80 mm

12 With the correct shim fitted, release the cam follower depressing tool. Turn the engine back so that the cam lobes are again pointing upwards and check that the clearance is now correct.

13 Repeat the process for the remaining valves, turning the engine each time to bring a pair of cam lobes upwards.

14 It will be helpful for future adjustment if a record is kept of the thickness of shim fitted at each position. The shims required can be purchased in advance once the clearances and the existing shim thicknesses are known.

15 It is permissible to interchange shims between cam followers to achieve the correct clearances but it is not advisable to turn the camshaft with any shims removed, since there is a risk that the cam lobe will jam in the empty cam follower.

16 When all the clearances are correct, refit the glow plugs (Chapter 5A Section 12), then refit the oil baffle plate and tighten the nuts to the specified torque. Refit the cylinder head cover as described in Section 4.

17 Refit the wheel arch liner and engine undertray, then refit the roadwheel and lower the car to the ground. Tighten the wheel nuts to the specified torque.

6 Crankshaft pulley – removal and refitting

Removal

1 Disconnect the battery negative lead as described in Chapter 5A Section 4.

2 Loosen the right-hand front roadwheel nuts, then raise the front of the vehicle, and support securely on axle stands (see 'Jacking and vehicle support'). Remove the roadwheel.

3 Undo the fasteners and withdraw the engine undertray from under the car.

4 Remove the auxiliary drivebelt, as described in Chapter 1B Section 24.

5 The centre bolt which secures the crankshaft pulley must now be slackened. This bolt is tightened to a very high torque, and it is first of all essential to ensure that the car is adequately supported, as considerable effort will be needed.

To make a pulley or sprocket holding tool, obtain two lengths of steel strip about 6 mm thick by about 30 mm wide or similar, one 600 mm long, the other 200 mm long (all dimensions are approximate). Bolt the two strips together to form a forked end, leaving the bolt slack so that the shorter strip can pivot freely. At the other end of each 'prong' of the fork, drill a suitable hole and fit a nut and bolt to allow the tool to engage with the holes in the pulley or sprocket.

6 Ford technicians use a special holding tool (205-072) which locates in the holes of the pulley and prevents it from turning. If this tool is not available, a home-made tool can easily be fabricated (see **Tool Tip**).

7 Unscrew the bolt securing the pulley to the crankshaft, and remove the pulley. It is essential to obtain a new bolt for reassembly **(see illustration)**.

8 With the pulley removed, it is advisable to check the crankshaft oil seal for signs of oil leakage. If necessary, fit a new seal as described in Section 16.

Refitting

9 Refit the pulley to the crankshaft sprocket, then fit the new pulley securing bolt and tighten it as far as possible before the crankshaft starts to rotate.

10 Holding the pulley against rotation as for removal, first tighten the bolt to the specified Stage 1 torque.

11 Stage 2 involves tightening the bolt though

7.4a Unclip the fuel pipes from the timing belt cover

6.7 Unscrew the crankshaft pulley bolt and remove the pulley

an angle, rather than to a torque. The bolt must be rotated through the specified angle – special angle gauges are available from tool outlets. As a guide, a 180° angle is equivalent to a half-turn, and this is easily judged by assessing the start and end positions of the socket handle or torque wrench.

12 Refit the auxiliary drivebelt as described in Chapter 1B Section 24.

13 Refit the engine undertray.

14 Refit the roadwheel, lower the vehicle to the ground, and reconnect the battery negative lead as described in Chapter 5A Section 4. Tighten the wheel nuts to the specified torque.

7 Timing belt – removal and refitting

Removal

1 Disconnect the battery negative lead as described in Chapter 5A Section 4.

2 Remove the cylinder head cover as described in Section 4.

3 Referring to the information in Section 3, set the engine to TDC on No 1 cylinder. The timing pin described must be used, to ensure accuracy.

4 Unclip the fuel pipes, then undo the nut, slacken the clamps and remove the intercooler air outlet duct from the right-hand end of the engine **(see illustrations)**.

5 Ford recommend that the engine is further

7.4b Intercooler duct-to-throttle housing clamp (arrowed)

7.8 Engine mounting nuts and bolts (arrowed)

7.9a Using a suitable socket on the Torx end fitting...

7.9b... unscrew and remove the engine mounting front stud

prevented from turning by fitting another special tool, to lock the flywheel ring gear (this prevents the fuel pump sprocket from moving). This tool (Ford No 303-393) is also available from Ford dealers, and is quite simple. With the starter motor removed, as described in Chapter 5A Section 4, the tool bolts across the starter motor aperture in the bellhousing, and a peg on the back of the tool engages and locks the flywheel ring gear. A substitute for this tool could be made, or the ring gear jammed using another suitable tool.

6 Before unbolting the engine mounting, it is recommended that the right-hand wheel is refitted, and the car lowered to the ground (assuming the car has been raised as part of setting the engine to TDC).

7 The engine must now be supported before the right-hand mounting is removed. Ford technicians use an engine support bar, which locates in the channels at the top of each inner wing, and a further beam attached to this, which rests on the front crossmember. If such an arrangement is not available, use an engine crane; either way, use a suitable length of chain and hooks to attach the lifting gear to the engine lifting eye. If the engine must be supported from below (and this is not recommended), use a large piece of wood on a trolley jack to spread the load and reduce the chance of damage to the sump.

8 With the weight of the engine supported, unscrew the two nuts and two bolts securing the engine right-hand mounting, and lift the mounting off the two studs (see illustration).

9 Before the timing belt outer cover can be removed, the stud fitted to the front of the engine mounting must be unscrewed and removed. This can be achieved using a socket on the Torx end fitting provided (see illustrations).

10 Unscrew the three bolts (and one stud/bolt at the top), and remove the timing belt outer cover (see illustration).

11 If the timing belt is not being fitted straight away (or if the belt is being removed as part of another procedure, such as cylinder head removal), temporarily refit the engine right-hand mounting and tighten the bolts securely.

12 Before proceeding further, check once more that the engine is positioned at TDC on No 1 cylinder, as described in Section 3.

13 Slacken the timing belt tensioner bolt, and remove the tensioner completely. Slip the timing belt from the sprockets, and remove it (see illustrations).

14 The camshaft sprocket must be removed – this is necessary as part of setting up the new timing belt, to ensure that the correct valve timing is preserved. Not only will a method for holding the sprocket stationary be required, but the sprocket itself is mounted on a taper, so a puller will be needed to free it from the camshaft. Due to its design, the sprocket cannot readily be removed using an ordinary puller, so either the Ford tool (303-651) must be obtained, or a suitable alternative fabricated.

15 Holding the camshaft sprocket using a suitable tool (see **Tool Tip** in Section 6),

7.10 Remove the timing belt outer cover

7.13a Slacken the tensioner bolt...

7.13b... and slip the timing belt from its sprockets

7.15 Using a forked holding tool, unscrew the camshaft sprocket bolt

7.16a Fit Ford tool 303-651 to the camshaft sprocket

7.16b Using the special Ford puller, free the sprocket from its taper…

7.16c… then remove the sprocket bolt and washer…

7.16d… and finally remove the camshaft sprocket

loosen the sprocket bolt **(see illustration)**. **Note:** *Do not rely on the TDC setting bar engaged in the slot at the opposite end of the camshaft to hold it stationary – not only is this dangerous, it could well result in damage to the camshaft.*

16 Using a suitable puller, release the camshaft sprocket from the taper, and remove it **(see illustrations)**.

17 Do not be tempted to re-use the old timing belt under any circumstances – even if it is known to have covered less mileage than the renewal interval indicated in Chapter 1B Section 23. Ford state that, once a new timing belt has been run on the engine, it is considered worn, and should be discarded. In any case, given the potential expense involved should the belt fail in service, re-using an old belt would be a false economy.

18 Before disposing of the old belt, however, examine it for evidence of contamination by coolant or lubricant. If there are any signs of contamination, find the source of the contamination before progressing any further. If an oil leak is evident, this will most likely be from the camshaft seal. Cure the problem, then wash down the whole area (including the sprockets) with degreaser and allow to dry before fitting the new belt.

19 Spin the tensioner pulley, and check for signs of sticking or roughness, indicating bearing wear. Many professional mechanics will fit a new tensioner as a matter of course when fitting a new timing belt. This should be considered a good idea, especially if the engine has completed a high mileage.

Refitting

20 Ensure that the crankshaft and camshaft are still set to TDC on No 1 cylinder, as described in Section 3.

21 Refit the camshaft sprocket to the

camshaft, tightening the bolt by hand only **(see illustration)**. The sprocket must be able to rotate independently of the camshaft.

22 Fit the timing belt tensioner into position, noting that the adjustment arm must be set pointing as shown **(see illustration)**. Fit the retaining bolt, tightening it finger-tight only at this stage.

23 Fit the new timing belt over the sprockets and above the tensioner pulley, ensuring that the fuel pump sprocket does not move (the camshaft sprocket must be free to turn – remember that the camshaft itself is locked

7.21 Refit the camshaft sprocket bolt, hand-tight at first

7.22 Note that the adjustment arm (arrowed) must be approximately pointing as shown

7.24a Rotate the tensioner arm anti-clockwise…

7.24b… until the pointer is between the sides of the 'window' (arrowed)

9.6 Remove the camshaft bearing shells

by the tool fitted to its slotted end). Where applicable, ensure the arrow on the back of the belt points in the direction of engine rotation.

24 Using an Allen key in the adjuster arm, maintain the tensioner's position whilst the retaining bolt is slackened, then rotate the adjuster arm anti-clockwise until the pointer is positioned between the sides of the adjustment 'window' **(see illustrations)**. Fully tighten the tensioner retaining bolt.

25 Hold the camshaft sprocket against rotation, and tighten the sprocket retaining bolt.

26 Remove the locking tools from the engine, so that it can be turned; these may include the timing pin, the plate fitted into the camshaft slot, and the tool used to lock the flywheel.

27 Mark the TDC position of the crankshaft pulley, using paint or typist's correction fluid, to give a rough indication of TDC, and so that the number of turns can be counted.

28 Using a spanner or socket on the crankshaft pulley centre bolt, turn the engine forwards (clockwise, viewed from the timing belt end) through two full turns, bringing the engine almost up to the TDC position on completion.

29 Using the information in Section 3, set the engine to TDC on No 1 cylinder. Make sure that the timing pin and camshaft locking tools are refitted – also lock the flywheel against rotation, using the same method used previously (see paragraph 5). If the special tools cannot be refitted, go back to paragraph 20 and repeat the setting procedure.

30 Check the position of the timing belt automatic tensioner pointer. If the pointer is still within the two sides of the 'window', proceed to next paragraph. If the pointer is outside the 'window', repeat the tensioning procedure.

31 Remove the locking tools from the engine; these may include the timing pin, the plate fitted into the camshaft slot, and the tool used to lock the flywheel.

32 If the engine right-hand mounting had been temporarily refitted as described in paragraph 11, support the engine once more, and remove the mounting.

33 Refit the timing belt outer cover, and tighten the retaining bolts securely.

34 Refit the front stud to the engine mounting, and tighten it securely, using a similar method to that used for the stud's removal.

35 Refit the engine right-hand mounting, and tighten the nuts and bolts to the specified torque.

36 With the engine securely supported by its mounting once more, the engine supporting tools can be carefully removed.

37 Refit the cylinder head cover as described in Section 4.

38 Refit the intercooler outlet duct and reclip the fuel pipes.

39 Reconnect the battery negative lead as described in Chapter 5A Section 4.

8 Timing belt tensioner and sprockets – removal, inspection and refitting

Timing belt tensioner

1 The timing belt tensioner is removed as part of the timing belt renewal procedure, in Section 7.

Camshaft sprocket

2 The camshaft sprocket is removed as part of the timing belt renewal procedure, in Section 7.

Fuel pump sprocket

3 Removal of the fuel pump sprocket is described as part of the high-pressure fuel pump removal procedure, in Chapter 4B Section 9. Note that the sprocket is sealed to the pump using two types of sealant/locking compound.

9 Camshaft and cam followers – removal, inspection and refitting

Note: *A new camshaft oil seal will be required on refitting.*

Removal

1 Remove the timing belt and camshaft sprocket as described in Section 7.

2 Remove the camshaft oil seal. The seal is quite deeply recessed – Ford dealers have

a special seal extractor for this (tool No 303-293). In the absence of this tool, do not use any removal method which might damage the sealing surfaces, or a leak will result when the new seal is fitted.

3 Unscrew and remove the nuts securing the oil baffle plate to the top of the engine, noting that these nuts also secure Nos 2 and 4 camshaft bearing caps. Lift off the baffle plate, and recover the bearing caps – if no identification numbers are evident on the caps, mark them for position, as they must be refitted to the correct locations.

4 Progressively unscrew (by half a turn at a time) the nuts securing the remaining bearing caps (Nos 1, 3 and 5) until the camshaft is free.

5 Lift off each bearing cap and bearing shell in turn, and mark it for position if necessary – all the caps must be refitted in their original positions.

6 Carefully lift out the camshaft, and place it somewhere safe – the lobes must not be scratched. Remove the lower part of the bearing shells in turn, and mark them for position **(see illustration)**.

7 Before lifting out the cam followers and shims, give some thought to how they will be stored while they are removed. Unless new components are being fitted, the cam followers and shims must be identified for position. The best way to do this is to take a box, and divide it into eight compartments, each with a clearly-marked number; taking No 1 cam follower and shim as being that nearest the timing belt end of the engine, lift out each cam follower and shim, and place it in the box. Alternatively, keep the cam follower/shim assemblies in line, in fitted order, as they are removed – mark No 1 to avoid confusion.

Inspection

8 With the camshaft removed, examine the bearing caps and the bearing locations in the cylinder head for signs of obvious wear or pitting. If evident, a new cylinder head will probably be required. Also check that the oil supply holes in the cylinder head are free from obstructions. (New bearing shells should be used on reassembly.)

9 Visually inspect the camshaft for evidence of wear on the surfaces of the lobes and

9.16 Lubricate the cam followers before refitting

journals. Normally their surfaces should be smooth and have a dull shine; look for scoring, erosion or pitting and areas that appear highly polished, indicating excessive wear. Accelerated wear will occur once the hardened exterior of the camshaft has been damaged, so always renew worn items. **Note:** *If these symptoms are visible on the tips of the camshaft lobes, check the corresponding cam follower/shim, as it will probably be worn as well.*

10 If suitable precision measuring equipment (such as a micrometer) is available, the camshaft bearing journals can be checked for wear, by comparing the values measured with those specified.

11 If the machined surfaces of the camshaft appear discoloured or blued, it is likely that it has been overheated at some point, probably due to inadequate lubrication. This may have distorted the shaft, in which case the runout should be checked; Ford do not quote a runout tolerance, so if this kind of damage is suspected, an engine reconditioning specialist should be consulted. In the case of inadequate lubrication, distortion is unlikely to be the only damage which has occurred, and a new camshaft will probably be needed.

12 To measure the camshaft endfloat, temporarily refit the camshaft to the cylinder head, then fit Nos 1 and 5 bearing caps and tighten the retaining nuts to the specified torque setting. Anchor a DTI gauge to the timing belt end of the cylinder head. Push the camshaft to one end of the cylinder head as far as it will travel, then rest the DTI gauge probe on the end face of the camshaft, and zero the gauge. Push the camshaft as far as it will go to the other end of the cylinder head, and record the gauge reading. Verify the reading by pushing the camshaft back to its original position and checking that the gauge indicates zero again. **Note:** *The cam followers must not be fitted whilst this measurement is being taken.*

13 Check that the camshaft endfloat measurement is within the limit listed in the Specifications. If the measurement is outside the specified limit, wear is unlikely to be confined to any one component, so renewal of the camshaft, cylinder head and bearing caps must be considered.

9.17 Refit the brake vacuum pump pushrod before refitting the camshaft

14 Inspect the cam followers and shims for obvious signs of wear or damage, and renew if necessary.

Refitting

15 Make sure that the top surfaces of the cylinder head, and in particular the camshaft bearings and the mating surfaces for the camshaft bearing caps, are completely clean.

16 Smear some clean engine oil onto the sides of the cam followers, and offer each one into position in their original bores in the cylinder head, together with its respective shim **(see illustration)**. Push them down until they contact the valves, then lubricate the top surface of each shim.

17 Lubricate the camshaft and cylinder head bearing journals with clean engine oil. If the pushrod which operates the brake vacuum pump has been removed from the cylinder head **(see illustration)**, refit it now – once the camshaft is in position, the pushrod cannot be refitted.

18 Carefully lower the camshaft into position in the cylinder head, making sure that the cam lobes for No 1 cylinder are pointing upwards. Also use the position of the locking tool slot at the end of the camshaft as a guide to correct alignment when refitting – the slot should be flush to the top surface of the cylinder head (the larger 'semi-circle' created by the offset slot should be uppermost).

19 Prior to refitting the No 1 camshaft bearing cap, the front halves of the flat sealing surface must be coated with a smear of suitable sealant, as shown **(see illustration)**.

20 Lubricate Nos 1, 3 and 5 bearing caps and shells with clean oil (taking care not to get any on the sealant-coated surfaces of No 1 cap), then place them into their correct positions. Refit the bearing cap nuts, and tighten them progressively to the specified torque wrench setting.

21 The outer edges of No 1 bearing cap must now be sealed to the cylinder head surface with a thin bead of suitable sealant.

22 Clean out the oil seal housing and the sealing surface of the camshaft by wiping it

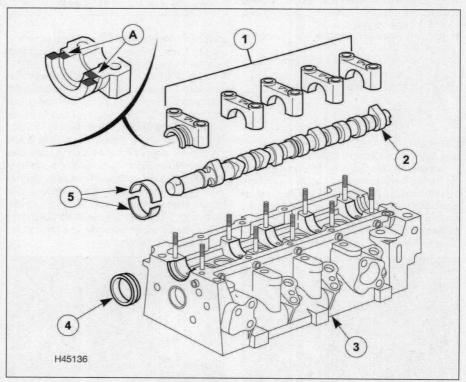

9.19 Camshaft refitting details

A Sealant application areas on No 1 bearing cap
1 Bearing caps (1 to 5)
2 Camshaft
3 Cylinder head
4 Camshaft oil seal
5 Bearing shells

10.4a Lubricate the oil seal before fitting over the camshaft…

10.4b… and use a suitable socket to tap the seal in squarely

11 Cylinder head – removal, inspection and refitting

Note: *Ford technicians remove the cylinder head complete with the inlet and exhaust manifolds. Whilst this may reduce the overall time spent, it makes the cylinder head assembly incredibly heavy and awkward to lift clear (the head is of cast iron, and is quite heavy enough on its own). We felt that, for the DIY mechanic at least, removing the manifolds would be the more sensible option.*

Removal

1 Disconnect the battery negative lead as described in Chapter 5A Section 4.

2 Remove the air cleaner assembly, as described in Chapter 4B Section 5.

3 Remove the cylinder head cover as described in Section 4.

4 Using the information in Section 3, bring the engine round to just before the TDC position on No 1 cylinder. Do not insert any of the locking tools at this stage.

5 Firmly apply the handbrake, then jack up the front of the vehicle and support it securely on axle stands (see *'Jacking and vehicle support'*).

6 Drain the cooling system as described in Chapter 1B Section 30.

7 Remove the turbocharger/exhaust manifold and the inlet manifold as described in Chapter 4B Section 17.

8 Remove the timing belt as described in Section 7.

9 Remove the bolt securing the timing belt backplate to the cylinder head, and the seven nuts around the fuel pump sprocket **(see illustrations)**. While this does not allow the backplate to be removed, it makes it possible to bend the plate enough for the camshaft's tapered end to pass as the head is lifted. If the backplate is to be removed completely, this requires that the fuel pump sprocket and its oil seal housing are also removed, as described in Chapter 4B Section 9.

10 Disconnect the wiring connector from each glow plug and the glow plug supply lead in front of the dipstick tube, and move the wiring harness to one side **(see illustration)**.

with a lint-free cloth. Remove any swarf or burrs that may cause the seal to leak.

23 Apply a little oil to the new camshaft oil seal, and fit it over the end of the camshaft, lips facing inwards. To avoid damaging the seal lips, wrap a little tape over the end of the camshaft. Ford dealers have a special tool (No 303-199A) for fitting the seal, but if this is not available, a deep socket of suitable size can be used. It is important that the seal is fitted square to the shaft, and is fully seated.

24 Refit the camshaft sprocket and timing belt as described in Section 7.

25 Check the valve clearances as described in Section 5.

26 Oil the bearing surfaces of Nos 2 and 4 bearing caps, then refit them and the oil baffle plate to the engine. Tighten the bearing cap nuts to the specified torque.

27 Refit the cylinder head cover as described in Section 4.

28 Further refitting is a reversal of removal.

10 Camshaft oil seal – renewal

1 Remove the timing belt and camshaft sprocket as described in Section 7. Access to the seal is hampered by the presence of the timing belt backplate, but this can only be removed after taking off the fuel pump sprocket; it should not prove necessary to remove the backplate in practice.

2 Remove the camshaft oil seal. The seal is quite deeply recessed – Ford dealers have

a special seal extractor for this (tool No 303-293). In the absence of this tool, do not use any removal method which might damage the sealing surfaces, or a leak will result when the new seal is fitted (see **Haynes Hint**).

3 Clean out the seal housing and the sealing

> **HAYNES HINT** *One of the best ways to remove an oil seal is to carefully drill or punch two holes through the seal opposite each other (taking care not to damage the surface behind the seal as this is done). Two self-tapping screws are then screwed into the holes; by pulling on the screw heads alternately with a pair of pliers, the seal can be extracted.*

surface of the camshaft by wiping it with a lint-free cloth. Remove any swarf or burrs that may cause the seal to leak.

4 Apply a little oil to the new camshaft oil seal, and fit it over the end of the camshaft, lips facing inwards. To avoid damaging the seal lips, wrap a little tape over the end of the camshaft. Ford dealers have a special tool (No 303-199A) for fitting the seal, but if this is not available, a deep socket of suitable size can be used. **Note:** *Select a socket that bears only on the hard outer surface of the seal, not the inner lip which can easily be damaged. It is important that the seal is fitted square to the shaft, and is fully-seated* **(see illustrations)**.

5 Refit the camshaft sprocket and timing belt as described in Section 7.

11.9a Remove the timing belt backplate bolt from the cylinder head…

11.9b… and the 7 nuts around the fuel pump sprocket

11.10 Unscrew the nut securing the glow plug supply lead

11.11a Disconnect the breather hoses...

11.11b... unscrew the mounting bolt...

11.11c... disconnect the oil pressure warning light switch...

11 Release the clips from the crankcase ventilation hoses as necessary, and disconnect the wiring plug from the oil pressure switch, then unbolt and remove the oil separator from the left-hand end of the cylinder head **(see illustrations)**.

12 Unclip and disconnect the wiring plug for the cylinder head temperature sensor, next to the brake vacuum pump **(see illustration)**.

13 Disconnect the vacuum hose and the oil return pipe from the vacuum pump at the left-hand end of the cylinder head (left as seen from the driver's seat). Unscrew the top mounting bolt, and loosen the lower bolt – the lower mounting is slotted, to make removal easier – and lift off the pump. Recover the large O-ring seal – a new one must be used on reassembly **(see illustrations)**.

14 Remove the screw securing the glow plug supply lead to the thermostat housing.

11.11d... and remove the oil separator from the end of the cylinder head

Remove the two bolts securing the thermostat housing to the front of the head, then pull the housing forwards and rest it clear of the head without disconnecting any further pipework **(see illustrations)**. Note that a new

11.12 Disconnect the cylinder head temperature sensor wiring plug

thermostat housing gasket will be needed for reassembly.

15 Clean the area around the high-pressure fuel pipes from the pump to the accumulator rail, and from the injectors to the accumulator rail.

11.13a Unscrew the vacuum hose union...

11.13b... release the hose clip and disconnect the oil return pipe...

11.13c... then unbolt...

11.13d... and remove the vacuum pump – recover the O-ring

11.14a Remove the glow plug supply lead securing bolt

11.14b Unscrew the thermostat housing bolts

11.18 Note their positions, then remove the pipe clamps

11.19 Disconnect the pressure sensor wiring plug

16 Disconnect the fuel return pipes from the injectors (see Chapter 4B Section 3). Cover or plug the openings to prevent dirt ingress.

17 Disconnect the wiring plugs from each injector.

18 Make a note of their exact fitted positions, then remove the high-pressure pipe clamps **(see illustration)**.

19 Disconnect the wiring plug from the pressure sensor on the accumulator rail **(see illustration)**.

20 Unscrew the union nuts and remove the high-pressure fuel pipes from the accumulator rail to the injectors. When unscrewing the unions, counter-hold the adapters with one spanner, and loosen the unions with another. Cover over the end fittings on the accumulator rail and on the injectors to keep the dirt out **(see illustrations)**. Ford insist that the

high-pressure fuel pipes are not re-used – discard the pipes.

21 Undo the bolt/nut and remove the bracket supporting the high-pressure fuel pipe from the pump to the accumulator rail **(see illustration)**.

22 Unscrew the union nuts and remove the high-pressure fuel pipe from the pump to the accumulator rail – again, counter-hold the adapters with a second spanner. Note its fitted position, then remove the clamp from the pipe, Cover or plug the openings to prevent dirt ingress. Ford insist that the pipe is not re-used – discard it.

23 Remove the three bolts securing the accumulator rail bracket to the engine, and withdraw the rail complete with the bracket.

24 If not already done, it is recommended before removing the cylinder head that the

engine right-hand mounting is refitted, and the engine supporting tools removed. This will improve working room if a hoist or engine support bar was used, and avoids the risk of the engine slipping if it was supported from below.

25 Remove the four nuts securing the oil baffle plate, and carefully lift the plate off the engine. Note that these nuts are also used to secure Nos 2 and 4 camshaft bearing caps, which will then be loose. Once the plate is removed, refit the nuts by hand, to keep the caps in place.

26 Check around the head and the engine bay that there is nothing still attached to the cylinder head, nor anything which would prevent it from being lifted away.

27 Working in the reverse order of the tightening sequence(see illustration 11.53), loosen the cylinder head bolts by half a turn at a time, until they are all loose. Remove the head bolts, and discard them – Ford state that they must not be re-used, even if they appear to be serviceable **(see illustrations)**. Note the fitted positions of the two shorter bolts, which should be the two nearest the timing belt end of the engine.

28 Bend the timing belt backplate gently away from the head sufficiently for the camshaft stub to clear it. Lift the cylinder head away; use assistance if possible, as it is a very heavy assembly.

29 If the head is stuck (as is possible), be careful how you choose to free it. Striking the head with tools carries the risk of damage, and the head is located on two dowels, so its movement will be limited. Do not, under any circumstances, lever the head between the mating surfaces, as this will certainly damage the sealing surfaces for the gasket, leading to leaks.

30 Once the head has been removed, recover the gasket from the two dowels. The gasket is manufactured from laminated steel, and cannot be re-used, but see paragraph 32.

Inspection

31 If required, dismantling and inspection of the cylinder head is covered in Part D of this Chapter.

11.20a Use a second spanner to counter-hold the adapters whilst undoing the union nuts at the injectors...

11.20b... and at the accumulator rail

11.21 Remove the pipe support bracket (arrowed)

11.27a Working in the reverse of the tightening sequence, unscrew...

11.27b... and remove the cylinder head bolts

11.36 Measure piston projection with a dial test indicator (DTI)

Cylinder head gasket selection

32 Examine the old cylinder head gasket for manufacturer's identification markings. These will be in the form of notches (two to seven) on the front edge of the gasket, which indicate the gasket's thickness(see illustration 11.49).
33 Unless new components have been fitted, or the cylinder head has been machined (skimmed), the new cylinder head gasket must be of the same type as the old one. Purchase the required gasket, and proceed to paragraph 40.
34 If the head has been machined, or if new pistons have been fitted, it is likely that a head gasket of different thickness to the original will be needed.
35 Gasket selection is made on the basis of the measured piston protrusion above the cylinder head gasket surface. If the head has not been machined, and the pistons, connecting rods, and crankshaft have not been disturbed, use a new head gasket with the same number of notches as the old one.
36 To measure the piston protrusion, anchor a dial test indicator (DTI) to the top face (cylinder head gasket mating face) of the cylinder block, and zero the gauge on the gasket mating face **(see illustration)**.
37 Rest the gauge probe above No 1 piston crown, and turn the crankshaft slowly by hand until the piston reaches TDC (its maximum height). Measure and record the maximum piston projection at TDC.
38 Repeat the measurement for the remaining pistons, and record the results.
39 Note the greatest piston protrusion measurement, and use this to determine the correct cylinder head gasket thickness required (see Specifications). The series of notches/holes on the side of the gasket are used for thickness identification **(see illustration 11.49)**.

Preparation for refitting

40 The mating faces of the cylinder head and cylinder block must be perfectly clean before refitting the head. Use a hard plastic or wooden scraper to remove all traces of gasket and carbon; also clean the piston crowns.
Note: *The new head gasket has rubber-coated surfaces, which could be damaged from sharp edges or debris left by a metal scraper.*

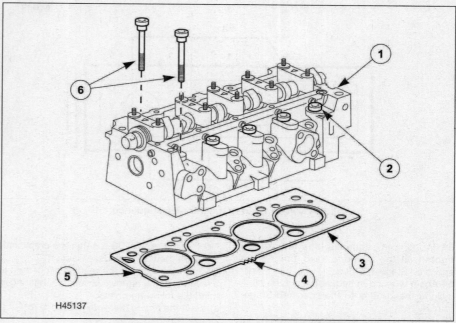

11.49 Cylinder head bolt positions and gasket details

1 Cylinder head
2 Longer bolts (eight, 177 mm long)
3 Cylinder head gasket
4 Thickness markings (notches)
5 Position marking (cut-out)
6 Shorter bolts (two, 137 mm long)

41 Take particular care when cleaning the piston crowns, as the soft aluminium alloy is easily damaged.
42 Make sure that the carbon is not allowed to enter the oil and water passages – this is particularly important for the lubrication system, as carbon could block the oil supply to the engine's components. Using adhesive tape and paper, seal the water, oil and bolt holes in the cylinder block.
43 To prevent carbon entering the gap between the pistons and bores, smear a little grease in the gap. After cleaning each piston, use a small brush to remove all traces of grease and carbon from the gap, then wipe away the remainder with a clean rag. Clean all the pistons in the same way.
44 Check the mating surfaces of the cylinder block and the cylinder head for nicks, deep scratches and other damage (refer to the Note in paragraph 40). If slight, they may be removed carefully with a file, but if excessive, machining may be the only alternative to renewal.
45 If warpage of the cylinder head gasket surface is suspected, use a straight-edge to check it for distortion. Refer to Part D of this Chapter if necessary.
46 Ensure that the cylinder head bolt holes in the crankcase are clean and free of oil. Syringe or soak up any oil left in the bolt holes. This is most important in order that the correct bolt tightening torque can be applied, and to prevent the possibility of the block being cracked by hydraulic pressure when the bolts are tightened.

Refitting

47 Turn the crankshaft anti-clockwise all the pistons at an equal height, approximately halfway down their bores from the TDC position (see Section 3). This will eliminate any risk of piston-to-valve contact as the cylinder head is refitted.
48 To guide the cylinder head into position, screw two long studs (or old cylinder head bolts with the heads cut off, and slots cut in the ends to enable the bolts to be unscrewed) into the end cylinder head bolt locations on the exhaust manifold side of the cylinder block.
49 Ensure that the cylinder head locating dowels are in place at the front corners of the cylinder block, then fit the new cylinder head gasket over the dowels, ensuring that the OBEN/TOP marking is uppermost, and the notches are at the front (there is a further cut-out at the timing belt end of the gasket)**(see illustration)**. Take care to avoid damaging the gasket's rubber coating.
50 Lower the cylinder head into position on the gasket, ensuring that it engages correctly over the guide studs and dowels.
51 Fit the new cylinder head bolts to the eight remaining bolt locations (remember that the two shorter bolts are fitted at the timing belt end of the engine) and screw them in as far as possible by hand. Do not apply oil to the bolts.
52 Unscrew the two guide studs from the exhaust side of the cylinder block, then screw in the two remaining new cylinder head bolts as far as possible by hand.

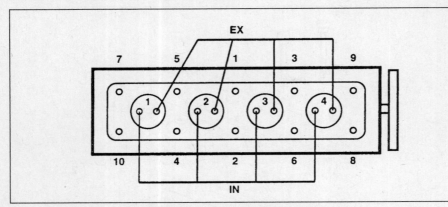

11.53 Cylinder head bolt tightening sequence

11.55 The 2 shorter bolts are tightened through less of an angle than the longer bolts

53 Working in sequence (see illustration), tighten all the cylinder head bolts to the specified Stage 1 torque.
54 Again working in sequence, tighten all the cylinder head bolts to the specified Stage 2 torque.
55 Stages 3 and 4 involve tightening the bolts though an angle, rather than to a torque (see illustration). Each bolt in sequence must be rotated through the specified angle – special angle gauges are available from tool outlets. As a guide, a 90° angle is equivalent to a quarter-turn, and this is easily judged by assessing the start and end positions of the socket handle or torque wrench. Note: *The two shorter bolts at the timing belt end of the engine are tightened through a smaller angle than the remaining eight bolts – do not get confused when following the tightening sequence.*
56 After finally tightening the cylinder head bolts, turn the crankshaft forwards to bring

No 1 piston up to TDC, so that the crankshaft contacts the timing pin (see Section 3).
57 The remainder of the refitting procedure is a reversal of the removal procedure, bearing in mind the following points:
a) *Refit the timing belt with reference to Section 7.*
b) *Reconnect the exhaust front section to the exhaust manifold with reference to Chapter 4B Section 18.*
c) *Refit the accumulator rail and new high-pressure fuel pipes as described in Chapter 4B Section 10 and Section 4B Section 2.*
d) *Refit the cylinder head cover with reference to Section 4.*
e) *Refit the air cleaner as described in Chapter 4B Section 5.*
f) *Refill the cooling system as described in Chapter 1B Section 30.*
g) *Check and if necessary top-up the engine oil level and power steering fluid level as described in 'Weekly checks'.*
h) *Before starting the engine, read through the section on engine restarting after overhaul, in Chapter 2D Section 20.*

12 Sump – removal and refitting

Note: *The full procedure outlined below must be followed so that the mating surfaces can be cleaned and prepared to achieve an oil-tight joint on reassembly.*

Removal

1 Firmly apply the handbrake, then jack up the front of the vehicle and support it securely on axle stands (see *'Jacking and vehicle support'*).
2 Referring to Chapter 1B Section 6 if necessary, drain the engine oil, then clean and refit the engine oil drain plug, tightening it to the specified torque wrench setting. Although not strictly necessary as part of the dismantling procedure, owners are advised to remove and discard the oil filter, so that it can be renewed with the oil.

3 A conventional sump gasket is not used, and sealant is used instead.
4 Progressively unscrew the sump retaining bolts, and the two retaining nuts (the bolts are of different lengths, but it will be obvious where they fit on reassembly). Break the joint by striking the sump with the palm of the hand, then lower the sump away, turning it as necessary.
5 Unfortunately, the use of sealant can make removal of the sump more difficult. If care is taken not to damage the surfaces, the sealant can be cut around using a sharp knife. On no account lever between the mating faces, as this will almost certainly damage them, resulting in leaks when finished. Ford technicians have a tool comprising a metal rod which is inserted through the sump drain hole, and a handle to pull the sump downwards.

Refitting

6 On reassembly, thoroughly clean and degrease the mating surfaces of the cylinder block/crankcase and sump, removing all traces of sealant, then use a clean rag to wipe out the sump and the engine's interior.
7 If the two studs have been removed, they must be refitted before the sump is offered up, to ensure that it is aligned correctly. If this is not done, some of the sealant may enter the blind holes for the sump bolts, preventing the bolts from being fully fitted.
8 Referring to the accompanying illustration, apply silicone sealant (Ford part No WSE-M4G323-A4) to the sump flange, making sure the bead is around the inside edge of the bolt holes. Do not allow sealant to enter the bolts holes. Ford specify that the sealant must be applied in a bead of 2.5 mm diameter (see illustration). Note: *The sump must be refitted within 10 minutes of applying the sealant.*
9 Fit the sump over the studs, and insert the sump bolts and two nuts, tightening them by hand only at this stage.
10 Tighten all the bolts and nuts in the sequence shown (see illustration 12.8).
11 Lower the car to the ground. Wait at least 1 hour for the sealant to cure (or whatever time is indicated by the sealant manufacturer) before refilling the engine with oil. If removed, fit a new oil filter with reference to Chapter 1B Section 6.

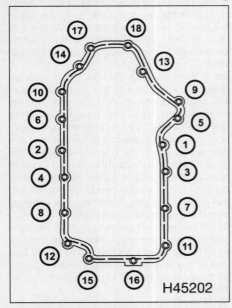

12.8 Sump bolt tightening sequence and sealant application details

Dotted line – 2.5 mm diameter bead of sealant

13.8 Undo the retaining bolts and remove the rotor cover

13.9 Check the condition of the pressure relief valve and clean out the oilways

13.10 Check the clearance between the inner and outer rotor

13 Oil pump – removal, inspection and refitting

Removal

1 Remove the crankshaft pulley as described in Section 6.
2 Unbolt the auxiliary drivebelt idler pulley in front of the crankshaft pulley location.
3 Remove the timing belt and camshaft sprocket as described in Section 7.
4 Remove the fuel pump sprocket and oil seal housing as described in Chapter 4B Section 9.
5 Unbolt and remove the timing belt backplate from the engine.
6 The oil pump is secured by 7 studs and 12 bolts – note their positions carefully for refitting. The studs can be unscrewed using a spanner on the hex provided.
7 Once all the fasteners have been removed, carefully lift the pump from its location. Recover the main gasket, and the smaller spacer ring from below the injection pump. Neither gasket may be re-used – obtain new ones for reassembly.

Inspection

8 Undo the retaining screws and remove the

13.12 Align the dots on the 2 rotors (arrowed)

cover from the oil pump(see illustration). Note the location of the identification marks on the inner and outer rotors for refitting.
9 Unscrew the plug and remove the pressure relief valve, spring and plunger, clean out and check condition of components (see illustration).
10 The clearance between the inner and outer rotors can be checked using feeler blades, and compared with the value given in the Specifications (see illustration).
11 Check the general condition of the oil pump, and in particular, its mating face to the cylinder block. If the mating face is damaged

13.15 Fit a new metal gasket and spacer ring (arrowed) in position

significantly, this may lead to oil loss (and a resulting drop in oil pressure).
12 Inspect the rotors for obvious signs of wear or damage; it is not clear at the time of writing whether individual components are available separately. Lubricate the rotors with fresh engine oil and refit them into the body, making sure that the identification marks are positioned as noted on removal (see illustration).
13 If the oil pump has been removed as part of a major engine overhaul, it is assumed that the engine will have completed a substantial mileage. In this case, it is often considered good practice to fit a new (or reconditioned) pump as a matter of course. In other words, if the rest of the engine is being rebuilt, the engine has completed a large mileage, or there is any question as to the old pump's condition, it is preferable to fit a new oil pump.

Refitting

14 Before fitting the oil pump, ensure that the mating faces on the pump and the engine block are completely clean.
15 Lay the main metal gasket and a new spacer ring in position on the engine – in the case of the spacer ring, 'stick' it in position with a little oil or grease if required (see illustration).
16 Offer the pump into position, and secure it with the studs and bolts, tightened only loosely at this stage (see illustration).
17 Ford technicians use a special tool (303-652) to align the oil pump as it is being

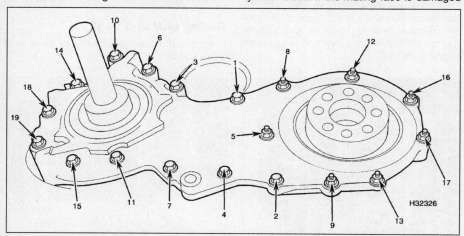

13.16 Oil pump nut/bolt tightening sequence – note special tool 303-652 used to align the pump

13.17 Tool used to align the oil pump before tightening the bolts fully

fitted and tightened **(see illustration)**. The tool is basically a circular socket, which fits over the end of the crankshaft, and ensures that the corresponding hole in the oil pump is centrally located over the end of the crankshaft. In the absence of the tool, this alignment could be confirmed visually, or a large socket/piece of tubing (perhaps wrapped with tape) could be used instead.

18 Ensuring that the correct alignment of the pump is maintained, tighten the pump securing studs and bolts to the specified Stage 1 torque, in sequence **(see illustration 13.16)**.

19 When all the fasteners have been tightened to the Stage 1 torque, go around again in the sequence, and tighten them all to the specified Stage 2 torque.

20 Refit the timing belt backplate to the engine.

21 Refit the fuel pump sprocket and oil seal housing as described in Chapter 4B Section 9.

22 Refit the timing belt and camshaft sprocket as described in Section 7.

23 Refit the auxiliary drivebelt idler pulley, and tighten the bolt to the specified torque.

24 Refit the crankshaft pulley as described in Section 6.

25 When the engine is next started, check for correct oil pump operation (at least, as indicated by the oil pressure warning light going out).

14 Oil pressure warning light switch – removal and refitting

Removal

1 The switch is screwed into the left-hand (flywheel) end of the cylinder head, behind the vacuum pump.

2 Disconnect the battery negative lead as described in Chapter 5A Section 4.

3 To improve access to the switch, it will be necessary to remove (or partially remove) the air cleaner inlet duct and the intercooler right-hand air duct, using the information in Chapter 4B Section 5 and Section 4B Section 16. It will also be helpful to release the

14.4 Disconnect the wiring from the oil pressure warning light switch

hoses and remove the crankcase ventilation system oil separator from the left-hand end of the cylinder head.

4 Unplug the wiring from the switch and unscrew it; be prepared for some oil loss **(see illustration)**.

Refitting

5 Refitting is the reverse of the removal procedure; apply a thin smear of suitable sealant to the switch threads, and tighten it to the specified torque wrench setting.

6 Refit all components removed for access to the switch.

7 Check the engine oil level and top-up as necessary (see 'Weekly checks').

8 Check for correct warning light operation, and for signs of oil leaks, once the engine has been restarted and warmed-up to normal operating temperature.

15 Oil cooler – removal and refitting

Removal

1 The oil cooler is mounted next to the oil filter on the rear of the cylinder block. Access to the oil cooler is best obtained from below.

2 Firmly apply the handbrake, then jack up the front of the vehicle and support it securely on axle stands (see 'Jacking and vehicle support'). Undo the screws and remove the engine undertray.

15.5 Disconnect the turbocharger oil supply union bolt (arrowed)

3 Position a container beneath the oil filter to catch escaping oil and coolant. To improve access to the coolant hoses, unscrew and remove the oil filter, making sure that the filter sealing ring is removed with the filter cartridge – anticipate a small loss of engine oil as the filter is removed. Provided the filter is not due for renewal, it can be refitted on completion.

4 Clamp the oil cooler coolant hoses to minimise spillage, then remove the clips, and disconnect the hoses from the oil cooler. Be prepared for coolant spillage.

5 Loosen the turbocharger oil supply union bolt at the top of the cooler **(see illustration)**, and separate the pipe (be prepared for oil spillage). Recover the copper washers from the union – new ones must be used on reassembly.

6 Unscrew the four bolts securing the oil cooler, noting their positions, as they are of different lengths. Remove the oil cooler from the engine, and recover the gasket (a new gasket must be used on refitting).

Refitting

7 Refitting is a reversal of removal, bearing in mind the following points:

a) Use a new gasket **(see illustration)**.

b) Fit the oil cooler mounting bolts to the positions noted on removal, and tighten them securely. Refit the oil filter if removed – apply a little oil to the filter sealing ring, and tighten the filter securely by hand (do not use any tools).

c) Use new copper washers when reconnecting the oil supply union at the top of the cooler, and tighten the union bolt securely.

d) On completion, refit the engine undertray and lower the car to the ground. Check and if necessary top-up the oil and coolant levels, then start the engine and check for signs of oil or coolant leakage.

16 Crankshaft oil seals – renewal

Timing belt end seal

1 Remove the crankshaft pulley as described in Section 6.

15.7 Renew the oil cooler gasket

2 Note the fitted depth of the oil seal as a guide for fitting the new one.

3 Using a screwdriver or similar tool, carefully prise the oil seal from its location. Take care not to damage the oil seal contact surfaces or the oil seal seating. An alternative method of removing the seals is to drill a small hole in the seal (taking care not to drill any deeper than necessary), then insert a self-tapping screw and use pliers to pull out the seal.

4 Wipe clean the oil seal contact surfaces and seating, and clean up any sharp edges or burrs which might damage the new seal as it is fitted, or which might cause the seal to leak once in place.

5 The new oil seal should be supplied fitted with a locating sleeve, which must not be removed prior to fitting. No oil should be applied to the oil seal, which is made of PTFE.

6 Ford technicians use a special seal-fitting tool (303-652), but an adequate substitute can be achieved using a large socket or piece of tubing of sufficient size to bear on the outer edge of the new seal.

7 Locate the new seal (lips facing inwards) over the end of the crankshaft, using the tool **(see illustration)**, socket, or tubing to press the seal squarely and fully into position, to the previously-noted depth. Once the seal is fully fitted, remove the locating sleeve, if necessary.

8 The remainder of reassembly is the reverse of the removal procedure, referring to the relevant text for details where required. Check for signs of oil leakage when the engine is restarted.

Flywheel end seal

9 Remove the transmission as described in Chapter 7A Section 7, and the clutch assembly as described in Chapter 6 Section 6.

10 Remove the flywheel as described in Section 17.

11 Unbolt and remove the oil seal carrier; the seal is renewed complete with the carrier, and is not available separately. A complete set

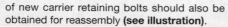

16.7 Use a locating tool to press the seal in squarely (locating sleeve not required when using this tool)

of new carrier retaining bolts should also be obtained for reassembly **(see illustration)**.

12 Clean the end of the crankshaft, polishing off any burrs or raised edges, which may have caused the seal to fail in the first place. Clean also the seal carrier mating face on the engine block, using a suitable solvent for degreasing if necessary.

13 The new oil seal is supplied fitted with a locating sleeve, which must not be removed prior to fitting (it will drop out on its own when the carrier is bolted into position). No oil should be applied to the oil seal, which is made of PTFE.

14 Offer up the carrier into position, feeding the locating sleeve over the end of the crankshaft. Insert the new seal carrier retaining bolts, and tighten them all by hand **(see illustrations)**.

15 Ford technicians use a special tool (308-204) to centre the oil seal carrier around the end of the crankshaft. In the absence of the tool, this alignment could be confirmed visually, or a large socket/piece of tubing (perhaps wrapped with tape) could be used instead.

16 Ensuring that the correct alignment of the carrier is maintained, tighten the retaining bolts to the specified torque. If the seal

16.11 The oil seal is renewed complete with the carrier

locating sleeve is still in position, remove it now.

17 The remainder of the reassembly procedure is the reverse of dismantling, referring to the relevant text for details where required. Check for signs of oil leakage when the engine is restarted.

17 Flywheel – removal, inspection and refitting

Removal

1 Remove the transmission as described in Chapter 7A Section 7, and the clutch assembly as described in Chapter 6 Section 6.

2 Use a centre-punch or paint to make alignment marks on the flywheel and crankshaft, to ensure correct alignment during refitting.

3 Prevent the flywheel from turning by locking the ring gear teeth, or by bolting a strap between the flywheel and the cylinder block/crankcase. Slacken the bolts evenly until all are free.

4 Remove each bolt in turn and ensure that new ones are obtained for reassembly; these bolts are subjected to severe stresses and so

16.14a Fit the new seal assembly, complete with guide sleeve over the end of the crankshaft...

16.14b... then remove the guide sleeve

17.10 Align the bolts holes in the crankshaft – they will only line up in one position

17.11 Tool (arrowed) fabricated to lock the flywheel

must be renewed, regardless of their apparent condition, whenever they are disturbed.

5 Withdraw the flywheel, remembering that it is very heavy – do not drop it.

Inspection

6 Clean the flywheel to remove grease and oil. Inspect the surface for cracks, rivet grooves, burned areas and score marks. Light scoring can be removed with emery cloth. Check for cracked and broken ring gear teeth. Lay the flywheel on a flat surface and use a straight-edge to check for warpage.

7 Clean and inspect the mating surfaces of the flywheel and the crankshaft. If the crankshaft seal is leaking, renew it (see Section 16) before refitting the flywheel. If the engine has covered a high mileage, it may be worth fitting a new seal as a matter if course, given the amount of work needed to access it.

8 Thoroughly clean the threaded bolt holes in the crankshaft, removing all traces of locking compound.

9 Note that on models fitted with a dual-mass flywheel, the maximum travel of the primary mass in relation to the secondary must not exceed 15 teeth.

Refitting

10 On refitting, fit the flywheel to the crankshaft so that all bolt holes align – it will fit only one way – check this using the marks made on removal **(see illustration)**. If the new bolts are not already pre-coated, apply thread-locking compound to their threads and insert them.

11 Lock the flywheel by the method used on dismantling **(see illustration)**. Working in a diagonal sequence, tighten the bolts to the specified Stage 1 torque wrench setting.

12 Stage 2 involves tightening the bolts though an angle, rather than to a torque. Each bolt must be rotated through the specified angle – special angle gauges are available from tool outlets.

13 The remainder of reassembly is the reverse of the removal procedure, referring to the relevant text for details where required.

18 Engine/transmission mountings – inspection and renewal

1 Refer to Chapter 2A, Section 16, but note the different torque wrench settings given in the Specifications at the beginning of this Chapter.

Chapter 2 Part C
2.0 litre diesel engine in-car repair procedures

Contents

Degrees of difficulty

Easy, suitable for novice with little experience	Fairly easy, suitable for beginner with some experience	Fairly difficult, suitable for competent DIY mechanic	Difficult, suitable for experienced DIY mechanic	Very difficult, suitable for expert DIY or professional

Specifications

General

Engine type.	Four-cylinder, in-line, double overhead camshaft, aluminium cylinder head and cast iron engine block
Designation	Duratorq TDCi
Engine codes: *	
Engines to emission level Stage III/IV.	AZBA and QXBA
Engines to emission level Stage V	TXBA, TXBB, TYBA, UFBA, UKBA and UKBB
Output:	
Power:	
Engine code AZBA	96 kW (130 PS) @ 4000 rpm
Engine code QXBA	103 kW (140 PS) @ 4000 rpm
Engine code QXBB.	102 kW (138 PS) @ 4000 rpm
Engine code TXBA	120 kW (163 PS) @ 4000 rpm
Engine code TXBB	120 kW (163 PS) @ 4000 rpm
Engine codes KLBA, LPBA, TYBA	85 kW (115 PS) @ 4000 rpm
Engine code UFBA	103 kW (140 PS) @ 4000 rpm
Engine code UFBB.	103kW (140ps) @ 4000 rpm
Engine code UKBA.	100 kW (136 PS) @ 4000 rpm
Torque	320 Nm @ 1750 rpm
Capacity	1997 cc
Bore	85.0 mm
Stroke	88.0 mm
Compression ratio	18: 1
Firing order	1-3-4-2 (No 1 cylinder at transmission end)
Direction of crankshaft rotation	Clockwise (seen from right-hand side of vehicle)

* For details of engine code location, see 'Vehicle identification' in the Reference Chapter.

Cylinder head

Piston protrusion:	Thickness of cylinder head gasket
0.55 to 0.60 mm	1.21 to 1.29 mm (1 hole)
0.61 to 0.65 mm	1.26 to 1.34 mm (2 holes)
0.66 to 0.70 mm	1.31 to 1.39 mm (3 holes)
0.71 to 0.75 mm	1.36 to 1.44 mm (4 holes)
Valve clearances.	Hydraulic adjusters – no adjustment necessary

Camshaft

Camshaft bearing journal diameter	25.059 to 25.080 mm
Camshaft endfloat	0.070 to 0.168 mm

Lubrication

Engine oil type/specification	See *Lubricants and fluids* on page 0•18
Engine oil capacity	See Chapter 1B
Oil pressure – minimum (engine at operating temperature):	
At 2000 rpm	2.0 bar
At 4000 rpm	4.0 bar

Torque wrench settings

	Nm	lbf ft
Engines to emission level Stage III/IV		
Air conditioning compressor bolts	28	21
Big-end bearing cap nuts: *		
Stage 1	20	15
Stage 2	Angle-tighten a further 70°	
Camshaft sprocket bolt:		
Stage 1	20	15
Stage 2	Angle-tighten a further 60°	
Crankshaft oil seal carrier	14	10
Crankshaft pulley bolt: *		
Stage 1	70	52
Stage 2	Angle-tighten a further 60°	
Cylinder head lower section-to-block bolts: *		
Stage 1	60	44
Stage 2	Angle-tighten a further 220°	
Cylinder head upper section-to-lower section bolts:		
Stage 1	5	4
Stage 2	10	7
Cylinder head cover/inlet manifold:		
Stage 1	5	4
Stage 2	10	7
Driveplate bolts*	66	49
Engine mountings:		
Left-hand mounting (transmission):		
Mounting-to-body bolts	25	18
Mounting-to-body nuts	80	59
Mounting-to-transmission bracket centre bolt	133	98
Rear mounting (roll restrictor) bolts	80	59
Right-hand mounting-to-engine bracket nuts	80	59
Right-hand mounting–to-body bolts	90	66
Right-hand mounting engine bracket bolts	56	41
Engine-to-transmission bolts	48	35
Engine oil drain plug	34	25
Flywheel bolts*	48	35
Fuel accumulator rail mounting bolts	22	16
Fuel injector mounting studs	10	7
Fuel pump mounting bolts	20	15
High-pressure fuel pipe unions	30	22
Main bearing cap bolts:		
Stage 1	30	22
Stage 2	Angle-tighten a further 63°	
Oil pump bolts	16	12
Oil pump pick-up tube bolts	12	9
Roadwheel nuts	140	103
Subframe cross-brace retaining bolts	30	22
Subframe mounting bolts: *		
Stage 1	150	111
Stage 2	Angle-tighten a further 90°	
Sump bolts:		
Sump to cylinder block	16	12
Sump to transmission	48	35
Thermostat housing to cylinder head	10	7
Timing belt idler pulley	56	41
Timing belt tensioner	21	15
Timing chain tensioner	6	4
Vacuum pump mounting bolts	10	7

Torque wrench settings (continued)
Engines to emission level Stage V

	Nm	lbf ft
Big-end bearing cap nuts: *		
Stage 1	20	15
Stage 2	Angle-tighten a further 70°	
Camshaft sprocket bolt:		
Stage 1	20	15
Stage 2	Angle-tighten a further 60°	
Crankshaft oil seal carrier.	14	10
Crankshaft pulley bolt: *		
Stage 1	70	52
Stage 2	Angle-tighten a further 60°	
Cylinder head lower section-to-block bolts: *		
Stage 1	60	44
Stage 2	Angle-tighten a further 220°	
Cylinder head upper section-to-lower section bolts:		
Stage 1	5	4
Stage 2	10	7
Cylinder head cover/inlet manifold to cylinder head:		
Stage 1	5	4
Stage 2	10	7
Driveplate bolts: *		
Stage 1	20	15
Stage 2	66	49
Engine mountings:		
Left-hand mounting (transmission):		
Mounting-to-body bolts	25	18
Mounting-to-body nuts.	80	59
Mounting-to-transmission bracket centre bolt	133	98
Rear mounting (roll restrictor) bolts	80	59
Right-hand mounting-to-engine bracket nuts	133	98
Right-hand mounting–to-body bolts	90	66
Right-hand mounting engine bracket bolts	56	41
Engine-to-transmission bolts	48	35
Engine oil drain plug.	34	25
Flywheel bolts: *		
Stage 1	20	15
Stage 2	48	35
Fuel accumulator rail mounting bolts	22	16
Fuel pump mounting bolts	20	15
High-pressure fuel pipe unions	30	22
Inlet manifold upper section-to-lower section bolts.	8	6
Inlet manifold lower section-to-cylinder head nuts:		
Left-hand side nut	8	6
Right-hand side nut/bolt	20	15
Lower crankcase bolts:		
Stage 1	10	7
Stage 2	16	12
Main bearing cap bolts:		
Stage 1	10	7
Stage 2	30	22
Stage 3	Angle-tighten a further 82°	
Oil pump bolts	16	12
Roadwheel nuts	140	103
Subframe cross-brace retaining bolts	30	22
Subframe mounting bolts: *		
Stage 1	150	111
Stage 2	Angle-tighten a further 90°	
Sump bolts.	10	7
Thermostat housing to cylinder head.	10	7
Timing belt idler pulley	56	41
Timing belt tensioner	21	15
Timing chain tensioner	6	4
Vacuum pump mounting bolts	10	7

* Use new fasteners

1 General Information

How to use this Chapter

1 This Part of Chapter 2 is devoted to in-car repair procedures on the 2.0 litre Duratorq TDCi diesel engines. All procedures concerning engine removal, refitting, and overhaul can be found in Chapter 2D.

2 Refer to Vehicle identification 13 Section 3 for details of engine code locations.

3 Most of the operations included in this Chapter are based on the assumption that the engine is still installed in the car. Therefore, if this information is being used during a complete engine overhaul, with the engine already removed, many of the steps included here will not apply.

Engine description

4 The engine is a result of a joint venture between Ford and Peugeot. This DOHC (Double Overhead Camshaft) 16-valve engine features common rail direct injection, and a VNT (Variable Nozzle Turbine) turbocharger.

5 All major components are made from aluminium, apart from the cast-iron cylinder block – no liners are fitted, the cylinders are bored directly into the block. Engines to emission level Stage V have a lower crankcase which is bolted to the underside of the cylinder block/crankcase, with a sump bolted under that. This arrangement offers greater rigidity than the normal sump arrangement, and helps to reduce engine vibration.

6 The crankshaft runs in five main bearings, thrustwashers are fitting either side of the No 2 cylinder main bearings to control crankshaft endfloat. The connecting rods rotate on horizontally-split bearing shells at their big-ends. The pistons are attached to the connecting rods by gudgeon pins which are a floating fit in the connecting rod small-end eyes, secured by circlips. The aluminium alloy pistons are fitted with three piston rings: two compression rings and an oil control ring. After manufacture, the cylinder bores and piston skirts are measured and classified into four weight grades, which must be carefully matched together to ensure the correct piston/cylinder clearance; no oversizes are available to permit reboring.

7 The inlet and exhaust valves are each closed by coil springs; they operate in guides which are shrink-fitted into the cylinder head, as are the valve seat inserts.

8 A rubber-toothed belt, driven by the crankshaft sprocket, rotates the coolant pump and the exhaust camshaft sprocket. The inlet camshaft is driven by a short timing chain from the exhaust camshaft.

9 The camshafts operate the 16 valves via roller-rocker arms with hydraulic clearance adjusters. The camshafts rotate in five bearings that are line-bored directly into the two sections of the cylinder head.

10 The vacuum pump (used for the brake servo and other vacuum actuators) is driven from the end of the inlet camshaft, whilst the high-pressure fuel pump is driven from the end of the exhaust camshaft.

Lubrication system

11 The oil pump is mounted under the cylinder block, and is chain-driven from a crankshaft sprocket. The pump forces oil through an externally-mounted full-flow cartridge-type filter. From the filter, the oil is pumped into a main gallery in the cylinder block/crankcase, from where it is distributed to the crankshaft (main bearings) and cylinder head. An oil cooler is fitted next to the oil filter, at the rear of the block. The cooler is supplied with coolant from the engine cooling system.

12 While the crankshaft and camshaft bearings receive a pressurised supply, the camshaft lobes and valves are lubricated by splash, as are all other engine components. The undersides of the pistons are cooled by oil, sprayed from nozzles fitted above the upper main bearing shells. The turbocharger receives its own pressurised oil supply.

Operations with engine in car

13 The following major repair operations can be accomplished without removing the engine from the vehicle. However, owners should note that any operation involving the removal of the sump requires careful forethought, depending on the level of skill and the tools and facilities available; refer to the relevant text for details.

a) *Compression pressure – testing.*

b) *Cylinder head cover – removal and refitting.*

c) *Timing belt covers – removal and refitting.*

d) *Timing belt/chain – renewal.*

e) *Timing belt tensioner and sprockets – removal and refitting.*

f) *Camshaft oil seal – renewal.*

g) *Camshafts, rocker arms and hydraulic adjusters – removal and refitting.*

h) *Cylinder head – removal, overhaul and refitting.*

i) *Cylinder head and pistons – decarbonising.*

j) *Sump – removal and refitting.*

k) *Crankshaft oil seals – renewal.*

l) *Oil pump – removal and refitting.*

m) *Piston/connecting rod assemblies – removal and refitting (but see note below).*

n) *Flywheel/driveplate – removal and refitting.*

o) *Engine/transmission mountings – removal and refitting.*

Note: *It is possible to remove the pistons and connecting rods (after removing the cylinder head and sump) without removing the engine, however, this is not recommended. Work of this nature is more easily and thoroughly completed with the engine on the bench, as described in Chapter 2D Section 6.*

2 Compression and leakdown tests – description and interpretation

Compression test

Note: *A compression tester suitable for use with diesel engines will be required for this test.*

1 When engine performance is down, or if misfiring occurs which cannot be attributed to the fuel or emissions systems, a compression test can provide diagnostic clues as to the engine's condition. If the test is performed regularly, it can give warning of trouble before any other symptoms become apparent.

2 The engine must be fully warmed-up to normal operating temperature, the battery must be fully-charged and the glow plugs must be removed. The aid of an assistant will be required.

3 Note that it is necessary to disconnect the glow plug relay to allow the compression test to be performed. This will log a fault code in the engine management powertrain control module when the engine is turned over on the starter, and the fault code will have to be cleared, using Ford diagnostic equipment or a compatible alternative, on completion of the test. Unless you have access to the necessary diagnostic equipment it may be preferable to have the compression test carried out by a Ford dealer or suitably-equipped garage. Should you wish to proceed, the procedure is as follows.

4 Remove the glow plug relay from the engine compartment fuse/relay box **(see illustration)**.

5 Pull the plastic cover on the top of the engine upwards to release it from its mountings.

6 Disconnect the wiring plugs from the injectors.

7 Remove the glow plugs as described in Chapter 5A Section 12.

8 Fit a compression tester to the No 1 cylinder glow plug hole. The type of tester which screws into the plug thread is preferred.

9 Crank the engine for several seconds on the starter motor. After one or two revolutions, the compression pressure should build-up to a maximum figure and then stabilise. Record the highest reading obtained.

2.4 Glow plug relay (arrowed)

3.3a Release the clamps and disconnect the breather hose (arrowed) from the cylinder head cover...

3.3b... the EGR pipe (arrowed) from the inlet manifold...

3.3c... then depress the clip and disconnect the breather hose from the rear of the cylinder head cover

10 Repeat the test on the remaining cylinders, recording the pressure in each.

11 The cause of poor compression is less easy to establish on a diesel engine than on a petrol engine. The effect of introducing oil into the cylinders (wet testing) is not conclusive, because there is a risk that the oil will sit in the recess on the piston crown, instead of passing to the rings. However, the following can be used as a rough guide to diagnosis.

12 All cylinders should produce very similar pressures. Any great difference indicates the existence of a fault. Note that the compression should build-up quickly in a healthy engine. Low compression on the first stroke, followed by gradually increasing pressure on successive strokes, indicates worn piston rings. A low compression reading on the first stroke, which does not build-up during successive strokes, indicates leaking valves or a blown head gasket (a cracked head could also be the cause). Deposits on the undersides of the valve heads can also cause low compression.

13 A low reading from two adjacent cylinders is almost certainly due to the head gasket having blown between them and the presence of coolant in the engine oil will confirm this.

14 If the compression reading is unusually high, the cylinder head surfaces, valves and pistons are probably coated with carbon deposits. If this is the case, the cylinder head should be removed and decarbonised (see Part D).

15 On completion, remove the compression tester, and refit the glow plugs.

16 Reconnect the injector wiring plugs and the plastic cover over the top of the engine.

17 Refit the glow plug relay, then clear the fault code from the powertrain control module.

Leakdown test

18 A leakdown test measures the rate at which compressed air fed into the cylinder is lost. It is an alternative to a compression test, and in many ways it is better, since the escaping air provides easy identification of where pressure loss is occurring (piston rings, valves or head gasket).

19 The equipment required for leakdown testing is unlikely to be available to the home mechanic. If poor compression is suspected, have the test performed by a suitably-equipped garage.

---

3 Cylinder head cover – removal and refitting

Engines to emission level Stage III/IV

Removal

1 The cylinder head cover is integral with the inlet manifold. Begin by removing the plastic cover from the top of the engine by pulling it straight up from its mountings at the right-hand rear corner, right-hand front corner and left-hand front corner, then sliding it forwards.

2 Disconnect the battery negative lead as described in Chapter 5A Section 4.

3 Disconnect the crankcase ventilation hoses from the inlet manifold/cover, then release the clamp and disconnect the EGR pipe from the inlet manifold **(see illustrations)**.

4 Undo the bolts and remove the throttle housing/anti-shudder valve and retaining bracket **(see illustration)**.

5 Undo the remaining bolts and remove the EGR pipe.

6 Release the clips and detach the wiring harness and fuel pipes from the timing belt upper cover.

7 Undo the bolt and remove the wiring bracket from the right-hand rear corner of the cylinder head.

8 Undo the bolts, slacken the nut, then remove the timing belt upper cover.

9 Disconnect the wiring plug, undo the retaining bolt and remove the camshaft position sensor **(see illustration)**. Note that a new sensor will be required for refitting.

10 Disconnect the injector wiring plugs, then detach the harness duct from the inlet manifold/cover and position it to one side **(see illustration)**.

11 Release the glow plug's wiring harness from the two clips on the manifold.

12 Unclip the fuel temperature sensor (located on underside the inlet manifold).

3.4 Anti-shudder valve/throttle housing bolts (arrowed)

3.9 Undo the bolt (arrowed) and remove the camshaft position sensor

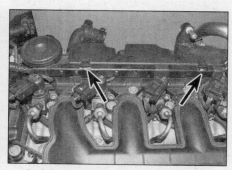

3.10 Release the clips (arrowed) and detach the injector wiring harness duct

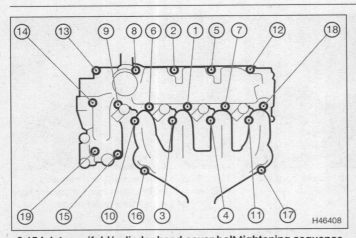

3.15 Inlet manifold/cylinder head cover bolt tightening sequence

Note that the 55 mm bolt is fitted to position 14, and 70 mm bolts are fitted to positions 16 and 17

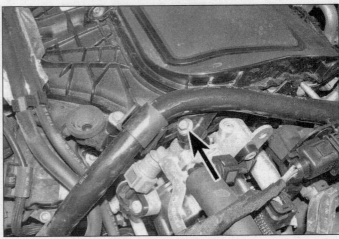

3.19 Undo the bolt (arrowed) securing the crankcase ventilation pipe to the top of the inlet manifold/cover

13 Undo the manifold/cover retaining bolts in the reverse of the sequence shown **(see illustration 3.15)**. Discard the gaskets, new ones must be fitted.

Refitting

14 Clean the sealing surfaces of the manifold/cover and the head.

15 Fit the new seals to the inlet manifold/cover, then fit it to the cylinder head. Use a little petroleum jelly on the manifold O-rings to ease assembly. Tighten the bolts to the specified torque in sequence **(see illustration)**.

16 The remainder of refitting is a reversal of removal, noting the following points:

a) *Tighten all fasteners to their specified torque where given.*

b) *The new camshaft position sensor must be fitted as described in Chapter 4B Section 12, otherwise it will not function correctly.*

Engines to emission level Stage V

⚠️ *Warning: Refer to the information contained in Chapter 4B, Section 2, before proceeding.*

Note 1: *A complete new set of high-pressure fuel pipes will be required for refitting.*

Note 2: *It will be necessary to prime and bleed the fuel system after completing this procedure. This entails the use of special tools and can, in some instances, be a difficult operation. Read through the priming and bleeding information contained in Chapter 4B Section 4 before proceeding.*

Removal

17 The cylinder head cover is integral with the inlet manifold. Begin by removing the plastic cover from the top of the engine by pulling it straight up from its mountings at the right-hand rear corner, right-hand front corner and left-hand front corner, then sliding it forwards.

18 Disconnect the battery negative lead as described in Chapter 5A Section 4.

19 Undo the bolt securing the crankcase ventilation pipe to the top of the inlet manifold/cover **(see illustration)**.

20 Disconnect the quick-release fittings at each end of the pipe and remove the pipe from the engine **(see illustrations)**.

21 Undo the two bolts securing the plastic cover to the top of the inlet manifold. Lift the cover up at the front, disengage the locating tags at the rear and remove the cover **(see illustrations)**.

3.20a Disconnect the lower quick-release fitting (arrowed)…

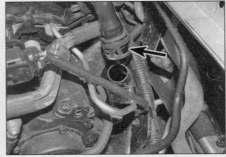

3.20b… and the upper quick-release fitting (arrowed)…

3.20c… then remove the crankcase ventilation pipe

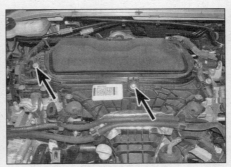

3.21a Undo the two bolts (arrowed) securing the plastic cover to the inlet manifold

3.21b Lift the cover up at the front, disengage the locating tags at the rear and remove the cover

3.22a Unscrew the high-pressure fuel pipe unions at the accumulator rail (arrowed)...

3.22b... and at the fuel pump (arrowed)

22 Clean the area around the high-pressure fuel pipes to and from the accumulator rail, then unscrew the fuel pump-to-accumulator rail pipe unions **(see illustrations)**. Remove the pipe.

23 Repeat the procedure on the accumulator rail-to-injector fuel pipes **(see illustrations)**. Note their fitted locations and remove the pipes.

24 Plug the openings in the accumulator rail and fuel pump to prevent dirt ingress.

25 Disconnect the fuel pressure sensor wiring plug from the accumulator rail **(see illustration)**.

26 Unscrew the three accumulator rail mounting bolts, and lift the rail off the manifold **(see illustration)**.

27 Release the three fuel injector wiring harness retaining clips from the manifold supports **(see illustration)**.

28 Depress the tabs on the undersides of the two injector wiring harness block connectors and slide the connectors out of their supports on the manifold **(see illustration)**.

29 Disconnect the wiring plugs from the four injectors and move the wiring harness to one side **(see illustration)**.

30 Thoroughly clean the fuel return hose connections on the injectors and fuel pump. Pull out the locking tab and disconnect the

3.23a Unscrew the injector high-pressure fuel pipe unions at the accumulator rail...

3.23b... and at the injectors

3.25 Disconnect the fuel pressure sensor wiring plug from the accumulator rail

3.26 Accumulator rail mounting bolts (arrowed)

3.27 Release the injector wiring harness retaining clips (arrowed) from the manifold supports

3.28 Depress the tabs on the undersides of the wiring harness block connectors and slide the connectors out of their supports

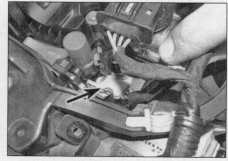

3.29 Disconnect the wiring plugs (arrowed) from the four injectors

3.30a Pull out the locking tab…

3.30b… and disconnect the return hose connector from each injector…

3.30c… and from the fuel pump

3.31 Lift the engine oil filler tube support clip (arrowed) out of the bracket on the manifold

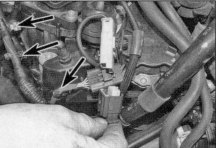

3.32 Disconnect the wiring harness connectors, then release the harness from the cable clips (arrowed)

return hose connector from each injector and from the fuel pump (see illustrations). Plug the openings to prevent dirt ingress and remove the return hose.

31 Lift the engine oil filler tube support clip out of the bracket on the manifold and move the tube to one side (see illustration).

32 Disconnect the wiring harness connectors at the sensors and block connectors, then release the harness from the cable clips around the front of the manifold (see illustration). Move the harness to one side.

33 Slacken the retaining clamp and disconnect the intercooler charge air hose from the inlet manifold lower section (see illustration).

34 Undo the three bolts securing the inlet manifold upper section to the lower section (see illustration).

35 Undo the three nuts securing the inlet manifold lower section to the cylinder head and remove the lower section from the car (see illustrations).

36 Undo the two bolts securing the manifold-to-EGR valve pipe to the EGR valve elbow. Separate the joint and collect the metal gasket (see illustration).

37 Disconnect the wiring plug, undo the retaining bolt and remove the camshaft position sensor (see illustration). Note that a new sensor will be required for refitting.

38 At the rear of the inlet manifold, undo the two nuts securing the air intake duct and

3.33 Slacken the retaining clamp (arrowed) and disconnect the intercooler charge air hose from the manifold lower section

3.34 Undo the three bolts (arrowed) securing the inlet manifold upper section to the lower section

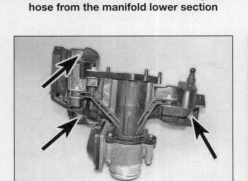

3.35a Undo the three nuts (arrowed) securing the manifold lower section to the cylinder head (shown with manifold removed)…

3.35b… and remove the lower section from the car

3.36 Undo the two bolts and separate the EGR valve pipe from the EGR valve elbow

3.37 Undo the retaining bolt and remove the camshaft position sensor

3.39 Undo the two bolts (arrowed) securing the timing belt upper cover to the inlet manifold

3.40 Undo the retaining bolts and lift off the inlet manifold/cylinder head cover

3.41a Fit the new rubber gasket...

43 The remainder of refitting is a reversal of removal, noting the following points:
a) Tighten all fasteners to their specified torque where given.
b) Refit the accumulator rail and the new high-pressure fuel pipes in accordance with the information given in Chapter 4BSection 10.
c) The new camshaft position sensor must be fitted as described in Chapter 4B Section 12, otherwise it will not function correctly.
d) Ensure all wiring connectors and harnesses are correctly refitting and secured.
e) On completion, prime and bleed the fuel system as described in Chapter 4B Section 4.

4 Crankshaft pulley – removal and refitting

Note: *Ford special tools or suitable alternatives will be required to lock the flywheel/driveplate and to retain the crankshaft and camshaft at the TDC position during this procedure.*
Note: *A new crankshaft pulley retaining bolt will be required for refitting.*

Removal

1 Disconnect the battery negative lead as described in Chapter 5A Section 4.
2 Pull the plastic cover on top of the engine straight up from its mountings at the right-hand rear corner, right-hand front corner and left-hand front corner, then slide it forwards.
3 Remove the auxiliary drivebelt as described in Chapter 1B Section 24.
4 Remove the starter motor as described in Chapter 5A Section 8.
5 Release the wiring harness from the timing belt upper cover, then unclip the fuel pipes.
6 Undo the bolt securing the air conditioning refrigerant hose to the support bracket in front of the timing belt upper cover. Undo the

the bolt securing the pipe and hose support bracket. Disconnect the vacuum hoses from the manifold and vacuum pipe stub.
39 Undo the two bolts securing the timing belt upper cover to the inlet manifold **(see illustration)**.
40 Working in the reverse of the sequence shown **(see illustration 3.42)** undo the 22 bolts securing the inlet manifold/cylinder head cover to the cylinder head, noting the locations of the various bolt lengths. Lift the inlet manifold/cover off the cylinder head

and collect the rubber gasket and seals **(see illustration)**.

Refitting

41 Clean the sealing surfaces of the manifold/cover and the head then fit the new rubber gasket and sealing rings **(see illustrations)**.
42 Fit the inlet manifold/cover to the cylinder head using a little petroleum jelly on the manifold sealing rings to ease assembly. Tighten the bolts to the specified torque in the sequence shown **(see illustration)**.

3.41b... and sealing rings

3.42 Inlet manifold/cylinder head cover bolt tightening sequence

4.6a Undo the bolt securing the air conditioning refrigerant hose to the support bracket...

4.6b... then undo the retaining nut (arrowed)...

4.6c... and remove the support bracket

4.7a Undo the three upper bolts (arrowed)...

4.7b... and the lower nut (arrowed)...

4.7c... and remove the timing belt upper cover

4.9 On engines to emission level Stage V, remove the rubber cover from the crankshaft pulley

retaining nut and remove the support bracket (see illustrations).

7 Undo the 3 bolts and 1 nut, and remove the upper timing belt cover (see illustrations).

8 Two special tools are now required to set the engine at TDC (Top Dead Centre) for No 1 cylinder (at the transmission end). Ford tool No 303-1059 locates through a hole in the rear flange of the cylinder block into a corresponding hole in the rear of the flywheel/driveplate, whilst tool No 303-735 locates through a hole in the exhaust camshaft sprocket into a hole in the cylinder head casting. In the absence of these tools, use an 8 mm diameter drill bit to lock the camshaft sprocket, and an 8 mm diameter rod to lock the flywheel/driveplate. Note: The flywheel/driveplate locking bolt must be flat (not tapered at all) at the end.

9 On engines to emission level Stage V,

remove the rubber cover from the centre of the crankshaft pulley (see illustration).

10 Using a spanner or socket on the crankshaft pulley bolt, rotate the engine in a clockwise direction (viewed from the timing belt end of the engine) until the hole in the camshaft sprocket begins to align with the corresponding hole in the cylinder head.

11 Insert the crankshaft setting tool though the hole in the cylinder block flange and press it against the back of the flywheel/driveplate. Have an assistant very slowly rotate the crankshaft clockwise, and the tool should slide into the flywheel/driveplate as the holes align (see illustrations).

12 It should now be possible to insert the camshaft locking tool (303-735) or equivalent through the hole in the camshaft sprocket into the hole in the cylinder head (see illustration).

4.11a The crankshaft setting tool fits through the hole in the cylinder block flange...

4.11b... and into a hole in the rear of the flywheel/driveplate

4.12 The camshaft locking tool fits through the hole in the camshaft sprocket, into the timing hole in the cylinder head

Note that it may be necessary to rotate the camshaft sprocket backwards or forwards very slightly to be able to insert the tool.

13 The centre bolt which secures the crankshaft pulley must now be slackened. This bolt is tightened to a very high torque, and it is first of all essential to ensure that the car is adequately supported, as considerable effort will be needed.

14 Ford technicians use a special holding tool (303-393/303-393-01) which bolts to the transmission housing and engages with the starter ring gear teeth **(see illustration)**. The use of this tool, or an equivalent, is strongly recommended. Do not rely on the crankshaft and camshaft setting/locking tools to prevent the crankshaft rotating.

15 Unscrew the bolt securing the pulley to the crankshaft, and remove the pulley. It is essential to obtain a new bolt for refitting. If required, remove the TDC sensor ring/spacer **(see illustrations)**. **Note:** *Handle the sensor ring with care.*

Refitting

16 Refit the TDC sensor ring/spacer and crankshaft pulley to the crankshaft, then fit the new pulley securing bolt and tighten it to the specified Stage 1 torque using a torque wrench.

17 Stage 2 involves tightening the bolt though an angle, rather than to a torque. The bolt must be rotated through the specified angle – special angle gauges are available from tool outlets.

18 The remainder of refitting is a reversal of removal.

5 Timing belt and tensioner – removal and refitting

Removal

1 Remove the crankshaft pulley as described in Section 4.

2 Disconnect the crankshaft position sensor wiring plug, then release the wiring harness from the clips on the timing belt lower cover.

3 Undo the three bolts and remove the lower cover **(see illustrations)**.

4.14 Crankshaft holding tool (arrowed) engaged with the ring gear teeth

4.15b... remove the crankshaft pulley...

4 Relieve the timing belt tension by slackening the bolt/nut in the centre of the tensioner pulley **(see illustration)**.

5 Remove the timing belt from the sprockets. Note that the belt must not be re-used.

5.3a Undo the three bolts (arrowed)...

5.4 Slacken the tensioner pulley bolt (arrowed)

4.15a Undo the retaining bolt...

4.15c... followed by the TDC sensor ring

6 Undo the engine mounting bracket lower rear retaining bolt and slide the idler pulley, together with the bolt, down and out through the slot in the bracket **(see illustrations)**.

7 Undo the bolt or the nut in the centre of the

5.3b... and remove the timing belt lower cover

5.6a Undo the engine mounting bracket lower rear retaining bolt (arrowed)...

5.6b... and slide the idler pulley, together with the bolt, down and out through the slot in the bracket

5.10 Ensure that the slot in the tensioner backplate engages over the dowel (arrowed) on the cylinder block

5.11 Timing belt routing

5.13a Using an Allen key in the tensioner arm hole (arrowed)…

5.13b… rotate the arm anti-clockwise until the pointer is between the sides of the adjustment 'window' (arrowed)

tensioner and remove the tensioner. Discard both the tensioner and idler pulleys – new ones must be fitted.

Refitting

8 Ensure that the crankshaft and camshaft are still set to TDC on No 1 cylinder, with the setting/locking tools in position (see Section 4).

9 Insert the bolt into the new idler pulley, then slide the pulley and bolt into position in the engine mounting bracket. Screw in the bolt and tighten it to the specified torque.

10 Locate the new timing belt tensioner into position, ensuring that the slot in the tensioner backplate engages over the dowel on the cylinder block **(see illustration)**. Tighten the retaining bolt/nut finger-tight only at this stage.

11 Fit the new timing belt over the various sprockets in the following order: crankshaft, idler pulley, camshaft, tensioner and coolant pump **(see illustration)**. Pay attention to any arrows on the belt indicating direction of rotation.

12 New tensioners are usually supplied with a locking pin holding the tensioner in the released position. If so, pull out the locking pin and allow the tensioner pulley to move into contact with the timing belt.

13 Using a 6 mm Allen key inserted in the tensioner arm, rotate the arm anti-clockwise

until the pointer is positioned between the sides of the adjustment 'window' **(see illustrations)**. Fully-tighten the tensioner retaining bolt.

14 Refit the timing belt lower cover and tighten the bolts securely.

15 Refit the sensor ring/spacer and the crankshaft pulley, then tighten the old pulley bolt to 50 Nm (37 lbf ft).

16 Remove the crankshaft and camshaft setting/locking tools, then rotate the crankshaft 4 complete revolutions clockwise, until the crankshaft setting tool can be re-inserted. Check that the camshaft locking tool can also be inserted.

17 Check position of the tensioner pointer, and if necessary slacken the retaining bolt and use the Allen key to align the pointer in the centre of the adjustment 'window'. Tighten the retaining bolt securely.

18 Remove the old crankshaft pulley bolt, and fit the new one. Tighten the bolt to the specified Stage 1 torque, then through the specified Stage 2 angle using the flywheel locking tool to prevent the crankshaft from rotating. Where applicable, refit the rubber cover to the centre of the crankshaft pulley

19 Remove the crankshaft and camshaft setting/locking tools.

20 The remainder of refitting is a reversal of removal, remembering to tighten all fasteners to their specified torque where given.

6 Timing chain and tensioner – removal and refitting

Timing chain

1 Removal of the timing chain is included in the camshaft removal and refitting procedure, as described in Section 7.

Tensioner

2 Remove the cylinder head cover as described in Section 3.

3 Press the tensioner upper guide rail upwards into the housing, then insert a 2.0 mm locking pin/drill bit to secure the rail in position **(see illustration)**.

4 Undo the 3 retaining bolts and withdrawn the tensioner **(see illustration)**.

5 Begin refitting by ensuring the tensioner and cylinder head mating faces are clean and free of debris.

6 Install the tensioner and tighten the retaining bolts to the specified torque.

7 Press the tensioner upper guide rail into the housing, pull out the locking pin/drill bit, then slowly release the guide rail.

8 Refit the cylinder head cover as described in Section 3.

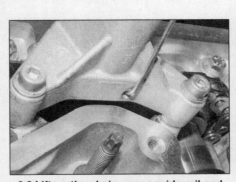

6.3 Lift up the chain upper guide rail and insert a 2.0 mm diameter rod/drill bit into the hole in the tensioner housing

6.4 Undo the tensioner retaining bolts (2 of 3 arrowed)

7.4a Depress the release tab (arrowed) and disconnect the servo hose from the pump

7.4b Undo the nut (arrowed) securing the EGR pipe and fuel hose

7.4c Vacuum pump securing bolts (arrowed)

7 Camshafts, rocker arms and hydraulic adjusters – removal, inspection and refitting

Note: *A new camshaft oil seal will be required for refitting.*

Engines to emission level Stage III/IV

Removal

1 Remove the timing belt as described in Section 5.

2 Remove the timing chain tensioner as described in Section 6.

3 Remove the following components as described in Chapter 4B :

a) *Air cleaner assembly.*

b) *Fuel injectors.*

c) *Fuel pump.*

4 Working at the left-hand end of the

cylinder head, depress the release tab and disconnect the hose from the vacuum pump, undo the nut securing the EGR pipe and fuel supply hose, then undo the 3 Allen bolts and remove the pump from the cylinder head **(see illustrations)**. Check the condition of the pump O-ring seals and renew if necessary.

5 Undo the retaining bolt and pull the sprocket from the exhaust camshaft. Ford technicians use a special holding tool (205-072) which locates in the holes of the sprocket and prevents it from turning as the bolt is undone. If this tool is not available, a home-made tool can easily be fabricated **(see Tool Tip)**.

6 Undo the bolts securing the timing belt inner cover to the cylinder head **(see illustration)**.

7 Undo the 2 bolts and remove the EGR pipe from over the left-hand end of the cylinder head.

8 Unscrew the injector mounting studs using a Torx socket.

9 Working in the reverse of the sequence given **(see illustration 7.22)**, gradually and evenly remove the bolts securing the upper section of the cylinder head to the lower section.

10 Carefully tap around the edge of the cylinder head upper section and lift it from position. Note that the cover will probably be reluctant to lift due to the sealant used, and possible corrosion around the two locating dowels at the front edge.

11 Lift the camshafts from position, disengage the timing chain from the sprockets, and remove the exhaust camshaft seal.

12 Have ready a box, filled with engine oil and

divided into 16 segments, or some containers or other means of storing and identifying the rockers arms and hydraulic adjusters after removal. It's essential that if they are to be refitted, they return to their original positions. Mark the segments in the box or the containers with the cylinder number for each rocker arm/adjuster, and left or right, for the particular cylinder.

13 Lift out the rockers arms and hydraulic adjusters, Keep them identified for position, and place them in their respective positions in the box or container **(see illustration)**. The hydraulic adjusters must be totally submerged in the oil to prevent air entering them.

Inspection

14 With the camshafts removed, examine the bearing surfaces in the upper and lower sections of the cylinder head for signs of obvious wear or pitting. If evident, a new cylinder head will probably be required. Also check that the oil supply holes in the cylinder head are free from obstructions.

15 Visually inspect the camshafts for evidence of wear on the surfaces of the lobes and journals. Normally their surfaces should be smooth and have a dull shine; look for scoring, erosion or pitting and areas that appear highly polished, indicating excessive wear. Accelerated wear will occur once the hardened exterior of the camshaft has been damaged, so always renew worn items. **Note:** *If these symptoms are visible on the tips of the camshaft lobes, check the rocker arm, as it will probably be worn as well.*

TOOL TIP

To make a camshaft sprocket holding tool, obtain two lengths of steel strip about 6 mm thick by 30 mm wide or similar, one 600 mm long, the other 200 mm long (all dimensions are approximate). Bolt the two strips together to form a forked end, leaving the bolt slack so that the shorter strip can pivot freely. Drill holes and insert bolts of a suitable size in the ends of the fork to engage in the sprocket spokes. Hold the bolts at the ends firmly in place by using a nut on the other side of the steel strip.

7.6 Remove the bolts (arrowed) securing the belt inner cover

7.13 Lift out the rocker arms and hydraulic adjusters

7.18 Fit the secondary timing chain lower guide rail

7.19a Apply clean oil to the hydraulic adjusters...

7.19b... and refit them to their original positions

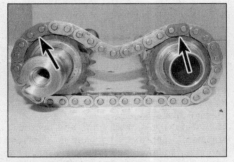

7.20a Align the coloured links on the chain (arrowed) with the marks on the camshaft sprockets...

7.20b... the mark on the sprockets is a dot and a line...

7.20c... then fit the camshafts with the mark on the inlet camshaft (arrowed) in the 12 o'clock position

16 If any doubt exists as to the condition of the camshafts or cylinder head, have them examined at a Ford dealer workshop or suitably-equipped automotive repair facility.

17 Inspect the rocker arms and hydraulic adjusters for obvious signs of wear or damage, and renew if necessary.

Refitting

18 Make sure that the top surfaces of the cylinder head, and in particular the camshaft bearings and the mating surfaces are completely clean. Ensure the secondary timing chain lower guide rail is in place **(see illustration)**.

19 Smear some clean engine oil onto the sides of the hydraulic adjusters, and offer each one into position in their original bores in the cylinder head, together with its rocker arm **(see illustrations)**.

20 Locate the timing chain on the camshaft sprockets, aligning the two coloured chain links with the marks on the camshaft sprockets, then lubricate the camshaft and cylinder head bearing journals with clean engine oil, and lower the camshafts into position **(see illustrations)**. The mark on the inlet camshaft must be in the 12 o'clock position.

21 Apply a thin bead of silicone sealant (Ford part No WSE-M4G323-A4) to the mating surface of the cylinder head lower section. Take great care to ensure the chain tensioner oil supply hole is free from sealant **(see illustrations)**.

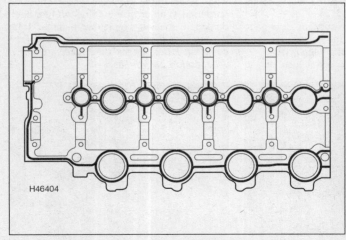

7.21a Apply a thin bead of sealant as indicated by the heavy black line

7.21b We inserted a tapered rod (arrowed) into the tensioner oil supply hole to prevent any sealant from entering

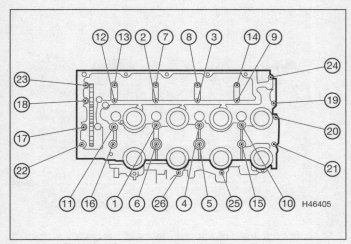

7.22 Cylinder head upper section bolt tightening sequence

7.33 Disconnect the wiring connectors at the solenoid valves and at the loom connector above the fuel pump location (arrowed)

22 Lower the upper section of the cylinder head into place, and tighten the retaining bolts to the specified torque in the sequence shown **(see illustration)**.

23 Refit the fuel injector mounting studs and tighten them to the specified torque.

24 Refit the camshaft timing chain tensioner assembly, and tighten the retaining bolts to the specified torque. Press the tensioner guide rail up into the housing and pull out the locking pin/drill bit. Slowly release the guide rail to tension the chain.

25 Fit a new exhaust camshaft oil seal as described in Section 8.

26 Refit the 2 bolts securing the timing belt inner cover to the cylinder head, and the single bolt to the cylinder block, then tighten the bolts securely.

27 Slide the exhaust camshaft sprocket into place, aligning the integral key with the camshaft and fit the camshaft sprocket locking tool **(see illustration 4.12)**.

28 Fit the sprocket retaining bolt and tighten it to the specified torque, preventing the sprocket from turning using the tool used during removal.

29 The remainder of refitting is a reversal of removal, noting the following points:

a) *When refitting the vacuum pump, use a new gasket and ensure the drive coupling is aligned with the slot in the camshaft.*

b) *Refit the fuel pump, fuel injectors and air cleaner assembly as described in Chapter 4B.*

c) *Fit the new timing belt, tensioner and idler pulley as described in Section 5.*

d) *Tighten all fasteners to their specified torque, where given.*

e) *Check the engine oil and coolant levels as described in 'Weekly checks'.*

Engines to emission level Stage V

Removal

30 Remove the timing belt as described in Section 5.

31 Remove the timing chain tensioner as described in Section 6.

32 Remove the following components as described in Chapter 4B :

a) *Air cleaner assembly.*

b) *Fuel injectors.*

c) *Fuel pump.*

33 Working at the left-hand end of the cylinder head, disconnect the wiring connectors at the two solenoid valves and at the loom connector above the fuel pump location **(see illustration)**. Undo the three bolts securing the solenoid valve mounting bracket to the vacuum pump and move the bracket and valves to one side. Release the vacuum hoses and wiring harness from the cable clips as necessary.

34 Depress the tabs and disconnect vacuum hoses at the quick-release connectors on the vacuum pump. Undo the 3 bolts and remove the vacuum pump from the cylinder head **(see illustration)**. Recover the gasket and obtain a new one for refitting.

35 Undo the retaining bolt and pull the sprocket from the exhaust camshaft. Ford technicians use a special holding tool (205-072) which locates in the holes of the sprocket and prevents it from turning as the bolt is undone. If this tool is not available, a

home-made tool can easily be fabricated **(see Tool Tip)**.

36 Undo the bolts securing the timing belt inner cover to the cylinder head **(see illustration 7.6)**.

37 Working in the reverse of the sequence given **(see illustration 7.22)**, gradually and evenly remove the bolts securing the upper section of the cylinder head to the lower section.

38 Carefully tap around the edge of the cylinder head upper section and lift it from position. Note that the cover will probably be reluctant to lift due to the sealant used, and possible corrosion around the two locating dowels at the front edge.

39 Lift the camshafts from position, disengage the timing chain from the sprockets, and remove the exhaust camshaft seal **(see illustration)**.

40 Have ready a box, filled with engine oil and divided into 16 segments, or some containers or other means of storing and identifying the rockers arms and hydraulic adjusters after removal. It's essential that if they are to be refitted, they return to their original positions. Mark the segments in the box or the containers with the cylinder number for each rocker arm/adjuster, and left or right, for the particular cylinder.

7.34 Vacuum pump retaining bolts (arrowed)

7.39 Lift the camshafts from position and disengage the timing chain from the sprockets

7.46 Place the new gasket in position on the cylinder head lower section

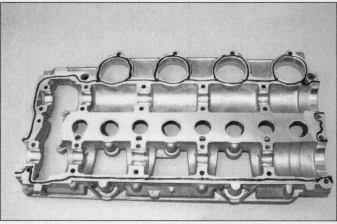

7.47 Apply a thin bead of silicone sealant to the mating surface of the cylinder head upper section

41 Lift out the rockers arms and hydraulic adjusters, Keep them identified for position, and place them in their respective positions in the box or container **(see illustration 7.13)**. The hydraulic adjusters must be totally submerged in the oil to prevent air entering them.

Inspection

42 Proceed as described in paragraphs 14 to 17.

Refitting

43 Make sure that the top surfaces of the cylinder head, and in particular the camshaft bearings and the mating surfaces are completely clean. Ensure the secondary timing chain lower guide rail is in place **(see illustration 7.18)**.

44 Smear some clean engine oil onto the sides of the hydraulic adjusters, and offer each one into position in their original bores in the cylinder head, together with its rocker arm **(see illustrations 7.19a and 7.19b)**.

45 Locate the timing chain on the camshaft sprockets, aligning the two coloured chain links

with the marks on the camshaft sprockets, then lubricate the camshaft and cylinder head bearing journals with clean engine oil, and lower the camshafts into position **(see illustrations 7.20a, 7.20b and 7.20c)**. The mark on the inlet camshaft must be in the 12 o'clock position.

46 Place the new gasket in position between the two camshafts on the cylinder head lower section **(see illustration)**.

47 Apply a thin bead of silicone sealant (Ford part No WSE-M4G323-A4) to the mating surface of the cylinder head upper section**(see illustration)**.

48 Lower the upper section of the cylinder head into position, keeping the gasket aligned as you do so. To temporarily retain the gasket in alignment, insert two of the fuel injector clamp bolts into their locations for No 1 and No 4 injector **(see illustrations)**.

49 Refit the cylinder head upper section retaining bolts and tighten them to the specified torque in the sequence shown **(see illustration 7.22)**.

50 Remove the two injector clamp bolts used to align the gasket.

51 Refit the camshaft timing chain tensioner assembly, and tighten the retaining bolts to the specified torque. Press the tensioner guide rail up into the housing and pull out the locking pin/drill bit. Slowly release the guide rail to tension the chain.

52 Fit a new exhaust camshaft oil seal as described in Section 8.

53 Refit the bolts securing the timing belt inner cover to the cylinder head and tighten the bolts securely.

54 Slide the exhaust camshaft sprocket into place, aligning the integral key with the camshaft and fit the camshaft sprocket locking tool **(see illustration 4.12)**.

55 Fit the sprocket retaining bolt and tighten it to the specified torque, preventing the sprocket from turning using the tool used during removal.

56 The remainder of refitting is a reversal of removal, noting the following points:

a) *When refitting the vacuum pump, use a new gasket and ensure the drive coupling is aligned with the slot in the camshaft.*

b) *Refit the fuel pump, fuel injectors and air*

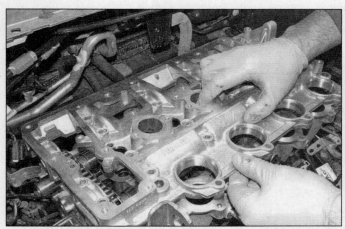

7.48a Lower the upper section of the cylinder head into position, keeping the gasket aligned

7.48b Insert two of the fuel injector clamp bolts (arrowed) to maintain the gasket alignment

8.4a Apply a little clean oil to the oil seal inner lip…

8.4b… then use a socket (or similar) to drive the seal into place…

8.4c… until the seal is flush with the casing surface

cleaner assembly as described in Chapter 4B.

c) Fit the new timing belt, tensioner and idler pulley as described in Section 5.

d) Tighten all fasteners to their specified torque, where given.

e) Check the engine oil and coolant levels as described in 'Weekly checks'.

8 Camshaft oil seal – renewal

1 Remove the timing belt as described in Section 5, and the camshaft sprocket as described in paragraph 5 of the previous Section.

2 Carefully prise or pull the seal from position (see **Haynes Hint**).

One of the best ways to remove an oil seal is to carefully drill or punch two holes through the seal opposite each other (taking care not to damage the surface behind the seal as this is done). Two self-tapping screws are then screwed into the holes; by pulling on the screw heads alternately with a pair of pliers, the seal can be extracted.

3 Clean out the seal housing and the sealing surface of the camshaft by wiping it with a lint-free cloth. Remove any swarf or burrs that may cause the seal to leak.

4 Apply a little oil to the new camshaft oil seal, and fit it over the end of the camshaft, lips facing inwards. To avoid damaging the seal lips, wrap a little tape over the end of the camshaft. Ford dealers have a special tool (No 303-684/1) for fitting the seal, but if this is not available, a deep socket of suitable size can be used. **Note:** *Select a socket that bears only on the hard outer surface of the seal, not the inner lip which can easily be damaged. It is important that the seal is fitted square to the shaft, and is fully-seated***(see illustrations)**.

5 Refit the camshaft sprocket (Section 7) and timing belt as described in Section 5.

9 Cylinder head – removal, inspection and refitting

Removal

1 Disconnect the battery negative lead as described in Chapter 5A Section 4.

2 Drain the cooling system as described in Chapter 1B Section 30.

3 Remove the thermostat as described in Chapter 3 Section 3.

4 Remove the camshafts, rocker arms and hydraulic adjusters as described in Section 7.

5 Remove the turbocharger/exhaust manifold as described in Chapter 4B Section 17.

6 On engines to emission level Stage III/IV, disconnect the wiring plug from the pressure sensor on the underside of the fuel accumulator rail at the front of the cylinder head.

7 On engines to emission level Stage III/IV, undo the retaining bolts, and remove the oil filler pipe support bracket.

8 On engines to emission level Stage V, remove the EGR valve cooler as described in Chapter 4C Section 3.

9 Position a jack under the sump, with a large block of wood between the jack head and the sump, then carefully raise the engine just enough to take the weight off the right-hand engine/transmission mounting.

10 Unscrew the two locking nuts securing the mounting to the engine bracket, then undo the two bolts securing the mounting to the inner wing panel. Remove the mounting, then undo the three bolts and remove the engine bracket.

11 Working in the reverse order of the tightening sequence **(see illustration 9.35)**, gradually and evenly slacken and remove the cylinder head bolts. Discard the bolts, new ones must be fitted.

12 Lift the cylinder head away; use assistance if possible, as it is a very heavy assembly. Do not place the cylinder head flat on its sealing surface, as the ends of the glow plugs may be damaged – support the ends of the cylinder head on wooden blocks.

13 If the head is stuck (as is possible), be careful how you choose to free it. Striking the head with tools carries the risk of damage, and the head is located on two dowels, so its movement will be

limited. Do not, under any circumstances, lever the head between the mating surfaces, as this will certainly damage the sealing surfaces for the gasket, leading to leaks.

14 Once the head has been removed, recover the gasket from the two dowels.

15 Do not discard the gasket at this stage – it will be needed for correct identification of the new gasket.

Inspection

16 If required, dismantling and inspection of the cylinder head is covered in Part D of this Chapter.

Cylinder head gasket selection

17 Examine the old cylinder head gasket for manufacturer's identification markings. These will be in the form of holes on the front edge of the gasket, which indicate the gasket's thickness.

18 Unless new components have been fitted, or the cylinder head has been machined (skimmed), the new cylinder head gasket must be of the same type as the old one. Purchase the required gasket, and proceed to paragraph 25.

19 If the head has been machined, or if new pistons have been fitted, it is likely that a head gasket of different thickness to the original will be needed.

20 Gasket selection is made on the basis of the measured piston protrusion above the cylinder head gasket surface.

21 To measure the piston protrusion, anchor a dial test indicator (DTI) to the top face (cylinder head gasket mating face) of the cylinder block, and zero the gauge on the gasket mating face **(see illustration)**.

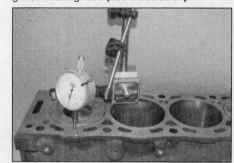

9.21 Zero the DTI on the gasket face

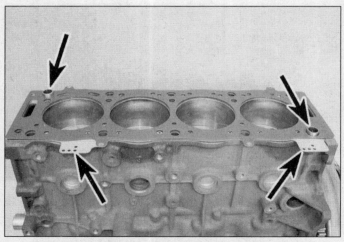

9.32 Fit the new gasket over the dowels, with the thickness identification holes at the front (arrowed)

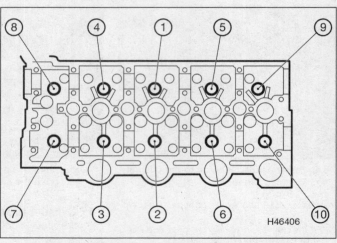

9.35 Cylinder head lower section bolt tightening sequence

22 Rest the gauge probe above No 1 piston crown, and turn the crankshaft slowly by hand until the piston reaches TDC (its maximum height). Measure and record the maximum piston projection at TDC.

23 Repeat the measurement for the remaining pistons, and record the results.

24 If the measurements differ from piston to piston, take the highest figure, and use this to determine the thickness of the head gasket required. Refer to the Specifications for details of cylinder head gasket thicknesses.

Preparation for refitting

25 The mating faces of the cylinder head and cylinder block must be perfectly clean before refitting the head. Use a hard plastic or wooden scraper to remove all traces of gasket and carbon; also clean the piston crowns. **Note:** *The new head gasket has rubber-coated surfaces, which could be damaged from sharp edges or debris left by a metal scraper. Take particular care when cleaning the piston crowns, as the soft aluminium alloy is easily damaged.*

26 Make sure that the carbon is not allowed to enter the oil and water passages – this is particularly important for the lubrication system, as carbon could block the oil supply

to the engine's components. Using adhesive tape and paper, seal the water, oil and bolt holes in the cylinder block.

27 To prevent carbon entering the gap between the pistons and bores, smear a little grease in the gap.

28 After cleaning each piston, use a small brush to remove all traces of grease and carbon from the gap, then wipe away the remainder with a clean rag. Clean all the pistons in the same way.

29 Check the mating surfaces of the cylinder block and the cylinder head for nicks, deep scratches and other damage (refer to the Note in paragraph 25). If slight, they may be removed carefully with a file, but if excessive, machining may be the only alternative to renewal.

30 If warpage of the cylinder head gasket surface is suspected, use a straight-edge to check it for distortion. Refer to Part D of this Chapter if necessary.

31 Ensure that the cylinder head bolt holes in the crankcase are clean and free of oil. Syringe or soak up any oil left in the bolt holes. This is most important in order that the correct bolt tightening torque can be applied, and to prevent the possibility of the block being cracked by hydraulic pressure when the bolts are tightened.

Refitting

32 Ensure that the cylinder head locating dowels are in place at the corners of the cylinder block, then fit the new cylinder head gasket over the dowels, ensuring that the identification holes are at the front**(see illustration)**. Take care to avoid damaging the gasket's rubber coating.

33 Lower the cylinder head into position on the gasket, ensuring that it engages correctly over the dowels.

34 Fit the new cylinder head bolts and screw them in as far as possible by hand.

35 Working in sequence**(see illustration)**, tighten all the cylinder head bolts to the

specified Stage 1 torque using an E14 Torx socket.

36 Stage 2 involves tightening the bolts though an angle, rather than to a torque **(see illustration)**. Each bolt in sequence must be rotated through the specified angle – special angle gauges are available from tool outlets.

37 The remainder of refitting is a reversal of the removal procedure, bearing in mind the following points:

a) *Refit the turbocharger/exhaust manifold as described in Chapter 4B Section 17.*

b) *Refit the camshafts, rocker arms and hydraulic adjusters as described in Section 7.*

c) *Refit the thermostat as described in Chapter 3 Section 3.*

d) *Refill the cooling system as described in Chapter 1B Section 30.*

e) *Check and if necessary top-up the engine oil level as described in 'Weekly checks'.*

f) *Before starting the engine, read through the section on engine restarting after overhaul, in Chapter 2D Section 20.*

10 Sump – removal and refitting

Removal

1 Firmly apply the handbrake, then jack up the front of the vehicle and support it securely on axle stands (see *'Jacking and vehicle support'*). Undo the fasteners and remove the engine undertray.

2 Pull the plastic cover on the top of the engine upwards from its mountings.

3 Referring to Chapter 1B Section 6 if necessary, drain the engine oil, then clean and refit the engine oil drain plug, tightening it to the specified torque wrench setting. We strongly advise renewing the oil filter element, also described in Chapter 1B Section 6.

4 Slacken the hose clamps, undo the bracket

9.36 Use an angle gauge for the Stage 2 torque setting

10.4 Undo the charge air pipe bracket bolt (arrowed)

10.6a Undo the 2 bolts securing the sump to the transmission (arrowed)...

10.6b... access to the sump end bolts is through the holes (arrowed)

10.9 Apply sealant around the inside of the bolt holes

allow the sealant to enter the bolt holes **(see illustration). Note:** *The sump must be refitted within 4 minutes of applying the sealant.*

10 Refit the sump and fit the retaining bolts, tightening them by hand only at this stage.

11 On engines to emission level Stage III/IV, tighten the 2 bolts securing the sump to the transmission casing to the specified torque first.

12 Tighten the sump-to-cylinder block bolts gradually and evenly to the specified torque.

13 On engines to emission level Stage III/IV, refit the air conditioning compressor, then refit the auxiliary drivebelt as described in Chapter 1B Section 24.

14 Refit the engine undertray, then lower the car to the ground. Wait at least 1 hour for the sealant to cure (or whatever time is indicated by the sealant manufacturer) before refilling the engine with oil. If removed, fit a new oil filter with reference to Chapter 1B Section 6.

15 On completion, refit the plastic cover on the top of the engine.

11 Oil pump – removal, inspection and refitting

Engines to emission level Stage III/IV

Removal

1 Remove the timing belt as described in Section 5, then slide off the crankshaft sprocket **(see illustrations).**

2 Remove the sump as described in Section 10.

3 Undo the retaining bolts and remove the crankshaft oil seal carrier. Note the original locations of the cover bolts – they are of different lengths.

4 Undo the bolt securing the oil level pipe **(see illustration).**

5 Pull out the key from the crankshaft sprocket, then undo the pump mounting bolts, slide the pump, chain, and crankshaft

bolt and remove the charge air pipe from the underside of the engine **(see illustration).**

5 On engines to emission level Stage III/IV, remove the auxiliary drivebelt as described in Chapter 1B Section 24, then undo the mounting bolts and move the air conditioning compressor to one side without disconnecting the refrigerant pipes. Suspend the compressor from the radiator crossmember using wires or straps.

6 Progressively unscrew and remove the sump retaining bolts. On engines to emission level Stage III/IV, don't forget the 2 bolts securing the sump to the transmission housing, and the 4 bolts at the left-hand end accessed through the holes **(see illustrations).**

7 Break the joint by carefully inserting a putty knife (or similar) between the sump and cylinder block. Take care not to damage the sealing surfaces.

Refitting

8 On reassembly, thoroughly clean and degrease the mating surfaces of the cylinder block/crankcase and sump, removing all traces of sealant, then use a clean rag to wipe out the sump and the engine's interior.

9 Apply a 3 mm thick bead of sealant (Ford part No WSE-M4G323-A4) to the sump flange, making sure the bead is around the inside edge of the bolt holes. Do not

11.1a Slide off the crankshaft sprocket...

11.1b... and recover the crankshaft key

11.4 Oil level pipe bracket bolt (arrowed)

11.5a Remove the sprocket key...

11.5b... undo the oil pump mounting bolts (arrowed), slide the assembly from the crankshaft...

11.5c... and recover the O-ring between the sprocket and crankshaft (arrowed)

sprocket from the end of the engine **(see illustrations)**. Recover the O-ring between the sprocket and crankshaft.

Inspection

6 Undo the retaining bolts and remove the cover from the oil pump **(see illustration)**. Note the location of any identification marks on the inner and outer rotors for refitting.

7 Unscrew the plug and remove the pressure relief valve, spring and plunger, clean out and check condition of components **(see illustration)**.

8 No specifications for the pump internal components are given by Ford.

9 Check the general condition of the oil pump, and in particular, its mating face to the cylinder block. If the mating face is damaged significantly, this may lead to oil loss (and a resulting drop in available oil pressure).

10 Inspect the rotors for obvious signs of wear or damage; at the time of writing, no new parts are available. If the pump is faulty, it must be renewed as a complete unit. Lubricate the rotors with fresh engine oil and refit them into the body, making sure that the identification marks are positioned as noted on removal.

11 If the oil pump has been removed as part of a major engine overhaul, it is assumed that the engine will have completed a substantial mileage. In this case, it is often considered good practice to fit a new (or reconditioned) pump as a matter of course. In other words,

if the rest of the engine is being rebuilt, the engine has completed a large mileage, or there is any question as to the old pump's condition, it is preferable to fit a new oil pump.

Refitting

12 Before fitting the oil pump, ensure that the mating faces on the pump and the cylinder block are completely clean.

13 Fit the O-ring to the end of the crankshaft **(see illustration)**.

14 Engage the drive chain with the oil pump and crankshaft sprockets, then slide the crankshaft sprocket into place (aligning the slot in the sprocket with the keyway in crankshaft) as the pump is refitted. Refit the crankshaft key.

15 Refit the mounting bolts and tighten them to the specified torque. Note that the front, left-hand bolt is slightly longer than the others.

16 Thoroughly clean the oil seal carrier and its mating face on the cylinder block.

17 Apply a 3 mm wide bead of silicone sealant (Ford part No WSE-M4G323-A4) to the oil seal carrier flange. Refit the carrier and tighten the bolts to the specified torque. Note that the bolts must be tightened within 4 minutes of the sealant being applied.

18 Fit a new oil seal to the carrier as described in Section 14.

19 Refit the bolt securing the oil level pipe.

20 The remainder of refitting is a reversal of removal.

Engines to emission level Stage V

Removal

21 Remove the timing belt as described in Section 5, then slide off the crankshaft sprocket **(see illustrations 11.1a and 11.1b)**.

22 Remove the sump as described in Section 10.

23 Undo the bolt securing the crankshaft position sensor to the crankshaft oil seal carrier and position the sensor to one side.

24 Slacken the retaining clamp and disconnect the intercooler charge air hose from the inlet manifold lower section **(see illustration 3.33)**.

25 Undo the three bolts securing the inlet manifold upper section to the lower section **(see illustration 3.34)**.

26 Undo the three nuts securing the inlet manifold lower section to the cylinder head and remove the lower section from the car **(see illustrations 3.35a and 3.35b)**.

27 Undo the 3 bolts and remove the engine oil level dipstick tube and oil filler tube.

28 Progressively unscrew the 20 bolts securing the lower crankcase to the cylinder block. Break the joint by carefully inserting a putty knife (or similar) between the lower crankcase and cylinder block. Take care not to damage the sealing surfaces.

29 Undo the retaining bolts and remove the crankshaft oil seal carrier. Note the original

11.6 Oil pump cover bolts

11.7 Oil pressure relief valve plug

11.13 Fit the O-ring to the end of the crankshaft

locations of the cover bolts – they are of different lengths.
30 Remove the oil baffle plate from the underside of the cylinder block.
31 Pull out the key from the crankshaft sprocket, then undo the pump mounting bolts, slide the pump, chain, and crankshaft sprocket from the end of the engine. Recover the O-ring between the sprocket and crankshaft.

Inspection

32 Proceed as described in paragraphs 6 to 11.

Refitting

33 Before fitting the oil pump, ensure that the mating faces on the pump and the cylinder block are completely clean.
34 Fit the O-ring to the end of the crankshaft **(see illustration 11.13)**.
35 Engage the drive chain with the oil pump and crankshaft sprockets, then slide the crankshaft sprocket into place (aligning the slot in the sprocket with the keyway in the crankshaft) as the pump is refitted. Refit the crankshaft key.
36 Refit the mounting bolts and tighten them to the specified torque.
37 Thoroughly clean the oil seal carrier and its mating face on the cylinder block.
38 Apply a 3 mm wide bead of silicone sealant (Ford part No WSE-M4G323-A4) to the oil seal carrier flange. Refit the carrier and tighten the bolts to the specified torque. Note that the bolts must be tightened within 4 minutes of the sealant being applied.
39 Fit a new oil seal to the carrier as described in Section 14.
40 Refit the oil baffle plate to the underside of the cylinder block.
41 Thoroughly clean the lower crankcase and its mating face on the cylinder block.
42 Apply a 3 mm wide bead of silicone sealant (Ford part No WSE-M4G323-A4) to the lower crankcase flange. Refit the lower

crankcase and progressively tighten the bolts to the specified torque in two stages. Note that the bolts must be tightened within 4 minutes of the sealant being applied.
43 The remainder of refitting is a reversal of removal.

12 Oil pressure warning light switch – removal and refitting

Removal

1 The switch is screwed into the oil filter housing **(see illustration)**. Access is from under the vehicle.
2 Firmly apply the handbrake, then jack up the front of the vehicle and support it securely on axle stands (see *'Jacking and vehicle support'*). Undo the fasteners and remove the engine undertray.
3 To further improve access, Remove the auxiliary drivebelt as described in Chapter 1B Section 24, then undo the mounting bolts and move the air conditioning compressor to one side. Suspend the compressor from the radiator crossmember using wire or straps. There is no need to disconnect the refrigerant pipes.
4 Disconnect the switch wiring plug.
5 Unscrew the switch from the housing; be prepared for some oil loss.

Refitting

6 Refitting is the reverse of the removal procedure; fit a new pressure switch sealing washer, and tighten the switch securely.
7 Reconnect the switch wiring plug.
8 Refit all components removed for access to the switch.
9 Check the engine oil level and top-up as necessary (see *'Weekly checks'*).
10 Check for correct warning light operation,

and for signs of oil leaks, once the engine has been restarted and warmed-up to normal operating temperature.

13 Oil cooler – removal and refitting

Note: *New sealing rings will be required on refitting – check for availability prior to commencing work.*

Removal

1 The cooler is fitted to the oil filter housing on the front of the cylinder block. Access is from under the vehicle.
2 Firmly apply the handbrake, then jack up the front of the vehicle and support it securely on axle stands (see *'Jacking and vehicle support'*). Undo the fasteners and remove the engine undertray.
3 To further improve access, remove the auxiliary drivebelt as described in Chapter 1B Section 24, then undo the mounting bolts and move the air conditioning compressor to one side. Suspend the compressor from the radiator crossmember using wire or straps. There is no need to disconnect the refrigerant pipes.
4 Undo the 4 retaining bolts and detach the cooler from the housing **(see illustration)**. Recover the sealing rings and be prepared for oil/coolant spillage.

Refitting

5 Refitting is a reversal of removal, bearing in mind the following points:
a) Use new sealing rings.
b) Tighten the cooler mounting bolts securely
c) Refit all components removed for access to the cooler.
d) On completion, refit the engine undertray, then lower the car to the ground. Check

12.1 Oil pressure warning switch (arrowed)

13.4 Oil cooler retaining bolts (arrowed)

14.4a Drill a small hole in the seal...

14.4b... insert a self-tapping screw and pull out the seal

14.7a Locate the new seal and guide over the end of the crankshaft...

14.7b... then drive the seal home until it's flush with the cover

and if necessary top-up the oil and coolant levels (see 'Weekly checks'), then start the engine and check for signs of oil or coolant leakage.

14 Crankshaft oil seals – renewal

Timing belt end seal

1 Remove the timing belt as described in Section 5.

2 Slide the belt sprocket from the crankshaft, and recover the locating key from the groove on the crankshaft **(see illustrations 11.1a and 11.1b)**.

3 Note the fitted depth of the oil seal as a guide for fitting the new one.

4 Using a screwdriver or similar tool, carefully prise the oil seal from its location. Take care not to damage the oil seal contact surfaces or crankshaft. Alternatively, drill a small hole in the seal (taking care not to drill any deeper than necessary), then insert a self-tapping screw and use pliers to pull out the seal **(see illustrations)**.

5 Wipe clean the oil seal contact surfaces and seating, and clean up any sharp edges or burrs which might damage the new seal as it is fitted, or which might cause the seal to leak once in place.

6 No oil should be applied to the oil seal, which is made of PTFE. Ford technicians use a special seal-fitting tool (303-255/303-395), but an adequate substitute can be achieved using a large socket or piece of tubing of sufficient size to bear on the outer edge of the new seal. Note that the new seal is supplied with a guide which fits over the end of the crankshaft.

7 Locate the new seal (with guide still fitted) over the end of the crankshaft, using the tool **(see illustrations)**, socket, or tubing to press the seal squarely and fully into position, to the previously-noted depth. Remove the guide from the end of the crankshaft.

8 The remainder of reassembly is the reverse of the removal procedure, referring to the relevant text for details where required. Check for signs of oil leakage when the engine is restarted.

Flywheel/driveplate end seal

9 Remove the flywheel/driveplate as described in Section 15.

10 Using a screwdriver or similar, carefully prise the oil seal from place. Take great care not to damage the seal seating area or the crankshaft sealing surface. Alternatively, punch or drill two small holes opposite each other in the oil seal, then screw a self-tapping screw into each hole, and pull the screws with pliers to extract the seal**(see illustrations)**.

11 Clean the end of the crankshaft, polishing off any burrs or raised edges, which may have caused the seal to fail in the first place. Clean also the seal mating face on the engine block, using a suitable solvent for degreasing if necessary.

12 The new oil seal is supplied fitted with a locating sleeve, which must not be removed prior to fitting (it will drop out on its own when the seal is fitted). Do not lubricate the seal.

13 Offer the new seal into position, feeding the locating sleeve over the end of the crankshaft **(see illustration)**.

14 Ford technicians use a special tool (205-307) to pull the seal into position. In the absence of the tool, use a large socket/piece of tubing which bears only on the hard outer

14.10a Drill a hole in the seal...

14.10b... then insert a self-tapping screw and pull out the seal

14.13 Locate the seal and locating sleeve over the end of the crankshaft

14.14 Press the seal in until it's flush with the surface

15.2 A simple home-made tool to lock the flywheel

15.3 Flywheel retaining bolts

edge of the seal, and carefully tap the seal into position **(see illustration)**.

15 If the seal locating sleeve is still in position, remove it now.

16 The remainder of the reassembly procedure is the reverse of dismantling, referring to the relevant text for details where required. Check for signs of oil leakage when the engine is restarted.

15 Flywheel/driveplate – removal, inspection and refitting

Note: *New flywheel/driveplate retaining bolts will be required for refitting.*

Removal

Manual transmission models

1 Remove the transmission as described in Chapter 7A Section 7 then remove the clutch assembly as described in Chapter 6 Section 6.

2 Prevent the flywheel from turning by locking the ring gear teeth with a similar arrangement to that shown **(see illustration)**. Alternatively, bolt a strap between the flywheel and the cylinder block/crankcase. Make alignment marks between the flywheel and crankshaft using paint or a suitable marker pen.

3 Slacken and remove the retaining bolts and remove the flywheel **(see illustration)**. Do not drop it, as it is very heavy.

Automatic transmission models

4 Remove the transmission as described in Chapter 7B Section 12 then remove the driveplate as described in paragraphs 2 and 3.

Inspection

5 On manual transmission models, examine the flywheel for scoring of the clutch face. If the clutch face is scored, the flywheel may be surface-ground, but renewal is preferable.

6 On automatic transmission models closely examine the driveplate and ring gear teeth for signs of wear or damage and check the driveplate surface for any signs of cracks.

7 If there is any doubt about the condition of the flywheel/driveplate, seek the advice of a Ford dealer or engine reconditioning specialist. They will be able to advise if it is possible to recondition it or whether renewal is necessary.

Refitting

Manual transmission models

8 Clean the mating surfaces of the flywheel and crankshaft.

9 Unless they are already pre-coated, apply a drop of locking compound to each of the new retaining bolt threads then offer up the flywheel, if the original is being refitted align the marks made prior to removal. Screw in the retaining bolts.

10 Lock the flywheel by the method used on removal, and tighten the retaining bolts to the specified torque in two stages.

11 Refit the clutch as described in Chapter 6 Section 6 then remove the locking tool, and refit the transmission as described in Chapter 7A Section 7.

Automatic transmission models

12 Clean the mating surfaces of the driveplate and crankshaft.

13 Unless they are already pre-coated, apply a drop of locking compound to each of the new retaining bolt threads then offer up the driveplate, if the original is being refitted align the marks made prior to removal. Screw in the retaining bolts.

14 Lock the driveplate by the method used on removal, and tighten the retaining bolts to the specified torque in two stages.

15 Remove the locking tool and refit the transmission as described in Chapter 7B Section 12.

16 Engine/transmission mountings – inspection and renewal

1 Refer to Chapter 2A, Section 16, but note the different torque wrench settings given in the Specifications at the beginning of this Chapter.

Chapter 2 Part D
Engine removal and overhaul procedures

Contents

Degrees of difficulty

Easy, suitable for novice with little experience	Fairly easy, suitable for beginner with some experience 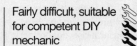	Fairly difficult, suitable for competent DIY mechanic	Difficult, suitable for experienced DIY mechanic	Very difficult, suitable for expert DIY or professional

Specifications

Engine type

2.0 litre (1998 cc) DOHC 16-valve petrol engine	AOBA and AOBC
1.8 litre (1753 cc) SOHC 8-valve diesel engine	FFBA, KHBA and QYBA

Manufacturer's engine codes*

2.0 litre (1998 cc) DOHC 16-valve diesel engine:

Engines to emission level Stage III/IV	AZBA and QXBA
Engines to emission level Stage V	TXBA, TYBA, UFBA and UKBA

* For details of engine code location, see 'Vehicle identification' in the Reference Chapter.

Petrol engines

Cylinder head

Maximum gasket face distortion	0.10 mm

Valves

Stem diameter:

Inlet valves	5.470 to 5.485 mm
Exhaust valves	5.465 to 5.480 mm

Torque wrench settings

Refer to Chapter 2A Specifications2A,

Diesel engines

Cylinder head
Maximum gasket face distortion: . . . .
   1.8 litre engines . . . . 0.06 mm
   2.0 litre engines . . . . 0.03 mm

Valves
Valve stem diameter: . . . .
   1.8 litre engines . . . . Not available
   2.0 litre engines . . . .
      Inlet valves . . . . .5.978 ± 0.009 mm
      Exhaust valves . . . . .5.968 ± 0.009 mm

Cylinder block
Cylinder bore diameter (nominal): . . . .
   1.8 litre engines . . . . 82.50 mm
   2.0 litre engines . . . . 85.00 mm

Piston rings
End gaps: . . . .
   1.8 litre engines: . . . .
      Top compression ring . . . . 0.31 to 0.50 mm
      Second compression ring. . . . . 0.31 to 0.50 mm
      Oil control ring . . . . 0.25 to 0.58 mm
   2.0 litre engines: . . . .
      Top compression ring . . . . 0.20 to 0.35 mm
      Second compression ring. . . . . 0.80 to 1.00 mm
      Oil control ring . . . . 0.25 to 0.50 mm

Crankshaft
Endfloat:
   1.8 litre engines . . . . 0.11 to 0.37 mm
   2.0 litre engines . . . . 0.07 to 0.32 mm
Maximum bearing journal out-of-round (all engines) . . . . 0.007 mm

Torque wrench settings
Refer to Specifications in Chapter 2A or Chapter 2B.

1 General Information

1 Included in this Part of Chapter 2 are details of removing the engine/transmission from the car and general overhaul procedures for the cylinder head, cylinder block/crankcase and all other engine internal components. **Note:** *On all petrol engines covered by this manual, it is not possible to remove the intermediate/ main bearing section or to remove the crankshaft or pistons. No separate parts are available, and replacement/exchange units are supplied with crankshaft, pistons, connecting rods, etc, already fitted. Consult a Ford dealer or parts specialist for further information.*
2 The information given ranges from advice concerning preparation for an overhaul and the purchase of parts, to detailed step-by-step procedures covering removal, inspection, renovation and refitting of engine internal components (where possible).
3 After Section 6, all instructions are based on the assumption that the engine has been removed from the car. For information concerning in-car engine repair, as well as the removal and refitting of those external

components necessary for full overhaul, refer to Parts A to C of this Chapter (as applicable) and to Section 6. Ignore any preliminary dismantling operations described in Parts A to C that are no longer relevant once the engine has been removed from the car.
4 Apart from torque wrench settings, which are given at the beginning of Parts A to C (as applicable), all specifications relating to engine overhaul are at the beginning of this Part of Chapter 2.

2 Engine overhaul – general information

1 It is not always easy to determine when, or if, an engine should be completely overhauled, as a number of factors must be considered.
2 High mileage is not necessarily an indication that an overhaul is needed, while low mileage does not preclude the need for an overhaul. Frequency of servicing is probably the most important consideration. An engine which has had regular and frequent oil and filter changes, as well as other required maintenance, will most likely give many thousands of miles of reliable service. Conversely, a neglected

engine may require an overhaul very early in its life.
3 Excessive oil consumption is an indication that piston rings, valve stem oil seals and/ or valves and valve guides are in need of attention. Make sure that oil leaks are not responsible before deciding that the rings and/or guides are to blame. Perform a cylinder compression check to determine the likely cause of the problem.
4 Check the oil pressure with a gauge fitted in place of the oil pressure switch, and compare it with the value given in the Specifications. If it is extremely low, the main and big-end bearings and/or the oil pump are probably worn out.
5 Loss of power, rough running, knocking or metallic engine noises, excessive valve gear noise and high fuel consumption may also point to the need for an overhaul, especially if they are all present at the same time. If a complete tune-up does not remedy the situation, major mechanical work is the only solution.
6 An engine overhaul involves restoring the internal parts to the specifications of a new engine. During an overhaul, the pistons and rings are renewed, and the cylinder bores are reconditioned. New main bearings, connecting rod bearings and camshaft bearings are

generally fitted, and if necessary, the crankshaft may be reground to restore the journals. The valves are also serviced as well, since they are usually in less-than-perfect condition at this point. While the engine is being overhauled, other components, such as the starter and alternator, can be overhauled as well. The end result should be a like-new engine that will give many trouble-free miles. **Note:** *Critical cooling system components such as the hoses, drivebelts, thermostat and coolant pump should be renewed when an engine is overhauled. The radiator should be checked carefully, to ensure that it is not clogged or leaking. Also, it is a good idea to renew the oil pump whenever the engine is overhauled.*

7 Before beginning the engine overhaul, read through the entire procedure to familiarise yourself with the scope and requirements of the job. Overhauling an engine is not difficult if you follow all of the instructions carefully, have the necessary tools and equipment, and pay close attention to all specifications; however, it can be time-consuming. Plan on the car being tied up for a minimum of two weeks, especially if parts must be taken to an engineering works for repair or reconditioning. Check on the availability of parts, and make sure that any necessary special tools and equipment are obtained in advance. Most work can be done with typical hand tools, although a number of precision measuring tools are required for inspecting parts to determine if they must be renewed. Often the engineering works will handle the inspection of parts, and offer advice concerning reconditioning and renewal.

8 Always wait until the engine has been completely dismantled, and all components, especially the engine block, have been inspected before deciding what service and repair operations must be performed by an engineering works. Since the condition of the block will be the major factor to consider when determining whether to overhaul the original engine or buy a reconditioned unit, do not purchase parts or have overhaul work done on other components until the block has been thoroughly inspected. As a general rule, time is the primary cost of an overhaul, so it does not pay to fit worn or substandard parts.

9 As a final note, to ensure maximum life and minimum trouble from a reconditioned engine, everything must be assembled with care, and in a spotlessly-clean environment.

3 Engine removal –
methods and precautions

⚠️ **Warning:** *Always be extremely careful when removing and refitting the engine. Serious injury can result from careless actions. Plan ahead, take your time, and you will find that a job of this nature, although major, can be accomplished successfully.*

1 If you have decided that an engine must be removed for overhaul or major repair work, several preliminary steps should be taken.

2 Locating a suitable place to work is extremely important. Adequate work space, along with storage space for the car, will be needed. If a garage is not available, at the very least a flat, level, clean work surface is required.

3 Cleaning the engine compartment and engine before beginning the removal procedure will help keep tools clean and organised.

4 The engine is removed complete with the transmission, by lowering it out of the car; the car's body must be raised and supported securely, sufficiently high that the engine/transmission can be unbolted as a single unit and lowered to the ground. An engine hoist will therefore be necessary. Make sure the equipment is rated in excess of the combined weight of the engine and transmission. Safety is of primary importance, considering the potential hazards involved in lifting the engine out of the car.

5 If the engine is being removed by a novice, an assistant should be available. Advice and aid from someone more experienced would also be helpful. There are many instances when one person cannot simultaneously perform all of the operations required when removing the engine from the car.

6 Plan the operation ahead of time. Arrange for, or obtain, all of the tools and equipment you will need, prior to beginning the job. Some of the equipment necessary to perform engine removal and installation safely and with relative ease are (in addition to an engine hoist) a heavy-duty trolley jack, complete sets of spanners and sockets as described at the end of this manual, wooden blocks, and plenty of rags and cleaning solvent for mopping-up spilled oil, coolant and fuel. If the hoist must be hired, make sure that you arrange for it in advance, and perform all of the operations possible without it beforehand. This will save you money and time.

7 Plan for the car to be out of use for quite a while. An engineering works will be required to perform some of the work which the do-it-yourselfer cannot accomplish without special equipment. These places often have a busy schedule, so it would be a good idea to consult them before removing the engine, in order to accurately estimate the amount of time required to rebuild or repair components that may need work.

8 During the engine/transmission removal procedure, it is advisable to make notes of the locations of all brackets, cable-ties, earthing points, etc, as well as how the wiring harnesses, hoses and electrical connections are attached and routed around the engine and engine compartment. An effective way of doing this is to take a series of photographs of the various components

before they are disconnected or removed; the resulting photographs will prove invaluable when the engine/transmission is refitted.

Note: *Such is the complexity of the power unit arrangement on these vehicles, and the variations that may be encountered according to model and optional equipment fitted, that the procedures given in Sections 4 and 5 should be regarded as a guide to the work involved, rather than an accurate step-by-step procedure. Where differences are encountered, or additional component disconnection or removal is necessary, make notes of the work involved as an aid to refitting.*

4 Petrol engine – removal, separation and refitting

Note: *This procedure describes removing the engine and transmission a complete assembly downwards out the of the engine compartment. When raising the vehicle bear in mind that the front underside of the vehicle must be at least 700 mm above the ground to provide sufficient clearance.*

Removal

1 Remove the plastic cover over the top of the engine.

2 Depressurise the fuel system with reference to Chapter 4A Section 2.

3 Remove the air cleaner assembly as described in Chapter 4A Section 5.

4 Remove the battery and battery tray as described in Chapter 5A Section 4.

5 Remove the right-hand headlight unit as described in Chapter 12 Section 7.

6 Jack up the front of the car, and support it on axle stands (see *'Jacking and vehicle support'*). Although not essential immediately, it would pay at this stage to raise the car sufficiently to allow the engine and transmission to be withdrawn from underneath.

7 Remove the auxiliary drivebelt as described in Chapter 1A Section 25.

8 Drain the cooling system as described in Chapter 1A Section 30.

9 If the engine is being dismantled, drain the engine oil with reference to Chapter 1A Section 7.

10 Undo the retaining nut and disconnect the engine positive supply lead from the battery positive terminal connector.

11 Disconnect the reversing light switch wiring connector and the earth leads at the engine/transmission left-hand mounting and at the left-hand chassis member. Release the wiring from the cable clips and ties.

12 Taking precautions against fluid spillage, prise up the spring clip and disconnect the clutch slave cylinder fluid pipe from on top of

4.12 Prise out the clip and disconnect the clutch slave cylinder hose

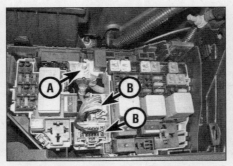

4.13 Undo the nut (A) and disconnect the positive leads, then disconnect the two wiring connectors (B)

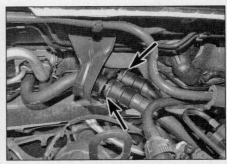

4.15 Prise up the spring clips (arrowed) and disconnect the heater coolant hoses

the transmission **(see illustration)**. Unclip the pipe, and tie it up to the bulkhead to reduce further fluid spillage.

13 Disconnect the engine wiring harness from the engine compartment fuse/relay box**(see illustration)**. Using a small screwdriver, release the two retaining tabs and lift up the front section of the fuse/relay carrier. Release the wiring harness from the fuse/relay box so it is free to be removed with the engine.

14 Disconnect the gearchange cables from the transmission as described in Chapter 7A Section 3.

15 Prise up the spring clips and disconnect the heater coolant hoses at the quick-release connectors **(see illustration)**.

16 Disconnect the radiator bottom hose and expansion tank hose at the coolant outlet housing on the left-hand end of the cylinder head.

17 Disconnect the wiring connector and vapour hose from the carbon canister purge valve on the left-hand side of the engine.

18 Disconnect the fuel supply hose quick-release connection from the fuel rail at the front of the engine.

19 Release the carbon canister vapour hose and the fuel supply hose from the clips at the front and sides of the cylinder head and move the hoses aside.

20 Disconnect the oxygen sensor wiring connectors **(see illustration)**.

21 Disconnect the wiring connector at the radiator cooling fan.

22 Disconnect the coolant hose from the expansion tank and the top hose from the radiator.

4.20 Disconnect the oxygen sensor wiring connectors (arrowed)

23 Disconnect the brake servo vacuum hose from the inlet manifold.

24 Disconnect the wiring connector from the pressure switch on the power steering pump, then undo the three bolts securing the power steering pump to the engine. Move the pump to one side as far as the hoses will allow and secure it with cable-ties or similar.

25 Remove both driveshafts as described in Chapter 8.

26 Remove the front subframe as described in Chapter 10 Section 7.

27 Remove the exhaust manifold as described in Chapter 4A Section 11.

28 Undo the two nuts and remove the heat shield from the rear of the alternator.

29 Disconnect the wiring connector from the air conditioning compressor. Undo the three bolts securing the compressor to the block, and secure the compressor to one side using cable-ties – do not disconnect any of the hoses.

30 Refer to Chapter 4A Section 10 and disconnect the three wiring connectors from the engine management powertrain control module (PCM).

31 Undo the nut securing the air conditioning refrigerant pipe support bracket to the stud below the right-hand engine/transmission mounting.

32 Make a final check round the engine and transmission, to make sure nothing (apart from the left- and right-hand mountings) remains attached or in the way which will prevent it from being lowered out. Also make sure there is enough room under the front of the car for the engine/transmission to be lowered out and withdrawn.

33 Securely attach the engine/transmission unit to a suitable engine crane or hoist, and raise it so that the weight is just taken off the two remaining engine mountings. It is helpful at this stage to have an assistant available, either to work the crane or to guide the engine out.

34 With the engine securely supported, remove the centre bolt from the engine left-hand mounting (on top of the transmission).

35 Similarly, remove the two nuts and two bolts from the engine right-hand mounting, on the driver's side of the engine compartment.

36 With the help of an assistant, carefully lower

the assembly from the engine compartment, making sure it clears the surrounding components and bodywork. Be prepared to steady the engine when it touches down, to stop it toppling over. Withdraw the assembly from under the car, and remove it to wherever it will be worked on.

Separation

37 To separate the transmission from the engine, first remove the starter motor with reference to Chapter 5A Section 8.

38 Remove the bolts securing the transmission to the engine. Note the fitted positions of any brackets.

39 With the aid of an assistant, draw the transmission off the engine. Once it is clear of the dowels, do not allow it to hang on the input shaft.

Refitting

40 Make sure that the clutch is correctly centred and that the clutch release components are fitted to the bellhousing. Do not apply any grease to the transmission input shaft, the guide sleeve, or the release bearing itself, as these components have a friction-reducing coating which does not require lubrication.

41 Manoeuvre the transmission squarely into position, and engage it with the engine dowels. Refit the bolts securing the transmission to the engine, and tighten them to the specified torque. Refit the starter motor.

42 The remainder of refitting is a reversal of removal, noting the following additional points:

a) *Make sure that all mating faces are clean, and use new gaskets where necessary.*

b) *Tighten all nuts and bolts to the specified torque setting, where given.*

c) *Check and if necessary adjust the gearchange cables as described in Chapter 7A Section 3.*

d) *Refill the transmission with lubricant if necessary as described in Chapter 1A Section 28.*

e) *Top-up and bleed the clutch hydraulic system as described in Chapter 6 Section 5.*

f) *Refill the engine with coolant and oil as described in Chapter 1A.*

5 Diesel engine – removal, separation and refitting

⚠ *Warning: The diesel injection system operates at extremely high pressures when the pump is running. Wait at least one minute after stopping the engine before working on the fuel injection system components.*
Note: *This procedure describes removing the engine and transmission a complete assembly downwards out the of the engine compartment. When raising the vehicle bear in mind that the front underside of the vehicle must be at least 700 mm above the ground to provide sufficient clearance.*

Removal

1 Remove the plastic cover over the top of the engine.
2 Remove the air cleaner assembly as described in Chapter 4B Section 5.
3 Remove the battery and battery tray as described in Chapter 5A Section 4.
4 Remove the right-hand headlight unit as described in Chapter 12 Section 7.
5 Jack up the front of the car, and support it on axle stands (see 'Jacking and vehicle support'). Although not essential immediately, it would pay at this stage to raise the car sufficiently to allow the engine and transmission to be withdrawn from underneath.
6 Undo the fasteners and remove the engine undertray.
7 Remove the auxiliary drivebelt as described in Chapter 1B Section 24.
8 Drain the cooling system as described in Chapter 1B Section 30.
9 If the engine is being dismantled, drain the engine oil with reference to Chapter 1B Section 6.
10 Slacken the hose clamps, undo the bracket bolt and remove the charge air pipe from the underside of the engine **(see illustration)**.
11 Undo the retaining nut and disconnect the engine positive supply lead from the battery positive terminal connector.
12 Disconnect the reversing light switch wiring connector and the earth leads at the engine/transmission left-hand mounting and at the left-hand chassis member. Release the wiring from the cable clips and ties.
13 On automatic transmission models, disconnect the wiring connector at the transmission control module, then release the wiring harness from the cable clips and ties.
14 On manual transmission models, taking precautions against fluid spillage, prise up the spring clip and disconnect the clutch slave cylinder fluid pipe from on top of the transmission**(see illustration 4.12)**. Unclip the pipe, and tie it up to the bulkhead to reduce further fluid spillage.
15 Disconnect the engine wiring harness from the engine compartment fuse/relay box**(see**

illustration 4.13). Using a small screwdriver, release the two retaining tabs and lift up the front section of the fuse/relay carrier. Release the wiring harness from the fuse/relay box so it is free to be removed with the engine.
16 Disconnect the transmission gearchange/selector cable(s) from the transmission as described in Chapter 7A Section 3 or Chapter 7B Section 4, as applicable.
17 On 1.8 litre engines, release the clamps, undo the retaining bolt, disconnect the MAP sensor wiring plug, then remove the intercooler outlet pipe.
18 Disconnect the radiator top and bottom hoses, expansion tank hose, heater matrix coolant hoses and EGR cooler hoses.
19 On automatic transmission models, disconnect the two transmission fluid pipes from the fluid cooler by pressing the two tabs on the quick-release connectors and pulling the connectors off the fluid cooler pipe stubs. Be prepared for fluid spillage.
20 Disconnect the fuel supply and return pipes at the quick-release connectors on the fuel filter (1.8 litre engines) or on the right-hand side of the engine (2.0 litre engines). Suitably cover or plug the disconnected unions, then release the fuel pipes from their retaining clips.
21 Disconnect the wiring connector at the radiator cooling fan.
22 Disconnect the brake servo vacuum hose from the vacuum pump.
23 Undo the bolts securing the power steering pump to the engine, then move the pump to one side as far as the hoses will allow and secure it with cable-ties or similar.
24 Remove both driveshafts as described in Chapter 8.
25 Remove the front subframe as described in Chapter 10 Section 7.
26 Remove the catalytic converter as described in Chapter 4B Section 18.
27 Disconnect the wiring connector from the air conditioning compressor. Undo the three bolts securing the compressor to the block, and secure the compressor to one side using cable-ties – do not disconnect any of the hoses.
28 Refer to Chapter 4B Section 12 and disconnect the three wiring connectors from the engine management powertrain control module (PCM)
29 Make a final check round the engine and transmission, to make sure nothing (apart from the left- and right-hand mountings) remains attached or in the way which will prevent it from being lowered out. Also make sure there is enough room under the front of the car for the engine/transmission to be lowered out and withdrawn.
30 Securely attach the engine/transmission unit to a suitable engine crane or hoist, and raise it so that the weight is just taken off the two remaining engine mountings. It is helpful at this stage to have an assistant available, either to work the crane or to guide the engine out.
31 With the engine securely supported, undo the nuts and bolts and remove the engine/transmission left-hand mounting.

5.10 Undo the charge air pipe bracket bolt (arrowed)

32 Similarly, remove the two nuts and two bolts from the engine right-hand mounting, on the driver's side of the engine compartment.
33 With the help of an assistant, carefully lower the assembly from the engine compartment, making sure it clears the surrounding components and bodywork. Be prepared to steady the engine when it touches down, to stop it toppling over. Withdraw the assembly from under the car, and remove it to wherever it will be worked on.

Separation

34 Remove the starter motor with reference to Chapter 5A Section 8.

Manual transmission models

35 Remove the bolts securing the transmission to the engine. Note the fitted positions of any brackets.
36 With the aid of an assistant, draw the transmission off the engine. Once it is clear of the dowels, do not allow it to hang on the input shaft.

Automatic transmission models

37 Remove the access cover over the starter motor aperture.
38 Rotate the crankshaft, using a socket on the pulley nut, until one of the torque converter-to-driveplate retaining bolts/nuts becomes accessible through the opening on the rear facing side of the engine. Working through the opening, undo the bolt. Rotate the crankshaft as necessary and remove the remaining bolts in the same way, there are six bolts in total. Note that new bolts will be required for refitting.
39 Remove the bolts securing the transmission to the engine.
40 With the aid of an assistant, draw the transmission squarely off the engine dowels making sure that the torque converter remains in position on the transmission. Use the access hole in the transmission housing to hold the converter in place.

Refitting

Manual transmission models

41 Make sure that the clutch is correctly centred and that the clutch release components are fitted to the bellhousing. Do not apply any grease to the transmission input shaft, the guide sleeve, or the release bearing itself, as these components have a friction-reducing coating which does not require lubrication.

42 Manoeuvre the transmission squarely into position, and engage it with the engine dowels. Refit the bolts securing the transmission to the engine, and tighten them to the specified torque. Refit the starter motor.

Automatic transmission models

43 Clean the contact surfaces on the torque converter and driveplate, and the transmission and engine mating faces. Lightly lubricate the torque converter guide projection and the engine/transmission locating dowels with grease.

44 Manoeuvre the transmission squarely into position, and engage it with the engine dowels. Refit the bolts securing the transmission to the engine and tighten lightly first in a diagonal sequence, then again to the specified torque.

45 Attach the torque converter to the driveplate using new bolts. Rotate the crankshaft for access to the bolts as was done for removal, then rotate the torque converter by means of the access hole in the transmission housing. Fit and tighten all the bolts hand-tight first, then tighten again to the specified torque. Refit the starter motor.

All models

46 The remainder of refitting is a reversal of removal, noting the following additional points:
a) *Make sure that all mating faces are clean, and use new gaskets where necessary.*
b) *Tighten all nuts and bolts to the specified torque setting, where given.*
c) *On manual transmission models, check and if necessary adjust the gearchange cables as described in Chapter 7A Section 3.*
d) *On automatic transmission models, reconnect and adjust the selector cable as described in Chapter 7B Section 4.*
e) *Refill the transmission with lubricant if necessary as described in the relevant parts of Chapter 7A Section 6 and Chapter 7B Section 2.*
f) *On manual transmission models, top-up and bleed the clutch hydraulic system as described in Chapter 6 Section 5.*
g) *Refill the engine with coolant and oil as described in Chapter 1A Section 7 or Chapter 1B Section 6.*

6 Engine overhaul – dismantling sequence

Note: *On all petrol engines covered by this manual, it is not possible to remove the intermediate/main bearing section or to remove the crankshaft or pistons. No separate parts are available, and replacement/*

exchange units are supplied with crankshaft, pistons, connecting rods, etc, already fitted. Consult a Ford dealer or parts specialist for further information.

1 It is much easier to dismantle and work on the engine if it is mounted on a portable engine stand. These stands can often be hired from a tool hire shop. Before the engine is mounted on a stand, the flywheel/driveplate should be removed from the engine, so that the engine stand bolts can be tightened into the end of the cylinder block.

2 If a stand is not available, it is possible to dismantle the engine with it blocked up on a sturdy workbench or on the floor. Be extra careful not to tip or drop the engine when working without a stand.

3 If you're going to obtain a reconditioned ('recon') engine, all external components must be removed first, to be transferred to the new engine (just as they will if you are doing a complete engine overhaul yourself). **Note:** *When removing the external components from the engine, pay close attention to details that may be helpful or important during refitting. Note the fitted position of gaskets, seals, spacers, pins, washers, bolts and other small items. These external components include the following:*

Petrol engines
a) *Ignition system HT components including ignition coils, spark plugs and wiring as applicable.*
b) *All electrical switches and sensors.*
c) *Thermostat housing.*
d) *Fuel system components.*
e) *Inlet and exhaust manifolds.*
f) *Oil filter.*
g) *Engine mountings and lifting brackets.*
h) *Ancillary component mounting brackets.*
i) *Oil filler tube and dipstick.*
j) *Coolant pipes and hoses.*
k) *Flywheel.*

Diesel engines
a) *All electrical switches and sensors.*
b) *Fuel system components and glow plugs.*
c) *Thermostat housing.*
d) *Inlet and exhaust manifolds.*
e) *Oil cooler.*
f) *Engine lifting brackets, hose brackets and wiring brackets.*
g) *Ancillary component mounting brackets.*
h) *Wiring harnesses and brackets.*
i) *Coolant pipes and hoses.*
j) *Oil filler tube and dipstick.*
k) *Flywheel/driveplate.*

4 If you are obtaining a 'short' motor (which consists of the engine cylinder block, crankshaft, pistons and connecting rods all assembled), then the timing belt/chain, cylinder head, sump and oil pump will have to be removed also.

5 If you are planning a complete overhaul (diesel engines only) the engine can be

disassembled and the internal components removed in the following order:
a) *Engine external components (including inlet and exhaust manifolds).*
b) *Timing belt and sprockets.*
c) *Cylinder head.*
d) *Flywheel/driveplate.*
e) *Sump.*
f) *Oil pump.*
g) *Pistons and connecting rods.*
h) *Crankshaft and main bearings.*

6 Before beginning the disassembly and overhaul procedures, make sure that you have all of the correct tools necessary. Refer to the reference section at the end of this manual for further information.

7 Cylinder head – dismantling

Note: *New and reconditioned cylinder heads are available from the manufacturers and from engine overhaul specialists. Due to the fact that some specialist tools are required for the dismantling and inspection procedures, and new components may not be readily available, it may be more practical and economical for the home mechanic to purchase a reconditioned head rather than dismantle, inspect and recondition the original head.*

1 Remove the cylinder head as described in Part A, B or C of this Chapter (as applicable).

2 If not already done, remove the inlet and exhaust manifolds with reference to Chapter 4A Section 11 or Chapter 4B Section 17. Also remove all external fittings, unions, pipes, sensors, brackets and elbows.

3 Proceed as follows according to engine type.

Petrol engines

4 Tap each valve stem smartly, using a light hammer and drift, to free the spring and associated items.

5 Fit a deep-reach type valve spring compressor to each valve in turn, and compress each spring until the collets are exposed **(see illustration)**. Lift out the collets; a small screwdriver, a magnet or a pair of tweezers may be useful. Carefully release the spring compressor and remove it.

7.5 Compress the valve spring with a suitable valve spring compressor

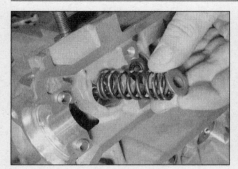

7.6 Remove the spring retainer and the valve spring

7.7 Special pliers are available specifically designed to remove valve stem seals

7.8 Place each valve and its associated components in a labelled bag

6 Remove the spring retainer and the valve spring **(see illustration)**. Pull the valve out of its guide.

7 Pull off the valve stem oil seal with a pair of long-nosed pliers **(see illustration)**. It may be necessary to use a tool such as a pair of electrician's wire strippers, the 'legs' of which will engage under the seal, if the seal is tight.

8 It is essential that each valve is stored together with its collets, retainer, spring and spring seat. The valves should also be kept in their correct sequence, unless they are so badly worn or burnt that they are to be renewed. If they are going to be kept and used again, place each valve assembly in a labelled polythene bag or similar container

(see illustration). Note that No 1 valve is nearest to the timing chain end of the engine.

9 Continue removing all the remaining valves in the same way.

Diesel engines

10 On 1.8 litre engines, remove the camshaft, cam followers and shims as described in Part B of this Chapter. On 2.0 litre engines, remove the camshaft drive chain guide from the cylinder head **(see illustration)**.

11 Tap each valve stem smartly, using a light hammer and drift, to free the spring and associated items.

12 Using a valve spring compressor, compress each valve spring in turn until the

split collets can be removed. Release the compressor, and lift off the spring retainer, spring and, where fitted, the spring seat **(see illustrations)**. Pull the valve out of its guide.

13 Using a pair of pliers, carefully extract the valve stem oil seal from the top of the guide. On 2.0 litre engines, the valve stem oil seal also forms the spring seat and is deeply recessed in the cylinder head. It is also a tight fit on the valve guide making it difficult to remove with pliers or a conventional valve stem oil seal removal tool. It can be easily removed, however, using a self-locking nut of suitable diameter screwed onto the end of a bolt and locked with a second nut. Push the nut down onto the top of the seal; the locking

7.10 Remove the camshaft drive chain guide – 2.0 litre diesel engines

7.12a Compress the valve spring using a spring compressor…

7.12b… then extract the collets and release the spring compressor

7.12c Remove the spring retainer…

7.12d… followed by the valve spring…

7.12e… and the spring seat (not all models)

7.13a Remove the valve stem oil seal using a pair of pliers...

7.13b... alternatively, secure a self-locking nut of suitable diameter to a long bolt, then use the tool to removethe valve stem seal

portion of the nut will grip the seal allowing it to be withdrawn from the top of the valve guide **(see illustrations)**.

14 It is essential that each valve is stored together with its collets, retainer, spring, and spring seat. The valves should also be kept in their correct sequence, unless they are so badly worn or burnt that they are to be renewed. If they are going to be kept and used again, place each valve assembly in a labelled polythene bag or similar small container **(see illustration 7.8)**. Note that No 1 valve is nearest to the timing belt end of the engine on 1.8 litre engines, and nearest to the transmission (flywheel/driveplate) end on 2.0 litre engines.

15 Continue removing all the remaining valves in the same way.

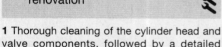

8 Cylinder head and valves
– cleaning, inspection and renovation

1 Thorough cleaning of the cylinder head and valve components, followed by a detailed inspection, will enable you to decide how much valve service work must be carried out during the engine overhaul.

Cleaning

2 Scrape away all traces of old gasket material and sealing compound from the cylinder head. Take care not to damage the cylinder head surfaces.

3 Scrape away the carbon from the combustion chambers and ports, then wash the cylinder head thoroughly with paraffin or a suitable solvent.

4 Scrape off any heavy carbon deposits that may have formed on the valves, then use a power-operated wire brush to remove deposits from the valve heads and stems.

5 If the head is extremely dirty, it should be steam cleaned. On completion, make sure that all oil holes and oil galleries are cleaned.

Inspection and renovation

Note: *Be sure to perform all the following inspection procedures before concluding that the services of an engine overhaul specialist are required. Make a list of all items that require attention.*

Cylinder head

6 Inspect the head very carefully for cracks, evidence of coolant leakage and other damage. If cracks are found, a new cylinder head should be obtained.

7 Use a straight-edge and feeler blade to check that the cylinder head surface is not distorted **(see illustration)**. If the specified distortion limit is exceeded, machining of the gasket face is not recommended by the manufacturers, so the only course of action is to renew the cylinder head.

8 Examine the valve seats in each of the combustion chambers. If they are severely pitted, cracked or burned, then they will need to be renewed or recut by an engine overhaul specialist. If they are only slightly pitted, this

can be removed by grinding the valve heads and seats together with coarse, then fine, grinding paste as described below.

9 If the valve guides are worn, indicated by a side-to-side motion of the valve in the guide, new guides must be fitted. If necessary, insert a new valve in the guides to determine if the wear is on the guide or valve. If new guides are to be fitted, the valves must be renewed as a matter of course. Valve guides may be renewed using a press and a suitable mandrel, and the work is best carried out by an engine overhaul specialist, since if it is not done skilfully, there is a risk of damaging the cylinder head.

10 Where applicable, check the cam follower bores in the cylinder head for wear. If excessive wear is evident, the cylinder head must be renewed.

11 Examine the camshaft bearing surfaces in the cylinder head as described in Chapter 2A Section 9, Chapter 2B Section 9 or Chapter 2C Section 7.

Valves

12 Examine the head of each valve for pitting, burning, cracks and general wear, and check the valve stem for scoring and wear ridges. Rotate the valve, and check for any obvious indication that it is bent. Look for pits and excessive wear on the end of each valve stem.

13 If the valve appears satisfactory at this stage, measure the valve stem diameter at several points using a micrometer **(see illustration)**. Any significant difference in the readings obtained indicates wear of the valve stem. Should any of these conditions be apparent, the valve(s) must be renewed.

14 If the valves are in satisfactory condition, or if new valves are being fitted, they should be ground (lapped) into their respective seats to ensure a smooth gas-tight seal.

15 Valve grinding is carried out as follows. Place the cylinder head upside-down on a bench, with a block of wood at each end to give clearance for the valve stems. Where applicable, take care to protect the camshaft bearing surfaces.

16 Smear a trace of coarse carborundum paste on the seat face, and press a suction grinding tool onto the valve head. With a semi-rotary action, grind the valve head to its

8.7 Check the cylinder head gasket surface for distortion

8.13 Measure the valve stem diameter with a micrometer

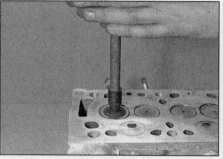

8.16 Grinding-in a valve

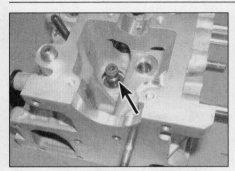

9.1a Locate the valve stem oil seal (arrowed) on the valve guide…

9.1b… and press the seal firmly onto the guide using a suitable socket

9.1c On some engines, the valve stem oil seal is integral with the spring seat

seat, lifting the valve occasionally to redistribute the grinding paste (see illustration).

17 When a dull-matt even surface is produced on both the valve seat and the valve, wipe off the paste and repeat the process with fine carborundum paste. A light spring placed under the valve head will greatly ease this operation.

18 When a smooth unbroken ring of light grey matt finish is produced on both the valve and seat, the grinding operation is complete. Be sure to remove all traces of grinding paste, using paraffin or a suitable solvent, before reassembly of the cylinder head.

Valve components

19 Examine the valve springs for signs of damage and discoloration, and also measure their free length by comparing the existing spring with a new component.

20 Stand each spring on a flat surface, and check it for squareness. If any of the springs are damaged, distorted or have lost their tension, obtain a complete new set of springs. It is normal to renew the springs as a matter of course during a major overhaul.

21 Renew the valve stem oil seals regardless of their apparent condition.

9 Cylinder head – reassembly

1 Working on the first valve assembly, refit the spring seat then dip the new valve stem oil seal in fresh engine oil. Locate the seal on the valve guide and press the seal firmly

onto the guide using a suitable socket (see illustrations).

2 Lubricate the stem of the first valve, and insert it in the guide (see illustration).

3 Locate the valve spring on top of its seat, then refit the spring retainer.

4 Compress the valve spring, and locate the split collets in the recess in the valve stem. Release the compressor, then repeat the procedure on the remaining valves. Ensure that each valve is inserted into its original location. If new valves are being fitted, insert them into the locations to which they have been ground.

> **HAYNES HINT** *Use a little dab of grease to hold the collets in position on the valve stem while the spring compressor is released.*

5 With all the valves installed, support the cylinder head and, using a hammer and interposed block of wood, tap the end of each valve stem to settle the components.

6 The previously-removed components can now be refitted with reference to Section 7.

10 Fuel pump drive (1.8 litre engines) – removal, inspection and refitting

Removal

Note: *The high-pressure fuel pump will be driven either by a double-row chain*

or a toothed belt, depending on year of manufacture. The following procedures are applicable to both arrangements.

1 With the engine removed from the vehicle, proceed as follows.

2 Remove the oil pump as described in Chapter 2B Section 13.

3 At the rear of the engine block, locate the drive hydraulic tensioner (below and behind the coolant pump). Using the hex in the top of the tensioner body, unscrew and extract the tensioner from the block (see illustration). Be prepared for a small amount of oil spillage as this is done.

4 Unscrew the two bolts securing the chain/belt guides, then carefully slide the two sprockets simultaneously from their locations, and remove the complete chain/belt, guide and sprocket assembly from the engine.

Inspection

5 Examine the guides for scoring or wear ridges, and for chipping or wear of the sprocket teeth (see illustration).

6 On engines with a chain driven fuel pump, check the chains for wear, which will be evident in the form of excess play between the links. If the chains can be lifted at either 'end' of their run so that the sprocket teeth are visible, they have stretched excessively. If the chains have covered more than 150 000 miles, they must be renewed regardless of condition. On engines with a belt driven fuel pump, do not be tempted to re-use the old belt under any circumstances – even if it is known to have covered less than the 150 000 mile recommended renewal interval. Ford state that, once a drive belt has

9.2 Lubricate the stem of the valve and insert it into the guide

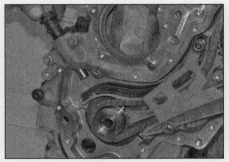

10.3 Unscrew the chain tensioner from the housing

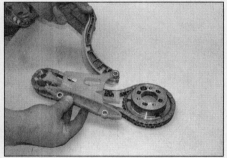

10.5 Examine the chain guides for wear

10.8 Tighten the chain guide retaining bolts

11.3 Remove the big-end bearing shell and cap

been run on an engine, it is considered worn, and should be discarded. In any case, given the potential expense involved should the belt fail in service, re-using an old belt would be a false economy.

7 Check the chain tensioner for signs of wear, and renew if required.

Refitting

8 Refitting is a reversal of removal, noting the following points:
a) Tighten the chain/belt guide retaining bolts securely to the specified torque **(see illustration)**.
b) Especially if a new chain and sprocket assembly has been fitted, lubricate it thoroughly with fresh engine oil.
c) Refit the tensioner, and tighten it to the specified torque.
d) Refit the oil pump as described in Chapter 2B Section 13.

11 Piston/connecting rod assemblies (diesel engines) – removal

1 Remove the cylinder head, sump, oil pump pick-up tube, oil pump and baffle plate, as applicable, with reference to Chapter 2A or Chapter 2B.
2 Rotate the crankshaft so that No 1 big-end cap is at the lowest point of its travel. If the big-end cap and rod are not already numbered, mark them with a marker pen. Mark both cap and rod to identify the cylinder they operate in.

3 Unscrew and remove the big-end bearing cap bolts/nuts, and withdraw the cap complete with shell bearing from the connecting rod **(see illustration)**. Make sure that the shell remains in the cap and if necessary identify it for position.
4 If only the bearing shells are being attended to, push the connecting rod up and off the crankpin, and remove the upper bearing shell. Keep the bearing shells and cap together in their correct sequence if they are to be refitted.
5 If the piston is being removed, push the connecting rod up and remove the piston and rod from the top of the bore. Note that if there is a pronounced wear ridge at the top of the bore, there is a risk of damaging the piston as the rings foul the ridge. However, it is reasonable to assume that a rebore (where possible) and new pistons will be required in any case if the ridge is so pronounced.
6 Repeat the procedure for the remaining piston/connecting rod assemblies. Ensure that the caps and rods are marked before removal, as described previously, and keep all components in order.

12 Crankshaft (diesel engines) – removal

1 Remove the pistons and connecting rods, as described in Section 10. If no work is to be done on the pistons and connecting rods, there is no need to remove the cylinder head, or to push the pistons out of the cylinder

bores. The pistons should just be pushed far enough up the bores so that they are positioned clear of the crankshaft journals.
2 Check the crankshaft endfloat as described in Section 15, then proceed as follows.

1.8 litre engines

3 Check the main bearing caps, to see if they are marked to indicate their locations. They should be numbered consecutively from the timing belt end of the engine – if not, mark them with number-stamping dies or a centre-punch. The caps will also have an embossed arrow pointing to the timing belt end of the engine **(see illustration)**. Noting, where applicable, the different fasteners (for the oil baffle nuts) used on caps 2 and 4, slacken the cap bolts a quarter-turn at a time each, starting with the left- and right-hand end caps and working toward the centre, until they can be removed by hand.
4 Gently tap the caps with a soft-faced hammer, then separate them from the cylinder block/crankcase. If necessary, use the bolts as levers to remove the caps. Try not to drop the bearing shells if they come out with the caps.
5 Carefully lift the crankshaft out of the engine. It may be a good idea to have an assistant available, since the crankshaft is quite heavy. With the bearing shells in place in the cylinder block/crankcase and main bearing caps, return the caps to their respective locations on the block, or refit the lower crankcase, and tighten the bolts finger-tight. Leaving the old shells in place until reassembly will help prevent the bearing recesses from being accidentally nicked or gouged. New shells should be used on reassembly.

2.0 litre engines

6 The main bearing caps should be numbered 1 to 5, starting from the transmission (flywheel/driveplate) end of the engine **(see illustration)**. If not, mark them accordingly using quick-drying paint. Also note the correct fitted depth of the crankshaft oil seal in the bearing cap.
7 Slacken and remove the main bearing cap retaining bolts, and lift off each bearing cap. Recover the lower bearing shells, and tape them to their respective caps for safe-keeping. Also recover the lower thrustwasher halves from the side of No 2 main bearing cap **(see illustration)**. Remove the rubber sealing strips

12.3 Main bearing caps are marked with cylinder number and arrowhead

12.6 Main bearing cap identification markings (arrowed)

12.7 Note the thrustwasher (arrowed) fitted to the No 2 main bearing cap

12.8 Lift out the crankshaft

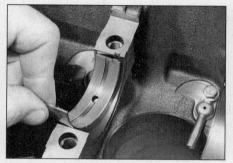

12.9 Remove the upper main bearing shells

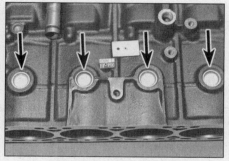

13.1 Cylinder block core plugs (arrowed)

from the sides of No 1 main bearing cap, and discard them.

8 Lift out the crankshaft, and discard the oil seal **(see illustration)**.

9 Recover the upper bearing shells from the cylinder block, and tape them to their respective caps for safe-keeping **(see illustration)**. Remove the upper thrustwasher halves from the side of No 2 main bearing, and store them with the lower halves.

13 Cylinder block/crankcase (diesel engines) – cleaning and inspection

Cleaning

1 For complete cleaning, the core plugs should be removed. Drill a small hole in them, then insert a self-tapping screw and pull out the plugs using pliers or a slide-hammer **(see illustration)**. Also remove all external components and senders (if not already done), noting their locations.

2 Scrape all traces of gasket or sealant from the cylinder block, taking care not to damage the head and sump mating faces.

3 If the block is extremely dirty, it should be steam-cleaned.

4 After the block has been steam-cleaned, clean all oil holes and oil galleries one more time. Flush all internal passages with warm water until the water runs clear, dry the block thoroughly and wipe all machined surfaces with a light rust-preventative oil. If you have access to compressed air, use it to speed up

the drying process and to blow out all the oil holes and galleries.

 Warning: Wear eye protection when using compressed air.

5 If the block is not very dirty, you can do an adequate cleaning job with hot soapy water and a stiff brush. Take plenty of time, and do a thorough job. Regardless of the cleaning method used, be sure to clean all oil holes and galleries very thoroughly, dry the block completely and coat all machined surfaces with light oil.

6 The threaded holes in the block must be clean to ensure accurate torque wrench readings during reassembly. Run the proper-size tap into each of the holes to remove rust, corrosion, thread sealant or sludge, and to restore damaged threads. If possible, use compressed air to clear the holes of debris produced by this operation.

7 After coating the mating surfaces of the new core plugs with suitable sealant, refit them in the cylinder block. Make sure that they are driven in straight and seated properly, or leakage could result. Special tools are available for this purpose, but a large socket, with an outside diameter that will just slip into the core plug, will work just as well **(see illustration)**.

8 Where applicable, remove the oil spray jets from their locations in the crankcase and clean them **(see illustration)**. After cleaning the cylinder block, refit the jets.

9 If the engine is not going to be reassembled right away, cover it with a large plastic bag to keep it clean and prevent it rusting.

Inspection

10 Visually check the block for cracks, rust and corrosion. Look for stripped threads in the threaded holes. It's also a good idea to have the block checked for hidden cracks by an engine reconditioning specialist that has the equipment to do this type of work, especially if the vehicle had a history of overheating or using coolant. If defects are found, have the block repaired, if possible, or renewed.

11 If in any doubt as to the condition of the cylinder block, have it inspected and measured by an engine reconditioning specialist. If the bores are worn or damaged, a new cylinder block will be required. If the bores are in a satisfactory condition, they will be able to carry out the necessary honing and supply appropriate pistons, etc.

12 Refit all external components and senders in their correct locations, as noted before removal.

14 Piston/connecting rod assemblies (diesel engines) – inspection and reassembly

Inspection

1 Before the inspection process can begin, the piston/connecting rod assemblies must be cleaned, and the original piston rings removed from the pistons.

2 Carefully expand the old rings over the top of the pistons. The use of two or three old feeler blades will be helpful in preventing the rings dropping into empty grooves **(see illustration)**.

13.7 A large socket on an extension can be used to drive in new core plugs

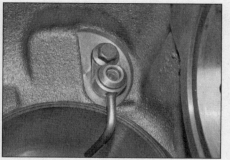

13.8 Piston cooling jets may be fitted to the base of each cylinder bore

14.2 Remove the piston rings with the aid of feeler gauges

Note that the oil control scraper ring is in two sections.

3 Scrape away all traces of carbon from the top of the piston. A hand-held wire brush or a piece of fine emery cloth can be used once the majority of the deposits have been scraped away.

4 Remove the carbon from the ring grooves in the piston by cleaning them using an old ring. Break the ring in half to do this. Be very careful to remove only the carbon deposits; do not remove any metal, or scratch the sides of the ring grooves. Protect your fingers – piston rings are sharp.

5 Once the deposits have been removed, clean the piston/connecting rod assembly with paraffin or a suitable solvent, and dry thoroughly. Make sure the oil return holes in the ring grooves are clear.

6 If the pistons and cylinder bores are not damaged or worn excessively, the original pistons can be re-used. Normal piston wear appears as even vertical wear on the piston thrust surfaces, and slight looseness of the top ring in its groove. New piston rings, however, should always be used when the engine is reassembled.

7 Carefully inspect each piston for cracks around the skirt, at the gudgeon pin bosses, and at the piston ring lands (between the piston ring grooves).

8 Look for scoring and scuffing on the sides of the skirt, holes in the piston crown, and burned areas at the edge of the crown. If the skirt is scored or scuffed, the engine may have been suffering from overheating and/or abnormal combustion, which caused excessively-high operating temperatures. The cooling and lubricating systems should be checked thoroughly.

9 Scorch marks on the sides of the pistons show that blow-by has occurred and the rings are not sealing correctly. A hole in the piston crown is an indication that abnormal combustion (pre-ignition, knocking or detonation) has been occurring. If any of the above problems exist, the causes must be corrected, or the damage will occur again.

10 Corrosion of the piston, in the form of small pits, indicates that coolant is leaking into the combustion chamber and/or the crankcase.

Again, the cause must be corrected, or the problem may persist in the rebuilt engine.

11 If in any doubt as to the condition of the pistons and connecting rods, have them inspected and measured by an engine reconditioning specialist. If new parts are required, they will be able to supply and fit appropriate-sized pistons/rings, and hone the cylinder block.

Reassembly

12 Before refitting the rings to the pistons, check their end gaps by inserting each of them in their cylinder bores. Use the piston to make sure that they are square. Using feeler blades, check that the gaps are within the tolerances given in the Specifications. Genuine rings are supplied pre-gapped; no attempt should be made to adjust the gaps by filing.

13 Install the new rings by fitting them over the top of the piston, starting with the oil control scraper ring sections. Use feeler blades in the same way as when removing the old rings. New rings generally have their top surfaces identified, and must be fitted the correct way round **(see illustration)**. Note that the first and second compression rings have different sections. Be careful when handling the compression rings; they will break if they are handled roughly or expanded too far. With all the rings in position, space the ring gaps at 120° to each other (unless otherwise specified). The oil control scraper ring expander must also be positioned opposite to the actual ring.

---

15 Crankshaft (diesel engines) – inspection

Checking endfloat

1 If the crankshaft endfloat is to be checked, this must be done when the crankshaft is installed in the cylinder block/crankcase, but is free to move.

2 Check the endfloat using a dial gauge in contact with the end of the crankshaft. Push the crankshaft fully one way, and then zero the gauge. Push the crankshaft fully the

other way, and check the endfloat. The result can be compared with the specified amount, and will give an indication as to whether new thrustwashers are required **(see illustration)**.

3 If a dial gauge is not available, feeler gauges can be used. First push the crankshaft fully towards the flywheel end of the engine, then use feeler gauges to measure the gap between the web and the thrustwasher **(see illustration)**.

Inspection

4 Clean the crankshaft using paraffin or a suitable solvent, and dry it, preferably with compressed air if available. Be sure to clean the oil holes with a pipe cleaner or similar probe, to ensure that they are not obstructed.

⚠️ *Warning: Wear eye protection when using compressed air.*

5 Check the main and big-end bearing journals for uneven wear, scoring, pitting and cracking.

6 Big-end bearing wear is accompanied by distinct metallic knocking when the engine is running (particularly noticeable when the engine is pulling from low revs), and some loss of oil pressure.

7 Main bearing wear is accompanied by severe engine vibration and rumble – getting progressively worse as engine revs increase – and again by loss of oil pressure.

8 Check the bearing journal for roughness by running a finger lightly over the bearing surface. Any roughness (which will be accompanied by obvious bearing wear) indicates that the crankshaft requires regrinding.

9 Have the crankshaft journals measured by an engine reconditioning specialist. If the crankshaft is worn or damaged, they may be able to regrind the journals and supply suitable undersize bearing shells. If no undersize shells are available and the crankshaft has worn beyond the specified limits, it will have to be renewed. Consult your Ford dealer or engine reconditioning specialist for further information on parts availability.

10 If the crankshaft has been reground, check for burrs around the crankshaft oil holes (the holes are usually chamfered, so burrs should

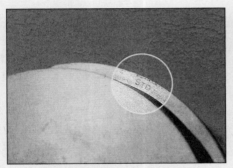

14.13 Look for etched markings identifying the piston ring top surface

15.2 Check the crankshaft endfloat using a DTI gauge...

15.3... or with feeler gauges

not be a problem unless regrinding has been carried out carelessly). Remove any burrs with a fine file or scraper, and thoroughly clean the oil holes as described previously.

16 Main and big-end bearings (diesel engines) – inspection

1 Even though the main and big-end bearings should be renewed during the engine overhaul, the old bearings should be retained for close examination, as they may reveal valuable information about the condition of the engine. The size of the bearing shells is stamped on the back metal, and this information should be given to the supplier of the new shells.

2 Bearing failure occurs because of lack of lubrication, the presence of dirt or other foreign particles, overloading the engine, and corrosion. Regardless of the cause of bearing failure, it must be corrected before the engine is reassembled, to prevent it from happening again (see illustration).

3 When examining the bearings, remove them from the engine block, the main bearing caps, the connecting rods and the rod caps, and lay them out on a clean surface in the same general position as their location in the engine. This will enable you to match any bearing problems with the corresponding crankshaft journal.

4 Dirt and other foreign particles get into the engine in a variety of ways. Dirt may be left in the engine during assembly, or it may pass through filters or the crankcase ventilation system. It may get into the oil, and from there into the bearings. Metal chips from machining operations and normal engine wear are often present. Abrasives are sometimes left in engine components after reconditioning, especially when parts are not thoroughly cleaned using the proper cleaning methods.

5 Whatever the source, these foreign objects often end up embedded in the soft bearing material, and are easily recognised. Large particles will not embed in the bearing, and will score or gouge the bearing and journal. The best prevention for this cause of bearing failure is to clean all parts thoroughly, and keep everything spotlessly-clean during engine assembly. Frequent and regular engine oil and filter changes are also recommended.

6 Lack of lubrication (or lubrication breakdown) has a number of interrelated causes. Excessive heat (which thins the oil), overloading (which squeezes the oil from the bearing face) and oil leakage (from excessive bearing clearances, worn oil pump or high engine speeds) all contribute to lubrication breakdown. Blocked oil passages, which usually are the result of misaligned oil holes in a bearing shell, will also oil-starve a bearing and destroy it. When lack of lubrication is the cause of bearing failure, the bearing material is wiped or extruded from the steel backing of

the bearing. Temperatures may increase to the point where the steel backing turns blue from overheating.

7 Driving habits can have a definite effect on bearing life. Full-throttle, low-speed operation (labouring the engine) puts very high loads on bearings, which tends to squeeze out the oil film. These loads cause the bearings to flex, which produces fine cracks in the bearing face (fatigue failure). Eventually, the bearing material will loosen in pieces and tear away from the steel backing. Short-trip driving leads to corrosion of bearings, because insufficient engine heat is produced to drive off the condensed water and corrosive gases. These products collect in the engine oil, forming acid and sludge. As the oil is carried to the engine bearings, the acid attacks and corrodes the bearing material.

8 Incorrect bearing installation during engine assembly will lead to bearing failure as well. Tight-fitting bearings leave insufficient bearing oil clearance, and will result in oil starvation. Dirt or foreign particles trapped behind a bearing shell result in high spots on the bearing which lead to failure.

9 Do not touch any shell's bearing surface with your fingers during reassembly; there is a risk of scratching the delicate surface, or of depositing particles of dirt on it.

10 As mentioned at the beginning of this Section, the bearing shells should be renewed as a matter of course during engine overhaul; to do otherwise is false economy.

17 Engine overhaul – reassembly sequence

1 Before reassembly begins, ensure that all new parts have been obtained and that all necessary tools are available. Read through the entire procedure to familiarise yourself with the work involved, and to ensure that all items necessary for reassembly of the engine are at hand. In addition to all normal tools and materials, jointing and thread locking compound will be needed during engine reassembly. Do not use any kind of silicone-based sealant on any part of the fuel system or inlet manifold, and never use exhaust sealants upstream (on the engine side) of the catalytic converter.

2 In order to save time and avoid problems, engine reassembly can be carried out in the following order.

a) Crankshaft and main bearings (diesel engines).

b) Pistons/connecting rods (diesel engines).

c) Oil pump.

d) Sump.

e) Flywheel/driveplate.

f) Cylinder head.

g) Timing sprockets and belt.

h) Engine external components (including inlet and exhaust manifolds).

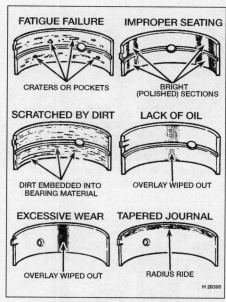

16.2 Typical bearing failures

3 Ensure that everything is clean prior to reassembly. As mentioned previously, dirt and metal particles can quickly destroy bearings and result in major engine damage. Use clean engine oil to lubricate during reassembly.

18 Crankshaft (diesel engines) – refitting

Selection of new bearing shells

1 Have the crankshaft inspected and measured by a Ford dealer or engine reconditioning specialist. They will be able to carry out any regrinding/repairs, and supply suitable main and big-end bearing shells.

Refitting

1.8 litre engines

Note: New main bearing cap bolts must be used on refitting.

2 If they're still in place, remove the old bearing shells from the block and the main bearing caps. Wipe the bearing recesses with a clean, lint-free cloth. They must be kept spotlessly clean.

3 Clean the backs of the new main bearing shells. Fit the shells with an oil groove in each main bearing location in the block. Note the thrustwashers integral with the No 3 (centre) upper main bearing shell, or the thrustwasher halves fitted either side of No 3 upper main bearing location. Fit the other shell from each bearing set in the corresponding main bearing cap. Make sure the tab on each bearing shell fits into the notch in the block or cap/lower crankcase. Also, the oil holes in the block must line up with the oil holes in the bearing

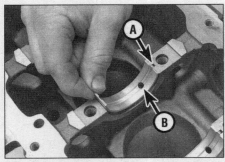

18.3a Ensure the tab (A) and oil hole (B) are correctly aligned when refitting the shells

18.3b Note the thrustwashers fitted to the No 3 main bearing shell

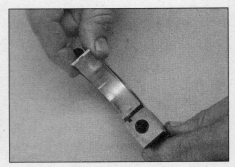

18.3c Make sure the tab on the cap bearing shell engages correctly

18.4 Oil the bearing shells before fitting the crankshaft

18.6 Lower the crankshaft gently into place

18.7 Tighten the main bearing cap bolts

shell **(see illustrations)**. Don't hammer the shells into place, and don't nick or gouge the bearing faces.

4 Clean the bearing surfaces of the shells in the block, then apply a thin, uniform layer of clean molybdenum disulphide-based grease, engine assembly lubricant, or clean engine oil to each surface **(see illustration)**. Coat the thrustwasher surfaces as well.

5 Lubricate the crankshaft oil seal journals with molybdenum disulphide-based grease, engine assembly lubricant, or clean engine oil.

6 Make sure the crankshaft journals are clean, then lay the crankshaft back in place in the block**(see illustration)**.

7 Refit and tighten the main bearing caps as follows:

a) *Clean the bearing surfaces of the shells in the caps, then lubricate them. Refit the*

caps in their respective positions, with the arrows pointing to the timing belt end of the engine.

b) *Working on one cap at a time, from the centre main bearing outwards (and ensuring that each cap is tightened down squarely and evenly onto the block), tighten the main bearing cap bolts to the specified torque then through the specified angle* **(see illustration)**.

8 Rotate the crankshaft a number of times by hand, to check for any obvious binding.

9 Check the crankshaft endfloat (see Section 15). It should be correct if the crankshaft thrustwashers/thrust control bearing(s) aren't worn or damaged, or have been renewed.

10 Refit the crankshaft left-hand oil seal carrier and install a new seal as described in Part B of this Chapter.

11 Refit the piston/connecting rod assemblies to the crankshaft as described in Section 19.

2.0 litre engines

12 Using a little grease, stick the upper thrustwashers to each side of the No 2 main bearing upper location. Ensure that the oilway grooves on each thrustwasher face outwards (away from the cylinder block) **(see illustration)**.

13 Place the bearing shells in their locations. If new shells are being fitted, ensure that all traces of protective grease are cleaned off using paraffin. Wipe dry the shells and connecting rods with a lint-free cloth. Liberally lubricate each bearing shell in the cylinder block/crankcase and cap with clean engine oil.

14 Lower the crankshaft into position so that Nos 2 and 3 cylinder crankpins are at TDC; Nos 1 and 4 cylinder crankpins will be at BDC, ready for fitting No 1 piston. Check the crankshaft endfloat, referring to Section 15.

15 Lubricate the lower bearing shells in the main bearing caps with clean engine oil. Make sure that the locating lugs on the shells engage with the corresponding recesses in the caps.

16 Fit main bearing caps Nos 2 to 5 to their correct locations, ensuring that they are fitted the correct way round (the bearing shell tab recesses in the block and caps must be on the same side). Insert the bolts/nuts, tightening them only loosely at this stage.

17 Apply a small amount of sealant to the No 1 main bearing cap mating face on the cylinder block, around the sealing strip holes **(see illustration)**.

18.12 Ensure the oil grooves on each thrustwasher are facing outwards from the No 2 main bearing location

18.17 Apply sealant to the No 1 main bearing cap mating face on the cylinder block, around the sealing strip holes in the corners

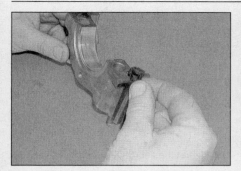

18.18 Fit the sealing strips to the No 1 main bearing cap

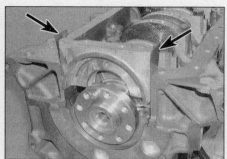

18.19 Use 2 metal strips (arrowed) to hold the sealing strips in place as the bearing cap is fitted

18.20 Trim off the ends of the bearing cap sealing strips, so that they protrude by approximately 1.0 mm

18 Locate the tab of each sealing strip over the pins on the base of No 1 bearing cap, and press the strips into the bearing cap grooves. It is now necessary to obtain two thin metal strips, of 0.25 mm thickness or less, in order to prevent the strips moving when the cap is being fitted. Ford garages use the tool shown, which acts as a clamp. Metal strips (such as old feeler blades) can be used, provided all burrs which may damage the sealing strips are first removed **(see illustration)**.

19 Where applicable, oil both sides of the metal strips, and hold them on the sealing strips. Fit the No 1 main bearing cap, insert the bolts loosely, then carefully pull out the metal strips in a horizontal direction, using a pair of pliers **(see illustration)**.

20 Tighten all the main bearing cap bolts evenly to the specified torque, then through the specified angle. Using a sharp knife, trim off the ends of the No 1 bearing cap sealing strips, so that they protrude above the cylinder block/crankcase mating surface by approximately 1.0 mm **(see illustration)**.

21 Fit a new crankshaft left-hand oil seal as described in Part C of this Chapter.

22 Refit the piston/connecting rod assemblies to the crankshaft as described in Section 19.

19 Piston/connecting rod assemblies (diesel engines) – refitting

Note: *New big-end cap bolts/nuts must be used on refitting.*

1 Note that the following procedure assumes that the crankshaft and main bearing caps are in place.

2 Clean the backs of the bearing shells, and the bearing locations in both the connecting rod and bearing cap.

3 Press the bearing shells into their locations, ensuring that the tab on each shell engages in the notch in the connecting rod and cap. Take care not to touch any shell's bearing surface with your fingers **(see illustration)**.

4 Lubricate the cylinder bores, the pistons, and piston rings, then lay out each piston/connecting rod assembly in its respective position.

5 Start with assembly No 1. Make sure that the piston rings are still spaced as described in Section 14, then clamp them in position with a piston ring compressor.

6 Insert the piston/connecting rod assembly into the top of cylinder No 1, ensuring the piston is correctly positioned as follows.

On 1.8 litre engines, ensure that the DIST mark or arrow on the piston crown is towards the timing belt end of the engine.

On 2.0 litre engines, ensure that the valve recesses on the piston crown are towards the rear of the cylinder block.

7 Once the piston is correctly positioned, using a block of wood or hammer handle against the piston crown, tap the assembly into the cylinder until the piston crown is flush with the top of the cylinder/liner **(see illustration)**.

8 Ensure that the bearing shell is still correctly installed. Liberally lubricate the crankpin and both bearing shells. Taking care not to mark the cylinder bores, pull the piston/connecting rod assembly down the bore and onto the crankpin. Refit the big-end bearing cap and fit the new bolts/nuts, tightening them finger-tight at first **(see illustration)**. Note that the faces with the identification marks must match (which means that the bearing shell locating tabs abut each other).

9 Tighten the bearing cap retaining bolts/nuts evenly and progressively to the specified torque setting, then through the specified angle(s).

10 Once the bearing cap retaining bolts/nuts have been correctly tightened, rotate the crankshaft. Check that it turns freely; some stiffness is to be expected if new components have been fitted, but there should be no signs of binding or tight spots.

11 Refit the components removed in paragraph 1 of Section 11.

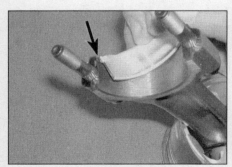

19.3 Ensure the bearing shell tab (arrowed) locates correctly in the cut-out

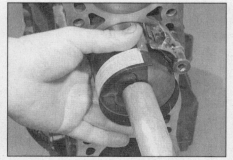

19.7 Tap the piston into the bore using a hammer handle

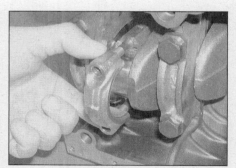

19.8 Fit the big-end bearing cap, ensuring it is fitted the right-way around, and fit the new nuts

20 Engine –
initial start-up after overhaul

1 With the engine refitted in the vehicle, double-check the engine oil and coolant levels. Make a final check that everything has been reconnected, and that there are no tools or rags left in the engine compartment.

2 On diesel engines, prime and bleed the fuel system as described in Chapter 4B Section 4.

3 Start the engine, noting that this may take a little longer than usual. Make sure that the oil pressure warning light goes out.

4 While the engine is idling, check for fuel, water and oil leaks. Don't be alarmed if there are some odd smells and smoke from parts getting hot and burning off oil deposits.

5 Assuming all is well, run the engine until it reaches normal operating temperature, then switch off the engine.

6 After a few minutes, recheck the oil and coolant levels as described in 'Weekly checks', and top-up as necessary.

7 Note that there is no need to retighten the cylinder head bolts once the engine has first run after reassembly.

8 If new pistons, rings or crankshaft bearings have been fitted, the engine must be treated as new, and run-in for the first 600 miles. Do not operate the engine at full-throttle, or allow it to labour at low engine speeds in any gear. It is recommended that the oil and filter be changed at the end of this period.

Chapter 3
Cooling, heating and air conditioning systems

Contents

Degrees of difficulty

Easy, suitable for novice with little experience	Fairly easy, suitable for beginner with some experience	Fairly difficult, suitable for competent DIY mechanic	Difficult, suitable for experienced DIY mechanic	Very difficult, suitable for expert DIY or professional

Specifications

Coolant
Antifreeze type . . . . See *Lubricants and fluids*
Cooling system capacity . . . . See Chapter 1A or 1B

Expansion tank filler cap
Pressure rating . . . . 1.3 to 1.5 bars approximately – see cap for actual value

Thermostat
Starts to open . . . . 92°C
Fully-open . . . . 99°C

Air conditioning system
Refrigerant R134a
Refrigerant quantity:
  Manual transmission models . . . . 510 to 530 g
  Automatic transmission models . . . . 580 to 600 g
Refrigerant oil . . . . Ford WSH-M1C231-B
Refrigerant oil capacity when refilling . . . . 200 ml

Torque wrench settings

	Nm	lbf ft
Air conditioning compressor mounting bolts	24	18
Coolant pump bolts:		
Petrol engines	10	7
1.8 litre diesel engines:		
Lower bolt	23	17
Upper bolts	10	7
2.0 litre diesel engines	16	12
Coolant pump pulley bolts:		
Petrol engines	20	15
1.8 litre diesel engines	23	17
Coolant temperature sensor	12	9
Cylinder head temperature sensor	20	15
Radiator crossmember bolts	25	18
Refrigerant lines:		
To compressor	24	18
To condensor	24	18
To expansion valve	8	6
Thermostat cover/housing bolts/nuts	10	7

1 General information and precautions

1 The cooling system is of pressurised type, comprising a pump driven by the auxiliary drivebelt (petrol engines and 1.8 litre diesel engines) or the timing belt (2.0 litre diesel engines), an aluminium crossflow radiator, electric cooling fan, and a thermostat. The system functions as follows. Cold coolant from the radiator passes through the hose to the coolant pump, where it is pumped around the cylinder block and head passages. After cooling the cylinder bores, combustion surfaces and valve seats, the coolant reaches the underside of the thermostat, which is initially closed. The coolant passes through the heater, and is returned via the cylinder block to the coolant pump.

2 When the engine is cold, the thermostat is shut, and the coolant circulates only through the cylinder block, cylinder head and heater. When the coolant reaches a predetermined temperature, the thermostat opens and the coolant passes through to the radiator. As the coolant circulates through the radiator, it is cooled by the inrush of air when the car is in forward motion. Airflow is supplemented by the action of the electric cooling fan when necessary. Once the coolant has passed through the radiator, and has cooled, the cycle is repeated.

3 The temperature gauge and cooling fan are controlled by the engine coolant temperature sensor or, on 1.8 litre diesel engines, the cylinder head temperature sensor which transmits a signal to the engine management powertrain control module (PCM) to operate them.

4 An expansion tank is fitted to allow for the expansion of the coolant when hot. On models fitted with an engine oil cooler or automatic transmission fluid cooler, the coolant is also passed through the oil/fluid cooler.

5 Refer to Sections 8 and 11 for information on the heater/ventilation system and air conditioning system.

 Warning: Do not attempt to remove the expansion tank filler cap, or disturb any part of the cooling system, while the engine is hot; there is a high risk of scalding. If the expansion tank filler cap must be removed before the engine and radiator have fully cooled (even though this is not recommended) the pressure in the cooling system must first be relieved. Cover the cap with a thick layer of cloth, to avoid scalding, and slowly unscrew the filler cap until a hissing sound can be heard. When the hissing has stopped, indicating that the pressure has reduced, slowly unscrew the filler cap until it can be removed; if more hissing sounds are heard, wait until they have stopped before unscrewing the cap completely. At all times, keep well away

from the filler cap opening and protect your hands.

 Warning: Do not allow antifreeze to come into contact with skin, or with the painted surfaces of the car. Rinse off spills immediately, with plenty of water. Never leave antifreeze lying around in an open container, or in a puddle on the driveway or garage floor. Children and pets are attracted by its sweet smell, but antifreeze can be fatal if ingested.

 Warning: If the engine is hot, the electric cooling fan may start rotating even if the engine is not running; be careful to keep hands, hair and loose clothing well clear when working in the engine compartment.

 Warning: Refer to Section 11 for precautions to be observed when working on models equipped with air conditioning.

2 Cooling system hoses – disconnection and renewal

Note: *Refer to the warnings given in Section 1 of this Chapter before proceeding. Do not attempt to disconnect any hose while the system is still hot.*

1 If the checks described in Chapter 1A Section 10 or Chapter 1B Section 8 reveal a faulty hose, it must be renewed as follows.

2 First drain the cooling system (see Chapter 1A Section 30 or Chapter 1B Section 30). If the coolant is not due for renewal, it may be re-used if it is collected in a clean container.

3 Before disconnecting a hose, first note its routing in the engine compartment, and whether it is secured by any additional retaining clips or cable-ties. Use a pair of pliers to release the clamp-type clips, or a screwdriver to slacken the screw-type clips, then move the clips along the hose, clear of the relevant inlet/outlet union. Carefully work the hose free.

2.4 On quick-release hose fittings, lift the wire retaining clip with a screwdriver, then withdraw the hose

4 Depending on engine, some of the hose attachments may be of the quick-release type. Where this type of hose is encountered, lift the wire retaining clip with a screwdriver, then withdraw the hose from the inlet/outlet union **(see illustration)**.

5 Note that the radiator inlet and outlet unions are fragile; do not use excessive force when attempting to remove the hoses. If a hose proves to be difficult to remove, try to release it by rotating the hose ends before attempting to free it.

 If all else fails, cut the coolant hose with a sharp knife, then slit it so that it can be peeled off in two pieces. Although this may prove expensive if the hose is otherwise undamaged, it is preferable to buying a new radiator.

6 When fitting a hose, first slide the clips onto the hose, then work the hose into position. If clamp-type clips were originally fitted, it is a good idea to use screw-type clips when refitting the hose. If the hose is stiff, use a little soapy water (washing-up liquid is ideal) as a lubricant, or soften the hose by soaking it in hot water.

7 Work the hose into position, checking that it is correctly routed and secured. Slide each clip along the hose until it passes over the flared end of the relevant inlet/outlet union, before tightening the clips securely.

8 Refill the cooling system with reference to Chapter 1A Section 30 or Chapter 1B Section 30.

9 Check thoroughly for leaks as soon as possible after disturbing any part of the cooling system.

3 Thermostat – removal, testing and refitting

Note: *Refer to the warnings given in Section 1 of this Chapter before proceeding.*

Removal

1 Disconnect the battery negative lead as described in Chapter 5A Section 4.

2 Drain the cooling system (see Chapter 1A Section 30 or Chapter 1B Section 30). If the coolant is relatively new or in good condition, drain it into a clean container and re-use it.

Petrol engines

3 Remove the plastic cover from the top of the engine.

4 Remove the right-hand headlight unit as described in Chapter 12 Section 7.

5 Release the clips and disconnect the

3.5 Release the clips and disconnect the coolant hoses from the thermostat cover

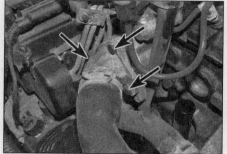

3.9 Undo the thermostat cover bolts (arrowed)

3.14 Undo the nuts and move the support bracket to one side

coolant hoses from the thermostat cover **(see illustration)**.

6 Slacken and remove the three bolts from the thermostat cover and withdraw it from the thermostat housing. Twist the thermostat to release it from the cover retainers and remove the thermostat from the cover.

7 Check the condition of the cover rubber seal and renew it if necessary.

1.8 litre diesel engines

8 Remove the plastic cover from the top of the engine.

9 The thermostat cover is located at the front of the engine cylinder block. Undo the 3 retaining bolts and move the cover to one side **(see illustration)**.

10 Note the position of the air bleed valve (where fitted), and how the thermostat is installed (ie, which end is facing outwards), then pull the thermostat and rubber seal from the housing.

11 Check the condition of the cover rubber seal and renew it if necessary.

2.0 litre diesel engines

12 Remove the plastic cover from the top of the engine. The thermostat housing is located at the left-hand end of the cylinder head.

13 Remove the air cleaner assembly as described in Chapter 4B Section 5.

14 Undo the retaining nuts and move the support bracket at the left-hand end of the thermostat housing to one side **(see illustration)**.

15 Release the clamps and disconnect the hoses from the thermostat housing.

16 Disconnect the wiring plug(s) from the thermostat housing.

17 Undo the 4 retaining nuts/bolts and remove the housing. Examine the rubber seal and renew if necessary **(see illustrations)**. Note that the thermostat is integral with the housing – if faulty the complete assembly must be renewed.

Testing

General

18 Before assuming the thermostat is to blame for a cooling system problem, check the coolant level (see Weekly checks Section), the auxiliary drivebelt tension and condition (see Chapter 1A Section 11 or Chapter 1B Section 9) and the temperature gauge operation.

19 If the engine seems to be taking a long time to warm up (based on heater output or temperature gauge operation), the thermostat may be stuck open. Renew the thermostat.

20 Equally, a lengthy warm-up period might suggest that the thermostat is missing – it may have been removed or inadvertently omitted by a previous owner or mechanic. Don't drive the vehicle without a thermostat – the engine management system's PCM will stay in warm-up mode for longer than necessary, causing emissions and fuel economy to suffer.

21 If the engine runs hot, use your hand to check the temperature of the radiator top hose. If the hose isn't hot, but the engine is, the thermostat is probably stuck closed, preventing the coolant inside the engine from escaping to the radiator – renew the thermostat.

22 If the radiator top hose is hot, it means that the coolant is flowing and the thermostat is open. Consult the Fault finding Section at the end of this manual to assist in tracing possible cooling system faults.

Thermostat test

23 If the thermostat remains in the open position at room temperature, it is faulty, and must be renewed as a matter of course.

24 To test it fully, suspend the (closed) thermostat on a length of string in a container of cold water, with a thermometer beside it; ensure that neither touches the side of the container.

25 Heat the water, and check the temperature at which the thermostat begins to open; compare this value with that specified. Remove the thermostat and allow it to cool down; check that it closes fully.

26 If the thermostat does not open and close as described, if it sticks in either position, or if it does not open at the specified temperature, it must be renewed.

Refitting

27 Refitting is the reverse of the removal procedure, noting the following points:

a) Clean the mating surfaces carefully and, where necessary renew the thermostat's sealing ring.

b) Fit the thermostat in the same position as noted on removal.

c) Tighten the thermostat cover/housing bolts/ nuts to the specified torque wrench setting

d) Remake all the coolant hose connections, then refill the cooling system as described in Chapter 1A Section 30 or Chapter 1B Section 30.

e) Start the engine and allow it to reach normal operating temperature, then check for leaks and proper thermostat operation.

3.17a Thermostat housing retaining nuts (arrowed)

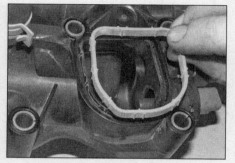

3.17b Renew the thermostat housing sealing ring

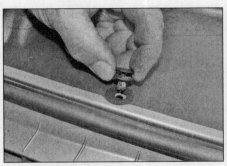

4.9 Remove the plastic rivet each side securing the radiator cover panel to the top of the bumper

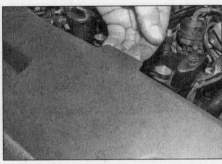

4.10a Pull up on the tabs at the rear of the radiator cover panel each side...

4.10b... to release the retaining clips (arrowed)...

4.10c... then lift the cover panel off the car

4.11a Rotate the two radiator upper guide pins a quarter-turn anti-clockwise...

4.11b... and remove them from the front panel

4 Radiator electric cooling fan – testing, removal and refitting

Note: *Refer to the warnings given in Section 1 of this Chapter before proceeding.*

Testing

1 The radiator cooling fan is controlled by the engine management system's PCM, acting on the information received from the cylinder head temperature sensor (1.8 litre diesel engines) or engine coolant temperature sensor.

2 First, check the relevant fuses and relays (see Chapter 12 Section 3).

3 To test the fan motor, unplug the electrical connector, and use fused jumper wires to connect the fan directly to the battery. If the fan still does not work, renew the motor.

4 If the motor proved sound, the fault lies in the engine coolant temperature sensor or cylinder head temperature sensor (see Section 5), in the wiring loom (see Chapter 12 Section 2 for testing details) or in the engine management system (see Chapter 4A Section 9 or Chapter 4B Section 12).

Removal

5 Disconnect the battery negative lead as described in Chapter 5A Section 4.

6 Firmly apply the handbrake, then jack up the front of the vehicle and support it securely on axle stands (see *'Jacking and vehicle support'*).

7 Undo the fasteners and remove the engine undertray (where fitted), followed by the shield under the radiator.

8 Drain the cooling system as described in Chapter 1A Section 30 or Chapter 1B Section 30.

9 Prise up the centre section, then remove the plastic rivet each side securing the radiator cover panel to the top of the bumper **(see illustration)**.

10 Pull up on the tabs at the rear of the radiator cover panel each side to release the retaining clips, then lift the cover panel off the car **(see illustrations)**.

11 Rotate the two radiator upper guide pins a quarter-turn anti-clockwise and remove them from the front panel **(see illustrations)**.

12 Loosely secure the radiator to the front panel each side using a cable-tie, to enable it to be lowered by approximately 70 mm **(see illustration)**.

13 Release the quick-release fittings and disconnect the top and bottom coolant hoses from the radiator **(see illustrations)**.

4.12 Loosely secure the radiator to the front panel each side using a cable-tie (arrowed)

4.13a Release the quick-release fittings and disconnect the top...

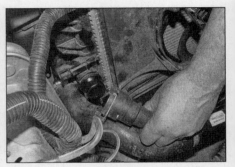

4.13b... and bottom coolant hoses from the radiator

4.14 Release the coolant hose from the retaining clip on the fan shroud

4.15 Unclip the expansion tank hose from the top of the fan shroud

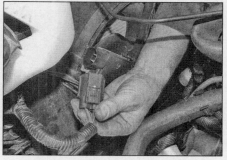

4.16a Unplug the cooling fan electrical connector...

14 Release the coolant hose from the retaining clip on the fan shroud **(see illustration)**.

15 Unclip the expansion tank small-bore hose(s) from the top of the fan shroud **(see illustration)**.

16 Unplug the cooling fan electrical connector, and release the wiring loom from the fan shroud **(see illustrations)**.

17 From under the car, undo the two bolts each side securing the radiator crossmember to the underbody **(see illustration)**. Lower the radiator, condenser and cooling fan assembly by approximately 70 mm then retain it in this position by tightening the cable-ties.

18 Using a screwdriver, push back the tab on the fan shroud upper mounting each side, while at the same time lifting the shroud upwards **(see illustration)**.

19 Once the fan shroud mountings are released from the radiator, manoeuvre the fan and shroud upwards and withdraw the assembly from the engine compartment **(see illustration)**.

20 To remove the fan motor from the shroud, undo the retaining nut and remove the fan from the motor spindle. Undo the three retaining bolts and lift the motor off the shroud. Disconnect the wiring connector and remove the motor **(see illustrations)**.

Refitting

21 Refitting is the reverse of the removal procedure. Refill the cooling system as described in Chapter 1A Section 30 or Chapter 1B Section 30 on completion.

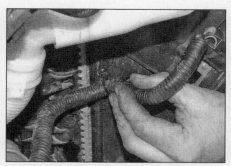

4.16b... and release the wiring loom from the fan shroud

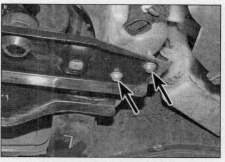

4.17 Undo the two bolts each side (arrowed) securing the radiator crossmember to the underbody

4.18 Push back the tab (arrowed) on the fan shroud upper mounting each side and lift the shroud upwards

4.19 Manoeuvre the fan and shroud upwards and out of the engine compartment

---

5 Cooling system electronic components – removal and refitting

Cylinder head temperature sensor

Note: *Only the 1.8 litre diesel engine is fitted with this sensor.*

1 Remove the plastic cover from the top of the engine.

2 Disconnect the hoses, then undo the retaining bolt and remove the crankcase

4.20a Undo the nut (arrowed) and remove the fan...

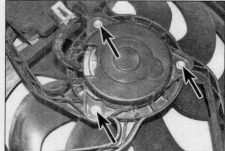

4.20b... then undo the three bolts (arrowed) and lift the motor off the shroud

5.2 Remove the crankcase ventilation oil separator

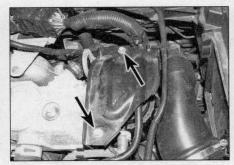

5.3 Undo the two bolts (arrowed) and remove the crash shield

5.5 Disconnect the wiring plug then unscrew the cylinder head temperature sensor (arrowed)

ventilation oil separator from the end of the cylinder head **(see illustration)**.

3 Where fitted, undo the two retaining bolts and remove the crash shield above the fuel filter **(see illustration)**.

4 Disconnect the fuel filter wiring plug, then release the clips securing the fuel hoses and move the fuel filter to one side.

5 Disconnect the wiring plug, unclip the plug from the bracket, then unscrew the cylinder head temperature sensor from place **(see illustration)**.

6 Refitting is a reversal of removal. Tighten the sensor to the specified torque.

Coolant temperature sensor

Note: *Refer to the warnings given in Section 1 of this Chapter before starting work.*

 Warning: Ensure the coolant is cold before attempting this procedure.

Petrol engines

7 The sensor is located at the coolant outlet housing at the left-hand end of the cylinder head.

8 Remove the plastic cover from the top of the engine.

9 Disconnect the wiring connector from the sensor.

10 Two different types of sensor may be fitted. The first type is screwed into the coolant outlet housing, and the second type is clipped into place. Unscrew the sensor from the housing, or pull out the clip as applicable **(see illustrations)**. Be prepared for coolant spillage and have rag or a rubber plug handy to force into the sensor aperture. This way only a little coolant will be lost.

11 Refitting is the reverse of the removal procedure, noting the following points:

a) *Renew the sensor seal if necessary.*

b) *Screw the sensor into position and tighten it to the specified torque, or refit the sensor and insert the clip, as applicable.*

c) *Top-up or refill the cooling system as described in 'Weekly checks' or Chapter 1A Section 30.*

Diesel engines

12 The sensor is located in the thermostat housing at the left-hand end of the cylinder head.

13 Remove the plastic cover from the top of the engine.

14 Remove the air cleaner assembly and intake duct as described in Chapter 4B Section 5.

15 Prise out the retaining clip, and disconnect the coolant hose from the heater to the thermostat housing.

16 Disconnect the sensor wiring plug, pull out the retaining clip, and remove the engine coolant temperature sensor **(see illustration 5.10b)**. Be prepared for coolant spillage and have rag or a rubber plug handy to force into the sensor aperture. This way only a little coolant will be lost.

17 Refitting is the reverse of the removal procedure, noting the following points:

a) *Renew the sensor seal if necessary.*

b) *Top-up or refill the cooling system as described in 'Weekly checks' or Chapter 1B Section 30*

---

6 Radiator – removal, inspection and refitting

Note: *Refer to the warnings given in Section 1 of this Chapter before starting work.*

Note: *If leakage is the reason for removing the radiator, bear in mind that minor leaks can often be cured using a radiator sealant added to the coolant with the radiator in situ.*

Removal

1 Remove the radiator electric cooling fan and shroud assembly as described in Section 4.

2 On diesel engines, remove the intercooler as described in Chapter 4B Section 16.

3 Remove the right-hand headlight unit as described in Chapter 12 Section 7.

4 Undo the bolt securing the air conditioning condenser to the right-hand side of the radiator **(see illustration)**.

5 Depress the tabs and disconnect the

5.10a Unscrew the coolant temperature sensor (arrowed)...

5.10b... or pull out the retaining clip (arrowed) followed by the sensor

6.4 Undo the bolt (arrowed) securing the condenser to the radiator

6.5 Depress the tabs and disconnect the expansion tank hose from the top of the radiator

6.7 Disengage the two condenser mounting lugs each side from the radiator guides

6.9 Use an open-ended spanner to prise the mounting bushes off the radiator mounting pegs

expansion tank small-bore hose(s) from the top of the radiator **(see illustration)**.

6 Engage the help of an assistant to support the radiator as it is removed.

7 Lift the condenser slightly and disengage the two mounting lugs each side from the guides on the radiator **(see illustration)**. Secure the condenser to the front panel each side using a cable-tie.

8 Cut off the cable-ties used to support the radiator during removal of the cooling fan and shroud. Lower the radiator and radiator crossmember assembly down and remove it from under the car.

9 To remove the crossmember from the radiator, spray the radiator lower rubber mounting bushes with a little penetrating oil, then carefully prise the crossmember free. Use an open-ended spanner to prise the mounting bushes off the radiator mounting pegs **(see illustration)**.

Inspection

10 With the radiator removed, it can be inspected for leaks and damage. If it needs repair, have a radiator specialist or dealer service department perform the work, as special techniques are required.

11 Insects and dirt can be removed from the radiator with a garden hose or a soft brush. Take care not to damage the cooling fins as this is being done.

Refitting

12 Refitting is the reverse of the removal procedure, noting the following points:
a) *Be sure the mounting bushes are seated properly at the base of the radiator.*
b) *After refitting, refill the cooling system with the recommended coolant as described in Chapter 1A Section 30 or Chapter 1B Section 30.*
c) *Start the engine, and check for leaks. Allow the engine to reach normal operating temperature, indicated by the radiator top hose becoming hot. Once the engine has cooled (ideally, leave overnight), recheck the coolant level, and add more if required.*

7 Coolant pump – checking, removal and refitting

Note: *Refer to the warnings given in Section 1 of this Chapter before starting work.*

Checking

1 A failure in the coolant pump can cause serious engine damage due to overheating.

2 There are three ways to check the operation of the coolant pump while it's installed on the engine. If the pump is defective, fit a new or rebuilt unit.

3 With the engine running at normal operating temperature, squeeze the radiator top hose. If

the coolant pump is working properly, a pressure surge should be felt as the hose is released.

4 Coolant pumps are equipped with weep or vent holes. If a failure occurs in the pump seal, coolant will leak from the hole. In most cases you'll need an electric torch to find the hole on the coolant pump from underneath to check for leaks. It will also be necessary to remove the timing belt upper cover on 2.0 litre diesel engines (Chapter 2C Section 5).

5 If the coolant pump shaft bearings fail, there may be a howling sound at the drivebelt end of the engine while it's running. Shaft wear can be felt if the coolant pump pulley or sprocket is rocked up and down.

6 Don't mistake drivebelt slippage, which causes a squealing sound, for coolant pump bearing failure.

Removal

7 Drain the cooling system (see Chapter 1A Section 30 or Chapter 1B Section 30).

Petrol engines

8 Remove the plastic cover from the top of the engine.

9 Slacken the coolant pump pulley bolts, then remove the auxiliary drivebelt as described in Chapter 1A Section 25.

10 Unscrew the bolts and remove the coolant pump pulley.

11 Undo the 3 bolts and remove the coolant pump. Remove the O-ring seal and discard it **(see illustrations)**.

7.11a Unscrew the mounting bolts (arrowed)...

7.11b... remove the coolant pump...

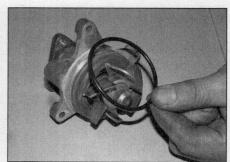

7.11c... and remove the O-ring seal

7.16 Remove the coolant pump from the cylinder block

7.18a Coolant pump retaining bolts (arrowed)

7.18b Renew the coolant pump gasket

1.8 litre diesel engines

12 Slacken the coolant pump pulley bolts, then remove the auxiliary drivebelt as described in Chapter 1B Section 24.

13 Unbolt and remove the coolant pump pulley.

14 Remove the timing belt cover and engine right-hand mounting as described in Chapter 2B. The engine must be supported as the engine mounting is disconnected; support the engine from above with a hoist or engine support bar, if available. If the engine is supported from below with a trolley jack, use a wide block of wood between the jack head and the sump, to spread the load.

15 Remove the four bolts securing the engine front mounting bracket to the block, then lift the engine up by approximately 20 mm.

16 Unscrew the seven coolant pump securing bolts and withdraw the pump **(see illustration)**. Recover the gasket. **Note:** *Take care not to damage or contaminate the timing belt as the pump is removed. Place some stiff cardboard around the belt in the pump area.*

2.0 litre diesel engines

17 Remove the timing belt as described in Chapter 2C Section 5.

18 Undo the retaining bolts and remove the coolant pump. Recover the gasket **(see illustrations)**.

Refitting

19 Clean the pump mating surfaces carefully; the gasket/O-ring must be renewed whenever it is disturbed. Refit the pump and tighten the bolts to the specified torque wrench setting.

9.4a Undo the three bolts (arrowed)…

20 The remainder of the refitting procedure is the reverse of dismantling, noting the following points:

a) *Tighten all fixings to the specified torque wrench settings (where given).*
b) *Where applicable, check the timing belt for contamination and renew if required, as described in Chapter 2C Section 5.*
c) *On completion, refill the cooling system as described in Chapter 1A Section 30 or Chapter 1B Section 30.*

8 Heating and ventilation system – general information

1 The heater/ventilation system consists of a blower fan and heater matrix (housed behind the facia), face-level vents in the centre and at each end of the facia, and air ducts to the front (and on some models, the rear) footwells.

2 The control unit is located in the facia, and the controls operate flap valves, to deflect and mix the air flowing through the various parts of the heater/ventilation system. The flap valves are contained in the air distribution housing, which acts as a central distribution unit, passing air to the various ducts and vents.

3 Incoming fresh air for the ventilation system passes through a pollen filter mounted in the air distribution housing (see Chapter 1A Section 9 or Chapter 1B Section 7) – this ensures that most particles will be removed before the air enters the cabin. However, it is vital that the pollen filter is changed regularly, since a blocked filter will significantly reduce

9.4b… and remove the air recirculation flap housing

airflow to the cabin, leading to ineffective de-misting.

4 The air (boosted by the blower fan if required) then flows through the various ducts, according to the settings of the controls. Stale air is expelled through ducts at the rear of the car. If warm air is required, the cold air is passed through the heater matrix, which is heated by the engine coolant.

5 A recirculation switch enables the outside air supply to be closed off, while the air inside the car is recirculated. This can be useful to prevent unpleasant odours entering from outside the car, but should only be used briefly, as the recirculated air inside the car will soon deteriorate.

9 Heater/ventilation components – removal and refitting

Heater blower motor

Note: *This is a difficult procedure requiring patience and dexterity to release the blower motor retaining clip. It's much easier if the facia is removed as described in Chapter 11 Section 29.*

Removal

1 Disconnect the battery negative lead as described in Chapter 5A Section 4.

2 Remove the glovebox from the facia as described in Chapter 11 Section 27.

3 Remove the clutch pedal as described in Chapter 6 Section 2.

4 Working through the glovebox aperture, disconnect the wiring connector, then undo the three bolts and remove the air recirculation flap housing **(see illustrations)**.

5 The blower motor fan is an extremely fragile component and can be easily damaged during removal of the motor. Ford technicians use a special tool (412-131) which fits over the motor spindle, allowing the motor to be removed without placing any strain on the fan. In the absence of the special tool, an E22 Torx socket on a short extension is a snug fit over the spindle and serves as a suitable alternative.

6 Fit the special tool or the alternative Torx socket over the motor spindle.

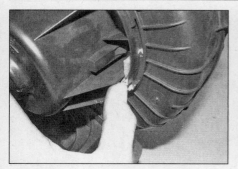

9.8a Depress the release clip, and rotate the blower motor clockwise...

9.8b... then using the special tool, withdraw the motor and fan from the passenger's side of the housing

9.12 Remove the blower motor resistor from the air distribution housing

7 Disconnect the blower motor wiring connector and release the wiring from the clip on the housing.

8 Depress the release clip, and rotate the blower motor clockwise to release it from the housing. Using the special tool or alternative Torx socket, carefully withdraw the motor and fan from the passenger's side of the housing **(see illustrations)**. Take great care not to damage the motor fan. Do not pull on the fan, or allow the motor to rest on the fan.

Refitting

9 Refitting is the reverse of the removal procedure.

Blower motor resistor

Removal

10 Disconnect the battery negative lead as described in Chapter 5A Section 4.

11 Remove the glovebox from the facia as described in Chapter 11 Section 27.

12 Working through the glovebox aperture, disconnect the wiring connector(s), then undo the bolt (two bolts on early models) and remove the resistor from the air distribution housing **(see illustration)**.

Refitting

13 Refitting is the reverse of the removal procedure.

Air distribution housing

Note: *This is an involved and complex operation and it is suggested that the contents of this Section, and the relevant Sections in Chapter 11 are studied carefully to gain an understanding of the work involved, before proceeding.*

Removal

14 Have the air conditioning system refrigerant discharged at a dealer service department or an automotive air conditioning repair facility.

15 Drain the cooling system as described in Chapter 1A Section 30 or Chapter 1B Section 30.

16 The heater matrix coolant hoses must now be disconnected from within the engine compartment. Access to the hose connections at the matrix pipe stubs on the bulkhead is virtually impossible and it is

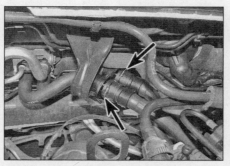

9.16 Disconnect the heater matrix coolant hoses at the quick-release connectors (arrowed) – petrol engine shown

9.17 Undo the nut (arrowed) and disconnect the air conditioning refrigerant pipes at the expansion valve

preferable to disconnect the other end of each hose at the quick-release connectors **(see illustration)**.

17 On early models, undo the two nuts and disconnect the air conditioning refrigerant pipes at the expansion valve on the engine compartment bulkhead. On later models, undo the single nut and remove the plastic surround **(see illustration)**. On all models, discard the seals – new ones must be used when refitting. Suitably cap the open fittings immediately to keep moisture and contamination out of the system.

18 Remove the facia and facia crossmember as described in Chapter 11 Section 30.

19 Disconnect the evaporator water drain tube from the floor connection at the right-hand side of the distribution housing **(see illustration)**.

20 With the help of an assistant, lift the air distribution housing from its location and remove it from the car **(see illustration)**. Guide the heater matrix hoses through the bulkhead as the housing is withdrawn, being prepared for coolant spillage.

Refitting

21 Refitting is the reverse of the removal procedure, bearing in mind the following points:

a) *Refit the facia crossmember and facia as described in Chapter 11 Section 30.*

b) *Renew all disturbed refrigerant pipe seals.*

c) *Refill the cooling system as described in Chapter 1A Section 30 or Chapter 1B Section 30.*

d) *Have the air conditioning system evacuated, charged and leak-tested by the specialist who discharged it.*

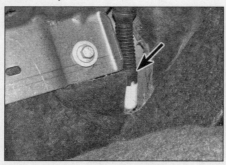

9.19 Disconnect the evaporator water drain tube (arrowed) from the floor connection

9.20 Lift the air distribution housing from its location and remove it from the car

9.24a Undo the two retaining bolts...

9.24b... and remove the expansion valve from the refrigerant pipe stubs

9.25a Remove the expansion valve retaining plate...

9.25b... then lift off the foam pad

9.26a Undo the two screws (arrowed)...

seals for the refrigerant pipes will be required for refitting. Suitably plug or cover the disconnected pipes.

25 Remove the expansion valve retaining plate, then lift off the foam pad **(see illustrations)**.

26 Undo the two screws securing the two halves of the bulkhead closure plate together. Separate the plate and recover the pipe spacer **(see illustrations)**.

27 Carefully withdraw the matrix and heater pipe assembly from the air distribution housing **(see illustration)**.

Refitting

28 Refitting is the reverse of the removal procedure.

Pollen filter

29 Refer to Chapter 1A Section 9 or Chapter 1B Section 7.

9.26b... separate the bulkhead closure plate...

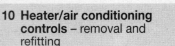

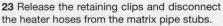

9.26c... and recover the pipe spacer

| 10 | Heater/air conditioning controls – removal and refitting |

1 Disconnect the battery negative (earth) lead (see Chapter 5A Section 4).
2 Remove the facia-mounted audio unit as described in Chapter 12 Section 17

Manual temperature control

3 On models from 04/2010, undo the two lower bolts securing the ashtray to the facia.
4 On all models, pull the ashtray from its location, disconnect the wiring connectors and remove the ashtray.
5 Undo the ten bolts and remove the audio unit mounting frame from the facia.
6 Withdraw the heater/air conditioning control panel from its location.
7 Taking careful note of all their locations, disconnect the various wiring connectors from the rear of the panel and unclip the heater operating cables from the temperature and direction controls. Remove the control panel.
8 Refitting is the reverse of the removal procedure.

Automatic temperature control

9 Lift out the centre console trim pad located under the ashtray **(see illustration)**.

Heater matrix

Removal

22 Remove the air distribution housing as described previously in this Section.

23 Release the retaining clips and disconnect the heater hoses from the matrix pipe stubs.
24 Undo the two retaining bolts and remove the expansion valve from the refrigerant pipe stubs **(see illustrations)**. Note that new

9.27 Withdraw the matrix and heater pipe assembly from the housing

10.9 Lift out the centre console trim pad located under the ashtray

10.10a Unscrew the gear lever knob...

10.10b... unclip the gear lever gaiter trim surround...

10.10c... and lift the gaiter and the gear lever reverse detent mechanism off the gear lever shaft

10 On manual transmission models, unscrew the gear lever knob then unclip the gear lever gaiter trim surround. Lift the gaiter and the gear lever reverse detent mechanism off the gear lever shaft **(see illustrations)**.

11 On automatic transmission models, unclip the selector lever trim surround from the centre console.

12 Starting at the rear, carefully pull up the centre console upper section to release the retaining clips, then disengage the front tabs and remove the upper section**(see illustration)**. Where applicable, disconnect the switch wiring connectors. On automatic transmission models, feed the selector lever trim surround through the aperture as the console upper section is removed.

13 On models up to 04/2010, carefully prise out the two triangular trim covers at each upper corner of the facia centre panel. Where applicable, disconnect the wiring connector from the power switch **(see illustration)**. On models from 04/2010, carefully unclip the side trim around and below the facia centre panel. Where applicable, disconnect the wiring connector from the power switch.

14 Undo the six retaining screws and withdraw the centre panel from the facia. Disconnect the wiring connectors and remove the panel **(see illustrations)**.

15 Undo the four screws and remove the heater/air conditioning control panel from the rear of the facia centre panel **(see illustrations)**.

16 Refitting is the reverse of the removal procedure.

10.12 Carefully pull up the centre console upper section to release the retaining clips

10.13 Carefully prise out the triangular trim covers at each upper corner of the facia centre panel

10.14a Undo the six retaining screws(arrowed)...

10.14b... withdraw the centre panel from the facia...

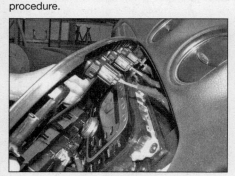

10.14c... and disconnect the wiring connectors

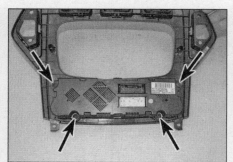

10.15a Undo the four screws (arrowed)...

10.15b... and remove the heater/air conditioning control panel from the facia centre panel

Climate control

17 The climate control function is built-into the DVD navigation touch screen. Removal of the screen assembly is described in Chapter 12 Section 17.

11 Air conditioning system – general information and precautions

General information

1 The air conditioning system consists of a condenser mounted in front of the radiator, an evaporator mounted adjacent to the heater matrix, a compressor driven by the auxiliary drivebelt, an accumulator/dehydrator, and the plumbing connecting all of the above components. The system enables the temperature of incoming air to be lowered, and also dehumidifies the air, which makes for rapid demisting and increased comfort.

2 The cooling side of the system works in the same way as a domestic refrigerator. Refrigerant gas is drawn into the compressor, and passes into the condenser where it loses heat and becomes liquid. The liquid passes through an expansion valve to an evaporator, where it changes from liquid under high pressure to gas under low pressure. This change is accompanied by a drop in temperature, which cools the evaporator. The refrigerant returns to the compressor, and the cycle begins again.

3 Air blown through the evaporator passes to the heater assembly, where it is mixed with hot air blown through the heater matrix, to achieve the desired temperature in the passenger compartment.

4 The heating side of the system works in the same way as on models without air conditioning (see Section 8).

Air conditioning service ports

Note: *The air conditioning service port location varies slightly according to model. The following is a general description of service port location.*

5 The high-pressure service port is the larger of the two service port connections and is located to the rear of the radiator on the right-hand side **(see illustration)**.

11.5 Air conditioning high-pressure service port (arrowed)...

6 The low-pressure service port is located at the rear right-hand side of the engine compartment **(see illustration)**.

Precautions

⚠️ **Warning: The air conditioning system is under high pressure. Do not loosen any fittings or remove any components until after the system has been discharged. Air conditioning refrigerant should be properly discharged at a dealer service department or an automotive air conditioning repair facility capable of handling R134a refrigerant. Always wear eye protection when disconnecting air conditioning system fittings.**

7 When an air conditioning system is fitted, it is necessary to observe the following special precautions whenever dealing with any part of the system, its associated components, and any items which necessitate disconnection of the system:

● While the refrigerant used is less damaging to the environment than the previously-used R12, it is still a very dangerous substance. It must not be allowed into contact with the skin or eyes, or there is a risk of frostbite. It must also not be discharged in an enclosed space – while it is not toxic, there is a risk of suffocation. The refrigerant is heavier than air, and so must never be discharged over a pit.

● The refrigerant must not be allowed to come in contact with a naked flame, otherwise a poisonous gas will be created – under certain circumstances, this can form an explosive mixture with air. For similar reasons, smoking in the presence of refrigerant is highly dangerous, particularly if the vapour is inhaled through a lighted cigarette.

● Never discharge the system to the atmosphere – R134a is not an ozone-depleting ChloroFluoroCarbon (CFC) like R12, but is instead a hydrofluorocarbon, which causes environmental damage by contributing to the 'greenhouse effect' if released into the atmosphere.

● R134a refrigerant must not be mixed with R12; the system uses different seals (now

11.6... and low-pressure service port (arrowed)

green-coloured, previously black) and has different fittings requiring different tools, so that there is no chance of the two types of refrigerant becoming mixed accidentally.

● If for any reason the system must be discharged, entrust this task to your Ford dealer or an air conditioning specialist.

● It is essential that the system be professionally discharged prior to using any form of heat – welding, soldering, brazing, etc – in the vicinity of the system, before having the vehicle oven-dried at a temperature exceeding 70°C after repainting, and before disconnecting any part of the system.

12 Air conditioning system components – removal and refitting

⚠️ **Warning: The air conditioning system is under high pressure. Do not loosen any fittings or remove any components until after the system has been discharged. Air conditioning refrigerant should be properly discharged into an approved type of container at a dealer service department or an automotive air conditioning repair facility capable of handling R134a refrigerant. Cap or plug the pipe lines as soon as they are disconnected to prevent the entry of moisture. Always wear eye protection when disconnecting air conditioning system fittings.**
Note: *This Section refers to the components of the air conditioning system itself – refer to Sections 9 and 10 for details of components common to the heating/ventilation system.*

Condenser

Removal

1 Have the refrigerant discharged at a dealer service department or an automotive air conditioning repair facility.

2 Disconnect the battery negative lead as described in Chapter 5A Section 4.

3 Remove the right-hand headlight unit as described in Chapter 12 Section 7.

4 Undo the bolt securing the condenser to the right-hand side of the radiator **(see illustration 6.4)**.

5 Undo the two bolts securing the refrigerant pipes to the right-hand side of the condenser. Discard the seals – new ones must be used when refitting. Suitably cap the open fittings immediately to keep moisture and contamination out of the system.

6 Prise up the centre section, then remove the plastic rivet each side securing the radiator cover panel to the top of the bumper **(see illustration 4.9)**.

7 Pull up on the tabs at the rear of the radiator cover panel each side to release the retaining clips each side, then lift the cover panel off the car **(see illustrations 4.10a, 4.10b and 4.10c)**.

12.15a Undo the three screws (arrowed)…

12.15b… and remove the evaporator cover panel

12.16 Withdraw the evaporator from the air distribution housing

8 Firmly apply the handbrake, then jack up the front of the vehicle and support it securely on axle stands (see *'Jacking and vehicle support'*).

9 Undo the fasteners and remove the engine undertray (where fitted), followed by the shield under the radiator.

10 On diesel engines, remove the intercooler as described in Chapter 4B Section 16.

11 Lift the condenser slightly and disengage the two mounting lugs each side from the guides on the radiator **(see illustration 6.7)**. Lower the condenser and remove it from under the car.

Refitting

12 Refitting is the reverse of removal. Renew the O-rings and lubricate with refrigerant oil.

13 Have the system evacuated, charged and leak-tested by the specialist who discharged it.

Evaporator

Removal

14 Remove the heater matrix as described in Section 9.

15 Undo the three screws and remove the evaporator cover panel from the side of the air distribution housing**(see illustrations)**.

16 Withdraw the evaporator from the air distribution housing **(see illustration)**.

Refitting

17 Refitting is the reverse of the removal procedure.

Compressor

Removal

18 Have the refrigerant discharged at a dealer service department or an automotive air conditioning repair facility.

19 Disconnect the battery negative lead as described in Chapter 5A Section 4.

20 Firmly apply the handbrake, then jack up the front of the vehicle and support it securely on axle stands (see *'Jacking and vehicle support'*).

21 Undo the fasteners and remove the engine undertray (where fitted).

22 Remove the auxiliary drivebelt as described in Chapter 1A Section 25 or Chapter 1B Section 24.

23 Unscrew the clamping bolts to disconnect the refrigerant lines from the compressor **(see illustration)**. Plug the line connections to prevent entry of any dirt or moisture. Discard the O-ring seals, new ones must be fitted.

24 Unbolt the compressor from the cylinder block/crankcase, unplug its electrical connector, then withdraw the compressor from the vehicle. **Note:** *Keep the compressor level during handling and storage. If the compressor has seized, or if you find metal particles in the refrigerant lines, the system must be flushed out by an air conditioning technician, and the accumulator/dehydrator must be renewed.*

Refitting

25 Refitting is the reverse of the removal procedure. Renew the O-rings and lubricate with refrigerant oil.

26 Have the system evacuated, charged and leak-tested by the specialist who discharged it.

Accumulator/dehydrator

Removal

27 Have the refrigerant discharged at a dealer service department or an automotive air conditioning repair facility.

28 Disconnect the battery negative lead as described in Chapter 5A Section 4.

29 Remove the right-hand headlight unit as described in Chapter 12 Section 7.

12.23 Unscrew the clamping bolts (arrowed) to disconnect the refrigerant lines from the compressor

30 Undo the bolt securing the condenser to the right-hand side of the radiator**(see illustration 6.4)**.

31 Prise up the centre section, then remove the plastic rivet each side securing the radiator cover panel to the top of the bumper **(see illustration 4.9)**.

32 Pull up on the tabs at the rear of the radiator cover panel each side to release the retaining clips each side, then lift the cover panel off the car **(see illustrations 4.10a, 4.10b and 4.10c)**.

33 Firmly apply the handbrake, then jack up the front of the vehicle and support it securely on axle stands (see *'Jacking and vehicle support'*).

34 Undo the fasteners and remove the engine undertray (where fitted), followed by the shield under the radiator.

35 On diesel engines, remove the intercooler as described in Chapter 4B Section 16.

36 Lift the condenser slightly and disengage the two mounting lugs each side from the guides on the radiator **(see illustration 6.7)**.

37 Unscrew the retaining cap from the base of the condenser on the left-hand side and withdraw the accumulator/dehydrator from the condenser **(see illustration)**.

Refitting

38 Refitting is the reverse of removal. Have the system evacuated, charged and leak-tested by the specialist who discharged it.

12.37 Unscrew the retaining cap (arrowed) and withdraw the accumulator/dehydrator from the condenser

13.3a Remove the bulbholder from the footwell air duct on the driver's side...

13.3b... then remove the duct

13.4 Undo the nut and five bolts (arrowed) and remove the facia crossmember support bracket

13 Electric booster heater – general information, removal and refitting

General information

1 Because diesel engines give off low residual heat, an electric booster heating element is fitted into the air distribution housing above the heater matrix. At engine coolant temperatures of less than 60°C and ambient temperatures of less than 10°C, when the high temperature setting is selected, the GEM (see Section 13) provides power to the heating element. Power is cut to the element when the engine coolant temperature exceeds 70°C or the ambient temperature exceeds 20°C.

Removal

2 Remove the facia as described in Chapter 11 Section 29.

3 Remove the footwell illumination bulbholder from the footwell air duct on the driver's side then remove the duct (see illustrations).

4 Undo the nut and five bolts and remove the facia crossmember support bracket at the right-hand side of the air distribution housing (see illustration). Note the location of the earth lead on the upper centre bolt.

5 Disconnect the booster heater wiring connectors then release the connector blocks from the floor bracket (see illustrations).

6 Release the booster heater wiring harness from the clip on the air distribution housing, undo the two retaining bolts and withdraw the booster heater from the housing (see illustration).

Refitting

7 Refitting is the reversal of removal.

13.5a Disconnect the booster heater wiring connectors...

13.5b... then release the connector blocks from the floor bracket

13.6a Release the booster heater wiring harness from the clip on the air distribution housing...

13.6b... undo the two retaining bolts (arrowed)...

13.6c... and withdraw the booster heater from the housing

Chapter 4 Part A
Fuel and exhaust systems – petrol models

Contents

Degrees of difficulty

Easy, suitable for novice with little experience	Fairly easy, suitable for beginner with some experience	Fairly difficult, suitable for competent DIY mechanic 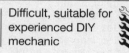	Difficult, suitable for experienced DIY mechanic	Very difficult, suitable for expert DIY or professional

Specifications

General

System type . . . . Sequential multiport fuel injection
Fuel octane requirement. . . . . 95 RON unleaded
Regulated fuel pressure (nominal) . . . . 3.6 to 4.0 bar

Torque wrench settings

	Nm	lbf ft
Accelerator pedal assembly nuts.	8	6
Alternator heat shield nuts	20	15
Camshaft position sensor	8	6
Catalytic converter support bracket bolts	25	18
Crankshaft position sensor	8	6
Engine rear mounting (roll restrictor):		
Bolts	80	59
Nuts	48	35
Engine right-hand mounting-to-body bolts	90	66
Engine right-hand mounting-to-engine nuts*	80	59
Exhaust manifold:		
Manifold nuts (to cylinder head)	55	41
Flexible section to exhaust centre section	48	35
Exhaust manifold heat shield bolts	10	7
Fuel rail mounting nuts.	25	18
Fuel tank strap retaining bolts	25	18
Inlet manifold to cylinder head	18	13
Oxygen sensors	48	35
Subframe cross-brace bolts.	60	44
Throttle housing retaining bolts	10	7

Use new nuts

1 General information and precautions

1 The fuel system consists of a fuel tank (mounted under the floor, beneath the rear seats), fuel hoses, an electric fuel pump mounted in the fuel tank, and a sequential electronic fuel injection system controlled by an engine management electronic control unit (powertrain control module).

2 The electric fuel pump supplies fuel under pressure to the fuel rail, which distributes fuel to the injectors. A pressure regulator integral with the pump controls the system pressure. From the fuel rail, fuel is injected into the inlet ports, just above the inlet valves, by four fuel injectors. The fuel rail is mounted to the cylinder head, just above the plastic inlet manifold.

3 The amount of fuel supplied by the injectors is precisely controlled by the powertrain control module (PCM). The module uses the signals from the crankshaft position sensor and the camshaft position sensor to trigger each injector separately in cylinder firing order (sequential injection), with benefits in terms of better fuel economy and leaner exhaust emissions.

4 The powertrain control module is the heart of the entire engine management system, controlling the fuel injection, ignition and emissions control systems. The module receives information from various sensors which is then computed and compared with preset values stored in its memory to determine the required period of injection.

5 Information on crankshaft position and engine speed is generated by a crankshaft position sensor. The inductive head of the sensor runs adjacent to the crankshaft pulley and scans a series of protrusions on the pulley periphery. As the crankshaft rotates, the sensor transmits a pulse to the system's ignition module every time a protrusion passes it. There is one missing protrusion at a point corresponding to 90° BTDC. The ignition module recognises the absence of a pulse from the crankshaft position sensor at this point to establish a reference mark for crankshaft position. Similarly, the time interval between absent pulses is used to determine engine speed. This information is then fed to the powertrain control module for further processing.

6 On early models, a camshaft position sensor is located in the cylinder head so that it registers with a lobe on the camshaft. The sensor functions in the same way as the crankshaft position sensor, producing a series of pulses; this gives the powertrain control module a reference point, to enable it to determine the firing order and operate the injectors in the appropriate sequence. On later models a camshaft position sensor is not used and the firing order is determined by the different current rises of the two sparked cylinders 1 and 3.

7 Engine temperature information is supplied by the coolant temperature sensor. The sensor is an NTC (Negative Temperature Coefficient) thermistor – that is, a semi-conductor whose electrical resistance decreases as its temperature increases. The sensor provides the powertrain control module with a constantly-varying (analogue) voltage signal, corresponding to the temperature of the engine coolant. This is used to refine the calculations made by the module when determining the correct amount of fuel required to achieve the ideal air/fuel mixture ratio.

8 Inlet air temperature and density information for air/fuel mixture ratio calculations is provided by a temperature and manifold absolute pressure (TMAP) sensor. The TMAP sensor is located on the throttle housing, and consists of a pressure transducer and a temperature sensor which directly supersedes the mass airflow and inlet air temperature sensors. The TMAP sensor provides information to the powertrain control module relating to inlet manifold vacuum and barometric pressure, and the temperature of the air in the inlet manifold. When the ignition is switched on with the engine stopped, the sensor calculates barometric pressure and, when the engine is running, the sensor calculates inlet manifold vacuum.

9 The throttle valve inside the throttle housing is controlled by the driver via the position of the accelerator pedal. As the valve opens, the amount of air that can pass through the system increases. As the throttle valve opens further, the TMAP sensor signal alters, and the powertrain control module opens each injector for a longer duration, to increase the amount of fuel delivered to the inlet ports.

10 All models feature a throttle which is electronically-controlled – an accelerator cable is not fitted. Instead, a throttle position sensor fitted to the accelerator pedal provides the powertrain control module with the throttle opening signal, and this is relayed to a motor-driven throttle valve. This system also enables the PCM to control the engine idle speed, varying the throttle opening as required by changes in engine temperature and load.

11 On all models, roadspeed is monitored by the ABS wheel speed sensors.

12 The clutch pedal position is monitored by a switch fitted to the pedal bracket. This sends a signal to the powertrain control module.

13 A pressure-operated switch is screwed into the power steering system's high-pressure pipe. The switch sends a signal to the powertrain control module to increase engine speed to maintain idle speed as pressure in the system rises – typically, when the steering is near full-lock.

14 Oxygen sensors in the exhaust system provides the module with constant feedback – 'closed-loop' control – which enables it to adjust the mixture to provide the best possible operating conditions for the catalytic converter. A further sensor is fitted, downstream of the converter, to monitor the converter's operation, and this provides an even finer degree of emission control.

15 The air inlet side of the system consists of an air cleaner housing, an inlet hose and duct, and a throttle housing.

16 Both the idle speed and mixture are under the control of the powertrain control module, and cannot be adjusted.

Precautions

17 Before disconnecting any of the fuel injection system sensor wiring plugs, ensure at least that the ignition is switched off (ideally, disconnect the battery – refer to Chapter 5A Section 4). If this is not done, it could result in a fault code being logged in the system memory, and may even cause damage to the component concerned.

18 Residual pressure will remain in the fuel lines long after the car was last used. When disconnecting any fuel line, first depressurise the fuel system as described in Section 2.

 Warning: Many of the procedures in this Chapter require the removal of fuel lines and connections, which may result in some fuel spillage. Before carrying out any operation on the fuel system, refer to the precautions given in Safety First! at the beginning of this manual, and follow them implicitly. Petrol is a highly-dangerous and volatile liquid, and the precautions necessary when handling it cannot be overstressed.

2 Fuel system – depressurisation

 Warning: The following procedure will merely relieve the pressure in the fuel system – remember that fuel will still be present in the system components, and take precautions accordingly before disconnecting any of them.

Note: *Refer to the warning note in Section 1 before proceeding.*

1 The fuel system referred to in this Chapter is defined as the fuel tank and tank-mounted fuel pump/fuel gauge sender unit, the fuel injector, and the metal pipes and flexible hoses of the fuel lines between these components. All these contain fuel, which will be under pressure while the engine is running and/or while the ignition is switched on.

2 The pressure will remain for some time after the ignition has been switched off, and must be relieved before any of these components is disturbed for servicing work.

3 The simplest depressurisation method is to disconnect the fuel pump electrical supply by removing the fuel pump fuse (refer to the wiring diagrams or the label on the engine compartment fusebox for exact location) and starting the engine; allow the engine to idle until it stops through lack of fuel. Turn the engine over once or twice on the starter to ensure that all pressure is released, then switch off the ignition; do not forget to refit the fuse when work is complete.

4 Note that, once the fuel system has been depressurised and drained (even partially), it will take significantly longer to restart the engine – perhaps several seconds of cranking – before the system is refilled and pressure restored.

3 Unleaded petrol – general information and usage

1 All petrol models are designed to run on fuel with a minimum octane rating of 95 (RON). All models have a catalytic converter, and so must be run on unleaded fuel only. Under no circumstances should leaded fuel (UK '4-star' or LRP) be used, as this will damage the converter.
2 Super unleaded petrol (98 or 99 octane) can also be used in all models if wished, though there is no advantage in doing so.

4 Fuel lines and fittings – general information

Note: *Refer to the warning note in Section 1 before proceeding.*

Quick-release couplings

1 Quick-release couplings are employed at many of the unions in the fuel feed and return lines.
2 Before disconnecting any fuel system component, relieve the residual pressure in the system (see Section 2), and equalise tank pressure by removing the fuel filler cap.

 Warning: This procedure will merely relieve the increased pressure necessary for the engine to run – remember that fuel will still be present in the system components, and take precautions accordingly before disconnecting any of them.

3 Release the protruding locking lugs on each union by squeezing them together and carefully pulling the coupling apart. Note that on some quick-release couplings it will be necessary to release a retaining collar, using a small screwdriver, to disconnect the coupling. Use rag to soak up any spilt fuel. Where the unions are colour-coded, the pipes cannot be confused. Where both unions are the same colour, note carefully which pipe is connected to which, and ensure that they are correctly reconnected on refitting.
4 To reconnect one of these couplings, press them firmly together. Switch the ignition on and off five times to pressurise the system, and check for any sign of fuel leakage around the disturbed coupling before attempting to start the engine.

Checking fuel lines

5 Checking procedures for the fuel lines are included in Chapter 1A Section 10.

Component renewal

6 If any damaged sections are to be renewed, use original-equipment hoses or pipes, constructed from exactly the same material as the section being renewed. Do not install substitutes constructed from inferior or inappropriate material; this could cause a fuel leak or a fire.
7 Before detaching or disconnecting any part of the fuel system, note the routing of all hoses and pipes, and the orientation of all clamps and clips. New sections must be installed in exactly the same manner.
8 Before disconnecting any part of the fuel system, be sure to relieve the fuel system pressure (see Section 2), and equalise tank pressure by removing the fuel filler cap. Also disconnect the battery negative lead as described in Chapter 5A Section 4. Cover the fitting being disconnected with a rag, to absorb any fuel that may spray out.

5 Air cleaner assembly – removal and refitting

Removal

1 Remove the plastic cover from the top of the engine by pulling it upwards from its mountings.
2 Remove the left-hand headlight unit as described in Chapter 12 Section 7.
3 Loosen the clips and disconnect the air outlet duct from the air cleaner cover and throttle housing. Similarly, disconnect the resonator air duct from the air cleaner cover and resonator **(see illustrations)**.
4 Reach down and detach the air inlet duct from the front of the air cleaner housing.
5 Pull the air cleaner upwards from its rubber mountings. Squeeze together the sides of the collar and disconnect the crankcase ventilation hose from the air cleaner housing as it's withdrawn.

5.3a Loosen the clips (arrowed) and disconnect the air outlet duct from the air cleaner cover and throttle housing...

Refitting

6 When refitting, locate the pegs on the base of the air cleaner housing into the mounting grommets and push the housing firmly downwards.

6 Accelerator pedal – removal and refitting

Removal

1 Disconnect the wiring plug from the throttle position sensor, then unscrew the three mounting nuts and remove the pedal/sensor assembly from the bulkhead studs. Note that the sensor is not available separately from the pedal assembly.

Refitting

2 Refitting is a reversal of the removal procedure.

7 Fuel tank – removal, inspection and refitting

Note: *Refer to the warning note in Section 1 before proceeding.*

Removal

1 Run the fuel level as low as possible prior to removing the tank. There is no drain plug fitted (and siphoning may prove difficult) but it may be possible to partially drain the tank.
2 Relieve the residual pressure in the fuel system (see Section 2), and equalise tank pressure by removing the fuel filler cap.
3 Disconnect the battery negative lead as described in Chapter 5A Section 4.
4 Chock the front wheels, then jack up the rear of the car and support it on axle stands (see 'Jacking and vehicle support'). Remove the rear roadwheels.
5 Unhook the exhaust system mounting rubbers from the centre and rear hangers, and allow the exhaust system to rest on the rear suspension crossmember.
6 Undo the nuts and bolts and remove the

5.3b... similarly, disconnect the resonator air duct from the air cleaner cover and resonator

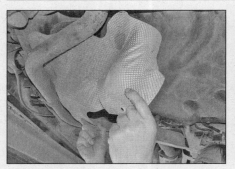

7.6 Undo the nuts and bolts and remove the exhaust heat shield from under the fuel tank

7.7 Release the clip (arrowed) and disconnect the fuel tank filler pipe

7.8 Disconnect the fuel supply pipe and canister purge valve pipe at the quick-release connectors

7.9 Disconnect the fuel and vent pipes at the quick-release connectors (arrowed) on the carbon canister

car, it should be placed in a safe area where sparks or open flames cannot ignite the fumes coming out of the tank. Be especially careful inside garages where a natural-gas type appliance is located, because the pilot light could cause an explosion.

Refitting

16 Refitting is a reversal of the removal procedure, noting the following points:
a) *Ensure that all pipe and wiring connections are securely fitted.*
b) *When refitting the quick-release couplings, press them together until the locking lugs snap into their groove.*
c) *Tighten the tank strap retaining bolts to the specified torque.*
d) *If evidence of contamination was found, do not return any previously-drained fuel to the tank unless it is carefully filtered first.*

8 Fuel pump/fuel gauge sender unit – removal and refitting

Note: *Refer to the warning note in Section 1 before proceeding. Ford specify the use of their service tool 310-069 (a large socket with projecting teeth to engage the fuel pump/ sender unit retaining rings raised edges) for this task. Suitable alternatives to this tool are readily available from accessory stores and motor factor outlets.*

Removal

1 A combined fuel pump and fuel gauge sender unit is located in the top face of the fuel tank. The combined unit can only be detached and withdrawn from the tank after the tank is released and lowered from under the car. Refer to Section 7 and remove the fuel tank, then proceed as follows.
2 With the fuel tank removed, disconnect the fuel supply pipe from the stub by squeezing the quick-release lugs.
3 Unscrew and remove the special retaining ring, by unscrewing it with the Ford tool or a suitable alternative.
4 Check that alignment marks are visible on the fuel pump/gauge sender unit and fuel tank. There should be an arrow on the sender unit aligned with raised projections on the tank (**see illustration**). If no marks are visible,

exhaust heat shield from under the fuel tank (**see illustration**).
7 Release the clip and disconnect the fuel tank filler pipe(**see illustration**). Discard the pipe clip and obtain a worm-drive hose clip for refitting. Be prepared for fuel spillage and observe all relevant safety precautions.
8 Disconnect the fuel supply pipe and canister purge valve pipe at the quick-release connectors in front of the fuel tank (**see illustration**).
9 Disconnect the fuel and vent pipes at the quick-release connectors on the carbon canister (**see illustration**).
10 Disconnect the wiring for the fuel pump/ gauge sender unit at the connector located in front of the carbon canister.
11 Support the tank using a trolley jack and a large sheet of wood to spread the load.
12 Undo the front and rear bolt each side

securing the fuel tank retaining straps to the underbody (**see illustrations**).
13 Slowly and carefully lower the fuel tank to the ground, checking all the way down that no pipes or wiring are under any strain. Remove the tank from under the car.

Inspection

14 Whilst removed, the fuel tank can be inspected for damage or deterioration. Removal of the fuel pump/fuel gauge sender unit (see Section 8) will allow a partial inspection of the interior. If the tank is contaminated with sediment or water, swill it out with clean fuel. Do not under any circum-stances undertake any repairs on a leaking or damaged fuel tank; this work must be carried out by a professional who has experience in this critical and potentially-dangerous work.
15 Whilst the fuel tank is removed from the

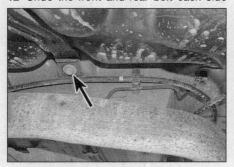

7.12a Fuel tank retaining strap front mounting bolt (arrowed)...

7.12b... and rear mounting bolt (arrowed)

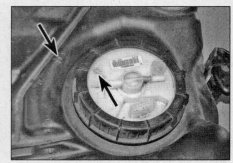

8.4 Align the arrow on the top of the module with the mark on the tank (arrowed)

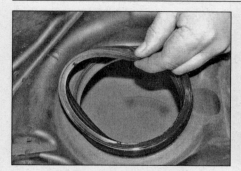

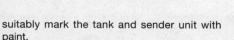
8.6 Renew the rubber seal

9.2 Diagnostic connector (arrowed)

suitably mark the tank and sender unit with paint.

5 Carefully lift out the fuel pump/gauge sender unit from the tank. Take care that the sender unit float and arm are not damaged as the unit is removed.

6 Lift out the rubber seal and obtain a new seal for refitting **(see illustration)**.

7 At the time of writing it was not clear whether the fuel gauge sender unit was available separately. If a new part can be sourced, the sender unit can be removed from the pump by disconnecting the wiring connector, releasing the retaining catch and withdrawing the unit from the side of the pump.

Refitting

8 Refitting is a reversal of removal, but fit a new rubber seal and tighten the retaining ring securely, aligning the arrow on the top of the module with the mark on the top of the tank. Refit the fuel tank as described in Section 7.

9 Fuel injection system – checking

Note: *Refer to the warning note in Section 1 before proceeding.*

1 If a fault appears in the fuel injection system, first ensure that all the system wiring connectors are securely connected and free of corrosion – also refer to paragraphs 5 to 8 below. Then ensure that the fault is not due to poor maintenance; ie, check that the air cleaner filter element is clean, the spark plugs are in good condition and correctly gapped, the cylinder compression pressures are correct, the ignition system wiring is in good condition and securely connected, and the engine breather hoses are clear and undamaged, referring to Chapter 1A, Chapter 2A and Chapter 5B.

2 If these checks fail to reveal the cause of the problem, the car should be taken to a suitably-equipped Ford dealer or diagnostic specialist for testing. A diagnostic connector is fitted under the facia on the driver's side into which dedicated electronic test equipment can be plugged **(see illustration)**. The test equipment is capable of 'interrogating' the

engine management system powertrain control module (PCM) electronically and accessing its internal fault log (reading fault codes).

3 Fault codes can only be extracted from the PCM using a dedicated fault code reader. A Ford dealer will obviously have such a reader, but they are also available from other suppliers. It is unlikely to be cost-effective for the private owner to purchase a fault code reader, but a well-equipped local garage or auto-electrical specialist will have one.

4 Using this equipment, faults can be pinpointed quickly and simply, even if their occurrence is intermittent. Testing all the system components individually in an attempt to locate the fault by elimination is a time-consuming operation that is unlikely to be fruitful (particularly if the fault occurs dynamically), and carries a high risk of damage to the PCM's internal components.

Limited Operation Strategy

5 Certain faults, such as failure of one of the engine management system sensors, will cause the system will revert to a backup (or 'limp-home') mode, referred to by Ford as 'Limited Operation Strategy' (LOS). This is intended to be a 'get-you-home' facility only – the engine management warning light will come on when this mode is in operation.

6 In this mode, the signal from the defective sensor is substituted with a fixed value (it would normally vary), which may lead to loss of power, poor idling, and generally-poor running, especially when the engine is cold.

7 However, the engine may in fact run quite well in this situation, and the only clue (other than the warning light) would be that the exhaust CO emissions (for example) will be higher than they should be.

8 Bear in mind that, even if the defective sensor is correctly identified and renewed, the engine will not return to normal running until the fault code is erased, taking the system out of LOS. This also applies even if the cause of the fault was a loose connection or damaged piece of wire – until the fault code is erased, the system will continue in LOS.

10 Fuel injection system components – removal and refitting

Note: *Refer to the precautions in Section 1 before proceeding.*

Throttle housing

1 Remove the plastic cover on top of the engine.

2 Release the clamps and remove the ducting between the air cleaner and the throttle housing **(see illustration 5.3a)**.

3 Disconnect the wiring plug, then undo the four bolts and remove the throttle housing **(see illustrations)**.

4 Refitting is a reversal of removal. Use a new seal if necessary, and tighten the mounting bolts to the specified torque.

5 After refitting the throttle housing, turn the ignition key to position II (or press the power button) and wait for 1 minute for the throttle housing to initialise, then turn the ignition off. Do not press the accelerator pedal during this procedure.

Fuel rail and injectors

6 Relieve the residual pressure in the fuel system (see Section 2), and equalise tank pressure by removing the fuel filler cap.

⚠️ *Warning: This procedure will merely relieve the increased pressure necessary for the engine to run – remember that fuel will still be present in the system components, and take precautions accordingly before disconnecting any of them.*

10.3a Disconnect the throttle housing wiring plug...

10.3b... then undo the four bolts (arrowed)

10.10 Push in the collar (arrowed) and pull the connector from the fuel rail

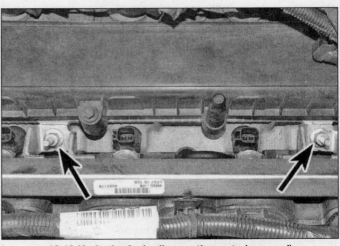

10.12 Undo the fuel rail mounting nuts (arrowed)

7 Disconnect the battery negative lead as described in Chapter 5A Section 4.

8 Remove the plastic cover from the top of the engine.

9 Depress the clips and disconnect the wiring plugs from the injectors, then unclip the wiring harness.

10 Disconnect the fuel supply pipe from the fuel rail by pushing the collar into the connector(see illustration).

11 Release the fuel pipes from the retaining clips on the fuel rail and adjacent components.

12 Unscrew the mounting nuts, then lift the fuel rail from the cylinder head – there will be some resistance from the injector O-ring seals (see illustration).

13 To remove the injectors, first lift the retaining clips at the top, then slide them off sideways. Now pull the injectors out of the fuel rail.

14 Refitting is the reverse of the removal procedure, noting the following points:

a) Fit new injector O-rings, and lubricate them with clean engine oil to aid refitting.

b) Tighten the fuel rail mounting nuts to the specified torque.

c) Ensure that the hoses and wiring are routed correctly, and secured on reconnection by any clips or ties provided.

d) On completion, switch the ignition on to activate the fuel pump and pressurise the system, without cranking the engine. Check for signs of fuel leaks around all disturbed unions and joints before attempting to start the engine.

TMAP sensor

15 The sensor is located beneath the throttle housing. Remove the plastic cover from the top of the engine.

16 With the ignition switched off, disconnect the sensor wiring plug, then remove the mounting bolt and withdraw it from the manifold. Check the condition of the sensor O-ring seal, and obtain a new one if necessary (see illustration).

17 Refitting is a reversal of removal. Use a new seal if necessary, and tighten the mounting bolt securely, to prevent air leaks.

Powertrain control module

Note: The module is fragile. Take care not to drop it, or subject it to any other kind of impact. Do not subject it to extremes of temperature, or allow it to get wet.

Note: If a new PCM is to be fitted, the configuration information stored within the module must be uploaded to Ford diagnostic equipment prior to the module being removed, and downloaded to the new PCM once installed. Entrust this task to a Ford dealer or suitably-equipped specialist.

18 Disconnect the battery negative lead as described in Chapter 5A Section 4.

19 Firmly apply the handbrake, then jack up the front of the vehicle and support it securely on axle stands (see 'Jacking and vehicle support'). Remove the left-hand front roadwheel.

20 Release the fasteners and remove the left-hand front wheel arch liner (see illustration).

21 The PCM is fitted under the front bumper. To gain access, undo the retaining bolts and remove the plastic cover (see illustrations).

10.16 The TMAP sensor is located at the lower, left-hand edge of the manifold (arrowed)

10.20 Release the fasteners and remove the left-hand front wheel arch liner

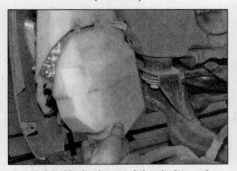

10.21a Undo the retaining bolts and remove the plastic cover...

10.21b... to gain access to the PCM

22 Undo the three mounting bolts and withdraw the PCM from its location.

23 Suitably support the PCM and centre-punch a hole in the centre of the security shield retaining shear-bolt.

24 Drill a 3.5 mm diameter hole in the shear bolt, then tap a T20 Torx bit into the hole **(see illustrations)**. Unscrew the Torx bit to remove the shear bolt. Note that a new shear bolt will be required for refitting.

25 Remove the security shield, then lever over the locking catches and disconnect the wiring plugs from the PCM.

26 Refitting is a reversal of removal. Tighten the new shear-bolt until the heads shear off.

Crankshaft position sensor

27 The sensor is located adjacent to the crankshaft pulley. Firmly apply the handbrake, then jack up the front of the vehicle and support it securely on axle stands (see 'Jacking and vehicle support').

28 Disconnect the sensor wiring plug **(see illustration)**.

29 Undo the two retaining bolts and remove the sensor.

30 Refitting is a reversal of removal. Tighten the sensor retaining bolts to the specified torque.

Camshaft position sensor

Note: *The camshaft position sensor is only fitted to engines built up to 12/2007.*

31 Remove the plastic cover on the top of the engine.

32 Disconnect the wiring plug, then undo the retaining bolt and remove the sensor **(see illustration)**.

33 Refitting is a reversal of removal. Tighten the retaining bolt to the specified torque.

Coolant temperature sensor

34 Refer to Chapter 3 Section 5.

Knock sensor

35 Refer to Chapter 5B Section 5.

Clutch pedal switches

36 Refer to Chapter 6 Section 7.

Oxygen sensors

37 Refer to Chapter 4C.

10.24a Drill a 3.5 mm diameter hole in the shear bolt...

10.28 Crankshaft position sensor

10.24b... then tap a T20 Torx bit into the hole

10.32 Camshaft position sensor (arrowed)

11 Manifolds – removal and refitting

Note: *Refer to the warning note in Section 1 before proceeding.*

Inlet manifold

1 Depressurise the fuel system as described in Section 2. On completion, disconnect the battery negative lead (refer to Chapter 5A Section 4).

2 Remove the plastic cover on the top of the engine.

3 Disconnect the battery as described in Chapter 5A Section 4.

4 Remove the air cleaner assembly as described in Section 5.

5 Remove the right-hand headlight unit as described in Chapter 12 Section 7.

6 Remove the throttle housing as described in Section 10.

7 Remove the engine oil level dipstick guide tube upper and lower retaining bolts **(see illustrations)**.

8 Remove the inlet manifold lower retaining bolt **(see illustration)**.

9 Disconnect the wiring plug from the TMAP sensor (on the manifold), then unclip the wiring harnesses and all related vacuum hoses from the manifold.

10 Disconnect the following around the manifold:

a) *Crankcase breather hose at the base of the manifold.*

b) *Brake servo vacuum pipe from the manifold.*

11.7a Oil level dipstick guide tube upper bolt (arrowed)...

11.7b... and lower bolt (arrowed)

11.8 Manifold lower retaining bolt (arrowed)

11.13 Undo the nuts and bolts (arrowed) and remove the engine right-hand mounting

11.15 Renew the inlet manifold gaskets

11.20 Disconnect the oxygen sensor wiring connectors (arrowed)

11 Firmly apply the handbrake, then jack up the front of the vehicle and support it securely on axle stands (see *Jacking and vehicle support*). 13 Section 5

12 Undo the retaining nuts and bolts and remove the engine/transmission rear mounting (roll restrictor) from the subframe and engine bracket.

13 Support the engine using a trolley jack and block of wood beneath the sump, then unscrew the nuts/bolts securing the engine/transmission right-hand mounting bracket and remove the mounting from the engine **(see illustration)**. Note that new nuts will be required for refitting.

14 Check carefully around the manifold, unclipping any remaining wiring or pipework which may still be attached to it.

15 Undo the bolts securing the manifold to the cylinder head. Carefully move the right-hand side of the engine rearward and raise or lower it as necessary to provide sufficient clearance to remove the manifold. Recover the gaskets **(see illustration)**.

16 Refitting is a reversal of removal, noting the following points:

a) *Ensure that the mating faces are clean, and use new manifold gaskets if necessary.*

b) *Tighten all fixings to the specified torque (where given).*

c) *On completion, switch the ignition on to activate the fuel pump and pressurise the system, without cranking the engine. Check for signs of fuel leaks around all disturbed unions and joints before attempting to start the engine.*

Exhaust manifold

 Warning: Do not attempt this procedure until the engine is completely cool – ideally, the car should be left overnight before starting work.

17 The exhaust manifold is integral with the catalytic converter.

18 Disconnect the battery negative lead as described in Chapter 5A Section 4.

19 Remove the plastic cover on the top of the engine.

20 Disconnect the oxygen sensors' wiring connectors behind the left-hand side of the engine **(see illustration)**. Release the wiring from the cable clips so it is free to be removed with the manifold.

21 Undo the four bolts and remove the exhaust manifold heat shield**(see illustration)**.

22 Working in a diagonal sequence, loosen and remove the seven exhaust manifold nuts. The manifold will remain in position for now, located on the cylinder head studs – do not try and slide it off the studs yet. **Note:** *If all of the studs come out with the nuts, leave two of them in place to support the manifold.*

23 Firmly apply the handbrake, then jack up the front of the vehicle and support it securely on axle stands (see '*Jacking and vehicle support*').

24 Undo the two bolts each side and remove the subframe cross-brace**(see illustration)**.

25 Undo the two nuts and remove the alternator heat shield.

26 To prevent damage to the exhaust flexible section, support it by attaching a pair of splints either side (two scrap strips of wood, plant canes, etc) using some cable-ties **(see illustration)**.

27 Unscrew the nuts securing the centre section to the flexible section flange, and separate the joint. Recover the gasket.

28 Unhook the two rubber mountings from beneath the flexible section.

29 Undo the two bolts securing the catalytic converter to the support bracket on its underside, and with the help of an assistant, slide the manifold off the cylinder head studs (or completely unscrew any remaining studs), and lower it down to remove it, taking care not to damage the sensors or their wiring **(see illustration)**. Recover and discard the gasket.

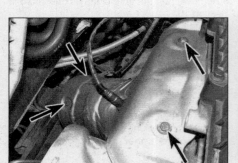

11.21 Undo the four bolts (arrowed) and remove the exhaust manifold heat shield

11.24 Undo the two bolts each side and remove the subframe cross-brace

11.26 Make a 'splint' to support the flexible section of the exhaust

11.29 Undo the two bolts (arrowed) securing the catalytic converter to the support bracket

30 Unscrew the oxygen sensors from the manifold and catalytic converter.
31 Refitting is a reversal of removal, noting the following points:
a) *Ensure that the mating faces are clean, and use new manifold gaskets.*
b) *Use new manifold/catalytic converter nuts/ bolt.*
c) *Do not fully tighten the manifold/catalytic converter mounting nuts/bolts until the centre section flange joint has been reconnected and the rubber mountings refitted.*
d) *Tighten the manifold nuts in a diagonal sequence, to the specified torque.*
e) *Tighten all fixings to the specified torque*

12 Exhaust system – general information, removal and refitting

Caution: Any work on the exhaust system should only be attempted once the system is completely cool – this may take several hours, especially in the case of the forward sections, such as the manifold and catalytic converter.

General information

1 The exhaust system consists of the exhaust manifold with integral catalytic converter, and the centre section incorporating the front and rear silencers. A flexible ('mesh') section is fitted to allow for engine movement. The flexible section is located just after the catalytic converter, upstream of the centre section-to-catalytic converter flange joint.
2 When fitted in the factory, the exhaust system from the centre section flange joint to the end of the tail pipe is one piece. However, if the rear silencer is to be renewed, new silencers should be available – check with your parts supplier. It will be necessary to cut through the centre section using a hacksaw if a new rear silencer is to be fitted.
3 The system is suspended throughout its entire length by rubber mountings.

Removal

4 To remove a part of the system, first jack up the front or rear of the car, and support it on axle stands (see *'Jacking and vehicle support'*). Alternatively, position the car over an inspection pit, or on car ramps.

Manifold and catalytic converter

5 Refer to Section 11.

Centre section

6 Remove the rear silencer as described later in this Section.
7 Unscrew the nuts securing the centre section to the catalytic converter, and separate the joint. Recover the gasket.
8 Unhook the centre section's rubber mountings, and remove it from under the car.

Rear silencer

9 If the original one-piece exhaust system is still fitted, it will be necessary to cut off the old rear silencer to enable fitment of the new unit. Using the new rear silencer as a pattern, mark the exhaust centre section to determine the cut point. Ensure that the cut point will allow a sufficient length of centre section to fit into the new rear silencer.
10 Using a hacksaw, cut through the centre section at the marked cut point. Unhook the rear silencer's rubber mountings, and remove it from under the car.
11 If a replacement rear silencer has already been fitted, unbolt the clamp securing the silencer to the centre section, and separate the pipes. Usually, this will require some effort – the most successful method involves twisting the silencer from side to side, to break the joint. Unfortunately, if the pipe at the rear of the centre section has suffered from corrosion, it's very likely that the centre section will be damaged beyond repair in removing the silencer. A less-destructive method of removal involves heating the two pipes, but this carries the risk of damaging the underbody components, and even a risk of fire from the fuel tank and lines.
12 Unhook the silencer rubber mountings, and remove it from under the car.

Heat shields

13 The heat shields are secured to the underside of the body by special nuts. Each shield can be removed separately, but note that they may overlap, making it necessary to loosen another section first. If a shield is being removed to gain access to a component located behind it, it may prove sufficient in some cases to remove the retaining nuts and/or bolts, and simply lower the shield, without disturbing the exhaust system. Otherwise, remove the exhaust section as described earlier.

Refitting

14 In all cases, refitting is a reversal of removal, but note the following points:
a) *Always use new gaskets, nuts and clamps (as applicable), and coat all threads with copper grease. Make sure any new clamps are the same size as the original – overtightening a clamp which is too big will not seal the joint.*
b) *On a sleeved joint (such as that between the centre section and rear silencer), use a smear of exhaust jointing paste to achieve a gas-tight seal.*
c) *If any of the exhaust mounting rubbers are in poor condition, fit new ones.*
d) *Make sure that the exhaust is suspended properly on its mountings, and will not come into contact with the floor or any suspension parts. The rear silencer especially must be aligned correctly before tightening the clamp nuts*
e) *Tighten all nuts/bolts to the specified torque, where given.*

Chapter 4 Part B
Fuel and exhaust systems – diesel models

Contents

Degrees of difficulty

Easy, suitable for novice with little experience	Fairly easy, suitable for beginner with some experience	Fairly difficult, suitable for competent DIY mechanic	Difficult, suitable for experienced DIY mechanic	Very difficult, suitable for expert DIY or professional

Specifications

General

System type:

1.8 litre engines . . . . Siemens direct injection common rail with a chain-driven high-pressure delivery pump, variable nozzle turbocharger and intercooler

2.0 litre engines:

To emission level Stage III/IV . . . . Siemens direct injection common rail with a camshaft-driven high-pressure delivery pump, variable nozzle turbocharger, and intercooler

To emission level Stage V. . . . . Delphi direct injection common rail with a camshaft-driven high-pressure delivery pump, variable nozzle turbocharger, and intercooler

Firing order:

1.8 litre engines . . . . 1-3-4-2 (No 1 at timing belt end)
2.0 litre engines . . . . 1-3-4-2 (No 1 at flywheel end)
Fuel system operating pressure. . . . . 200 to 1350 bars (according to engine speed)

Torque wrench settings

	Nm	lbf ft
1.8 litre engines		
Accumulator rail mounting bolts	25	18
Catalytic converter:		
To turbocharger	25	18
Support bracket nuts	25	18
Exhaust manifold nuts/bolts.	20	15
Exhaust system flange joint nuts	48	35
Fuel high-pressure pipe union nuts: *†		
To accumulator rail.	38	28
To fuel pump.	25	18
To fuel injectors.	25	18
Fuel injector clamp retaining bolts: †		
Stage 1	5	4
Stage 2	Angle-tighten a further 90°	

Torque wrench settings (continued)

	Nm	lbf ft
1.8 litre engines (continued)		
High-pressure fuel pump:		
Drive chain sprocket bolts	24	18
Mounting bolts	20	15
Oil seal housing nuts	10	7
Support bracket bolts	23	17
Timing belt sprocket bolts	42	31
Subframe cross-brace bolts	60	44
Turbocharger oil return pipe bolts	10	7
Turbocharger oil supply pipe banjo bolts	35	26
Turbocharger-to-support bracket bolts	25	18
2.0 litre engines to emission level Stage III/IV		
Accumulator rail mounting nuts	22	16
Catalytic converter:		
To turbocharger clamp	25	18
Support bracket nuts	25	18
Exhaust manifold nuts	30	22
Exhaust system flange joint nuts	48	35
Fuel high-pressure pipe union nuts: *†		
Stage 1	19	14
Stage 2	30	22
Fuel injector clamp retaining nuts: †		
Stage 1	5	4
Stage 2	Angle-tighten a further 45°	
High-pressure fuel pump mounting bolts	20	15
Particulate filter temperature sensor	30	22
Subframe cross-brace bolts	60	44
Turbocharger oil return pipe bolts	10	7
Turbocharger oil supply pipe banjo bolts:		
To cylinder block	40	30
To turbocharger	28	21
Turbocharger support bracket bolts	15	11
Turbocharger-to-manifold nuts	25	18
2.0 litre engines to emission level Stage V		
Accumulator rail mounting bolts	22	16
Catalytic converter:		
Mounting rubber support bracket bolts	25	18
To turbocharger clamp	25	18
Support bracket nuts	25	18
Exhaust manifold heat shield bolts	10	7
Exhaust manifold nuts:		
Stage 1	10	7
Stage 2	20	15
Exhaust system flange joint nuts	48	35
Fuel high-pressure pipe union nuts: *†		
Stage 1	18	13
Stage 2	27	20
Fuel injector clamp retaining bolts: †		
Stage 1	7	5
Stage 2	Angle-tighten a further 55°	
High-pressure fuel pump mounting bolts	20	15
Inlet manifold lower section-to-cylinder head nuts:		
Left-hand side nut	8	6
Right-hand side nut/bolt	20	15
Inlet manifold upper section-to-lower section	8	6
Particulate filter temperature sensor	30	22
Subframe cross-brace bolts	60	44
Turbocharger coolant outlet pipe-to-cylinder block	38	28
Turbocharger oil supply pipe banjo bolts:		
To cylinder block	40	30
To turbocharger	38	28
Turbocharger-to-support bracket bolt	25	18
Turbocharger-to-manifold nuts	25	18

These torque settings are using special crow's-foot adapters – see Section 2
† Do not re-use

1 General information and system operation

1 The fuel system consists of a rear-mounted fuel tank, a fuel filter with integral water separator and fuel heater (to avoid fuel waxing in cold conditions), and an electronically-controlled high-pressure diesel injection system, together with a turbocharger.

2 The exhaust system is conventional, but to meet the latest emission levels, a catalytic converter and an exhaust gas recirculation system are fitted to all models. On 2.0 litre engines, a diesel particulate filter is also incorporated in the exhaust system.

3 The high-pressure diesel injection system (generally known as a 'common-rail' system) derives its name from the fact that a common-rail (referred to as an accumulator rail), or fuel reservoir, is used to supply fuel to all the fuel injectors. Instead of an in-line or distributor type injection pump, which distributes the fuel directly to each injector, a high-pressure pump is used, which generates a very high fuel pressure (1500 bars at high engine speed) in the accumulator rail. The accumulator rail stores fuel, and maintains a constant fuel pressure with the aid of a pressure control valve. Each injector is supplied with high-pressure fuel from the accumulator rail, and the injectors are individually controlled via signals from the system electronic control unit (powertrain control module, or PCM). The injectors are electromagnetically-operated.

4 In addition to the various sensors used on previous diesel engines with a conventional fuel injection pump, common-rail systems also have a fuel pressure sensor. The fuel pressure sensor allows the PCM to maintain the required fuel pressure, via the pressure control valve.

System operation

5 For the purposes of describing the operation of a common-rail injection system, the components can be divided into three sub-systems; the low-pressure fuel system, the high-pressure fuel system, and the electronic control system.

Low-pressure fuel system

6 The low-pressure fuel system consists of the following components:
a) Fuel tank.
b) Fuel transfer pump.
c) Fuel filter/water trap/heater.
d) Low-pressure fuel lines.

7 The low-pressure system (fuel supply system) is responsible for supplying clean fuel to the high-pressure fuel system.

High-pressure fuel system

8 The high-pressure fuel system consists of the following components:
a) High-pressure fuel pump with pressure control valve.
b) High-pressure fuel accumulator rail.
c) Fuel injectors.
d) High-pressure fuel lines.

9 Fuel is drawn from the fuel tank, through the fuel filter, by means of a fuel transfer pump incorporated into the high-pressure pump. After passing through the transfer pump, the fuel is supplied through internal passages to the high-pressure pump, which forces it into the accumulator rail. As diesel fuel has a certain elasticity, the pressure in the accumulator rail remains constant, even though fuel leaves the rail each time one of the injectors operates. Additionally, a pressure control valve mounted on the high-pressure pump ensures that the fuel pressure is maintained within preset limits.

10 The pressure control valve is operated by the PCM. When the valve is opened, fuel is returned from the high-pressure pump to the tank, via the fuel return lines, and the pressure in the accumulator rail falls. To enable the PCM to trigger the pressure control valve correctly, the pressure in the accumulator rail is measured by a fuel pressure sensor.

11 The electromagnetically-controlled fuel injectors are operated individually, via signals from the PCM, and each injector injects fuel directly into the relevant combustion chamber. The fact that high fuel pressure is always available allows very precise and highly flexible injection in comparison to a conventional injection pump: for example combustion during the main injection process can be improved considerably by the pre-injection of a very small quantity of fuel.

Electronic control system

12 The electronic control system consists of the following components:
a) Powertrain control module (PCM).
b) Crankshaft speed/position sensor.
c) Camshaft position sensor.
d) Accelerator pedal position sensor.
e) Cylinder head temperature sensor (1.8 litre engines).
f) Coolant temperature sensor (2.0 litre engines).
g) Inlet air temperature sensor.
h) Mass airflow sensor.
i) Manifold absolute pressure sensor.
j) Inlet air shut-off throttle (2.0 litre engines).
k) Fuel pressure sensor.
l) ABS wheel speed sensors.
m) Brake and clutch pedal position switches.

13 The information from the various sensors is passed to the PCM, which evaluates the signals. The PCM contains electronic 'maps' which enable it to calculate the optimum quantity of fuel to inject, the appropriate start of injection, and even pre- and post-injection fuel quantities, for each individual engine cylinder under any given condition of engine operation.

14 Additionally, the PCM carries out monitoring and self-diagnostic functions. Any faults in the system are stored in the PCM memory, which enables quick and accurate fault diagnosis using appropriate diagnostic equipment (such as a suitable fault code reader).

System components

High-pressure pump

15 The high-pressure pump is mounted on the engine in the position normally occupied by the conventional distributor fuel injection pump. The pump is driven at half engine speed, and is lubricated by the fuel which it pumps.

16 The fuel transfer pump (integral with the high-pressure pump) forces the fuel into the high-pressure pump chamber, via a safety valve.

17 The high-pressure pump consists of three radially-mounted pistons and cylinders. The pistons are operated by an eccentric cam mounted on the pump drive spindle. As a piston moves down, fuel enters the cylinder through an inlet valve. When the piston reaches bottom dead centre (BDC), the inlet valve closes, and as the piston moves back up the cylinder, the fuel is compressed. When the pressure in the cylinder reaches the pressure in the accumulator rail, an outlet valve opens, and fuel is forced into the accumulator rail. When the piston reaches top dead centre (TDC), the outlet valve closes, due to the pressure drop, and the pumping cycle is repeated. The use of multiple cylinders provides a steady flow of fuel, minimising pulses and pressure fluctuations.

18 As the pump needs to be able to supply sufficient fuel under full-load conditions, it will supply excess fuel during idle and part-load conditions. This excess fuel is returned from the high-pressure circuit to the low-pressure circuit (to the tank) via the pressure control valve.

19 The pump incorporates a facility to effectively switch off one of the cylinders to improve efficiency and reduce fuel consumption when maximum pumping capacity is not required. When this facility is operated, a solenoid-operated needle holds the inlet valve in the relevant cylinder open during the delivery stroke, preventing the fuel from being compressed.

Accumulator rail

20 As its name suggests, the accumulator rail acts as an accumulator, storing fuel and preventing pressure fluctuations. Fuel enters the rail from the high-pressure pump, and each injector has its own connection to the rail. The fuel pressure sensor is mounted in the rail, and the rail also has a connection to the fuel pressure control valve on the pump.

Fuel pressure control valve

21 The pressure control valve is operated by the PCM, and controls the system pressure. The valve is integral with the high-pressure pump and cannot be separated.

22 If the fuel pressure is excessive, the valve opens, and fuel flows back to the tank. If the pressure is too low, the valve closes, enabling the high-pressure pump to increase the pressure.

23 The valve is an electromagnetically-operated ball valve. The ball is forced against its seat, against the fuel pressure, by a powerful spring, and also by the force provided by the electromagnet. The force generated by the electromagnet is directly proportional to the current applied to it by the PCM. The desired pressure can therefore be set by varying the current applied to the electromagnet. Any pressure fluctuations are damped by the spring.

Fuel metering valve

24 To improve engine efficiency, the fuel metering valve adjusts the quantity of fuel to the high-pressure pump elements as a function of engine operating conditions.

25 The fuel metering valve is controlled by the PCM using pulse-width modulation.

26 The fuel metering valve is closed when de-energised.

Fuel pressure sensor

27 The fuel pressure sensor is mounted in the accumulator rail, and provides very precise information on the fuel pressure to the PCM.

Fuel injectors

28 The injectors are mounted on the engine in a similar manner to conventional diesel fuel injectors. The injectors are electromagnetically-operated via signals from the PCM, and fuel is injected at the pressure existing in the accumulator rail. The injectors are high-precision instruments and are manufactured to very high tolerances.

29 Fuel flows into the injector from the accumulator rail, via an inlet valve and an inlet throttle, and an electromagnet causes the injector nozzle to lift from its seat, allowing injection. Excess fuel is returned from the injectors to the tank via a return line. The injector operates on a hydraulic servo principle: the forces resulting inside the injector due to the fuel pressure effectively amplify the effects of the electromagnet, which does not provide sufficient force to open the injector nozzle directly. The injector functions as follows. Five separate forces are essential to the operation of the injector:

a) *A nozzle spring forces the nozzle needle against the nozzle seat at the bottom of the injector, preventing fuel from entering the combustion chamber.*

b) *In the valve at the top of the injector, the valve spring forces the valve ball against the opening to the valve control chamber. The fuel in the chamber is unable to escape through the fuel return.*

c) *When triggered, the electromagnet exerts a force which overcomes the valve spring force, and moves the valve ball away from its seat. This is the triggering force for the start of injection. When the valve ball moves off its seat, fuel enters the valve control chamber.*

d) *The pressure of the fuel in the valve control chamber exerts a force on the valve control plunger, which is added to the nozzle spring force.*

e) *A slight chamfer towards the lower end of the nozzle needle causes the fuel in the control chamber to exert a force on the nozzle needle.*

30 When these forces are in equilibrium, the injector is in its rest (idle) state, but when a voltage is applied to the electromagnet, the forces work to lift the nozzle needle, injecting

fuel into the combustion chamber. There are four phases of injector operation as follows:

a) *Rest (idle) state – all forces are in equilibrium. The nozzle needle closes off the nozzle opening, and the valve spring forces the valve ball against its seat.*

b) *Opening – the electromagnet is triggered which opens the nozzle and triggers the injection process. The force from the electromagnet allows the valve ball to leave its seat. The fuel from the valve control chamber flows back to the tank via the fuel return line. When the valve opens, the pressure in the valve control chamber drops, and the force on the valve plunger is reduced. However, due to the effect of the input throttle, the pressure on the nozzle needle remains unchanged. The resulting force in the valve control chamber is sufficient to lift the nozzle from its seat, and the injection process begins.*

c) *Injection – within a few milliseconds, the triggering current in the electromagnet is reduced to a lower holding current. The nozzle is now fully open, and fuel is injected into the combustion chamber at the pressure present in the accumulator rail.*

d) *Closing – the electromagnet is switched off, at which point the valve spring forces the valve ball firmly against its seat, and in the valve control chamber, the pressure is the same as that at the nozzle needle. The force at the valve plunger increases, and the nozzle needle closes the nozzle opening. The forces are now in equilibrium once more, and the injector is once more in the idle state, awaiting the next injection sequence.*

PCM and sensors

31 The PCM and sensors are described earlier in this Section – see Electronic control system.

Inlet air shut-off throttle housing

32 The inlet air shut-off throttle housing controls the volume of air drawn into the engine according to driving conditions, and thus influences the composition of the recirculated exhaust gases. It is activated by the PCM. In addition, the unit ensures that the engine does not run-on after switching off the ignition.

2.4 Typical plastic plug and cap set for sealing disconnected fuel pipes and components

2 High-pressure diesel injection system – special information

Warnings and precautions

1 It is essential to observe strict precautions when working on the fuel system components, particularly the high-pressure side of the system. Before carrying out any operations on the fuel system, refer to the precautions given in *Safety First!* at the beginning of this manual, and to the following additional information.

• Do not carry out any repair work on the high-pressure fuel system unless you are competent to do so, have all the necessary tools and equipment required, and are aware of the safety implications involved.

• Before starting any repair work on the fuel system, wait at least 30 seconds after switching off the engine to allow the fuel circuit pressure to reduce.

• Never work on the high-pressure fuel system with the engine running.

• Keep well clear of any possible source of fuel leakage, particularly when starting the engine after carrying out repair work. A leak in the system could cause an extremely high pressure jet of fuel to escape, which could result in severe personal injury.

• Never place your hands or any part of your body near to a leak in the high-pressure fuel system.

• Do not use steam-cleaning equipment or compressed air to clean the engine or any of the fuel system components.

Procedures and information

2 Strict cleanliness must be observed at all times when working on any part of the fuel system. This applies to the working area in general, the person doing the work, and the components being worked on.

3 Before working on the fuel system components, they must be thoroughly cleaned with a suitable degreasing fluid. Specific cleaning products may be obtained from dealers. Alternatively, a suitable brake cleaning fluid may be used. Cleanliness is particularly important when working on the fuel system connections at the following components:

a) *Fuel filter.*

b) *High-pressure fuel pump.*

c) *Accumulator rail.*

d) *Fuel injectors.*

e) *High-pressure fuel pipes.*

4 After disconnecting any fuel pipes or components, the open union or orifice must be immediately sealed to prevent the entry of dirt or foreign material. Plastic plugs and caps in various sizes are available in packs from motor factors and accessory outlets, and are particularly suitable for this application **(see illustration)**. Fingers cut from disposable rubber gloves should be used to protect components such as fuel pipes, fuel injectors and wiring connectors, and can be secured in place using elastic bands. Suitable gloves of this type are available at no cost from most filling station forecourts.

5 Whenever any of the high-pressure fuel pipes are disconnected or removed, new pipes must be obtained for refitting.

6 On the completion of any repair on the high-pressure fuel system, the use of a leak-detecting compound is recommended. This is a powder which is applied to the fuel pipe unions and connections, which is white when dry. Any leak in the system will cause the product to darken, indicating the source of the leak.

7 The torque wrench settings given in the Specifications must be strictly observed when tightening component mountings and connections. This is particularly important when tightening the high-pressure fuel pipe unions. To use a torque wrench on the fuel pipe unions, two crow's-foot adapters are required – these are available from motor factors and accessory outlets **(see illustration)**.

3 Fuel injection system – checking

Note: *Refer to the warnings and precautions in Section 2 before proceeding.*

1 If a fault appears in the fuel injection system, first ensure that all the system wiring connectors are securely connected and free of corrosion – also refer to paragraphs 5 to 8 below. Then ensure that the fault is not due to poor maintenance; ie, check that the air cleaner filter element is clean, the cylinder compression pressures are correct, the wiring is in good condition and securely connected, and the engine breather hoses are clear and undamaged, referring to Chapter 1B, and Chapter 2B and Chapter 2C.

2 If these checks fail to reveal the cause of the problem, the car should be taken to a suitably-equipped Ford dealer or diagnostic specialist for testing. A diagnostic connector is fitted under the facia on the driver's side into which dedicated electronic test equipment can be plugged **(see illustration)**. The test equipment is capable of 'interrogating' the

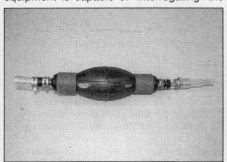

4.3 Typical hand-priming pump

engine management system powertrain control module (PCM) electronically and accessing its internal fault log (reading fault codes).

3 Fault codes can only be extracted from the PCM using a dedicated fault code reader. A Ford dealer will obviously have such a reader, but they are also available from other suppliers. It is unlikely to be cost-effective for the private owner to purchase a fault code reader, but a well-equipped local garage or auto-electrical specialist will have one.

4 Using this equipment, faults can be pinpointed quickly and simply, even if their occurrence is intermittent. Testing all the system components individually in an attempt to locate the fault by elimination is a time-consuming operation that is unlikely to be fruitful (particularly if the fault occurs dynamically), and carries a high risk of damage to the PCM's internal components.

Limited Operation Strategy

5 Certain faults, such as failure of one of the engine management system sensors, will cause the system will revert to a backup (or 'limp-home') mode, referred to by Ford as 'Limited Operation Strategy' (LOS). This is intended to be a 'get-you-home' facility only – the engine management warning light will come on when this mode is in operation.

6 In this mode, the signal from the defective sensor is substituted with a fixed value (it would normally vary), which may lead to loss of power, poor idling, and generally-poor running, especially when the engine is cold.

7 However, the engine may in fact run quite

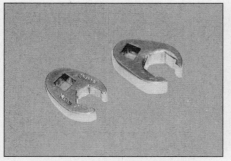

2.7 Two crow's-foot adapters will be necessary for tightening the fuel pipe unions

4.7 Disconnect the fuel return pipe at the quick-release connection on the filter (arrowed)

well in this situation, and the only clue (other than the warning light) would be that the exhaust CO emissions (for example) will be higher than they should be.

8 Bear in mind that, even if the defective sensor is correctly identified and renewed, the engine will not return to normal running until the fault code is erased, taking the system out of LOS. This also applies even if the cause of the fault was a loose connection or damaged piece of wire – until the fault code is erased, the system will continue in LOS.

4 Diesel fuel system – priming and bleeding

Note: *Refer to the warnings and precautions in Section 2 before proceeding.*

1 After disconnecting any part of the fuel system or running out of fuel, it is necessary to prime the fuel system and bleed off any air which may have entered the system components.

2 In some circumstances, the system will self-bleed by operating the starter for a maximum of 10 seconds. If the engine does not start within this time, wait 30 seconds and repeat the procedure. If, after two or three attempts, the engine still will not start, proceed as follows.

3 It will be necessary to obtain the special Ford priming hose (kit No 310-110A) or a suitable alternative hand-priming pump, together with various adapters to enable the pump to be connected to the fuel lines. Hand-priming pump and adapter kits are readily available from motor factors and tool supply outlets at moderate cost **(see illustration)**.

1.8 litre engines

4 Remove the plastic cover on the top of the engine.

5 If fitted, undo the bolts and remove the metal shield over the top of the fuel filter.

6 Disconnect the wiring plug from the top of the filter housing.

7 Disconnect the fuel return pipe at the quick-release connection on the filter **(see illustration)**.

3.2 Diagnostic connector (arrowed)

4.10a Disconnect the fuel return pipe at the quick-release connection (arrowed) on engines to emission level Stage III/IV...

4.10b... and on engines to emission level Stage V

4.11 Using the adapters supplied, connect the pump between the fuel return pipe and the filter

8 Using the adapters supplied with the hand priming pump, connect the pump between the fuel return pipe and the filter. Ensure that the arrow on the pump is pointing away from the filter.

2.0 litre engines

9 Remove the plastic cover on the top of the engine.
10 Disconnect the fuel return pipe at the quick-release connection at the right-hand side of the engine (see illustrations). Note that the fuel return pipe is the smaller diameter of the two adjacent pipes.
11 Using the adapters supplied with the hand priming pump, connect the pump into the fuel return pipe (see illustration). Ensure that the arrow on the pump is pointing towards the fuel tank.

All engines

12 Squeeze and release the pump to draw fuel from the tank, through the filter, through the high-pressure fuel pump and back to the tank via the fuel return line. Continue to squeeze and release the pump until fuel without air bubbles can be seen flowing through the clear plastic adapter on the pump. Note that it may take some time before the fuel flow is completely free of air bubbles.
13 When no more air bubbles can be seen, operate the starter for a maximum of 10 sec- onds, waiting 30 seconds between each attempt. If the engine does not start after two attempts, continue operating the priming pump as there may still be air in the system.
14 Once the engine starts and runs satisfactorily, switch it off, disconnect the priming pump and reconnect the fuel return pipe.

15 On 1.8 litre engines, reconnect the filter wiring connector, refit the metal shield over the filter (where applicable).
16 On all engines, refit the plastic engine cover.

5 Air cleaner assembly – removal and refitting

Removal

1 Remove the plastic cover from the top of the engine by pulling it upwards from its mountings.
2 Pull out the locking tab and disconnect the wiring connector from the mass airflow sensor (see illustrations).
3 Loosen the clip and disconnect the air outlet duct from the air cleaner cover (see illustration).
4 Reach down and detach the air inlet duct from the front of the air cleaner housing.
5 Pull the air cleaner upwards from its rubber mountings(see illustration).

Refitting

6 When refitting, locate the pegs on the base of the air cleaner housing into the mounting grommets and push the housing firmly downwards.

6 Accelerator pedal – removal and refitting

1 Refer to Chapter 4A Section 6.

7 Fuel tank – removal, inspection and refitting

Note: Refer to the warnings and precautions in Section 2 before proceeding.
1 Refer to Chapter 4A Section 7. Fuel tank removal and refitting is the same as for petrol models, with the exception that an evaporative emissions charcoal canister is not fitted to diesel models. Note also that on 2.0 litre diesel engine models, it will be necessary to disconnect the two fuel lines at the quick-release connectors on the fuel filter.

5.2a Pull out the locking tab...

5.2b... and disconnect the wiring connector from the mass airflow sensor

5.3 Loosen the clip and disconnect the air outlet duct from the air cleaner cover

5.5 Pull the air cleaner upwards from its rubber mountings

8 Fuel gauge sender unit – removal and refitting

Note: *Refer to the warnings and precautions in Section 2 before proceeding.*

1 On diesel engine models, the fuel gauge sender unit is located in the same in-tank module as used for the fuel pump on petrol models. The only difference is that there is no fuel pump, just the sender unit.

2 Refer to Chapter 4A. but note that there are two fuel pipe quick-release connection on the sender unit.

9 High-pressure fuel pump – removal and refitting

⚠️ **Warning: Refer to the information contained in Section 2 before proceeding.**

1.8 litre engines

Note: *A new fuel pump-to-accumulator rail high- pressure fuel pipe will be required for refitting.*

Removal

1 Disconnect the battery negative lead as described in Chapter 5A Section 4.

2 Remove the timing belt as described in Chapter 2B Section 7.

3 Slacken the three bolts securing the fuel pump timing belt sprocket, and remove the sprocket from the pump. The sprocket may need to be prevented from turning as this is done – it should prove sufficient to select a gear and apply the handbrake, but Ford technicians use a special holding tool (205-072) which locates in the holes of the sprocket and prevents it from turning. If this tool is not available, a home-made tool can easily be fabricated (see **Tool Tip**). The sprocket is sealed to the inner sprocket using RTV sealant, and may need to be prised free; recover the metal gasket.

4 Remove the seven nuts which secure the fuel pump oil seal housing, and withdraw the seal housing from around the pump

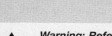

To make a sprocket holding tool, obtain two lengths of steel strip about 6 mm thick by 30 mm wide or similar, one 600 mm long, the other 200 mm long (all dimensions are approximate). Bolt the two strips together to form a forked end, leaving the bolt slack so that the shorter strip can pivot freely. Drill holes and insert bolts of a suitable size in the ends of the fork to engage in the sprocket spokes. Hold the bolts at the ends firmly in place by using a nut on the other side of the steel strip.

inner sprocket (**see illustration**). Withdraw the timing belt backplate from the oil pump housing studs, noting which way round it fits.

5 Ensure the area around fuel pipe connections on the pump and accumulator rail are absolutely clean, place rags over the top of the alternator to protect it from fuel spillage. Slacken the unions, clean the pipes once the unions nuts have been moved along the pipe, then remove the pump-to-accumulator rail high-pressure fuel pipe (**see illustration**). Plug or cap the openings to prevent dirt ingress.

6 Note their fitted positions, then disconnect all wiring plugs from the pump.

7 Undo the four bolts securing the support bracket to the rear of the pump.

8 Depress the locking tabs and disconnect the fuel return pipe from the pump(**see illustration**). Plug or cap the opening to prevent dirt ingress.

9 Prise out the locking catch, then using a small screwdriver, prise out the clip and

9.4 Remove the oil seal housing retaining nuts

disconnect the fuel supply pipe from the pump. Plug or cap the opening to prevent dirt ingress.

10 Unscrew and remove the four bolts securing the drive chain sprocket to the injection pump. As with removal of its timing belt sprocket, it may be necessary to prevent the sprocket from turning as the bolts are loosened.

11 Undo the three bolts securing the pump to the engine casing. It may not be possible to remove the bolts completely. The sprocket and chain remain in place on the engine.

12 Manoeuvre the pump from the engine.

Refitting

13 With a new gasket and seal, refit the pump to the front engine casing, and tighten the bolts to the specified torque.

14 Refit the four chain sprocket bolts and tighten them to the specified torque.

15 Remove the blanking plugs/cap (if not already done so), and reconnect the fuel return and supply pipes to the pump.

16 Reconnect the wiring plugs to the pump.

17 Remove the blanking plugs/caps and fit the new pump-to-accumulator rail rigid metal fuel pipe. Only finger-tighten the unions at this stage.

18 Refit the pump rear support bracket, and tighten the bolts securely.

19 Using a crow's-foot adapter, tighten the rigid metal pipe unions to the specified torque, starting at the accumulator rail first. Ensure the spanner acts upon the part of the union where there is the most metal, to avoid damage to the union (**see illustration**).

9.5 Pump-to-accumulator rail high-pressure fuel pipe unions (arrowed)

9.8 Depress the locking tabs and disconnect the fuel return pipe (arrowed) from the pump

9.19 Place the spanner on the thickest section of the union nut (arrowed)

9.27a Release the clamp (arrowed) and disconnect the EGR pipe from the manifold...

9.27b... then undo the bolt (arrowed) securing the pipe support bracket to the vacuum pump

9.29 Undo the unions and remove the high-pressure fuel pipe (arrowed) between the pump and the accumulator rail

20 Fit a new metal gasket to the pump drive chain sprocket. Apply a coating of Loctite RTV 5910 sealant to the sprocket (avoiding the three sprocket bolt holes). The three bolts should be cleaned, then lightly coated with Loctite 518 locking fluid. Offer up the timing belt sprocket, aligning the bolt holes carefully, then fit the three bolts and tighten to the specified torque.

21 Refit the timing belt as described in Chapter 2B Section 7.

22 With everything reassembled and reconnected, prime the fuel system as described in Section 4. Observing the precautions listed in Section 2, start the engine and allow it to idle. Check for leaks at the high-pressure fuel pipe unions with the engine idling. If satisfactory, increase the

engine speed to 4000 rpm and check again for leaks.

23 Take the car for a short road test, and check for leaks once again on return. If any leaks are detected, obtain and fit another new high-pressure fuel pipe. Do not attempt to cure even the slightest leak by further tightening of the pipe unions.

2.0 litre engines to emission level Stage III/IV

Note: A new fuel pump-to-accumulator rail high-pressure fuel pipe will be required for refitting.

Removal

24 Disconnect the battery negative lead as described in Chapter 5A Section 4.

25 Remove the plastic cover from the top of the engine.

26 Remove the air cleaner assembly as described in Section 5.

27 Release the clamp and disconnect the EGR pipe from the inlet manifold. Undo the bolt securing the EGR pipe support bracket to the vacuum pump, then undo the bolts and disconnect the other end of the pipe from the EGR cooler (see illustrations). Remove the pipe from the engine.

28 At the rear of the engine, undo the bolt securing the air outlet duct to the support bracket and the two bolts securing the duct and resonator to the turbocharger. Release the vacuum hose from the clips on the duct and remove the duct and resonator from the engine.

29 Ensure the area around fuel pipe connections on the pump and accumulator rail are absolutely clean. Undo the unions and remove the high-pressure fuel pipe between the pump and the accumulator rail (see illustration). Discard the pipe, a new one must be fitted.

30 Note their fitted positions, depress the release tabs, and disconnect the fuel supply and return pipes from the pump (see illustrations). Be prepared for fuel spillage. Plug the openings to prevent contamination.

31 Note their fitted positions, and disconnect the wiring plugs from the pump.

32 Undo the three retaining bolts and pull the pump from the cylinder head (see illustration). Discard the gasket.

Refitting

33 Ensure that the mating surfaces of the pump and cylinder head are clean and dry, and fit the new gasket.

34 Ensure the slot in the end of the camshaft and the pump drive dog are aligned, then refit the pump, tightening the mounting bolts to the specified torque (see illustration).

35 Reconnect the fuel supply and return pipes to the pump, and the wiring plugs.

36 Fit the new high-pressure fuel pipe between the pump and accumulator rail, then tighten to the specified torque, using a crow's-foot adapter.

37 The remainder of refitting is a reversal of removal.

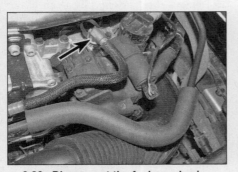

9.30a Disconnect the fuel supply pipe (arrowed)...

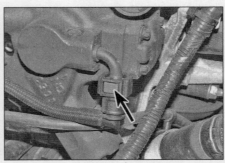

9.30b... and return pipe (arrowed) from the pump

9.32 Undo the three retaining bolts (arrowed) and remove the pump

9.34 Ensure the pump drive dog (arrowed) is aligned with the slot in the end of the camshaft

9.42 Undo the bolt (arrowed) securing the crankcase ventilation pipe to the inlet manifold/cylinder head cover

9.43a Disconnect the lower quick-release fitting...

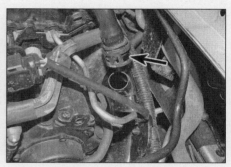

9.43b... and upper quick-release fitting...

9.43c... and remove the crankcase ventilation pipe

9.44a Undo the two bolts (arrowed)...

9.44b... and remove the plastic cover from the engine

38 With everything reassembled and re-connected, prime the fuel system as described in Section 4. Observing the precautions listed in Section 2, start the engine and allow it to idle. Check for leaks at the high-pressure fuel pipe unions with the engine idling. If satisfactory, increase the engine speed to 4000 rpm and check again for leaks.

39 Take the car for a short road test, and check for leaks once again on return. If any leaks are detected, obtain and fit another new high-pressure fuel pipe. Do not attempt to cure even the slightest leak by further tightening of the pipe unions.

2.0 litre engines to emission level Stage V

Note: *A new fuel pump-to-accumulator rail high-pressure fuel pipe will be required for refitting.*

Removal

40 Disconnect the battery negative lead as described in Chapter 5A Section 4.

41 Remove the plastic cover from the top of the engine.

42 Undo the bolt securing the crankcase ventilation pipe to the top of the inlet manifold/cylinder head cover **(see illustration)**.

43 Disconnect the quick-release fittings at each end of the pipe and remove the pipe from the engine **(see illustrations)**.

44 Undo the two bolts securing the plastic cover to the top of the inlet manifold. Lift the cover up at the front, disengage the locating tags at the rear and remove the cover **(see illustrations)**.

45 Ensure the area around fuel pipe connections on the pump and accumulator rail are absolutely clean, then unscrew the fuel pipe unions **(see illustrations)**. Remove and discard the pipe, a new one must be fitted.

46 Plug the openings in the accumulator rail and fuel pump to prevent dirt ingress.

47 Loosen the clips and disconnect the air outlet duct connecting the air cleaner cover to the rigid duct at the rear of the engine.

48 Note their fitted positions, depress the release tabs, and disconnect the fuel supply and return pipes from the pump **(see illustration)**. Be prepared for fuel spillage. Plug the openings to prevent contamination.

49 Thoroughly clean the fuel injector return hose connection at the rear of the fuel pump.

9.45a Unscrew the fuel pipe union (arrowed) at the accumulator rail...

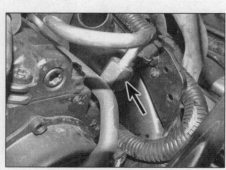

9.45b... and at the fuel pump (arrowed)

9.48 Disconnect the fuel supply and return pipes from the pump

9.49 Pull out the locking tab and disconnect the injector return hose connector from the pump

9.50 Disconnect the wiring plugs from the pump

9.51 Undo the three retaining bolts and remove the pump from the cylinder head

Pull out the locking tab and disconnect the return hose connector from the pump **(see illustration)**.

50 Note their fitted positions, and disconnect the two wiring plugs from the pump **(see illustration)**.

51 Undo the three retaining bolts and pull the pump from the cylinder head **(see illustration)**. Discard the gasket.

Refitting

52 Ensure that the mating surfaces of the pump and cylinder head are clean and dry, and fit the new gasket.

53 Ensure the slot in the end of the camshaft and the pump drive dog are aligned, then refit the pump, tightening the mounting bolts to the specified torque.

54 Reconnect the fuel supply and return pipes to the pump, and the wiring plugs.

55 Fit the new high-pressure fuel pipe between the pump and accumulator rail, then tighten to the specified torque, using a crow's-foot adapter.

56 The remainder of refitting is a reversal of removal.

57 With everything reassembled and reconnected, prime the fuel system as described in Section 4. Observing the precautions listed in Section 2, start the engine and allow it to idle. Check for leaks at the high-pressure fuel pipe unions with the engine idling. If satisfactory, increase the engine speed to 4000 rpm and check again for leaks.

58 Take the car for a short road test, and

check for leaks once again on return. If any leaks are detected, obtain and fit another new high-pressure fuel pipe. Do not attempt to cure even the slightest leak by further tightening of the pipe unions.

10 Accumulator rail – removal and refitting

> ⚠️ **Warning: Refer to the information contained in Section 2 before proceeding.**

1.8 litre engines

Note: *A complete new set of high-pressure fuel pipes will be required for refitting.*

Removal

1 Disconnect the battery negative lead as described in Chapter 5A Section 4.

2 Remove the plastic cover on the top of the engine.

3 Undo the four bolts securing the support bracket to the rear of the high-pressure fuel pump.

4 Clean the area around the high-pressure fuel pipes to and from the accumulator rail, then unscrew the fuel pump-to-accumulator rail pipe unions. Remove the pipe.

5 Repeat the procedure on the accumulator rail-to-injector fuel pipes. Use a second spanner to counter-hold the unions screwed into the injectors – these unions must not be

allowed to move. Note their fitted locations and remove the pipes.

6 Plug the openings in the accumulator rail and fuel pump to prevent dirt ingress.

7 Disconnect the fuel pressure sensor wiring plug from the accumulator rail **(see illustration)**.

8 Unscrew the two accumulator rail mounting bolts, and manoeuvre it out **(see illustration)**. **Note:** *The fuel pressure sensor on the accumulator rail must not be removed.*

Refitting

9 Locate the accumulator rail in position, refit and finger-tighten the mounting bolts.

10 Reconnect the fuel pressure sensor wiring plug.

11 Fit the new fuel pump-to-accumulator rail high-pressure fuel pipe, and only finger-tighten the pipe unions at this stage.

12 Fit the new set of accumulator rail-to-injector high-pressure fuel pipes, and finger-tighten the pipe unions.

13 Tighten the accumulator rail mounting bolts to the specified torque.

14 Using a crow's-foot adapter, tighten all the high-pressure pipe unions to the specified torque. Use a second spanner to counter-hold the injector unions.

15 Refit the support bracket to the rear of the high-pressure fuel pump and tighten the retaining bolts to the specified torque.

16 With everything reassembled and reconnected, prime the fuel system as described in Section 4. Observing the precautions listed in Section 2, start the engine and allow it to idle. Check for leaks at the high-pressure fuel pipe unions with the engine idling. If satisfactory, increase the engine speed to 4000 rpm and check again for leaks.

17 Take the car for a short road test, and check for leaks once again on return. If any leaks are detected, obtain and fit another new high-pressure fuel pipe. Do not attempt to cure even the slightest leak by further tightening of the pipe unions.

2.0 litre engines to emission level Stage III/IV

Note: *A complete new set of high-pressure fuel pipes will be required for refitting.*

10.7 Disconnect the fuel pressure sensor wiring plug (arrowed) from the accumulator rail

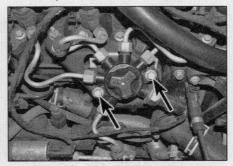

10.8 Accumulator rail mounting bolts (arrowed)

Removal

18 Remove the cylinder head cover as described in Chapter 2C Section 3.

19 Remove the rubber covers from the high-pressure fuel pipe unions at the fuel injectors.

20 Clean the area around the high-pressure fuel pipes to and from the accumulator rail, then unscrew the fuel pump-to-accumulator rail pipe unions. Unscrew the bolt securing the pipe to the support bracket and remove the pipe.

21 Repeat the procedure on the accumulator rail-to-injector fuel pipes. Use a second spanner to counter-hold the unions screwed into the injectors – these unions must not be allowed to move **(see illustration)**. Note their fitted locations and remove the pipes.

22 Plug the openings in the accumulator rail and fuel pump to prevent dirt ingress.

23 Disconnect the fuel pressure sensor wiring plug from the accumulator rail **(see illustration)**.

24 Unscrew the two accumulator rail retaining nuts, and manoeuvre it out. **Note:** *The fuel pressure sensor on the accumulator rail must not be removed.*

Refitting

25 Locate the accumulator rail in position, refit and finger-tighten the two retaining nuts.

26 Reconnect the fuel pressure sensor wiring plug.

27 Fit the new fuel pump-to-accumulator rail high-pressure fuel pipe, and only finger-tighten the pipe unions at this stage.

28 Fit the new set of accumulator rail-to-injector high-pressure fuel pipes, and finger-tighten the pipe unions.

29 Tighten the accumulator rail retaining nuts to the specified torque.

30 Using a crow's-foot adapter, tighten all the high-pressure pipe unions to the specified torque. Use a second spanner to counter-hold the injector unions.

31 Refit and tighten the bolt securing the fuel pump-to-accumulator rail fuel pipe to the support bracket.

32 Refit the rubber covers to the fuel pipe unions at the fuel injectors.

33 Refit the cylinder head cover as described in Chapter 2C Section 3.

34 With everything reassembled and

10.21 Use a second spanner to counter-hold the injector port when slackening the union nut

reconnected, prime the fuel system as described in Section 4. Observing the precautions listed in Section 2, start the engine and allow it to idle. Check for leaks at the high-pressure fuel pipe unions with the engine idling. If satisfactory, increase the engine speed to 4000 rpm and check again for leaks.

35 Take the car for a short road test, and check for leaks once again on return. If any leaks are detected, obtain and fit another new high-pressure fuel pipe. Do not attempt to cure even the slightest leak by further tightening of the pipe unions.

2.0 litre engines to emission level Stage V

Note: *A complete new set of high-pressure fuel pipes will be required for refitting.*

Removal

36 Disconnect the battery negative lead as described in Chapter 5A Section 4.

37 Remove the plastic cover from the top of the engine.

38 Undo the bolt securing the crankcase ventilation pipe to the top of the inlet manifold/cylinder head cover **(see illustration 9.42)**.

39 Disconnect the quick-release fittings at each end of the pipe and remove the pipe from the engine **(see illustrations 9.43a, 9.43b and 9.43c)**.

40 Undo the two bolts securing the plastic cover to the top of the inlet manifold. Lift the cover up at the front, disengage the locating tags at the rear and remove the cover **(see illustrations 9.44a and 9.44b)**.

10.23 The fuel pressure sensor (arrowed) is located on the underside of the accumulator rail

41 Clean the area around the high-pressure fuel pipes to and from the accumulator rail, then unscrew the fuel pump-to-accumulator rail pipe unions **(see illustrations 9.45a and 9.45b)**. Remove the pipe.

42 Repeat the procedure on the accumulator rail-to-injector fuel pipes **(see illustration)**. Note their fitted locations and remove the pipes.

43 Plug the openings in the accumulator rail and fuel pump to prevent dirt ingress.

44 Disconnect the fuel pressure sensor wiring plug from the accumulator rail **(see illustration)**.

45 Unscrew the three accumulator rail retaining bolts, and manoeuvre it out **(see illustration)**. **Note:** *The fuel pressure sensor on the accumulator rail must not be removed.*

Refitting

46 Locate the accumulator rail in position, refit and finger-tighten the three retaining bolts.

47 Reconnect the fuel pressure sensor wiring plug.

48 Fit the new fuel pump-to-accumulator rail high-pressure fuel pipe, and only finger-tighten the pipe unions at this stage.

49 Fit the new set of accumulator rail-to-injector high-pressure fuel pipes, and finger-tighten the pipe unions.

50 Tighten the accumulator rail retaining bolts to the specified torque.

51 Using a crow's-foot adapter, tighten all the high-pressure pipe unions to the specified torque.

10.42 Unscrew the accumulator rail-to-injector fuel pipe unions

10.44 Disconnect the fuel pressure sensor wiring plug from the accumulator rail

10.45 Accumulator rail retaining bolts (arrowed)

11.3 Disconnect the breather hoses (arrowed) from the cylinder head cover

11.5a Disconnect the fuel temperature sensor wiring plug (arrowed)

11.5b Depress the clip (arrowed) and disconnect the injector wiring plugs

52 The remainder of refitting is a reversal of removal.

53 With everything reassembled and reconnected, prime the fuel system as described in Section 4. Observing the precautions listed in Section 2, start the engine and allow it to idle. Check for leaks at the high-pressure fuel pipe unions with the engine idling. If satisfactory, increase the engine speed to 4000 rpm and check again for leaks.

54 Take the car for a short road test, and check for leaks once again on return. If any leaks are detected, obtain and fit another new high-pressure fuel pipe. Do not attempt to cure even the slightest leak by further tightening of the pipe unions.

11 Fuel injectors – removal and refitting

> ⚠ **Warning: Refer to the information contained in Section 2 before proceeding.**

Note: *The following procedure describes the removal and refitting of the injectors as a complete set. However, each injector may be removed individually if required. New copper washers, upper seals, injector clamp retaining nuts/bolts and a high-pressure fuel pipe will be required for each disturbed injector when refitting.*

1.8 litre engines

Removal

1 Disconnect the battery negative lead as described in Chapter 5A Section 4.

2 Remove the plastic cover on the top of the engine.

3 Release the clamps and disconnect the breather hoses from the cylinder head cover **(see illustration)**.

4 Disconnect the wiring plugs from the high-pressure fuel pump and the accumulator rail.

5 Disconnect the wiring plug from the fuel temperature sensor, then disconnect the wiring plug from each injector**(see illustrations)**. Move the wiring harness to one side.

6 Ensure the areas around the injection pipes and unions is absolutely clean.

7 Slacken and unscrew the pipe unions at the injectors and the accumulator rail, but keep the metal pipes in contact with the injectors and accumulator rail until the unions have been moved along the pipe and the areas at the ends of the pipes cleaned. Use a second spanner to counter-hold the unions at the injectors. Be prepared for fuel spillage.

8 With any dirt/debris removed, detach the pipes from the injectors and accumulator rail, then plug the openings to prevent dirt ingress. Discard the pipes, new ones must be fitted.

9 Carefully prise down the lower edge of the retaining clips, then disconnect the fuel return hoses from the injectors. Take care not to drop the retaining clips as they are removed, and check the condition of the O-ring seals – renew if necessary.

10 Slacken the injector clamps retaining bolts, and pull the injectors from place **(see**

illustrations)**. Discard the clamp bolts – new ones must be fitted. If the original injectors are to be refitted, it is absolutely essential that they are refitted in to their original positions.

11 Discard the injectors sealing washers – new ones must be fitted.

Refitting

12 If new injectors are being fitted, take of note of the identification numbers **(see illustration)**. These need to be downloaded into the PCM on completion of the work.

13 Fit a new sealing washer onto each injector **(see illustration)**.

14 Fit the injectors and clamps into the cylinder head, then tighten the new clamp bolts finger-tight only at this stage.

15 Working on one fuel injector at a time, remove the blanking plugs from the fuel pipe unions on the accumulator rail and the

11.10a Slacken the injector clamp bolts...

11.10b... and pull the injectors from place

11.12 Take note of the identification numbers of the new injectors, these need to be downloaded into the PCM

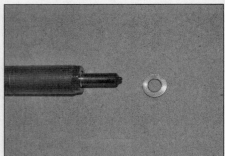

11.13 Fit a new sealing washer onto each injector

11.17 Tighten the high-pressure pipe union nuts using a 'crow's-foot' adapter

11.25a Prise down the lower edge of the retaining clip (shown with the return hose disconnected for clarity)...

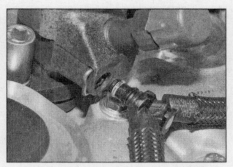

11.25b... then pull the return hoses from the injectors

relevant injector. Locate a new high-pressure fuel pipe over the unions and screw on the union nuts. Take care not to cross-thread the nuts or strain the fuel pipes as they are fitted. Once the union nut threads have started, finger-tighten the nuts only at this stage to the ends of the threads.

16 When all the fuel pipes are in place, tighten the injector clamp retaining bolts to the specified torque and through the specified angle.

17 Using an open-ended spanner, hold each fuel pipe union in turn and tighten the union nut to the specified torque using a torque wrench and crow's-foot adapter **(see illustration)**. Tighten all the disturbed union nuts in the same way.

18 If new injectors have been fitted, their classification numbers must be programmed into the engine management PCM using dedicated diagnostic equipment. If this equipment is not available, entrust this task to a Ford dealer or suitably-equipped repairer. Note that it should be possible to drive the vehicle, albeit with reduced performance/ increased emissions, to a repairer for the numbers to be programmed.

19 The remainder of refitting is a reversal of removal.

20 With everything reassembled and reconnected, prime the fuel system as described in Section 4. Observing the precautions listed in Section 2, start the engine and allow it to idle. Check for leaks at the high-pressure fuel pipe unions with

the engine idling. If satisfactory, increase the engine speed to 4000 rpm and check again for leaks.

21 Take the car for a short road test, and check for leaks once again on return. If any leaks are detected, obtain and fit another new high-pressure fuel pipe. Do not attempt to cure even the slightest leak by further tightening of the pipe unions.

2.0 litre engines to emission level Stage III/IV

Removal

22 Remove the cylinder head cover as described in Chapter 2C Section 3.

23 Remove the rubber covers from the high-pressure fuel pipe unions at the fuel injectors.

24 Make sure the areas around the high-pressure fuel pipe unions from the accumulator rail to the injectors is scrupulously clean and free from debris, etc. If possible, use a vacuum cleaner and a degreaser to clean the area.

25 Carefully prise down the lower edge of the retaining clips, then disconnect the fuel return hoses from the injectors **(see illustrations)**. Take care not to drop the retaining clips as they are removed, and check the condition of the O-ring seals – renew if necessary.

26 Undo the unions, then remove the high-pressure fuel pipes from the fuel rail to the injectors. Use a second spanner to counter-hold the unions screwed into the injectors – these unions must not be allowed

to move **(see illustration 10.21)**. Discard the fuel pipes, new ones must be fitted.

27 Plug the openings in the accumulator rail and fuel injectors to prevent dirt ingress.

28 Unscrew the two nuts securing each injector clamp, and carefully remove the injectors. If the original injectors are to be refitted, it is absolutely essential that they are refitted in to their original positions. Slide the copper sealing washer and upper seal from each injector. Discard the sealing washers – new ones must be fitted **(see illustration)**.

Refitting

29 If new injectors are being fitted, take of note of the identification numbers. These need to be downloaded into the PCM on completion of the work.

30 Locate a new upper seal on the body of each injector, and place a new copper washer on the injector nozzle **(see illustration)**.

31 Place the injector clamp in the slot on each injector body and refit the injectors to the cylinder head. Guide the clamp over the mounting stud and onto the locating dowel as each injector is inserted. Ensure the upper injector seals are correctly located in the cylinder head.

32 Fit the washer and a new injector clamp retaining nut to each mounting stud. Tighten the nuts finger-tight only at this stage.

33 Working on one fuel injector at a time, remove the blanking plugs from the fuel pipe unions on the accumulator rail and the relevant injector. Locate a new high-pressure fuel pipe over the unions and screw on the union nuts. Take care not to cross-thread the nuts or strain the fuel pipes as they are fitted. Once the union nut threads have started, finger-tighten the nuts only at this stage to the ends of the threads.

34 When all the fuel pipes are in place, tighten the injector clamp retaining nuts to the specified torque and through the specified angle.

35 Using an open-ended spanner, hold each fuel pipe union in turn and tighten the union nut to the specified torque using a torque wrench and crow's-foot adapter **(see illustration 11.17)**. Tighten all the disturbed union nuts in the same way.

11.28 Injector clamp bolts (arrowed)

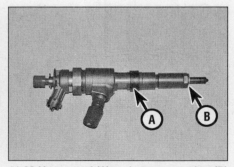

11.30 Upper seal (A) and copper washer (B)

11.41 Release the injector wiring harness retaining clips (arrowed) from the manifold supports

11.42 Depress the tabs on the injector wiring block connectors and slide the connectors out of their supports

11.43 Disconnect the wiring plugs from the four injectors

36 If new injectors have been fitted, their classification numbers must be programmed into the engine management PCM using dedicated diagnostic equipment/scanner. If this equipment is not available, entrust this task to a Ford dealer or suitably-equipped repairer. Note that it should be possible to drive the vehicle, albeit with reduced performance/increased emissions, to a repairer for the numbers to be programmed.

37 The remainder of refitting is a reversal of removal.

38 With everything reassembled and reconnected, prime the fuel system as described in Section 4. Observing the precautions listed in Section 2, start the engine and allow it to idle. Check for leaks at the high-pressure fuel pipe unions with the engine idling. If satisfactory, increase the

engine speed to 4000 rpm and check again for leaks.

39 Take the car for a short road test, and check for leaks once again on return. If any leaks are detected, obtain and fit another new high-pressure fuel pipe. Do not attempt to cure even the slightest leak by further tightening of the pipe unions.

2.0 litre engines to emission level Stage V

Removal

40 Remove the accumulator rail as described in Section 10.

41 Release the three fuel injector wiring harness retaining clips from the manifold supports (see illustration).

42 Depress the tabs on the undersides of the

two injector wiring harness block connectors and slide the connectors out of their supports on the manifold (see illustration).

43 Disconnect the wiring plugs from the four injectors and move the wiring harness to one side (see illustration).

44 Thoroughly clean the fuel return hose connections on the injectors and high-pressure fuel pump. Pull out the locking tab and disconnect the return hose connector from each injector and from the fuel pump (see illustrations). Plug the openings to prevent dirt ingress and remove the return hose.

45 Unscrew the bolt securing each injector clamp, withdraw the clamps from the injectors and lift the injectors out of the cylinder head (see illustrations). If the original injectors are to be refitted, it is absolutely essential that

11.44a Pull out the locking tab...

11.44b... and disconnect the return hose connector from each injector...

11.44c... and from the fuel pump

11.45a Unscrew the bolt securing each injector clamp...

11.45b... withdraw the clamps from the injectors...

11.45c... and lift the injectors out of the cylinder head

11.47a Locate a new upper seal in the injector location in the cylinder head...

11.47b... and place a new copper washer on the injector nozzle

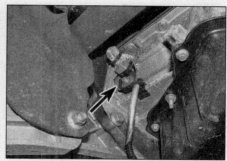

12.1 Crankshaft position sensor – 1.8 litre engines

they are refitted in to their original positions. Slide the copper sealing washer from the end of each injector and remove the upper seal from the injector location in the cylinder head. Discard the seals and washers – new ones must be fitted.

Refitting

46 If new injectors are being fitted, take note of the identification numbers. These need to be downloaded into the PCM on completion of the work.

47 Locate a new upper seal in the injector location in the cylinder head, and place a new copper washer on the injector nozzle **(see illustrations)**.

48 Refit the injectors to the cylinder head, place the clamps in position and screw in the clamp retaining bolts. Tighten the clamp retaining bolts to the specified torque and through the specified angle.

49 Reconnect the fuel return hose to each injector and to the fuel pump, and push in the locking tabs at each connection.

50 Reconnect the wiring plugs to each injector, reconnect the wiring harness block connectors and secure the harness in the manifold clips.

51 Refit the accumulator rail as described in Section 10.

52 If new injectors have been fitted, their classification numbers must be programmed into the engine management PCM using dedicated diagnostic equipment/scanner. If this equipment is not available, entrust this task to a Ford dealer or suitably-equipped

repairer. Note that it should be possible to drive the vehicle, albeit with reduced performance/increased emissions, to a repairer for the numbers to be programmed.

12 Engine management system components – removal and refitting

Crankshaft position/ speed sensor

1.8 litre engines

Note: *Ford specify that, after removal, a new sensor must always be fitted.*

1 The sensor is located at the flywheel end of the engine, low down at the rear **(see illustration)**. For improved access, apply the handbrake then jack up the front of the vehicle and support it on axle stands (see *'Jacking and vehicle support'*).

2 Undo the fasteners and remove the engine undertray.

3 Disconnect the wiring plug from the sensor.

4 Unscrew the retaining bolt, then slide the sensor towards the timing belt end of the engine and withdraw it.

5 If the new sensor has a raised projection on the sensor tip, fit the sensor and push it into contact with the flywheel. Refit the retaining bolt and tighten it securely.

6 If the new sensor has a flat tip, fit the sensor and push it into contact with the flywheel. Using feeler blades measure the gap between the sensor body and the sensor housing. Add

1.2 mm to this measurement and select feeler blades equal to the total measurement. Place the feeler blades against the sensor housing and push the sensor into contact with the feeler blades. Hold the sensor in this position, refit the retaining bolt and tighten it securely.

7 Reconnect the sensor wiring plug, refit the engine undertray and lower the car to the ground.

2.0 litre engines

8 The sensor is located at the front of the engine, adjacent to the crankshaft pulley. For improved access, apply the handbrake then jack up the front of the vehicle and support it on axle stands (see *'Jacking and vehicle support'*).

9 Undo the fasteners and remove the engine undertray.

10 Undo the sensor retaining bolt, disconnect the wiring connector and remove the sensor **(see illustration)**.

11 Refitting is the reverse of removal, tightening the retaining bolt securely.

Mass airflow (MAF) sensor

12 The mass airflow sensor is fitted to the air cleaner cover outlet.

13 Using a small screwdriver, lift the locking catch and disconnect the sensor wiring plug **(see illustrations)**.

14 Undo the two bolts then remove the airflow sensor from the air cleaner cover, along with its sealing ring.

15 Refitting is the reverse of removal, lubricating the sealing ring.

12.10 Crankshaft position sensor retaining bolt – 2.0 litre engines

12.13a Lift the locking catch...

12.13b... and disconnect the MAF sensor wiring plug

12.21 Disconnect the MAP sensor wiring plug – 1.8 litre engines

12.24 MAP sensor location – 2.0 litre engines to Stage III/IV emission level

12.31 Disconnect the MAP sensor wiring plug – 2.0 litre engines to Stage V emission level

Coolant temperature sensor

Note: *A coolant temperature sensor is only fitted to 2.0 litre engines.*
16 Refer to Chapter 3 Section 5 for removal and refitting details.

Cylinder head temperature sensor

Note: *A cylinder head temperature sensor is only fitted to 1.8 litre engines.*
17 Refer to Chapter 3 Section 5 for removal and refitting details.

Accelerator pedal position sensor

18 The sensor is secured to the accelerator pedal. Refer to Section 6 of this Chapter for pedal removal and refitting. Note that at the time of writing, the sensor was not available separately from the pedal assembly.

Manifold absolute pressure (MAP) sensor

1.8 litre engines

19 The manifold absolute pressure sensor is fitted to the top of the cylinder head cover.
20 Remove the plastic cover on the top of the engine.
21 Disconnect the sensor wiring plug, followed by the vacuum hose **(see illustration)**.
22 Undo the two mounting bracket bolts and remove the sensor from the cylinder head cover.
23 Refitting is the reverse of removal, tightening the retaining bolts securely.

2.0 litre engines to emission level Stage III/IV

24 The sensor is mounted on the inlet air shut-off throttle **(see illustration)**.
25 Remove the plastic cover on the top of the engine.
26 Disconnect the sensor wiring plug.
27 Slacken and remove the retaining bolt and remove the sensor from the inlet air shut-off throttle.
28 Refitting is the reverse of removal, tightening the retaining bolt securely.

2.0 litre engines to emission level Stage V

29 The sensor is mounted on the inlet manifold upper section.
30 Remove the plastic cover on the top of the engine.
31 Disconnect the sensor wiring plug **(see illustration)**.
32 Slacken and remove the retaining bolt and remove the sensor from the manifold.
33 Refitting is the reverse of removal, tightening the retaining bolt securely.

Brake and clutch pedal position switches

34 The powertrain control module receives a signal from the brake and clutch pedal position switches which indicates when the brakes are being applied or the clutch pedal is depressed. Switch removal and refitting details can be found in Chapter 9 Section 17 and Chapter 6 Section 7 respectively.

ABS wheel speed sensors

35 Refer to Chapter 9 Section 20 for removal and refitting details.

Powertrain control module (PCM)

Note: *The module is fragile. Take care not to drop it, or subject it to any other kind of impact. Do not subject it to extremes of temperature, or allow it to get wet.*
Note: *If a new PCM is to be fitted, the configuration information stored within the module must be uploaded to Ford diagnostic equipment prior to the module being removed, and downloaded to the new PCM once installed. Entrust this task to a Ford dealer or suitably-equipped specialist.*
36 Disconnect the battery negative lead as described in Chapter 5A Section 4.
37 Firmly apply the handbrake, then jack up the front of the vehicle and support it securely on axle stands (see *'Jacking and vehicle support'*). Remove the left-hand front roadwheel.
38 Release the fasteners and remove the left-hand front wheel arch liner **(see illustration)**.
39 The PCM is fitted under the front bumper. To gain access, undo the retaining bolts and remove the plastic cover **(see illustrations)**.
40 Undo the three mounting bolts and withdraw the PCM from its location.
41 Suitably support the PCM and centre-punch a hole in the centre of the security shield retaining shear-bolt.
42 Drill a 3.5 mm diameter hole in the shear-bolt, then tap a T20 Torx bit into the

12.38 Release the fasteners and remove the left-hand front wheel arch liner

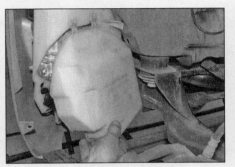

12.39a Undo the retaining bolts and remove the plastic cover…

12.39b… to gain access to the PCM

12.42a Drill a 3.5 mm diameter hole in the shear bolt...

12.42b... then tap a T20 Torx bit into the hole

12.47 Disconnect the inlet air temperature sensor wiring plug – 1.8 litre engines

hole **(see illustrations)**. Unscrew the Torx bit to remove the shear-bolt. Note that a new shear-bolt will be required for refitting.

43 Remove the security shield, then lever over the locking catches and disconnect the wiring plugs from the PCM.

44 Refitting is a reversal of removal. Tighten the new shear-bolt until the head breaks off.

Inlet air temperature sensor

1.8 litre engines

45 The inlet air temperature sensor is located in the intercooler air outlet duct on the right-hand end of the engine.

46 Remove the plastic cover on the top of the engine.

47 Disconnect the sensor wiring plug **(see illustration)**.

48 Undo the retaining bolt and withdraw the sensor from the duct.

49 Apply a little petroleum jelly to ease the sensor in to place, then tighten the retaining bolt securely.

50 Reconnect the sensor wiring plug and refit the engine cover.

2.0 litre engines to emission level Stage III/IV

51 The sensor is mounted on the inlet air shut-off throttle **(see illustration)**.

52 Remove the plastic cover on the top of the engine.

53 Disconnect the sensor wiring plug.

54 Slacken and remove the retaining bolt and remove the sensor from the inlet air shut-off throttle.

55 Refitting is the reverse of removal, tightening the retaining bolt securely.

Fuel pressure sensor

56 It is not possible to renew the sensor separately from the fuel accumulator rail. Ford advise that no attempt should be made to remove it. If the sensor is faulty, renew the accumulator rail as described in Section 10.

Camshaft position sensor

1.8 litre engines

57 Remove the plastic cover on the top of the engine.

58 The sensor is located on the cylinder head cover. Disconnect the sensor wiring plug **(see illustration)**.

59 Undo the bolt and pull the sensor from the cylinder head cover.

60 Refitting is a reversal of removal, tightening the retaining bolt securely.

2.0 litre engines

Note: *Ford specify that after removal, a new sensor must always be fitted.*

61 The camshaft position sensor is mounted on the right-hand end of the cylinder head cover, directly behind the camshaft sprocket.

62 Remove the upper timing belt cover, as described in Chapter 2C Section 5.

63 Unplug the sensor wiring connector.

64 Undo the retaining bolt and pull the sensor from its location **(see illustration)**.

65 Using a socket or spanner on the crankshaft pulley, turn the engine in the normal direction of rotation until the back of

12.51 Inlet air temperature sensor location (arrowed) – 2.0 litre engines to Stage III/IV emission level

one of the webs on the camshaft sprocket is directly in line with the camshaft position sensor hole in the timing belt inner cover.

66 Place the sensor in position and push it in so that the raised projection on the sensor tip is in contact with the camshaft sprocket. Fit the retaining bolt and tighten it securely.

67 Reconnect the sensor wiring plug, then refit the upper timing belt cover as described in Chapter 2C Section 5.

Turbocharger boost pressure regulator valve

Note: *A turbocharger boost pressure regulator valve is only fitted to 2.0 litre engines.*

68 Remove the plastic cover on the top of the engine.

69 Disconnect the wiring plug, then undo the two regulator retaining nuts **(see illustration)**.

12.58 Camshaft position sensor location (arrowed) – 1.8 litre engines

12.64 Camshaft position sensor location (arrowed) – 2.0 litre engines

12.69 Turbocharger boost pressure regulator valve location (arrowed) – 2.0 litre engines

12.76 Intake air shut-off throttle bolts (arrowed) – 2.0 litre engines to Stage III/IV emission level

12.79 Lift the oil filler tube out of the bracket on the manifold – 2.0 litre engines to Stage V emission level

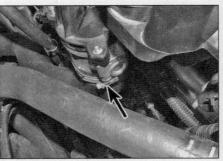

12.80 Disconnect the wiring harness connectors at the manifold – 2.0 litre engines to Stage V emission level

70 Note their fitted locations and disconnect the vacuum hoses as the regulator is withdrawn.

71 Refitting is a reversal of removal, tightening the retaining nuts securely.

Fuel pressure control valve and fuel metering valve

72 These valves are fitted to the high-pressure fuel pump. They are not available as separate items, and can only be renewed along with the pump. Ford advise that no attempt should be made to remove the valves.

Inlet air shut-off throttle

Note: *An inlet air shut-off throttle is only fitted to 2.0 litre engines.*

Engines to emission level Stage III/IV

73 Remove the plastic cover on the top of the engine.

74 To remove the throttle body, note their fitted positions, and disconnect wiring plugs and vacuum hoses from the various sensors/ motors fitted to the throttle body.

75 Slacken the clamp, and disconnect the intercooler charge air hose from the throttle body.

76 Undo the mounting bolts and remove the throttle body **(see illustration)**.

77 Refitting is a reversal of removal, tightening the retaining bolts securely.

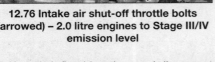

12.81 Disconnect the charge air hose (arrowed) from the shut-off throttle – 2.0 litre engines to Stage V emission level

Engines to emission level Stage V

78 Remove the plastic cover on the top of the engine.

79 Lift the engine oil filler tube support clip out of the bracket on the inlet manifold and move the tube to one side **(see illustration)**.

80 Disconnect the wiring harness connectors at the sensors and block connectors, then release the harness from the cable clips around the front of the manifold **(see illustration)**. Move the harness to one side.

81 Slacken the retaining clamp and disconnect the intercooler charge air hose

12.82 Undo the three inlet manifold upper section bolts (arrowed) – 2.0 litre engines to Stage V emission level

from the inlet air shut-off throttle body **(see illustration)**.

82 Undo the three bolts securing the inlet manifold upper section to the lower section **(see illustration)**.

83 Undo the three nuts/bolts securing the inlet manifold lower section to the cylinder head and remove the lower section from the car **(see illustrations)**.

84 Undo the three bolts and remove the shut-off throttle body from the manifold lower section **(see illustration)**.

85 Refitting is a reversal of removal, tightening all retaining nuts/bolts to the specified torque, where given.

12.83a Undo the three nuts (arrowed) securing the manifold lower section to the cylinder head (shown with manifold removed)...

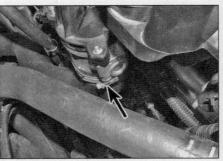

12.83b... and remove the lower section from the car – 2.0 litre engines to Stage V emission level

12.84 Undo the three bolts (arrowed) and remove the shut-off throttle – 2.0 litre engines to Stage V emission level

13 Turbocharger – description and precautions

Description

1 A turbocharger increases engine efficiency by raising the pressure in the inlet manifold above atmospheric pressure. Instead of the air simply being sucked into the cylinders, it is forced in. Additional fuel is supplied by the injection pump in proportion to the increased air inlet.

2 Energy for the operation of the turbocharger comes from the exhaust gas. The gas flows through a specially-shaped housing (the turbine housing) and in so doing, spins the turbine wheel. The turbine wheel is attached to a shaft, at the end of which is another vaned wheel known as the compressor wheel. The compressor wheel spins in its own housing and compresses the inducted air on the way to the inlet manifold.

3 The compressed air passes through an intercooler. This is an air-to-air heat exchanger, mounted with the radiator at the front of the vehicle. The purpose of the intercooler is to remove from the inducted air some of the heat gained in being compressed. Because cooler air is denser, removal of this heat further increases engine efficiency.

4 The turbocharger has adjustable guide vanes controlling the flow of exhaust gas into the turbine. On 2.0 litre engines, the vanes are swivelled by a vacuum unit on the turbocharger, controlled by the boost pressure regulator valve, controlled in turn by the engine management PCM. On 1.8 litre engines, the position of the vanes is controlled by an electric motor attached to the turbocharger, again, controlled by the PCM. At lower engine speeds, the vanes close together, giving a smaller exhaust gas entry port, and therefore higher gas speed, which increases boost pressure at low engine speed. At high engine speed, the vanes are turned to give a larger exhaust gas entry port, and therefore lower gas speed, effectively maintaining a reasonably constant boost pressure over the engine rev range. This is known as a Variable Nozzle Turbocharger (VNT).

5 The turbo shaft is pressure-lubricated by an oil feed pipe from the main oil gallery. The shaft 'floats' on a cushion of oil. A drain pipe returns the oil to the sump.

Precautions

6 The turbocharger operates at extremely high speeds and temperatures. Certain precautions must be observed to avoid premature failure of the turbo or injury to the operator.

● Do not operate the turbo with any parts exposed. Foreign objects falling onto the rotating vanes could cause excessive damage and (if ejected) personal injury.
● Do not race the engine immediately after start-up, especially if it is cold. Give the oil a few seconds to circulate.
● Always allow the engine to return to idle speed before switching it off – do not blip the throttle and switch off, as this will leave the turbo spinning without lubrication.
● Allow the engine to idle for several minutes before switching off after a high-speed run.
● Observe the recommended intervals for oil and filter changing, and use a reputable oil of the specified quality (see *Lubricants and fluids*). Neglect of oil changing, or use of inferior oil, can cause carbon formation on the turbo shaft and subsequent failure.

14 Turbocharger – removal and refitting

Note: *The turbocharger should only be removed with the engine completely cool.*

1.8 litre engines

Removal

1 Disconnect the battery negative lead as described in Chapter 5A Section 4.
2 Remove the catalytic converter as described in Section 18.
3 Remove the air cleaner and inlet duct as described in Section 5.
4 Remove the EGR cooler, as described in Chapter 4C Section 3.
5 Disconnect the inlet and outlet charge air ducts from the turbocharger.
6 Undo the nuts and remove the turbocharger-to-exhaust manifold retaining clamp.
7 Disconnect the wiring plug from the turbocharger electronic vane adjustment solenoid.
8 Undo the nut securing the turbocharger oil supply pipe support bracket.
9 Undo the banjo bolt and disconnect the oil supply pipe from the cylinder block. Note that the banjo bolt cannot be removed from the pipe.
10 Undo the bolts and remove the oil return pipe from the underside of the turbocharger. Discard the gaskets.
11 Undo the two bolts securing the turbocharger to the support bracket, and manoeuvre it from position.

14.19 Turbocharger inlet hose support bracket bolt (arrowed)

12 No further dismantling of the turbocharger is recommended. Interfering with the wastegate setting may lead to a reduction in performance, or could result in engine damage. No parts appear to be available separately for the turbocharger.

13 If on inspection there are any signs of internal oil contamination on the turbine or compressor wheels, this indicates failure of the turbocharger oil seals. Renewing these seals is a job best left to a turbocharger specialist. In the event of any problem with the turbocharger, one of these specialists will usually be able to rebuild a defective unit, or offer a rebuilt unit on an exchange basis, either of which will prove cheaper than a new unit.

Refitting

14 Refitting is a reversal of removal, noting the following points:
a) Use new gaskets for the turbocharger oil return connections.
b) Refer to Chapter 4C Section 3 when refitting the EGR cooler.
c) Refer to Section 18 when refitting the catalytic converter.
d) Refill the cooling system as described in Chapter 1B Section 30.

2.0 litre engines to emission level Stage III/IV

Removal

15 Disconnect the battery negative lead as described in Chapter 5A Section 4.
16 Remove the plastic cover from the top of the engine.
17 Drain the cooling system as described in Chapter 1B Section 30.
18 Depress the release button and disconnect the engine breather hose from the inlet manifold.
19 Undo the bolt securing the turbocharger inlet hose support bracket **(see illustration)**.
20 Slacken the clamp and disconnect the outlet pipe from the turbocharger.
21 Remove the catalytic converter as described in Section 18.
22 Remove the catalytic converter support bracket.
23 Undo the nuts/bolts and remove the support bracket from the underside of the turbocharger **(see illustration)**.

14.23 Undo the bolts/nuts and remove the bracket under the turbocharger (arrowed)

14.24 Turbocharger vane position sensor/ actuator wiring plug and vacuum hose (arrowed)

14.25 Undo the two bolts (arrowed) securing the inlet hose

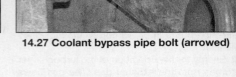

14.27 Coolant bypass pipe bolt (arrowed)

24 Note their fitted positions, then disconnect the vacuum hose and wiring plug from the vane position sensor/actuator **(see illustration)**.

25 Undo the bolts and detach the inlet hose from the turbocharger. Depress the release clip and detach the pipe from the cylinder head cover **(see illustration)**.

26 Release the clamp and disconnect the heater core-to-bypass coolant hose.

27 Slacken the clamp, remove the support bracket bolt, undo the connection bolts and remove the bypass hose **(see illustration)**. Recover the O-ring seal, and renew if necessary.

28 Undo the banjo bolts securing the oil supply pipe to the cylinder block. Renew the sealing washers. Note that a small filter is fitted into the banjo bolt – renew it **(see illustration)**.

29 Undo the two bolts securing the oil return hose to the underside of the turbocharger **(see illustration)**. Renew the gasket.

30 Undo the nuts and separate the turbo-charger from the manifold **(see illustration)**.

31 If required, undo the banjo bolt and detach the oil supply pipe from the turbocharger. Renew the seals.

Refitting

32 Refitting is a reversal of removal, noting the following points:

Ensure all mating surfaces are clean and dry.

a) *Renew all O-rings, seals and gaskets.*

b) *Tighten all fasteners to the specified torque where available.*

c) *Refer to Section 18 when refitting the catalytic converter.*

d) *Refill the cooling system as described in Chapter 1B Section 30.*

2.0 litre engines to emission level Stage V

Removal

33 Disconnect the battery negative lead as described in Chapter 5A Section 4.

34 Remove the plastic cover from the top of the engine.

35 Drain the cooling system as described in Chapter 1B Section 30.

36 Remove the catalytic converter as described in Section 18.

37 Release the clip and disconnect the coolant inlet hose from the turbocharger coolant pipe.

38 Undo the bolt and disconnect the coolant outlet pipe from the cylinder block.

39 Undo the banjo bolt securing the oil supply pipe to the cylinder block. Renew the sealing washers. Note that a small filter is fitted into the banjo bolt – renew it **(see illustration 14.28)**.

40 Undo the two bolts securing the oil return hose to the underside of the turbocharger. Renew the gasket.

41 Undo the ten nuts securing the exhaust manifold to the cylinder head.

42 Undo the bolt securing the turbocharger to the support bracket. Ease the exhaust manifold off the mounting studs and

manipulate the manifold and turbocharger down and out from under the car. Recover the manifold gasket.

43 Undo the bolt securing the coolant pipe to the manifold, and the four nuts securing the turbocharger to the manifold. Separate the turbocharger from the manifold and recover the gasket.

Refitting

44 Refitting is a reversal of removal, noting the following points:

a) *Ensure all mating surfaces are clean and dry.*

b) *Renew all O-rings, seals and gaskets.*

c) *Tighten all fasteners to the specified torque where available.*

d) *Refer to Section 18 when refitting the catalytic converter.*

e) *Refill the cooling system as described in Chapter 1B Section 30.*

15 Turbocharger – examination and overhaul

1 With the turbocharger removed, inspect the housing for cracks or other visible damage.

2 Spin the turbine or the compressor wheel to verify that the shaft is intact and to feel for excessive shake or roughness. Some play is normal since in use the shaft is 'floating' on a film of oil. Check that the wheel vanes are undamaged.

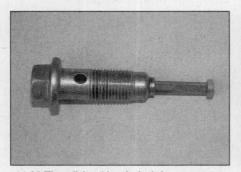

14.28 The oil feed banjo bolt incorporates a filter

14.29 Turbocharger oil return hose retaining bolts (arrowed)

14.30 Undo the nuts (arrowed) securing the turbocharger to the manifold

3 The wastegate and actuator are integral with the turbocharger, and cannot be checked or renewed separately. Consult a Ford dealer or other specialist if it is thought that the wastegate may be faulty.

4 If the exhaust or induction passages are oil-contaminated, the turbo shaft oil seals have probably failed. (On the induction side, this will also have contaminated the intercooler, where applicable, which if necessary should be flushed with a suitable solvent.)

5 No DIY repair of the turbo is possible. A new unit may be available on an exchange basis.

16 Intercooler –
removal and refitting

Removal

1 Raise the front of the vehicle and support it securely on axle stands (see 'Jacking and vehicle support').

2 Undo the fasteners and remove the engine undertray, followed by the splash shield under the radiator.

3 Slacken the clamps and disconnect the inlet and outlet hoses from the intercooler.

4 Undo the bolt each side securing the intercooler to the base of the radiator and lower the intercooler out from under the car (see illustration).

Refitting

5 Refitting is a reversal of removal. Ensure the inside of the inlet and outlet hoses are clean where they attach to the intercooler.

17 Manifolds –
removal and refitting

Inlet manifold

1.8 litre engines

1 The manifold is integral with the EGR valve – refer to Chapter 4C Section 3.

2.0 litre engines

2 The manifold is integral with the cylinder head cover – refer to Section 17.

Exhaust manifold removal

1.8 litre engines

3 Remove the turbocharger as described in Section 14.

4 Remove the EGR cooler as described in Chapter 4C Section 3.

5 Undo the retaining nuts and bolts and withdraw the manifold from the cylinder head studs. Recover the gasket.

2.0 litre engines to emission level Stage III/IV

6 Remove the turbocharger as described in Section 14.

7 Remove the EGR cooler as described in Chapter 4C Section 3.

8 Pull the manifold heat shield upwards to release the two retaining clips.

9 Undo the nuts securing the exhaust manifold to the cylinder head, and recover the spacers **(see illustration)**. Pull the manifold from the mounting studs. If the manifold is being removed to renew the gasket, no further dismantling is required. Remove the gasket.

2.0 litre engines to emission level Stage V

10 The manifold is removed complete with the turbocharger, and the two components are then separated on the bench. Refer to the turbocharger removal and refitting procedures contained in Section 14.

Exhaust manifold refitting

11 Examine the studs for signs of damage and corrosion; remove traces of corrosion, and repair or renew any damaged studs.

12 Ensure the mating surfaces of the exhaust manifold and cylinder head are clean and dry. Position the new gasket, and refit the exhaust manifold to the cylinder head. Tighten the nuts/bolts to the specified torque.

13 The remainder of refitting is a reversal of removal, noting the following points:

a) Tighten all fasteners to their specified torque where available.

b) Apply a little high-temperature anti-seize grease (Copperslip) to the manifold studs.

c) Top-up the cooling system as described in 'Weekly checks'.

d) Check and, if necessary, top-up the oil level as described in Chapter 1B Section 6.

18 Exhaust system –
general information, removal and refitting

Caution: Any work on the exhaust system should only be attempted once the system is completely cool – this may take several hours, especially in the case of the forward sections.

General information

1 The exhaust system consists of the catalytic converter, and the centre section incorporating the silencer. On 2.0 litre engines a diesel particulate filter (DPF) is fitted between the catalytic converter and the centre section.

2 A flexible ('mesh') section is fitted to allow for engine movement. The flexible section is located just after the catalytic converter, upstream of the catalytic converter flange joint.

3 When fitted in the factory, the exhaust system from the centre section flange joint to the end of the tail pipe is one piece. However, if the rear silencer is to be renewed, new silencers should be available – check with your parts supplier. It will be necessary to cut through the centre section using a hacksaw if a new rear silencer is to be fitted.

4 The system is suspended throughout its entire length by rubber mountings.

Removal

5 To remove a part of the system, first jack up the front or rear of the car, and support it on axle stands (see 'Jacking and vehicle support'). Alternatively, position the car over an inspection pit, or on car ramps.

6 Undo the fasteners and remove the engine undertray.

Catalytic converter – 1.8 litre engines

7 Undo the two bolts each side and remove the subframe cross-brace **(see illustration)**.

8 Attach wooden 'splints' each side of the exhaust flexible section using cable-ties. This is to prevent excessive bending of the section as it's disconnected. Undo the nuts securing the flexible section to the centre section. Pull the centre section rearwards, and allow the exhaust to hang down.

16.4 Intercooler left-hand retaining bolt (arrowed)

17.9 Undo the nuts and recover the manifold spacers – 2.0 litre engines to Stage III/IV emission level

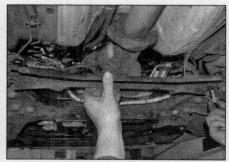

18.7 Undo the two bolts each side and remove the subframe cross-brace

18.9 Catalytic converter-to-turbocharger nuts (arrowed) – 1.8 litre engines

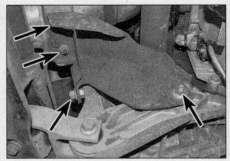

18.10 Catalytic converter support bracket nuts (arrowed) – 1.8 litre engines

18.14 Catalytic converter-to-turbocharger clamp (arrowed) – 2.0 litre engines to Stage III/IV emission level

9 Undo the nuts securing the catalytic converter to the turbocharger **(see illustration)**.

10 Undo the catalytic converter support bracket nuts, release the mounting rubbers, and manoeuvre the catalytic converter out from under the car **(see illustration)**.

Catalytic converter – 2.0 litre engines to emission level Stage III/IV

11 Undo the two bolts each side and remove the subframe cross-brace **(see illustration 18.7)**.

12 Attach wooden 'splints' each side of the exhaust flexible section using cable-ties. This is to prevent excessive bending of the section as it's disconnected.

13 Disconnect the wiring plug, then unscrew the temperature sensor from the front section of the catalytic converter.

14 Slacken the clamp securing the catalytic converter to the turbocharger **(see illustration)**.

15 Undo the nuts securing the flexible section to the particulate filter. Pull the particulate filter rearwards, and allow the exhaust to hang down.

16 Release the mounting rubbers, then undo the two bolts and remove the mounting rubber support bracket from the subframe **(see illustration)**.

17 Undo the retaining nuts and remove the catalytic converter support bracket.

18 Manoeuvre the catalytic converter out from under the car.

Catalytic converter – 2.0 litre engines to emission level Stage V

19 Undo the bolt securing the crankcase ventilation pipe to the top of the inlet manifold/cylinder head cover **(see illustration 9.42)**.

20 Disconnect the quick-release fittings at each end of the pipe and remove the pipe from the engine **(see illustrations 9.43a, 9.43b and 9.43c)**.

21 Slacken the clip and disconnect the air cleaner outlet duct from the rigid plastic air duct at the rear of the engine.

22 Slacken the clip and disconnect the other end of the duct from the turbocharger. Release the wiring and hoses from the retaining clips, undo the two nuts and remove the duct from the engine.

23 Disconnect the particulate filter temperature sensor wiring block connector at the left-hand side of the engine **(see illustration)**.

24 Slacken the two clips, undo the bolt and remove the turbocharger outlet duct from under the engine.

25 Undo the two bolts each side and remove the subframe cross-brace **(see illustration 18.7)**.

26 Attach wooden 'splints' each side of the exhaust flexible section using cable-ties. This is to prevent excessive bending of the section as it's disconnected.

27 Note their fitted positions, then disconnect the vacuum hose and wiring plug from the turbocharger wastegate control assembly.

28 Undo the four bolts and remove the exhaust manifold heat shield.

29 Undo the two bolts securing the mounting rubber support bracket to the subframe.

30 Undo the retaining nuts and remove the catalytic converter support bracket.

31 Undo the nuts securing the flexible section to the particulate filter. Pull the particulate filter rearwards, and allow the exhaust to hang down.

32 Slacken the clamp securing the catalytic converter to the turbocharger, then manoeuvre the catalytic converter out from under the car.

Centre section

33 Remove the rear silencer as described later in this Section.

34 Unscrew the nuts securing the centre section to the catalytic converter or particulate filter, and separate the joint. Recover the gasket.

35 Unhook the centre section's rubber mountings, and remove it from under the car.

Particulate filter

36 Attach wooden 'splints' each side of the exhaust flexible section using cable-ties. This is to prevent excessive bending of the section as it's disconnected. Undo the nuts securing the flexible section to the particulate filter.

37 Note their fitted positions, and disconnect the pressure pipes from the front of the particulate filter **(see illustration)**.

18.16 Mounting rubber support bracket retaining bolts (arrowed) – 2.0 litre engines to Stage III/IV emission level

18.23 Disconnect the temperature sensor wiring block connector (arrowed) – 2.0 litre engines to Stage V emission level

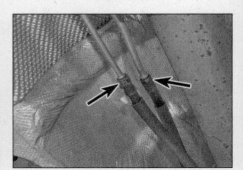

18.37 Disconnect the pressure pipes (arrowed) from the front of the particulate filter

38 Disconnect the temperature sensor wiring connector(s).

39 Undo the nuts securing the rear exhaust section to the particulate filter, release the mounting rubber and manoeuvre the filter from position.

Rear silencer

40 If the original one-piece exhaust system is still fitted, it will be necessary to cut off the old rear silencer to enable fitment of the new unit. Using the new rear silencer as a pattern, mark the exhaust centre section to determine the cut point. Ensure that the cut point will allow a sufficient length of centre section to fit into the new rear silencer.

41 Using a hacksaw, cut through the centre section at the marked cut point. Unhook the rear silencer's rubber mountings, and remove it from under the car.

42 If a replacement rear silencer has already been fitted, unbolt the clamp securing the silencer to the centre section, and separate the pipes. Usually, this will require some effort – the most successful method involves twisting the silencer from side to side, to break the joint. Unfortunately, if the pipe at the rear of the centre section has suffered from corrosion, it's very likely that the centre section will be damaged beyond repair in removing the silencer. A less-destructive method of removal involves heating the two pipes, but this carries the risk of damaging the underbody components, and even a risk of fire from the fuel tank and lines.

43 Unhook the silencer rubber mountings, and remove it from under the car.

Heat shields

44 The heat shields are secured to the underside of the body by special nuts. Each shield can be removed separately, but note that they may overlap, making it necessary to loosen another section first. If a shield is being removed to gain access to a component located behind it, it may prove sufficient in some cases to remove the retaining nuts and/ or bolts, and simply lower the shield, without disturbing the exhaust system. Otherwise, remove the exhaust section as described earlier.

Refitting

45 In all cases, refitting is a reversal of removal, but note the following points:

a) *Always use new gaskets, nuts and clamps (as applicable), and coat all threads with copper grease. Make sure any new clamps are the same size as the original – overtightening a clamp which is too big will not seal the joint.*

b) *On a sleeved joint (such as that between the centre section and rear silencer), use a smear of exhaust jointing paste to achieve a gas-tight seal.*

c) *If any of the exhaust mounting rubbers are in poor condition, fit new ones.*

d) *Make sure that the exhaust is suspended properly on its mountings, and will not come into contact with the floor or any suspension parts. The rear silencer especially must be aligned correctly before tightening the clamp nuts.*

e) *Tighten all nuts/bolts to the specified torque, where given.*

Chapter 4 Part C
Emission control systems

Contents

Degrees of difficulty

Easy, suitable for novice with little experience	Fairly easy, suitable for beginner with some experience	Fairly difficult, suitable for competent DIY mechanic	Difficult, suitable for experienced DIY mechanic	Very difficult, suitable for expert DIY or professional

Specifications

Torque wrench settings	Nm	lbf ft
Petrol engines		
EGR valve/solenoid bolts	25	18
Oxygen (lambda) sensors	48	35
Diesel engines		
Inlet manifold (1.8 litre engines)	25	18

1 General Information

Petrol engines

Crankcase emission control

1 To reduce the emission of unburned hydrocarbons from the crankcase into the atmosphere, the engine is sealed and the blow-by gases and oil vapour are drawn from inside the crankcase, through an oil separator and regulating (PCV – positive crankcase ventilation) valve, into the inlet manifold to be burned by the engine during normal combustion.

2 Under all conditions the gases are forced out of the crankcase by the (relatively) higher crankcase pressure.

Evaporative emission control

3 To minimise the escape into the atmosphere of unburned hydrocarbons, an evaporative emissions control system is also fitted to all models. The fuel tank filler cap is sealed, and a charcoal canister is mounted at the rear of the fuel tank. The canister collects the petrol vapours generated in the tank when the car is parked, and stores them until they can be cleared from the canister (under the control of the fuel injection/ignition system PCM) via the purge valve into the inlet tract to be burned by the engine during normal combustion.

4 To ensure that the engine runs correctly when it is cold and/or idling and to protect the catalytic converter from the effects of an over-rich mixture, the EVAP valve is not opened by the PCM until the engine has warmed-up, and the engine is under load; the valve solenoid is then modulated on and off to allow the stored vapour to pass into the inlet tract.

Exhaust emission control

5 To minimise the amount of pollutants which escape into the atmosphere, all models are fitted with a catalytic converter in the exhaust system. The system is of the closed-loop type, in which an oxygen (lambda) sensor in the exhaust manifold provides the fuel injection/ignition system powertrain control module (PCM) with constant feedback, enabling the PCM to adjust the mixture to provide the best possible conditions for the converter to operate.

6 The oxygen sensor has a heating element built-in that is controlled by the PCM through a relay to quickly bring the sensor's tip to an efficient operating temperature. The sensor's tip is sensitive to oxygen and sends the PCM a varying voltage depending on the amount of oxygen in the exhaust gases; if the inlet air/fuel mixture is too rich, the exhaust gases are low in oxygen so the sensor sends a low-voltage signal, the voltage rising as the mixture weakens and the amount of oxygen rises in the exhaust gases.

7 Peak conversion efficiency of all major pollutants occurs if the inlet air/fuel mixture is maintained at the chemically-correct ratio for the complete combustion of petrol of 14.7 parts (by weight) of air to 1 part of fuel (the 'stoichiometric' ratio). The sensor output voltage alters in a large step at this point, the PCM using the signal change as a reference point and correcting the inlet air/fuel mixture accordingly by altering the fuel injector pulse width.

8 A second sensor is fitted downstream of the catalytic converter, to monitor the converter's efficiency, and to fine-tune the information being sent back to the PCM, so that emissions are kept even more tightly under control.

Exhaust gas recirculation system

9 This system is designed to recirculate small quantities of exhaust gas into the inlet tract, and therefore into the combustion process. This reduces the level of oxides of nitrogen present in the final exhaust gas which is released into the atmosphere.

10 The volume of exhaust gas recirculated is controlled by an electrically-operated solenoid valve. The solenoid and valve is mounted at the left-hand end of the cylinder head. The EGR system is controlled by the engine management PCM, which receives

information on engine operating parameters from its various sensors.

Diesel engines

Crankcase emission control

11 To reduce the emission of unburned hydrocarbons from the crankcase into the atmosphere, the engine is sealed and the blow-by gases and oil vapour are drawn from inside the crankcase, through an oil separator and into the inlet manifold to be burned by the engine during normal combustion.

Exhaust emission control

12 To minimise the level of exhaust pollutants released into the atmosphere, a catalytic converter is fitted in the exhaust system of all models.
13 The catalytic converter consists of a canister containing a fine mesh impregnated with a catalyst material, over which the hot exhaust gases pass. The catalyst speeds up the oxidation of harmful carbon monoxide, unburnt hydrocarbons and soot, effectively reducing the quantity of harmful products released into the atmosphere via the exhaust gases.
14 On 2.0 litre engines, a diesel particulate filter is incorporated in the exhaust system and contains a silicon carbide honeycomb block containing microscopic channels in which the exhaust gases flow. As the gases flow through the honeycomb channels, soot particles are deposited on the channel walls. To prevent clogging of the honeycomb channels, the soot particles are burned off at regular intervals during what is known as a 'regeneration phase'. Under the control of the engine management system PCM, the injection characteristics are altered to raise the temperature of the exhaust gases to approximately 600°C. At this temperature, the soot particles are effectively burned off the honeycomb walls as the exhaust gases pass through. A differential pressure sensor and temperature sensors are used to inform the PCM of the condition of the particulate filter, and the temperature of the exhaust gases during the regeneration phase. When the PCM detects that soot build-up is reducing the efficiency of the particulate filter, it will instigate the regeneration process. This

2.5 Oil separator components and attachments

occurs at regular intervals under certain driving conditions and will normally not be detected by the driver.

Exhaust gas recirculation system

15 An exhaust gas recirculation (EGR) system is fitted to all diesel-engined models. This reduces the level of nitrogen oxides produced during combustion by introducing a proportion of the exhaust gas back into the inlet manifold, under certain engine operating conditions, via an electrically-operated valve. The system is controlled electronically by the engine management system. A cooler is fitted to the EGR valve, through which engine coolant is passed. This lowers the temperature of the recirculated gas, thus reducing the formation of NOx (oxides of nitrogen) in the exhaust gases.

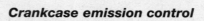

2 Petrol engine emission control systems – checking and component renewal

Crankcase emission control

Checking

1 The components of this system require no attention, other than to check that the hoses are clear and undamaged.

Oil separator renewal

2 Remove the inlet manifold as described in Chapter 4A Section 11.
3 The oil separator is located on the front

2.12 Disconnect the hoses (arrowed) from the charcoal canister

facing side of the cylinder block, below the inlet manifold. Disconnect the breather hose from the top of the separator.
4 Depress the clip each side of the PCV valve and remove the valve from the top of the separator.
5 Undo the bolts and remove the separator **(see illustration)**. Recover the gasket.
6 On reassembly, fit a new gasket and tighten the bolts securely.

Evaporative emission control

Checking

7 Poor idle, stalling and poor driveability can be caused by an inoperative canister vacuum valve, a damaged canister, split or cracked hoses, or hoses connected to the wrong fittings. Check the fuel filler cap for a damaged or deformed gasket.
8 Fuel loss or fuel odour can be caused by liquid fuel leaking from fuel lines, a cracked or damaged canister, an inoperative canister vacuum valve, and disconnected, misrouted, kinked or damaged vapour or control hoses.
9 Inspect each hose attached to the canister for kinks, leaks and cracks along its entire length. Repair or renew as necessary.
10 Inspect the canister. If it is cracked or damaged, renew it. Look for fuel leaking from the bottom of the canister. If fuel is leaking, renew the canister, and check the hoses and hose routing.

Charcoal canister renewal

11 The canister is located under the rear of the vehicle, attached to the rear subframe.
12 Note their fitted locations, then press in the release buttons, and disconnect the hoses from the canister **(see illustration)**.
13 Undo the two retaining bolts and lower the canister from under the car**(see illustration)**.
14 Refitting is a reversal of removal.

Canister purge valve (EVAP) renewal

15 The canister purge valve is mounted in the engine compartment, on the left-hand end of the cylinder head **(see illustration)**.
16 Note their fitted positions, then disconnect the vacuum pipes and wiring plug from the valve.
17 Unclip the valve from the bracket.
18 Refitting is a reversal of removal.

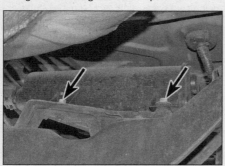

2.13 Undo the two retaining bolts (arrowed) and lower the canister from under the car

2.15 Canister purge valve location (arrowed)

2.21 Disconnect the oxygen sensor wiring plugs (arrowed) at the rear of the engine

2.22a An oxygen sensor is fitted to the exhaust manifold...

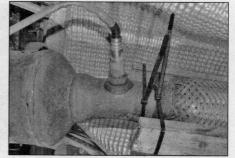

2.22b... and the front section of the exhaust pipe

Exhaust emission control

Checking

19 Checking of the system as a whole entails a close visual inspection of all hoses, pipes and connections for condition and security. Apart from this, any known or suspected faults should be attended to by a Ford dealer or suitably-equipped specialist.

Catalytic converter renewal

20 The catalytic converter is integral with the exhaust manifold – refer to Chapter 4A Section 11 for details.

Oxygen (lambda) sensors renewal

Note: *The oxygen sensor is delicate and will not work if it is dropped or knocked, if its power supply is disrupted, or if any cleaning materials are used on it.*

21 Disconnect the oxygen sensor wiring plugs at the rear of the engine **(see illustration)**.
22 Unscrew the sensors from the manifold or exhaust section as applicable **(see illustrations)**.
23 On refitting, clean the sealing washer (where fitted) and renew it if it is damaged or worn. Apply a smear of anti-seize compound to the sensor's threads, then refit the sensor, tightening it to the specified torque. Reconnect the wiring and secure with cable-ties where applicable.

EGR solenoid/valve renewal

24 Remove the plastic cover on the top of the engine by pulling it straight up from its mountings.

25 Remove the air cleaner assembly as described in Chapter 4A Section 5.
26 Drain the coolant as described in Chapter 1A Section 30. Alternatively, use hose clamps prior to disconnecting the coolant hoses from the EGR valve.
27 Disconnect the EGR valve/solenoid wiring plug **(see illustration)**.
28 Release the clamps and disconnect the coolant hoses from the EGR valve.
29 Undo the two bolts and remove the EGR valve/solenoid. Recover the gasket.
30 Refitting is a reversal of removal, renewing the gasket where applicable.

---

3 Diesel engine emission control systems – checking and component renewal

Crankcase emission control

Checking

1 The components of this system require no attention other than to check that the hoses are clear and undamaged.

Oil separator renewal – 1.8 litre engines

2 The oil separator is located at the left-hand end of the cylinder head. Pull the plastic cover on the top of the engine upwards from its mountings at the front and right-hand edges, then pull it forwards.
3 Release the clamps and disconnect the breather hoses from the separator.

4 Undo the retaining bolts and remove the oil separator **(see illustrations)**.
5 Refitting is a reversal of removal.

Oil separator renewal – 2.0 litre engines

6 The oil separator is integral with the cylinder head cover/inlet manifold – refer to Chapter 2C Section 3.

Exhaust emission control

Checking

7 Checking of the system as a whole entails a close visual inspection of all hoses, pipes and connections for condition and security. Apart from this, any known or suspected faults should be attended to by a Ford dealer or suitably-equipped specialist.

Catalytic converter renewal

8 Refer to Chapter 4B Section 17.

Diesel particulate filter renewal

9 Refer to Chapter 4B Section 18.

EGR solenoid/valve renewal – 1.8 litre engines

10 Disconnect the battery negative lead as described in Chapter 5A Section 4.
11 Pull the plastic cover on the top of the engine upwards from its mountings at the front and right-hand edges, then pull it forwards.
12 Remove the exhaust manifold as described in Chapter 4B Section 17.
13 Disconnect the vacuum hose from the MAP sensor on the inlet manifold.

2.27 The EGR valve (arrowed) is located at the left-hand end of the cylinder head

3.4a Unscrew the mounting bolts...

3.4b... and remove the separator from the engine – 1.8 litre engines

3.14 Disconnect the wiring plug from the EGR valve (arrowed) –
1.8 litre engines

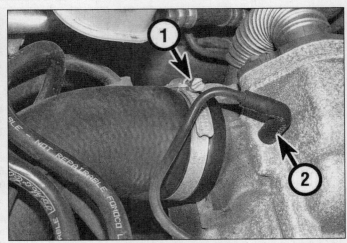

3.16 Air inlet hose clamp (1) and MAP sensor vacuum hose (2) –
1.8 litre engines

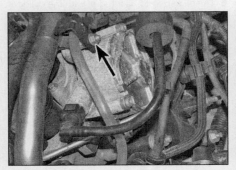

3.22 Undo the nut (arrowed) and remove
the stud securing the EGR pipe support
bracket – 2.0 litre engines to emission level
Stage III/IV

3.23a Release the EGR pipe clamp
(arrowed)…

EGR solenoid/valve renewal – 2.0 litre engines to emission level Stage III/IV

19 Disconnect the battery negative lead as described in Chapter 5A Section 4.

20 Pull the plastic cover on the top of the engine upwards from its mountings at the front and right-hand edges, then pull it forwards.

21 Remove the air cleaner assembly as described in Chapter 4B Section 5.

22 Undo the EGR pipe support bracket retaining nut (**see illustration**).

23 Release the clamp securing the EGR pipe to the inlet manifold, and the two bolts securing the pipe to the EGR valve (**see illustrations**).

24 Disconnect the wiring plug from the EGR valve.

25 Undo the bolts securing the EGR cooler to the valve (**see illustration**).

26 Slacken the EGR valve lower retaining bolt

27 Undo the two remaining retaining bolts and remove the valve. Note that if a new valve is fitted, the base setting must be programmed using Ford specialist diagnostic equipment.

14 Note their fitted positions, then disconnect the various wiring plugs from the EGR valve/inlet manifold (**see illustration**).

15 Unclip the EGR cooler coolant hose from the support bracket.

16 Slacken the clamp and disconnect the air hose from the inlet manifold (**see illustration**).

17 Undo the retaining nuts/bolts and remove the inlet manifold. Note that the EGR valve is integral with the manifold.

18 Refitting is a reversal of removal, tightening the retaining bolts securely.

3.23b… and undo the two bolts securing the pipe to the valve – 2.0
litre engines to emission level Stage III/IV

3.25 EGR cooler-to-valve bolts (arrowed) – 2.0 litre engines to
emission level Stage III/IV

28 Refitting is a reversal of removal, tightening the retaining bolts securely.

EGR solenoid/valve renewal – 2.0 litre engines to emission level Stage V

29 The EGR solenoid/valve is an integral part of the EGR cooler and must not be separated. EGR cooler removal and refitting procedures are described later in this Section.

EGR cooler renewal – 1.8 litre engines

30 Disconnect the battery negative lead as described in Chapter 5A Section 4.
31 Pull the plastic cover on the top of the engine upwards from its mountings at the front and right-hand edges, then pull it forwards.
32 Drain the cooling system as described in Chapter 1B Section 30.
33 Disconnect the inlet air temperature sensor wiring plug. Unclip the fuel pipes, then undo the nut, slacken the clamps and remove the intercooler air outlet duct from the right-hand end of the engine (see illustrations).
34 Release the clamps and disconnect the coolant hoses from the EGR cooler.
35 Undo the bolts securing the cooler to the exhaust manifold and inlet manifold, then manoeuvre it from position.
36 Refitting is a reversal of removal tightening the retaining bolts securely. Refill the cooling system as described in Chapter 1B Section 30.

EGR cooler renewal – 2.0 litre engines to emission level Stage III/IV

37 Disconnect the battery negative lead as described in Chapter 5A Section 4.
38 Pull the plastic cover on the top of the engine upwards from its mountings at the front and right-hand edges, then pull it forwards.
39 Drain the cooling system as described in Chapter 1B Section 30.
40 Release the clamp and disconnect the turbocharger inlet pipe breather hose.
41 Prise out the wire clip and disconnect the heater-to-EGR cooler hose, then release the clamp and disconnect the coolant

3.33a Disconnect the inlet air temperature sensor wiring plug...

3.33b... unclip the fuel pipes...

3.33c... then undo the nut, slacken the clamps and remove the air outlet duct – 1.8 litre engines

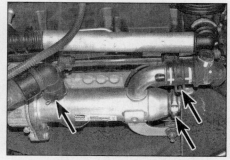

3.41 EGR cooler pipe clamp and coolant hose clamps (arrowed) – 2.0 litre engines to emission level Stage III/IV

bypass-to-EGR cooler hose (see illustration).
42 Undo the nuts and remove the EGR tube heat shield.
43 Release the clamp, undo the two retaining nuts, and remove the EGR cooler 'elbow' connecting pipe (see illustration). Renew the gasket.
44 Undo the nut and the two retaining bolts, and remove the EGR cooler.
45 Refitting is a reversal of removal, tightening the retaining bolts securely. Refill the cooling system as described in Chapter 1B Section 30.

EGR cooler renewal – 2.0 litre engines to emission level Stage V

46 Disconnect the battery negative lead as described in Chapter 5A Section 4.
47 Pull the plastic cover on the top of the engine upwards from its mountings at the front and right-hand edges, then pull it forwards.
48 Lift the engine oil filler tube support clip out of the bracket on the manifold and move the tube to one side (see illustration).
49 Disconnect the wiring harness connectors at the sensors and block connectors, then release the harness from the cable clips

3.43 EGR elbow-to-manifold nuts (arrowed) – 2.0 litre engines to emission level Stage III/IV

3.48 Lift the oil filler tube support clip (arrowed) out of the bracket on the manifold – 2.0 litre engines to emission level Stage V

3.49 Disconnect the connectors, then release the harness from the cable clips (arrowed) – 2.0 litre engines to emission level Stage V

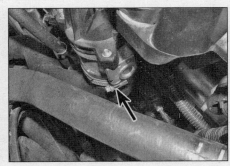

3.50 Slacken the clamp (arrowed) and disconnect the intercooler charge air hose – 2.0 litre engines to emission level Stage V

3.51 Undo the bolts (arrowed) securing the manifold upper section to the lower section – 2.0 litre engines to emission level Stage V

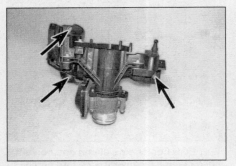

3.52a Undo the three nuts (arrowed) securing the manifold lower section to the cylinder head (shown with manifold removed)…

3.52b… and remove the lower section from the car – 2.0 litre engines to emission level Stage V

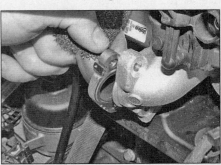

3.53 Undo the manifold-to-EGR valve pipe-to-elbow bolts, then separate the joint and collect the metal gasket – 2.0 litre engines to emission level Stage V

around the front of the inlet manifold (see illustration). Move the harness to one side.

50 Slacken the retaining clamp and disconnect the intercooler charge air hose from the inlet manifold lower section (see illustration).

51 Undo the three bolts securing the inlet manifold upper section to the lower section(see illustration).

52 Undo the three nuts securing the inlet manifold lower section to the cylinder head, and remove the lower section from the car (see illustrations).

53 Undo the two bolts securing the manifold-to-EGR valve pipe to the EGR valve elbow. Separate the joint and collect the metal gasket (see illustration).

54 Release the clip and disconnect the

coolant hose from the base of the EGR cooler (see illustration).

55 Disconnect the wiring connectors and vacuum hose from the EGR valve.

56 Undo the nut securing the engine oil dipstick guide tube to the cooler (see illustration).

57 Undo the upper right-hand bolt, and the left-hand nut and two bolts securing the

3.54 Release the clip and disconnect the coolant hose from the base of the EGR cooler – 2.0 litre engines to emission level Stage V

3.56 Undo the nut (arrowed) securing the engine oil dipstick guide tube to the cooler – 2.0 litre engines to emission level Stage V

3.57a Undo the upper right-hand bolt (arrowed)...

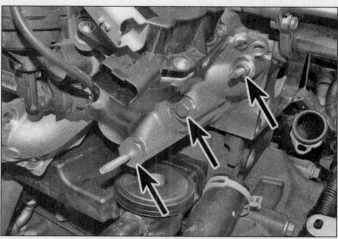

3.57b... and the left-hand nut and two bolts (arrowed) securing the cooler to the cylinder head – 2.0 litre engines to emission level Stage V

3.58a Withdraw the cooler and EGR valve assembly from the cylinder head...

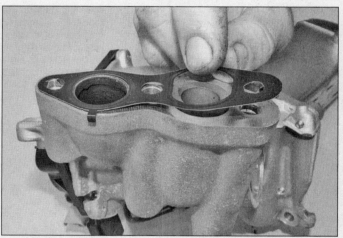

3.58b... and recover the gasket – 2.0 litre engines to emission level Stage V

cooler to the cylinder head (see illustrations). Unscrew the stud at the upper left-hand mounting.

58 Withdraw the cooler and EGR valve assembly from the cylinder head and recover the gasket (see illustrations). No further dismantling is possible.

59 Refitting is a reversal of removal using a new gasket and tightening the retaining bolts securely. Refill the cooling system as described in Chapter 1B Section 30.

4 Catalytic converter – general information and precautions

1 The catalytic converter reduces harmful exhaust emissions by chemically converting the more poisonous gases to ones which (in theory at least) are less harmful. The chemical reaction is known as an 'oxidising' reaction, or one where oxygen is 'added'.

2 Inside the converter is a honeycomb structure, made of ceramic material and coated with the precious metals palladium, platinum and rhodium (the 'catalyst' which promotes the chemical reaction). The chemical reaction generates heat, which itself promotes the reaction – therefore, once the car has been driven several miles, the body of the converter will be very hot.

3 The ceramic structure contained within the converter is understandably fragile, and will not withstand rough treatment. Since the converter runs at a high temperature, driving through deep standing water (in flood conditions, for example) is to be avoided, since the thermal stresses imposed when plunging the hot converter into cold water may well cause the ceramic internals to fracture, resulting in a 'blocked' converter – a common cause of failure. A converter which has been damaged in this way can be checked by shaking it (do not strike it) – if a rattling noise is heard, this indicates probable failure.

Precautions

4 Always renew seals and gaskets upstream of the catalytic converter (between the engine and converter) whenever they are disturbed.

5 The catalytic converter is a reliable and simple device which needs no maintenance in itself, but there are some facts of which an owner should be aware if the converter is to function properly for its full service life:

Petrol engines

a) DO NOT use leaded petrol (or lead-replacement petrol, LRP) in a car equipped with a catalytic converter – the lead (or other additives) will coat the precious metals, reducing their converting efficiency and will eventually destroy the converter.

b) Always keep the ignition and fuel systems well-maintained in accordance with the manufacturer's schedule (see Chapter 1A Section 2).

c) If the engine develops a misfire, do not

4C•8 Emission control systems

drive the car at all (or at least as little as possible) until the fault is cured.

d) DO NOT push- or tow-start the car – this will soak the catalytic converter in unburned fuel, causing it to overheat when the engine does start.

e) DO NOT switch off the ignition at high engine speeds – ie, do not 'blip' the throttle immediately before switching off the engine.

f) DO NOT use fuel or engine oil additives – these may contain substances harmful to the catalytic converter.

g) DO NOT continue to use the car if the engine burns oil to the extent of leaving a visible trail of blue smoke.

h) Remember that the catalytic converter operates at very high temperatures. DO NOT, therefore, park the car in dry undergrowth, over long grass or piles of dead leaves after a long run.

i) As mentioned above, driving through deep water should be avoided if possible. The sudden cooling effect may fracture the ceramic honeycomb, damaging it beyond repair.

j) Remember that the catalytic converter is FRAGILE – do not strike it with tools during servicing work, and take care handling it when removing it from the car for any reason.

k) In some cases, a sulphurous smell (like that of rotten eggs) may be noticed from the exhaust. This is common to many catalytic converter-equipped cars, and has more to do with the sulphur content of the brand of fuel being used than the converter itself.

l) If a substantial loss of power is experienced, remember that this could be due to the converter being blocked. This can occur simply as a result of high mileage, but may be due to the ceramic element having fractured and collapsed internally (see paragraph 3). A new converter is the only cure in this instance.

m) The catalytic converter, used on a well-maintained and well-driven car, should last at least 100 000 miles – if the converter is no longer effective, it must be renewed.

Diesel engines

6 The catalytic converter fitted to diesel models is simpler than that fitted to petrol models, but it still needs to be treated with respect to avoid problems:

a) DO NOT use fuel or engine oil additives – these may contain substances harmful to the catalytic converter.

b) DO NOT continue to use the car if the engine burns (engine) oil to the extent of leaving a visible trail of blue smoke.

c) Remember that the catalytic converter operates at very high temperatures. DO NOT, therefore, park the car in dry undergrowth, over long grass or piles of dead leaves after a long run.

d) As mentioned above, driving through deep water should be avoided if possible. The sudden cooling effect will fracture the ceramic honeycomb, damaging it beyond repair.

e) Remember that the catalytic converter is FRAGILE – do not strike it with tools during servicing work, and take care handling it when removing it from the car for any reason.

f) If a substantial loss of power is experienced, remember that this could be due to the converter being blocked. This can occur simply as a result of high mileage, but may be due to the ceramic element having fractured and collapsed internally (see paragraph 3). A new converter is the only cure in this instance.

g) The catalytic converter, used on a well-maintained and well-driven car, should last at least 100 000 miles – if the converter is no longer effective, it must be renewed.

Chapter 5 Part A
Starting and charging systems

Contents

Degrees of difficulty

Easy, suitable for novice with little experience	Fairly easy, suitable for beginner with some experience	Fairly difficult, suitable for competent DIY mechanic	Difficult, suitable for experienced DIY mechanic 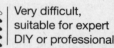	Very difficult, suitable for expert DIY or professional

Specifications

System type .... 12 volt, negative earth

Battery

Type .... Low-maintenance or maintenance-free sealed for life

Torque wrench settings

	Nm	lbf ft
Air conditioning compressor bolts (1.8 litre diesel engines)	25	18
Alternator mounting bolts/nuts:		
Petrol engines	47	35
1.8 litre diesel engines	25	18
2.0 litre diesel engines	47	25
Alternator pulley bracket bolts (1.8 litre diesel engines)	25	18
Battery negative lead-to-body retaining bolt	25	18
Glow plugs:		
1.8 litre engines	15	11
2.0 litre engines	10	7
Starter motor mounting bolts	40	30

1 General information and precautions

1 The engine electrical system consists mainly of the charging and starting systems. Because of their engine-related functions, these components are covered separately from the body electrical devices such as the lights, instruments, etc (which are covered in Chapter 12). Information on the ignition system is covered in Part B of this Chapter.

2 The electrical system is of the 12 volt negative earth type.

3 The battery is of the low-maintenance or maintenance-free (sealed for life) type, and is charged by the alternator, which is belt-driven from the crankshaft pulley.

4 The starter motor is of the pre-engaged type, incorporating an integral solenoid. On starting, the solenoid moves the drive pinion into engagement with the flywheel ring gear before the starter motor is energised. Once the engine has started, a one-way clutch prevents the motor armature being driven by the engine until the pinion disengages from the flywheel.

5 Further details of the various systems are given in the relevant Sections of this Chapter. While some repair procedures are given, the usual course of action is to renew the component concerned.

 Warning: It is necessary to take extra care when working on the electrical system to avoid damage to semi-conductor devices (diodes and transistors), and to avoid the risk of personal injury. In addition to the precautions given in Safety First!, observe the following when working on the system:

• Always remove rings, watches, etc, before working on the electrical system. Even with the battery disconnected, capacitive discharge could occur if a component's live terminal is earthed through a metal object. This could cause a shock or nasty burn.

• Do not reverse the battery connections. Components such as the alternator, electronic control units, or any other components having semi-conductor circuitry could be irreparably damaged.

• Never disconnect the battery terminals, the alternator, any electrical wiring or any test instruments when the engine is running.

• Do not allow the engine to turn the alternator when the alternator is not connected.

• Never test for alternator output by 'flashing' the output lead to earth.

• Always ensure that the battery negative lead is disconnected when working on the electrical system.

• If the engine is being started using jump leads and a slave battery, connect the batteries positive-to-positive and negative-to-negative (see Jump starting). This also applies when connecting a battery charger.

• Never use an ohmmeter of the type incorporating a hand-cranked generator for circuit or continuity testing.

• Before using electric-arc welding equipment on the car, disconnect the battery, alternator and components such as the electronic control units to protect them from the risk of damage.

2 Electrical fault finding – general information

1 Refer to Chapter 12 Section 2.

3 Battery – testing and charging

Testing

Standard and low-maintenance battery

1 If the car covers a small annual mileage, it is worthwhile checking the specific gravity of the electrolyte every three months to determine the state of charge of the battery. Use a hydrometer to make the check and compare the results with the following table. Note that the specific gravity readings assume an electrolyte temperature of 15°C; for every 10°C below 15°C subtract 0.007. For every 10°C above 15°C add 0.007.

	Ambient temperature	
	Above 25°C	Below 25°C
Fully-charged	1.210 to 1.230	1.270 to 1.290
70% charged	1.170 to 1.190	1.230 to 1.250
Discharged	1.050 to 1.070	1.110 to 1.130

2 If the battery condition is suspect, first check the specific gravity of electrolyte in each cell. A variation of 0.040 or more between any cells indicates loss of electrolyte or deterioration of the internal plates.

3 If the specific gravity variation is 0.040 or more, the battery should be renewed. If the cell variation is satisfactory but the battery is discharged, it should be charged as described later in this Section.

Maintenance-free battery

4 In cases where a 'sealed for life' maintenance-free battery is fitted, topping-up and testing of the electrolyte in each cell is not possible. The condition of the battery can therefore only be tested using a battery condition indicator or a voltmeter.

5 Certain models are fitted with a maintenance-free battery with a built-in charge condition indicator. The indicator is located in the top of the battery casing, and indicates the condition of the battery from its colour. The charge conditions denoted by the colour of the indicator should be printed on a label attached to the battery – if not, consult a Ford dealer or automotive electrician for advice.

All battery types

6 If testing the battery using a voltmeter, connect the voltmeter across the battery and note the voltage. The test is only accurate if the battery has not been subjected to any kind of charge for the previous six hours. If this is not the case, switch on the headlights for 30 seconds, then wait four to five minutes before testing the battery after switching off the headlights. All other electrical circuits must be switched off, so check that the doors and tailgate are fully shut when making the test.

7 If the voltage reading is less than 12.2 volts, then the battery is discharged, whilst a reading of 12.2 to 12.4 volts indicates a partially-discharged condition.

8 If the battery is to be charged, remove it from the vehicle and charge it as described later in this Section.

Charging

Note: *The following is intended as a guide only. Always refer to the manufacturer's recommendations (often printed on a label attached to the battery) before charging a battery.*

Standard and low-maintenance battery

9 Charge the battery at a rate equivalent to 10% of the battery capacity (eg, for a 45 Ah battery charge at 4.5 A) and continue to charge the battery at this rate until no further rise in specific gravity is noted over a four-hour period.

10 Alternatively, a trickle charger charging at the rate of 1.5 amps can safely be used overnight.

11 Specially rapid boost charges which are claimed to restore the power of the battery in 1 to 2 hours are not recommended, as they can cause serious damage to the battery plates through overheating. If the battery is completely flat, recharging should take at least 24 hours.

12 While charging the battery, note that the

temperature of the electrolyte should never exceed 38°C.

Maintenance-free battery

13 This battery type takes considerably longer to fully recharge than the standard type, the time taken being dependent on the extent of discharge, but it can take anything up to three days.

14 A constant voltage type charger is required, to be set, when connected, to 13.9 to 14.9 volts with a charger current below 25 amps. Using this method, the battery should be useable within three hours, giving a voltage reading of 12.5 volts, but this is for a partially-discharged battery and, as mentioned, full charging can take far longer.

15 If the battery is to be charged from a fully-discharged state (condition reading less than 12.2 volts), have it recharged by your Ford dealer or local automotive electrician, as the charge rate is higher, and constant supervision during charging is necessary.

4 Battery – disconnection, removal and refitting

Disconnection

Caution: Wait at least 5 minutes after turning off the ignition switch before disconnecting the battery. This is to allow sufficient time for the various control modules to store information.

Note: *Ensure you have the audio unit security code. This code will need to be inputted after reconnecting the battery – refer to the owner's handbook supplied with the vehicle.*

1 The battery is located on the left-hand side of the engine compartment, partially concealed under the windscreen cowl panel.

2 The location of the battery is such that access to the negative (earth) lead terminal clamp on the battery itself is impossible with the battery installed. It is therefore necessary to disconnect the negative lead at its connection on the body (see illustration).

3 Unscrew the negative lead retaining bolt while at the same time pulling upward on the lead to keep it in contact with the body (there is a small tab on the underside of the lead which maintains contact while the bolt is

4.2 Battery negative lead connection on the body (arrowed)

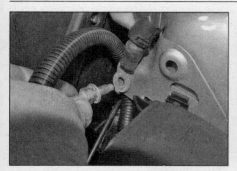

4.3 Unscrew the negative lead retaining bolt and pull the lead sharply away from the body

4.4 Cover the lead end fitting with a piece of rubber or plastic tubing

4.7a Release the two clips...

undone). With the bolt removed, pull the lead sharply away from the body **(see illustration)**.
4 Cover the lead end fitting with a piece of rubber or plastic tubing (such as a small piece of garden hose) to prevent accidental contact with the body **(see illustration)**. Alternatively wrap tape around the end fitting.

Removal

5 Disconnect the battery negative lead as described previously.
6 Remove the air cleaner assembly as described in Chapter 4A Section 5 or Chapter 4B Section 5, as applicable.
7 Release the two clips and remove the battery cover**(see illustrations)**.
8 Slacken the clamp nut and disconnect the battery positive lead terminal **(see illustration)**.
9 Unscrew the retaining bolt and remove the battery clamp plate **(see illustration)**.
10 Cut the cable-tie securing one of the battery positive leads to the base of the battery tray, and lift the other positive lead out of the battery tray guide **(see illustrations)**.
11 Move the positive leads clear, then slide the battery forward to gain access to the battery negative lead terminal. Slacken the clamp nut, disconnect the negative lead terminal and lift off the lead **(see illustration)**.
12 Lift the battery out of the engine compartment.
13 To remove the battery tray, undo the 3 bolts and lift the battery tray from the support platform **(see illustration)**.

4.7b... and remove the battery cover

4.8 Slacken the clamp nut and disconnect the battery positive lead terminal

4.9 Unscrew the retaining bolt and remove the battery clamp plate

4.10a Cut the cable-tie securing one of the battery positive leads to the battery tray...

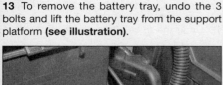

4.10b... and lift the other positive lead out of the battery tray guide

4.11 Slide the battery forward, slacken the clamp nut and disconnect the negative lead terminal

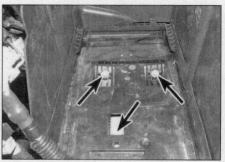

4.13 Battery tray retaining bolts (arrowed)

Refitting

14 If removed, place the battery tray in position and refit the three retaining bolts, tightening them securely.

15 Position the battery on the battery tray.

16 Reconnect the battery negative lead to the terminal and securely tighten the clamp nut. Smear a little petroleum jelly on the terminal.

17 Slide the battery back into its fitted position, then refit the clamp plate and tighten the bolt securely.

18 Reconnect the battery positive lead to the terminal and securely tighten the clamp nut. Smear a little petroleum jelly on the terminal.

19 Secure the positive lead with a new cable-tie and position the other positive lead in the battery tray guide.

20 Refit the battery cover.

21 Refit the air cleaner assembly as described in Chapter 4A Section 5 or Chapter 4B Section 5, as applicable.

22 Reconnect the battery negative lead to body as follows.

Reconnection

23 Ensure no-one is inside the vehicle whilst the battery negative lead is reconnected. Remove the rubber or plastic tubing or tape used to cover the negative lead end fitting and place the lead in position on the body. Hold the lead in contact with the body and fit the retaining bolt. Tighten the bolt to the specified torque.

24 Enter the audio unit security code and any preset radio frequencies.

25 Reset the clock to the correct time.

Powertrain control module initialisation

26 Carry out the following to allow the powertrain control module to relearn various engine operating parameters:
a) *Start the engine and allow it to run at idle for approximately 3 minutes.*
b) *Increase the engine speed to 1200 rpm and maintain this speed for approximately 2 minutes.*
c) *Drive the car for approximately 5 miles of varied driving. Note that during this time the engine may run erratically as the PCM relearns its parameters.*

Electric windows initialisation

27 Re-initialise the electric windows as follows:
a) *With the engine running, press and hold the window control close button until the window is fully closed.*
b) *Release the button, then press it again 3 times for 1 second each time.*
c) *Briefly press the open button to the second detent, then release it. The window should open automatically.*
d) *Briefly press the close button to the second detent, then release it. If the*

window does not close automatically, repeat the complete procedure.
e) *Repeat this procedure on each electric window.*

Sunroof initialisation

28 On models with an electric sunroof, re-initialise the sunroof as follows:
a) *With the ignition switched on, press the sunroof control button to the up/close position to tilt the rear of the sunroof as far as possible, then release the button.*
b) *Press and hold the same button again for 30 seconds until you see the sunroof move.*
c) *Release the button and immediately press and hold it again. The sunroof will close, open fully, then close again. Do not release the button until the sunroof has closed for the second time.*

---

5 Charging system – testing

Note: *Refer to the warnings given in* Safety First! *and in Section 1 of this Chapter before starting work.*

1 If the ignition/no charge warning light fails to illuminate when the ignition is switched on, first check the alternator wiring connections for security. If all is satisfactory, the alternator may be at fault and should be renewed or taken to an auto-electrician for testing and repair.

2 If the ignition warning light illuminates when the engine is running, stop the engine and check that the drivebelt is intact and correctly tensioned (see Chapter 1A Section 11 or Chapter 1B Section 9) and that the alternator connections are secure. If all is so far satisfactory, have the alternator checked by an auto-electrician for testing and repair.

3 If the alternator output is suspect even though the warning light functions correctly, the regulated voltage may be checked as follows.

4 Connect a voltmeter across the battery terminals and start the engine.

5 Increase the engine speed until the voltmeter reading remains steady; the reading should be between 13.5 and 14.8 volts.

6 Switch on as many electrical accessories (eg, the headlights, heated rear window and heater blower) as possible, and check that the alternator maintains the regulated voltage between 13.5 and 14.8 volts.

7 If the regulated voltage is not as stated, the fault may be due to worn brushes, weak brush springs, a faulty voltage regulator, a faulty diode, a severed phase winding, or worn or damaged slip-rings. At the time of writing, it would appear that no parts were available for the alternator. If faulty the complete assembly must be renewed. If in doubt, the alternator should be renewed or taken to an auto-electrician for testing.

---

6 Alternator – removal and refitting

Removal

1 Disconnect the battery negative lead (see Section 4).

2 Remove the auxiliary drivebelt as described in Chapter 1A Section 25 or Chapter 1B Section 24, as applicable.

Petrol engines

3 Remove the plastic cover on the top of the engine by pulling it straight upwards from its mountings.

4 If not already done, raise the vehicle and support it securely on axle stands (see 'Jacking and vehicle support'). Where fitted, undo the fasteners and remove the engine undertray.

5 Disconnect the wiring plug, then prise out the rubber cap and disconnect the lead from the rear of the alternator. Unclip the alternator wiring harness and move it to one side.

6 Undo the two nuts and remove the exhaust manifold heat shield.

7 Undo the alternator upper mounting nut and the lower mounting bolt and mounting nut, then remove the alternator from below.

1.8 litre diesel engines

8 Remove the plastic cover on the top of the engine by pulling it straight upwards from its mountings.

9 If not already done, raise the vehicle and support it securely on axle stands (see 'Jacking and vehicle support'). Where fitted, undo the fasteners and remove the engine undertray.

10 Disconnect the air conditioning compressor wiring connector, then undo the three bolts and move the compressor to one side.

Caution: Do not disconnect the refrigerant pipes.

11 Disconnect the wiring plug, then prise out the rubber cap and disconnect the lead from the rear of the alternator **(see illustration)**. Unclip the alternator wiring harness and move it to one side.

12 Undo the three alternator pulley bracket

6.11 Prise up the plastic cover (arrowed) then disconnect the alternator wiring

bolts, then slacken the three alternator decoupler bolts and remove the decoupler **(see illustrations)**.

13 Unscrew the alternator mounting bolts and carefully lift the alternator from the engine

2.0 litre diesel engines

14 Remove the plastic cover on the top of the engine by pulling it straight upwards from its mountings.

15 If not already done, raise the vehicle and support it securely on axle stands (see *'Jacking and vehicle support'*). Where fitted, undo the fasteners and remove the engine undertray.

16 Undo the three retaining bolts and move the power steering pump to one side.

17 Disconnect the wiring plug, then prise out the rubber cap and disconnect the lead from the rear of the alternator.

18 Slacken the alternator lower mounting clamp bolt, then undo the upper mounting bolts, slide the alternator to the right, and manoeuvre it from its location**(see illustration)**.

Refitting

19 Refitting is a reversal of removal. Remembering to tighten the various fasteners to their specified torque where given.

6.12a Undo the three pulley bracket bolts...

6.12b... slacken the three decoupler bolts...

6.12c... and remove the decoupler from the alternator

6.18 Undo the upper bolts, and slacken the lower Allen bolt (arrowed)

---

7 Starting system – testing

Note: *Refer to the precautions given in* Safety First! *and in Section 1 of this Chapter before starting work.*

1 If the starter motor fails to operate when the ignition key is turned to the appropriate position, or the start/stop button is pressed, the following possible causes may be to blame:

a) *The anti-theft system does not recognise the ignition key code or the passive key code.*

b) *The clutch pedal is not depressed (manual transmission models).*

c) *The gear selector lever is not in the P or N position and the brake pedal is not depressed (automatic transmission models).*

d) *The battery is faulty.*

e) *The electrical connections between the switch, solenoid, battery and starter motor are somewhere failing to pass the necessary current from the battery through the starter to earth.*

f) *The solenoid is faulty.*

g) *The starter motor is mechanically or electrically defective.*

2 To check the battery, switch on the headlights. If they dim after a few seconds, this indicates that the battery is discharged – recharge (see Section 3) or renew the battery. If the headlights glow brightly, operate the ignition switch or start/stop button and

observe the lights. If they dim, then this indicates that current is reaching the starter motor, therefore the fault must lie in the starter motor. If the lights continue to glow brightly (and no clicking sound can be heard from the starter motor solenoid), this indicates that there is a fault in the circuit or solenoid – see following paragraphs. If the starter motor turns slowly when operated, but the battery is in good condition, then this indicates that either the starter motor is faulty, or there is considerable resistance somewhere in the circuit.

3 If a fault in the circuit is suspected, disconnect the battery leads (see Section 4), the starter/solenoid wiring and the engine/transmission earth connections. Thoroughly clean the connections, and reconnect the leads and wiring, then use a voltmeter or test light to check that full battery voltage is available at the battery positive lead connection to the solenoid, and that the earth is sound. Smear petroleum jelly around the battery terminals to prevent corrosion – corroded connections are amongst the most frequent causes of electrical system faults.

4 If the battery and all connections are in good condition, check the circuit by disconnecting the wire from the solenoid blade terminal. Connect a voltmeter or test light between the wire end and a good earth (such as the battery negative lead connection on the body), and check that the wire is live when the ignition switch is turned to the start position or the stop/start button is pressed.

If it is, then the circuit is sound – if not, the circuit wiring can be checked as described in Chapter 12 Section 2.

5 The solenoid contacts can be checked by connecting a voltmeter or test light between the battery positive feed connection on the starter side of the solenoid, and earth. When the ignition switch is turned to the start position or the start/stop button is pressed, there should be a reading or lighted bulb, as applicable. If there is no reading or lighted bulb, the solenoid is faulty and should be renewed.

6 If the circuit and solenoid are proved sound, the fault must lie in the starter motor. In this event, it may be possible to have the starter motor overhauled by a specialist, but check on the cost of spares before proceeding, as it may prove more economical to obtain a new or exchange motor.

---

8 Starter motor – removal and refitting

Removal

1 Disconnect the battery negative lead (see Section 4).

Petrol engines

2 Raise the front of the vehicle and support it securely on axle stands (see *'Jacking and vehicle support'*).

8.3 Undo the nut (arrowed) and slide the wiring terminal from the stud

8.4 Remove the wiring harness bracket from the starter motor retaining studs/bolts

8.9 Remove the wiring connectors from the starter motor

3 Disconnect the wiring from the starter solenoid **(see illustration)**.

4 Undo the retaining nuts and move the wiring bracket to one side **(see illustration)**.

5 Undo the mounting stud bolts and remove the starter motor. Discard the gasket and obtain a new one for refitting.

1.8 litre diesel engines

6 Remove the air cleaner assembly as described in Chapter 4B Section 5.

7 Undo the support bracket nuts and bolts and move the intercooler charge air pipe to one side.

8 Raise the front of the vehicle and support it securely on axle stands (see *'Jacking and vehicle support'*). Undo the fasteners and remove the engine undertray.

9 Undo the nuts, and disconnect the wiring connections from the starter motor **(see illustration)**.

10 Undo the three mounting bolts and remove the starter downwards.

2.0 litre diesel engines

11 Pull the plastic cover on the top of the engine upwards to release its mountings.

12 Undo the nuts and disconnect the wiring from the starter motor solenoid **(see illustration)**.

13 Undo the 3 mounting bolts, and remove the starter motor **(see illustration)**. Check the locating dowel is still in place in the starter motor mounting face.

Refitting

14 Refitting is a reversal of removal. Tighten

all fasteners to their specified torque where given.

9 Starter motor – testing and overhaul

1 If the starter motor is thought to be suspect, it should be removed from the vehicle and taken to an auto-electrician for testing. Most auto-electricians will be able to supply and fit brushes at a reasonable cost. However, check on the cost of repairs before proceeding, as it may prove more economical to obtain a new or exchange motor.

10 Preheating system – general information

1 To assist cold starting, diesel engine models are fitted with a preheating system, which comprises a relay, and four glow plugs. The system is controlled by the engine management powertrain control module (PCM), using information provided by the coolant temperature sensor or cylinder head temperature sensor (see Chapter 3 Section 5).

2 The glow plugs are miniature electric heating elements, encapsulated in a metal case with a probe at one end, and an electrical connection at the other. The combustion chambers have a glow plug threaded into it. When the glow plug is energised, it heats

up rapidly causing the temperature of the air charge drawn into each of the combustion chambers to rise. Each glow plug probe is positioned directly in line with the incoming spray of fuel from the injector. Hence the fuel passing over the glow plug probe is also heated, allowing its optimum combustion temperature to be achieved more readily.

3 The duration of the preheating period is governed by the engine management PCM, using information provided by the coolant temperature or cylinder head temperature sensor (see Chapter 3 Section 5). The PCM alters the preheating time (the length for which the glow plugs are supplied with current) to suit the prevailing conditions.

4 A warning light informs the driver that preheating is taking place. The light extinguishes when sufficient preheating has taken place to allow the engine to be started, but power will still be supplied to the glow plugs for a further period, known as post-heating, to reduce exhaust emissions. If no attempt is made to start the engine, the power supply to the glow plugs is switched off to prevent battery drain and glow plug burn-out.

11 Preheating system – testing

1 Full testing of the system can only be carried out using specialist diagnostic equipment which is connected to the engine management system diagnostic connector (see Chapter 4B Section 12). If the preheating system is thought to be faulty, some preliminary checks of the glow plug operation may be made as described in the following paragraphs.

2 Connect a voltmeter or 12 volt test lamp between the glow plug supply cable, and a good earth point on the engine.

Caution: Make sure that the live connection is kept well clear of the engine and bodywork.

3 Have an assistant activate the preheating system by turning the ignition key to the second position, or pressing the start/stop button, and check that battery voltage is applied to the glow plug electrical connection.

Note: *The supply voltage will be less than*

8.12 Undo the nuts (arrowed) and disconnect the wiring

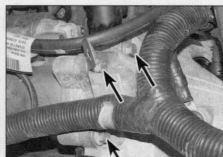

8.13 Starter motor bolts (arrowed)

12.5 Undo the nuts (right-hand side glow plugs arrowed) and disconnect the supply cable

12.8 Undo the nuts (arrowed) securing the electrical connections to the glow plugs

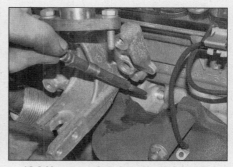

12.9 Unscrew the glow plugs from the cylinder head

battery voltage initially, but will rise and settle as the glow plug heats up. It will then drop to zero when the preheating period ends and the safety cut-out operates.

4 If no supply voltage can be detected at the glow plug, then the glow plug relay or the supply cable may be faulty.

5 To locate a faulty glow plug, measure the electrical resistance between the glow plug terminal and the engine earth, and compare it with the resistance of the other glow plugs, or a known working example. If the reading is significantly different, the glow plug is probably defective.

6 If no problems are found, take the vehicle to a Ford dealer or specialist for testing using the appropriate diagnostic equipment.

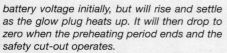

12 Glow plugs – removal, inspection and refitting

Removal

1 Disconnect the battery negative lead as described in Section 4.

1.8 litre engines

2 Pull the plastic cover on the top of the engine upwards to release it from the mountings.

3 Release the clamps and disconnect the two engine breather hoses from the front of the cylinder head cover.

4 Undo the bolt securing the engine oil level dipstick guide tube.

5 Undo the nuts and disconnect the electrical supply cable from the top of each glow plug **(see illustration)**.

6 Using a deep socket, carefully unscrew each glow plug from the cylinder head.

2.0 litre engines

7 Remove the EGR valve cooler as described in Chapter 4B Section 18.

8 Undo the nuts (where fitted) and disconnect the electrical supply cable from the top of each glow plug **(see illustration)**.

9 Unscrew each glow plug from the cylinder head using a deep socket **(see illustration)**.

Inspection

10 Inspect the glow plugs for signs of damage. Burt or eroded glow plug tips can be caused by a bad injector spray pattern. Have the injectors checked if this sort of damage is found.

11 If the glow plugs are in good condition, check them electrically, as described in Section 11.

12 The glow plugs can be energised by applying 12 volts to them to verify that they

heat up evenly and in the required time. Observe the following precautions:

a) *Support the glow plug by clamping it carefully in a vice or self-locking pliers. Remember it will be red hot.*

b) *Make sure that the power supply or test lead incorporates a fuse or overload trip to protect against damage from a short-circuit*

c) *After testing, allow the glow plug to cool for several minutes before attempting to handle it.*

13 A glow plug in good condition will start to glow red at the tip after drawing current for 5 seconds or so. Any plug which takes much longer to start glowing, or which starts glowing in the middle instead of at the tip, is probably defective.

Refitting

14 Thoroughly clean the glow plugs, and the glow plug seating areas in the cylinder head.

15 Apply a smear of anti-seize compound to the glow plug threads, then refit the glow plug and tighten it to the specified torque.

16 Reconnect the wiring to the glow plug and tighten the nut securely.

17 The remainder of refitting is a reversal of removal.

Notes

Chapter 5 Part B
Ignition system – petrol models

Contents

Degrees of difficulty

Easy, suitable for novice with little experience	Fairly easy, suitable for beginner with some experience	Fairly difficult, suitable for competent DIY mechanic	Difficult, suitable for experienced DIY mechanic	Very difficult, suitable for expert DIY or professional

Specifications

General

System type .... Electronic distributorless ignition system controlled by engine management system Powertrain Control Module (PCM)

Firing order 1-3-4-2
Location of No 1 cylinder .... Timing chain end of engine

Ignition system data

Ignition timing .... Controlled by the powertrain control module (PCM)
Ignition coil resistances .... Not available

Torque wrench settings

	Nm	lbf ft
Ignition coil	10	7
Knock sensor	20	15

1 Ignition system – general information and precautions

General information

1 The ignition system is integrated with the fuel injection system to form a combined engine management system under the control of the powertrain control module (PCM) (see Chapter 4A Section 10 for further information). The main ignition system components include the ignition switch, the battery, the crankshaft speed/position sensor, the ignition coils, the camshaft position sensor, the knock sensor, and the spark plugs.

2 A distributorless ignition system (DIS) is fitted where the main functions of the conventional distributor are superseded by a computerised module within the PCM. One ignition coil is fitted for each spark plug. The coil fits above the spark plug, and has an integral power stage and HT cap.

3 The crankshaft speed/position sensor signal provides the basis for ignition timing calculations within the PCM. From an ignition map, the PCM determines the ignition timing settings according to engine operating conditions. Once the ignition timing is determined, the PCM interrupts the current supply to the ignition coil primary circuit, thereby producing an ignition spark which passes to the cylinder via the spark plug.

4 The ignition coils are activated in pairs (cylinders 1 and 4, and cylinders 2 and 3) and provide a strong primary spark to the cylinder on the compression stroke and a weak secondary spark to the cylinder on the exhaust stroke. The primary spark is generated automatically in the cylinder on the compression stroke, because a higher resistance exists between the spark plug electrodes due to the high compression. On one spark plug, a spark jumps from the centre electrode to the earth electrode, and on the other spark plug from the earth electrode to the centre electrode.

5 The information contained in this Chapter concentrates on the ignition-related components of the engine management system. Information covering the fuel, exhaust and emission control components can be found in the applicable Parts of Chapter 4A.

Precautions

6 The following precautions must be observed, to prevent damage to the ignition system components and to reduce risk of personal injury.

a) Do not keep the ignition on for more than 10 seconds if the engine will not start.
b) Ensure that the ignition is switched off before disconnecting any of the ignition wiring.
c) Ensure that the ignition is switched off before connecting or disconnecting any ignition test equipment.
d) Do not earth the coil primary or secondary circuits.

⚠ **Warning: Due to the high voltages produced by the electronic ignition system, extreme care must be taken when working on the system with the ignition switched on. Persons with surgically-implanted cardiac pacemaker devices should keep well clear of the ignition circuits, components and test equipment.**

3.2 Press down the clip and disconnect the coil wiring plug

3.3 Undo the bolt and pull the coil from the cylinder head

5.4 The knock sensor (arrowed) is located under the inlet manifold

2 Ignition system – testing

General

1 The components of the ignition system are normally very reliable; most faults are far more likely to be due to loose or dirty connections, or to tracking of HT voltage due to dirt, dampness or damaged insulation, than to the failure of any of the system's components. Always check all wiring thoroughly before condemning an electrical component, and work methodically to eliminate all other possibilities before deciding that a particular component is faulty.

2 The old practice of checking for a spark by holding the live end of an HT cap a short distance away from the engine is not recommended; not only is there a high risk of a powerful electric shock, but the PCM or HT coil may be damaged. Similarly, never try to diagnose misfires by pulling off one HT coil at a time.

3 The following tests should be carried out when an obvious fault such as non-starting or a clearly detectable misfire exists. Some faults, however, are more obscure and are often disguised by the fact that the PCM will adopt an emergency programme (limp-home) mode to maintain as much driveability as possible. Faults of this nature usually appear in the form of excessive fuel consumption, poor idling characteristics, lack of performance, knocking or pinking noises from the engine under certain conditions, or a combination of these conditions. Where problems such as this are experienced, the best course is to refer the car to a suitably-equipped garage for diagnostic testing using dedicated test equipment.

Engine will not start

Note: *Remember that a fault with the anti-theft alarm or immobiliser will give rise to apparent starting problems. Make sure that the alarm or immobiliser has been deactivated, referring to the vehicle handbook for details.*

4 If the engine either will not turn over at all, or only turns very slowly, check the battery and starter motor. Connect a voltmeter across the battery terminals (meter positive probe to battery positive terminal) then note the voltage reading obtained while turning the engine over on the starter for (no more than) ten seconds. If the reading obtained is less than approximately 9.5 volts, first check the battery, starter motor and charging system as described in Part A of this Chapter.

Engine misfires

5 An irregular misfire is probably due to a loose connection to one of the ignition coils or system sensors.

6 With the ignition switched off, check carefully through the system, ensuring that all connections are clean and securely fastened.

7 If these checks fail to reveal the cause of the problem, the car should be taken to a suitably-equipped Ford dealer or engine management diagnostic specialist for testing. A diagnostic socket is incorporated in the engine management circuit into which a fault code reader or other suitable test equipment can be connected (see Chapter 4A Section 10). By using the code reader or test equipment, the engine management PCM can be interrogated, and any stored fault codes can be retrieved. This will allow the fault to be quickly and simply traced, alleviating the need to test all the system components individually, which is a time-consuming operation that carries a risk of damaging the PCM.

3 HT coil(s) – removal and refitting

Removal

1 Remove the plastic cover from the top of the engine, by pulling it upwards from the mountings.

2 Disconnect the ignition coil(s) wiring plug(s) **(see illustration)**. It is safest to work on one coil at a time. However, if the coils and the wiring plugs are marked for position, all four could be removed at once.

3 Each coil is secured by one bolt. Undo the bolt and pull the coil from the cylinder head **(see illustration)**.

Refitting

4 Refitting is a reversal of removal. Tighten the retaining bolts to the specified torque.

4 Ignition timing – checking and adjustment

1 Due to the nature of the ignition system, the ignition timing is constantly being monitored and adjusted by the engine management PCM, and nominal values cannot be given. Therefore, it is not possible for the home mechanic to check the ignition timing.

2 The only way in which the ignition timing can be checked is using special electronic test equipment, connected to the engine management system diagnostic connector (refer to Chapter 4A Section 10). No adjustment of the ignition timing is possible. Should the ignition timing be incorrect, then a fault must be present in the engine management system.

5 Knock sensor – removal and refitting

Removal

1 The knock sensor is located on the front facing side of the cylinder block under the inlet manifold.

2 Refer to Chapter 4A Section 11 and remove the inlet manifold.

3 Disconnect the wiring connector from the knock sensor.

4 Note the fitted position of the sensor, it is essential that it is refitted to its original position. Undo the retaining bolt and remove the sensor **(see illustration)**.

Refitting

5 Refitting is a reversal of removal, noting the following points:

a) *The sensor must be refitted in its original position, with the wiring harness angle exactly as before.*

b) *Tightening the retaining bolt to the specified torque is absolutely essential. Failure to do so could impair the performance of the sensor, causing engine damage.*

Chapter 6
Clutch

Contents

Degrees of difficulty

Easy, suitable for novice with little experience	Fairly easy, suitable for beginner with some experience	Fairly difficult, suitable for competent DIY mechanic 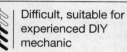	Difficult, suitable for experienced DIY mechanic	Very difficult, suitable for expert DIY or professional

Specifications

General

Clutch type . . . . Single dry plate, diaphragm spring, hydraulically-operated release mechanism

Driven plate

Driven plate minimum thickness:
Petrol engines	5.7 mm
1.8 litre diesel engines	5.0 mm
2.0 litre diesel engines	5.7 mm

Torque wrench settings

	Nm	lbf ft
Clutch cover/pressure plate to flywheel*	29	21
Clutch pedal bracket nuts	28	21
Clutch slave cylinder mounting bolts*	10	7

*Do not re-use

1 General Information

1 All manual transmission models are equipped with a single dry plate diaphragm spring clutch assembly. The pressure plate assembly consists of a steel cover (doweled and bolted to the flywheel face), the pressure plate, and a diaphragm spring.

2 The driven plate is free to slide along the splines of the transmission input shaft, and is held in position between the flywheel and the pressure plate by the pressure of the diaphragm spring. Friction lining material is riveted to the driven plate (friction disc), which on some models, has a spring-cushioned hub, to absorb transmission shocks and help ensure a smooth take-up of the drive. On other models, a dual-mass flywheel is fitted, where the flywheel is split into two masses – a primary mass (incorporating the starter ring gear) secured to the engine crankshaft, and secondary mass which is the driving surface mated to the clutch driven plate. Between these two masses are rubber/spring elements which absorb the power pulses from the engine as well as the transmission shocks.

3 The clutch release bearing contacts the fingers of the diaphragm spring. Depressing the clutch pedal pushes the release bearing against the diaphragm fingers, so moving the centre of the diaphragm spring inwards. As the centre of the spring is pushed inwards, the outside of the spring pivots outwards, so moving the pressure plate backwards and disengaging its grip on the driven plate.

4 When the pedal is released, the diaphragm spring forces the pressure plate back into contact with the friction linings on the driven plate. The plate is now firmly held between the pressure plate and the flywheel, thus transmitting engine power to the transmission. On some models, a self-adjusting clutch (SAC) is fitted, where an adjustment ring rotates in the pressure plate assembly, adjusting the diaphragm spring fingers pivot points as the driven plate wears. This maintains the clutch pedal 'bite point'.

5 All Mondeo models have a hydraulically-operated clutch. A master cylinder is mounted below the clutch pedal, and takes its hydraulic fluid supply from a separate chamber in the brake fluid reservoir. Depressing the clutch pedal operates the master cylinder pushrod, and the fluid pressure is transferred along the fluid lines to a slave cylinder mounted inside the bellhousing. The slave cylinder is incorporated into the release bearing – when the slave cylinder operates, the release bearing moves against the diaphragm spring fingers and disengages the clutch.

6 The hydraulic clutch offers several advantages over a cable-operated clutch – it is completely self-adjusting, requires less pedal effort, and is less subject to wear problems.

⚠️ *Warning: The hydraulic fluid used in the system is brake fluid, which is poisonous. Take care to keep it off bare skin, and in particular out of your eyes. The fluid also attacks paintwork, and may discolour carpets, etc – keep spillages to a minimum, and wash any off immediately with cold water. Finally, brake fluid is highly inflammable, and should be handled with the same care as petrol.*

2 Clutch pedal –
removal and refitting

⚠️ *Warning: Hydraulic fluid is poisonous; wash off immediately and thoroughly in the case of skin contact, and seek immediate medical advice if any fluid is swallowed or gets into the eyes. Certain types of hydraulic fluid are inflammable, and may ignite when allowed into contact with hot components; when servicing any hydraulic system, it is safest to assume that the fluid IS inflammable, and to take precautions against the risk of fire as though it is petrol that is being handled. Hydraulic fluid is also an effective paint stripper, and will attack plastics; if any is spilt, it should be washed off immediately, using copious quantities of clean water. Finally, it is hygroscopic (it absorbs moisture from the air) – old fluid may be contaminated and unfit for further use. When topping-up or renewing the fluid, always use the recommended type, and ensure that it comes from a freshly-opened sealed container.*

Note: *If the clutch master cylinder is to be separated from the pedal bracket, a new master cylinder pushrod-to-clutch pedal retaining clip will be required for refitting.*

Removal

1 Remove the steering column as described in Chapter 10 Section 16.
2 Unscrew the filler cap from the brake

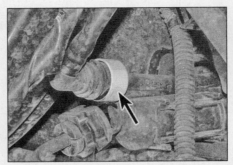
2.3 Pull back the collar (arrowed) and disconnect the fluid supply pipe

2.4 Prise down the clip and pull the pressure pipe from the clutch master cylinder

2.5a Disconnect the wiring connector at the clutch pedal actuation switch (arrowed)...

2.5b... and at the clutch pedal position switch (arrowed)

master cylinder reservoir on top of the brake master cylinder, and siphon the hydraulic fluid from the reservoir until it is at the MIN mark (below the outlet to the clutch master cylinder). Alternatively, open the slave cylinder bleed screw, and gently pump the clutch pedal to expel the fluid through a plastic tube connected to the screw; tighten the screw when all the fluid has been removed.

⚠️ *Warning: Do not siphon the fluid by mouth, as it is poisonous; use a syringe or an old poultry baster.*

3 Trace the fluid supply hose to the master cylinder connection on the bulkhead. Depress the release button, pull back the collar and disconnect the hose from the master cylinder **(see illustration)**. There will be some loss of fluid as the hose is removed – wipe up any spillage, and rinse any painted surfaces with

water (avoid getting water inside the clutch master cylinder).
4 Similarly, extract the retaining clip and disconnect the supply pipe to the clutch slave cylinder from the master cylinder connection on the bulkhead (this is the connection below the one just removed) **(see illustration)**.
5 From inside the car, disconnect the wiring connectors at the clutch pedal switches located on the pedal mounting bracket. Release the wiring from the clips on the pedal bracket **(see illustrations)**.
6 Undo the three retaining nuts and manoeuvre the clutch pedal complete with the bracket and master cylinder out from under the facia **(see illustrations)**.
7 To separate the master cylinder from the pedal bracket, prise off the retaining clip and pull the pushrod from the pedal **(see illustration)**.

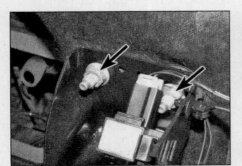
2.6a Clutch pedal mounting bracket upper retaining nuts (arrowed)...

2.6b... and lower retaining nut (arrowed)

2.7 Clutch master cylinder pushrod retaining clip (arrowed)

2.8 Rotate the master cylinder 60° anti-clockwise and pull it from the pedal bracket

Note that a new retaining clip will be required for refitting.

8 Rotate the master cylinder 60° anti-clockwise (as viewed from the pushrod side) and pull it from the bracket **(see illustration)**.

Refitting

9 Refitting is a reversal of removal, noting the following points:

a) Tighten the pedal bracket retaining nuts to the specified torque.

b) Renew the seal between the master cylinder and the bulkhead if necessary.

c) Bleed the clutch hydraulic system as described in Section 5.

d) Refit the steering column as described in Chapter 10 Section 16.

3 Clutch master cylinder – removal and refitting

Note: *At the time of writing, it would appear that master cylinder internal components are not available separately, and therefore no repair or overhaul of the cylinder is possible. In the event of a hydraulic system fault, or any sign of visible fluid leakage on or around the master cylinder or clutch pedal, the unit should be renewed – consult a Ford dealer or specialist.*

1 Removal and refitting of the master cylinder is included in the pedal removal and refitting procedure described previously.

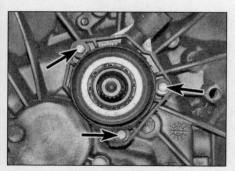

4.4 Slave cylinder mounting bolts (arrowed)

4 Clutch slave cylinder and release bearing – removal and refitting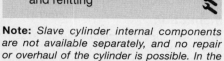

Note: *Slave cylinder internal components are not available separately, and no repair or overhaul of the cylinder is possible. In the event of a hydraulic system fault, or any sign of fluid leakage, the unit should be renewed.*
Note: *Refer to the warning at the beginning of Section 2 before proceeding.*

Removal

1 Remove the transmission as described in Chapter 7A Section 7. The internal slave cylinder cannot be removed with the transmission in place.

2 Wrap adhesive tape around the transmission input shaft splines to protect the slave cylinder oil seal lips during removal.

3 Release the rubber seal from the transmission.

4 Remove the mounting bolts securing the cylinder and release bearing assembly to the transmission, and remove the assembly, feeding the fluid pipe in through the transmission aperture **(see illustration)**. Discard the retaining bolts and obtain new ones for refitting.

Refitting

5 Ensure the release bearing/slave cylinder and transmission casing mating surfaces are clean. Apply a bead of sealant (Ford specification WSK-M2G348-A5) to the bearing/cylinder as shown **(see illustration)**.

6 Lubricate the inner lips of the seal with a little grease, then position the release bearing/slave cylinder on the input shaft, and tighten the new bolts to the specified torque. Take care not to damage the seal lips with the input shaft splines.

7 Refit the rubber seal around the pipes, ensuring it is correctly positioned.

8 The remainder of refitting is a reversal of removal, noting the following points:

a) Remove the adhesive tape from the input shaft splines.

b) Refit the transmission as described in Chapter 7A Section 7.

c) Bleed the clutch hydraulic system as described in Section 5.

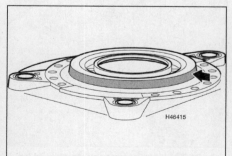

4.5 Apply a bead of sealant to the slave cylinder around the edge (arrowed)

5 Clutch hydraulic system – bleeding

Note: *Refer to the warning at the beginning of Section 2 before proceeding.*

1 The clutch hydraulic system will not normally require bleeding, and this task should only be necessary when the system has been opened for repair work. However, as with the brake pedal, if the clutch pedal feels at all spongy or unresponsive in operation, this may indicate the need for bleeding.

2 The system bleed screw is located on top of the transmission bellhousing **(see illustration)**.

3 To gain access to the bleed screw, remove the air cleaner as described in the relevant Part of Chapter 4A Section 5. Move the pipework and wiring harness to one side as necessary for access.

4 Remove the bleed screw dust cap.

5 Bleeding the clutch is much the same as bleeding the brakes – refer to Chapter 9 Section 2. Ensure that the level in the brake fluid reservoir is maintained well above the MIN mark at all times, otherwise the clutch and brake hydraulic systems will both need bleeding.

6 If conventional bleeding does not work, it may be necessary to use a hand operated-pressure pump. Siphon some of the fluid out of the reservoir until the level is at the MIN mark, remove the bleed screw dust cap and connect the hose from the hand pump. Fill the hand pump reservoir with new hydraulic fluid, open the bleed screw, and pump the fluid backwards through the slave cylinder/release bearing up to the reservoir until it reaches its MAX mark.

7 On completion, tighten the bleed screw securely, and top-up the brake fluid level to the MAX mark. If possible, test the operation of the clutch before refitting all the components removed for access.

8 Failure to bleed correctly may point to a leak in the system, or to a worn master or slave cylinder.

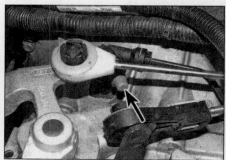

5.2 Clutch hydraulic system bleed screw (arrowed)

6 Clutch components – removal, inspection and refitting

Warning: Dust created by clutch wear and deposited on the clutch components may contain asbestos, which is a health hazard. DO NOT blow it out with compressed air, and do not inhale any of it. DO NOT use petrol or petroleum-based solvents to clean off the dust. Brake system cleaner or methylated spirit should be used to flush the dust into a suitable receptacle. After the clutch components are wiped clean with rags, dispose of the contaminated rags and cleaner in a sealed, marked container.

Removal

1 Access to the clutch may be gained in one of two ways. The engine/transmission unit can be removed, as described in Chapter 2D Section 4 or Chapter 2D Section 5, and the transmission separated from the engine on the bench. Alternatively, the engine may be left in the vehicle and the transmission removed independently, as described in Chapter 7A Section 7.

2 Having separated the transmission from the engine, check if there are any marks identifying the relation of the clutch pressure plate to the flywheel. If not, make your own marks using a dab of paint or a scriber. These marks will be used if the original pressure plate is refitted, and will help to maintain the balance of the unit. A new pressure plate may be fitted in any position allowed by the locating dowels.

3 Unscrew the six clutch pressure plate retaining bolts, working in a diagonal sequence, and slackening the bolts only a turn at a time **(see illustration)**. If necessary, the flywheel may be held stationary using a wide-bladed screwdriver, inserted in the teeth of the starter ring gear and resting against part of the cylinder block. Ford state that new pressure plate bolts must be used when refitting.

4 Ease the clutch pressure plate off its locating dowels. Be prepared to catch the clutch driven plate, which will drop out as the pressure plate is removed. Note which way round the driven plate is fitted.

Inspection

Note: *On models equipped with a self-adjusting clutch, Ford insist that if a new driven plate is fitted, the pressure plate must also be renewed.*

5 The most common problem which occurs in the clutch is wear of the clutch driven plate (friction disc). However, all the clutch components should be inspected at this time, particularly if the engine has covered a high mileage. Unless the clutch components are known to be virtually new, it is worth renewing them all as a set (driven plate, pressure plate and release bearing). Renewing a worn driven plate by itself is not always satisfactory, especially if the old one was slipping and causing the pressure plate to overheat.

6 Examine the linings of the driven plate for wear and loose rivets, and the plate hub and rim for distortion, cracks, broken torsion springs, and worn splines (where applicable). The surface of the friction linings may be highly glazed, but as long as the friction material pattern can be clearly seen, and the rivet heads are at least 1 mm below the lining surface, this is satisfactory. The plate must be renewed if the lining thickness has worn down to the minimum thickness given in the Specifications.

7 If there is any sign of oil contamination, indicated by shiny black discoloration, the driven plate must be renewed, and the source of the contamination traced and rectified. This will be a leaking crankshaft oil seal or transmission input shaft oil seal. The renewal procedure for the former is given in the relevant Part of Chapter 2A Section 10. The renewal procedure for the transmission input shaft oil seal is contained in Chapter 7A Section 4.

8 Check the machined faces of the flywheel and pressure plate. If either is grooved, or heavily scored, renewal is necessary. The pressure plate must also be renewed if any cracks are apparent, or if the diaphragm spring is damaged or its pressure suspect. Pay particular attention to the tips of the spring fingers, where the release bearing acts upon them.

9 With the transmission removed, it is also advisable to check the condition of the release bearing, although having got this far, it is almost certainly worth renewing it. Note that the release bearing is integral with the slave cylinder – the two must be renewed together; however, given that access to the slave cylinder is only possible with the transmission removed, not to renew it at this time is probably a false economy.

Refitting

10 It is important that no oil or grease is allowed to come into contact with the friction material of the driven plate or the pressure plate and flywheel faces. To ensure this, it is advisable to refit the clutch assembly with clean hands, and to wipe down the pressure plate and flywheel faces with a clean dry rag before assembly begins.

11 Ford technicians use a special tool for centralising the driven plate at this stage. The tool holds the driven plate centrally on the pressure plate, and locates in the middle of the diaphragm spring fingers. If the tool is not available, it will be necessary to centralise the driven plate after assembling the pressure plate loosely on the flywheel, as described in the following paragraphs.

12 Place the driven plate against the flywheel, ensuring that it is the right way round **(see illustrations)**. It may be marked FLYWHEEL SIDE, but if not, position it so that the raised hub with the cushion springs is facing away from the flywheel.

13 Place the clutch pressure plate over the dowels. Fit the new retaining bolts, and tighten them finger-tight so that the driven plate is gripped lightly, but can still be moved.

14 The driven plate must now be centralised so that, when the engine and transmission are mated, the splines of the transmission input shaft will pass through the splines in the centre of the driven plate hub.

15 Centralisation can be carried out by inserting a round bar through the hole in the centre of the driven plate, so that the end of the bar rests in the hole in the rear end of

6.3 Undo the pressure plate retaining bolts

6.12a The clutch driven plate should be marked to indicate which side faces the transmission or flywheel

6.12b Position the driven plate using a clutch aligning tool

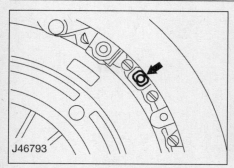

6.17 Check the 'stop-pin' (arrowed) is moveable as the bolts are tightened

7.2 Disconnect the clutch pedal actuation switch wiring connector

7.3 Push the tab (arrowed) to the left, then push the switch body down to disengage the two lugs

the crankshaft. Move the bar sideways or up-and-down, to move the driven plate in whichever direction is necessary to achieve centralisation. Centralisation can then be checked by removing the bar and viewing the driven plate hub in relation to the diaphragm spring fingers, or by viewing through the side apertures of the pressure plate, and checking that the disc is central in relation to the outer edge of the pressure plate.

16 An alternative and more accurate method of centralisation is to use a commercially-available clutch-aligning tool, obtainable from most accessory shops **(see illustration 6.12b)**.

17 Once the clutch is centralised, progressively tighten the pressure plate bolts in a diagonal sequence to the torque setting given in the Specifications. **Note:** *On models with a self-adjusting clutch, Check that the 'stop-pin' is moveable during the tightening of the bolts***(see illustration)**.

18 Ensure that the input shaft splines and driven plate splines are clean. Apply a thin smear of high melting-point grease to the input shaft splines – do not apply excessively,

however, or it may end up on the driven plate, causing the new clutch to slip.

19 Refit the transmission to the engine.

7 Clutch switches – removal, refitting and adjustment

Removal

Clutch pedal actuation switch

1 The clutch pedal actuation switch is located at the top of the clutch pedal mounting bracket.

2 Disconnect the switch wiring connector **(see illustration)**.

3 Push the tab at the top of the switch to the left, then push the switch body down to disengage the two locating lugs from the slots in the pedal bracket **(see illustration)**. Lift the switch out from its location.

Clutch pedal position switch

4 The clutch pedal position switch is located at the lower right-hand side of the clutch pedal mounting bracket**(see illustration)**.

7.4 Clutch pedal position switch (arrowed)

5 Disconnect the switch wiring connector.

6 Rotate the switch anti-clockwise by a quarter-turn, and withdraw it from the pedal bracket. Do not depress the clutch pedal during the removal or refitting procedure – the pedal must be 'at rest'.

Refitting and adjustment

7 Refitting is a reversal of the removal procedure. Both switches are automatically adjusted/calibrated by the vehicle system.

Chapter 7 Part A
Manual transmission

Contents

Degrees of difficulty

Easy, suitable for novice with little experience	Fairly easy, suitable for beginner with some experience	Fairly difficult, suitable for competent DIY mechanic	Difficult, suitable for experienced DIY mechanic	Very difficult, suitable for expert DIY or professional

Specifications

General

Transmission type	Five or six forward gears and one reverse. Synchromesh on all gears
Designation:	
5-speed	MTX 75
6-speed	MMT 6
Transmission oil type	See *Lubricants, fluids and tyre pressures*
Transmission oil capacity	See Chapter 1A or 1B Specifications

Gear ratios

Petrol engine models

1st	3.667: 1
2nd	2.136: 1
3rd	1.483: 1
4th	1.114: 1
5th	0.854: 1
Reverse	3.727: 1
Final drive	4.067: 1

1.8 litre diesel engine models

	5-speed transmission	6-speed transmission
1st	3.800: 1	3.583: 1
2nd	2.048: 1	1.952: 1
3rd	1.258: 1	1.241: 1
4th	0.865: 1	0.868: 1
5th	0.674: 1	0.943: 1
6th	N/A	0.789: 1
Reverse	3.727: 1	1.423: 1
Final drive	3.563: 1	

2.0 litre diesel engine models

1st	3.583: 1
2nd	1.952: 1
3rd	1.241: 1
4th	0.868: 1
5th	0.943: 1
6th	0.789: 1
Reverse	1.423: 1

Torque wrench settings

	Nm	lbf ft
Engine/transmission mountings	See Chapter 2A, 2B or 2C	
Oil filler/drain plugs	35	26
Reversing light switch	25	18
Roadwheel nuts	140	103
Transmission-to-engine bolts	48	35

2.2a Depress the buttons in the centre of the gearchange inner cable end fittings...

2.2b... and disengage the end fittings from the balljoints on the levers

2.3 Pull back the retaining collars (arrowed) and detach the gearchange outer cables from the gear lever housing

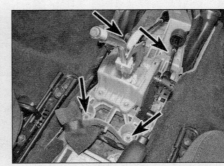

2.4 Gear lever housing retaining nuts (arrowed)

1 General Information

1 The manual transmission and final drive are housed in an aluminium casing, bolted directly to the left-hand side of the engine. Gear selection is by a remotely-sited lever assembly, operating the transmission selector mechanism via cables. Synchromesh is fitted to all gears.

2 The Ford transmission code for the 5-speed transmission is MTX 75. MT standing for Manual Transmission, X for transaxle (front-wheel drive), and 75 being the distance between the input and output shafts in mm. On certain 1.8 litre diesel models and all 2.0 litre diesel models a 6-speed transmission is fitted, with the designation MMT 6.

3 Because of the complexity of the assembly, possible unavailability of new parts and special tools necessary, internal repair procedures for the transmission are not recommended for the home mechanic. The bulk of the information in this Chapter is devoted to removal and refitting procedures.

2 Gear lever housing – removal and refitting

Removal

1 Remove the centre console as described in Chapter 11 Section 27, 28.

2 Depress the buttons in the centre of the gearchange inner cable end fittings and disengage the end fittings from the balljoints on the levers **(see illustrations)**.

3 Pull back the retaining collars and detach the gearchange outer cables from their locations on the gear lever housing **(see illustration)**.

4 Undo the four nuts and lift out the gear lever housing assembly **(see illustration)**.

Refitting

5 Refitting is a reversal of removal. On completion, adjust the cables as described in Section 3.

3 Selector cables – removal, refitting and adjustment

Removal

1 Remove the air cleaner assembly as described in Chapter 4A Section 5 or Chapter 4B Section 5, as applicable.

2 Remove the centre console as described in Chapter 11 Section 28.

3 Depress the release button in the centre of the selector inner cable end fitting and pull the end fitting from the transmission lever balljoint**(see illustration)**. Repeat this procedure with the shift cable.

4 Pull back the retaining collars and detach the selector and shift outer cables from the bracket on the transmission **(see illustration)**.

5 Firmly apply the handbrake, then jack up the front of the vehicle and support it securely

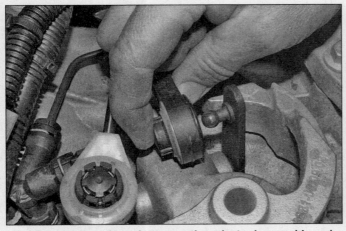

3.3 Depress the release button on the selector inner cable end fitting and pull the end fitting from the transmission lever

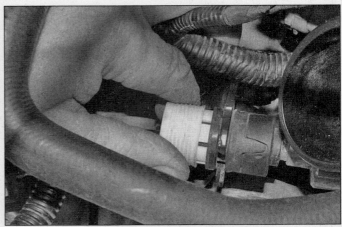

3.4 Pull back the retaining collars and detach the outer cables from the transmission bracket

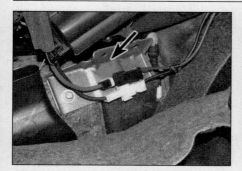

3.9 Undo the retaining bolts and remove the facia lower support bracket (arrowed)

3.20 Unlock the selector cable by prising up the coloured insert (arrowed)

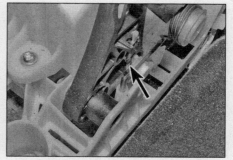

3.21 Insert a 4 mm drill bit (arrowed) through the lug on the side of the lever mechanism and into the hole in the gear lever base

on axle stands (see *'Jacking and vehicle support'*).

6 Undo the fasteners, and slide the heat shield above the intermediate section of the exhaust pipe rearwards. On later models it will also be necessary to release the wiring and cable retaining clips on the side of the heat shield to enable it to be slid rearwards.

7 Release the selector cables from the retaining clips on the underside of the floor.

8 Disconnect the selector cables from the gear lever as described in Section 2.

9 Disconnect the wiring connectors, where applicable, then undo the retaining bolts and remove the facia lower support bracket on each side **(see illustration)**.

10 Fold back the carpet each side of the centre console area, and carefully cut away the sound insulation around the cable grommet, located just in front of the heater housing. Remove the sound insulation.

11 Undo the 2 nuts securing the cable grommet to the floor, and lift the grommet from the mounting studs.

12 Manoeuvre the cable assembly into the passenger compartment, then out of the vehicle.

Refitting

13 Manoeuvre the cable assembly into position, through the hole in the floor, up to the transmission, then fit the grommet over the mounting studs and tighten the retaining nuts securely.

14 Reposition the sound insulation around the grommet, and tape over the cuts.

15 Reconnect the selector cables to the gear lever and housing.

16 Reclip the cables to the underside of the floor.

17 Refit the heat shield above the exhaust system.

18 Adjust the selector cable as described later in this Section.

Adjustment

19 If not already done, remove the air cleaner assembly as described in Chapter 4A Section 5 or Chapter 4B Section 5, and the centre console as described in Chapter 11 Section 28.

5-speed transmission

Note: *A 4 mm drill bit will be required for this adjustment.*

20 Working at the transmission end of the cable, unlock the selector cable by prising the coloured insert upwards, and move the transmission selector lever (not the gear lever inside the car) to the 4th gear position by moving it forwards or backwards as necessary **(see illustration)**.

21 From inside the car, move the gear lever to the 4th gear position, then insert a 4 mm drill bit through the lug on the side of the lever mechanism and into the hole in the gear lever base, making sure that it is fully inserted **(see illustration)**.

22 Check that the selector lever on the transmission is still in the 4th gear position, then lock the selector cable by pushing the coloured insert back in.

23 Remove the drill bit then refit the centre console and air cleaner assembly using a reversal of the removal procedure.

24 Start the engine, keeping the clutch pedal depressed, and check for correct gear selection.

6-speed transmission (up to 10/2007)

Note: *2.5 mm and 4 mm drill bits will be required for this adjustment.*

25 Working at the transmission end of the cables, depress the release button in the centre of each inner cable end fitting and pull the end fittings from the transmission lever balljoints **(see illustration 3.3)**. Unlock the selector cable by prising up the coloured insert on the cable end fitting.

26 From inside the car, move the gear lever to the 4th gear position, then insert a 4 mm drill bit through the lug on the side of the lever mechanism and into the hole in the gear lever base, making sure that it is fully inserted**(see illustration 3.21)**.

27 Insert a 2.5 mm drill bit into the centre of the roll-pin securing the selector mechanism preload sleeve, set the vertical distance of 44 mm, and turn the selector arm to engage 4th gear.

28 Reattach the gearchange cables to the transmission lever balljoints, then lock the

selector cable by pushing the coloured insert back in.

29 Remove the two drill bits then refit the centre console and air cleaner assembly using a reversal of the removal procedure.

30 Start the engine, keeping the clutch pedal depressed, and check for correct gear selection.

6-speed transmission (from 10/2007)

Note: *A 4 mm drill bit will be required for this adjustment.*

31 Working at the transmission end of the cable, depress the release button in the centre of the selector inner cable end fitting and pull the end fitting from the transmission lever balljoint **(see illustration 3.3)**. Unlock the selector cable by prising up the coloured insert on the cable end fitting.

32 From inside the car, move the gear lever to the 4th gear position, then insert a 4 mm drill bit through the lug on the side of the lever mechanism and into the hole in the gear lever base, making sure that it is fully inserted **(see illustration 3.21)**.

33 Move the selector lever on the transmission to the 4th gear position by moving it forwards or backwards as necessary

34 Reattach the selector cable to the transmission lever balljoint, then lock the selector cable by pushing the coloured insert back in.

35 Remove the drill bit then refit the centre console and air cleaner assembly using a reversal of the removal procedure.

36 Start the engine, keeping the clutch pedal depressed, and check for correct gear selection.

4 Oil seals – renewal

Driveshaft seals

1 Remove the left- or right-hand driveshaft (as appropriate) with reference to Chapter 8.

2 Drain the transmission oil as described in Section 6.

3 Using a large screwdriver or suitable lever, carefully prise the oil seal out of the

4.3 Carefully prise out the driveshaft oil seal

4.6 Drive in the new oil seal using a socket which bears only on the hard, outer edge of the seal

4.11 Insert a self-tapping screw and pull the seal from its location

transmission casing, taking care not to damage the casing **(see illustration)**.

4 Wipe clean the oil seal seating in the transmission casing.

5 Apply a small amount of general purpose grease to the new seal lips, then press it a little way into the casing by hand, making sure that it is square to its seating.

6 Using suitable tubing or a large socket, care- fully drive the oil seal fully into position until it is flush with the casing edge **(see illustration)**.

7 Refit the driveshaft(s) as described in Chapter 8.

8 Replenish the transmission oil as described in Section 6.

Input shaft oil seal

5-speed transmission

9 The input shaft seal is integral with the clutch slave cylinder/release bearing. Renew the cylinder/bearing as described in Chapter 6 Section 4.

6-speed transmission

10 Remove the clutch release bearing/slave cylinder as described in Chapter 6 Section 4.

11 Note its fitted depth, then drill a small hole in the hard outer surface of the seal, insert a self-tapping screw, and use pliers to extract the seal **(see illustration)**.

12 Lubricate the new seal with grease and fit it to the bellhousing, lips pointing to the transmission side. Use a deep socket or suitable tubing to seat it **(see illustration)**.

13 Refit the release bearing/slave cylinder using a reversal of removal.

5 Reversing light switch – removal and refitting

Removal

5-speed transmission

1 Remove the air cleaner assembly as described in Chapter 4A Section 5 or Chapter 4B Section 5.

2 Disconnect the wiring plug, then unscrew the switch from the top of the transmission casing **(see illustration)**.

6-speed transmission

3 The reversing light switch is located on the upper face of the transmission, between the two gear selector levers. Remove the air cleaner assembly as described in Chapter 4B Section 5.

4 Clean around the switch, disconnect the wiring connector **(see illustration)** and unscrew the switch.

Refitting

5 Refit by reversing the removal operations.

6 Manual transmission oil – draining and refilling

Note: *Renewal of the transmission oil is not a service requirement and will normally only be necessary if the unit is removed for overhaul or renewal. However, if the car has completed a high mileage, or is used under arduous conditions (eg, extensive towing or taxi work), it would be advisable to change the oil as a precaution, especially if the gearchange quality has deteriorated.*

Draining

1 Slacken the left-hand front roadwheel nuts, then jack up the front of the vehicle and support it securely on axle stands (see *'Jacking and vehicle support'*). Remove the roadwheel.

2 Release the fasteners and remove the engine undertray (where fitted), then position a suitable container beneath the transmission.

5-speed transmission

3 On the right-hand side of the transmission casing, you will see the drain plug. Unscrew

4.12 Drive the new seal squarely into place to its original depth

5.2 Reversing light switch (arrowed) – 5-speed transmission

5.4 Reversing light switch (arrowed) – 6-speed transmission

6.3 Transmission drain plug – 5-speed transmission

6.4 Transmission drain plug (A) and oil filler/level plug (B) – 6-speed transmission

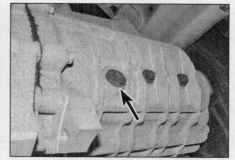

6.6 Oil filler/level plug (arrowed) – 5-speed transmission

and remove the drain plug and allow the oil to drain into the container **(see illustration)**. Check the condition of the drain plug sealing washer, and renew if necessary.

6-speed transmission

4 The drain plug is located on the left-hand side of the differential casing. Unscrew and remove the drain plug and allow the oil to drain into the container **(see illustration)**. Check the condition of the drain plug sealing washer (where fitted), and renew if necessary.

All models

5 When all the oil has drained, refit the drain plug and tighten it to the specified torque.

Refilling

Note: *For the level check to be accurate, the car must be completely level. If the front of the car has been jacked up, the rear should be jacked up also.*

5-speed transmission

6 Unscrew the level/filler plug located on the front of the transmission casing **(see illustration)**. Discard the sealing washer, a new one must be fitted.

7 Add oil of the correct specification (see Lubricants and fluids0,6) until oil begins to trickle out of the filler/level plug.

8 Fit a new sealing washer to the filler plug and tighten it to the specified torque.

6-speed transmission

9 Wipe clean the area around the filler/

level plug, and unscrew the plug from the casing**(see illustration 6.4)**.

10 Fill the transmission through the filler/level plug orifice with the correct type of oil (see Lubricants and fluids0,6) until the oil begins to run out of the orifice.

11 Refit the filler/level plug with a new seal (where fitted), and tighten it to the specified torque.

All models

12 Dispose of the old oil safely in accordance with environmental regulations. Refit the undertray (where applicable) and the roadwheel, then lower the vehicle to the ground.

---

7 Manual transmission – removal and refitting

⚠️ *Warning: The hydraulic fluid used in the clutch system is brake fluid, which is poisonous. Take care to keep it off bare skin, and in particular out of your eyes. The fluid also attacks paintwork, and may discolour carpets, etc – keep spillages to a minimum, and wash any off immediately with cold water. Finally, brake fluid is highly inflammable, and should be handled with the same care as petrol.*

Note: *Arrangements must be made to support the engine from above. The best way to support the engine is with a bar resting*

in the bonnet channels with an adjustable hook appropriately placed. Trolley jacks and the help of an assistant will also be required throughout the procedure.

Removal

1 Remove the plastic cover from the top of the engine.

2 Remove the air cleaner assembly as described in Chapter 4A Section 5 or Chapter 4B Section 5, and all relevant inlet ducting around the left-hand side of the engine.

3 Remove the battery and battery tray as described in Chapter 5A Section 4.

4 Disconnect the gearchange selector cables at the transmission as described in Section 3.

5 Note the fitted position of any earth leads on the top/front of the transmission (where fitted), then disconnect the lead, along with the reversing light switch wiring plug **(see illustration)**.

6 Release the wiring harness, pipes and hoses from the clips and cable ties on the top and front of the transmission.

7 Undo the transmission-to-engine bolts which are accessible from above.

8 Remove the front subframe as described in Chapter 10 Section 7.

9 Remove both driveshafts as described in Chapter 8.

10 On diesel engines, remove the catalytic converter as described in Chapter 4B Section 18.

11 On petrol engines, undo the nuts securing the intermediate section flange joint, and separate the joint. Recover the gasket, and discard it.

12 Remove the starter motor as described in Chapter 5A Section 8.

13 Taking adequate precautions against brake fluid spillage (refer to the Warning at the start of this Section), prise out the retaining clip and disconnect the clutch hydraulic fluid pipe from the junction at the transmission bellhousing, then pull the pipe's rubber bush upwards from the bracket on the transmission. Plug or seal the openings to prevent contamination.

14 Support the engine from above (see the note at the start of this Section), then undo the nuts/bolts and remove the left-hand engine/transmission mounting and bracket **(see illustration)**.

7.5 Note the earth connection on the top of the transmission housing (arrowed)

7.14 Undo the bolts/nuts and remove the left-hand transmission mounting and bracket

15 Taking care that nothing which is still attached to the engine is placed under strain, lower the engine/transmission as far as possible.

16 Remove the lower transmission-to-engine bolts. The bolts are of different lengths, so note their positions carefully for refitting.

17 Securely and safely support the transmission from below on a trolley jack.

18 Undo the remaining bolts securing the transmission to the engine. Withdraw the transmission squarely off the engine dowels, taking care not to allow the weight of the transmission to hang on the input shaft. Lower the engine slightly as the transmission is withdrawn to clear the chassis sidemember.

19 Lower the jack and remove the unit from under the car.

Refitting

20 Ensure the transmission input shaft is clean and free of rust or grease, then apply a little grease (Ford specification ESD-M1C220-A) to the splines of the input shaft – wipe off any excess grease. Check to make sure all locating dowels are in good condition and fitted correctly.

21 Manoeuvre the transmission squarely into position, and engage it with the engine dowels. Refit the lower bolts securing the transmission to the engine, and tighten them to the specified torque.

22 Raise the engine to its approximate fitted position. Refit the left-hand engine mounting bracket and mounting, and secure with the bolts/nuts tightened to the specified torque.

23 The remainder of refitting is a reversal of removal, noting the following points:

a) *Tighten all fasteners to their specified torque where given.*

b) *Refit the starter motor as described in Chapter 5A Section 8.*

c) *Refit the disturbed exhaust system components as described in Chapter 4A Section 12 or Chapter 4B Section 18, as applicable.*

d) *Refit the driveshafts as described in Chapter 8.*

e) *Refit the front subframe as described in Chapter 10 Section 7.*

f) *Reconnect and adjust the gearchange selector cables as described in Section 3.*

g) *Refit the battery tray and battery as described in Chapter 5A Section 4.*

h) *Refit the air cleaner assembly and inlet ducting as described in Chapter 4A Section 5 or Chapter 4B Section 5, as applicable.*

i) *Top-up the transmission oil as described in Section 6 of this Chapter.*

j) *Bleed the clutch hydraulic system as described in Chapter 6 Section 5.*

8 Manual transmission overhaul – general information

1 Overhauling a manual transmission is a difficult job for the do-it-yourselfer. It involves the dismantling and reassembly of many small parts. Numerous clearances must be precisely measured and, if necessary, changed with selected spacers and circlips. As a result, if transmission problems arise, while the unit can be removed and refitted by a competent do-it-yourselfer, overhaul should be left to a transmission specialist. Rebuilt transmissions may be available – check with your dealer parts department, motor factors, or transmission specialists. At any rate, the time and money involved in an overhaul is almost sure to exceed the cost of a rebuilt unit.

2 Nevertheless, it's not impossible for an experienced mechanic to rebuild a transmission, providing the special tools are available, and the job is done in a deliberate step-by-step manner, so nothing is overlooked.

3 The tools necessary for an overhaul include: internal and external circlip pliers, a bearing puller, a slide hammer, a set of pin punches, a dial test indicator, and possibly a hydraulic press. In addition, a large, sturdy workbench and a vice or transmission stand will be required.

4 During dismantling of the transmission, make careful notes of how each part comes off, where it fits in relation to other parts, and what holds it in place.

5 Before taking the transmission apart for repair, it will help if you have some idea what area of the transmission is malfunctioning. Certain problems can be closely tied to specific areas in the transmission, which can make component examination and renewal easier. Refer to the Fault finding section at the rear of this manual for information regarding possible sources of trouble.

Chapter 7 Part B
Automatic transmission

Contents

Degrees of difficulty

Easy, suitable for novice with little experience	Fairly easy, suitable for beginner with some experience	Fairly difficult, suitable for competent DIY mechanic	Difficult, suitable for experienced DIY mechanic	Very difficult, suitable for expert DIY or professional

Specifications

General

Type	Electronically-controlled adaptive automatic, six forward speeds and reverse, with sequential manual gear selection capability
Manufacturer's designation	AWF21

Lubrication

Lubricant type	See *Lubricants, fluids and tyre pressures*
Lubricant capacity	See Chapter 1B

Torque wrench settings

	Nm	lbf ft
Automatic transmission fluid drain/filler plugs:		
Drain plug	47	35
Filler plug	40	30
Level checking plug	8	6
Engine-to-transmission bolts	See Chapter 2C	
Engine/transmission mountings	See Chapter 2C	
Fluid pan bolts	25	18
Oil cooler pipes	14	10
Roadwheel nuts	140	103
Selector shaft lever to transmission selector shaft	16	12
Torque converter-to-driveplate bolts*	36	27
Transmission control module mounting bolts	25	18

* Use new bolts

1 General Information

1 2.0-litre diesel engine models are optionally available with a six-speed, electronically-controlled automatic transmission. The transmission consists of a torque converter, an epicyclic geartrain, and hydraulically-operated clutches and brakes. The unit is controlled by the transmission control module (TCM) and engine management powertrain control module (PCM). In addition to the fully automatic operation, the transmission can also be operated manually with a six-speed sequential gear selection.

2 The torque converter provides a fluid coupling between engine and transmission, which acts as an automatic clutch, and also provides a degree of torque multiplication when accelerating. The torque converter incorporates a lock-up function whereby the engine and transmission can be directly coupled by means of a clutch unit inside the torque converter. The lock-up function is controlled by the TCM according to operating conditions.

3 The epicyclic geartrain provides either of the six forward or one reverse gear ratios, according to which of its component parts are held stationary or allowed to turn. The components of the geartrain are held or released by hydraulically-actuated brakes and clutches. A fluid pump within the transmission provides the necessary hydraulic pressure to operate the brakes and clutches.

4 In automatic mode, the transmission is fully adaptive, whereby the shift points are dependent on driver input, roadspeed, engine speed and vehicle operating conditions. The PCM receives inputs from various engine and drivetrain related sensors, and determines the appropriate shift point for each gear. If the selector lever is moved to the S position, the transmission unit is switched into sport mode. In sport mode, the transmission shifts up only at high engine speeds, giving improved acceleration and overtaking performance.

5 Driver control of the transmission is by a five-position selector lever. The gear selector includes the normal P, R, N and D positions together with an additional S position for sport mode and manual gear selection. The drive D position, allows automatic changing throughout the range of forward gear ratios. An automatic kickdown facility shifts the transmission down a gear if the accelerator pedal is fully depressed. If the selector lever is moved to the S position, the gear selector lever can be used to shift the transmission up or down each gear sequentially.

6 The unit has been designed to have a low maintenance requirement, the fluid level being checked periodically (see Chapter 1B Section 27). The fluid is intended to last the life of the transmission, and is cooled by a separate fluid cooler.

7 Due to the complexity of the automatic transmission, any repair or overhaul work must be left to a Ford dealer or transmission specialist with the necessary special equipment for fault diagnosis and repair. The contents of the following Sections are therefore confined to supplying general information, and any service information and instructions that can be used by the owner.

2 Transmission fluid – draining and refilling

Draining

1 Position the vehicle over an inspection pit, on vehicle ramps, or jack it up and support it securely on axle stands (see 'Jacking and vehicle support'), but make sure that it is level. Remove the clips and bolts and remove the undertray from beneath the engine.

2 Position a container under the combined drain plug/level checking plug at the base of the transmission. Note that the drain plug and level checking plug are incorporated into one unit – the drain plug is the larger of the two plugs, with the level checking plug screwed into the centre of it **(see illustration)**.

3 Unscrew the level checking plug and remove it, along with its sealing washer, from the centre of the drain plug. Now unscrew the

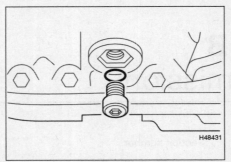

2.2 Automatic transmission fluid level checking plug

drain plug and remove it, along with its sealing washer, from the transmission. Allow the fluid to drain completely into the container.

 Warning: If the fluid is hot, take precautions against scalding.

4 When the fluid has finished draining, clean the drain plug and level checking plug threads and those of the transmission casing. Fit a new sealing washer and refit the drain plug, tightening it to the specified torque. Now refit the level checking plug together with a new sealing washer and tighten it to the specified torque also.

Refilling

5 Remove the air cleaner assembly as described in Chapter 4B Section 5.

6 Wipe clean the area around the transmission fluid filler plug, located on the top of the transmission housing, adjacent to the selector cable **(see illustration)**. Unscrew and remove the filler plug along with its sealing washer.

7 Slowly refill the transmission with the specified type and quantity of fluid, via the filler plug aperture. Use a funnel with a fine mesh gauze, to avoid spillage, and to ensure that no foreign matter enters the transmission.

8 Once the transmission has been filled, refit the filler plug with a new sealing washer, and tighten the plug to the specified torque.

9 Refit the engine undertray and lower the vehicle to the ground.

10 Refit the air cleaner assembly as described in Chapter 4B Section 5.

11 Take the vehicle on a journey of approximately 8 to 10 miles to warm the transmission up to normal operating temperature.

12 On your return, check the transmission fluid level as described in Chapter 1B Section 27.

3 Selector cable – adjustment

Note: If the battery is discharged, or is disconnected with the selector lever in the P (park) position, the lever will be locked in position. To manually release the lever, remove the centre trim panel under the facia on the

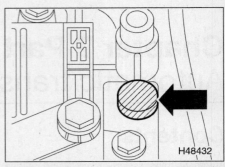

2.6 Automatic transmission fluid filler plug

driver's side by extracting the expanding rivet and releasing the retaining clips. Insert a flat-bladed screwdriver into the slot on the yellow emergency release lever, and turn the screwdriver 90° clockwise. The selector lever can now be moved to the N (neutral) position.

1 Operate the selector lever throughout its entire range and check that the transmission engages the correct gear indicated on the selector lever position indicator. If adjustment is necessary, continue as follows.

2 From inside the car, move the selector lever to the D (drive) position.

3 To gain access to the transmission end of the selector cable, remove the air cleaner assembly as described in Chapter 4B Section 5.

4 Depress the release button in the centre of the selector cable end fitting and pull the end fitting from the transmission selector shaft lever balljoint **(see illustration)**.

5 Move the transmission selector lever fully forwards (to the P position) then move it three notches backwards (to the D position).

6 Unlock the selector cable by prising the coloured insert in the end fitting upwards**(see illustration)**.

7 Reconnect the selector cable end fitting to the transmission selector shaft lever balljoint, then push the coloured insert back in to lock the cable.

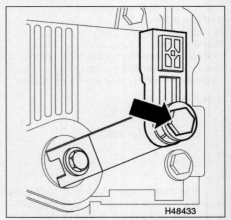

3.4 Depress the release button (arrowed) and pull the selector cable end fitting from the selector shaft lever

8 Refit the air cleaner assembly as described in Chapter 4B Section 5, then check the operation of the selector lever and, if necessary, repeat the adjustment procedure.

---

4 Selector cable – removal and refitting

Removal

1 Remove the centre console as described in Chapter 11 Section 28.

2 To gain access to the transmission end of the selector cable, remove the air cleaner assembly as described in Chapter 4B Section 5.

3 Depress the release button in the centre of the selector cable end fitting and pull the end fitting from the transmission selector shaft lever balljoint (see illustration 3.4).

4 Pull back the retaining collar and detach the selector outer cable from the bracket on the transmission.

5 Firmly apply the handbrake, then jack up the front of the vehicle and support it securely on axle stands (see *'Jacking and vehicle support'*). Remove the clips and bolts and remove the undertray from beneath the engine.

6 Undo the fasteners, and slide the heat shield above the intermediate section of the exhaust pipe approximately 500 mm rearwards.

7 Release the selector cable from the retaining clips on the underside of the floor.

8 From inside the car, depress the release button in the centre of the selector inner cable end fitting and disengage the end fitting from the balljoint on the selector lever.

9 Pull back the retaining collar and detach the selector outer cable from the selector lever housing.

10 Disconnect the wiring connectors, undo the retaining bolts and remove the facia lower support bracket on each side (see illustration).

11 Fold back the carpet each side of the centre console area, and carefully cut away the sound insulation around the cable grommet, located just in front of the heater housing. Remove the sound insulation.

12 Undo the 2 nuts securing the cable

6.4 Carefully prise out the driveshaft oil seal

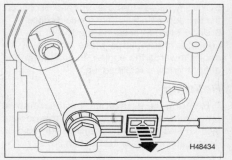

3.6 Unlock the selector cable by prising the coloured insert in the end fitting upwards

grommet to the floor, and lift the grommet from the mounting studs.

13 Manoeuvre the cable assembly into the passenger compartment, then out of the vehicle.

Refitting

14 Manoeuvre the cable assembly into position, through the hole in the floor, up to the transmission, then fit the grommet over the mounting studs and tighten the retaining nuts securely.

15 Reposition the sound insulation around the grommet, and tape over the cuts.

16 Reconnect the selector cable to the selector lever and housing.

17 Reclip the cables to the underside of the floor.

18 Refit the heat shield above the exhaust system.

19 Refit the engine undertray, then lower the vehicle to the ground.

20 Refit the centre console as described in Chapter 11 Section 28.

21 Adjust the selector cable as described in Section 3.

---

5 Selector lever assembly – removal and refitting

Removal

1 Remove the centre console as described in Chapter 11 Section 28.

2 From inside the car, depress the release

6.5 Drive in the new oil seal using a socket which bears only on the hard, outer edge of the seal

---

4.10 Undo the retaining bolts and remove the facia lower support bracket (arrowed)

button in the centre of the selector inner cable end fitting and disengage the end fitting from the balljoint on the selector lever.

3 Pull back the retaining collar and detach the selector outer cable from the selector lever housing.

4 Disconnect the wiring connector, undo the four nuts and lift out the selector lever housing assembly.

Refitting

5 Refitting is a reversal of removal. On completion, adjust the cable as described in Section 3.

---

6 Oil seals – renewal

Driveshaft oil seals

1 Firmly apply the handbrake, then jack up the front of the car and support it securely on axle stands (see *'Jacking and vehicle support'*). Remove the clips and bolts and remove the undertray from beneath the engine.

2 Drain the transmission fluid as described in Section 2.

3 Remove the relevant driveshaft as described in Chapter 8.

4 Note the correct fitted depth of the seal in its housing then carefully prise it out of position using a large flat-bladed screwdriver (see illustration).

5 Remove all traces of dirt from the area around the oil seal aperture, then lubricate the new oil seal with automatic transmission fluid. Ensure the seal is correctly positioned, with its sealing lip facing inwards, and tap it squarely into position, using a suitable tubular drift (such as a socket) which bears only on the hard outer edge of the seal (see illustration). Ensure the seal is fitted at the same depth in its housing that the original was.

6 Refit the driveshaft as described in Chapter 8.

7 Refill the transmission with the specified type and amount of fluid, as described in Section 2.

Torque converter oil seal

8 Remove the transmission as described in Section 12.

9 Carefully slide the torque converter off of the transmission shaft whilst being prepared for fluid spillage.

10 Note the correct fitted depth of the seal in the oil pump housing then carefully lever the seal out of position taking care not to mark the housing or input shaft.

11 Remove all traces of dirt from the area around the oil seal aperture then press the new seal into position, to the depth noted during removal, ensuring its sealing lip is facing inwards.

12 Lubricate the seal with clean transmission fluid then carefully ease the torque converter into position. Slide the torque converter onto the transmission shaft by turning it until it fully engages with the oil pump.

13 Check that the torque converter is fully entered inside the transmission bellhousing by measuring the distance from the flange to the bolt holes in the torque converter, using a straight-edge and vernier calipers. The distance measured must be greater than 34.5 mm.

14 Refit the transmission as described in Section 12.

7 Fluid cooler – removal and refitting

Removal

1 The transmission fluid cooler is located behind the radiator on the left-hand side.

2 Drain the cooling system as described in Chapter 1B Section 30.

3 Remove the air cleaner assembly as described in Chapter 4B Section 5.

4 Disconnect the two transmission fluid pipes from the fluid cooler by pressing the two tabs on the quick-release connectors and pulling the connectors off the fluid cooler pipe stubs **(see illustration)**. Be prepared for fluid spillage.

5 Similarly, release the hose clips and disconnect the two coolant hoses from the fluid cooler.

6 Undo the bolt securing the top of the fluid cooler to the radiator. Move the top of the cooler towards the engine, then lift it up and out of the lower retaining lug.

Refitting

7 Refitting is a reversal of the removal procedure. On completion refill the cooling system and top-up the transmission fluid as described in Chapter 1B Section 30.

8 Selector lever position switch – removal and refitting

1 The selector lever position switch is an integral part of the transmission control module and cannot be separated. Removal and refitting procedures for the transmission control module are contained in Section 10.

9 Transmission input/output speed sensors – removal and refitting

1 The input and output shaft speed sensors are located internally within the transmission and are not individually available. If one or both speed sensors are diagnosed as faulty, it will be necessary to obtain a complete new transmission.

10 Transmission control module (TCM) – removal and refitting

Note: *If a new TCM is to be fitted, this work must be entrusted to a Ford dealer or suitably-equipped specialist. It is necessary to reset the transmission electronic control system prior to removal, and to programme the new TCM after installation. This work requires the use of dedicated Ford diagnostic equipment or a compatible alternative.*

Removal

1 The combined TCM and selector lever position switch are located on the top of the transmission housing.

2 Ensure the handbrake is fully applied, then move the gear selector lever to the N (neutral) position.

3 Remove the air cleaner assembly as described in Chapter 4B Section 5.

4 Depress the release button in the centre of the selector cable end fitting and pull the end fitting from the transmission selector shaft lever balljoint **(see illustration 3.4)**.

5 Disconnect the wiring harness connector from the TCM.

6 Unscrew the retaining nut and remove the lever from the transmission selector shaft.

7 Unscrew and remove the three mounting bolts, then carefully lift the TCM upwards and remove it from the transmission **(see illustration)**. Take great care not to damage the wiring connector pins on the underside of the TCM as it is lifted off.

Refitting

8 Prior to refitting, first make sure that the transmission selector shaft is still in the N (neutral) position. If there is any doubt, temporarily engage the selector shaft lever with the transmission selector shaft and move the lever fully forwards (to the P position) then move it two notches backwards.

9 Set the selector lever position switch on the TCM to the N position by turning the switch until the two arrows are aligned.

10 Check that the transmission wiring harness is correctly located, then carefully place the TCM in position. Take great care not to damage the wiring connector pins as the TCM is fitted.

11 Refit the three bolts and tighten to the specified torque.

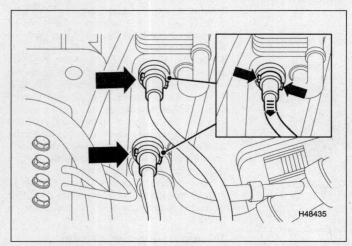

7.4 Press the two tabs on the quick-release connectors and pull the fluid pipes off the fluid cooler pipe stubs

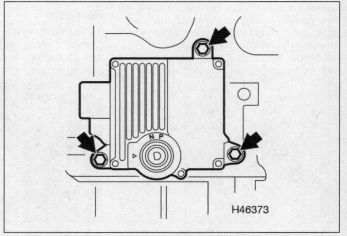

10.7 Transmission control module mounting bolts (arrowed)

12 Refit the selector lever to the shaft and tighten its retaining nut to the specified torque.
13 Reconnect the selector cable end fitting to the transmission selector shaft lever balljoint.
14 Reconnect the TCM wiring harness connector.
15 Adjust the selector cable as described in Section 3.

11 Fluid pan – removal and refitting

Note: *This procedure is provided principally to cure any leak developing from the fluid pan joint. It is not advisable for the DIY mechanic to remove the fluid pan for any other reason, since it gives access to internal transmission components, servicing of which is considered beyond the scope of this Manual.*

Removal

1 Firmly apply the handbrake, then jack up the front of the vehicle and support it securely on axle stands (see 'Jacking and vehicle support'). Remove the clips and bolts and remove the undertray from beneath the engine.
2 Drain the transmission oil as described in Section 2.
3 Undo the two bolts and disconnect the fluid cooler pipes from the front of the transmission.
4 Place a suitable container below the fluid pan, then progressively unscrew and remove the 12 fluid pan retaining bolts.
5 The fluid pan is 'stuck' to the front face of the transmission by a bead of sealant, so it is unlikely that the pan will fall off once the bolts are removed. Care must now be taken to break the sealant without damaging the mating surfaces. Do not prise the pan away, as this may bend it, or damage the sealing surfaces. The most successful method found is to run a sharp knife around the joint – this should cut through sufficiently to make removal possible without excess effort.

Refitting

6 With the fluid pan removed, clean off all traces of sealant from the pan and the mating face on the transmission. Again, take care not to mark either mating surface. Also clean off all traces of thread-locking compound from the fluid pan retaining bolts.
7 Apply a 2.0 mm thick bead of silicone sealant (Ford specification WSS-M4G320-A3, or equivalent) to the fluid pan mating face, running the bead on the inside of the bolt holes. Do not apply excess sealant, or a bead much thicker than suggested, since the excess could end up inside the pan, and contaminate the internal components.
8 Apply thread-locking compound (Ford specification WSK-M2G349-A7, or equivalent) to the threads of the fluid pan retaining bolts.
9 Offer the pan up into position, and insert a few of the bolts to locate it. Refit

all the remaining bolts, and tighten them progressively to the specified torque. Give the sealant time to cure, then trim off any excess with a knife.
10 Reconnect the two fluid cooler pipes to the front of the transmission and tighten the retaining bolts to the specified torque.
11 Refit the engine undertray, then lower the vehicle to the ground.
12 Refill the transmission with the specified type and amount of fluid, as described in Section 2.

12 Automatic transmission – removal and refitting

Note: *New torque converter-to-driveplate bolts will be required for refitting.*

Removal

1 Apply the handbrake, place the selector lever in the N (neutral) position. then jack up the front of the vehicle and support it on axle stands (see 'Jacking and vehicle support'). Allow sufficient working room to remove the transmission from under the left-hand side of the engine compartment. Remove both front roadwheels then undo the retaining clips/screws and remove the engine undertray. Also remove the engine top cover.
2 Drain the transmission fluid as described in Section 2, then refit the drain plug and tighten it to the specified torque.
3 Remove the battery and battery tray as described in Chapter 5A Section 4.
4 Disconnect the transmission control module wiring connector, then release the wiring harness from the retaining clips and cable-ties over the top of the transmission.
5 Depress the release button in the centre of the selector cable end fitting and pull the end fitting from the transmission selector shaft lever balljoint **(see illustration 3.4)**.
6 Pull back the retaining collar and detach the selector outer cable from the bracket on the transmission.
7 Remove the starter motor as described in Chapter 5A Section 8.
8 Unscrew and remove the upper bolts securing the transmission to the rear of the engine.
9 Remove both driveshafts as described in Chapter 8.
10 Remove the front subframe assembly as described in Chapter 10 Section 7, ensuring that the engine unit is securely supported by connecting a hoist to the engine assembly. If available, the type of support bar which locates in the engine compartment side channels is to be preferred.
11 Slacken the hose clips, undo the two retaining bolts and remove the intercooler charge air pipe from under the engine.
12 Slacken the hose clip and detach the intercooler charge air pipe from the anti-shudder control valve at the front of the engine.

13 Disconnect the two transmission fluid pipes from the fluid cooler by pressing the two tabs on the quick-release connectors and pulling the connectors off the fluid cooler pipe stubs **(see illustration 7.4)**. Be prepared for fluid spillage.
14 Undo the two bolts and remove the cover plate below the starter motor aperture.
15 Using a socket and extension bar, turn the crankshaft pulley until one of the bolts securing the torque converter to the driveplate becomes accessible through the starter motor aperture. Slacken and remove the bolt, then turn the crankshaft pulley as necessary, and undo the remaining bolts as they become accessible. There are six securing bolts in total. Discard the bolts, new ones must be used on refitting.
16 Place a jack with a block of wood beneath the transmission, and raise the jack to take the weight of the transmission.
17 Mark the nut/bolt positions for correct refitting, then unscrew the four nuts and two bolts securing the left-hand engine/transmission mounting to the body. Unscrew the centre bolt securing the mounting to the transmission bracket and remove the mounting **(see illustration)**.
18 Unscrew the four bolts and remove the left-hand engine/transmission mounting bracket from the transmission.
19 By manipulating the engine hoist and the jack under the transmission, lower the engine/transmission approximately 50 mm. Ensure that the various coolant hoses and wiring harnesses are not stretched.
20 Slacken and remove the remaining bolts securing the transmission to the engine and sump flange. Note the correct fitted positions of each bolt, and the relevant brackets, as they are removed to use as a reference on refitting. Make a final check that all components have been disconnected, and are positioned clear of the transmission so that they will not hinder the removal procedure.
21 With all the bolts removed, move the trolley jack and transmission, to free it from its locating dowels. Once the transmission is free, lower the jack and manoeuvre the unit out from under the car, taking care to ensure that the torque converter does not fall off. Remove

12.17 Undo the bolts/nuts and remove the left-hand transmission mounting and bracket

the locating dowels from the transmission or engine if they are loose, and keep them in a safe place. Retain the torque converter while the transmission is removed by bolting a strip of metal across the transmission bellhousing end face.

Refitting

22 The transmission is refitted by a reversal of the removal procedure, bearing in mind the following points.

a) *Prior to refitting, remove all traces of old locking compound from the torque converter threads by running a tap of the correct thread diameter and pitch down the holes. In the absence of a suitable tap, use one of the old bolts with slots cut in its threads.*

b) *Ensure the engine/transmission locating dowels are correctly positioned and apply a smear of molybdenum disulphide grease to the torque converter locating pin and its centering bush in the crankshaft end.*

c) *Check that the torque converter is fully entered inside the transmission bellhousing by measuring the distance from the flange to the bolt holes in the torque converter, using a straight-edge and vernier calipers. The distance measured must be greater than 34.5 mm.*

d) *Once the transmission and engine are correctly joined, refit the securing bolts, tightening them to the specified torque setting.*

e) *Fit the new torque converter to driveplate bolts and tighten them lightly only to start, then go around and tighten them to the specified torque setting in a diagonal sequence.*

f) *Tighten all nuts and bolts to the specified torque (where given).*

g) *Refit the starter motor as described in Chapter 5A Section 8.*

h) *Renew the driveshaft oil seals (see Section 8) and refit the driveshafts to the transmission as described in Chapter 8.*

i) *Refit the front subframe assembly as described in Chapter 10 Section 7.*

j) *On completion, refill the transmission with the specified type and quantity of fluid as described in Section 2, and adjust the selector cable as described in Section 3*

13 Automatic transmission overhaul – general information

1 In the event of a fault occurring with the transmission, it is first necessary to determine whether it is of a mechanical, electrical or hydraulic nature, and to do this, special test equipment is required. It is therefore essential to have the work carried out by a Ford dealer or suitably-equipped specialist if a transmission fault is suspected.

2 Do not remove the transmission from the car for possible repair before professional fault diagnosis has been carried out, since most tests require the transmission to be in the vehicle.

Chapter 8
Driveshafts

Contents

Degrees of difficulty

Easy, suitable for novice with little experience	Fairly easy, suitable for beginner with some experience	Fairly difficult, suitable for competent DIY mechanic	Difficult, suitable for experienced DIY mechanic	Very difficult, suitable for expert DIY or professional

Specifications

General

Driveshaft type . . . . Solid steel shafts with inner and outer constant velocity (CV) joints, both outer joints are of the ball-and-cage type and the inner joints of the tripod (spider-and-yoke) type. The right-hand driveshaft is fitted with a support bearing

Lubricant

Type/specification. . . . . Special grease (Ford specification WSS-M1C259-A1) supplied in sachets with gaiter kits – joints are otherwise prepacked with grease and sealed

Quantity per joint (approximate):
Inner joint . . . . 180 g
Outer joint. . . . . 150 g

Torque wrench settings

	Nm	lbf ft
Brake caliper mounting bracket to swivel hub	200	148
Driveshaft retaining bolt: *		
Stage 1	45	33
Stage 2	Angle-tighten a further 80°	
Headlight levelling sensor bracket to lower arm	8	6
Lower arm balljoint retaining nut	100	74
Right-hand driveshaft support bearing cap nuts*	25	18
Roadwheel nuts	140	103

Use new fastenings

1 General Information

1 Drive is transmitted from the differential to the front wheels by means of two solid-steel, equal-length driveshafts equipped with constant velocity (CV) joints at their inner and outer ends. Due to the position of the transmission, an intermediate shaft and support bearing are incorporated into the right-hand driveshaft assembly.

2 A ball-and-cage type CV joint is fitted to the outer end of each driveshaft. The joint has an outer member, which is splined at its outer end to accept the wheel hub, and is threaded so that it can be fastened to the hub by a large bolt. The joint contains six balls within a cage, which engage with the inner member. The complete assembly is protected by a flexible gaiter secured to the driveshaft and joint outer member.

3 At the inner end, the driveshaft is splined to engage a tripod type CV joint, containing needle roller bearings and cups. On the left-hand side, the driveshaft inner CV joint engages directly with the differential sun wheel. On the right-hand side, the inner joint is integral with the intermediate shaft, the inner end of which engages with the differential sun wheel. As on the outer joints, a flexible gaiter secured to the driveshaft and CV joint outer member protects the complete assembly.

2 Driveshafts – removal and refitting

Note: *Ford special tool 204-607 (or a compatible alternative) will be needed to separate the lower arm balljoint shank from the swivel hub.*

Removal

1 Firmly apply the handbrake, then jack up the front of the car and support it securely on axle stands (see *'Jacking and vehicle support'*). Remove the relevant front roadwheel. Where applicable, remove the engine undertray.

2 Refit at least two roadwheel nuts to the

2.2 Using a fabricated tool to hold the front hub stationary whilst the driveshaft retaining bolt is slackened

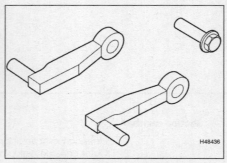

2.6 Ford special tool 204-607 used for separating the lower arm balljoint from the swivel hub

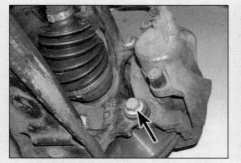

2.7 Undo and remove the lower bolt (arrowed) securing the brake caliper mounting bracket to the swivel hub

2.9 Home-made method of releasing the lower arm – wood block, long pole and length of chain

front hub, and tighten them securely. Have an assistant firmly depress the brake pedal to prevent the front hub from rotating, then using a socket and extension bar, slacken the driveshaft retaining bolt. Alternatively, a tool can be fabricated from two lengths of steel strip (one long, one short) and a nut and bolt; the nut and bolt forming the pivot of a forked tool. Attach the tool to the hub using two wheel nuts, and hold the tool to prevent the hub from rotating as the driveshaft retaining bolt is slackened**(see illustration)**. Note that this bolt is extremely tight – ensure that the tools used to loosen it are of good quality, and a good fit.

3 Unscrew and remove the previously-slackened driveshaft retaining bolt. Discard the bolt – a new one must be fitted.

4 Using a hammer and suitable drift, tap the end of the driveshaft approximately 15 to 20

mm into the wheel hub flange.

5 Undo the bolt/nut and detach the headlight levelling sensor bracket from the lower arm (where applicable).

6 The design of the lower arm balljoint and swivel hub assembly is such that using a conventional balljoint separator tool to release the balljoint shank from the swivel hub is likely to damage the balljoint rubber boot. It is therefore necessary to use Ford special tool 204-607 (or a compatible alternative) to separate the balljoint shank from the hub as follows **(see illustration)**.

7 Unscrew the lower arm balljoint retaining nut two turns, then undo and remove the lower bolt securing the brake caliper mounting bracket to the swivel hub **(see illustration)**. Bolt the special tool to the caliper mounting bracket and position the other end of the tool under, and in

contact with, the steering arm on the swivel hub. Unscrew the lower arm balljoint retaining nut until it contacts the special tool, then continue unscrewing the nut to release the balljoint shank taper from the swivel hub.

8 Once the balljoint shank taper releases, fully unscrew the retaining nut, then remove the special tool. Refit the caliper mounting bracket lower retaining bolt and tighten it to the specified torque.

9 Lever down the lower arm to free the balljoint from the swivel hub **(see illustration)**, then move the swivel hub to one side, taking care not to damage the balljoint rubber boot.

10 The driveshaft can be separated from the hub by having an assistant pull the swivel hub and suspension strut outwards, while the splined end of the shaft is pulled clear of the hub **(see illustration)**. Do not bend the driveshaft excessively at any stage, or the joints may be damaged – the inner and outer joints should not be bent through more than 18° and 45° respectively. Do not let the driveshaft hang down under its own weight – tie it up level if necessary.

11 Proceed as follows, according to which driveshaft is being removed.

Left-hand driveshaft

12 Insert a lever between the driveshaft inner joint and the transmission housing, positioning a thin piece of wood between the lever and housing to protect it. Also position a container below the inner joint, to catch the transmission oil/fluid which may be lost as the driveshaft is removed. Carefully lever the driveshaft inner joint out of the differential, taking great care not to damage the transmission housing or the oil seal **(see illustration)**.

13 Manoeuvre the driveshaft out of position, ensuring that the constant velocity joints are not placed under excessive strain, and remove the driveshaft from underneath the car. Whilst the driveshaft is removed, plug the differential aperture with a clean, lint-free cloth to prevent the entry of dirt.

14 Extract the circlip from the groove on the inner end of the driveshaft, and obtain a new one.

Right-hand driveshaft

15 Unscrew the nuts securing the inter-mediate shaft support bearing cap to the rear of the cylinder block and remove the support bearing cap from the studs **(see illustration)**.

2.10 Pull the swivel hub and suspension strut outwards and withdraw the driveshaft

2.12 Carefully lever the driveshaft inner joint out of the differential

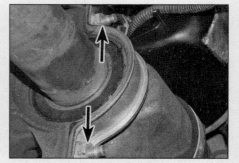

2.15 Undo the two nuts (arrowed) and remove the intermediate shaft support bearing cap

Note that a new bearing cap and nuts must be used when refitting.

16 Position a container below the transmission, to catch the transmission oil/fluid which may be lost as the driveshaft is removed. Taking care to ensure that the constant velocity joints are not placed under excessive strain, pull the intermediate shaft out of the transmission, and remove the driveshaft assembly from underneath the car. **Note:** *Do not pull the outer shaft from the intermediate shaft – the coupling will separate. Whilst the driveshaft is removed, plug the differential aperture with a clean, lint-free cloth to prevent the entry of dirt.*

Both driveshafts

17 Check the condition of the differential oil seals, and if necessary renew them as described in Chapter 7A Section 4 or Chapter 7B Section 6.

Refitting

Right-hand driveshaft

18 Use a special sleeve to protect the differential oil seal as the intermediate shaft is inserted. If the sleeve is not used, take great care to avoid damaging the seal. (Installation sleeves are supplied with new oil seals, where required.)

19 Carefully refit the intermediate shaft in the support bearing and into the transmission. Turn the intermediate shaft until it engages the splines on the differential gears.

20 Fit the new support bearing cap and nuts and tighten the nuts to the specified torque. Proceed to paragraph 24.

Left-hand driveshaft

21 Locate the new circlip in the groove on the inner end of the driveshaft **(see illustration)**.

22 Use a special sleeve to protect the differential oil seal as the driveshaft is inserted. If the sleeve is not used, take great care to avoid damaging the seal. (Installation sleeves are supplied with new oil seals, where required.)

23 Insert the driveshaft inner joint into the transmission, and push it fully home. Try pulling the joint out, to make sure the circlip is fully engaged.

Both driveshafts

24 Pull the suspension strut outwards, and insert the outer end of the driveshaft through the hub. Turn the driveshaft to engage the splines in the hub, and fully push on the hub.

25 Screw in the new driveshaft retaining bolt, and use it to draw the driveshaft fully through the hub.

26 Locate the suspension lower arm balljoint shank in the bottom of the swivel hub. Screw on the retaining nut, and tighten it to the specified torque. Use an Allen key inserted in the centre of the balljoint shank to prevent rotation as the nut is tightened.

27 Using the method employed on removal to prevent rotation, tighten the driveshaft retaining bolt to the specified torque and through the specified angle.

28 Where applicable, refit the headlight levelling sensor bracket to the lower arm.

29 Check, and if necessary top-up the transmission oil/fluid level as described in Chapter 1A Section 28 or Chapter 7B Section 2.

30 Where applicable, refit the engine undertray, then refit the wheel, and lower the car to the ground. Tighten the wheel nuts to the specified torque.

3 Outer constant velocity joint gaiter – renewal

1 Dismantle the inner constant velocity joint as described in Section 4.

2 Using a screwdriver, release the gaiter inner and outer retaining clips, then slide the gaiter down and off the shaft to expose the outer constant velocity joint **(see illustrations)**.
Caution: Do not disassemble the outer CV joint.

3 Scoop out as much grease as possible from the joint.

4 Inspect the ball tracks on the inner and outer members. If the tracks have widened, the balls will no longer be a tight fit. At the same time, check the ball cage windows for wear or cracking between the windows. If the joints appear worn, complete renewal may be the only option – check with a Ford dealer or specialist.

5 If the joint is in satisfactory condition, obtain a repair kit from your Ford dealer, consisting of new inner and outer gaiters, retaining clips, driveshaft retaining bolt, circlips and grease.

6 Position the retaining clips on the new gaiter, then slide the gaiter onto the shaft **(see illustration)**.

7 Pack the joint with half the specified amount of the grease supplied, working it well into the ball tracks **(see illustrations)**.

2.21 Fit a new circlip to the driveshaft groove

3.2a Release the gaiter inner…

3.2b… and outer retaining clips…

3.2c… then slide the gaiter down and off the driveshaft

3.6 Position the retaining clips on the new gaiter, then slide the gaiter onto the shaft

3.7a Pack the joint with half the specified amount of the grease supplied…

3.7b... working it well into the ball tracks

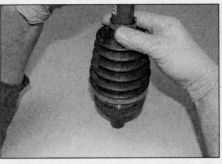

3.9a Locate the outer lip of the gaiter in the groove on the joint outer member

3.9b Ensure that the retaining clip is correctly positioned, then compress the raised section using a special pair of pincers

8 Apply the remaining grease to the joint and the inside of the gaiter.

9 Locate the outer lip of the gaiter in the groove on the joint outer member. Ensure that the retaining clip is correctly positioned,

then remove any slack in the clip by carefully compressing the raised section using a special pair of pincers **(see illustrations)**. **Note:** *Ensure no grease is on the surfaces between the gaiter and the joint housing.*

10 Use a small screwdriver to lift the inner lip of the gaiter, allowing the air pressure inside the gaiter to equalise, then fit the inner clip to the gaiter **(see illustrations)**.

11 Reassembly the inner constant velocity joint as described in Section 4.

4 Inner constant velocity joint gaiter – renewal

1 Remove the driveshaft as described in Section 2.

2 Using quick-drying paint (such as correction fluid) mark the driveshaft in relation to the joint housing, to ensure correct refitting.

3 Using a screwdriver, release and remove the gaiter inner and outer retaining clips **(see illustrations)**.

4 Withdraw the inner joint housing from the tripod **(see illustration)**.

5 Tip the bearing rollers sideways and remove them from the tripod **(see illustration)**. Once the bearing rollers are removed, handle them carefully. The inner bearing race, together with the needle rollers, can easily fall out.

6 Scoop out as much grease as possible from the joint and gaiter, then extract the circlip retaining the tripod on the driveshaft **(see illustration)**.

7 Make alignment marks on the driveshaft and the edge of the tripod, to ensure correct refitting.

8 Using a puller, remove the tripod from the end of the driveshaft **(see illustration)**.

3.10a Use a small screwdriver to lift the inner lip of the gaiter, allowing the air pressure inside to equalise...

3.10b... then locate the inner clip on the gaiter and compress the raised section

4.3a Using a screwdriver, release the gaiter inner retaining clip...

4.3b... and outer retaining clip...

4.3c... and remove both clips from the gaiter

4.4 Withdraw the inner joint housing from the tripod

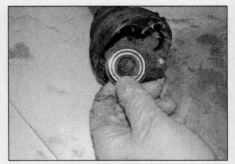

4.5 Tip the bearing rollers sideways and remove them from the tripod

4.6 Extract the circlip retaining the tripod on the driveshaft

4.8 Using a puller, remove the tripod from the end of the driveshaft

4.9a Remove the stiffening plate from inside the gaiter…

4.9b… then slide the gaiter off the driveshaft

4.12 Slide the new gaiter onto the shaft and locate the inner end against the driveshaft groove

4.13 Ensure that the retaining clip is correctly positioned, then compress the raised section using a special pair of pincers

9 Remove the stiffening plate from inside the gaiter, then slide the gaiter off the driveshaft **(see illustrations)**.

10 If the outer joint gaiter is also to be renewed, remove it and fit the new one as described in Section 3.

11 Clean the grease from the driveshaft, tripod, bearing rollers and housing, then obtain a repair kit from your Ford dealer, consisting of a new inner gaiter, retaining clips, driveshaft retaining bolt, circlips and grease.

12 Position the retaining clips on the new gaiter, then slide the gaiter onto the shaft. Locate the inner end of the gaiter against the groove in the driveshaft **(see illustration)**.

13 Check that the inner end retaining clip is correctly seated on the gaiter, then remove any slack in the clip by carefully compressing the raised section using a special pair of pincers **(see illustration)**.

14 Locate the stiffening plate inside the gaiter, then place the tripod in position on the driveshaft splines, ensuring that the previously-made marks are aligned **(see illustrations)**.

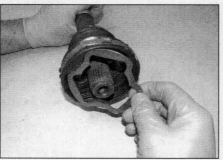

4.14a Locate the stiffening plate inside the gaiter…

15 Tap the tripod onto the driveshaft using a soft-faced mallet and a suitable drift, until the new circlip can be installed **(see illustrations)**. Ensure that the circlip is fully engaged in its groove.

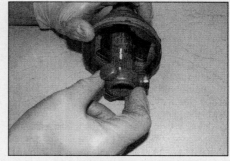

4.14b… then place the tripod in position on the driveshaft splines

4.15a Tap the tripod onto the driveshaft initially using a soft-faced mallet…

4.15b… then fully home using a hammer and suitable drift…

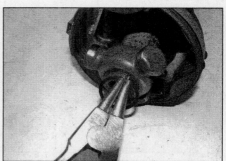

4.15c… until the new circlip can be installed

4.16 Tip the bearing rollers sideways and place them in position on the tripod

4.17a Pack the joint housing with half the specified amount of the grease supplied…

4.17b… then insert the tripod and driveshaft into the housing

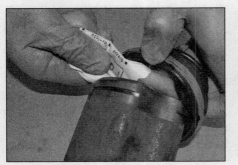

4.18a Fill the gaiter with the remainder of the grease…

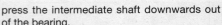

4.18b… then locate the outer lip of the gaiter in the groove on the joint housing

16 Tip the bearing rollers sideways and place them in position on the tripod **(see illustration)**.
17 Pack the joint housing with half the specified amount of the grease supplied, then insert the tripod and driveshaft into the housing**(see illustrations)**. Ensure that the previously-made marks on the driveshaft and housing are aligned.
18 Fill the gaiter with the remainder of the grease, then locate the outer lip of the gaiter in the groove on the joint housing **(see illustrations)**.
19 Insert a small screwdriver under the lip of the gaiter to allow trapped air to escape. Push the joint housing fully onto the tripod as far as it will go, then pull it back by 20 mm to its normal operating position. Using a ruler, check that the distance from one edge of the gaiter to the other edge is 95 mm, then remove the screwdriver **(see illustrations)**.

20 Check that the outer end retaining clip is correctly seated on the gaiter, then remove any slack in the clip by carefully compressing the raised section using a special pair of pincers **(see illustration)**.
21 Refit the driveshaft as described in Section 2.

5 Right-hand driveshaft support bearing – renewal

Note: *A hydraulic press, together with suitable mandrels will be needed for this operation.*
1 Dismantle the inner constant velocity joint as described in Section 4. Note that a new constant velocity joint gaiter repair kit will be required for reassembly.
2 Support the bearing on the press bed and

press the intermediate shaft downwards out of the bearing.
3 With the new bearing supported on its inner race, press the intermediate shaft back into the bearing until it is fully engaged.
4 Reassemble the inner constant velocity joint as described in Section 4.

6 Driveshaft overhaul – general information

1 Road test the car, and listen for a metallic clicking from the front as the car is driven slowly in a circle with the steering on full-lock. Repeat the check on full-left and full-right lock. This noise may also be apparent when pulling away from a standstill with lock applied. If a clicking noise is heard, this indicates wear in the outer constant velocity joints.
2 If vibration, consistent with roadspeed, is felt through the car when accelerating, there is a possibility of wear in the inner constant velocity joints.
3 If the joints are worn or damaged, it would appear at the time of writing that no parts are available, other than gaiter kits and right-hand driveshaft support bearing, and the complete driveshaft must be renewed. Exchange driveshafts may be available – check with a Ford dealer or specialist.
4 Continual noise from the right-hand driveshaft, increasing with roadspeed, may indicate wear in the support bearing. To renew this bearing, proceed as described in Section 5.

4.19a Insert a screwdriver under the gaiter lip to allow trapped air to escape, then push the housing fully onto the tripod

4.19b Pull the housing back until the distance from each edge of the gaiter is as specified

4.20 Ensure that the retaining clip is correctly positioned, then compress the raised section using a special pair of pincers

Chapter 9
Braking system

Contents

Degrees of difficulty

| Easy, suitable for novice with little experience | | Fairly easy, suitable for beginner with some experience | | Fairly difficult, suitable for competent DIY mechanic | | Difficult, suitable for experienced DIY mechanic | | Very difficult, suitable for expert DIY or professional | |

Specifications

Front brakes

Type	Ventilated disc, with single-piston sliding caliper
Disc diameter	300.0 mm
Minimum disc thickness......	26.0 mm
Maximum disc thickness variation............	0.008 mm
Maximum disc/hub run-out (installed)	0.1 mm
Brake pad friction material minimum thickness........	2.0 mm

Rear brakes

Type	Solid disc, with single-piston sliding caliper
Disc diameter	302.0 mm
Minimum disc thickness......	9.0 mm
Maximum disc thickness variation............	0.025 mm
Maximum disc/hub run-out (installed)	0.1 mm
Brake pad friction material minimum thickness........	1.5 mm

Torque wrench settings

	Nm	lbf ft
ABS hydraulic modulator:		
Mounting bracket bolts	10	7
To mounting bracket.	10	7
Brake fluid pipe and hose unions.	18	13
Brake master cylinder retaining nuts	25	18
Brake pedal mounting bracket nuts.	25	18
Exhaust flexible section flange nuts.	48	35
Front brake caliper:		
Guide bolts.	28	21
Mounting bracket bolts	200	148
Handbrake lever retaining nuts	25	18
Rear brake caliper:		
Guide pin bolts.	35	26
Mounting bracket bolts	110	81
Roadwheel nuts	140	103
Steering column shaft universal joint clamp bolt*	34	25
Vacuum pump mounting bolts (diesel engine models):		
1.8 litre engines	22	16
2.0 litre engines:		
To Stage III/IV emission level	22	16
To Stage V emission level.	10	7
Vacuum servo unit to brake pedal mounting bracket	25	18

* Use a new bolt

1 General Information

1 The braking system is of servo-assisted, dual-circuit hydraulic type split diagonally. The arrangement of the hydraulic system is such that each circuit operates one front and one rear brake from a tandem master cylinder. Under normal circumstances, both circuits operate in unison. However, in the event of hydraulic failure in one circuit, full braking force will still be available at two wheels.

2 All models are fitted with front and rear disc brakes. The front calipers are of single sliding piston design, and the rear calipers are of a single-piston floating design, both using asbestos-free pads.

3 The cable-operated handbrake provides an independent mechanical means of rear brake application.

4 On petrol engine models, the vacuum servo unit uses inlet manifold depression (generated only when the engine is running) to boost the effort applied by the driver at the brake pedal, and transmits this increased effort to the master cylinder pistons. Because there is no throttling of the inlet manifold on a diesel engine, it is not a suitable source of vacuum for brake servo operation. Vacuum is therefore derived from a separate camshaft-driven vacuum pump.

5 An anti-lock braking system (ABS) is fitted as standard equipment to all models. The system incorporates an electronic stability program (ESP) together with traction control. According to vehicle specification, additional functions such as emergency brake assist and hill start assist may also be supported by the system. Refer to Section 19 for further information on ABS operation.

⚠ *Warning: When servicing any part of the system, work carefully and methodically; also observe scrupulous cleanliness when overhauling any part of the hydraulic system. Always renew components (in axle sets, where applicable) if in doubt about their condition, and use only genuine Ford parts, or at least those of known good quality. Note the warnings given in Safety First! and at relevant points in this Chapter concerning the dangers of asbestos dust and hydraulic fluid.*

2 Hydraulic system – bleeding

⚠ *Warning: Hydraulic fluid is poisonous; wash off immediately and thoroughly in the case of skin contact, and seek immediate medical advice if any fluid is swallowed or gets into the eyes. Certain types of hydraulic fluid are inflammable, and may ignite when allowed into contact with hot components; when servicing any hydraulic system, it is safest to assume that the fluid is inflammable, and to take precautions against the risk of fire as though it is petrol that is being handled. Hydraulic fluid is also an effective paint stripper, and will attack plastics; if any is spilt, it should be washed off immediately, using copious quantities of fresh water. Finally, it is hygroscopic (it absorbs moisture from the air) – old fluid may be contaminated and unfit for further use. When topping-up or renewing the fluid, always use the recommended type, and ensure that it comes from a freshly-opened sealed container.*

General

1 The correct operation of any hydraulic system is only possible after removing all air from the components and circuit; this is achieved by bleeding the system.

2 During the bleeding procedure, add only clean, unused hydraulic fluid of the recommended type; never re-use fluid that has already been bled from the system. Ensure that sufficient fluid is available before starting work.

3 If there is any possibility of incorrect fluid being already in the system, the brake components and circuit must be flushed completely with uncontaminated, correct fluid, and new seals should be fitted to the various components.

4 If hydraulic fluid has been lost from the system, or air has entered because of a leak, ensure that the fault is cured before proceeding further.

5 Park the vehicle over an inspection pit or on car ramps. Alternatively, apply the handbrake then jack up the front and rear of the vehicle and support it on axle stands (see *'Jacking and vehicle support'*). For improved access with the vehicle jacked up, remove the roadwheels.

6 Check that all pipes and hoses are secure, unions tight and bleed screws closed. Clean any dirt from around the bleed screws.

7 Unscrew the master cylinder reservoir cap, and top the master cylinder reservoir up to the MAX level line; refit the cap loosely, and remember to maintain the fluid level at least above the MIN level line throughout the procedure, otherwise there is a risk of further air entering the system.

8 There are a number of one-man, do-it-yourself brake bleeding kits currently available from motor accessory shops. It is recommended that one of these kits is used whenever possible, as they greatly simplify the bleeding operation, and also reduce the risk of expelled air and fluid being drawn back into the system. If such a kit is not available, the basic (two-man) method must be used, which is described in detail below.

9 If a kit is to be used, prepare the vehicle as described previously, and follow the kit manufacturer's instructions, as the procedure may vary slightly according to the type being used; generally, they are as outlined below in the relevant sub-section.

10 Whichever method is used, the same sequence should be followed (paragraphs 11 and 12) to ensure the removal of all air from the system.

Bleeding sequence

11 If the system has been only partially disconnected, and suitable precautions were taken to minimise fluid loss, it should only be necessary to bleed that part of the system (ie, the primary or secondary circuit). If the master cylinder or main brake lines have been disconnected, then the complete system must be bled.

12 If the complete system is to be bled, then it should be done in the following sequence:
● Left-hand rear brake.
● Right-hand rear brake.
● Left-hand front brake.
● Right-hand front brake.

Bleeding

Basic (two-man) method

13 Collect together a clean glass jar, a suitable length of plastic or rubber tubing which is a tight fit over the bleed screw, and a ring spanner to fit the screw. The help of an assistant will also be required.

14 Remove the dust cap from the first bleed screw in the sequence **(see illustration)**. Fit the spanner and tube to the screw, place the other end of the tube in the jar, and pour in sufficient fluid to cover the end of the tube.

15 Ensure that the master cylinder reservoir fluid level is maintained at least above the MIN level line throughout the procedure.

16 Have the assistant fully depress the brake pedal several times to build-up pressure, then maintain it on the final downstroke.

17 While pedal pressure is maintained, unscrew the bleed screw (approximately one turn) and allow the compressed fluid and air to flow into the jar. The assistant should maintain pedal pressure, following it down to the floor if necessary, and should not release it until instructed to do so. When the flow stops, tighten the bleed screw again, have the assistant release the pedal slowly, and recheck the reservoir fluid level.

18 Repeat the steps given in paragraphs 16 and 17 until the fluid emerging from the bleed screw is free from air bubbles. If the master cylinder has been drained and refilled, and air is being bled from the first screw in the

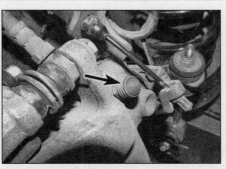

2.14 Remove the dust cap (arrowed) from the bleed screw

sequence, allow approximately five seconds between cycles for the master cylinder passages to refill.

19 When no more air bubbles appear, securely tighten the bleed screw, remove the tube and spanner, and refit the dust cap. Do not overtighten the bleed screw.

20 Repeat the procedure on the remaining screws in the sequence, until all air is removed from the system and the brake pedal feels firm again.

Using a one-way valve kit

21 As the name implies, these kits consist of a length of tubing with a one-way valve fitted, to prevent expelled air and fluid being drawn back into the system; some kits include a translucent container, which can be positioned so that the air bubbles can be more easily seen flowing from the end of the tube.

22 The kit is connected to the bleed screw, which is then opened. The user returns to the driver's seat, depresses the brake pedal with a smooth, steady stroke, and slowly releases it; this is repeated until the expelled fluid is clear of air bubbles.

23 Note that these kits simplify work so much that it is easy to forget the master cylinder reservoir fluid level; ensure that this is maintained at least above the MIN level line at all times.

Using a pressure-bleeding kit

24 These kits are usually operated by a reservoir of pressurised air contained in the spare tyre. However, note that it will probably be necessary to reduce the pressure to a lower level than normal; refer to the instructions supplied with the kit. You may have to borrow a friend's spare tyre if your car has a puncture kit instead of a spare tyre.

25 By connecting a pressurised, fluid-filled container to the master cylinder reservoir, bleeding can be carried out simply by opening each screw in turn (in the specified sequence), and allowing the fluid to flow out until no more air bubbles can be seen in the expelled fluid.

26 This method has the advantage that the large reservoir of fluid provides an additional safeguard against air being drawn into the system during bleeding.

27 Pressure-bleeding is particularly effective when bleeding 'difficult' systems, or when

bleeding the complete system at the time of routine fluid renewal.

All methods

28 When bleeding is complete, and firm pedal feel is restored, wash off any spilt fluid, securely tighten the bleed screws, and refit the dust caps.

29 Check the hydraulic fluid level in the master cylinder reservoir, and top-up if necessary (see 'Weekly checks').

30 Discard any hydraulic fluid that has been bled from the system; it will not be fit for re-use.

31 Check the feel of the brake pedal. If it feels at all spongy, air must still be present in the system, and further bleeding is required. Failure to bleed satisfactorily after a reasonable repetition of the bleeding procedure may be due to worn master cylinder seals.

---

3 Hydraulic pipes and hoses – renewal

Note: *Before starting work, refer to the note at the beginning of Section 2 concerning the dangers of hydraulic fluid.*

1 If any pipe or hose is to be renewed, minimise fluid loss by first removing the master cylinder reservoir cap and screwing it down onto a piece of polythene. Alternatively, flexible hoses can be sealed, if required, using a proprietary brake hose clamp. Metal brake pipe unions can be plugged (if care is taken not to allow dirt into the system) or capped immediately they are disconnected. Place a wad of rag under any union that is to be disconnected, to catch any spilt fluid.

2 If a flexible hose is to be disconnected, unscrew the brake pipe union nut before removing the spring clip which secures the hose to its mounting bracket. Where applicable, unscrew the hose from the caliper.

3 To unscrew union nuts, it is preferable to obtain a brake pipe spanner of the correct size; these are available from most motor accessory shops. Failing this, a close-fitting open-ended spanner will be required, though if the nuts are tight or corroded, their flats may be rounded-off if the spanner slips. In such a case, a self-locking wrench is often the only way to unscrew a stubborn union, but it follows that the pipe and the damaged nuts must be renewed on reassembly. Always clean a union and surrounding area before disconnecting it. If disconnecting a component with more than one union, make a careful note of the connections before disturbing any of them.

4 If a brake pipe is to be renewed, it can be obtained, cut to length and with the union nuts and end flares in place, from Ford dealers. All that is then necessary is to bend it to shape, following the line of the original, before fitting it to the car. Alternatively, most motor accessory shops can make up brake pipes from kits, but

this requires very careful measurement of the original, to ensure that the new one is of the correct length. The safest answer is usually to take the original to the shop as a pattern.

5 On refitting, do not overtighten the union nuts.

6 Ensure that the pipes and hoses are correctly routed, with no kinks, and that they are secured in the clips or brackets provided. Check also that the hoses are clear of all suspension components and underbody fittings, and will remain clear during movement of the suspension and steering.

7 After fitting, remove the polythene from the reservoir, and bleed the hydraulic system as described in Section 2. Wash off any spilt fluid, and check carefully for fluid leaks.

4.2a Use a flat-bladed screwdriver and a pair of grips to carefully prise off the caliper spring plate

4 Front brake pads – renewal

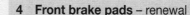

⚠ *Warning: Renew BOTH sets of front brake pads at the same time – NEVER renew the pads on only one wheel, as uneven braking may result. Note that the dust created by wear of the pads may contain asbestos, which is a health hazard. Never blow it out with compressed air, and do not inhale any of it. An approved filtering mask should be worn when working on the brakes. DO NOT use petroleum-based solvents to clean brake parts – use brake cleaner or methylated spirit only.*

1 Apply the handbrake, then jack up the front of the vehicle and support it on axle stands (see *'Jacking and vehicle support'*). Remove the front roadwheels.

2 Follow the accompanying photos (**illustrations 4.2a to 4.2s**) for the pad renewal procedure, bearing in mind the additional points listed below. Be sure to stay in order and read the caption under each illustration.

3 If the original brake pads are still serviceable, carefully clean them using a clean, fine wire brush or similar, paying particular attention to the sides and back of the metal backing plate. Clean out the grooves in the friction material, and pick out any large embedded

particles of dirt or debris. Carefully clean the pad locations in the caliper mounting bracket.

4 Prior to fitting the pads, inspect the dust seal around the piston for damage, and the piston for evidence of fluid leaks, corrosion or damage. If attention to any of these components is necessary, refer to Section 5.

5 If new brake pads are to be fitted, the caliper piston must be pushed back into the cylinder to allow for the extra pad thickness. Either use a G-clamp or similar tool, or use suitable pieces of wood as levers. Clamp off the flexible brake hose leading to the caliper then connect a brake bleeding kit to the caliper bleed screw. Open the bleed screw as the piston is retracted, the surplus brake fluid will then be collected in the bleed kit vessel (**see illustration 4.2k**). Close the bleed screw just before the caliper piston is pushed fully into the caliper. This should ensure no air enters the hydraulic system. **Note:** *The ABS unit contains hydraulic components that are very sensitive to impurities in the brake fluid. Even the smallest particles can cause the system to fail through blockage. The pad retraction method described here prevents any debris in the brake fluid expelled from the caliper from being passed back to the ABS hydraulic unit, as well as preventing any chance of damage to the master cylinder seals.*

6 With the brake pads installed, depress the brake pedal repeatedly, until normal (non-assisted) pedal pressure is restored, and the

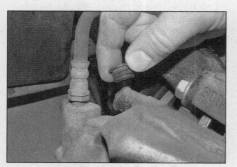

4.2b Prise out the upper...

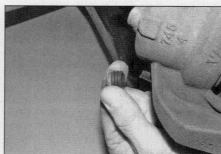

4.2c... and lower rubber caps...

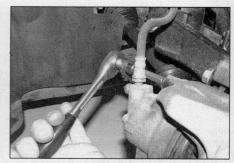

4.2d... then unscrew the upper and lower caliper guide bolts

4.2e Release the brake hydraulic hose from the bracket on the suspension strut

4.2f Slide the caliper and inner pad from the disc

4.2g Pull the inner brake pad from the caliper piston...

4.2h… and lift the outer pad from the caliper bracket

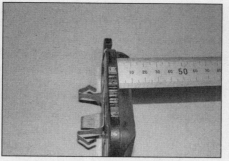

4.2i Measure the thickness of the pad's friction material. If it's 2.0 mm or less, renew all the front pads

4.2j Clean the pad mounting surfaces with a wire brush

4.2k If you're fitting new pads, push the piston back into the caliper using a piston retraction tool or G-clamp

4.2l Fit the outer pad to the caliper mounting bracket…

4.2m… then fit the inner pad to the caliper piston

4.2n Slide the caliper, with the inner pad fitted, over the disc and outer pad

4.2o Refit the caliper guide bolts and tighten them to the specified torque

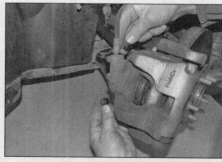

4.2p Press the rubber caps into position

4.2q Refit the brake hydraulic hose to the suspension strut bracket

4.2r Use a pair of grips to compress the caliper spring plate…

4.2s… and push the spring plate tabs fully into the holes in the caliper

pads are pressed into firm contact with the brake disc.

7 Repeat the above procedure on the remaining front brake caliper.

8 Refit the roadwheels, then lower the vehicle to the ground and tighten the roadwheel nuts to the specified torque setting.

9 Check the hydraulic fluid level as described in 'Weekly checks'.

Caution: New pads will not give full braking efficiency until they have bedded-in. Be prepared for this, and avoid hard braking as far as possible for the first hundred miles or so after pad renewal.

5 Front brake caliper – removal, overhaul and refitting

Note: *Before starting work, refer to the warnings at the beginning of Sections 2 and 4 concerning the dangers of hydraulic fluid and asbestos dust.*

Removal

1 Apply the handbrake, then jack up the front of the vehicle and support it on axle stands (see 'Jacking and vehicle support'). Remove the roadwheel.

2 Minimise fluid loss by first removing the master cylinder reservoir cap and screwing it down onto a piece of polythene. Alternatively, use a brake hose clamp to clamp the flexible hose leading to the brake caliper.

3 Loosen the union on the caliper end of the flexible brake hose. Once loosened, do not try to unscrew the hose at this stage.

4 Remove the brake pads as described in Section 4.

5 Support the caliper in one hand, and prevent the hydraulic hose from turning with the other hand. Unscrew the caliper from the hose, making sure that the hose is not twisted unduly or strained. Once the caliper is detached, plug the open hydraulic unions in the caliper and hose, to keep out dust and dirt.

6 If required, the caliper mounting bracket can be unbolted from the swivel hub.

Overhaul

Note: *Before starting work, check on the availability of parts (caliper overhaul kit/seals).*

7 With the caliper on the bench, brush away all traces of dust and dirt, but take care not to inhale any dust, as it may be harmful to your health.

8 Pull the dust cover rubber seal from the end of the piston.

9 Apply low air pressure to the fluid inlet union, to eject the piston. Only low air pressure is required for this, such as is produced by a foot-operated tyre pump.

Caution: The piston may be ejected with some force. Position a thin piece of wood between the piston and the caliper body, to prevent damage to the end face of the piston, in the event of it being ejected suddenly.

10 Using a suitable blunt instrument, prise the piston seal from the groove in the cylinder bore. Take care not to scratch the surface of the bore.

11 Clean the piston and caliper body with methylated spirit, and allow to dry. Examine the surfaces of the piston and cylinder bore for wear, damage and corrosion. If the piston alone is unserviceable, a new piston must be obtained, along with seals. If the cylinder bore is unserviceable, the complete caliper must be renewed. The seals must be renewed, regardless of the condition of the other components.

12 Coat the piston and seals with clean brake fluid, then manipulate the piston seal into the groove in the cylinder bore.

13 Push the piston squarely into its bore, taking care not to damage the seal.

14 Fit the dust cover rubber seal onto the piston and caliper, then depress the piston fully.

Refitting

15 Refit the caliper by reversing the removal operations. Make sure that the flexible brake hose is not twisted. Tighten the mounting bolts and wheel nuts to the specified torque.

16 Bleed the brake circuit according to the procedure given in Section 2, remembering to remove the brake hose clamp (where applicable) from the flexible hose. Make sure there are no leaks from the hose connections. Test the brakes carefully before returning the vehicle to normal service.

6 Front brake disc – inspection, removal and refitting

Note: *Before starting work, refer to the warning at the beginning of Section 4 concerning the dangers of asbestos dust. If either disc requires renewal, both should be renewed at the same time together with new pads, to ensure even and consistent braking.*

Inspection

1 Firmly apply the handbrake, then jack up the front of the vehicle and support it securely on axle stands (see 'Jacking and vehicle support'). Remove the roadwheel.

2 Release the brake hydraulic hose from the suspension strut bracket **(see illustration 4.2e)**.

3 Unscrew the bolts securing the brake caliper mounting bracket to the swivel hub, then slide the caliper/bracket assembly from the swivel hub and brake disc (there is no need to remove the brake pads) **(see illustration)**. Suspend the caliper/bracket assembly from the strut coil spring using wire or a cable-tie – do not allow the caliper to hang on the brake hose.

4 Temporarily refit two of the wheel nuts to diagonally-opposite studs, with the flat side of the nuts against the disc. Tighten the nuts progressively, to hold the disc firmly.

5 Scrape any corrosion from the disc. Rotate the disc, and examine it for deep scoring, grooving or cracks. Using a micrometer, measure the thickness of the disc in several places **(see illustration)**. The minimum thickness is given in the Specifications. Light wear and scoring is normal, but if

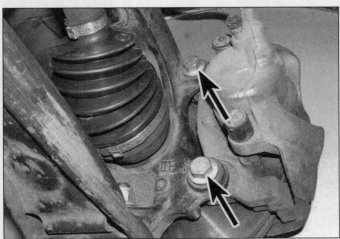

6.3 Unscrew the bolts (arrowed) then slide the caliper and mounting bracket assembly from the swivel hub and brake disc

6.5 Measure the thickness of the disc using a micrometer

6.6 Measuring the disc run-out with a dial gauge

11 Mark the disc in relation to the hub, if it is to be refitted, then withdraw the disc over the wheel studs **(see illustration)**.

Refitting

12 Make sure that the disc and hub mating surfaces are clean, then locate the disc on the wheel studs. Align the previously-made marks if the original disc is being refitted.
13 Refit the special retaining nuts to the wheel studs.
14 Refit the caliper mounting bracket complete with caliper and pads, and tighten the bolts to the specified torque.
15 Locate the brake hydraulic hose in the bracket on the suspension strut.
16 Refit the wheel, and lower the car to the ground. Tighten the wheel nuts to the specified torque.
17 Test the brakes carefully before returning the car to normal service.

| 7 | Rear brake pads – renewal | |

⚠ **Warning: Renew BOTH sets of rear brake pads at the same time – NEVER renew the pads on only one wheel, as uneven braking may result. Note that the dust created by wear of the pads may contain asbestos, which is a health hazard. Never blow it out with compressed air, and do not inhale any of it. An approved filtering mask should be worn when working on the brakes. DO NOT use petroleum-based solvents to clean brake parts – use brake cleaner or methylated spirit only.**

1 Chock the front wheels then jack up the rear of the car and securely support it on axle stands (see *'Jacking and vehicle support'*). Remove the rear roadwheels.
2 Follow the accompanying photos (illustrations 7.2a to 7.2t) for the pad renewal procedure, bearing in mind the additional points listed below. Be sure to stay in order

excessive, the disc should be removed, and either reground by a specialist, or renewed. If regrinding is undertaken, the minimum thickness must be maintained. Obviously, if the disc is cracked, it must be renewed.
6 Using a dial gauge or a flat metal block and feeler gauges, check that the disc run-out 10 mm from the outer edge does not exceed the limit given in the Specifications. To do this, fix the measuring equipment, and rotate the disc, noting the variation in measurement as the disc is rotated **(see illustration)**. The difference between the minimum and maximum measurements recorded is the disc run-out.
7 If the run-out is greater than the specified amount, check for variations of the disc thickness as follows. Mark the disc at eight positions 45° apart then, using a micrometer, measure the disc thickness at the eight positions, 15 mm in from the outer edge. If the

variation between the minimum and maximum readings is greater than the specified amount, the disc should be renewed.
8 The hub face run-out can also be checked in a similar way. First remove the disc as described later in this Section, fix the measuring equipment, then slowly rotate the hub, and check that the run-out does not exceed the amount given in the Specifications. If the hub face run-out is excessive, this should be corrected (by renewing the hub bearings – see Chapter 10 Section 2) before rechecking the disc run-out.

Removal

9 With the wheel and caliper removed, remove the wheel nuts which were temporarily refitted in paragraph 4.
10 Unscrew the special retaining nuts from the wheel studs **(see illustration)**.

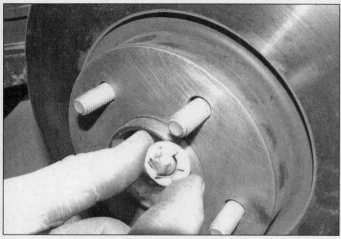

6.10 Unscrew the special retaining nuts from the wheel studs...

6.11... then withdraw the disc from the hub

and read the caption under each illustration. Note that if the old pads are to be refitted, ensure that they are identified so that they can be returned to their original positions.

3 If the original brake pads are still serviceable, carefully clean them using a clean, fine wire brush or similar, paying particular attention to the sides and back of the metal backing plate. Clean out the grooves in the friction material, and pick out any large embedded particles of dirt or debris. Carefully clean the pad locations in the caliper body/mounting bracket.

4 Prior to fitting the pads, check that the guide pins are a snug fit in the caliper mounting bracket. Brush the dust and dirt from the caliper and piston, but do not inhale it, as

it is injurious to health. Inspect the dust seal around the piston for damage, and the piston for evidence of fluid leaks, corrosion or damage. If attention to any of these components is necessary, refer to Section 8.

5 If new brake pads are to be fitted, it will be necessary to retract the piston fully into the caliper bore by rotating it in a clockwise direction. This can be achieved by using sturdy circlip pliers, noting that as well as being turned, the piston has to be pressed in very firmly. Special tools are readily available to achieve this with less effort. While the caliper is being retracted, clamp off the flexible brake hose leading to the caliper then connect a brake bleeding kit to the caliper

bleed screw. Open the bleed screw as the piston is retracted, the surplus brake fluid will then be collected in the bleed kit vessel **(see illustration 7.2k)**. Close the bleed screw just before the caliper piston is pushed fully into the caliper. This should ensure no air enters the hydraulic system. **Note:** *The ABS unit contains hydraulic components that are very sensitive to impurities in the brake fluid. Even the smallest particles can cause the system to fail through blockage. The pad retraction method described here prevents any debris in the brake fluid expelled from the caliper from being passed back to the ABS hydraulic unit, as well as preventing any chance of damage to the master cylinder seals.*

6 With the brake pads installed, depress the brake pedal repeatedly, until normal (non-assisted) pedal pressure is restored, and the pads are pressed into firm contact with the brake disc.

7 Repeat the above procedure on the remaining rear brake caliper.

8 Refit the roadwheels, then lower the vehicle to the ground and tighten the roadwheel nuts to the specified torque.

9 Check the hydraulic fluid level as described in *'Weekly checks'*.

Caution: New pads will not give full braking efficiency until they have bedded-in. Be prepared for this, and avoid hard braking as far as possible for the first hundred miles or so after pad renewal.

7.2a Unscrew the lower guide pin bolt while counter-holding the guide pin with a second spanner...

7.2b... then remove the guide pin bolt from the caliper

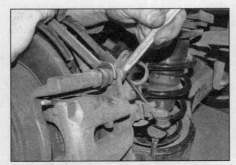

7.2c Unscrew the upper guide pin bolt in the same way until the caliper is released from the mounting bracket...

7.2d... but note that it is not possible to completely remove the upper guide pin bolt (arrowed)

7.2e Lift the caliper off the mounting bracket and suspend it from a suitable place under the wheel arch using a cable-tie or similar

7.2f Remove the outer pad...

7.2g... and inner pad from the caliper mounting bracket

7.2h Remove the lower guide plate...

7.2i... and upper guide plate from the caliper mounting bracket

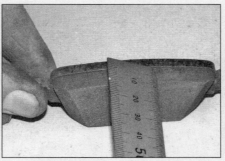

7.2j Measure the thickness of the pad's friction material. If it's 1.5 mm or less, renew all the rear pads

7.2k Using a caliper retracting tool to retract the piston as far as the stop

7.2l Brush the dust and dirt from the caliper, piston and mounting bracket

7.2m Refit the lower guide plate...

7.2n... and upper guide plate to the caliper mounting bracket

7.2o Fit the inner pad to the caliper mounting bracket

7.2p If present, remove the adhesive foil from the pad backing plate, then fit the outer pad to the caliper mounting bracket

7.2q Slide the caliper into position in the mounting bracket

7.2r Refit the upper guide pin bolt...

7.2s... followed by the lower guide pin bolt...

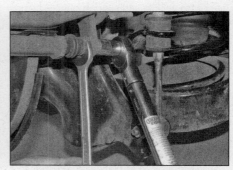

7.2t... and tighten them both to the specified torque

8.2 Move the handbrake operating lever upwards and detach the handbrake inner cable end fitting from the lever

8.3a Compress the tabs on the handbrake outer cable collar...

8.3b... and withdraw the cable from the mounting bracket

8.8 Rear brake caliper mounting bracket retaining bolts (arrowed)

8 Rear brake caliper – removal, overhaul and refitting

Note: *Before starting work, refer to the note at the beginning of Section 2 concerning the dangers of hydraulic fluid, and to the warning at the beginning of Section 7 concerning the dangers of asbestos dust.*

Removal

1 Chock the front wheels, then jack up the rear of the vehicle and support on axle stands (see 'Jacking and vehicle support'). Remove the roadwheel.

2 Move the handbrake operating lever on the caliper upwards and detach the handbrake inner cable end fitting from the lever **(see illustration)**.

3 Using pointed-nose pliers, compress the tabs on the handbrake outer cable collar and withdraw the cable from the mounting bracket **(see illustrations)**.

4 Minimise fluid loss by first removing the master cylinder reservoir cap and screwing it down onto a piece of polythene. Alternatively, use a brake hose clamp to clamp the flexible hose leading to the brake caliper.

5 Clean the area around the caliper brake hose union. Slacken (but do not completely unscrew) the union on the caliper end of the flexible hose.

6 Support the caliper in one hand, and prevent the flexible hose from turning with the other hand. Unscrew the caliper from the hose, making sure that the hose is not twisted unduly or strained.

7 Once the caliper is detached, plug the open hydraulic unions in the caliper and hose, to keep out dust and dirt.

8 If necessary, unbolt the caliper mounting bracket from the hub carrier **(see illustration)**.

Overhaul

9 No overhaul procedures, or parts, were available at the time of writing. Check the availability of spares before dismantling the caliper. Do not attempt to dismantle the handbrake mechanism inside the caliper; if the mechanism is faulty, the complete caliper assembly must be renewed.

Refitting

10 Refit the caliper by reversing the removal operations. Make sure that the flexible brake hose is not twisted. Tighten the mounting bolts and wheel nuts to the specified torque.

11 Bleed the brake circuit according to the procedure given in Section 2, remembering to remove the brake hose clamp (where applicable) from the flexible hose. Make sure there are no leaks from the hose connections. Test the brakes carefully before returning the vehicle to normal service.

9 Rear brake disc – inspection, removal and refitting

Inspection

1 Remove the rear brake pads as described in Section 7.

2 Temporarily refit two of the wheel nuts to diagonally-opposite studs, with the flat side of the nuts against the disc. Tighten the nuts progressively, to hold the disc firmly.

3 Scrape any corrosion from the disc. Rotate the disc, and examine it for deep scoring, grooving or cracks. Using a micrometer, measure the thickness of the disc in several places. The minimum thickness is given in the Specifications. Light wear and scoring is normal, but if excessive, the disc should be removed, and either reground by a specialist, or renewed. If regrinding is undertaken, the minimum thickness must be maintained. Obviously, if the disc is cracked, it must be renewed.

4 Using a dial gauge or a flat metal block and feeler gauges, check that the disc run-out 10 mm from the outer edge does not exceed the limit given in the Specifications. To do this, fix the measuring equipment, and rotate the disc, noting the variation in measurement as the disc is rotated. The difference between the minimum and maximum measurements recorded is the disc run-out.

5 If the run-out is greater than the specified amount, check for variations of the disc thickness as follows. Mark the disc at eight positions 45° apart then, using a micrometer,

9.11a Undo the securing screw (arrowed)…

9.11b… and withdraw the disc from the hub

measure the disc thickness at the eight positions, 15 mm in from the outer edge. If the variation between the minimum and maximum readings is greater than the specified amount, the disc should be renewed.

6 The hub face run-out can also be checked in a similar way. First remove the disc as described later in this Section, fix the measuring equipment, then slowly rotate the hub, and check that the run-out does not exceed the amount given in the Specifications. If the hub face run-out is excessive, this should be corrected (by renewing the hub bearings – see Chapter 10 Section 8) before rechecking the disc run-out.

Removal

7 If not already done, remove the rear brake pads as described in Section 7.

8 Where applicable, remove the wheel nuts which were temporarily refitted in paragraph 2.

9 Undo the two bolts securing the caliper mounting bracket to the hub carrier and remove the mounting bracket **(see illustration 8.8)**.

10 Mark the disc in relation to the hub, if it is to be refitted.

11 Remove the securing screw and withdraw the disc from the hub **(see illustrations)**.

Refitting

12 Make sure that the disc and hub mating surfaces are clean, then locate the disc on the wheel studs. Align the previously-made marks if the original disc is being refitted.

13 Refit and tighten the disc securing screw.

14 Refit the caliper mounting bracket and tighten the bolts to the specified torque.

15 Refit the rear brake pads as described in Section 7.

16 Refit the wheel, and lower the car to the ground. Tighten the wheel nuts to the specified torque.

17 Test the brakes carefully before returning the car to normal service.

---

10 Master cylinder –
removal and refitting

Note: *Before starting work, refer to the warning at the beginning of Section 2 concerning the dangers of hydraulic fluid.*

Removal

1 Remove the master cylinder reservoir cap, and siphon the hydraulic fluid from the reservoir. **Note:** *Do not siphon the fluid by mouth, as it is poisonous; use a syringe or an old hydrometer. Alternatively, open any convenient bleed screw in the system, and gently pump the brake pedal to expel the fluid through a plastic tube connected to the screw* (see Section 2).

2 Depress the tabs of the quick-release connector and disconnect the clutch master cylinder hydraulic hose from the base of the master cylinder reservoir **(see illustration)**.

3 Disconnect the brake fluid level sensor wiring connector from the underside of the reservoir.

4 Place cloth rags beneath the master cylinder to collect escaping brake fluid. Identify the brake lines for position, then unscrew the union nuts and move the lines to one side. Tape over or plug the line outlets.

5 Unscrew the mounting nuts and withdraw the master cylinder from the vacuum servo unit **(see illustration)**. Take care not to spill fluid on the vehicle paintwork.

6 Recover the gasket/seal from the master cylinder.

7 No further dismantling of the master cylinder is possible as the internal components are not available separately.

Refitting

8 Clean the contact surfaces of the master cylinder and servo and locate a new gasket/seal on the master cylinder.

9 Fit the master cylinder to the servo unit, ensuring that the servo unit pushrod enters the master cylinder piston centrally. Fit the retaining nuts and tighten them to the specified torque setting.

10 Refit the brake lines and tighten the union nuts securely.

11 Reconnect the clutch master cylinder hydraulic hose and the brake fluid level sensor wiring connector to the reservoir.

12 Remove the reservoir filler cap and top-up the reservoir with fresh hydraulic fluid to the MAX mark (see 'Weekly checks').

10.2 Disconnect the clutch master cylinder hydraulic hose (arrowed) from the base of the master cylinder reservoir

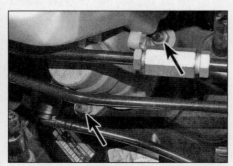

10.5 Master cylinder retaining nuts (arrowed)

11.6 Prise out the plastic clevis pin (arrowed) securing the brake pedal to the servo unit pushrod

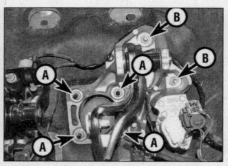

11.7 Vacuum servo unit retaining nuts (A) and pedal mounting bracket retaining nuts (B)

13 Bleed the hydraulic systems as described in Section 2 and Chapter 6 Section 5 then refit the filler cap. Thoroughly check the operation of the brakes and clutch before using the vehicle on the road.

11 Brake pedal – removal and refitting

Note: *The brake pedal is an integral part of the pedal mounting bracket assembly and cannot be individually removed. Should renewal of the pedal be required, due to wear of the pivot bushes or the pedal itself, it will be necessary to renew the complete mounting bracket assembly.*

Removal

1 Disconnect the battery negative lead as described in Chapter 5A Section 4.
2 Remove the steering column as described in Chapter 10 Section 16.
3 Remove the accelerator pedal as described in the relevant Part of Chapter 4A Section 6.
4 Remove the brake pedal position switch and brake light switch as described in Section 17.
5 Release the wiring harness from the clips on the brake pedal mounting bracket.
6 Using a screwdriver, prise out the plastic clevis pin securing the brake pedal to the servo unit pushrod**(see illustration)**. Note that the clevis pin will be damaged during

12.12 Unscrew and remove the engine lower mounting link through-bolt (arrowed)

removal and a new clevis pin will be required for refitting.
7 Undo the four nuts securing the vacuum servo unit to the brake pedal mounting bracket, and the two nuts securing the mounting bracket to the bulkhead **(see illustration)**.
8 Withdraw the brake pedal mounting bracket off the studs and remove it from inside the car.

Refitting

9 Refitting is a reversal of removal, noting the following points:
a) *Tighten the mounting bracket retaining nuts to the specified torque.*
b) *Reconnect the brake pedal to the servo unit pushrod using a new clevis pin.*
c) *Refit the brake pedal position switch and brake light switch as described in Section 17.*
d) *Refit the accelerator pedal as described in the relevant Part of Chapter 4A Section 6.*
e) *Refit the steering column as described in Chapter 10 Section 16.*
f) *Reconnect the battery negative lead as described in Chapter 5A Section 4.*

12 Vacuum servo unit – testing, removal and refitting

Testing

1 To test the operation of the servo unit, with the engine off, depress the footbrake several

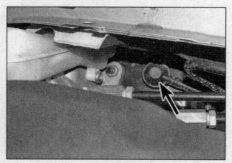

12.17 Carefully ease the vacuum hose (arrowed) out of the servo unit

times to exhaust the vacuum. Now start the engine, keeping the pedal firmly depressed. As the engine starts, there should be a noticeable 'give' in the brake pedal as the vacuum builds-up. Allow the engine to run for at least two minutes, then switch it off. The brake pedal should now feel normal, but further applications should result in the pedal feeling firmer, the pedal stroke decreasing with each application.
2 If the servo does not operate as described, first inspect the servo unit check valve as described in Section 13.
3 If the servo unit still fails to operate satisfactorily, the fault lies within the unit itself. Repairs to the unit are not possible; if faulty, the servo unit must be renewed.

Removal

Petrol engine models

4 Have the air conditioning system refrigerant discharged at a dealer service department or an automotive air conditioning repair facility.
5 Disconnect the battery negative lead as described in Chapter 5A Section 4.
6 Remove the brake master cylinder as described in Section 10.
7 Working in the driver's footwell, using a screwdriver, prise out the plastic clevis pin securing the brake pedal to the servo unit pushrod **(see illustration 11.6)**. Note that the clevis pin will be damaged during removal and a new clevis pin will be required for refitting.
8 Undo the four nuts securing the vacuum servo unit to the brake pedal mounting bracket **(see illustration 11.7)**.
9 Firmly apply the handbrake, then jack up the front of the vehicle and support it securely on axle stands (see '*Jacking and vehicle support*'). Where applicable, remove the engine undertray.
10 To prevent damage to the exhaust flexible section in subsequent operations, support it by attaching a pair of splints either side (two scrap strips of wood, plant canes, etc) using some cable-ties. Undo the nuts securing the flexible section flange to the intermediate section, and separate the joint. Recover the gasket, and discard it, a new gasket must be used for refitting.
11 Undo the two bolts securing the exhaust flexible section hanger bracket to the front subframe.
12 Unscrew and remove the engine lower mounting link through-bolt **(see illustration)**.
13 Undo the nut securing the air conditioning refrigerant pipes to the expansion valve on the bulkhead and withdraw the pipes from the valve. Discard the O-ring seals – new ones must be used when refitting. Suitably cap the open fittings immediately to keep moisture and contamination out of the system.
14 Undo the union nuts and disconnect the two brake pipes at the connectors adjacent to the servo unit.
15 The engine must now be supported, as the right-hand mounting (right as seen from

12.31 Left-hand engine/transmission mounting and bracket retaining nuts/bolts (arrowed)

12.32 Right-hand engine/transmission mounting retaining nuts/bolts (arrowed)

the driver's seat) must be unbolted from the body. Supporting the engine should ideally be done from above, using an engine crane or a special engine lifting beam. However, in the absence of these tools, the engine can be supported on the sump, using a trolley jack, providing a piece of wood is used to spread the load.

16 With the engine securely supported, undo the two bolts securing the right-hand engine mounting to the body.

17 Carefully ease the vacuum hose out of the servo unit, taking care not to displace the sealing grommet (see illustration).

18 Withdraw the servo unit from the bulkhead as far as the initial working clearance will allow. With the engine securely supported on the jack or crane, pull the engine forward on the right-hand side, until sufficient clearance exists to remove the servo unit from the engine compartment.

Diesel engine models

Note: *Arrangements must be made to support the engine/transmission assembly from above and enable it to be lowered by approximately 200 mm. The best way to support the engine/transmission is with a bar resting in the bonnet channels with an adjustable hook appropriately placed. Trolley jacks and the help of an assistant will also be required throughout the procedure.*

19 Have the air conditioning system refrigerant discharged at a dealer service department or an automotive air conditioning repair facility.

20 Remove the battery and battery tray as described in Chapter 5A Section 4.

21 Remove the brake master cylinder as described in Section 10.

22 Working in the driver's footwell, using a screwdriver, prise out the plastic clevis pin securing the brake pedal to the servo unit pushrod (see illustration 11.6). Note that the clevis pin will be damaged during removal and a new clevis pin will be required for refitting.

23 Undo the four nuts securing the vacuum servo unit to the brake pedal mounting bracket (see illustration 11.7).

24 Firmly apply the handbrake, then jack up the front of the vehicle and support it securely on axle stands (see *'Jacking and vehicle support'*). Ensure that the vehicle is raised sufficiently to allow the engine/transmission to be lowered by 200 mm.

25 Undo the retaining fasteners and remove the engine undertray.

26 Remove the front subframe as described in Chapter 10 Section 7.

27 Undo the nuts securing the exhaust flexible section flange to the intermediate section or diesel particulate filter, and separate the joint. Recover the gasket, and discard it, a new gasket must be used for refitting.

28 Undo the nut securing the air conditioning refrigerant pipes to the expansion valve on the bulkhead and withdraw the pipes from the valve. Discard the O-ring seals – new ones must be used when refitting. Suitably cap the open fittings immediately to keep moisture and contamination out of the system.

29 Undo the union nuts and disconnect the two brake pipes at the connectors adjacent to the servo unit.

30 Carefully ease the vacuum hose out of the servo unit, taking care not to displace the sealing grommet (see illustration 12.17).

31 Securely support the engine from above (see the note at the start of this sub-Section), then undo the nuts/bolts and remove the left-hand engine/transmission mounting and bracket (see illustration).

32 Undo the two bolts and two nuts and remove the right-hand engine/transmission mounting (see illustration).

33 Taking care that nothing attached to the engine is placed under strain, carefully lower the engine/transmission by approximately 200 mm.

34 Withdraw the servo unit from the bulkhead and manipulate it out of the engine compartment.

Refitting

Petrol engine models

35 Locate the vacuum servo unit in position on the bulkhead ensuring that the servo unit pushrod locates correctly around the brake pedal.

36 Refit the vacuum hose to the servo grommet, ensuring that the hose is correctly seated.

37 Move the engine back to its fitted position and refit the engine mounting retaining bolts. Tighten the bolts to the specified torque (see Chapter 2A Section 16). Remove the jack or crane used to support the engine.

38 Reconnect the two brake pipes at the connectors adjacent to the servo unit and tighten the union nuts securely.

39 Reconnect the air conditioning system refrigerant pipes using new O-ring seals and tighten the pipe retaining nut securely.

40 Refit the engine lower mounting link through-bolt and tighten the bolt to the specified torque (see Chapter 2A Section 16).

41 Refit and tighten the two bolts securing the exhaust flexible section hanger bracket to the front subframe.

42 Using a new gasket, reconnect the exhaust flexible section to the intermediate pipe and tighten the retaining nuts to the specified torque. Remove the support splints from the flexible section.

43 Where applicable, refit the engine undertray, then lower the car to the ground.

44 Refit the four nuts securing the vacuum servo unit to the brake pedal mounting bracket and tighten the nuts to the specified torque.

45 Reconnect the brake pedal to the servo unit pushrod using a new clevis pin.

46 Refit the brake master cylinder as described in Section 10, then reconnect the battery negative lead as described in Chapter 5A Section 4.

47 Have the air conditioning system

evacuated, charged and leak-tested by the specialist who discharged it.

Diesel engine models

48 Locate the vacuum servo unit in position on the bulkhead ensuring that the servo unit pushrod locates correctly around the brake pedal.

49 Refit the vacuum hose to the servo grommet, ensuring that the hose is correctly seated.

50 Raise the engine back to its fitted position and refit the left-hand and right-hand engine mountings. Tighten the retaining nuts/bolts to the specified torque (see Chapter 2B Section 18 or Chapter 2B Section 18 as applicable). Remove the jack or crane used to support the engine.

51 Reconnect the two brake pipes at the connectors adjacent to the servo unit and tighten the union nuts securely.

52 Reconnect the air conditioning system refrigerant pipes using new O-ring seals and tighten the pipe retaining nut securely.

53 Using a new gasket, reconnect the exhaust flexible section to the intermediate pipe or diesel particulate filter and tighten the retaining nuts to the specified torque.

54 Refit the front subframe as described in Chapter 10 Section 7.

55 Refit the engine undertray, then lower the car to the ground.

56 Refit the four nuts securing the vacuum servo unit to the brake pedal mounting bracket and tighten the nuts to the specified torque.

57 Reconnect the brake pedal to the servo unit pushrod using a new clevis pin.

58 Refit the brake master cylinder as described in Section 10.

59 Refit the battery tray and battery as described in Chapter 5A Section 4.

60 Have the air conditioning system evacuated, charged and leak-tested by the specialist who discharged it.

13 Vacuum servo unit check valve and hose – removal, testing and refitting

Removal

1 Carefully ease the vacuum hose out of the servo unit, taking care not to displace the sealing grommet **(see illustration 12.17)**.

2 Disconnect the hose quick-release fitting from the inlet manifold (petrol engines) or vacuum pump (diesel engines).

3 Release the vacuum hose from its clips and support brackets in the engine compartment, then remove the hose and check valve from the car.

Testing

4 Examine the check valve and hose for signs of damage, and renew if necessary. The valve may be tested by blowing through it in both directions. Air should flow through the valve

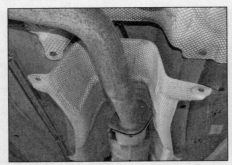

14.3 Undo the six bolts/nuts and remove the exhaust centre heat shield

in one direction only – when blown through from the servo unit end. If air flows in both directions, or not at all, renew the valve and hose as an assembly.

5 Examine the servo unit rubber sealing grommet for signs of damage or deterioration, and renew as necessary.

Refitting

6 Refitting is a reversal of removal ensuring that the quick-release connector audibly locks in position, and that the hose is correctly seated in the servo grommet.

7 On completion, start the engine and check that there are no air leaks.

14 Handbrake – adjustment

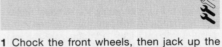

1 Chock the front wheels, then jack up the rear of the car, and support it securely on axle stands (see *'Jacking and vehicle support'*).

2 Unhook the rear section of the exhaust system from the three rubber mountings and allow it to rest on the rear subframe.

3 Undo the six bolts/nuts and remove the exhaust centre heat shield **(see illustration)**.

4 Apply the handbrake, then release it fully.

5 Working under the car, slacken the handbrake cable adjusting nut to the end of its threads **(see illustration)**.

6 Insert a 1.2 mm feeler gauge between the handbrake operating lever on the brake caliper and its abutment stop on both sides **(see illustration)**.

7 Tighten the handbrake cable adjusting nut until movement is observed on one of the operating levers (ie, until the feeler gauge drops out).

8 Remove the feeler gauge(s) and check that it is possible to rotate both rear wheels without brake drag.

9 If brake drag is felt, slacken the cable adjusting nut to the end of its threads again and repeat the adjustment procedure, but this time use 1.0 mm feeler gauges.

10 If brake drag is still felt, continue repeating the adjustment procedure, reducing the feeler gauge thickness by 0.2 mm each time.

11 When all is satisfactory, refit the heat

14.5 Handbrake cable adjusting nut (arrowed)

shield, hook the exhaust system back into its rubber mountings and lower the car to the ground.

15 Handbrake lever – removal and refitting

Removal

1 Remove the centre console as described in Chapter 11 Section 28.

2 Chock the front wheels, then jack up the rear of the car, and support it securely on axle stands (see *'Jacking and vehicle support'*).

3 Unhook the rear section of the exhaust system from the three rubber mountings and allow it to rest on the rear subframe.

4 Undo the six bolts/nuts and remove the exhaust centre heat shield**(see illustration 14.3)**.

5 Unscrew the handbrake cable adjusting nut and remove it from the short (front) handbrake cable **(see illustration 14.5)**.

6 Detach the handbrake cables from the compensator plate by sliding the end fittings down and out of the elongated holes in the plate. Remove the compensator plate from the short (front) handbrake cable.

7 Disconnect the wiring connector from the handbrake lever warning light switch and release the wiring from the clip on the lever base.

14.6 Insert a 1.2 mm feeler gauge (arrowed) between the handbrake operating lever and its abutment stop on both sides

8 Undo the three retaining bolts and remove the handbrake lever assembly from inside the car **(see illustration)**.

Refitting

9 Refitting is a reversal of removal, noting the following points:

a) *Adjust the handbrake as described in Section 14.*

b) *Refit the centre console as described in Chapter 11 Section 28.*

16 Handbrake cables – removal and refitting

Removal

1 Chock the front wheels, then jack up the rear of the car, and support it securely on axle stands (see *'Jacking and vehicle support'*). Remove both rear wheels.

2 Unhook the rear section of the exhaust system from the three rubber mountings and allow it to rest on the rear subframe.

3 Undo the bolts/nuts and remove the exhaust centre heat shield **(see illustration 14.3)**.

4 Similarly, undo the bolts/nuts and manipulate the rear heat shield from its location **(see illustration)**.

5 Unscrew the handbrake cable adjusting nut and remove it from the short (front) handbrake cable **(see illustration 14.5)**.

15.8 Handbrake lever retaining bolts (arrowed)

6 Detach the handbrake cables from the compensator plate by sliding the end fittings down and out of the elongated holes in the plate. Remove the compensator plate from the short (front) handbrake cable.

7 Depress the retaining tabs and push the handbrake cables rearwards out of the support bracket on the underbody **(see illustration)**.

8 Move the handbrake operating lever on each brake caliper upwards and detach the handbrake inner cable end fitting from the lever **(see illustration 8.2)**.

9 Using pointed-nose pliers, compress the tabs on the handbrake outer cable collar and withdraw the cable from the mounting bracket **(see illustrations 8.3a and 8.3b)**.

10 Slip the handbrake cable grommet out of the support bracket on the hub carrier **(see illustration)**.

11 Undo the bolts and detach the two handbrake cable guides from the lateral links each side **(see illustrations)**.

12 Release the handbrake cables from the four underbody retaining clips in front of the fuel tank and remove the cables from under the car **(see illustration)**.

Refitting

13 Refitting is a reversal of removal, noting the following points:

a) *Note that the cables cross over at the underbody support bracket* **(see illustration 16.7)**. *The left-hand cable has a black sleeve and the right-hand cable has a white sleeve.*

b) *Adjust the handbrake as described in Section 14.*

17 Brake switches – removal, refitting and adjustment

Removal

Brake light switch

1 Fully open the stowage compartment at the right-hand side of the facia for access to the brake pedal mounting bracket.

16.4 Undo the bolts/nuts and manipulate the exhaust rear heat shield from its location

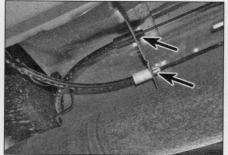

16.7 Depress the retaining tabs (arrowed) and push the handbrake cables rearwards out of the support bracket

16.10 Slip the handbrake cable grommet (arrowed) out of the support bracket on the hub carrier

16.11a Undo the rear bolt (arrowed)…

16.11b… and front bolt (arrowed) securing the handbrake cable guides to the lateral links each side

16.12 Release the handbrake cables from the underbody retaining clips (arrowed)

17.2 Disconnect the wiring connector from the brake light switch, located on the brake pedal mounting bracket

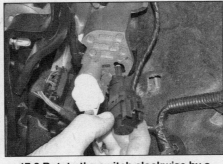

17.3 Rotate the switch clockwise by a quarter-turn, and withdraw it from the pedal bracket

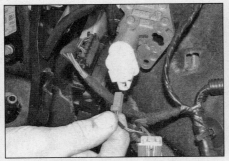

17.5 Disconnect the wiring connector from the brake pedal position switch

17.6 Rotate the switch anti-clockwise by a quarter-turn, and withdraw it from the pedal bracket

2 Reach through the stowage compartment aperture and disconnect the wiring connector from the brake light switch, located on the brake pedal mounting bracket **(see illustration)**. This is the switch on the right-hand side of the pedal mounting bracket, and is coloured black.

3 Rotate the switch clockwise by a quarter-turn, and withdraw it from the pedal bracket **(see illustration)**. Do not depress the brake pedal during the removal or refitting procedure – the pedal must be 'at rest'.

Brake pedal position switch

4 Remove the brake light switch as described previously. The wiring can be left connected to the switch and the switch just moved to one side.

5 Disconnect the wiring connector from the brake pedal position switch. This is the switch on the left-hand side of the pedal mounting bracket, and is coloured blue and white **(see illustration)**.

6 Rotate the switch anti-clockwise by a quarter-turn, and withdraw it from the pedal bracket **(see illustration)**. Do not depress the brake pedal during the removal or refitting procedure – the pedal must be 'at rest'.

Refitting and adjustment

7 Refitting is a reversal of the removal procedure. Both switches are automatically adjusted/calibrated by the vehicle system.

18 Handbrake warning light switch – removal and refitting

Removal

1 Remove the handbrake lever as described in Section 15.

2 Unscrew the mounting bolt and remove the switch from the underside of the handbrake lever bracket.

Refitting

3 Refitting is a reversal of removal.

19 Anti-lock braking and stability control systems – general information

1 The ABS system comprises a hydraulic modulator and electronic control unit together with four wheel speed sensors. The hydraulic modulator contains the electronic control unit (ECU), the hydraulic solenoid valves (one set for each brake) and the electrically-driven pump. The purpose of the system is to prevent the wheel(s) locking during heavy braking. This is achieved by automatic release of the brake on the relevant wheel, followed by re-application of the brake.

2 The solenoid valves are controlled by the ECU, which itself receives signals from the four wheel speed sensors which monitor the speed of rotation of each wheel. By comparing these signals, the ECU can determine the speed at which the vehicle is travelling. It can then use this speed to determine when a wheel is decelerating at an abnormal rate, compared to the speed of the vehicle, and therefore predicts when a wheel is about to lock. During normal operation, the system functions in the same way as a conventional braking system.

3 If the ECU senses that a wheel is about to lock, it operates the relevant solenoid valve(s) in the hydraulic unit, which then isolates from the master cylinder the relevant brake(s) on the wheel(s) which is/are about to lock, effectively sealing-in the hydraulic pressure.

4 If the speed of rotation of the wheel continues to decrease at an abnormal rate, the ECU operates the electrically-driven pump which pumps the hydraulic fluid back into the master cylinder, releasing the brake. Once the speed of rotation of the wheel returns to an acceptable rate, the pump stops, and the solenoid valves switch again, allowing the hydraulic master cylinder pressure to return to the caliper, which then re-applies the brake. This cycle can be carried out many times a second.

5 The action of the solenoid valves and return pump creates pulses in the hydraulic circuit. When the ABS system is functioning, these pulses can be felt through the brake pedal.

6 The electronic stability program (ESP) is a further development of ABS. Using additional sensors to monitor steering wheel position, vehicle yaw rate, acceleration and deceleration in conjunction with the ABS sensors, the ECU can intervene under conditions of vehicle instability and/or traction loss. Using the signals from the various sensors, the ECU can determine driver intent (steering wheel position, throttle position, vehicle speed and engine speed). From the sensor inputs from the wheel speed sensors, yaw rate sensors and acceleration sensors the ECU can calculate whether the vehicle is responding to driver input, or whether an unstable driving situation is occurring. If instability is detected, the ECU will intervene by applying or releasing the relevant front or rear brake, in conjunction with a power reduction, until vehicle stability returns.

7 The operation of the ABS and ESP is entirely dependent on electrical signals. To prevent the system responding to any inaccurate signals, a built-in safety circuit monitors all signals received by the ECU. If an inaccurate signal or low battery voltage is detected, the system is automatically shut down, and the relevant warning light on the instrument panel is illuminated, to inform the driver that the system is not operational. Normal braking is still available, however.

8 If a fault develops in the ABS/ESP system, the vehicle must be taken to a Ford dealer or diagnostic specialist for fault diagnosis and repair.

20 Anti-lock braking and stability control system components – removal and refitting

Note: *Faults on the ABS system can only be diagnosed using Ford diagnostic equipment or compatible alternative equipment.*
Note: *Before starting work, refer to the note at the beginning of Section 2 concerning the dangers of hydraulic fluid.*

Hydraulic modulator and ECU

Removal

1 The hydraulic modulator and ECU are located at the rear left-hand corner of the engine compartment. To gain access, remove the battery and battery tray as described in Chapter 5A Section 4.
2 Undo the retaining bolt and nut and lift out the battery tray support.
3 Remove the master cylinder reservoir cap, and siphon the hydraulic fluid from the reservoir. **Note:** *Do not siphon the fluid by mouth, as it is poisonous; use a syringe or an old hydrometer. Alternatively, open any convenient bleed screw in the system, and gently pump the brake pedal to expel the fluid through a plastic tube connected to the screw* (see Section 2).
4 Pull out the locking bar and disconnect the wiring harness plug from the ABS ECU on the hydraulic modulator **(see illustration)**. Release the wiring harness from the cable-tie on the modulator mounting bracket.
5 Note and record the fitted position of the brake pipes at the modulator, then unscrew the union nuts and release the pipes. As a precaution, place absorbent rags beneath the brake pipe unions when unscrewing them. Suitably plug or cap the disconnected unions to prevent dirt entry and fluid loss.
6 Unscrew the three mounting bracket retaining nuts and remove the hydraulic modulator together with the mounting bracket.
7 If necessary, undo the three retaining bolts and separate the modulator from the mounting bracket.

20.4 Disconnect the wiring harness plug (arrowed) from the ABS ECU on the hydraulic modulator

Refitting

8 Refitting is the reverse of the removal procedure, noting the following points:
a) *Tighten the modulator and mounting bracket retaining nuts/bolts to the specified torque.*
b) *Refit the brake pipes to their respective locations, and tighten the union nuts to the specified torque.*
c) *Ensure that the wiring is correctly routed, and that the ECU wiring harness plug is firmly pressed into position and secured with the locking bar.*
d) *Refit the battery tray and battery as described in Chapter 5A Section 4.*
e) *On completion, bleed the complete hydraulic system as described in Section 2. Ensure that the system is bled in the correct order, to prevent air entering the modulator return pump*

Electronic control unit (ECU)

Note: *If a new ECU is to be fitted, this work must be entrusted to a Ford dealer or suitably-equipped specialist as it is necessary to programme the new ECU after installation. This work requires the use of dedicated Ford diagnostic equipment or a compatible alternative.*

Removal

9 Remove the hydraulic modulator from the car as described previously in this Section.

10 Undo the four retaining bolts and carefully withdraw the ECU from the base of the hydraulic modulator.
11 Thoroughly clean the mating face of the hydraulic modulator.

Refitting

12 Ensuring that the seal is correctly located, carefully place the ECU in position, keeping it square and level.
13 Fit and moderately tighten the four retaining bolts.
14 On completion, refit the hydraulic modulator as described previously in this Section.

Front wheel speed sensors

Removal

15 Firmly apply the handbrake, then jack up the front of the car and support it securely on axle stands (see *'Jacking and vehicle support'*). Remove the appropriate front roadwheel.
16 Disconnect the wiring connector from the wheel speed sensor, located on top of the swivel hub **(see illustration)**.
17 Unscrew the wheel speed sensor retaining bolt, then withdraw the sensor from the swivel hub **(see illustration)**. **Note:** *The sensors can prove difficult to remove, due to corrosion – try soaking the sensor in maintenance spray. Do not use any great force to remove a sensor, or it may be damaged.*

Refitting

18 Refitting is a reversal of the removal procedure ensuring that the sensor and swivel hub sealing faces are clean.

Rear wheel speed sensors

Removal

19 Chock the front wheels, then jack up the rear of the vehicle, and support it securely on axle stands (see *'Jacking and vehicle support'*). Remove the appropriate rear roadwheel.
20 Disconnect the sensor wiring connector.
21 Unscrew the sensor mounting bolt, and withdraw the sensor **(see illustration)**. Withdraw the O-ring seal.

20.16 Disconnect the wiring connector from the front wheel speed sensor

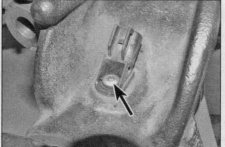

20.17 Unscrew the retaining bolt (arrowed), then withdraw the sensor from the swivel hub

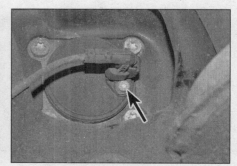

20.21 Rear wheel speed sensor retaining bolt (arrowed)

Refitting

22 Refitting is a reversal of the removal procedure ensuring that the sensor and hub sealing faces are clean. Fit a new O-ring seal to the hub carrier – not the sensor.

Yaw rate sensor/ accelerometer

Note: *The yaw rate sensor/accelerometer is only fitted to vehicles built up to mid-September 2010. On later vehicles, the sensor is an integral part of the restraints control module.*

Removal

23 The sensor is located beneath the driver's seat on the right-hand side of the car.

24 Remove the driver's seat and right-hand side B-pillar trim as described in Chapter 11 Section 25 and Chapter 11 Section 27.

25 Fold back the carpet to gain access to the sensor.

26 Disconnect the sensor wiring connector, then undo the two bolts and remove the sensor from the car.

Refitting

27 Refitting is the reversal of the removal procedure.

Steering angle sensor

28 The steering angle sensor is an integral part of the steering column control module and cannot be individually removed.

21 Vacuum pump (diesel engine models) – removal and refitting

Removal

1.8 litre engines

1 Remove the cylinder head cover as described in Chapter 2B Section 4.

2 Unscrew the union nut and disconnect the vacuum line from the top of the pump **(see illustration)**.

3 Using a suitable socket or spanner on the crankshaft pulley bolt, turn the crankshaft until the vacuum pump pushrod (operated by the eccentric on the camshaft end) is fully retracted into the cylinder head.

4 Disconnect the electrical connectors from the heater/glow plug, the engine temperature sensor and the oil pressure switch.

5 Release the retaining clips and disconnect the oil separator/return hose(s) from the pump. Be prepared for some oil spillage as the hose is disconnected and mop-up any spilt oil.

6 Evenly and progressively slacken the bolts securing the pump to the front of the cylinder head **(see illustration)**. Note that there is no need to remove the lower bolt completely, as the lower end of the pump is slotted.

7 Remove the pump from the engine compartment, along with its sealing ring **(see illustration)**. Discard the sealing ring, a new one should be used on refitting.

2.0 litre engines to Stage III/IV emission level

8 Remove the plastic cover from the top of the engine.

9 Release the quick-release fitting and disconnect the vacuum line from the pump – located at the left-hand end of the cylinder head **(see illustration)**.

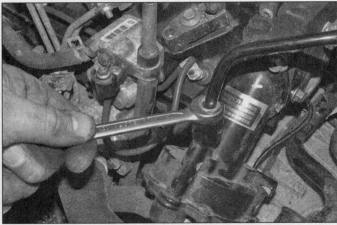

21.2 Unscrew the union nut and disconnect the vacuum line from the top of the pump

21.6 Slacken the bolts evenly, then remove the top bolt

21.7 Renew the sealing ring when refitting the vacuum pump

21.9 Release the quick-release fitting (arrowed) and disconnect the vacuum line from the pump

21.11a Undo the three bolts (arrowed) and remove the vacuum pump...

21.11b... then renew the O-ring seals (arrowed)

21.14 Release the quick-release fittings (arrowed) and disconnect the two vacuum lines from the pump

21.15 Undo the three bolts and move the vacuum solenoid's mounting bracket (arrowed) to one side

21.16a Undo the three bolts (arrowed) and remove the vacuum pump

21.16b Discard the gasket, a new one must be fitted

10 Undo the retaining bolt and release the fuel hose support bracket and EGR pipe support bracket from the pump.

11 Undo the three bolts and remove the vacuum pump. Discard the O-ring seals, new ones must be fitted **(see illustrations)**.

2.0 litre engines to Stage V emission level

12 Remove the plastic cover from the top of the engine.

13 Remove the air cleaner assembly and air inlet duct as described in Chapter 4B Section 5.

14 Release the quick-release fittings and disconnect the two vacuum lines from the pump – located at the left-hand end of the cylinder head **(see illustration)**.

15 Undo the three bolts and move the vacuum solenoid's mounting bracket to one side **(see illustration)**.

16 Undo the three bolts and remove the vacuum pump. Discard the gasket, a new one must be fitted **(see illustrations)**.

Refitting

17 Refitting is a reversal of removal, noting the following points:

a) Ensure the pump and cylinder head mating surfaces are clean and dry and fit the new gasket or O-ring seals to the pump.

b) On 1.8 litre engines, refit the cylinder head cover as described in Chapter 2B Section 4.

c) On 2.0 litre engines, ensure the drive coupling is aligned with the slot in the camshaft **(see illustration)**.

d) Start the engine and check for correct operation of the pump (check brakes have servo action) as described in Section 12.

e) Make sure all the hose connections are secure, and check for leaks.

21.17 On 2.0 litre engines, ensure the drive lugs engage with the slots in the camshaft (arrowed)

Chapter 10
Suspension and steering

Contents

Degrees of difficulty

Easy, suitable for novice with little experience	Fairly easy, suitable for beginner with some experience	Fairly difficult, suitable for competent DIY mechanic	Difficult, suitable for experienced DIY mechanic	Very difficult, suitable for expert DIY or professional

Specifications

Front suspension
Type . . . .   Independent, with MacPherson struts incorporating coil springs and telescopic shock absorbers. Anti-roll bar fitted to all models

Rear suspension
Type . . . .   Fully-independent, multilink with separate coil springs and hydraulic telescopic shock absorbers. Anti-roll bar fitted to all models

Steering
Type . . . .   Hydraulic power-assisted rack and pinion

Wheel alignment and steering angles
Front wheel:
  Camber angle:
    Tolerance range . . . .   0° 27' to -1° 59'
    Nominal setting. . . . .   -0° 43'
    Maximum permitted variation side-to-side. . . . .   1° 15'
  Castor angle:
    Tolerance range . . . .   4° 10' to 2° 06'
    Nominal setting. . . . .   3° 8'
    Maximum permitted variation side-to-side. . . . .   1°
  Toe setting:
    Tolerance range . . . .   0° 12' ± 0° 21' toe-in (1.4 ± 2.5 mm toe-in)
    Nominal setting. . . . .   0° 12' ± 0° 08' toe-in (1.4 ± 1.0 mm toe-in)
Rear wheel:
  Camber angle:
    Tolerance range . . . .   -2° 43' to -0° 11'
    Nominal setting. . . . .   -1° 27'
    Maximum permitted variation side-to-side. . . . .   1° 15'
  Toe setting:
    Tolerance range . . . .   0° 24' ± 0° 21' toe-in (2.8 ± 2.5 mm toe-in)
    Nominal setting. . . . .   0° 24' ± 0° 08' toe-in (2.8 ± 1.0 mm toe-in)

Tyres
Tyre pressures . . . .   See sticker on the driver's side door pillar

Torque wrench settings

	Nm	lbf ft
Front suspension		
Anti-roll bar clamp bolt nuts: *		
Stage 1	140	103
Stage 2	Angle-tighten a further 45°	
Anti-roll bar connecting link nuts: *		
Upper nut	60	44
Lower nut	70	52
Brake caliper mounting bracket to swivel hub	200	148
Driveshaft retaining bolt: *		
Stage 1	45	33
Stage 2	Angle-tighten a further 80°	
Engine lower mounting link through-bolt	80	59
Lower arm balljoint:		
Heat shield bolt.	10	7
Retaining nut	100	74
Lower arm mounting bolts: *		
Front mounting:		
Stage 1	80	59
Stage 2	Angle-tighten a further 120°	
Rear mounting:		
Stage 1	140	103
Stage 2	Angle-tighten a further 45°	
Subframe cross-brace retaining bolts	30	22
Subframe mounting bolts: *		
Stage 1	150	111
Stage 2	Angle-tighten a further 90°	
Suspension strut:		
Piston rod nut.	58	43
To swivel hub	110	81
Upper mounting to body	35	26
Rear suspension		
Anti-roll bar link:		
To anti-roll bar.	15	11
To hub carrier	60	44
Anti-roll bar-to-subframe bolts.	48	35
Lateral link/hub carrier to body	180	133
Lower control arm:		
To hub carrier	120	89
To subframe	103	76
Rear hub bearing assembly	110	81
Shock absorber:		
Lower mounting bolt:		
With standard suspension	175	129
With self-levelling suspension	280	207
Upper mounting bolts.	30	22
Subframe bolts.	110	81
Tie-rod to hub carrier/lateral link and subframe	130	96
Upper control arm to hub carrier/lateral link and subframe	130	96
Steering		
Power steering pump:		
High-pressure pipe union bolt	24	18
Mounting bolts.	24	18
Steering column:		
Mounting bolts*	24	18
Universal joint clamp bolt*	32	24
Steering rack:		
Fluid pipe clamp bolt	18	13
Mounting bolts.	120	89
Steering wheel bolt.	48	35
Track rod end:		
Balljoint nuts*	80	59
Locknuts.	90	66
Roadwheels		
Roadwheel nuts	140	103

* Use new fasteners

1 General Information

1 The independent front suspension is of the MacPherson strut type, incorporating coil springs and integral telescopic shock absorbers. The struts are located by transverse control arms, which are attached to the front subframe via rubber bushes at their inner ends, and incorporate a balljoint at their outer ends. The swivel hubs, which carry the hub bearings, brake calipers and the hub/disc assemblies, are bolted to the MacPherson struts, and connected to the control arms through the balljoints. A front anti-roll bar is fitted to all models, and is attached to the subframe and to the MacPherson struts via link arms.

2 The rear suspension is of the fully-independent, multilink type, consisting of an upper and lower control arm mounted via rubber bushes to the lateral link/hub carrier and rear subframe. The lateral link is attached to the vehicle body at the front end and incorporates the hub carrier at the rear. The assembly is located by a tie-rod each side. Coil springs are fitted between the lower control arm and the subframe. Separate hydraulic telescopic shock absorbers are fitted between the hub carrier between the lower control arm and the vehicle body.

3 Power assistance for the steering is derived from a hydraulic pump driven off the crankshaft pulley via the auxiliary drivebelt.

2 Front swivel hub and bearing – removal and refitting

Note: *The hub bearing is a sealed, pre-adjusted and pre-lubricated, double-row ball type, and is intended to last the car's entire service life without maintenance or attention. The hub flange and bearing are serviced as a complete assembly, and these components cannot be dismantled or renewed individually.*

Note: *Ford special tools (or compatible alternatives) will be needed for this procedure (see text).*

Removal

1 Firmly apply the handbrake, then jack up the front of the car and support it securely on axle stands (see 'Jacking and vehicle support'). Remove the relevant front roadwheel. Where applicable, remove the engine undertray.

2 Refit at least two roadwheel nuts to the front hub, and tighten them securely. Have an assistant firmly depress the brake pedal to prevent the front hub from rotating, then using a socket and extension bar, slacken the driveshaft retaining bolt. Alternatively, a tool

2.2 Using a fabricated tool to hold the front hub stationary whilst the driveshaft retaining bolt is slackened

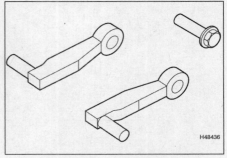

2.9 Ford special tool 204-607 used for separating the lower arm balljoint from the swivel hub

can be fabricated from two lengths of steel strip (one long, one short) and a nut and bolt; the nut and bolt forming the pivot of a forked tool. Attach the tool to the hub using two wheel nuts, and hold the tool to prevent the hub from rotating as the driveshaft retaining bolt is slackened **(see illustration)**. Note that this bolt is extremely tight – ensure that the tools used to loosen it are of good quality, and a good fit.

3 Unscrew and remove the previously-slackened driveshaft retaining bolt. Discard the bolt – a new one must be fitted.

4 Using a hammer and suitable drift, tap the end of the driveshaft approximately 15 to 20 mm into the wheel hub flange.

5 Undo the bolt/nut and detach the headlight levelling sensor bracket from the lower arm (where applicable).

6 On vehicles with dynamic suspension, disconnect the suspension strut wiring connector, and release the wiring grommets from the suspension strut and underbody brackets.

7 Disconnect the wiring plug, undo the bolt and remove the ABS wheel speed sensor from the swivel hub – refer to Chapter 9 Section 20 if necessary.

8 Undo the retaining nut, then disconnect the steering track rod end balljoint from the swivel hub. If necessary, use a balljoint separator tool **(see illustrations 21.3a and 21.3b)**.

9 The design of the lower arm balljoint and swivel hub assembly is such that using a conventional balljoint separator tool to release the balljoint shank from the swivel hub is likely to damage the balljoint rubber boot. It is therefore necessary to use Ford special tool 204-607 (or a compatible alternative) to separate the balljoint shank from the hub as follows **(see illustration)**.

10 Unscrew the lower arm balljoint retaining nut two turns, then undo and remove the lower bolt securing the brake caliper mounting bracket to the swivel hub **(see illustration)**. Bolt the special tool to the caliper mounting bracket and position the other end of the tool under, and in contact with, the steering arm on the swivel hub. Unscrew the lower arm balljoint retaining nut until it contacts the special tool, then continue unscrewing the nut to release the balljoint shank taper from the swivel hub.

11 Once the balljoint shank taper releases, fully unscrew the retaining nut, then remove the special tool.

12 Remove the front brake disc as described in Chapter 9 Section 6.

13 Undo the bolt and remove the lower arm balljoint heat shield.

14 Lever down the lower arm to free the balljoint from the swivel hub **(see illustration)**, then move the swivel hub to one side, taking care not to damage the balljoint rubber boot.

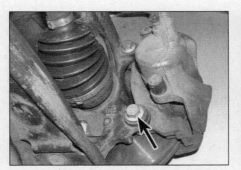

2.10 Undo and remove the lower bolt (arrowed) securing the brake caliper mounting bracket to the swivel hub

2.14 Home-made method of releasing the lower arm – wood block, long pole and length of chain

2.15 Pull the swivel hub and suspension strut outwards and withdraw the driveshaft CV joint

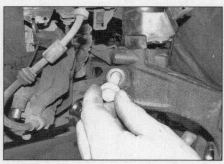

2.16 Remove the bolt securing the swivel hub to the suspension strut

2.17 Use an Allen key to spread the swivel hub where it clamps the lower end of the suspension strut

2.18 Tap the swivel hub assembly down and off the end of the suspension strut

2.19a Using the Ford special tool to support the swivel hub, press the hub flange and bearing out...

15 Pull the swivel hub assembly outwards, and withdraw the driveshaft CV joint from the hub flange **(see illustration)**.

16 Undo and remove the bolt securing the swivel hub to the suspension strut **(see illustration)**.

17 Insert a suitable Allen key into the gap and turn the Allen key slightly to spread the swivel hub where it clamps onto the lower end of the suspension strut **(see illustration)**. Alternatively, tap a chisel into the gap to spread the swivel hub.

18 Using a soft-faced mallet, tap the swivel hub assembly down and off the end of the suspension strut **(see illustration)**.

19 The hub and bearing must now be removed from the swivel hub as an assembly. Due to the design of the assembly, we found it impossible to press the new hub/bearing into the swivel hub without using Ford special tool No 204-348 **(see illustrations)**. The bearing will be rendered unserviceable by removal and cannot be re-used.

Refitting

20 Refitting is a reversal of removal, bearing in mind the following points:

a) *Ensure that the swivel hub is fully entered in the suspension strut, and that the lug at the rear of the strut is engaged with the gap in the swivel hub* **(see illustration)**.

b) *Use a new driveshaft retaining bolt and a new track rod end retaining nut.*

c) *Ensure that the hub and brake disc mating*

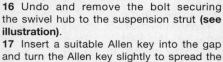

2.19b... then assemble the special tool around the new bearing/flange assembly

2.19c Position the swivel hub over the new bearing, and place the special tool on the swivel hub

2.19d Press the swivel hub...

2.19e... fully onto the bearing

2.20 Ensure that the lug (arrowed) at the rear of the strut is engaged with the gap in the swivel hub

faces are spotlessly clean, and refit the disc with the orientation marks aligned.

d) *Ensure that the ABS wheel speed sensor, and the sensor location in the swivel hub, are perfectly clean before refitting.*

e) *Tighten all nuts and bolts to the specified torque.*

f) *Use the method employed on removal to prevent rotation of the driveshaft as the retaining bolt is tightened.*

3 Front strut –
removal and refitting

Note: *Ford special tool 204-607 (or a compatible alternative) will be needed to separate the lower arm balljoint shank from the swivel hub.*

Removal

1 Remove the windscreen cowl panel as described in Chapter 11 Section 23.

2 Extract the plastic rivet and unclip the plastic panel over the suspension strut top mounting **(see illustration)**.

3 Firmly apply the handbrake, then jack up the front of the car and support it securely on axle stands (see *'Jacking and vehicle support'*). Remove the relevant front roadwheel.

4 On vehicles with dynamic suspension, disconnect the suspension strut wiring connector, and release the wiring grommets from the suspension strut and underbody brackets.

5 Release the brake hydraulic hose from the suspension strut bracket **(see illustration)**.

6 Unscrew and remove the nut securing the anti-roll bar connecting link to the suspension strut, while holding the link stub with an Allen key. Lift off the wheel speed sensor wiring harness support bracket, release the link from the strut and move it to one side **(see illustrations)**.

7 The design of the lower arm balljoint and swivel hub assembly is such that using a conventional balljoint separator tool to release the balljoint shank from the swivel hub is likely to damage the balljoint rubber boot. It is therefore necessary to use Ford special tool 204-607 (or a compatible alternative) to separate the balljoint shank from the hub as follows **(see illustration 2.9)**.

8 Unscrew the lower arm balljoint retaining nut two turns, then undo and remove the lower bolt securing the brake caliper mounting bracket to the swivel hub **(see illustration 2.10)**. Bolt the special tool to the caliper mounting bracket and position the other end of the tool under, and in contact with, the steering arm on the swivel hub. Unscrew the lower arm balljoint retaining nut until it contacts the special tool, then continue unscrewing the nut to release the balljoint shank taper from the swivel hub.

9 Once the balljoint shank taper releases, fully unscrew the retaining nut, then remove the special tool. Refit the caliper mounting bracket lower retaining bolt and tighten it to the specified torque.

10 Lever down the lower arm to free the balljoint from the swivel hub **(see illustration 2.14)**, then move the swivel hub to one side, taking care not to damage the balljoint rubber boot.

11 Undo and remove the bolt securing the swivel hub to the suspension strut **(see illustration 2.16)**.

12 Insert a suitable Allen key into the gap and turn the Allen key slightly to spread the swivel hub where it clamps onto the lower end of the suspension strut **(see illustration 2.17)**. Alternatively, tap a chisel into the gap to spread the swivel hub.

13 Using a soft-faced mallet, tap the swivel hub assembly down and off the end of the suspension strut **(see illustration 2.18)**.

14 With the help of an assistant, support the strut from under the wheel arch then, working in the engine compartment, unscrew the three suspension strut top mounting bolts. Remove the strut from under the wheel arch **(see illustrations)**.

Refitting

15 Refitting is a reversal of removal, bearing in mind the following points:

a) *Ensure that the swivel hub is fully entered in the suspension strut, and that the lug at the rear of the strut is engaged with the gap in the swivel hub* **(see illustration 2.20)**.

b) *Tighten all nuts and bolts to the specified torque.*

c) *Refit the windscreen cowl panel as described in Chapter 11 Section 23.*

3.2 Extract the plastic rivet and unclip the plastic panel over the suspension strut top mounting

3.5 Release the brake hydraulic hose from the suspension strut bracket

3.6a Unscrew the nut securing the anti-roll bar connecting link to the strut, while holding the link stub with an Allen key

3.6b Lift off the wiring harness support bracket, then release the link from the strut

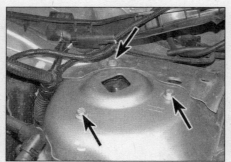

3.14a Unscrew the three suspension strut top mounting bolts (arrowed)...

3.14b... then remove the strut from under the wheel arch

4.2 Using a compressor tool, compress the coil spring to relieve the pressure on the spring seats

4.3 Counter-hold the strut piston rod and unscrew the piston rod nut

4.4 Remove the strut bearing, upper spring seat, dust cover and rubber bump stop as an assembly

4 Front strut – dismantling, inspection and reassembly

⚠️ **Warning: Before attempting to dismantle the suspension strut, a suitable tool to hold the coil spring in compression must be obtained. Adjustable coil spring compressors which can be positively secured to the spring coils are readily available, and are recommended for this operation. Any attempt to dismantle the strut without such a tool is likely to result in damage or personal injury.**

Dismantling

1 Remove the suspension strut from the car as described in Section 3.

2 With the suspension strut resting on a bench, or clamped in a vice, fit a spring compressor tool, and compress the coil spring to relieve the pressure on the spring seats. Ensure that the compressor tool is securely located on the spring, in accordance with the tool manufacturer's instructions **(see illustration)**.

3 Counter-hold the strut piston rod with an Allen key or hexagon bit and unscrew the piston rod nut **(see illustration)**.

4 Remove the piston rod nut, then remove the strut bearing, upper spring seat, dust cover and rubber bump stop as an assembly **(see illustration)**.

5 Lift off the dust cover, followed by the bump stop and upper spring seat from the strut bearing **(see illustrations)**.

6 Remove the spring (with compressor tool still fitted), followed by the lower spring seat **(see illustrations)**.

Inspection

7 With the strut assembly now completely dismantled, examine all the components for wear, damage or deformation. Renew any of the components as necessary.

8 Examine the shock absorber for signs of fluid leakage, and check the strut piston for signs of pitting along its entire length. Test the operation of the shock absorber, while holding it in an upright position, by moving the piston through a full stroke and then through short strokes of 50 to 100 mm. In both cases, the resistance felt should be smooth and continuous. If the resistance is jerky, or uneven, or if there is any visible sign of wear or damage, renewal is necessary.

9 If any doubt exists about the condition of the coil spring, gradually release the spring compressor, and check the spring for distortion and signs of cracking. Since no minimum free length is specified by Ford, the only way to check the tension of the spring is to compare it to a new component. Renew the spring if it is damaged or distorted, or if there is any doubt as to its condition.

10 Inspect all other components for signs of damage or deterioration, and renew any that are suspect.

11 If a new shock absorber is being fitted, hold it vertically and pump the piston a few times to prime it.

4.5a Lift off the dust cover...

4.5b... followed by the bump stop...

4.5c... and upper spring seat from the strut bearing

4.6a Remove the compressed spring...

4.6b... followed by the lower spring seat

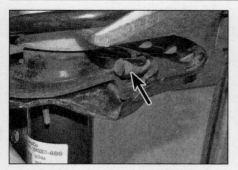

4.14 Position the lower end of the spring (arrowed) against the stop on the lower seat

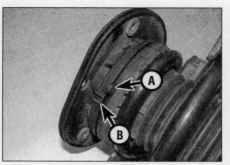

4.18 Position the upper spring seat so that the lug (A) on the seat is just to the side of the projection (B) on the strut bearing

4.19a Position the strut bearing so that the projection (A) on the bearing…

4.19b… is directly in line with the lug (B) at the base of the strut…

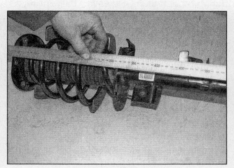

4.19c… and use a straight-edge to check the alignment

5.3 Unscrew the nut (arrowed) securing the connecting link to the anti-roll bar

Reassembly

12 Locate the lower spring seat on the strut ensuring that it is correctly positioned.

13 If the spring compressor tool has been removed from the spring, refit it and compress the spring sufficiently to enable it to be refitted to the strut.

14 Slide the spring over the strut, and position it so that the lower end of the spring is resting against the stop on the lower seat **(see illustration)**.

15 Refit the upper spring seat, rubber bump stop and dust cover to the strut bearing.

16 Slide the assembled strut bearing over the spring and into engagement with the strut piston.

17 Refit the piston rod nut, and tighten it to the specified torque. Counter-hold the piston rod using an Allen key or hexagon bit as during removal.

18 Position the upper spring seat so that the lug on the seat is just to the side of the projection on the strut bearing **(see illustration)**.

19 Maintaining the alignment between the upper spring seat and the strut bearing, position the strut bearing so that the projection on the bearing is directly in line with the lug at the base of the strut. If necessary, use a straight-edge to check this **(see illustrations)**. Slowly slacken the spring compressor tool to relieve the tension in the spring. Check that the lower end of the spring locates

correctly against the stop on the spring seat and the alignment between the projection on the upper bearing and lug on the strut is maintained. If necessary, turn the spring and the upper seat so that the components locate correctly before the compressor tool is removed. Remove the compressor tool when the spring is fully seated.

5 Front lower arm – removal, overhaul and refitting

Note: *Ford special tool 204-607 (or a compatible alternative) will be needed to separate the lower arm balljoint shank from the swivel hub.*

Removal

1 Firmly apply the handbrake, then jack up the front of the car and support it securely on axle stands (see *'Jacking and vehicle support'*). Remove the relevant front roadwheel.

2 Undo the bolt/nut and detach the headlight levelling sensor bracket from the lower arm (where applicable).

3 Unscrew and remove the nut securing the anti-roll bar connecting link to the anti-roll bar, while holding the link stub with an Allen key **(see illustration)**. Release the link from the anti-roll bar and move it to one side.

4 The design of the lower arm balljoint and

swivel hub assembly is such that using a conventional balljoint separator tool to release the balljoint shank from the swivel hub is likely to damage the balljoint rubber boot. It is therefore necessary to use Ford special tool 204-607 (or a compatible alternative) to separate the balljoint shank from the hub as follows **(see illustration 2.9)**.

5 Unscrew the lower arm balljoint retaining nut two turns, then undo and remove the lower bolt securing the brake caliper mounting bracket to the swivel hub **(see illustration 2.10)**. Bolt the special tool to the caliper mounting bracket and position the other end of the tool under, and in contact with, the steering arm on the swivel hub. Unscrew the lower arm balljoint retaining nut until it contacts the special tool, then continue unscrewing the nut to release the balljoint shank taper from the swivel hub.

6 Once the balljoint shank taper releases, fully unscrew the retaining nut, then remove the special tool. Refit the caliper mounting bracket lower retaining bolt and tighten it to the specified torque.

7 Lever down the lower arm to free the balljoint from the swivel hub**(see illustration 2.14)**, then move the swivel hub to one side, taking care not to damage the balljoint rubber boot.

8 Undo the lower arm front mounting bolt and the two rear mounting bolts, and remove the lower arm from the subframe **(see**

5.8a Lower arm front mounting bolt (arrowed)...

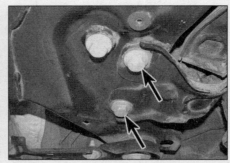

5.8b... and rear mounting bolts (arrowed)

illustrations). Note that new bolts will be required for refitting.

Overhaul

9 Thoroughly clean the lower arm and the area around the lower arm mountings. Inspect the arm for any signs of cracks, damage or distortion, and carefully check the inner pivot bushes for signs of swelling, cracks or deterioration of the rubber.

10 If either bush requires renewal, the work should be entrusted to a Ford dealer or specialist. A hydraulic press and suitable spacers are required to remove and refit the bushes, and a setting gauge is needed for accurate positioning of the bushes in the arm.

11 If the lower arm balljoint is worn, or the rubber boot is damaged, the complete lower arm must be renewed. At the time of writing, the balljoint could not be renewed separately

from the lower arm, as it is riveted in place during manufacture. However, balljoint repair kits have become available over time for other similarly-affected models – with these, the original rivets are drilled out, and the new balljoint is bolted onto the arm using the original rivet holes. Check the latest parts availability situation with Ford, and with reputable motor factors, before deciding.

Refitting

12 Refitting is a reversal of removal, bearing in mind the following points:
a) Use new lower arm mounting bolts.
b) Tighten all fixings to the specified torque and, where applicable, through the specified angle.
c) Have the front wheel toe-in (tracking) checked and adjusted at the earliest opportunity.

6.2 Undo the clamp bolt (arrowed) securing the steering column universal joint to the steering gear pinion

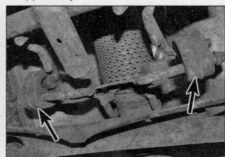

6.8 Exhaust front mounting rubbers (arrowed)

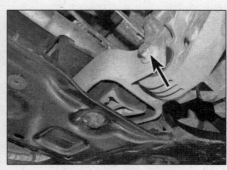

6.9 Exhaust front mounting bracket retaining bolts (arrowed) on Stage V emission level diesel engines

6.11 Engine lower mounting link through-bolt (arrowed)

6 Front anti-roll bar – removal and refitting

Note: *Ford special tool 205-316A (or a compatible alternative) will be needed to align the subframe with the body when refitting (see text).*

Removal

1 Make sure the front wheels (and steering wheel) are in the straight-ahead position. Lock the steering in this position using the steering column lock.

2 Working in the driver's footwell, undo the clamp bolt securing the steering column shaft universal joint to the steering gear pinion **(see illustration)**. Pull the shaft upwards and off the pinion, and move it to one side. Note that a new clamp bolt will be required for refitting.

3 Firmly apply the handbrake, then jack up the front of the vehicle and support it securely on axle stands (see *'Jacking and vehicle support'*). Remove both front roadwheels.

4 Undo the fasteners and remove the engine undertray, followed by the shield under the radiator.

5 Undo the bolt/nut and detach the headlight levelling sensor bracket from the suspension lower arm (where applicable).

6 Disconnect the two power steering fluid hoses at the quick-release connectors above the steering gear. Be prepared for fluid loss and cover or seal all disconnected unions.

7 Unscrew and remove the nut each side securing the anti-roll bar connecting link to the anti-roll bar, while holding the link stub with an Allen key **(see illustration 5.3)**.

8 Attach splints each side of the exhaust flexible section (two wooden strips secured by cable-ties will suffice) to prevent excessive bending. On all except 2.0 litre diesel engine models to Stage V emission level, unhook the exhaust mounting rubbers at the front **(see illustration)**.

9 On 2.0 litre diesel engine models to Stage V emission level, undo the two bolts securing the exhaust front mounting bracket to the rear of the subframe **(see illustration)**.

10 On 2.0 litre diesel engine models, release the cable clips securing the diesel particulate filter wiring harness and hoses to the subframe. According to equipment fitted, it may also be necessary to release additional cable clips, or unbolt support brackets, to release pipes and hoses that may be put under strain when the subframe is lowered.

11 Unscrew and remove the engine lower mounting link through-bolt **(see illustration)**.

12 Position a sturdy trolley jack beneath, and in contact with, the rear of the front subframe.

13 Undo the two rear bolts each side securing the subframe cross-brace to the underbody. With the subframe securely supported, undo the bolt each side securing the rear of the subframe and the cross-brace

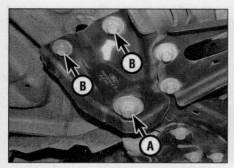

6.13 Subframe rear mounting bolt (A) and cross-brace mounting bolts (B)

6.26 Using an alignment tool (arrowed) to accurately position the subframe

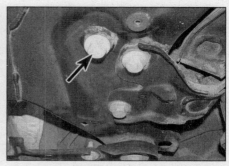

7.7 Steering rack left-hand mounting bolt (arrowed)

to the underbody and remove the cross-brace (see illustration). Note that new subframe mounting bolts will be required for refitting.

14 Position a second trolley jack beneath, and in contact with, the front of the subframe.

15 Undo the subframe front mounting bolt on each side. Note that new bolts will be required for refitting.

16 Engage the help of an assistant to steady the subframe, then carefully lower the jack and allow the subframe to drop slightly at the rear, so that the anti-roll bar clamp bolt nuts are accessible. Take care not to damage the power steering hoses.

17 Hold the bolts from below and unscrew the two nuts each side securing the anti-roll bar clamps to the subframe (see illus-tration 5.8b). Note that new nuts and bolts will be required for refitting.

18 Carefully manipulate the anti-roll bar out from under the car.

19 Note the position and orientation of each clamp, then lift the clamps off the mounting bushes. Similarly, note the position and orientation of the mounting bushes and remove them from the anti-roll bar. The bushes are split along their length to facilitate removal and refitting.

20 Examine the anti-roll bar for signs of damage or distortion, and the connecting links and mounting bushes for signs of deterioration of the rubber. Renew the anti-roll bar clamp nuts and bolts, the subframe mounting bolts and any other components as necessary.

Refitting

21 Fit the bushes to the anti-roll bar in the positions noted during removal. Do not use any lubricant when fitting the bushes.

22 Lubricate the anti-roll bar clamps with a little soapy water and push them into position over the bushes. The curved side of the clamp base, adjacent to the mounting bolt holes, must face toward the centre of the car.

23 Manipulate the anti-roll bar into position on the subframe. Fit the new clamp bolts and nuts and tighten them to the specified Stage 1 torque setting, then through the specified Stage 2 angle.

24 Raise the subframe into position and fit the new front mounting bolts. Tighten the bolts hand-tight only at this stage.

25 Place the subframe cross-brace in position and fit the two new subframe mounting bolts and the four cross-brace retaining bolts. Tighten the bolts hand-tight only at this stage.

26 The alignment of the subframe must be checked by inserting Ford alignment tools (part No 205-316A) or suitable alternatives through the holes in the sidemembers (see illustration).

27 With the subframe correctly aligned, tighten the four subframe mounting bolts to the specified Stage 1 torque setting, then through the specified Stage 2 angle. Tighten the four cross-brace retaining bolts to the specified torque.

28 The remainder of refitting is a reversal of removal bearing in mind the following points:
a) Tighten all fixings to the specified torque and, where applicable, through the specified angle.
b) Fill and bleed the power steering hydraulic system as described in Section 19
c) Have the front wheel toe-in (tracking) checked and adjusted at the earliest opportunity.

7 Front subframe – removal and refitting

Note: *Ford special tool 205-316A (or a compatible alternative) will be needed to align the subframe with the body when refitting (see text).*

Removal

1 Firmly apply the handbrake, then jack up the front of the vehicle and support it securely on axle stands (see 'Jacking and vehicle support'). Remove both front roadwheels.

2 Undo the fasteners and remove the engine undertray, followed by the shield under the radiator.

3 Undo the bolt/nut and detach the headlight levelling sensor bracket from the suspension lower arm (where applicable).

4 Attach splints each side of the exhaust flexible section (two wooden strips secured by cable-ties will suffice) to prevent excessive bending. On all except 2.0 litre diesel engine models to Stage V emission level, unhook the

exhaust mounting rubbers at the front (see illustration 6.8).

5 On 2.0 litre diesel engine models to Stage V emission level, undo the two bolts securing the exhaust front mounting bracket to the rear of the subframe (see illustration 6.9).

6 On 2.0 litre diesel engine models, release the cable clips securing the diesel particulate filter wiring harness and hoses to the subframe. According to equipment fitted, it may also be necessary to release additional cable clips, or unbolt support brackets, to release pipes and hoses that may be put under strain when the subframe is lowered.

7 Undo the two bolts securing the steering rack to the subframe (see illustration). Using cable-ties, secure the steering rack to suitable locations at the rear of the engine.

8 Hold the bolts from below and unscrew the two nuts each side securing the anti-roll bar clamps and suspension lower arm rear mountings to the subframe. Note that new nuts and bolts will be required for refitting.

9 Undo the suspension lower arm front mounting bolts and withdraw the lower arms from the subframe. Support the arms on axle stands to avoid placing undue strain on the outer balljoint.

10 Unscrew and remove the engine lower mounting link through-bolt (see illustration 6.11).

11 Position a sturdy trolley jack beneath, and in contact with, the rear of the front subframe.

12 Undo the two rear bolts each side securing the subframe cross-brace to the underbody. With the subframe securely supported, undo the bolt each side securing the rear of the subframe and the cross-brace to the underbody and remove the cross-brace (see illustration 6.13). Note that new subframe mounting bolts will be required for refitting.

13 Position a second trolley jack beneath, and in contact with, the front of the subframe.

14 Undo the subframe front mounting bolt on each side. Note that new bolts will be required for refitting.

15 Engage the help of an assistant to steady the subframe, then carefully lower the jacks. Remove the subframe from under the car.

16 Renewal of the subframe mounting bushes requires the use of Ford special tools and a

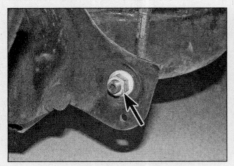

8.4 Anti-roll bar connecting link retaining nut (arrowed)

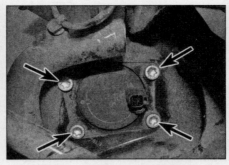

8.5a Undo the four retaining bolts (arrowed)…

8.5b… and remove the bearing assembly and brake backplate from the hub carrier

hydraulic press. Therefore it is recommended that this task should be entrusted to a Ford dealer or suitably-equipped specialist.

Refitting

17 Raise the subframe into position and fit the new front mounting bolts. Tighten the bolts hand-tight only at this stage.

18 Place the subframe cross-brace in position and fit the two new subframe mounting bolts and the four cross-brace retaining bolts. Tighten the bolts hand-tight only at this stage.

19 The alignment of the subframe must be checked by inserting Ford alignment tools (part No 205-316A) or suitable alternatives through the holes in the sidemembers **(see illustration 6.26)**.

20 With the subframe correctly aligned, tighten the four subframe mounting bolts to the specified

Stage 1 torque setting, then through the specified Stage 2 angle. Tighten the four cross-brace retaining bolts to the specified torque.

21 The remainder of refitting is a reversal of removal bearing in mind the following points:

a) *Tighten all fixings to the specified torque and, where applicable, through the specified angle.*

b) *Have the front wheel toe-in (tracking) checked and adjusted at the earliest opportunity.*

8 Rear hub bearings – renewal

1 The rear hub bearings cannot be renewed separately, and are supplied with the rear hub as a complete assembly.

2 Remove the rear brake disc as described in Chapter 9 Section 9.

3 Disconnect the wiring connector from the ABS wheel speed sensor.

4 To gain access to the rear hub retaining bolts, unscrew and remove the nut each side securing the anti-roll bar connecting links to the hub carriers, while holding the link stub with an Allen key **(see illustration)**. Swivel the anti-roll bar upwards as necessary.

5 Undo the four retaining bolts and remove the bearing assembly and brake backplate from the hub carrier **(see illustrations)**.

6 Fit the brake backplate and bearing assembly to the hub carrier then insert and tighten the bolts to the specified torque.

7 Refit the anti-roll bar connecting links and tighten the retaining nuts to the specified torque.

8 Reconnect the ABS wheel speed sensor wiring, then refit the brake disc described in Chapter 9 Section 9.

9 Rear hub carrier/lateral link – removal and refitting

Removal

1 Remove the rear hub as described in the previous Section.

2 Release the ABS wheel speed sensor wiring harness from the clips on the lateral link.

3 Undo the retaining nut and release the brake hose support bracket from the lateral link front mounting **(see illustration)**.

4 Undo the two bolts and detach the two handbrake cable guides from the lateral link **(see illustration)**.

5 Release the brake pipe, hose and wiring harness from the remaining clips on the lateral link.

6 Remove the relevant rear coil spring as described in Section 11.

7 Fabricate a spacer, 40 mm in diameter, and 226 mm long. Unscrew the suspension bump stop, insert the spacer between the lower control arm and the coil spring upper seat, then raise the lower control arm with a trolley jack until the spacer is lightly trapped **(see illustration)**. Ensure the spacer is vertical.

9.3 Undo the retaining nut (arrowed) and release the brake hose support bracket from the lateral link front mounting

9.4a Undo the rear bolt (arrowed)…

9.4b… and front bolt (arrowed) securing the handbrake cable guides to the lateral link

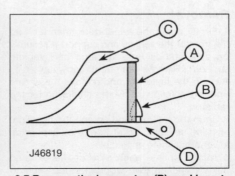

9.7 Remove the bump stop (B), and insert the spacer (A) between the lower control arm (D) and the spring upper seat (C)

9.10 Lateral link front mounting retaining bolts (arrowed)

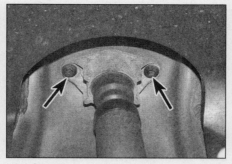

10.4 Shock absorber upper mounting bolts (arrowed)

10.5 Shock absorber lower mounting bolt (arrowed)

8 Undo the bolts securing the upper control arm and the tie-rod to the lateral link/hub carrier (see illustration 12.4a).

9 Undo the bolt and detach the lower control arm from the lateral link/hub carrier (see illustration 12.9b).

10 Undo the two bolts securing the lateral link front mounting to the vehicle body, and withdraw the hub carrier/lateral link from under the vehicle (see illustration).

11 Renewal of the bush at the front of the lateral link requires the use of Ford special tools and a hydraulic press. Therefore it is recommended that this task should be entrusted to a Ford dealer or suitably-equipped specialist.

Refitting

12 Manoeuvre the hub carrier/lateral link into position and tighten the two front mounting bolts to the specified torque.

13 Refit the upper control arm, lower control arm and tie-rod, but only tighten the bolts hand-tight at this stage.

14 Ensure the fabricated spacer (paragraph 7) is still in place between the lower control arm and the spring seat.

15 Tighten the upper control arm, lower control arm and tie-rod bolts to their specified torque. Remove the spacer, and refit the bump stop.

16 The remainder of refitting is a reversal of removal. Have the rear wheel toe-in (tracking) checked and adjusted at the earliest opportunity.

10 Rear shock absorber – removal and refitting

Removal

1 Chock the front wheels, then jack up the rear of the vehicle, and support it securely on axle stands (see 'Jacking and vehicle support'). Remove the relevant rear wheel.

2 Place a trolley jack under the hub carrier and raise the suspension a little to take the load off the shock absorber.

3 On vehicles with dynamic suspension, disconnect the shock absorber wiring connector, and release the wiring harness from the retaining clips.

4 Undo the two bolts securing the upper end of the shock absorber to the vehicle body (see illustration).

5 Undo the lower mounting bolt, and pull the shock absorber from the hub carrier (see illustration).

6 Check the condition of the shock absorber and renew as necessary.

Refitting

7 Refitting is a reversal of removal, tightening all nuts and bolts to the specified torque.

11 Rear coil spring – removal and refitting

Removal

1 Chock the front wheels, then jack up the rear of the vehicle, and support it securely on axle stands (see 'Jacking and vehicle support'). Remove the relevant rear wheel.

2 Unscrew nut securing the anti-roll bar connecting link to the hub carrier, while holding the link stub with an Allen key. Now undo the nut securing the upper end of the link to the anti-roll bar (see illustrations). Lift off the connecting link upper mounting bush and remove the link.

3 Place a trolley jack under the hub carrier and raise the suspension a little to take the load off the shock absorber.

4 Undo the shock absorber lower mounting bolt (see illustration 10.5).

5 Attach spring compressors to the spring and compress the spring. Ford specify tools No 204-167 and 204-167-01. Alternative spring compressors are available (see illustration).

6 Slowly lower the trolley jack, and remove the spring.

7 Examine all the components for wear or damage, and renew as necessary.

11.2a Unscrew nut securing the anti-roll bar connecting link to the hub carrier...

11.2b... then undo the nut (arrowed) securing the upper end of the link to the anti-roll bar

11.5 Remove the rear springs using spring compressors

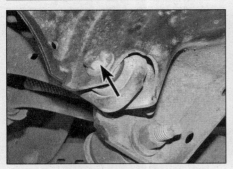

12.4a Tie-rod outer retaining bolt (arrowed)...

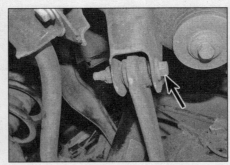

12.4b... and inner retaining bolt (arrowed)

Refitting

8 Refit the rubbers seats to the control arm and spring, ensuring the ends of the spring locate correctly.

9 Refit the compressed spring onto the seat in the lower control arm. Rotate the spring until the spring engages correctly in the control arm grooves.

10 Raise the control arm by means of the jack, and engage the upper end of the spring in its recess in the body.

11 Refit the shock absorber lower mounting bolt, securing it in place before removing the jack. Tighten all nuts and bolts to the specified torque.

12 Release and remove the spring compressor.

13 Refit the anti-roll bar connecting link tightening the nuts to the specified torque.

14 Refit the roadwheel and lower the car to the ground. Tighten the wheel nuts to the specified torque.

12 Rear link arms – removal and refitting

Removal

1 Chock the front wheels, then jack up the rear of the vehicle, and support it securely on axle stands (see *'Jacking and vehicle support'*). Remove the appropriate rear roadwheel(s).

Tie-rod

2 Remove the rear coil spring as described in Section 11.

3 Fabricate a spacer, 40 mm in diameter, and 226 mm long. Unscrew the suspension bump stop, insert the spacer between the lower control arm and the coil spring upper seat, then raise the lower control arm with a trolley jack until the spacer is lightly trapped **(see illustration 9.7)**. Ensure the spacer is vertical.

4 Undo the outer and inner bolts, then remove the tie-rod **(see illustrations)**.

Upper control arm

5 Remove the rear coil spring as described in Section 11.

6 Fabricate a spacer, 40 mm in diameter, and 226 mm long. Unscrew the suspension bump stop, insert the spacer between the lower control arm and the coil spring upper seat, then raise the lower control arm with a trolley jack until the spacer is lightly trapped **(see illustration 9.7)**. Ensure the spacer is vertical.

7 Undo the outer and inner bolts, then remove the control arm.

Lower control arm

8 Remove the rear coil spring as described in Section 11.

9 Mark the position of the inner bolt eccentric washer in relation to the arm then undo the inner and outer control arm nuts/bolts and remove the arm **(see illustrations)**.

10 Examine the condition of the metal-elastic bushes in the control arm. If renewal is necessary, the bushes must be pressed from

the arm and new ones pressed into place. This necessitates the use of an hydraulic press. Entrust this task to a Ford dealer or suitably-equipped garage.

Refitting

11 Refitting any of the control arms/tie-rods is essentially a reversal of removal, noting the following points:

a) Tighten all fasteners to their specified torque.

b) Before tightening any control arm/ tie-rod mounting bolts/nuts, ensure the suspension is in the 'normal' position using the fabricated spacer as described in the removal procedures.

c) When refitting the lower control arm, ensure that the inner mounting bolt eccentric washers are fitted in the positions marked on removal.

d) Have the rear wheel toe-in (tracking) checked and adjusted at the earliest opportunity.

13 Rear anti-roll bar – removal and refitting

Removal

1 Firmly apply the handbrake, then jack up the front of the vehicle and support it securely on axle stands (see *'Jacking and vehicle support'*). Remove both rear roadwheels.

2 Unscrew and remove the nut each side securing the anti-roll bar connecting links to the hub carriers, while holding the link stub with an Allen key **(see illustration 11.2a)**.

3 Undo the nut securing the upper end of the link to the anti-roll bar **(see illustration 11.2b)**. Lift off the connecting link upper mounting bush and remove the link.

4 Unscrew the two bolts each side securing the anti-roll bar clamps to the subframe **(see illustration)**.

5 Carefully manipulate the anti-roll bar out from under the car.

6 Note the position and orientation of each clamp, then lift the clamps off the mounting bushes. Similarly, note the position and orientation of the mounting bushes and

12.9a Mark the position of the eccentric washer (arrowed), then remove the lower control arm inner bolt...

12.9b... and outer bolt (arrowed)

13.4 Unscrew the two bolts each side (arrowed) securing the anti-roll bar clamps to the subframe

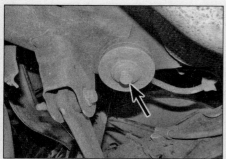

14.8a Subframe left-hand front mounting bolt (arrowed)...

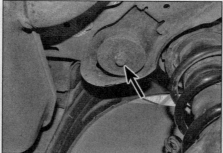

14.8b... and left-hand rear mounting bolt (arrowed)

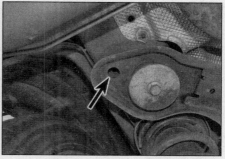

14.12 Subframe alignment tool locating hole (arrowed)

remove them from the anti-roll bar. The bushes are split along their length to facilitate removal and refitting.

7 Examine the anti-roll bar for signs of damage or distortion, and the connecting links and mounting bushes for signs of deterioration of the rubber. Renew any other components as necessary.

Refitting

8 Fit the bushes to the anti-roll bar in the positions noted during removal. Do not use any lubricant when fitting the bushes.

9 Lubricate the anti-roll bar clamps with a little soapy water and push them into position over the bushes.

10 Manipulate the anti-roll bar into position on the subframe. Fit the new clamp bolts and tighten them to the specified torque.

11 Refit the anti-roll bar connecting links and tighten the nuts to the specified torque.

12 Refit the roadwheels and lower the car to the ground. Tighten the wheel nuts to the specified torque.

14 Rear subframe – removal and refitting

Note: *Ford special tool 205-316A (or a compatible alternative) will be needed to align the subframe with the body when refitting (see text).*

Removal

1 Remove both rear coil springs as described in Section 11.

2 Remove the rear anti-roll bar as described in Section 13.

3 Mark the position of the lower control arm inner bolt eccentric washers on both sides in relation to the arms, then undo the inner control arm nuts/bolts **(see illustration 12.9a)**. Ease the control arms out of their location in the subframe.

4 Undo the upper control arm inner mounting bolts on each side and withdraw the arms from the subframe.

5 Similarly undo the tie-rod inner mounting bolts each side and withdraw the tie-rods from the subframe **(see illustration 12.4b)**.

6 Unhook the exhaust system mounting rubber from the subframe bracket.

7 Position a sturdy trolley jack beneath, and in contact with, the subframe.

8 With the subframe suitably supported, undo the two front and two rear subframe mounting bolts **(see illustrations)**.

9 Slowly lower the jack and manoeuvre the subframe out from under the car.

10 Renewal of the subframe mounting bushes requires the use of Ford special tools and a hydraulic press. Therefore it is recommended that this task should be entrusted to a Ford dealer or suitably-equipped specialist.

Refitting

11 Raise the subframe into position and refit the mounting bolts. Tighten the bolts hand-tight only at this stage.

12 The alignment of the subframe must be checked by inserting Ford alignment tools (part No 205-316A) or suitable alternatives through the holes adjacent to the rear mountings **(see illustration)**.

13 With the subframe correctly aligned, tighten the four subframe mounting bolts to the specified torque setting.

14 Refit the exhaust system rubber mounting to the subframe bracket.

15 Fabricate a spacer, 40 mm in diameter, and 226 mm long. Unscrew the suspension bump stop, insert the spacer between the lower control arm and the coil spring upper seat, then raise the lower control arm with a trolley jack until the spacer is lightly trapped

15.3 Disconnect the wiring connector for the steering wheel switches

(see illustration 9.7). Ensure the spacer is vertical.

16 Working on one side of the car at a time, engage the tie-rod with the subframe and fit the inner mounting bolt. Tighten the bolt to the specified torque. Similarly, engage the upper control arm with the subframe and refit the inner mounting bolt. Tighten the bolt to the specified torque.

17 Engage the lower control arm with the subframe and refit the inner mounting bolt eccentric washers and nut. Position the eccentric washers in the positions marked on removal and tighten the retaining nut to the specified torque.

18 Lower the jack and remove the spacer, then refit the suspension bump stop.

19 Insert the spacer between the lower control arm and spring upper seat on the other side of the car, then repeat the procedures described in paragraphs 16 and 17.

20 Lower the jack and remove the spacer, then refit the suspension bump stop.

21 Refit the rear anti-roll bar as described in Section 13.

22 Refit both rear coil springs as described in Section 11.

23 Have the rear wheel toe-in (tracking) checked and adjusted at the earliest opportunity.

15 Steering wheel – removal and refitting

⚠ Warning: *Make sure that the airbag safety recommendations given in Chapter 12 Section 23 are followed, to prevent personal injury.*

Removal

1 Remove the driver's airbag as described in Chapter 12 Section 24.

2 Make sure the front wheels (and steering wheel) are in the straight-ahead position. Lock the steering in this position using the steering column lock.

3 Disconnect the wiring connector for the steering wheel switches **(see illustration)**.

4 Prevent the steering wheel turning by

15.4 Unscrew and remove the steering wheel securing bolt

15.5 Remove the steering wheel and guide the wiring for the airbag through the aperture in the wheel

grasping the rim firmly, then unscrew and remove the steering wheel securing bolt **(see illustration)**. Do not rely on the steering column lock to prevent the wheel turning, as this may damage the lock.

5 Grip the steering wheel with both hands and carefully rock it from side-to-side to release it from the splines on the steering column. As the steering wheel is being removed, guide the wiring for the airbag through the aperture in the wheel, taking care not to damage the wiring connectors **(see illustration)**.

6 With the steering wheel removed, place a strip of adhesive tape across the top and front of the airbag rotary connector to prevent the connector rotating. To gain access to the rotary connector, use a small screwdriver to depress the retaining tabs on each side of the steering column shroud, and lift the upper shroud off the lower shroud **(see illustration)**.

Refitting

7 Make sure that the front wheels are pointing in the straight-ahead position, then remove the adhesive tape from the airbag rotary connector. Fit the steering column upper shroud back in position on the lower shroud.

8 Refit the steering wheel, routing the airbag wiring connectors through the steering wheel aperture.

9 Refit the steering wheel securing bolt, and tighten to the specified torque – again, do not rely on the steering column lock to hold the wheel as the bolt is tightened.

10 Reconnect the wiring connector for the steering wheel switches.

11 Release the steering lock, and refit the airbag as described in Chapter 12 Section 24.

16 Steering column –
removal and refitting

Removal

1 Remove the steering column shrouds as described in Chapter 11 Section 27.

2 Make sure the front wheels (and steering wheel) are in the straight-ahead position. Lock the steering in this position using the steering column lock.

3 Disconnect the battery negative lead as described in Chapter 5A Section 4.

4 Disconnect the wiring connectors at the steering column multifunction switches, ignition switch and airbag rotary connector, then release the wiring harness retaining clip **(see illustrations)**.

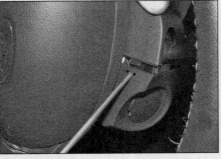

15.6 Depress the retaining tabs each side to release the steering column upper shroud from the lower shroud

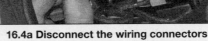

16.4a Disconnect the wiring connectors at the steering column multifunction switches...

16.4b... ignition switch...

16.4c... and airbag rotary connector...

16.4d... then release the wiring harness retaining clip

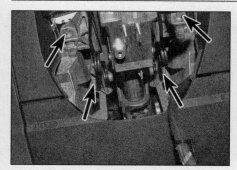

16.6a Undo the four retaining bolts (arrowed)…

16.6b… and manoeuvre the steering column from the vehicle

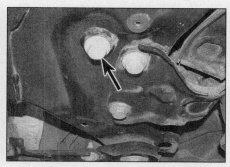

17.15 Steering rack left-hand mounting bolt (arrowed)

5 Working in the driver's footwell, undo the clamp bolt securing the steering column shaft universal joint to the steering gear pinion **(see illustration 6.2)**. Pull the shaft upwards and off the pinion. Note that a new clamp bolt will be required for refitting.

6 Undo the four retaining bolts and manoeuvre the column from the vehicle **(see illustrations)**.

7 With the column removed, prevent rotation of the steering wheel, by using masking tape to tape the wheel to the column.

Refitting

8 Refitting is a reversal of removal, using a new steering column shaft universal joint clamp bolt and tightening all bolts to the specified torque.

17 Steering rack – removal and refitting

Note: Ford special tool 205-316A (or a compatible alternative) will be needed to align the subframe with the body when refitting (see text).

Removal

1 Make sure the front wheels (and steering wheel) are in the straight-ahead position. Lock the steering in this position using the steering column lock.

2 Working in the driver's footwell, undo the clamp bolt securing the steering column shaft universal joint to the steering gear pinion **(see illustration 6.2)**. Pull the shaft upwards and off the pinion and move it to one side. Note that a new clamp bolt will be required for refitting.

3 Firmly apply the handbrake, then jack up the front of the vehicle and support it securely on axle stands (see *'Jacking and vehicle support'*). Remove both front roadwheels.

4 Undo the fasteners and remove the engine undertray, followed by the shield under the radiator.

5 Undo the bolt/nut and detach the headlight levelling sensor bracket from the suspension lower arm (where applicable).

6 Disconnect the two power steering fluid hoses at the quick-release connectors above

the steering gear. Be prepared for fluid loss and cover or seal all disconnected unions.

7 Undo the nut and detach the track rod end balljoint from the swivel hub on each side, using a balljoint separator tool as described in Section 21.

8 Unscrew and remove the nut each side securing the anti-roll bar connecting link to the anti-roll bar, while holding the link stub with an Allen key **(see illustration 5.3)**.

9 Attach splints each side of the exhaust flexible section (two wooden strips secured by cable-ties will suffice) to prevent excessive bending. On all except 2.0 litre diesel engine models to Stage V emission level, unhook the exhaust mounting rubbers at the front **(see illustration 6.8)**.

10 On 2.0 litre diesel engine models to Stage V emission level, undo the two bolts securing the exhaust front mounting bracket to the rear of the subframe **(see illustration 6.9)**.

11 On 2.0 litre diesel engine models, release the cable clips securing the diesel particulate filter wiring harness and hoses to the subframe. According to equipment fitted, it may also be necessary to release additional cable clips, or unbolt support brackets, to release pipes and hoses that may be put under strain when the subframe is lowered.

12 Unscrew and remove the engine lower mounting link through-bolt **(see illustration 6.11)**.

13 Undo the bolt securing the power steering fluid pipe clamp to the steering rack.

14 Undo the bolt, rotate the clamp plate and disconnect the power steering fluid pipes from the steering rack pinion housing. Be prepared for fluid loss and cover or seal all disconnected unions.

15 Undo the two bolts securing the steering rack to the subframe **(see illustration)**.

16 Position a sturdy trolley jack beneath, and in contact with, the rear of the subframe.

17 Undo the two rear bolts each side securing the subframe cross-brace to the underbody. With the subframe securely supported, undo the bolt each side securing the rear of the subframe and the cross-brace to the underbody and remove the cross-brace **(see illustration 6.13)**. Note that new subframe mounting bolts will be required for refitting.

18 Position a second trolley jack beneath, and in contact with, the front of the subframe.

19 Undo the subframe front mounting bolt on each side. Note that new bolts will be required for refitting.

20 Engage the help of an assistant to steady the subframe, then carefully lower the jack and allow the subframe to drop slightly at the rear.

21 When sufficient clearance exists, carefully manipulate the steering rack out from the driver's side of the car.

Refitting

22 Manipulate the steering rack into position on the subframe. Refit the retaining bolts and tighten them to the specified torque.

23 Raise the subframe into position and fit the new front mounting bolts. Tighten the bolts hand-tight only at this stage.

24 Place the subframe cross-brace in position and fit the two new subframe mounting bolts and the four cross-brace retaining bolts. Tighten the bolts hand-tight only at this stage.

25 The alignment of the subframe must be checked by inserting Ford alignment tools (part No 205-316A) or suitable alternatives through the holes in the sidemembers **(see illustration 6.26)**.

26 With the subframe correctly aligned, tighten the four subframe mounting bolts to the specified Stage 1 torque setting, then through the specified Stage 2 angle. Tighten the four cross-brace retaining bolts to the specified torque.

27 Engage the steering shaft universal joint with the pinion shaft, and push it fully home.

28 Fit the new universal joint clamp bolt and tighten it to the specified torque.

29 Refit the fluid pipes to the steering rack using new O-ring seals, and tighten the retaining bolt securely.

30 The remainder of refitting is a reversal of removal bearing in mind the following points:

a) *Tighten all fixings to the specified torque and, where applicable, through the specified angle.*

b) *Fill and bleed the power steering hydraulic system as described in Section 19.*

c) *Have the front wheel toe-in (tracking) checked and adjusted at the earliest opportunity.*

18 Steering rack gaiters – renewal

1 Remove the relevant track rod end as described in Section 21.
2 Count and record the number of exposed threads from the track rod end locknut to the end of the track rod, then unscrew the locknut.
3 Remove the inboard and outboard securing clips, then slide the gaiter off the end of the track rod.
4 Thoroughly clean the track rod, then slide the new gaiter into position.
5 Fit the gaiter securing clips, using new clips if necessary, making sure that the gaiter is not twisted.
6 Screw the track rod end locknut back onto the track rod and position it so that the same number of threads are exposed as was noted during removal.
7 Refit the track rod end as described in Section 21.

19 Power steering hydraulic system – bleeding

1 Wipe clean the area around the reservoir filler neck, and unscrew the filler cap from the reservoir.
2 If topping-up is necessary, use clean fluid of the specified type (see 'Weekly checks'). Check for leaks if frequent topping-up is required. Do not run the engine without fluid in the reservoir.
3 After component renewal, or if the fluid level has been allowed to fall so low that air has entered the hydraulic system, bleeding must be carried out as follows.
4 Fill the reservoir to the MAX mark as described in 'Weekly checks'. Note that the power steering fluid should be cold, and poured slowly into the reservoir to minimise aeration.

5 Raise the front of the vehicle until the tyres are just clear of the ground, then support the vehicle securely on axle stands (see 'Jacking and vehicle support').
6 Slowly turn the steering wheel from lock to lock, and add power steering fluid until the fluid level ceases to drop.
7 Start the engine, slowly turn the steering wheel from lock to lock, and add power steering fluid until the fluid level ceases to drop.
8 Switch off the engine and check the fluid level. Top-up if necessary.
9 Start the engine and turn the steering from lock to lock. If excessive noise is still apparent (indicating air in the system), leave the vehicle overnight, then try again.
10 If the steering is still noisy, it may be that the pump is faulty. Consult a Ford dealer or specialist.
11 On completion, stop the engine, lower the vehicle to the ground, and recheck the fluid level.

20 Power steering pump – removal and refitting

Removal

Petrol engine models

1 Remove the plastic cover over the top of the engine.
2 Remove the auxiliary drivebelt as described in Chapter 1A Section 25.
3 Undo the nut and release the hydraulic fluid pipe support bracket from the stud below the right-hand engine mounting.
4 Disconnect the wiring connector from the pressure switch on the hydraulic fluid supply pipe.
5 Position a suitable container beneath the power steering pump, then release the retaining clip and disconnect the reservoir supply hose from the pump outlet. Allow the fluid to drain into the container, then cover or seal the hose end and pump outlet.

6 Undo the retaining bolt and withdraw the high-pressure pipe from the side of the pump.
7 Undo the three mounting bolts and remove the pump from the engine.

Diesel engine models

8 Remove the plastic cover over the top of the engine.
9 Remove the auxiliary drivebelt as described in Chapter 1B Section 24.
10 Position a suitable container beneath the power steering pump, then release the retaining clip and disconnect the reservoir supply hose from the pump outlet **(see illustration)**. Allow the fluid to drain into the container, then cover or seal the hose end and pump outlet.
11 Undo the retaining bolt or retaining nut (as applicable) and withdraw the high-pressure pipe from the side of the pump.
12 Undo the three mounting bolts and remove the pump from the engine.

Refitting

13 Refitting is a reversal of removal, bearing in mind the following points:
a) Use a new O-ring on the high-pressure pipe union.
b) Tighten the mounting bolts to the specified torque.
c) Refill/top-up the fluid reservoir, and bleed the system as described in Section 19.

21 Track rod end – removal and refitting

Removal

1 Firmly apply the handbrake, then jack up the front of the vehicle and support it securely on axle stands (see 'Jacking and vehicle support'). Remove the appropriate front roadwheel.
2 Counter-hold the track rod, and slacken the track rod end locknut by half a turn **(see illustration)**. If the locknut is now left in this

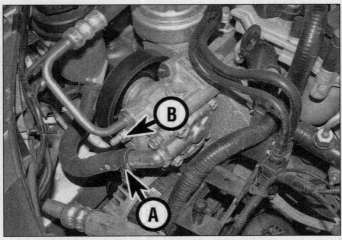

20.10 Power steering pump supply hose retaining clip (A) and high-pressure pipe retaining nut (B)

21.2 Slacken the track rod end locknut (arrowed) by half a turn

21.3a Unscrew the track rod end balljoint nut...

21.3b... then separate the balljoint from the steering arm with a proprietary balljoint separator

position, it will act as a further guide for refitting.

3 Unscrew the track rod end balljoint nut, using and Allen key to counter-hold the balljoint shank. Separate the balljoint from the steering arm with a proprietary balljoint separator, then remove the nut and disengage the balljoint from the arm **(see illustrations)**.

4 Unscrew the track rod end from the track rod, counting the number of turns needed to remove it. Make a note of the number of turns, so that the tracking can be reset (or at least approximated) on refitting.

Refitting

5 Screw the track rod end onto the track rod by the same number of turns noted during removal.

6 Engage the balljoint in the steering arm. Fit a new nut and tighten it to the specified torque.

7 Counter-hold the track rod and tighten the locknut.

8 Refit the front wheel, lower the car and tighten the wheel nuts to the specified torque.

9 Have the front wheel toe-in (tracking) checked and adjusted at the earliest opportunity.

22 Wheel alignment and steering angles – general information

1 A car's steering and suspension geometry is defined in four basic settings – all angles are expressed in degrees (toe settings are also expressed as a measurement); the relevant settings are camber, castor, steering axis inclination, and toe setting **(see illustration)**. On the models covered by this manual, only the front and rear wheel toe settings are adjustable. All other suspension and steering angles are set during manufacture, and no adjustment is possible. It can be assumed, therefore, that unless the vehicle has suffered accident damage, all the preset angles will be correct.

Camber

2 Camber is the angle at which the front wheels are set from the vertical when viewed from the front or rear of the car. Negative camber is the amount (in degrees) that the wheels are tilted inward at the top from the vertical.

Castor

3 Castor is the angle between the steering axis and a vertical line when viewed from each side of the car. Positive castor is when the steering axis is inclined rearward at the top.

Steering axis inclination

4 Steering axis inclination is the angle (when viewed from the front of the vehicle) between the vertical and an imaginary line drawn through the front suspension strut upper mounting and the control arm balljoint.

Toe setting

5 Toe setting (tracking) is the amount by which the distance between the front inside edges of the roadwheels (measured at hub height) differs from the diametrically opposite distance measured between the rear inside edges of the roadwheels. Toe-in is when the roadwheels point inwards, towards each other at the front, while toe-out is when they splay outwards from each other at the front.

6 The front wheel toe setting is adjusted by altering the length of the steering track rods on both sides.

7 The rear wheel toe setting is adjusted by rotating the lower control arm inner mounting bolt in the rear subframe. The bolt incorporates an eccentric washer, and the pivot point for the control arm varies as the bolt is rotated.

8 Special optical measuring equipment is necessary to accurately check and adjust the front and rear toe settings, and this work should be carried out by a Ford dealer or similar expert. Note that most tyre fitting shops now possess sophisticated checking equipment.

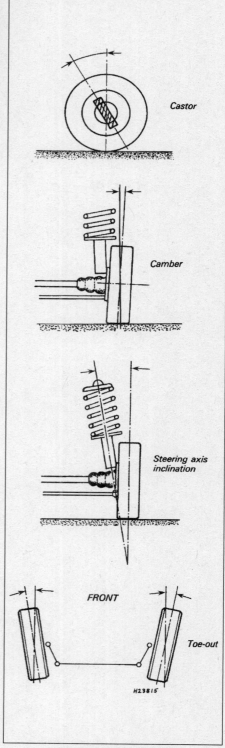

22.1 Front wheel geometry

Chapter 11
Bodywork and fittings

Contents

Degrees of difficulty

| Easy, suitable for novice with little experience | | Fairly easy, suitable for beginner with some experience | | Fairly difficult, suitable for competent DIY mechanic | | Difficult, suitable for experienced DIY mechanic | | Very difficult, suitable for expert DIY or professional | |

Specifications

Torque wrench settings	Nm	lbf ft
Boot lid-to-hinge bolts	23	17
Door-to-hinge bolts:		
Upper bolts.	35	26
Lower bolts.	47	35
Facia crossmember centre brace:		
Retaining bolts	25	18
Retaining nuts.	10	7
Facia crossmember mounting bolts:		
Front and centre bolts	25	18
Side bolts	80	59
Front seat mounting bolts	40	30
Seat belt mountings and anchorages	35	26
Tailgate-to-hinge bolts	22	16

1 General Information

1 The bodyshell is of four-door Saloon or five-door Hatchback and Estate configurations, and is made of pressed-steel sections. The bodyshell and underframe feature variable thickness steel, achieved by laser-welded technology, used to join steel panels of different gauges. This gives a stiffer structure, with mounting points being more rigid, which gives an improved crash performance.

2 An additional safety crossmember is incorporated between the A-pillars in the upper area of the bulkhead, and the facia and steering column are secured to it. The lower bulkhead area is reinforced by additional systems of members connected to the front of the vehicle. The body side rocker panels (sills) have been divided along the length of the vehicle by internal reinforcement, this functions like a double tube which increases its strength. All doors are reinforced and incorporate side impact protection, which is secured in the door structure. There are additional impact absorbers to the front and rear of the vehicle, behind the bumper assemblies.

3 All sheet metal surfaces which are prone to corrosion are galvanised. The painting process includes a base colour which closely matches the final topcoat, so that any stone damage is not as noticeable. The front wings are of a bolt-on type to ease their renewal if required.

4 Extensive use is made of plastic materials, mainly in the interior, but also in exterior components. The front and rear bumpers and the front grille are injection-moulded from a synthetic material which is very strong, and yet light. Plastic components such as wheel arch liners are fitted to the underside of the car, to improve the body's resistance to corrosion.

2 Maintenance – bodywork and underframe

1 The general condition of a car's bodywork is the one thing that significantly affects its value. Maintenance is easy, but needs to be regular. Neglect, particularly after minor damage, can lead quickly to further deterioration and costly repair bills. It is important also to keep watch on those parts of the car not immediately visible, for instance the underside, inside all the wheel arches, and the lower part of the engine compartment.

2 The basic maintenance routine for the bodywork is washing – preferably with a lot of water, from a hose. This will remove all the loose solids which may have stuck to the car. It is important to flush these off in such a way as to prevent grit from scratching the finish. The wheel arches and underframe need washing in the same way, to remove any accumulated mud which will retain moisture and tend to encourage rust. Paradoxically enough, the best time to clean the underframe and wheel arches is in wet weather, when the mud is thoroughly wet and soft. In very wet weather, the underframe is usually cleaned of large accumulations automatically, and this is a good time for inspection.

3 Periodically, except on models with a wax-based underbody protective coating, it is a good idea to have the whole of the underframe of the car steam-cleaned, engine compartment included, so that a thorough inspection can be carried out to see what minor repairs and renovations are necessary. Steam-cleaning is available at many garages, and is necessary for the removal of the accumulation of oily grime, which sometimes is allowed to become thick in certain areas. If steam-cleaning facilities are not available, there are one or two excellent grease solvents available, which can be brush-applied; the dirt can then be simply hosed off. Note that these methods should not be used on cars with wax-based underbody protective coating, or the coating will be removed. Such cars should be inspected annually, preferably just prior to Winter, when the underbody should be washed down, and any damage to the wax coating repaired. Ideally, a completely fresh coat should be applied. It would also be worth considering the use of such wax-based protection for injection into door panels, sills, box sections, etc, as an additional safeguard against rust damage, where such protection is not provided by the manufacturer.

4 After washing paintwork, wipe off with a chamois leather to give an unspotted clear finish. A coat of clear protective wax polish will give added protection against chemical pollutants in the air. If the paintwork sheen has dulled or oxidised, use a cleaner/polisher combination to restore the brilliance of the shine. This requires a little effort, but such dulling is usually caused because regular washing has been neglected. Care needs to be taken with metallic paintwork, as special non-abrasive cleaner/polisher is required to avoid damage to the finish. Always check that the door and ventilator opening drain holes and pipes are completely clear, so that water can be drained out. Brightwork should be treated in the same way as paintwork. Windscreens and windows can be kept clear of the smeary film which often appears, by the use of proprietary glass cleaner. Never use any form of wax, or other body or chromium polish, on glass.

3 Maintenance – upholstery and carpets

1 Mats and carpets should be brushed or vacuum-cleaned regularly, to keep them free of grit. If they are badly stained, remove them from the car for scrubbing or sponging, and make quite sure they are dry before refitting. Seats and interior trim panels can be kept clean by wiping with a damp cloth. If they do become stained (which can be more apparent on light-coloured upholstery), use a little liquid detergent and a soft nail brush to scour the grime out of the grain of the material. Do not forget to keep the headlining clean in the same way as the upholstery. When using liquid cleaners inside the car, do not over-wet the surfaces being cleaned. Excessive damp could get into the seams and padded interior, causing stains, offensive odours or even rot. If the inside of the car gets wet accidentally, it is worthwhile taking some trouble to dry it out properly, particularly where carpets are involved. Do not leave oil or electric heaters inside the car for this purpose.

4 Minor body damage – repair

Minor scratches

1 If the scratch is very superficial, and does not penetrate to the metal of the bodywork, repair is very simple. Lightly rub the area of the scratch with a paintwork renovator, or a very fine cutting paste, to remove loose paint from the scratch, and to clear the surrounding bodywork of wax polish. Rinse the area with clean water.

2 In the case of metallic paint, the most commonly-found scratches are not in the paint, but in the lacquer top coat, and appear white. If care is taken, these can sometimes be rendered less obvious by very careful use of paintwork renovator (which would other-wise not be used on metallic paintwork); otherwise, repair of these scratches can be achieved by applying lacquer with a fine brush.

3 Apply touch-up paint to the scratch using a fine paint brush; continue to apply fine layers of paint until the surface of the paint in the scratch is level with the surrounding paintwork. Allow the new paint at least two weeks to harden, then blend it into the surrounding paintwork by rubbing the scratch area with a paintwork renovator or a very fine cutting paste. Finally, apply wax polish.

4 Where the scratch has penetrated right through to the metal of the bodywork, causing the metal to rust, a different repair technique is required. Remove any loose rust from the bottom of the scratch with a penknife, then apply rust-inhibiting paint, to prevent the formation of rust in the future. Using a rubber or nylon applicator, fill the scratch with bodystopper paste. If required, this paste can be mixed with cellulose thinners, to provide a very thin paste which is ideal for filling narrow scratches. Before the stopper-paste in the scratch hardens, wrap a piece of smooth cotton rag around the top of a finger. Dip the finger in cellulose thinners, and quickly sweep it across the surface of the stopper-paste in the scratch; this will ensure that the surface of the stopper-paste is slightly hollowed. The scratch can now be painted over as described earlier in this Section.

Dents

5 When deep denting of the bodywork has taken place, the first task is to pull the dent out, until the affected bodywork almost attains its original shape. There is little point in trying to restore the original shape completely, as the metal in the damaged area will have stretched on impact, and cannot be reshaped fully to its original contour. It is better to bring the level of the dent up to a point which is about 3 mm below the level of the surrounding bodywork. In cases where the dent is very shallow anyway, it is not worth trying to pull it out at all. If the underside of the dent is accessible, it can be hammered out gently from behind, using a mallet with a wooden or plastic head. Whilst doing this, hold a suitable block of wood firmly against the outside of the panel, to absorb the impact from the hammer blows and thus prevent a large area of the bodywork from being 'belled-out'.

6 Should the dent be in a section of the bodywork which has a double skin, or some other factor making it inaccessible from behind, a different technique is called for. Drill several small holes through the metal inside the area – particularly in the deeper section. Then screw long self-tapping screws into the holes, just sufficiently for them to gain a good purchase in the metal. Now the dent can be pulled out by pulling on the protruding heads of the screws with a pair of pliers.

7 The next stage of the repair is the removal of the paint from the damaged area, and from an inch or so of the surrounding 'sound' bodywork. This is accomplished most easily by using a wire brush or abrasive pad on a power drill, although it can be done just as effectively by hand, using sheets of abrasive paper. To complete the preparation for filling, score the surface of the bare metal with a screwdriver or the tang of a file, or alternatively, drill small holes in the affected area. This will provide a really good 'key' for the filler paste.

8 To complete the repair, see the Section on filling and respraying.

Rust holes or gashes

9 Remove all paint from the affected area, and from an inch or so of the surrounding 'sound' bodywork, using an abrasive pad or a wire brush on a power drill. If these are not available, a few sheets of abrasive paper will do the job most effectively. With the paint removed, you will be able to judge the severity of the corrosion, and therefore decide whether to renew the whole panel (if this is possible) or to repair the affected area. New body panels are not as expensive as most people think, and it is often quicker and more satisfactory to fit a new panel than to attempt to repair large areas of corrosion.

10 Remove all fittings from the affected area, except those which will act as a guide to the original shape of the damaged bodywork (eg body side mouldings etc). Then, using tin snips or a hacksaw blade, remove all loose metal and any other metal badly affected by corrosion. Hammer the edges of the hole inwards, in order to create a slight depression for the filler paste.

11 Wire-brush the affected area to remove the powdery rust from the surface of the remaining metal. Paint the affected area with rust-inhibiting paint; if the back of the rusted area is accessible, treat this also.

12 Before filling can take place, it will be necessary to block the hole in some way. This can be achieved by the use of aluminium or plastic mesh, or aluminium tape.

13 Aluminium or plastic mesh, or glass-fibre matting, is probably the best material to use for a large hole. Cut a piece to the approximate size and shape of the hole to be filled, then position it in the hole so that its edges are below the level of the surrounding bodywork. It can be retained in position by several blobs of filler paste around its periphery.

14 Aluminium tape should be used for small or very narrow holes. Pull a piece off the roll, trim it to the approximate size and shape required, then pull off the backing paper (if used) and stick the tape over the hole; it can be overlapped if the thickness of one piece is insufficient. Burnish down the edges of the tape with the handle of a screwdriver or similar, to ensure that the tape is securely attached to the metal underneath.

Filling and respraying

15 Before using this Section, see the Sections on dent, deep scratch, rust holes and gash repairs.

16 Many types of bodyfiller are available, but generally speaking, those proprietary kits which contain a tin of filler paste and a tube of resin hardener are best for this type of repair. A wide, flexible plastic or nylon applicator will be found invaluable for imparting a smooth and well-contoured finish to the surface of the filler.

17 Mix up a little filler on a clean piece of card or board – measure the hardener carefully (follow the maker's instructions on the pack), otherwise the filler will set too rapidly or too slowly. Using the applicator, apply the filler paste to the prepared area; draw the applicator across the surface of the filler to achieve the correct contour and to level the surface. As soon as a contour that approximates to the correct one is achieved, stop working the paste – if you carry on too long, the paste will become sticky and begin to 'pick-up' on the applicator. Continue to add thin layers of filler paste at 20-minute intervals, until the level of the filler is just proud of the surrounding bodywork.

18 Once the filler has hardened, the excess can be removed using a metal plane or file. From then on, progressively-finer grades of abrasive paper should be used, starting with a 40-grade production paper, and finishing with a 400-grade wet-and-dry paper. Always wrap the abrasive paper around a flat rubber, cork, or wooden block – otherwise the surface of the filler will not be completely flat. During the smoothing of the filler surface, the wet-and-dry paper should be periodically rinsed in water. This will ensure that a very smooth finish is imparted to the filler at the final stage.

19 At this stage, the 'dent' should be surrounded by a ring of bare metal, which in turn should be encircled by the finely 'feathered' edge of the good paintwork. Rinse the repair area with clean water, until all of the dust produced by the rubbing-down operation has gone.

20 Spray the whole area with a light coat of – this will show up any imperfections in the surface of the filler. Repair these imperfections with fresh filler paste or bodystopper, and once more smooth the surface with abrasive paper. If bodystopper is used, it can be mixed with cellulose thinners, to form a really thin paste which is ideal for filling small holes. Repeat this spray-and-repair procedure until you are satisfied that the surface of the filler, and the feathered edge of the paintwork, are perfect. Clean the repair area with clean water, and allow to dry fully.

21 The repair area is now ready for final spraying. Paint spraying must be carried out in a warm, dry, windless and dust-free atmosphere. This condition can be created artificially if you have access to a large indoor working area, but if you are forced to work in the open, you will have to pick your day very carefully. If you are working indoors, dousing the floor in the work area with water will help to settle the dust which would otherwise be in the atmosphere. If the repair area is confined to one body panel, mask off the surrounding panels; this will help to minimise the effects of a slight mis-match in paint colours. Bodywork fittings (eg chrome strips, door handles etc) will also need to be masked off. Use genuine masking tape, and several thicknesses of newspaper, for the masking operations.

22 Before commencing to spray, agitate the aerosol can thoroughly, then spray a test area (an old tin, or similar) until the technique is mastered. Cover the repair area with a thick coat of primer; the thickness should be built up using several thin layers of paint, rather than one thick one. Using 400 grade wet-and-dry paper, rub down the surface of the primer until it is really smooth. While doing this, the work area should be thoroughly doused with water, and the wet-and-dry paper periodically rinsed in water. Allow to dry before spraying on more paint.

23 Spray on the top coat, again building up the thickness by using several thin layers of paint. Start spraying at the top of the repair area, and then, using a side-to-side motion, work downwards until the whole repair area and about 2 inches of the surrounding original paintwork is covered. Remove all masking material 10 to 15 minutes after spraying on the final coat of paint.

24 Allow the new paint at least two weeks to harden, then, using a paintwork renovator or a very fine cutting paste, blend the edges of the paint into the existing paintwork. Finally, apply wax polish.

Plastic components

25 With the use of more and more plastic body components by the car manufacturers (eg bumpers. spoilers, and in some cases major body panels), rectification of more serious damage to such items has become a matter of either entrusting repair work to a specialist in this field, or renewing complete components. Repair of such damage by the DIY owner is not really feasible, owing to the cost of the equipment and materials required for effecting such repairs. The basic technique involves making a groove along the line of the crack in the plastic, using a rotary burr in a power drill. The damaged part is then welded back together, using a hot air gun to heat up and fuse a plastic filler rod into the groove. Any excess plastic is then removed, and the area rubbed down to a smooth finish. It is important that a filler rod of the correct plastic is used, as body components can be made of a variety of different types (eg polycarbonate, ABS, polypropylene).

26 Damage of a less serious nature (abrasions, minor cracks etc) can be repaired by the DIY owner using a two-part epoxy filler repair. Once mixed in equal, this is used in similar fashion to the bodywork filler used on metal panels. The filler is usually cured in twenty to thirty minutes, ready for sanding and painting.

27 If the owner is renewing a complete component himself, or if he has repaired it with epoxy filler, he will be left with the problem of finding a suitable paint for finishing which is compatible with the type of plastic used. At one time, the use of a universal paint was not possible, owing to the complex range of plastics encountered in body component applications. Standard paints, generally speaking, will not bond to plastic or rubber satisfactorily, but suitable paints to match any plastic or rubber finish, can be obtained from dealers. However, it is now possible to obtain a plastic body parts finishing kit which consists of a preprimer treatment, a primer and coloured top coat. Full instructions are normally supplied with a kit, but basically, the method of use is to first apply the preprimer to the component concerned, and allow it to dry for up to 30 minutes. Then the primer is applied, and left to dry for about an hour before finally applying the special-coloured top coat. The result is a correctly-coloured component, where the paint will flex with the plastic or rubber, a property that standard paint does not normally posses.

5 Major body damage – repair

1 Where serious damage has occurred, or large areas need renewal due to neglect, it means that complete new panels will need welding-in, and this is best left to professionals. If the damage is due to impact, it will also be necessary to check completely the alignment of the bodyshell, and this can only be carried out accurately by a Ford dealer or accident repair specialist, using special jigs. If the body is left misaligned, it is primarily dangerous, as the car will not handle properly, and secondly, uneven stresses will be imposed on the steering, suspension and possibly transmission, causing abnormal wear, or complete failure, particularly to such items as the tyres.

6 Bumpers – removal and refitting

Front bumper

Removal

1 Remove the headlights as described in Chapter 12 Section 7.

2 Firmly apply the handbrake, then jack up the front of the vehicle and support it securely on axle stands (see *'Jacking and vehicle support'*).

3 Where fitted, undo the seven bolts and remove the engine undertray.

4 Undo the thirteen bolts, remove the six plastic rivets and remove the shield under the radiator **(see illustration)**.

5 Undo the fasteners and remove the wheel arch liner on both sides **(see illustration)**.

6 Prise up the centre section, then remove the plastic rivet each side securing the radiator cover panel to the top of the bumper **(see illustration)**.

6.4 Undo the fasteners and remove the shield under the radiator

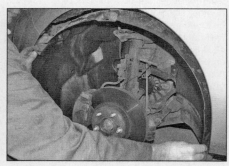

6.5 Remove the wheel arch liner on both sides

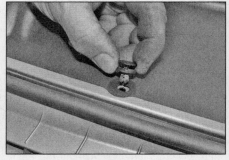

6.6 Remove the plastic rivet each side securing the radiator cover panel to the top of the bumper

6.7a Pull up on the tabs at the rear of the radiator cover panel each side...

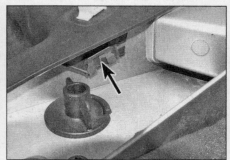

6.7b... to release the retaining clips (arrowed)...

6.7c... then lift the cover panel off the car

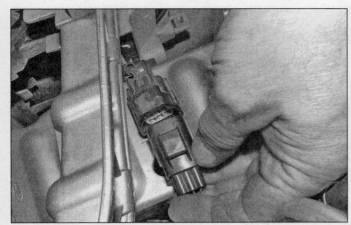

6.9a Where applicable, disconnect the parking sensor wiring harness connector...

6.9b... and the wiring connectors (arrowed) at the front foglights

6.11 Undo the two bolts each side (arrowed) securing the bumper to the front wing

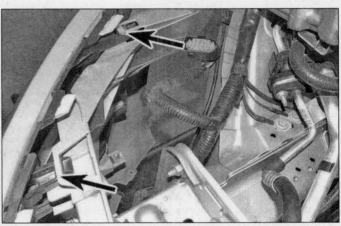

6.12 Lift the tabs (arrowed) to disengage the two bumper locating pegs each side

7 Pull up on the tabs at the rear of the radiator cover panel each side to release the retaining clips, then lift the cover panel off the car **(see illustrations).**
8 Unscrew the centre section and remove the two plastic rivets securing the radiator grille extensions to the front body panel.
9 Where applicable, disconnect the parking

sensor wiring harness connector, and the wiring connectors at the front foglights **(see illustrations).**
10 On models with headlight washers, disconnect the washer fluid hose.
11 Undo the two bolts each side securing the bumper to the front wing **(see illustration).**

12 With the help of an assistant, lift the tabs to disengage the two locating pegs each side, while at the same time pulling the bumper forward **(see illustration).**
13 Disengage the three upper centre locating pegs and remove the bumper from the car **(see illustration).**

Refitting

14 Refitting is a reversal of removal. Have an assistant available to help align the bumper with the locating pegs, and tighten the mounting bolts securely.

Rear bumper

Removal

15 Chock the front wheels, then jack up the rear of the vehicle, and support it securely on axle stands (see *'Jacking and vehicle support'*).
16 Undo the three screws each side securing the bumper to the wheel arch liner **(see illustration).**
17 Open the tailgate and undo the screw each

6.13 Disengage the three upper centre locating pegs and remove the front bumper

6.16 Undo the three screws each side (arrowed) securing the rear bumper to the wheel arch liner

6.17 Undo the screw each side (arrowed) in the tailgate aperture

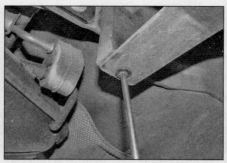

6.18a On Saloon and Hatchback models, unscrew the centre section...

6.18b... and remove the lower plastic rivet each side

6.19 On Estate models, undo the two lower centre retaining nuts (arrowed)

6.20 Where applicable, disconnect the parking sensor wiring harness connector (arrowed)

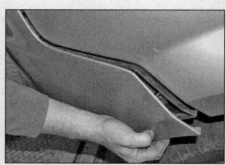

6.21 Pull the bumper lower section away from the body to disengage the side locating tabs

side (two screws each side on Estate models) in the tailgate aperture **(see illustration)**.

18 On Saloon and Hatchback models, remove the lower plastic rivet each side securing the bumper to the body, by unscrewing the centre section and withdrawing the rivet body **(see illustrations)**.

19 On Estate models, undo the two lower centre retaining nuts **(see illustration)**.

20 Where applicable, disconnect the parking sensor wiring harness connector located under the bumper on the right-hand side **(see illustration)**.

21 With the help of an assistant, pull the lower section of the bumper away from the body each side to disengage the side locating tabs **(see illustration)**.

22 Pull the bumper rearwards to disengage the three tabs under each rear light unit, and the upper locating tongue each side, then remove the bumper from the car **(see illustrations)**.

Refitting

23 Refitting is a reversal of removal. Have an assistant available to help align the bumper with the locating tabs.

7 Bonnet – removal, refitting and adjustment

Removal

1 Open the bonnet, and support it on its stay.
2 Prise out the retainers and remove the sound deadening pad from inside the bonnet **(see illustration)**.
3 Disconnect the windscreen washer hose at

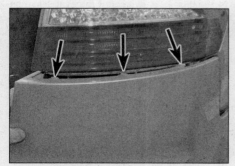

6.22a Pull the bumper rearwards to disengage the three tabs (arrowed) under each rear light unit...

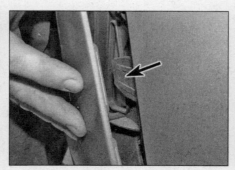

6.22b... and the upper locating tongue (arrowed) each side

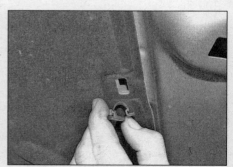

7.2 Prise out the retainers and remove the sound deadening pad from the bonnet

7.3a Disconnect the windscreen washer hose at the jet T-piece...

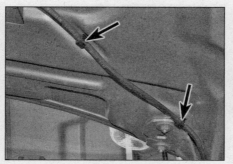

7.3b... and release the hose from the bonnet clips (arrowed)

7.4a On models with electrically-heated washer jets, extract the three fasteners (arrowed)...

7.4b... and remove the plastic panel above the right-hand front wing

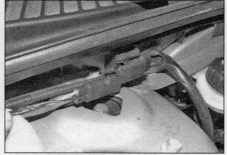

7.4c Disconnect the washer jet wiring at the connector above the suspension strut...

7.4d... and release the wiring from the clip on the bonnet hinge

the jet T-piece and release the hose from the clips on the bonnet (see illustrations).

4 On models with electrically-heated washer jets, extract the three fasteners and remove the plastic panel above the right-hand front wing. Disconnect the washer jet wiring at the connector above the right-hand suspension strut and release the wiring from the clip on the bonnet hinge (see illustrations).

5 Using a marker pen or paint, mark around the hinge positions on the bonnet.

6 With the aid of an assistant, support the bonnet, and unscrew the two nuts each side securing the bonnet to the hinges (see illustration).

7 Lift off the bonnet.

Refitting

8 Align the marks made on the bonnet with

the hinges, then refit and tighten the bonnet securing nuts.

9 Where applicable, reconnect the washer jet wiring connector, clip the wiring to the bonnet hinge and refit the plastic panel.

10 Feed the washer hose back across the bonnet, and reconnect it to the washer jet T-piece, then refit the sound deadening pad.

11 Check the bonnet adjustment as follows.

Adjustment

12 Close the bonnet, and check that there is an equal gap at each side between the bonnet and the wing panels. Check also that the bonnet sits flush in relation to the surrounding body panels.

13 The bonnet should close smoothly and positively without excessive pressure. If this is not the case, adjustment will be required.

14 To adjust the bonnet alignment, slacken the

bonnet securing nuts, and move the bonnet on the studs as required (the holes in the hinges are elongated). To adjust the bonnet closure, adjustable bump stops are fitted to the body front panel. These may be raised or lowered by screwing in or out as necessary.

8 Bonnet release cable – removal and refitting

Removal

1 The bonnet release lever is located under the facia on the left-hand side.

2 Remove the battery and battery tray as described in Chapter 5A Section 4.

3 Remove the left-hand headlight unit as described in Chapter 12 Section 7.

4 Remove the bonnet lock as described in Section 9.

5 Pull out the locking bar and disconnect the wiring harness plug from the ABS ECU on the hydraulic modulator.

6 Release the cable from the clips and brackets in the engine compartment, up to the cable entry grommet below the ABS hydraulic modulator.

7 Working inside the car, remove the A-pillar lower trim panel as described in Section 27.

8 Extract the trim cap from the centre of the bonnet release handle, then depress the two tabs and pull the release handle off the release lever assembly.

9 Undo the two screws and withdraw the release lever assembly from the A-pillar (see illustration).

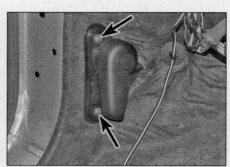

8.9 Bonnet release lever retaining screws (arrowed)

7.6 Unscrew the two nuts each side (arrowed) securing the bonnet to the hinges

9.4a Undo the two bolts securing the bonnet lock to the front body panel…

9.4b… and lift off the security shield

9.5a Disconnect the wiring connector…

9.5b… and withdraw the bonnet lock from the front body panel

9.6a Prise out the bonnet release outer cable end fitting from its slot in the bonnet lock…

9.6b… and unhook the inner cable from the lock operating lever

10 Disengage the bonnet release outer cable from the release lever assembly, then slip the inner cable end fitting out of the lever.

11 Fold back the carpet and trace the run of the release cable under the sound deadening material up to the cable grommet on the bulkhead. Note that it will be necessary to cut a slit in the sound deadening material, using a sharp knife, to gain access to the cable.

12 Tie a length of string to the end of the cable at the release lever inside the car, then carefully pull the cable through the bulkhead grommet into the engine compartment.

13 Untie the string from the end of the cable, and leave it in position to aid refitting.

Refitting

14 Refitting is a reversal of removal, but tie the string to the release lever end of the cable, and use the string to pull the cable into position. Ensure that the cable is routed as noted before removal, and make sure that the bulkhead grommet is correctly seated. Tape over the cut made in the sound deadening material.

---

9   Bonnet lock – removal and refitting

Removal

1 Open the bonnet, and support it on its stay.

2 Prise up the centre section, then remove the plastic rivet each side securing the

radiator cover panel to the top of the bumper **(see illustration 6.6)**.

3 Pull up on the tabs at the rear of the radiator cover panel each side to release the retaining clips, then lift the cover panel off the car **(see illustrations 6.7a, 6.7b and 6.7c)**.

4 Undo the two bolts securing the bonnet lock to the front body panel and lift off the security shield **(see illustrations)**.

5 Disconnect the wiring connector and withdraw the bonnet lock from the front body panel **(see illustrations)**.

6 Prise out the bonnet release outer cable end fitting from its slot in the bonnet lock and unhook the inner cable from the lock operating lever **(see illustrations)**. Remove the lock from the car.

Refitting

7 Refitting is a reversal of removal.

---

10   Boot lid – removal, refitting and adjustment

Removal

1 Remove the boot lid trim panel as described in Section 27.

2 Note their fitted positions, then disconnect the various wiring connectors on the inside of the boot lid.

3 Prise the rubber grommet from the left-hand corner of the boot lid, and pull the wiring loom through.

4 Mark the position of the hinge arms with a pencil. Place rags beneath each corner of the boot lid, to prevent damage to the paintwork.

5 With the help of an assistant to support the boot lid, prise off the spring clip and detach the support strut socket on each side from the ball stud on the boot lid.

6 Unscrew the mounting bolts and lift the boot lid from the car.

Refitting and adjustment

7 Refitting is a reversal of the removal procedure, noting the following points:

a) *Check that the boot lid is correctly aligned with the surrounding bodywork, with an equal clearance around its edge.*

b) *Adjustment can be made by loosening the hinge bolts, and moving the boot lid and hinges within the elongated mounting holes.*

c) *Check that the lock enters the striker centrally when the boot lid is closed.*

---

11   Boot lid lock components – removal and refitting

Lock assembly

Removal

1 Remove the boot lid trim panel as described in Section 27.

2 Disconnect the wiring plug from the lock assembly.

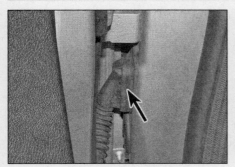

12.1a Release the rubber grommet (arrowed) from the door pillar...

12.1b... by pressing it down at the top and swivelling it outward...

12.1c... then disconnect the wiring block connectors

3 Using a Torx key, unscrew the lock mounting bolts, and withdraw the lock.

Refitting

4 Refitting is a reversal of the removal procedure.

Release and lock switches

Removal

5 Remove the boot lid trim panel as described in Section 27.

6 Using a plastic spatula, and starting at the upper right-hand corner, carefully prise up the boot lid exterior moulding above the number plate. Continue working across the top of the moulding until all the clips have been released then remove the moulding from the boot lid.

7 Undo the three screws securing the number plate light panel to the boot lid and withdraw the panel.

8 Disconnect the wiring connectors at the number plate lights and at the release and lock switches. Release the wiring from the cable-ties and clips and remove the number plate light panel.

9 Depress the tab at the side of the switch and remove the relevant switch from the panel.

Refitting

10 Refitting is a reversal of the removal procedure.

---

12 Door – removal, refitting and adjustment

Removal

1 Release the rubber grommet from the door pillar by pressing it down at the top and swivelling it outward, then disconnect the wiring block connectors **(see illustrations)**.

2 Support the door on a trolley jack using thick cloth or similar on the jack head to protect the paintwork. Engage the help of an assistant to support the door.

3 Ensure that the door is adequately supported, with the aid of an assistant, or using wooden blocks or similar under the

12.4a Door-to-hinge upper retaining bolts (arrowed)...

bottom edge of the door (take care not to damage the paintwork).

4 Mark the position of the hinges on the door, then unscrew the two upper bolts and single lower bolt, and remove the door from the car **(see illustrations)**.

Refitting and adjustment

5 Refitting is a reversal of the removal procedure, noting the following points:
a) *Check that the door is correctly aligned with the surrounding bodywork, with an equal clearance around its edge.*
b) *Adjustment can be made by loosening the hinge bolts, and moving the door within the elongated mounting holes.*
c) *Check that the lock enters the striker*

13.1a Prise up the front of the electric window/mirror control switch panel...

12.4b... and lower retaining bolt (arrowed)

centrally when the door is closed. If necessary, reposition the striker.

---

13 Door inner trim panel – removal and refitting

Front door

Removal

1 If working on the driver's door, using a plastic spatula or similar instrument, carefully prise up the front of the electric window/mirror control switch panel. Withdraw the switch panel and disconnect the wiring connector **(see illustrations)**.

13.1b... then withdraw the switch panel and disconnect the wiring connector

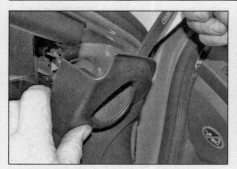

13.2a Prise free the speaker panel at the front of the door...

13.2b... then disconnect the wiring connector (arrowed) and remove the panel

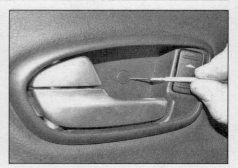

13.3a Remove the trim button from the centre of the inner door release handle trim panel...

13.3b... and undo the retaining screw now exposed

13.3c Operate the handle and manipulate the trim panel from the door

2 Again using a plastic spatula or similar, carefully prise free the speaker panel at the front of the door. Disconnect the speaker wiring connector and remove the panel **(see illustrations)**.

3 Using a small screwdriver, remove the circular trim button from the centre of the inner door release handle trim panel, and undo the retaining screw now exposed. Operate the handle and manipulate the trim panel from the door. Where applicable, disconnect the switch wiring connector and remove the panel **(see illustrations)**.

4 Using the plastic spatula or similar, carefully prise free and remove the door pull handle trim surround **(see illustration)**.

5 Undo the two screws securing the door pull handle to the door **(see illustration)**.

6 Undo the six screws securing the edges of the trim panel to the door. There are two screws at the rear, two screws at the bottom and two screws at the front **(see illustration)**.

7 Pull the panel away from the door and lift it upward to release it from the window aperture **(see illustration)**.

Refitting

8 Refitting is a reversal of removal.

Rear door

Removal

9 Where a manual window regulator is fitted, locate a cloth rag between the handle and the trim panel and pull it back and forth to release

13.3d Where applicable, disconnect the switch wiring connector and remove the panel

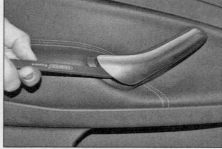

13.4 Carefully prise free and remove the door pull handle trim surround

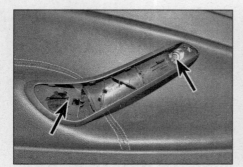

13.5 Undo the two screws (arrowed) securing the door pull handle to the door

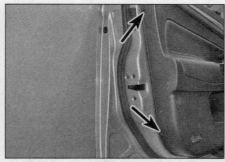

13.6 Door inner trim panel rear retaining screws (arrowed)

13.7 Pull the panel away from the door and lift it upward to release it from the window aperture

the spring clip. Alternatively use a proprietary regulator spring clip removal tool. Remove the handle from the splined shaft then remove the circular spacer **(see illustrations)**. Refit the spring clip to the handle.

10 Using a small screwdriver, remove the circular trim button from the centre of the inner door release handle trim panel, and undo the retaining screw now exposed. Operate the handle and manipulate the trim panel from the door. Where applicable, disconnect the switch wiring connector and remove the panel **(see illustrations 13.3a, 13.3b, 13.3c and 13.3d)**.

11 Using a plastic spatula or similar, carefully prise free and remove the door pull handle trim surround **(see illustration 13.4)**.

12 Undo the two screws securing the door pull handle to the door **(see illustration 13.5)**.

13 Undo the six screws securing the edges of the trim panel to the door. There are two screws at the rear, two screws at the bottom and two screws at the front **(see illustration)**.

14 Pull the panel away from the door and lift it upward to release it from the window aperture. Once the panel is free, disconnect the speaker wiring connector and remove the panel **(see illustrations)**.

Refitting

15 Refitting is a reversal of removal.

---

14 Door window glass –
    removal and refitting

Front door

Removal

1 Remove the door inner trim panel as described in Section 13.

2 Carefully prise up the door outer waist seal, starting at the rear and moving forward. Disengage the front of the waist seal from the door mirror housing and remove the seal **(see illustrations)**.

3 Disconnect the wiring connector, undo the three screws and remove the loudspeaker from the door.

4 Undo the retaining bolts and release the door control module from the door **(see illustration)**.

5 To gain access to the door components it is

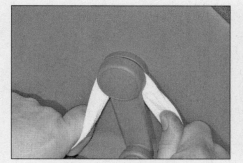

13.9a Use a clean cloth and a sawing motion to release the regulator handle retaining clip

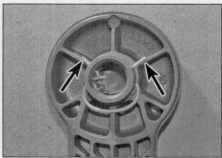

13.9b The ends of the clip (arrowed) must be pushed towards the handle

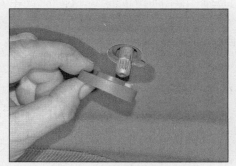

13.9c Recover the handle spacer

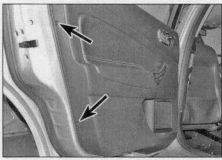

13.13 Door inner trim panel rear retaining screws (arrowed)

13.14a Pull the panel away from the door and lift it upward to release it from the window aperture

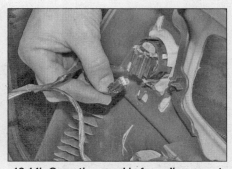

13.14b Once the panel is free, disconnect the speaker wiring connector

14.2a Carefully prise up the door outer waist seal, starting at the rear and moving forward...

14.2b... then disengage the front of the waist seal from the door mirror housing

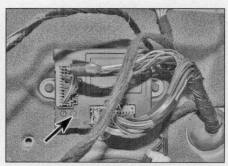

14.4 Undo the retaining bolts and release the door control module (arrowed) from the door

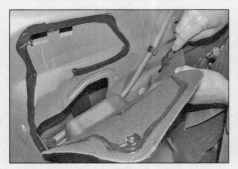

14.5 Carefully pull back the membrane while using a knife to cut along the bead of adhesive

14.7 Using a plastic spatula, spread the regulator fitting to disengage the glass

14.8 Tilt the glass up at the rear, and withdraw it from the outside of the door frame

necessary to remove the waterproof membrane. The membrane is attached to the door with a bead of mastic adhesive – carefully pull back the membrane without tearing it, while using a very sharp knife to cut along the bead of adhesive **(see illustration)**. Place the membrane to one side and protect the adhesive from dust and dirt so it can be used again.

6 Reconnect the electric window/mirror control switch panel wiring connector and lower the window glass approximately 200 mm until the glass-to-regulator attachment points are accessible through the door apertures.

7 The window glass is attached to the regulator in two places by means of a circular plastic fitting which engages with a hole in the glass. Using a plastic spatula or similar tool, reach behind the glass and spread the plastic fitting, while at the same time lifting the glass

upward **(see illustration)**. Release the other end of the glass in the same way.

8 Once the glass has been released from the regulator, tilt it up at the rear, and withdraw it from the outside of the door frame **(see illustration)**.

Refitting

9 Refitting is a reversal of removal, ensuring that the glass fully engages with the plastic fittings on the regulator.

Rear door

Removal

10 Fully lower the window.

11 Remove the door inner trim panel as described in Section 13.

12 Disconnect the wiring connector, undo the three screws and remove the loudspeaker from the door.

13 Undo the retaining bolts and release the door control module from the door **(see illustration)**.

14 To gain access to the door components it is necessary to remove the waterproof membrane. The membrane is attached to the door with a bead of mastic adhesive – carefully pull back the membrane without tearing it, while using a very sharp knife to cut along the bead of adhesive **(see illustration)**. Place the membrane to one side and protect the adhesive from dust and dirt so it can be used again.

15 Pull the lower ends of the door frame upper trim away from the frame at the front and rear to release the retaining clips **(see illustrations)**.

16 Carefully prise free the inner and outer waist seals from the door **(see illustrations)**.

14.13 Undo the retaining bolts and release the door control module (arrowed) from the door

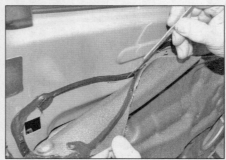

14.14 Carefully pull back the membrane while using a knife to cut along the bead of adhesive

14.15a Pull the lower ends of the door frame upper trim away from the frame at the front…

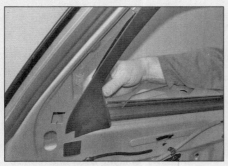

14.15b… and at the rear

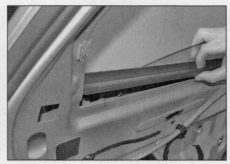

14.16a Carefully prise free the inner waist seal…

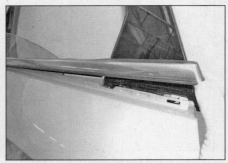

14.16b… and outer waist seal from the door

17 Release the window guide rubber from the door frame at the rear for access to the exterior trim panel attachments **(see illustration)**.

18 Undo the two screws securing the exterior trim panel to the door frame **(see illustration)**.

19 Extract the plastic fastener and remove the exterior trim panel from the door**(see illustrations)**.

20 Undo the screw from the regulator lifting channel clamp**(see illustration)**.

21 The window glass is attached to the regulator by means of a circular plastic fitting which engages with a hole in the glass. Using a plastic spatula or similar tool, reach behind the glass and spread the plastic fitting, while at the same time lifting the glass upward **(see illustration)**.

22 Once the glass has been released from the regulator, lift it up and withdraw it from the outside of the door frame **(see illustration)**.

Refitting

23 Refitting is a reversal of removal, ensuring that the glass fully engages with the plastic fitting on the regulator.

---

15 Door window regulator – removal and refitting

Front door

Removal

1 Remove the door inner trim panel as described in Section 13.

2 Release the door window glass from the regulator as described in Section 14 – the glass can be raised and taped to the door frame, as it does not have to be removed completely.

3 Disconnect the regulator wiring connector **(see illustration)**.

4 Slacken the five bolts securing the

14.17 Release the window guide rubber from the door frame at the rear

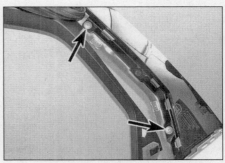

14.18 Undo the two screws (arrowed) securing the exterior trim panel to the door frame

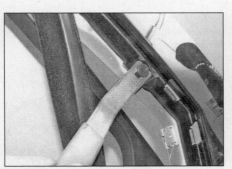

14.19a Extract the plastic fastener...

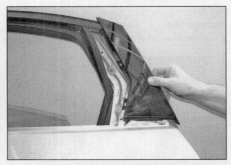

14.19b... and remove the exterior trim panel from the door

14.20 Undo the screw (arrowed) from the regulator lifting channel clamp

14.21 Using a plastic spatula, spread the regulator fitting to disengage the glass

14.22 Lift the glass up and withdraw it from the outside of the door frame

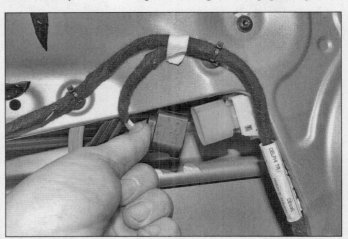

15.3 Disconnect the front door window regulator wiring connector

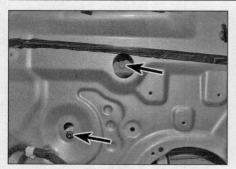

15.4a Slacken the window regulator upper rear retaining bolts (arrowed)…

15.4b… lower rear retaining bolt (arrowed)…

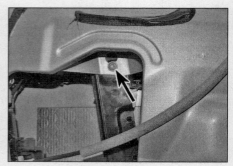

15.4c… upper front retaining bolt (arrowed)…

regulator to the door panel by two turns (see illustrations).

5 Lift the regulator to disengage the mounting

bolts from their elongated holes, then manipulate the regulator down and out of the door aperture (see illustration).

6 If required, the motor can be removed from the regulator after undoing the three retaining bolts (see illustration).

Refitting

7 Refitting is a reversal of removal.

Rear door

Removal

8 Remove the door inner trim panel as described in Section 13.

9 Release the door window glass from the regulator as described in Section 14 – the glass can be raised and taped to the door frame, as it does not have to be removed completely.

10 On models with electric windows, reach through the loudspeaker aperture and disconnect the regulator wiring connector (see illustration).

11 Slacken the five bolts (manually-operated windows) or three bolts (electrically-operated windows) securing the regulator to the door panel by two turns (see illustration).

12 Lift the regulator to disengage the mounting bolts from their elongated holes, then manipulate the regulator down and out of the door aperture (see illustration).

13 On models with electrically-operated windows, if required, the motor can be removed from the regulator after undoing the three retaining bolts (see illustration).

Refitting

14 Refitting is a reversal of removal.

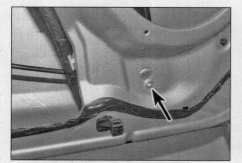

15.4d… and lower front retaining bolt (arrowed)

15.5 Manipulate the regulator down and out of the door aperture

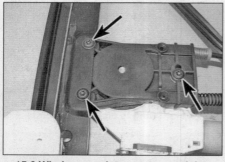

15.6 Window regulator motor retaining bolts (arrowed)

15.10 Disconnect the rear door window regulator wiring connector

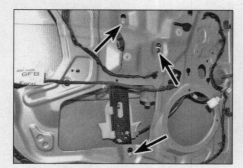

15.11 Window regulator retaining bolts (arrowed) – models with electric windows

15.12 Manipulate the regulator down and out of the door aperture

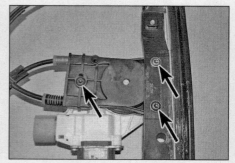

15.13 Window regulator motor retaining bolts (arrowed)

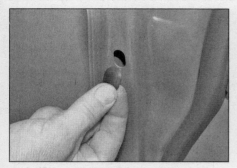

16.1 Prise out the rubber grommet from the end of the door

16.2a Slacken the handle retaining bolt...

16.2b... until the lock cylinder can be pulled from the door

16.3a Pull the exterior handle rearwards, and manoeuvre it from the door

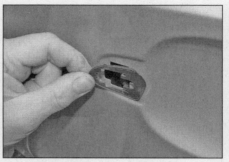

16.3b Recover the front seal...

16.3c... and rear seal between the handle and the door skin

16.4 On models with the Keyless Entry system, disconnect the wiring plug

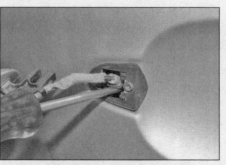

16.5 On models with the Keyless Entry system, lift the wiring connector with a small screwdriver and push it back into the door

Refitting

5 Refitting is a reversal of removal. When refitting the exterior handle on models with the Keyless Entry system, reconnect the wiring connector, then lift the connector with a small screwdriver and push it back into the door **(see illustration)**.

Rear door exterior handle

Removal

6 Prise out the rubber grommet from the end of the door adjacent to the exterior handle **(see illustration 16.1)**.

7 Working through the aperture, slacken the handle retaining bolt until the rear portion of the handle can be pulled from the door **(see illustrations)**.

8 Pull the exterior handle rearwards, and

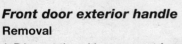
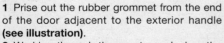

16 Door handles and lock components – removal and refitting

Front door exterior handle

Removal

1 Prise out the rubber grommet from the end of the door adjacent to the exterior handle **(see illustration)**.

2 Working through the aperture, slacken the handle retaining bolt until the lock cylinder can be pulled from the door **(see illustrations)**.

3 Pull the exterior handle rearwards, and manoeuvre it from the door. Recover the seals between the handle and the door skin **(see illustrations)**.

4 On models with the Keyless Entry system,

gently pull the handle wiring harness until an audible click is heard, and the harness connector is in the horizontal position. Disconnect the wiring plug **(see illustration)**.

16.7a Slacken the handle retaining bolt...

16.7b... until the rear portion of the handle can be pulled from the door

16.8 Pull the exterior handle rearwards, and manoeuvre it from the door

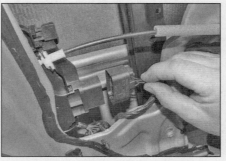

16.11a Disconnect the central locking motor wiring connector…

16.11b… and, where fitted, the Keyless Entry system wiring connector

manoeuvre it from the door (see illustration). Recover the seals between the handle and the door skin.

Refitting

9 Refitting is a reversal of removal.

Front door lock
Removal

10 Remove the door exterior handle as described previously in this Section.

11 Disconnect the central locking motor wiring connector from the lock. On models

with the Keyless Entry system, disengage the wiring connector from the clip on the door panel then disconnect the connector (see illustrations).

12 Undo the screw securing the interior handle to the door panel. Slide the handle forward to disengage the rear locating stud, then release the operating cable from the clip on the door panel (see illustrations).

13 Undo the three lock assembly retaining screws at the rear edge of the door and the single screw in the exterior handle aperture (see illustrations).

14 Remove the lock assembly, complete with interior handle, through the door aperture (see illustration).

15 To remove the operating cables, release the outer cable end fittings from their supports using a small screwdriver, then disengage the inner cable end fittings from the operating levers (see illustrations).

16.12a Undo the screw (arrowed) securing the interior handle to the door panel…

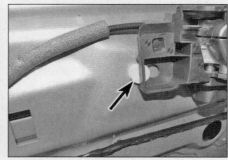

16.12b… slide the handle forward to disengage the rear locating stud (arrowed)…

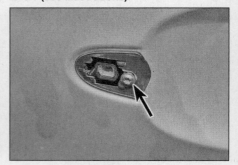

16.13b… and the single screw (arrowed) in the exterior handle aperture

16.12c… then release the operating cable from the clip (arrowed) on the door panel

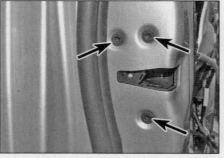

16.13a Undo the lock assembly retaining screws (arrowed) at the rear of the door…

16.14 Remove the lock assembly through the door aperture

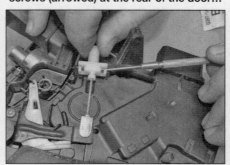

16.15a To remove the operating cables, release the outer cable end fittings…

16.15b… then disengage the inner cable end fittings from the operating levers

16.18a Disconnect the central locking motor wiring connector

16.18b On models with the Keyless Entry system, disengage the wiring connector…

16.18c… and wiring harness from the clips on the door panel…

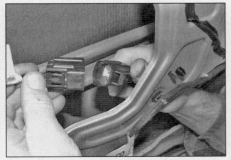

16.18d… then disconnect the connector

16.19a Undo the screw (arrowed) securing the interior handle to the door panel…

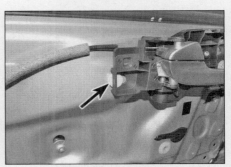

16.19b… slide the handle forward to disengage the rear locating stud (arrowed)…

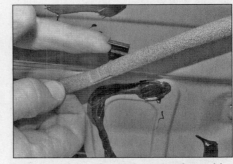

16.19c… then release the operating cable from the clip on the door panel

Refitting

16 Refitting is a reversal of removal.

Rear door lock

Removal

17 Remove the door exterior handle as described previously in this Section.

18 Disconnect the central locking motor wiring connector from the lock. On models with the Keyless Entry system, disengage the wiring connector and wiring harness from the clips on the door panel then disconnect the connector (see illustrations).

19 Undo the screw securing the interior handle to the door panel. Slide the handle forward to disengage the rear locating stud, then release the operating cable from the clip on the door panel (see illustrations).

20 Undo the four lock assembly retaining screws at the rear edge and inside the door,

and the single screw in the exterior handle aperture (see illustrations).

21 Remove the lock assembly, complete with interior handle, through the door aperture (see illustration).

22 To remove the operating cables, release the outer cable end fitting from the support using a small screwdriver, then disengage the inner cable end fitting from the operating lever (see illustrations 16.15a and 16.15b).

Refitting

23 Refitting is a reversal of removal.

Front lock cylinder

Removal

24 Prise out the rubber grommet from the end of the door adjacent to the exterior handle (see illustration 16.1).

25 Working through the aperture, slacken the handle retaining bolt until the lock cylinder can be pulled from the door (see illus-

trations 16.2a and 16.2b). If required, release the clip each side with a small screwdriver, and separate the lock cylinder from the trim

Refitting

26 Refitting is a reversal of removal.

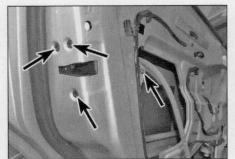

16.20a Undo the lock assembly retaining screws (arrowed)…

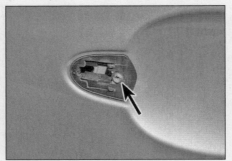

16.20b… and the single screw (arrowed) in the exterior handle aperture

16.21 Remove the lock assembly through the door aperture

17.3a Carefully prise up the tailgate exterior moulding above the number plate...

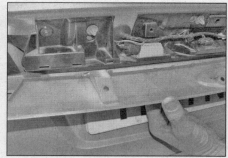

17.3b... then remove the moulding from the tailgate

17.4 Disconnect the wiring connectors at the number plate lights (arrowed) and tailgate lock switches

17 Tailgate and support struts – removal, refitting and adjustment

Tailgate – Hatchback models

Removal

1 Remove the tailgate trim panel as described in Section 27.

2 Remove the high-level brake light as described in Chapter 12 Section 7.

3 Using a plastic spatula, and starting at the upper right-hand corner, carefully prise up the tailgate exterior moulding above the number plate. Continue working across the top of the moulding until all the clips have been released then remove the moulding from the tailgate **(see illustrations)**.

4 With the moulding removed, disconnect the wiring connectors at the number plate lights and tailgate lock switches and free the harness from the retaining clips **(see illustration)**. Release the grommet from the tailgate inner panel and pull the wiring through.

5 Disconnect the wiring connectors at all the tailgate components and disconnect the washer tube at the connector at the top of the tailgate.

6 If the same tailgate is being refitted, tie a length of string to the wiring harness and washer tube beforehand – the string can then be untied when it emerges from the top of the tailgate, and left in place to pull the harness and washer tube back through. Prise out the rubber gaiters at the top of the tailgate, and carefully start to pull through the wiring and washer tube **(see illustration)**.

7 Using a pencil or marker pen, mark the position of the hinges on the tailgate to aid refitting.

8 Engage the help of an assistant to support the tailgate, then disconnect the support struts as described later in this Section.

9 Unscrew the four bolts securing the hinges to the tailgate, and lift the tailgate from the car **(see illustration)**.

Refitting and adjustment

10 Refitting is a reversal of removal, bearing in mind the following points:

a) Make sure that the hinges are aligned with the marks made before removal.

b) Use the string to pull the wiring harness and the washer fluid hose into position in the tailgate.

c) On completion, check the alignment of the tailgate with the surrounding body panels and, if necessary, adjust the position of the tailgate hinges and/or tailgate lock striker plate within the elongated holes until satisfactory alignment is achieved.

Tailgate – Estate models

Removal

11 Remove the tailgate trim panel as described in Section 27.

12 Remove the high-level brake light as described in Chapter 12 Section 7.

13 From inside the tailgate, undo the nuts securing the number plate light panel to the tailgate **(see illustration)**.

14 Undo the two outer screws and withdraw the number plate light panel from the tailgate **(see illustrations)**.

15 With the light panel released, disconnect

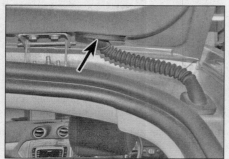

17.6 Prise out the rubber gaiters (arrowed) at the top of the tailgate

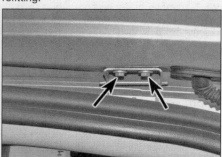

17.9 Tailgate retaining bolts (arrowed)

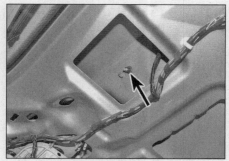

17.13 Number plate light panel retaining nut (arrowed)

17.14a Undo the two outer screws (arrowed)...

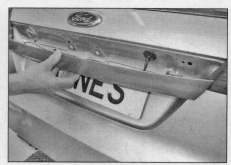

17.14b... and withdraw the number plate light panel from the tailgate

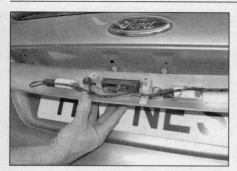

17.15 Disconnect the wiring connectors and free the harness from the retaining clips

the wiring connectors at the number plate lights and tailgate lock switches, and free the harness from the retaining clips **(see illustration)**. Release the grommet from the tailgate inner panel and pull the wiring through.

16 If the same tailgate is being refitted, tie a length of string to the wiring harness and washer tube beforehand – the string can then be untied when it emerges from the top of the tailgate, and left in place to pull the harness and washer tube back through. Disconnect the wiring connectors at all the tailgate components, then prise out the rubber gaiters at the top of the tailgate, and carefully start to pull through the wiring and washer tube **(see illustration 17.6)**.

17 Using a pencil or marker pen, mark the position of the hinges on the tailgate to aid refitting.

18.2a Disconnect the wiring plug (arrowed) from the lock assembly...

18.6a Number plate light panel left-hand retaining screws (arrowed)...

17.22 Lever off the retaining clip from the support strut

18 Engage the help of an assistant to support the tailgate, then disconnect the support struts as described later in this Section.

19 Unscrew the four bolts securing the hinges to the tailgate, and lift the tailgate from the car **(see illustration 17.9)**.

Refitting and adjustment

20 Refitting is a reversal of removal, bearing in mind the following points:
a) *Make sure that the hinges are aligned with the marks made before removal.*
b) *Use the string to pull the wiring harness and the washer fluid hose into position in the tailgate.*
c) *On completion, check the alignment of the tailgate with the surrounding body panels and, if necessary, adjust the position of the tailgate hinges and/or tailgate lock striker plate within the elongated holes until satisfactory alignment is achieved.*

18.2b... then unscrew the three lock mounting bolts, and withdraw the lock

18.6b... and right-hand retaining screws (arrowed)

Support struts

Removal

21 Open the tailgate, and support it in the open position, using a wooden prop or similar tool. Note that the tailgate is heavy, and will fall closed if either of the support struts are disconnected.

22 Working at the top end of the strut, lever off the retaining clip, and prise off the end of the strut from the lug on the tailgate **(see illustration)**.

23 Repeat the procedure at the bottom end of the strut, and withdraw the strut.

Refitting

24 Refitting is a reversal of removal.

---

18 Tailgate lock components – removal and refitting

Lock assembly

Removal

1 Remove the tailgate trim panel as described in Section 27.

2 Disconnect the wiring plug from the lock assembly, then unscrew the three lock mounting bolts, and withdraw the lock **(see illustrations)**.

Refitting

3 Refitting is a reversal of removal, but check the operation of the lock mechanism before refitting the tailgate trim panel.

Release and lock switches

Hatchback models

4 Remove the tailgate trim panel as described in Section 27.

5 Using a plastic spatula, and starting at the upper right-hand corner, carefully prise up the tailgate exterior moulding above the number plate. Continue working across the top of the moulding until all the clips have been released then remove the moulding from the tailgate **(see illustrations 17.3a and 17.3b)**.

6 Undo the four screws securing the number plate light panel to the tailgate and withdraw the panel **(see illustrations)**.

7 Disconnect the wiring connectors at the number plate lights and at the release and lock switches **(see illustration)**. Release

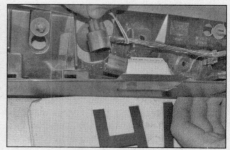

18.7 Disconnect the wiring connectors at the number plate lights and at the release and lock switches

18.8a Depress the tab at the side of the switch...

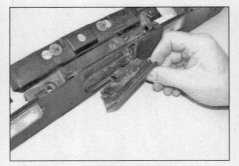

18.8b... and remove the relevant switch from the panel – Hatchback models

18.14 Depress the tab at the side of the switch and remove the relevant switch from the panel – Estate models

the wiring from the cable-ties and clips and remove the number plate light panel.

8 Depress the tab at the side of the switch and remove the relevant switch from the panel **(see illustrations)**.

9 Refitting is a reversal of removal, but check the operation of the lock mechanism before refitting the tailgate trim panel.

Estate models

10 Remove the tailgate trim panel as described in Section 27.

11 From inside the tailgate, undo the two nuts securing the number plate light panel to the tailgate **(see illustration 17.13)**.

12 Undo the two outer screws and withdraw the light panel from the tailgate **(see illustrations 17.14a and 17.14b)**.

13 Disconnect the wiring connectors at the number plate lights, and tailgate release and lock switches **(see illustration 17.15)**. Release the wiring from the cable-ties and clips, and remove the number plate light panel.

14 Depress the tab at the side of the switch and remove the relevant switch from the panel **(see illustration)**.

15 Refitting is a reversal of removal, but check the operation of the lock mechanism before refitting the tailgate trim panel.

19 Central locking system – testing, reprogramming, removal and refitting

Testing/reprogramming

1 Testing of the central locking/alarm system can only be carried out using Ford diagnostic test equipment.

2 Prior to reprogramming a remote locking transmitter, ensure the vehicle battery is fully-charged, and the alarm is not armed or triggered. Close all doors to ensure conflicting chimes do not sound during programming.

3 Turn the ignition switch from position 0 to position II four times within 6 seconds, then turn it back to position I.

4 A chime will be heard to indicate that the 'learning mode' has begun.

5 Within 10 seconds of the previous step,

press and hold any button on the remote transmitter until a further chime is heard. This indicates the process has been successful.

6 The system will now return to the 'learning mode' for a further 10 seconds and additional transmitters (up to a maximum of 8) can be programmed as described in paragraph 5. If no further transmitters are programmed, the system will return to normal mode after 10 sec- onds.

Removal

Door lock motors

7 The door lock motors are integral with the locks. Refer to Section 16.

Tailgate/boot lid lock motor

8 The tailgate/boot lid lock motor is integral with the lock. Refer to Section 18 or Section 11.

Generic electronic module (GEM)

Note: *If the GEM is to be renewed, the unit settings must be saved prior to removal, then initialised using Ford diagnostic test equipment.*

9 Removal and refitting of the GEM is described in Chapter 12 Section 22.

Keyless entry system module

Note: *If the module is to be renewed, the unit settings must be saved prior to removal, then initialised using Ford diagnostic test equipment.*

10 Remove the loadspace side trim on the right-hand side as described in Section 27.

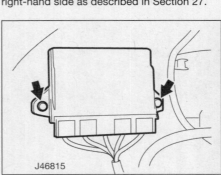

19.11 Keyless entry system module retaining bolts (arrowed)

11 Undo the two retaining bolts, and remove the module **(see illustration)**. Disconnect the wiring plugs as the module is withdrawn.

Keyless entry system front aerial

12 Remove the centre console as described in Section 28.

13 Disconnect the wiring plug from the aerial which is located in the centre of the facia, below the ashtray **(see illustration)**.

14 Undo the two retaining bolts and remove the aerial from its location.

Keyless entry system centre aerial

15 Remove the centre console as described in Section 28.

16 The aerial is located on the underside of the centre console at the rear. Undo the two retaining bolts and remove the aerial from its location.

Keyless entry system rear aerial

17 Remove the rear bumper as described in Section 6.

18 Disconnect the wiring plug from the aerial which is located in the centre of the rear bumper brace.

19 Undo the two retaining bolts and remove the aerial from its location.

Keyless entry system luggage compartment aerial

20 Remove the luggage compartment floor covering.

21 Disconnect the wiring plug from the aerial which is located in the centre of the luggage

19.13 Keyless entry system front aerial (arrowed)

compartment floor, just behind the rear seat backrest.

22 Undo the two retaining bolts and remove the aerial from its location.

Keyless entry system door aerial

23 Remove the front door exterior handle as described in Section 16.

24 Undo the screw at each end and separate the two halves of the handle **(see illustrations)**.

25 Free the wiring harness from the handle pivot, then lift out the aerial and release button assembly **(see illustration)**.

Refitting

26 In all cases, refitting is a reversal of removal.

---

20 Exterior mirrors and associated components – removal and refitting

Mirror

Removal

1 Remove the front door inner trim panel as described in Section 13.

2 Disconnect the mirror wiring from the connector on the inside of the door **(see illustration)**.

3 Suitably support the mirror and undo the mirror body retaining bolt **(see illustration)**.

4 Withdraw the mirror and wiring harness from the outside of the door **(see illustration)**.

Refitting

5 Refitting is a reversal of removal.

Mirror motor

6 The motor is integral with the mirror, and cannot be renewed separately. If faulty, the complete mirror assembly must be renewed.

Mirror switch

Removal

7 Using a plastic spatula or similar instrument, carefully prise up the front of the electric window/mirror control switch panel from the door inner trim panel. Withdraw the switch panel and disconnect the wiring connector **(see illustrations 13.1a and 13.1b)**.

Refitting

8 Refitting is a reversal of removal.

Mirror glass

Warning: If the mirror glass is broken, wear gloves to protect your hands.

Removal

9 Pull the outer edge of the glass rearwards, insert a plastic spatula or similar tool, and gently prise the glass from place **(see illustration)**.

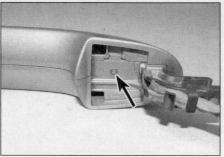

19.24a Undo the rear retaining screw (arrowed)...

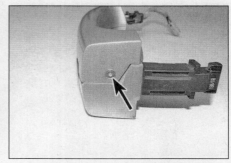

19.24b... and front retaining screw (arrowed)...

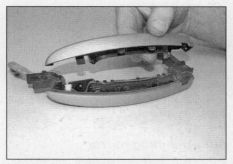

19.24c... and separate the two halves of the handle

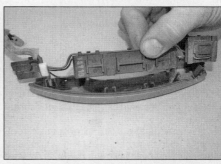

19.25 Free the wiring harness, then lift out the aerial and release button assembly

20.2 Disconnect the mirror wiring from the connector on the inside of the door

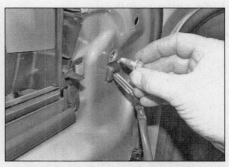

20.3 Undo the mirror body retaining bolt

20.4 Withdraw the mirror and wiring harness from the outside of the door

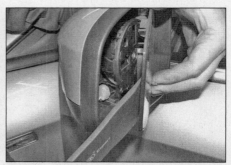

20.9 Insert a plastic spatula or similar tool, and gently prise the mirror glass from place

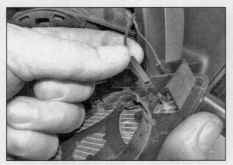

20.10 Withdraw the mirror glass and, where fitted, disconnect the wiring connectors

20.13a Using a plastic spatula or similar tool, release the internal retaining clips...

20.13b... and withdraw the cover from the mirror body

10 Withdraw the mirror glass and, where fitted, disconnect the wiring connectors for the heated mirrors **(see illustration)**.

Refitting

11 Refitting is a reversal of removal.

Mirror cover

Removal

12 Remove the mirror glass as described previously.

13 Using a plastic spatula or similar tool, release the internal retaining clips and withdraw the cover from the mirror body **(see illustrations)**.

Refitting

14 Refitting is a reversal of removal.

Side approach light

15 Refer to Chapter 12 Section 7.

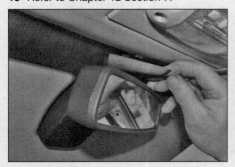

21.3 Squeeze together the sides, and slide up the mirror base upper cover

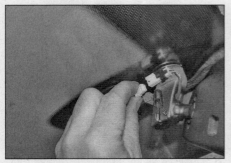

21.5 Where applicable, disconnect the mirror wiring plug

21 Interior mirror – removal and refitting

Basic mirror

1 Press the retaining clip away from the windscreen, then slide the mirror up from the base.

2 Refitting is a reversal of removal.

Auto-dimming mirror

3 Squeeze together the sides, and slide up the mirror base upper cover **(see illustration)**.

4 Pull apart the top edges and slide down the mirror base lower cover **(see illustration)**.

5 Where applicable, disconnect the mirror wiring plug **(see illustration)**.

6 Rotate the mirror base 60° anti-clockwise

21.4 Pull apart the top edges and slide down the mirror base lower cover

21.6 Rotate the mirror base 60° anti-clockwise and detach it from the mounting

and detach it from the mounting **(see illustration)**.

7 Refitting is a reversal of removal.

22 Windscreen, tailgate and fixed window glass – general information

1 These areas of glass are secured by the tight fit of the weatherseal in the body aperture, and are bonded in position with a special adhesive. Renewal of such fixed glass is a difficult, messy and time-consuming task, which is considered beyond the scope of the home mechanic. It is difficult, unless one has plenty of practise, to obtain a secure, waterproof fit. Furthermore, the task carries a high risk of breakage; this applies especially to the laminated glass windscreen. In view of this, owners are strongly advised to have this sort of work carried out by one of the many specialist windscreen fitters.

23 Body exterior fittings – removal and refitting

Radiator grille panel

Removal

1 Remove the front bumper as described in Section 6.

2 The radiator grille panel and the other detachable panels on the bumper are retained by a series of plastic clips, the location of which will become obvious on visual inspection.

3 Carefully disengage all the relevant clips using a small screwdriver, while at the same time pulling the panel from its location.

Refitting

4 Push the panel carefully into place ensuring that all the retaining clips engage fully.

Bumpers

5 Refer to Section 6.

Windscreen cowl panel

Removal

6 Remove the windscreen wiper arms as described in Chapter 12 Section 13.

23.7a Extract the three fasteners (arrowed)...

23.7b... and remove the plastic panel above the wing on both sides

23.8a Unscrew the cowl panel retaining screws...

23.8b... lift the panel away from the windscreen at the top...

23.8c... and remove the panel from the car

23.13 Pull the wheel arch liner down from the arch and remove it

7 Extract the three fasteners and remove the plastic panel above the wing on both sides **(see illustrations)**.

8 Unscrew the cowl panel retaining screws, lift the panel away from the windscreen at the top and remove the panel from the car **(see illustrations)**.

Refitting

9 Refitting is a reversal of removal.

Wheel arch liners

Removal

10 The wheel arch liners are secured by a combination of nuts, self-tapping screws and push-pin clips.

11 The push-pin clips are removed by prising out the centre expanding pin, then prising out the main clip body.

12 The metal star clips used to unscrew from their mounting studs – now the metal tabs have to be prised up at the centre with a small screwdriver to release them.

13 With all the fasteners removed, pull the liner down from the arch and remove it **(see illustration)**.

Refitting

14 Refitting is a reversal of removal.

Body trim strips and badges

15 The various body trim strips and badges are held in position with a special adhesive. Removal requires the trim/badge to be heated, to soften the adhesive, and then cut away from the surface. Due to the high risk of damage to the paintwork during this operation, it is recommended that this task should be entrusted to a Ford dealer.

24 Sunroof – general information

1 An electric sunroof is offered as an optional extra on most models, and is fitted as standard equipment on some models.

2 Due to the complexity of the sunroof mechanism, considerable expertise is needed to repair, renew or adjust the sunroof components successfully. Removal of the roof first requires the headlining to be removed, which is a complex and tedious operation in itself, and not a task to be undertaken lightly (see Section 27). Therefore, any problems with the sunroof should be referred to a Ford dealer.

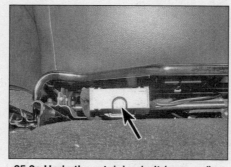

25.2a Undo the retaining bolt (arrowed)...

25 Seats – removal and refitting

Front seat

⚠ *Warning: Side airbags are built into the outer sides of the front seats. Refer to Chapter 12 Section 23 for the precautions which should be observed when dealing with an airbag system.*

1 Disconnect the battery negative lead as described in Chapter 5A Section 4, and wait a minimum of three minutes before proceeding.

2 Undo the retaining bolt and disconnect the wiring connector under the front of the seat **(see illustrations)**.

3 Slide the seat fully rearwards, then unscrew

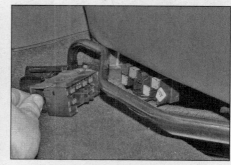

25.2b... and disconnect the wiring connector under the front of the seat

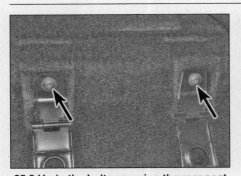

25.8 Undo the bolts securing the rear seat cushion hinges (arrowed)

25.11 Release the catch and lift the outer end of the backrest

25.12 Pull the backrest from the pivot to disengage the mounting pin

the two front Torx bolts securing the seat rails to the floor.

4 Slide the seat fully forwards, then unscrew the two rear Torx bolts.

5 Lift the seat, complete with mounting rails, and remove it from the car.

6 Refitting is a reversal of removal, but tighten the seat mounting bolts to the specified torque.

Rear seat

Cushion

7 Unclip the plastic trim from the hinges at the front of each seat cushion.

8 Unscrew and remove the Torx mounting bolts from the hinges **(see illustration)**, then

withdraw the seat cushion from inside the vehicle.

9 Refitting is a reversal of removal, but tighten the seat mounting bolts securely.

Backrest

10 Fold the rear seat cushion forwards (if not already removed), and fold the backrest forward.

11 Use a screwdriver to force the locking catch rearwards, and lift the outer end of the backrest from the hinge **(see illustration)**.

12 Pull the backrest from the centre pivot to disengage the mounting pin **(see illustration)**. If necessary, undo the seat belt stalk mounting bolt and manoeuvre the backrest from the vehicle.

13 Refitting is a reversal of removal.

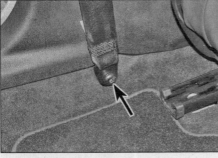

26.2 Front seat belt lower anchorage bolt (arrowed)

26.4 Front seat belt upper anchorage bolt (arrowed)

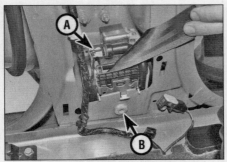

26.6 Front seat belt inertia reel wiring connector (A) and mounting bolt (B)

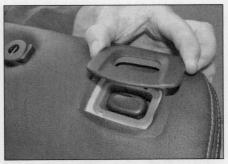

26.10 Undo and remove the bolt (arrowed) for the rear side seat belt lower anchorage – Saloon and Hatchback models

26 Seat belts – removal and refitting

Front seat belt

1 Disconnect the battery negative lead as described in Chapter 5A Section 4.

⚠️ *Warning: Before proceeding, wait a minimum of 3 minutes, as a precaution against accidental firing of the seat belt tensioner, incorporated in the inertia reel. This period ensures that any residual electrical energy is dissipated.*

⚠️ *Warning: There is a potential risk of the seat belt tensioning device firing during removal, so it should be handled carefully. Once removed, treat it with care – do not allow use chemicals on or near it, and do not expose it to high temperatures, or it may detonate.*

2 Undo and remove the bolt for the lower seat belt anchorage **(see illustration)**. Note that the spacer and washer are integral with the bolt.

3 Remove the B-pillar trim panel as described in Section 27.

4 Undo the seat belt upper anchorage bolt from the height adjuster **(see illustration)**.

5 Rotate the seat belt guide loop anticlockwise and remove it from the B-pillar.

6 Disconnect the inertia reel wiring connector, then unscrew the mounting bolt, and lift seat belt reel unit to remove it from the base of the pillar **(see illustration)**.

7 Refitting is a reversal of the removal procedure, tightening the mounting bolts to the specified torque.

Rear side seat belt

Saloon and Hatchback models

8 On Saloon models, remove the loadspace side trim as described in Section 27.

9 On Hatchback models, remove the parcel shelf support as described in Section 27.

10 Undo and remove the bolt for the seat belt lower anchorage **(see illustration)**. Note that the spacer and washer are integral with the bolt.

11 Undo the inertia reel mounting bolt and

26.11 Undo the inertia reel mounting bolt (arrowed) and remove the seat belt and reel – Saloon and Hatchback models

remove the seat belt and reel from the car **(see illustration)**.

12 Refitting is a reversal of the removal procedure, tightening the mounting bolts to the specified torque.

Estate models

13 Remove the loadspace side trim as described in Section 27.

14 Undo and remove the bolt for the seat belt lower anchorage **(see illustration 26.9)**. Note that the spacer and washer are integral with the bolt.

15 Lift off the trim cover and undo the seat belt upper anchorage bolt. Note that the spacer and washer are integral with the bolt.

16 Undo the three nuts and remove the inertia reel cover plate**(see illustrations)**.

17 Undo the inertia reel mounting bolt and remove the seat belt and reel from the car**(see illustration)**.

18 Refitting is a reversal of the removal procedure, tightening the mounting bolts to the specified torque.

Rear centre seat belt

19 The centre rear seat belt reel is attached to the rear seat backrest. Remove the backrest as described in Section 25.

20 Use a screwdriver to prise up the backrest release button surround trim, releasing the clips **(see illustration)**.

21 Push down the backrest padding and use a screwdriver to depress the clip on the side of the headrest guide tubes **(see illustrations)**. Pull the guide tubes from the backrest.

26.16a Undo the three nuts (arrowed)...

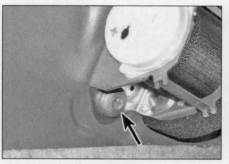

26.17 Undo the inertia reel mounting bolt (arrowed) and remove the seat belt and reel – Estate models

22 Prise free the front of the seat belt guide trim from the top of the backrest, then disengage the two rear locating tangs. Feed

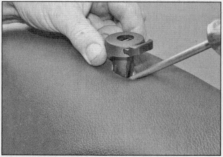

26.21a Push in the clip and pull the headrest guide tube from the backrest

26.16b... and remove the inertia reel cover plate – Estate models

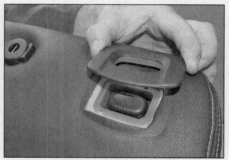

26.20 Prise up the backrest release button surround trim

the seat belt through the slot in the trim **(see illustrations)**.

23 Carefully prise out the beading securing

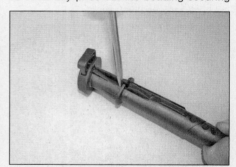

26.21b Depress the headrest guide tube clip (arrowed) – shown with the tube removed

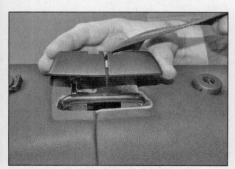

26.22a Prise free the front of the seat belt guide trim...

26.22b... disengage the two rear locating tangs...

26.22c... and feed the seat belt through the slot in the trim

26.23a Prise out the beading securing the top half of the backrest seat fabric...

26.23b... then peel back the fabric

26.24 Undo the bolt (arrowed) securing the inertia reel to the backrest

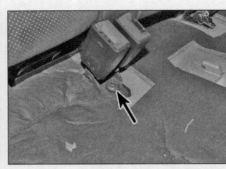

26.30 Rear seat belt buckle retaining bolt (arrowed)

the top half of the backrest seat fabric, then peel back the fabric to gain access to the inertia reel mounting bolt **(see illustrations)**.
24 Undo the bolt securing the inertia reel to the backrest **(see illustration)**.

25 Carefully pull the seat foam padding from the top part of the backrest and manoeuvre the seat belt reel from the seat backrest. Feed the seat belt through the seat backrest bracket as the reel is withdrawn.

26 Refitting is a reversal of the removal procedure, tightening the mounting bolts to the specified torque.

Front seat belt stalks

27 The front seat belt stalks are bolted to the seat frame and can be removed after removing the front seat as described in Section 25.
28 Refitting is a reversal of the removal procedure, tightening the mounting bolts to the specified torque.

Rear seat belt buckles

29 Remove the rear seat cushion as described in Section 25.
30 Undo the retaining bolt and remove the buckle(s) from the car **(see illustration)**.
31 Refitting is a reversal of the removal procedure, tightening the mounting bolts to the specified torque.

27 Interior trim and fittings – removal and refitting

General

1 The interior trim panels are secured by a combination of clips and screws, with easily-broken plastic clips featuring heavily. Removal and refitting is generally self-explanatory, noting that it may be necessary to remove or loosen surrounding panels to allow a particular panel to be removed. The following paragraphs describe the removal and refitting of the major panels in more detail.

Door inner trim panels

2 Refer to Section 13.

Steering column shrouds

Upper shroud

3 To release the upper shroud from the lower shroud, turn the steering wheel 90°, insert a thin screwdriver into the hole at each side of the column and release the retaining tabs. Lift the upper shroud from the column and unclip it from the bottom of the instrument panel **(see illustrations)**.
4 Refitting is a reversal of removal.

Lower shroud

5 Remove the upper shroud as described previously.
6 Undo the two retaining screws, then lower the steering column height adjuster lever, and withdraw the lower shroud. Disconnect the wiring connector (where applicable) and remove the shroud **(see illustrations)**.
7 Refitting is a reversal of removal.

Lower facia trim panel

Driver's side

⚠ *Warning: A knee airbag is incorporated in the lower facia trim panel. Refer to Chapter 12 Section 23 for the precautions which should be observed when dealing with an airbag system.*

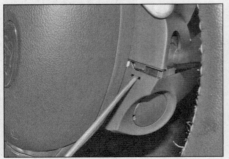

27.3a Release the retaining tabs...

27.3b... then lift off the upper shroud and unclip it from the instrument panel

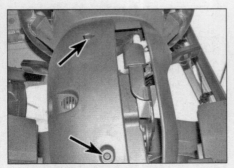

27.6a Undo the two screws (arrowed)...

27.6b... then withdraw the lower shroud and disconnect the wiring connector

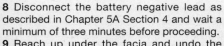

27.9 Undo the nuts from the studs (arrowed) securing the airbag to the facia frame – shown with trim panel removed

27.10 Pull the base of the panel away from the facia to release the clips along the lower edge...

27.11... then withdraw the panel and disconnect the wiring connector

8 Disconnect the battery negative lead as described in Chapter 5A Section 4 and wait a minimum of three minutes before proceeding.
9 Reach up under the facia and undo the two nuts securing the airbag to the facia frame **(see illustration)**.
10 Pull the base of the panel away from the facia to release the six retaining clips along the lower edge **(see illustration)**.
11 Withdraw the panel and disengage the upper locating tabs, then disconnect the wiring connector and remove the panel **(see illustration)**.
12 Refitting is a reversal of removal.

Passenger's side

13 Working in the passenger's side footwell, undo the retainer securing the outer edge of the panel to the base of the facia **(see illustration)**.
14 Unscrew the two plastic nuts securing the centre of the panel to the facia and remove the panel from under the facia **(see illustrations)**.

Sill trim panels

Front door sill panel

15 Pull away the rubber door seals in the vicinity of the sill trim panel to be removed.
16 Pull the panel up to release the three retaining clips and remove the panel from the car **(see illustration)**.
17 Refitting is a reversal of removal.

Rear door sill panel

18 Remove the rear door aperture trim panel as described later in this Section.
19 Pull away the rubber door seals in the vicinity of the sill trim panel to be removed.
20 Extract the clip securing the lower rear corner of the panel to the body **(see illustration)**.
21 Pull the panel up to release the retaining clips and remove the panel from the car **(see illustration)**.
22 Refitting is a reversal of removal.

A-pillar trim panels

Upper panel

23 Open the door, and carefully prise the rubber door seal from the edge of the door aperture.

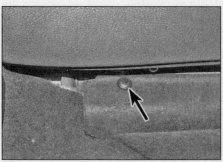

27.13 Undo the retainer (arrowed) securing the outer edge of the panel to the facia

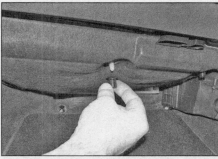

27.14a Unscrew the two plastic nuts...

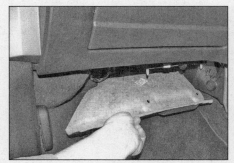

27.14b... and remove the panel from under the facia

27.16 Pull the sill panel up to release the three retaining clips

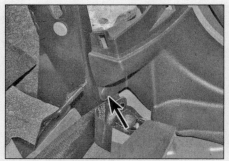

27.20 Extract the rear door sill panel retaining clip (arrowed)...

27.21... then pull the panel up to release the retaining clips

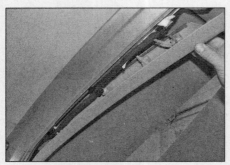

27.24 Pull the upper trim panel away from the A-pillar at the top and work down to disengage the upper retaining clips

24 Pull the panel away from the A-pillar at the top and work down to disengage the upper retaining clips(see illustration).
25 Once the panel is free, disengage the upper plastic strap from the panel, then lift the panel up to disengage the two lower locating lugs (see illustrations). Remove the panel from the car.
26 Refitting is a reversal of removal.

Lower panel

27 Remove the adjacent front door sill trim panel as described previously in this Section.
28 Pull the panel away from the A-pillar to disengage the retaining clips and remove the panel from the car(see illustration).
29 Refitting is a reversal of removal.

B-pillar trim panels

Upper panel

30 Detach the rubber weatherstrip from the B-pillar as necessary to free the edges of the trim panel.
31 Undo and remove the bolt for the lower seat belt anchorage(see illustration 26.2). Note that the spacer and washer are integral with the bolt.
32 Carefully prise out the trim cap at the top of the B-pillar and undo the retaining screw now exposed (see illustrations).
33 Pull the top of the panel away from the pillar to release the internal clips, then lift it up and off the lower panel. Feed the seat belt through the panel and remove the panel from the car (see illustrations).
34 Refitting is a reversal of removal. Tighten the seat belt anchorage bolt to the specified torque.

Lower panel

35 Remove the B-pillar upper trim panel and the front and rear door sill trim panels as described previously.
36 Undo the two screws securing the top of the panel to the B-pillar (see illustration).
37 Pull the panel away from the pillar to

27.25a Disengage the plastic strap from the panel...

27.25b... then lift the panel up to disengage the two lower locating lugs

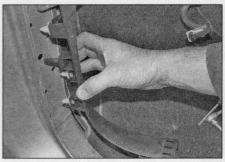

27.28 Pull the lower panel away from the A-pillar to disengage the retaining clips

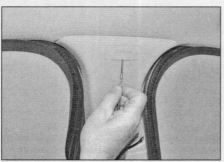

27.32a Prise out the trim cap at the top of the B-pillar...

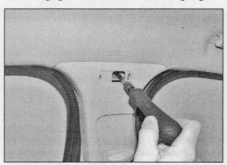

27.32b... and undo the retaining screw

27.33a Pull the top of the panel away from the pillar...

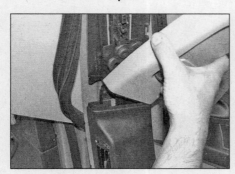

27.33b... lift it up and off the lower panel...

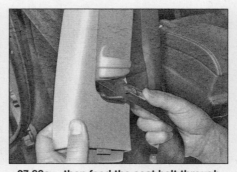

27.33c... then feed the seat belt through the panel opening

27.36 Undo the two screws securing the top of the lower panel to the B-pillar

27.37 Pull the panel away from the pillar to release the internal clips

27.41 Pull the rear door aperture trim panel away from the pillar to release the internal clips

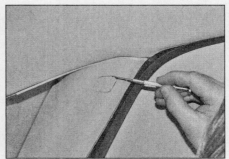

27.44a Prise out the trim cap at the top of the C-pillar…

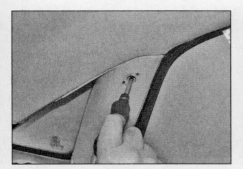

27.44b… and undo the retaining screw – Saloon and Hatchback models

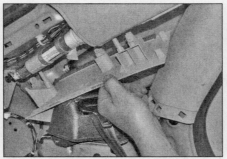

27.45a Pull the rear section of the panel away from the pillar to release the internal clips…

27.45b… then similarly remove the front section – Saloon and Hatchback models

release the internal clips, then remove the panel from the car **(see illustration)**.
38 Refitting is a reversal of removal.

Rear trim panels

Rear door aperture trim panel

39 Detach the rubber weatherstrip from the C-pillar as necessary to free the edges of the trim panel.
40 Tilt the rear seat backrest and cushion forward.
41 Pull the panel away from the pillar to release the internal clips, then remove the panel from the car **(see illustration)**.
42 Refitting is a reversal of removal.

C-pillar trim panel – Saloon and Hatchback models

43 Remove the D-pillar trim panel as described later in this Section.

44 Carefully prise out the trim cap at the top of the C-pillar and undo the retaining screw now exposed **(see illustrations)**.
45 Pull the rear section of the panel away from the pillar to release the internal clips, then similarly remove the front section **(see illustrations)**.
46 Refitting is a reversal of removal.

C-pillar trim panel – Estate models

47 Remove the parcel shelf support as described later in this Section.
48 Lift off the trim cover and undo the seat belt upper anchorage bolt**(see illustration)**. Note that the spacer and washer are integral with the bolt.
49 Carefully prise out the trim cap at the top of the C-pillar and undo the retaining screw now exposed **(see illustrations)**.
50 Pull the panel away from the pillar to

27.48 Lift off the trim cover and undo the seat belt upper anchorage bolt – Estate models

release the internal clips, then remove the panel from the car **(see illustration)**.
51 Refitting is a reversal of removal. Tighten

27.49a Prise out the trim cap at the top of the C-pillar…

27.49b… and undo the retaining screw – Estate models

27.50 Pull the panel away from the pillar to release the internal clips – Estate models

27.54a Removing the D-pillar trim panel on Saloon and Hatchback models...

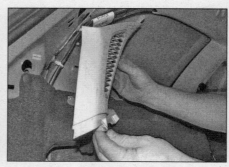

27.54b... and on Estate models

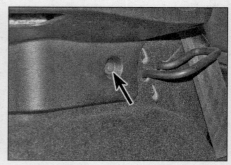

27.59a Undo the parcel shelf support front retaining screw (arrowed)...

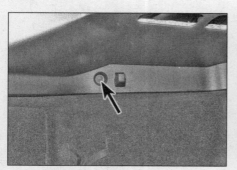

27.59b... and rear retaining screw (arrowed) – Hatchback models

27.60 Pull the panel away to release the internal clips – Hatchback models

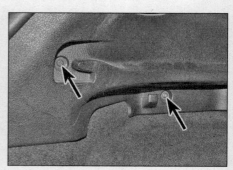

27.64a Undo the two rear retaining screws (arrowed)...

the seat belt anchorage bolt to the specified torque.

D-pillar trim panel

52 Remove the rear door aperture trim panel as described previously.

53 On Hatchback and Estate models, remove the parcel shelf support as described later in this Section.

54 Pull the panel away from the pillar to release the internal clips, then remove the panel from the car (see illustrations).

55 Refitting is a reversal of removal.

Parcel shelf support – Hatchback models

56 Remove the parcel shelf from the car.

57 Remove the rear door aperture trim panel as described previously.

58 Undo and remove the bolt for the rear seat belt lower anchorage. Note that the spacer and washer are integral with the bolt.

59 Undo the two screws securing the parcel shelf support to the body (see illustrations).

60 Pull the panel away to release the internal clips, feed the seat belt through the panel opening, then remove the panel from the car (see illustration).

61 Refitting is a reversal of removal. Tighten the seat belt anchorage bolt to the specified torque.

Parcel shelf support – Estate models

62 Remove the parcel shelf from the car.

63 Remove the rear door aperture trim panel as described previously.

64 Undo the three screws securing the parcel shelf support to the body (see illustrations).

65 Pull the panel away to release the internal clips, feed the seat belt through the panel opening, then remove the panel from the car(see illustrations).

66 Refitting is a reversal of removal.

Tailgate/boot lid aperture lower trim panel

67 Pull off the rubber seal from the tailgate/boot lid aperture, in the area adjoining the trim panel.

68 Prise out the plastic fasteners on the

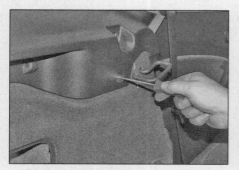

27.64b... and the front retaining screw – Estate models

27.65a Pull the panel away to release the internal clips...

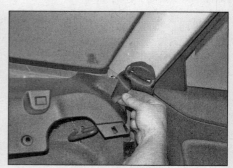

27.65b... then feed the seat belt through the panel opening

27.68 Prise out the plastic fasteners securing the tailgate/boot lid aperture lower trim panel

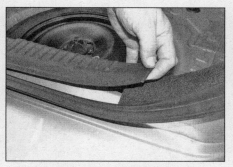

27.69a Pull the top of the panel up to release the internal clips...

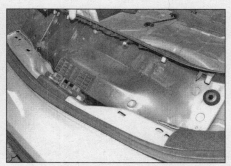

27.69b... then remove the panel from the car

inner side of the trim panel. There are four on Saloon and Estate models, and two on Hatchback models **(see illustration)**.
69 Pull the top of the panel up to release the internal clips, then remove the panel from the car **(see illustrations)**.
70 Refitting is a reversal of removal.

Loadspace side trim

71 On Hatchback and Estate models, remove the parcel shelf support and tailgate aperture lower trim panel as described previously in this Section.
72 On Saloon models, remove the boot lid aperture lower trim panel as described previously in this Section.
73 Prise out the plastic fastener securing the side trim to the body, then remove the trim from the car **(see illustrations)**.
74 Refitting is a reversal of removal.

Boot lid trim panel

75 Undo the trim panel retaining screws in the grab handle recess.
76 Pull the panel away from the boot lid to release the internal retaining clips and remove the panel from the car.
77 Refitting is a reversal of removal.

Tailgate trim panel

78 Pull the upper panel away from the tailgate to release the internal clips, then remove the panel from the car **(see illustration)**.
79 Similarly, remove the side panels in the same way **(see illustration)**.
80 On Hatchback models, undo the screws

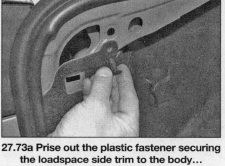

27.73a Prise out the plastic fastener securing the loadspace side trim to the body...

27.73b... then remove the trim from the car

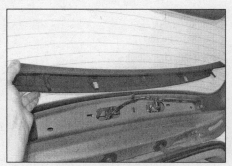

27.78 Pull the upper tailgate trim panel away from the tailgate to release the internal clips...

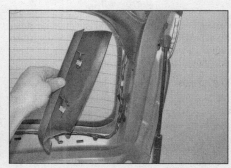

27.79... then remove the side panels in the same way

in the grab handle recesses **(see illustration)**.
81 On Estate models, prise out the plastic fasteners in the grab handle recesses and

remove the grab handles from the tailgate **(see illustrations)**.
82 Pull the main panel away from the

27.80 On Hatchback models, undo the screws in the grab handle recesses

27.81a On Estate models, prise out the plastic fasteners in the grab handle recesses...

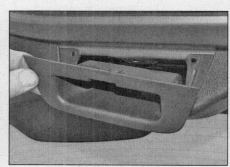

27.81b... and remove the grab handles from the tailgate

27.82 Pull the main panel away from the tailgate to release the internal retaining clips

27.88 Undo the two lower screws (arrowed) securing the glovebox to the facia

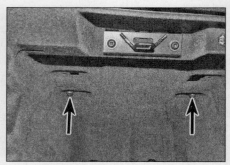

27.89a Undo the two central bolts (arrowed)...

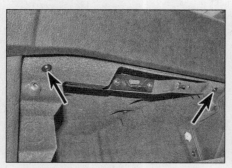

27.89b... and the two upper screws (arrowed)...

27.89c... then withdraw the glovebox from the facia

tailgate to release the internal retaining clips and remove the panel from the car **(see illustration)**.
83 Refitting is a reversal of removal.

Carpets

84 The passenger compartment floor carpet is in several pieces, and is secured along the edges by various types of clips.
85 Carpet removal and refitting is reasonably straightforward, but time-consuming, due to the fact that all adjoining trim panels must be released, and the seats and centre console must be removed.

Headlining

86 The headlining is clipped to the roof, and can be withdrawn only once all fittings such as the grab handles, sun visors, front, centre and rear pillar trim panels, and associated components have been removed. The door and tailgate weatherseals will also have to be prised clear.
87 Note that headlining removal requires

considerable skill and experience if it is to be carried out without damage, and is therefore best entrusted to an expert.

Glovebox

88 Open the glovebox lid and undo the two lower screws securing the glovebox to the facia **(see illustration)**.
89 Undo the two central bolts and the two upper screws, then withdraw the glovebox from the facia **(see illustrations)**.
90 Disconnect the wiring connectors and remove the glovebox from the car **(see illustration)**.
91 Refitting is a reversal of removal.

28 Centre console – removal and refitting

Removal

1 Lift out the centre console trim pad located under the ashtray **(see illustration)**.
2 On manual transmission models, unscrew the gear lever knob then unclip the gear lever

27.90 Disconnect the wiring connectors and remove the glovebox

28.1 Lift out the centre console trim pad located under the ashtray

28.2a Unscrew the gear lever knob...

28.2b... unclip the gear lever gaiter trim surround...

28.2c... and lift the gaiter and the gear lever reverse detent mechanism off the gear lever shaft

gaiter trim surround. Lift the gaiter and the gear lever reverse detent mechanism off the gear lever shaft (see illustrations).

3 On automatic transmission models, unclip the selector lever trim surround from the centre console.

4 Starting at the rear, carefully pull up the centre console upper section to release the retaining clips, then disengage the front tabs and remove the upper section (see illustration). Where applicable, disconnect the switch wiring connectors. On automatic transmission models, feed the selector lever trim surround through the aperture as the console upper section is removed.

5 On models from 04/2010, carefully unclip the side trim around and below the facia centre panel. Where applicable, disconnect the wiring connector from the power switch.

6 Release the upper edge of the handbrake lever gaiter trim surround from the centre console. Disengage the locating tab at the front, then fold the gaiter inside out and remove it from the handbrake lever (see illustrations).

7 Remove the centre trim panels under the facia on both sides by pulling out the centre pins and extracting the plastic rivet. Pull the panels away at the front and disengage the two pegs at the rear (see illustrations).

8 Undo the screw each side securing the

28.4 Carefully pull up the centre console upper section to release the retaining clips

28.6a Release the upper edge of the handbrake lever gaiter trim surround from the console...

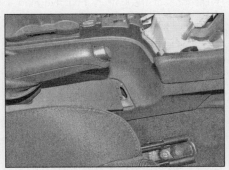

28.6b... disengage the locating tab at the front...

28.6c... then fold the gaiter inside out and remove it from the handbrake lever

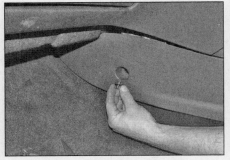

28.7a Extract the plastic rivet...

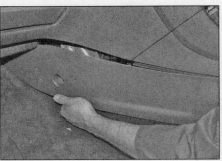

28.7b... pull the centre trim panel away at the front...

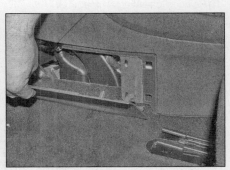

28.7c... and disengage the two pegs at the rear

28.8 Undo the screw each side securing the lower front corner of the console to the facia

28.9 Undo the screws (arrowed) securing the upper front corners of the console to the facia

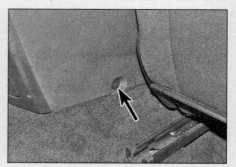

28.10 Undo the bolt each side (arrowed) securing the rear of the console to the floor bracket

28.11 Disconnect the wiring connectors adjacent to the gear/selector lever housing

28.12 Pull the console to the rear then lift it up and over the handbrake lever

lower front corner of the centre console to the base of the facia (see illustration).

9 Undo the screw each side, below the ashtray, securing the upper front corners of the centre console to the facia (see illustration).

10 Undo the bolt each side securing the rear of the centre console to the floor bracket(see illustration).

11 Disconnect the wiring connectors adjacent to the gear/selector lever housing and unclip the connectors from the centre console (see illustration).

12 Pull the console to the rear to disengage the two front locating lugs, then lift the console up and over the handbrake lever and remove it from the car (see illustration).

Refitting

13 Refitting is a reversal of removal.

29 Facia assembly – removal and refitting

Note: *This is an involved operation entailing the removal of numerous components and assemblies, and the disconnection of a multitude of wiring connectors. Make notes on the location of all disconnected wiring, or attach labels to the connectors, to avoid confusion when refitting. Taking a series of photographs throughout the removal procedure will prove invaluable when refitting.*

Removal

1 Disconnect the battery negative lead as described in Chapter 5A Section 4.

2 Remove the glovebox, the upper and lower

29.7a Undo the four upper bolts (arrowed)...

29.7c... and remove the audio unit mounting frame

A-pillar trim panels on both sides, the driver's lower facia trim panel, and the passenger's lower facia trim panel as described in Section 27.

3 Remove the centre console as described in Section 28.

4 Remove the steering column as described in Chapter 10 Section 16.

5 Remove the instrument panel, the headlight switch and the audio unit as described in Chapter 12.

6 Remove the heater/air conditioning control panel as described in Chapter 3 Section 10.

7 If not already done, undo the six bolts and remove the audio unit mounting frame from the facia (see illustrations).

8 Carefully prise up the grille panel from the upper centre of the facia. Disconnect the wiring connector for the sunlight sensor and remove the panel (see illustrations).

29.7b... and two lower bolts (arrowed)...

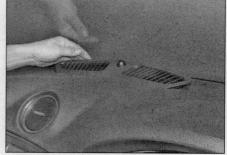

29.8a Prise up the grille panel from the upper centre of the facia...

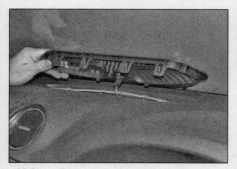

29.8b... disconnect the wiring connector and remove the panel

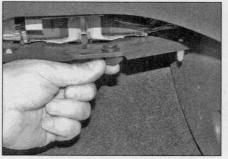

29.9a Turn the locking catch through 90°...

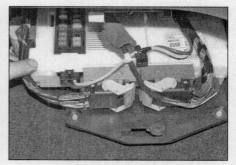

29.9b... and lower the generic electronics module (GEM) from its location

9 Turn the locking catch through 90° and lower the generic electronics module (GEM) from its location **(see illustrations)**. Lift the module from the two lower pivots and place it to one side.

10 Undo the two bolts (if still in place) and withdraw the ashtray from its location. Disconnect the wiring connectors and remove the ashtray.

11 Disconnect the wiring connector at the passenger's airbag, and at the servo motors and temperature sensors on the heater/air conditioning air distribution housing. Release the wiring harness from the clips and cable-ties so it is free to be withdrawn with the facia.

12 Undo the two bolts securing the passenger's airbag mounting bracket to the facia crossmember **(see illustration)**.

13 According to equipment fitted, disconnect

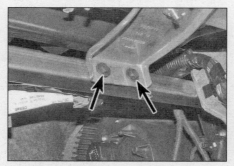

29.12 Undo the two bolts (arrowed) securing the passenger's airbag mounting bracket to the facia crossmember

29.14 Carefully prise off the facia end panels on each side

the remaining wiring connectors at the components attached to the facia and release the wiring harness from the clips and cable-ties.

14 Using a plastic spatula or similar tool, carefully prise off the facia end panels on each side **(see illustration)**.

15 Undo the facia retaining bolts from the following locations **(see illustrations)**:

a) *Two bolts each side securing the facia to the A-pillars.*

b) *Two bolts at the base of the glovebox aperture.*

c) *Two bolts at the lower centre of the facia.*

d) *Two bolts below the steering column location.*

e) *Two bolts in the instrument panel aperture.*

16 With the help of an assistant, carefully lift the facia from its location. Check that all wiring has been disconnected, then remove the facia out from the driver's side of the car.

Refitting

17 Refitting is a reversal of removal.

29.15a Undo the two bolts each side (arrowed) securing the facia to the A-pillars...

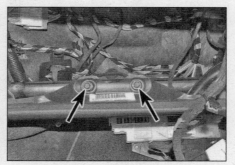

29.15b... the two bolts (arrowed) at the base of the glovebox aperture...

29.15c... the two bolts (arrowed) at the lower centre of the facia...

29.15d... the two bolts (arrowed) below the steering column location...

29.15e... and the two bolts (arrowed) in the instrument panel aperture

30.3 Disconnect the wiring connectors (arrowed) at the generic electronics module

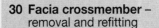

30 Facia crossmember –
removal and refitting

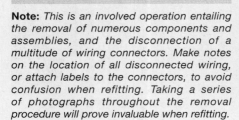

Note: *This is an involved operation entailing the removal of numerous components and assemblies, and the disconnection of a multitude of wiring connectors. Make notes on the location of all disconnected wiring, or attach labels to the connectors, to avoid confusion when refitting. Taking a series of photographs throughout the removal procedure will prove invaluable when refitting.*

Removal

1 Remove the facia assembly as described in Section 29.
2 Remove both front doors as described in Section 12.
3 Disconnect the wiring connectors at the generic electronics module **(see illustration)**.
4 Undo the two retaining bolts each side securing the facia centre brace to the facia crossmember. Release the wiring harnesses from the retaining clips around the brace and remove the brace from the car **(see illustrations)**.
5 Twist the bulbholder anti-clockwise and release the footwell illumination bulb from the footwell air duct on the driver's side **(see illustration)**.
6 Detach the footwell air ducts from each side of the air distribution housing **(see illustration)**.
7 Undo the nut and three bolts and remove the facia crossmember centre brace on the passenger's side **(see illustrations)**.
8 Disconnect the wiring at the connector on

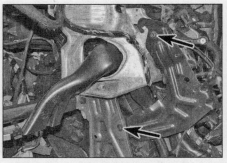

30.4a Undo the two bolts each side (arrowed) securing the facia centre brace to the crossmember...

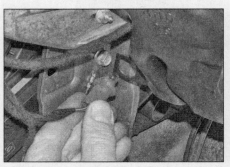

30.5 Release the footwell illumination bulb from the footwell air duct

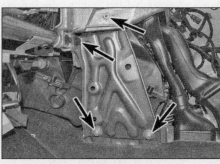

30.7a Undo the nut and three bolts (arrowed)...

the crossmember centre brace on the driver's side **(see illustration)**. Unclip the wiring connector from the brace.

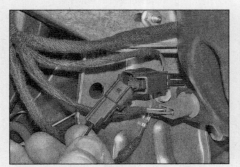

30.8 Disconnect the wiring at the connector on the crossmember centre brace on the driver's side

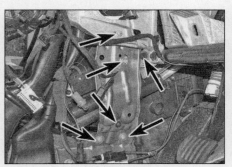

30.9a Undo the nut and five bolts (arrowed)...

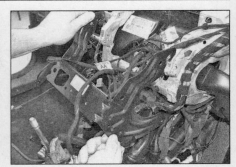

30.4b... then unclip the wiring harnesses and remove the brace

30.6 Detach the footwell air ducts from each side of the air distribution housing

30.7b... and remove the facia crossmember centre brace on the passenger's side

9 Undo the nut and five bolts and remove the crossmember centre brace on the driver's side **(see illustrations)**. Note the

30.9b... and remove the crossmember centre brace on the driver's side

30.10a Remove the front air ducts...

30.10b... rear air ducts...

30.10c... and connecting elbows

30.11 Disconnect the wiring connectors and release the wiring loom from the clips and cable-ties

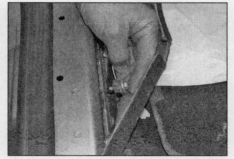

30.12a Undo the bolt and disconnect the earth lead from the inner sill...

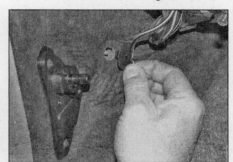

30.12b... then free the wiring from the retaining clip in the footwell

location of the earth lead on the upper centre bolt.

10 Remove the front and rear air ducts, and connecting elbows, from the air distribution housing and floor ducts (see illustrations).

11 Disconnect all the wiring connectors from the components located under the centre console. Release the wiring loom from the clips and cable-ties so it is free to be removed with the facia crossmember (see illustration).

12 Undo the bolt and disconnect the earth lead from the inner sill on the passenger's side. Trace the lead back to the retaining clip in the footwell and release the clip to free the wiring (see illustrations). Disconnect the earth lead on the driver's side in the same way.

13 Disconnect the two main wiring harness connectors in the passenger's footwell (see illustrations).

14 Disconnect the wiring connectors at the

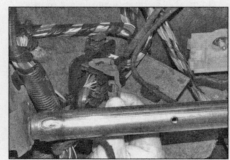

30.13a Disconnect the upper wiring harness connector...

30.13b... and the lower connector in the passenger's footwell

heater blower motor, blower motor resistor, air flap control servo motors and temperature sensors on the air distribution housing. Release the wiring loom from the clips and cable-ties around the air distribution housing, and from the cable-tie at the upper centre of the facia crossmember.

15 Undo the two upper bolts securing the air distribution housing to the facia crossmember (see illustration).

16 Disconnect the aerial lead at the connector on the driver's A-pillar, then release the lead retaining clip from the pillar (see illustrations).

30.15 Undo the two upper bolts (arrowed) securing the air distribution housing to the crossmember

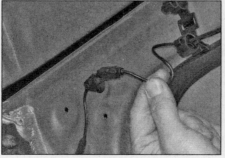

30.16a Disconnect the aerial lead at the A-pillar connector...

30.16b... then release the lead retaining clip

30.18a Undo the upper screw (arrowed)...

30.18b... and the lower screws (arrowed) each side...

30.18c... and lift away the air distribution housing top cover

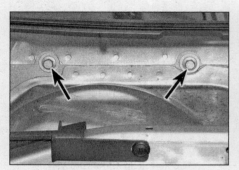

30.20 Undo the two bolts (arrowed) securing the facia crossmember to the bulkhead

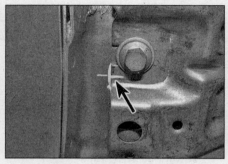

30.21 Make suitable alignment marks (arrowed) between the crossmember and the A-pillars

30.22a Extract the rubber grommets from the A-pillars...

17 On models with an electric booster heater, remove the booster heater as described in Chapter 3 Section 13.

18 Undo the three screws each side and lift away the air distribution housing top cover (see illustrations).

19 Remove the windscreen wiper motor and linkage as described in Chapter 12 Section 14.

20 Working in the windscreen wiper motor aperture, undo the two bolts securing the facia crossmember to the bulkhead (see illustration).

21 At each of the facia crossmember mounting bolt locations, make suitable alignment marks between the crossmember and the A-pillars (see illustration).

22 Extract the rubber grommet from the A-pillars on both sides, then using a socket and extension bar, undo and remove the facia crossmember side retaining bolts (see illustrations).

23 Undo the two bolts each side securing the facia crossmember to the A-pillars (see illustration).

24 With the help of an assistant, carefully lift the facia crossmember from its location. Check that all wiring has been disconnected, then remove the crossmember from the driver's side of the car (see illustration).

Refitting

25 Refitting is a reversal of removal, tightening the crossmember mounting bolts to the specified torque.

30.22b... then undo and remove the facia crossmember side retaining bolts

30.23 Undo the two bolts each side (arrowed) securing the facia crossmember to the A-pillars

30.24 Lift the facia crossmember from its location and remove it from the car

Chapter 12
Body electrical system

Contents

Degrees of difficulty

Easy, suitable for novice with little experience	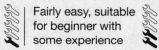	Fairly easy, suitable for beginner with some experience		Fairly difficult, suitable for competent DIY mechanic	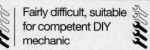	Difficult, suitable for experienced DIY mechanic		Very difficult, suitable for expert DIY or professional	

Specifications

General

System type . . . . 12 volt, negative earth

Fuses

Refer to the labels on the fuse/relay box covers and to the wiring diagrams at the end of this Chapter

Bulbs

	Type	Wattage
Approach light	W5	5
Brake/tail light	P21/5	21/5
Front direction indicator light	PY21W	21
Front direction indicator side repeater light	W5W	5
Front foglight*	H8/H11	35/55
Front sidelight.	W5W	5
Glovebox light	W5W	5
Headlight cornering light	H1	55
Headlight dipped beam	H7	55
Headlight main beam	H1	55
High-level brake light	W5W	5
Interior light	Festoon	10
Luggage compartment light	W5W	5
Map reading lights	BA9S	5
Number plate light	W5W	5
Rear direction indicator light	PY21W	21
Rear foglight.	P21/5	21/5
Reversing light	P21W	21
Tail light	P21/4W	4

* Fit a new bulb of the same wattage as the one removed

1 General information and precautions

⚠️ **Warning: Before carrying out any work on the electrical system, read through the precautions given in Safety First! at the beginning of this manual, and in Chapter 5A Section 1.**

1 The electrical system is of the 12 volt negative earth type. Power for the lights and all electrical accessories is supplied by a silver-calcium type battery, which is charged by the engine-driven alternator.

2 This Chapter covers repair and service procedures for the various electrical components not associated with the engine. Information on the battery, alternator and starter motor can be found in Chapter 5A.

3 It should be noted that, prior to working on any component in the electrical system, the battery negative lead should first be disconnected, to prevent the possibility of electrical short-circuits and/or fires.

Caution: Before proceeding, refer to Battery – disconnection, removal and refitting 5A Section 4.

2 Electrical fault finding – general information

Note: *Refer to the precautions given in Safety First! and in Section 1 before starting work. The following tests relate to testing of the main electrical circuits, and should not be used to test delicate electronic circuits (such as the anti-lock braking system or fuel injection system), particularly where an electronic control unit is used.*

General

1 A typical electrical circuit consists of an electrical component, any switches, relays, motors, fuses, fusible links or circuit breakers related to that component, and the wiring and connectors which link the component to both the battery and the vehicle body. To help to pinpoint a problem in an electrical circuit, wiring diagrams are shown at the end of this Chapter.

2 Before attempting to diagnose an electrical fault, first study the appropriate wiring diagram to obtain a complete understanding of the components included in the particular circuit concerned. The possible sources of a fault can be narrowed down by noting if other components related to the circuit are operating properly. If several components or circuits fail at one time, the problem is likely to be related to a shared fuse or earth connection.

3 Electrical problems usually stem from simple causes, such as loose or corroded connections, a faulty earth connection, a blown fuse, a melted fusible link, or a faulty relay. Inspect the condition of all fuses, wires and connections in a problem circuit before testing the components. Use the wiring diagrams to determine which terminal connections will need to be checked in order to pinpoint the trouble-spot.

4 The basic tools required for electrical fault finding include a circuit tester or voltmeter (a 12 volt bulb with a set of test leads can also be used for certain tests); a self-powered test light (sometimes known as a continuity tester); an ohmmeter (to measure resistance); a battery and set of test leads; and a jumper wire, preferably with a circuit breaker or fuse incorporated, which can be used to bypass suspect wires or electrical components. Before attempting to locate a problem with test instruments, use the wiring diagram to determine where to make the connections.

5 To find the source of an intermittent wiring fault (usually due to a poor or dirty connection, or damaged wiring insulation), a 'wiggle' test can be performed on the wiring. This involves wiggling the wiring by hand to see if the fault occurs as the wiring is moved. It should be possible to narrow down the source of the fault to a particular section of wiring. This method of testing can be used in conjunction with any of the tests described in the following sub-Sections.

6 Apart from problems due to poor connections, two basic types of fault can occur in an electrical circuit – open-circuit, or short-circuit.

7 Open-circuit faults are caused by a break somewhere in the circuit, which prevents current from flowing. An open-circuit fault will prevent a component from working, but will not cause the relevant circuit fuse to blow.

8 Short-circuit faults are caused by a 'short' somewhere in the circuit, which allows the current flowing in the circuit to 'escape' along an alternative route, usually to earth. Short-circuit faults are normally caused by a breakdown in wiring insulation, which allows a feed wire to touch either another wire, or an earthed component such as the bodyshell. A short-circuit fault will normally cause the relevant circuit fuse to blow.

Finding an open-circuit

9 To check for an open-circuit, connect one lead of a circuit tester or voltmeter to either the negative battery terminal or a known good earth.

10 Connect the other lead to a connector in the circuit being tested, preferably nearest to the battery or fuse.

11 Switch on the circuit, bearing in mind that some circuits are live only when the ignition switch is turned to a particular position.

12 If voltage is present (indicated either by the tester bulb lighting or a voltmeter reading, as applicable), this means that the section of the circuit between the relevant connector and the battery is problem-free.

13 Continue to check the remainder of the circuit in the same fashion.

14 When a point is reached at which no voltage is present, the problem must lie between that point and the previous test point with voltage. Most problems can be traced to a broken, corroded or loose connection.

Finding a short-circuit

15 To check for a short-circuit, first disconnect the load(s) from the circuit (loads are the components which draw current from a circuit, such as bulbs, motors, heating elements, etc).

16 Remove the relevant fuse from the circuit, and connect a circuit tester or voltmeter to the fuse connections.

17 Switch on the circuit, bearing in mind that some circuits are live only when the ignition switch is turned to a particular position.

18 If voltage is present (indicated either by the tester bulb lighting or a voltmeter reading, as applicable), this means that there is a short-circuit.

19 If no voltage is present, but the fuse still blows with the load(s) connected, this indicates an internal fault in the load(s).

Finding an earth fault

20 The battery negative terminal is connected to 'earth' – the metal of the engine/transmission unit and the car body – and most systems are wired so that they only receive a positive feed, the current returning via the metal of the car body. This means that the component mounting and the body form part of that circuit. Loose or corroded mountings can therefore cause a range of electrical faults, ranging from total failure of a circuit, to a puzzling partial fault. In particular, lights may shine dimly (especially when another circuit sharing the same earth point is in operation), motors (eg, wiper motors or the radiator cooling fan motor) may run slowly, and the operation of one circuit may have an apparently-unrelated effect on another. Note that on many vehicles, earth straps are used between certain components, such as the engine/transmission and the body, usually where there is no metal-to-metal contact between components, due to flexible rubber mountings, etc.

21 To check whether a component is properly earthed, disconnect the battery, and connect one lead of an ohmmeter to a known good earth point. Connect the other lead to the wire or earth connection being tested. The resistance reading should be zero; if not, check the connection as follows.

22 If an earth connection is thought to be faulty, dismantle the connection, and clean back to bare metal both the bodyshell and the wire terminal or the component earth connection mating surface. Be careful to remove all traces of dirt and corrosion, then use a knife to trim away any paint, so that a clean metal-to-metal joint is made. On reassembly, tighten the joint fasteners securely; if a wire terminal is being refitted, use serrated washers between the terminal

3.2a Lift the cover for access to the engine compartment fuse/relay box

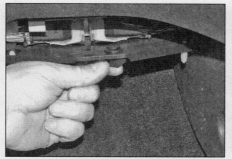

3.2b Turn the locking catch through 90°...

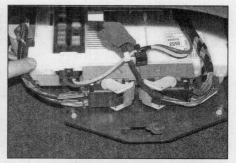

3.2c... and lower the generic electronics module from its location

and the bodyshell, to ensure a clean and secure connection. When the connection is remade, prevent the onset of corrosion in the future by applying a coat of petroleum jelly or silicone-based grease. Alternatively, at regular intervals, spray on a proprietary ignition sealer or a water-dispersant lubricant.

3.2d Turn the turnbuckles and remove the cover...

3.2e... for access to the luggage compartment fuse/relay box

3 Fuses and relays – general information

Fuses

1 Fuses are designed to break a circuit when a predetermined current is reached, in order to protect the components and wiring which could be damaged by excessive current flow. Any excessive current flow will be due to a fault in the circuit, usually a short-circuit (see Section 2).

2 There are three separate fuse/relay boxes on Mondeo models. One is located on the left-hand side of the engine compartment, another is located inside the car below the glovebox (also known as the generic electronics module) and the third is located on the left-hand side of the luggage compartment, behind a cover **(see illustrations)**. Refer to the information on the fuse/relay box lid and to the wiring diagrams at the end of Chapter 12 for details of the fuse locations and circuits protected.

3 A blown fuse can be recognised from its melted or broken wire**(see illustration)**.

4 To remove a fuse, first ensure that the relevant circuit is switched off – for maximum safety, disconnect the battery negative lead as described in Chapter 5A Section 4.

5 Pull the fuse from its location, using the tool provided or thin-nosed pliers **(see illustration)**.

6 Before renewing a blown fuse, trace and rectify the cause, and always use a fuse of the correct rating. Never substitute a fuse of a higher rating, or make temporary repairs using wire or metal foil; more serious damage, or even fire, could result.

7 If a new fuse blows immediately, find the

cause before renewing it again; a short to earth as a result of faulty insulation is most likely. Where a fuse protects more than one circuit, try to isolate the defect by switching on each circuit in turn (if possible) until the fuse blows again. Always carry a supply of spare fuses of each relevant rating on the vehicle, a spare of each rating should be clipped into the base of the fuse/relay box.

Relays

8 The main relays are located in the engine compartment fuse/relay box, in the generic electronics module located below the glovebox and in the luggage compartment fuse/relay box located on the left-hand side of the luggage compartment, behind a cover. Refer to paragraph 2 for further information.

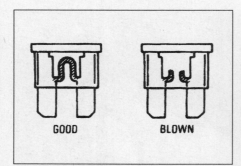

3.3 The fuses can be checked visually to see if they are blown

9 If a circuit or system controlled by a relay develops a fault, and the relay is suspect, operate the system. If the relay is functioning, it should be possible to hear it 'click' as it is energised. If this is the case, the fault lies with the components or wiring of the system. If the relay is not being energised, then either the relay is not receiving a main supply or a switching voltage, or the relay itself is faulty. Testing is by the substitution of a known good unit, but be careful – while some relays are identical in appearance and in operation, others look similar but perform different functions.

10 To remove a relay, first ensure that the relevant circuit is switched off. The relay can then simply be pulled out from the socket, and pushed back into position.

3.5 Pull the fuse from its location, using the tool provided or thin-nosed pliers

4.2 Disconnect the wiring plug and unclip the immobiliser tranceiver

4.4 Depress the locking pin at the front of the lock housing, and pull out the lock cylinder using the key

4 Switches – removal and refitting

Note: *Disconnect the battery negative lead as described in Chapter 5A Section 4 before removing any switch, and reconnect the lead after refitting.*

Ignition switch/steering lock

Steering column lock cylinder

1 Remove the steering column shrouds as described in Chapter 11 Section 27.

4.8 Release the switch retaining tabs then withdraw the ignition switch from the steering column

2 Disconnect the wiring plug, then unclip and withdraw the anti-theft immobiliser transceiver unit from the ignition switch/steering lock assembly **(see illustration)**.

3 Insert the ignition key, and turn it to position I.

4 Using a small screwdriver, depress the locking pin at the front of the lock housing, and pull out the lock cylinder using the key **(see illustration)**.

5 To refit the lock cylinder, push the assembly into the lock housing, until the locking pin engages, then turn the ignition key to position 0 and withdraw the key.

4.11 Undo the two screws (arrowed) securing the relevant switch to the switch housing

Ignition switch

Caution: Do not remove the ignition switch whilst the steering column lock cylinder is removed.

6 Remove the steering column shrouds as described in Chapter 11, Section 27.

7 Use a small screwdriver to lift the locking tab on the wiring connector at the back of the switch, then disconnect it.

8 The same screwdriver can now be used to release the switch retaining tabs at the top and bottom, then the switch is withdrawn from the steering column **(see illustration)**.

9 Refitting is a reversal of removal, but make sure that the switch engages correctly.

Steering column switches

10 Remove the steering column shrouds as described in Chapter 11, Section 27.

11 Undo the two screws securing the relevant switch to the switch housing **(see illustration)**.

12 Using a small screwdriver, lift the plastic catch at the top of the relevant switch, then slide the switch from the housing **(see illustrations)**.

13 Refitting is a reversal of removal.

Exterior light switch

14 Using a plastic spatula or similar tool, carefully prise off the facia end panel on the driver's side **(see illustration)**.

4.12a Lift the plastic catch at the top of the relevant switch...

4.12b... then slide the switch from the housing

4.14 Carefully prise off the facia end panel on the driver's side

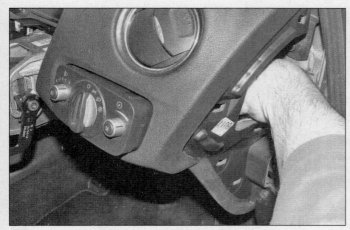

4.15a Reach in through the facia...

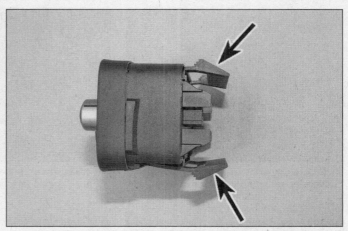

4.15b... and press together the light switch upper and lower retaining bars (arrowed) – shown with switch removed

15 Reach in through the opening in the end of the facia and press together the light switch upper and lower retaining bars **(see illustrations)**.

16 Withdraw the light switch from the facia, disconnect the wiring connector and remove the switch**(see illustration)**.

17 Refitting is a reversal of removal.

Facia upper centre switch panel

Note: *On models with a touch screen satellite navigation system, remove the audio unit with DVD player as described in Section 17.*

18 Lift out the centre console trim pad located under the ashtray **(see illustration)**.

19 On manual transmission models, unscrew the gear lever knob then unclip the gear lever gaiter trim surround. Lift the gaiter and the gear lever reverse detent mechanism off the gear lever shaft**(see illustrations)**.

20 On automatic transmission models, unclip the selector lever trim surround from the centre console.

21 Starting at the rear, carefully pull up the centre console upper section to release the retaining clips, then disengage the front tabs and remove the upper section **(see illustration)**. Where applicable, disconnect the switch wiring connectors. On automatic transmission models, feed the selector lever trim surround through the aperture as the console upper section is removed.

4.16 Withdraw the light switch and disconnect the wiring connector (arrowed)

4.18 Lift out the centre console trim pad located under the ashtray

4.19a Unscrew the gear lever knob...

4.19b... unclip the gear lever gaiter trim surround...

4.19c... and lift the gaiter and the gear lever reverse detent mechanism off the gear lever shaft

4.21 Carefully pull up the centre console upper section to release the retaining clips

4.22 Carefully prise out the triangular trim covers at each upper corner of the facia centre panel

4.23a Undo the six retaining screws (arrowed)...

4.23b... withdraw the centre panel...

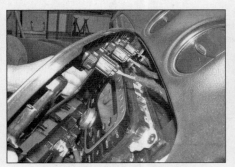

4.23c... and disconnect the wiring connectors

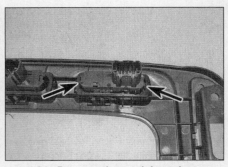

4.24a Depress the retaining tabs...

4.24b... and remove the switch from the panel

22 On models up to 04/2010, carefully prise out the two triangular trim covers at each upper corner of the facia centre panel. Where applicable, disconnect the wiring connector from the power switch **(see illustration)**. On models from 04/2010, carefully unclip the side trim around and below the facia centre panel. Where applicable, disconnect the wiring connector from the power switch.
23 Undo the six retaining screws and withdraw the centre panel from the facia. Disconnect the wiring connectors and remove the panel **(see illustrations)**.
24 Depress the tabs at the rear of the relevant switch and remove the switch from the panel **(see illustrations)**.
25 Refitting is a reversal of removal.

Centre console switches

26 Remove the centre console upper section as described previously in paragraphs 18 to 21.
27 Depress the tabs at the rear of the switch panel and remove the panel from the console upper section **(see illustration)**.
28 Refitting is a reversal of removal.

Air conditioning and recirculation switches

29 The switches are part of the heater/ air conditioning control panel which is removed as described in Chapter 3, Section 10.

Electric window switches

Driver's switches

30 Using a plastic spatula or similar instrument, carefully prise up the front of the electric window/mirror control switch panel from the door inner trim panel. Withdraw the switch panel and disconnect the wiring connector **(see illustrations)**.
31 Refitting is a reversal of removal.

Passenger's switches

32 Using a small screwdriver, remove the circular trim button from the centre of the inner door release handle trim panel, and undo the retaining screw now exposed. Operate the

4.27 Depress the tabs at the rear of the switch panel and remove the panel

4.30a Carefully prise up the front of the electric window/mirror control switch panel...

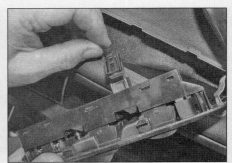

4.30b... then withdraw the panel and disconnect the wiring connector

handle and manipulate the trim panel from the door. Disconnect the switch wiring connector and remove the panel **(see illustrations)**.
33 Depress the tabs at the rear of the switch and withdraw the switch from the release handle trim panel **(see illustrations)**.
34 Refitting is a reversal of removal.

Electric mirror switch

35 The electric mirror switch is integral with the electric window/mirror control switch panel. Removal and refitting is described in paragraphs 30 and 31.

Power switch

Models up to 04/2010

36 Carefully prise out the triangular trim cover at the upper corner of the facia centre panel. Disconnect the wiring connector from the power switch **(see illustration 4.22)**.
37 Depress the tabs at the rear of the switch and withdraw the switch from the trim cover **(see illustrations)**.
38 Refitting is a reversal of removal.

Models from 04/2010

39 Remove the centre console upper section as described previously in paragraphs 18 to 21.
40 Carefully unclip the side trim around and below the facia centre panel. Disconnect the wiring connector from the power switch.
41 Depress the tabs at the rear of the switch and withdraw the switch from the side trim **(see illustrations 4.37a and 4.37b)**.
42 Refitting is a reversal of removal.

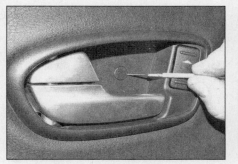
4.32a Remove the trim button from the centre of the inner door release handle trim panel...

4.32c Operate the handle and manipulate the trim panel from the door

Steering wheel switches

43 Remove the driver's airbag as described in Section 24.
44 Undo the screw at the front, and the

4.32b... and undo the retaining screw now exposed

4.32d Disconnect the switch wiring connector and remove the panel

two screws at the rear securing the relevant switch assembly to the steering wheel**(see illustrations)**.
45 Withdraw the relevant switch assembly

4.33a Depress the tabs at the rear of the switch...

4.37b... and withdraw the switch from the trim cover

4.33b... and withdraw the switch from the release handle trim panel

4.44a Steering wheel switches front securing screws (arrowed)...

4.37a Depress the tabs at the rear of the switch (arrowed)...

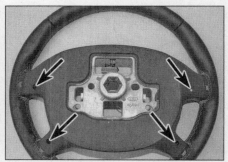
4.44b... and rear securing screws (arrowed)

from the steering wheel and disconnect the wiring connectors **(see illustrations)**.
46 Refitting is a reversal of removal.

Handbrake-on warning switch

47 Refer to Chapter 9, Section 18.

Brake light switch

48 Refer to Chapter 9, Section 17.

Brake pedal position switch

49 Refer to Chapter 9, Section 17.

Clutch pedal position switch

50 Refer to Chapter 6, Section 7.

Clutch pedal actuation switch

51 Refer to Chapter 6, Section 7.

---

5 Bulbs (exterior lights) – renewal

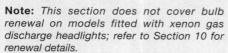

Note: *This section does not cover bulb renewal on models fitted with xenon gas discharge headlights; refer to Section 10 for renewal details.*
1 Whenever a bulb is renewed, note the following points:
a) *Make sure the switch is in the OFF position, for the bulb you are working on.*
b) *Remember that if the light has just been in use, the bulb may be extremely hot.*
c) *Always check the bulb contacts and holder, ensuring that there is clean metal-to-metal contact between the bulb and its*

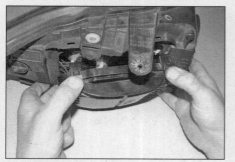

5.3 Depress the two tabs and remove the cover from the rear of the headlight unit

5.5 Withdraw the bulb from the light unit

4.45a Withdraw the relevant switch assembly from the steering wheel...

live(s) and earth. Clean off any corrosion or dirt before fitting a new bulb.
d) *Wherever bayonet-type bulbs are fitted, ensure that the live contact(s) bear firmly against the bulb contact.*
e) *Always ensure that the new bulb is of the correct rating, and that it is completely clean before fitting it; this applies particularly to headlight/foglight bulbs.*

Conventional headlight unit

2 Remove the relevant headlight as described in Section 7.

Halogen dipped beam

3 Depress the two tabs and remove the cover from the rear of the headlight unit **(see illustration)**.
4 Press the release tab at the base of the wiring plug and pull the plug from the rear of the bulb **(see illustrations)**.

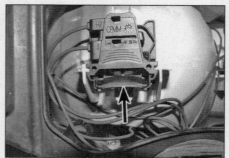

5.4a Press the release tab (arrowed)...

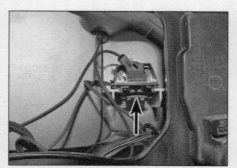

5.11 Press the release tab (arrowed) and pull the wiring plug from the main beam bulb

4.45b... and disconnect the wiring connectors

5 Withdraw the bulb from the rear of the light unit **(see illustration)**.
6 When handling the new bulb, use a tissue or clean cloth, to avoid touching the glass with the fingers; moisture and grease from the skin can cause blackening and rapid failure of this type of bulb. If the glass is accidentally touched, wipe it clean using methylated spirit.
7 Install the new bulb into the light unit, ensuring it is fully seated.
8 Reconnect the wiring plug, then refit the cover to the rear of the light unit.
9 Refit the headlight as described in Section 7.

Halogen main beam

10 Remove the cover from the rear of the headlight unit **(see illustration 5.3)**.
11 Press the release tab at the base of the wiring plug and pull the plug from the rear of the bulb **(see illustration)**.
12 Withdraw the bulb from the rear of the light unit **(see illustration)**.

5.4b... and pull the wiring plug from the dipped beam bulb

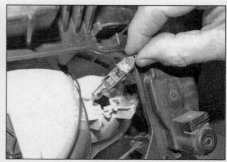

5.12 Withdraw the bulb from the light unit

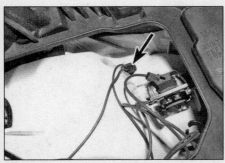

5.18 Using a small screwdriver, prise the sidelight bulbholder (arrowed) from the light unit

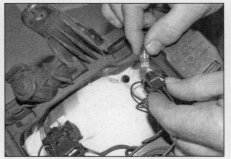

5.19 Pull out the capless bulb from the bulbholder

5.21 Twist the direction indicator bulbholder anti-clockwise and withdraw it from the headlight unit

13 When handling the new bulb, use a tissue or clean cloth, to avoid touching the glass with the fingers; moisture and grease from the skin can cause blackening and rapid failure of this type of bulb. If the glass is accidentally touched, wipe it clean using methylated spirit.
14 Install the new bulb into the light unit, ensuring it is fully seated.
15 Reconnect the wiring plug, then refit the cover to the rear of the light unit.
16 Refit the headlight as described in Section 7.

Sidelight

17 Remove the cover from the rear of the headlight unit (see illustration 5.3).
18 Using a small screwdriver, prise free the sidelight bulbholder from the light unit (see illustration).
19 Pull out the capless bulb from the holder, and fit a new one firmly into place (see illustration).
20 Refit the bulbholder and rear cover, then refit the headlight as described in Section 7.

Direction indicator light

21 Twist the holder anti-clockwise and withdraw it from the headlight unit (see illustration).
22 Depress and twist the bulb anti-clockwise to remove it (see illustration).
23 Fit the new bulb, then twist the bulbholder clockwise into the back of the headlight unit.

5.22 Depress and twist the bulb anti-clockwise to remove it

24 Refit the headlight as described in Section 7.

Projector headlight unit

25 Remove the relevant headlight as described in Section 7.

Halogen dipped beam

26 Depress the two tabs and remove the cover from the rear of the headlight unit (see illustration).
27 Pull the wiring plug from the rear of the bulb (see illustration).
28 Release the retaining clip, then remove the bulb from the light unit (see illustrations).
29 When handling the new bulb, use a tissue or clean cloth, to avoid touching the glass

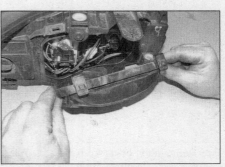

5.26 Depress the two tabs and remove the cover from the rear of the headlight unit

with the fingers; moisture and grease from the skin can cause blackening and rapid failure of this type of bulb. If the glass is accidentally touched, wipe it clean using methylated spirit.
30 Install the new bulb into the light unit, ensuring it is fully seated.
31 Secure the bulb with the retaining clip, then reconnect the wiring plug.
32 Refit the cover to the rear of the light unit then refit the headlight as described in Section 7.

Halogen main beam

33 Remove the cover from the rear of the headlight unit (see illustration 5.26).
34 Press up on the tab at the base of the

5.27 Pull the wiring plug from the rear of the bulb

5.28a Release the retaining clip...

5.28b... then remove the dipped beam bulb from the light unit

5.34a Press up on the tab at the base of the wiring plug…

5.34b… and remove the plug, complete with the main beam bulb

5.35 Hold the wiring plug and remove the bulb

5.39 Remove the cover from the side of the headlight unit

5.40a Press the release tab at the base of the wiring plug…

5.40b… and pull the plug from the cornering light bulb

wiring plug and remove the plug, complete with the bulb **(see illustrations)**.

35 Hold the wiring plug and remove the bulb **(see illustration)**.

36 When handling the new bulb, use a tissue or clean cloth, to avoid touching the glass with the fingers; moisture and grease from the skin can cause blackening and rapid failure of this type of bulb. If the glass is accidentally touched, wipe it clean using methylated spirit.

37 Install the new bulb into the wiring plug, then fit the wiring plug and bulb assembly into the headlight unit.

38 Refit the cover to the rear of the light unit then refit the headlight as described in Section 7.

Cornering light

39 Remove the cover from the side of the headlight unit **(see illustration)**.

40 Press the release tab at the base of the wiring plug and pull the plug from the rear of the bulb **(see illustrations)**.

41 Withdraw the bulb from the light unit **(see illustration)**.

42 When handling the new bulb, use a tissue or clean cloth, to avoid touching the glass with the fingers; moisture and grease from the skin can cause blackening and rapid failure of this type of bulb. If the glass is accidentally touched, wipe it clean using methylated spirit.

43 Install the new bulb into the light unit, ensuring it is fully seated.

44 Reconnect the wiring plug, then refit the cover to the side of the light unit.

45 Refit the headlight as described in Section 7.

Sidelight

46 Remove the cover from the rear of the headlight unit **(see illustration 5.26)**.

47 Prise free the sidelight bulbholder from the light unit **(see illustration)**.

48 Pull out the capless bulb from the holder, and fit a new one firmly into place **(see illustration)**.

49 Refit the bulbholder and rear cover, then refit the headlight as described in Section 7.

Direction indicator light

50 Twist the holder anti-clockwise and withdraw it from the headlight unit **(see illustration 5.26)**.

51 Depress and twist the bulb anti-clockwise to remove it **(see illustration 5.22)**.

52 Fit the new bulb, then twist the bulbholder clockwise into the back of the headlight unit.

5.41 Withdraw the bulb from the light unit

5.47 Prise free the sidelight bulbholder from the light unit

5.48 Pull out the capless bulb from the bulbholder

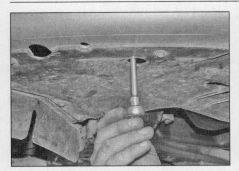

5.55a Slacken the foglight inner retaining bolt...

5.55b... and outer retaining bolt two turns

5.56 Using plastic spatulas, depress the retaining clips at each upper end of the light unit

5.57a Withdraw the foglight unit from the bumper...

5.57b... and disconnect the wiring connector

5.58 Turn the bulbholder anti-clockwise and remove it from the light unit

53 Refit the headlight as described in Section 7.

Front foglight

54 Firmly apply the handbrake, then jack up the front of the vehicle and support it securely on axle stands (see *'Jacking and vehicle support'*).

55 Working through the apertures at the base of the front bumper, slacken the two foglight retaining bolts approximately two turns **(see illustrations)**.

56 Using plastic spatulas, or similar tools inserted through the gap above the foglight, depress the retaining clips at each upper end of the light unit **(see illustration)**.

57 Withdraw the light unit from the bumper

and disconnect the foglight wiring connector **(see illustrations)**.

58 Turn the bulbholder anti-clockwise and remove it from the light unit **(see illustration)**. Note that the bulb cannot be separated from the bulbholder.

59 When handling the new bulb, use a tissue or clean cloth, to avoid touching the glass with the fingers; moisture and grease from the skin can cause blackening and rapid failure of this type of bulb. If the glass is accidentally touched, wipe it clean using methylated spirit.

60 Refitting is a reversal of removal.

Indicator side repeater light

In front wing

61 Using a plastic spatula or similar tool,

ease the light unit rearward and disengage it from the wing at the front **(see illustration)**.

62 Withdraw the light unit from the wing and turn the bulbholder anti-clockwise to remove it from the light unit **(see illustration)**.

63 Pull out the capless bulb from the holder, and fit a new one firmly into place **(see illustration)**.

64 Refitting is a reversal of removal.

In exterior mirror

65 Carefully prise the outer edge of the side repeater surround from the exterior mirror and withdraw the surround from the mirror body.

66 Withdraw the bulbholder from the surround.

67 Pull out the capless bulb, and press a new one into place.

68 Refitting is a reversal of removal.

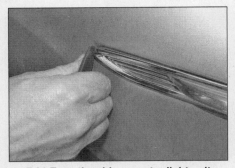

5.61 Ease the side repeater light unit rearward and disengage it from the wing at the front

5.62 Withdraw the light unit and turn the bulbholder anti-clockwise to remove it

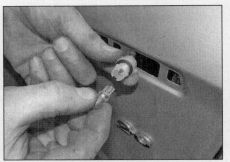

5.63 Pull out the capless bulb from the bulbholder

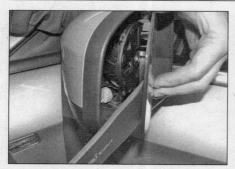

5.69 Using a plastic spatula or similar tool, gently prise free the mirror glass

5.70 Withdraw the approach light bulbholder from the mirror body

5.71 Pull out the capless bulb from the bulbholder

Side approach light

69 Pull the outer edge of the exterior mirror glass rearwards, insert a plastic spatula or similar tool, and gently prise the glass from place **(see illustration)**.

70 Withdraw the approach light bulbholder from the mirror body **(see illustration)**.

71 Pull out the capless bulb, and press a new one into place **(see illustration)**.

72 Refitting is a reversal of removal.

Rear lights

Direction indicator and brake/tail light

73 Remove the access panel from the loadspace side trim **(see illustration)**. If working on the left-hand side on Estate models, release the three catches and remove the side cover.

5.73 Remove the access panel from the loadspace side trim

74 Disconnect the wiring connector from the bulbholder on the rear of the light unit **(see illustration)**.

75 Squeeze together the two tabs on the

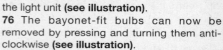

5.74 Disconnect the wiring connector from the bulbholder

bulbholder and withdraw the bulbholder from the light unit **(see illustration)**.

76 The bayonet-fit bulbs can now be removed by pressing and turning them anti-clockwise **(see illustration)**.

77 Fit the new bulb(s), then clip the bulbholder back onto the light unit, making sure that the clips engage securely.

78 Reconnect the wiring connector and refit the access panel/side cover.

Reversing light, tail light and foglight

79 Open the tailgate, and remove the access panel **(see illustration)**.

80 Squeeze together the two tabs on the bulbholder and withdraw the bulbholder from the light unit **(see illustrations)**.

81 The bayonet-fitting bulbs can now be

5.75 Squeeze together the two tabs and withdraw the bulbholder from the light unit

5.76 Depress and twist the bulb anti-clockwise to remove it

5.79 Open the tailgate, and remove the access panel

5.80a Squeeze together the two tabs on the bulbholder...

5.80b... and withdraw the bulbholder from the light unit

5.81 Depress and twist the bulb anti-clockwise to remove it

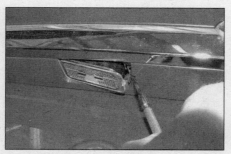

5.85 Insert a small screwdriver into the slot and carefully prise the number plate light unit from the tailgate

5.86 Remove the bulbholder from the light unit

5.87 Pull out the capless bulb from the bulbholder

5.91a Withdraw the high-level brake light unit…

5.91b… and disconnect the wiring connector

removed by pressing and turning them anti-clockwise **(see illustration)**.

82 Fit the new bulb(s), then clip the bulbholder back onto the light unit, making sure that the clips engage securely.

83 Refit the access panel to the tailgate.

Number plate light

84 To make access easier, open the boot lid/tailgate and hold it approximately half-open.

85 Insert a small screwdriver into the slot on the side of the light unit and carefully prise the light unit from its location **(see illustration)**.

86 Remove the bulbholder from the light unit **(see illustration)**.

87 Pull out the capless bulb, and press a new one into place **(see illustration)**.

88 Refit the bulbholder to the light unit, then press the light unit back into place.

High-level brake light

Saloon and Hatchback models

89 Remove the boot lid/tailgate trim panel as described in Chapter 11, Section 27.

90 Insert a screwdriver through the holes in the light unit bulbholder and carefully push the light unit from its location to release the internal retaining clips.

91 Once the clips are released, withdraw the light unit and disconnect the wiring connector **(see illustrations)**.

92 Again, using the screwdriver inserted through the holes in the bulbholder, pull the bulbholder from the light unit **(see illustrations)**.

93 Pull out the relevant capless bulb, and press a new one into place **(see illustration)**.

94 Press the bulbholder back into the light unit then reconnect the wiring connector and refit the light unit to the boot lid/tailgate.

95 Refit the boot lid/tailgate trim panel as described in Chapter 11, Section 27.

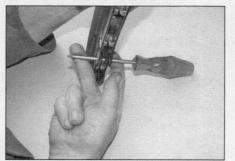

5.92a Insert a screwdriver through the holes in the bulbholder…

5.93 Pull out the relevant capless bulb from the bulbholder

Estate models

96 Open the tailgate and pull the upper trim panel away from the tailgate to release the internal clips **(see illustration)**.

97 Insert a screwdriver through the holes in

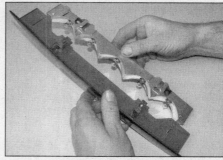

5.92b… and pull the bulbholder from the light unit

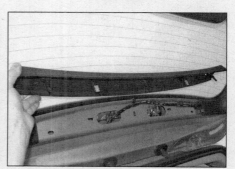

5.96 Pull the upper trim panel away from the tailgate to release the internal clips

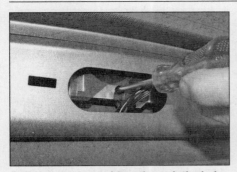

5.97 Insert a screwdriver through the holes in the bulbholder and push the light unit from its location

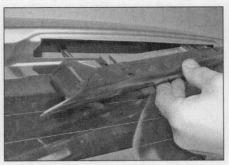

5.98a Withdraw the light unit...

5.98b... disconnect the wiring connector...

5.98c... and the tailgate washer hose

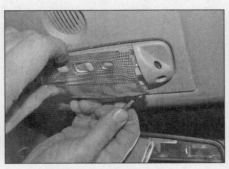

6.2a Unclip the interior light lens...

6.2b... and pull the festoon type bulb from the contacts

the light unit bulbholder and carefully push the light unit from its location to release the internal retaining clips **(see illustration)**.
98 Once the clips are released, withdraw the light unit and disconnect the wiring connector and the tailgate washer hose **(see illustrations)**.
99 Again, using the screwdriver inserted through the holes in the bulbholder, pull the bulbholder from the light unit **(see illustrations 5.92a and 5.92b)**.
100 Pull out the relevant capless bulb, and press a new one into place **(see illustration 5.93)**.

101 Press the bulbholder back into the light unit then reconnect the wiring connector and washer hose.
102 Refit the light unit to the tailgate, then refit the upper trim panel.

6 Bulbs (interior lights) – renewal

General

1 Refer to Section 5, paragraph 1.

Interior lights

2 Unclip the lens, and pull the interior light festoon type bulb from the contacts **(see illustrations)**.
3 Fit a new bulb using a reversal of the removal procedure.

Reading lights

4 Insert a small screwdriver into the slot in the front face of the light unit. Depress the clip and carefully prise the light unit from its location **(see illustrations)**.
5 Disconnect the wiring connectors and remove the light unit.

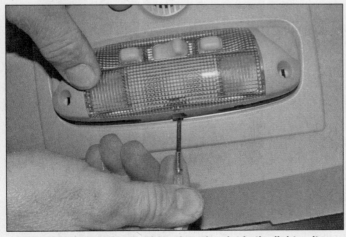

6.4a Insert a small screwdriver into the slot in the light unit...

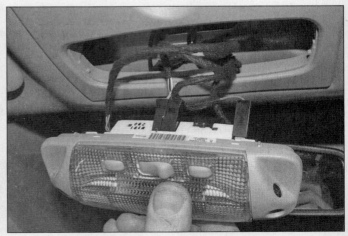

6.4b... then depress the clip and prise the light unit from its location

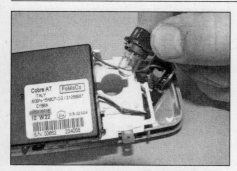

6.6 Turn the relevant bulbholder anti-clockwise and remove it from the light unit

6.7 Pull out the capless bulb from the bulbholder

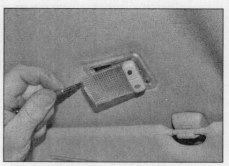

6.9 Carefully prise the light unit from its location

6 Turn the relevant bulbholder anti-clockwise and remove it from the light unit **(see illustration)**.

7 Pull out the capless bulb, and press a new one into place **(see illustration)**.

8 Refitting is a reversal of removal.

Sunvisor/vanity mirror light

9 Carefully prise the light unit from its location **(see illustration)**.

10 Pull the capless bulb from the bulbholder **(see illustration)**.

11 Fit the new bulb using a reversal of the removal procedure.

Glovebox/luggage area light

12 Carefully prise the light unit from its location **(see illustration)**.

13 Pull out the capless bulb from the bulbholder **(see illustration)**.

14 Fit the new bulb using a reversal of the removal procedure.

Instrument panel illumination

15 It is not possible to renew the instrument panel bulbs individually as they are of LED design and soldered to a printed circuit board. Where an LED is not functioning, the complete instrument panel must be renewed.

Switch illumination

16 The switches are illuminated by LEDs, and cannot be renewed separately. Refer to Section 4 and remove the relevant switch.

Heater/air conditioning control unit illumination

17 The control panel is illuminated by non-renewable LEDs. If defective, the control panel may need to be renewed.

Footwell illumination

18 Release the bulbholder from its location under the facia **(see illustration)**.

19 Pull out the capless bulb from the bulbholder.

20 Fit the new bulb using a reversal of the removal procedure.

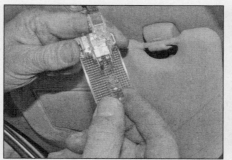

6.10 Pull the capless bulb from the bulbholder

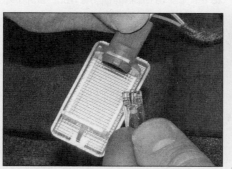

6.13 Pull out the capless bulb from the bulbholder

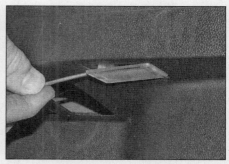

6.12 Carefully prise the light unit from its location

6.18 Release the footwell illumination bulbholder from its location under the facia

7 Exterior light units – removal and refitting

Headlight

Caution: On models equipped with xenon gas discharge headlights, disconnect the battery negative lead as described in Chapter 5A Section 4, prior to working on the headlights.

1 Open the bonnet and remove the plastic rivet securing the radiator grille extension to the front panel by unscrewing the centre section and withdrawing the rivet body.

2 Undo the headlight upper retaining screw and the lower retaining screw adjacent to the radiator grille.

3 Carefully pull the corner of the grille and bumper towards the front of the car.

4 Lift the corner of the headlight and move the unit as far as possible towards the rear of the car.

5 Pull the headlight towards the centre of the car, behind the grille and bumper, to disengage it from the lower outer attachment point.

6 Disconnect the wiring connector at the rear of the headlight and remove the unit from the car.

7 Refitting is a reversal of removal.

Front foglight

8 The procedure is described as part of the bulb renewal procedure in Section 5.

Indicator side repeater light

9 The procedure is described as part of the bulb renewal procedure in Section 5.

7.12a Undo the retaining screw (arrowed)…

7.12b… and remove the side approach light from the mirror body

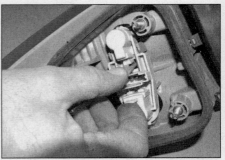

7.15 Squeeze together the two tabs and withdraw the bulbholder from the light unit

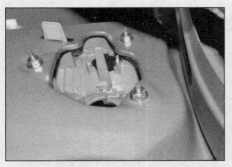

7.16 Undo the three nuts securing the light unit to the rear wing

7.17 Withdraw the light unit, then slide it to the rear to disengage the front retaining lug

Side approach light

10 Pull the outer edge of the exterior mirror glass rearwards, insert a plastic spatula or similar tool, and gently prise the glass from place **(see illustration 5.69)**.
11 Withdraw the approach light bulbholder from the mirror body **(see illustration 5.70)**.
12 Undo the retaining screw and remove the side approach light from the mirror body **(see illustrations)**.
13 Refitting is a reversal of removal.

Rear wing light unit

14 Remove the access panel from the loadspace side trim **(see illustration 5.73)**. If working on the left-hand side on Estate models, release the three catches and remove the side cover.
15 Squeeze together the two tabs on the bulbholder and withdraw the bulbholder from the light unit **(see illustration)**.
16 Undo the three nuts securing the light unit to the rear wing **(see illustration)**.
17 Withdraw the light unit from the wing, then slide it to the rear to disengage the front retaining lug **(see illustration)**.
18 Refitting is a reversal of removal.

Boot lid/tailgate light

Saloon and Hatchback models

19 Remove the tailgate trim panel as described in Chapter 11, Section 27.
20 Using a plastic spatula, and starting at the upper right-hand corner, carefully prise up the tailgate exterior moulding above the number plate. Continue working across the top of the moulding until all the clips have been released, then remove the moulding from the tailgate **(see illustrations)**.
21 Undo the four screws securing the number plate light panel to the tailgate and withdraw the panel **(see illustrations)**.
22 Disconnect the wiring connectors at the number plate lights, and at the release and

7.20a Carefully prise up the tailgate exterior moulding above the number plate…

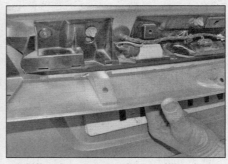

7.20b… then remove the moulding from the tailgate

7.21a Undo the two left-hand screws (arrowed)…

7.21b… and two right-hand screws (arrowed) securing the number plate light panel to the tailgate

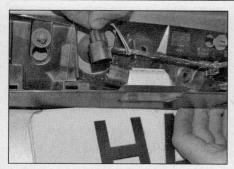

7.22 Disconnect the wiring connectors at the number plate lights, and at the release and lock switches

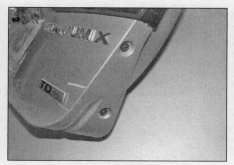

7.23a Undo the two screws at each end...

7.23b... and the two screws (arrowed) above the number plate securing the lower outer moulding

lock switches **(see illustration)**. Release the wiring from the cable-ties and clips and remove the number plate light panel.

23 Undo the two screws at each end, and the two screws above the number plate securing the lower outer moulding to the boot lid/tailgate **(see illustrations)**.

24 Pull the moulding to the rear on each side to disengage the clips at the base of the light unit **(see illustration)**.

25 Pull the moulding down to disengage the clips along the lower edge, securing the moulding to the boot lid/tailgate. Remove the moulding from the car.

26 Squeeze together the two tabs on the bulb- holder and withdraw the bulbholder from the light unit **(see illustrations 5.80a and 5.80b)**.

27 From inside the boot lid/tailgate, undo the two nuts securing the light unit to the boot lid/tailgate **(see illustration)**.

28 Withdraw the light unit, disengage the outer locating tabs and remove the unit from the car **(see illustrations)**.

29 Refitting is a reversal of removal.

Estate models

30 Remove the tailgate trim panel as described in Chapter 11, Section 27.

31 From inside the tailgate, undo the nuts securing the number plate light panel to the tailgate **(see illustration)**.

32 Undo the two outer screws and withdraw the number plate light panel from the tailgate **(see illustrations)**.

7.24 Pull the moulding to the rear on each side to disengage the clips at the base of the light unit

7.27 Undo the two nuts (arrowed) securing the light unit to the boot lid/tailgate

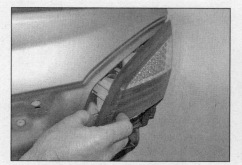

7.28a Withdraw the light unit...

7.28b... and disengage the outer locating tabs

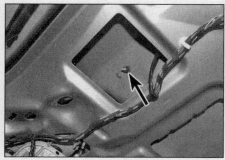

7.31 Number plate light panel retaining nut (arrowed)

7.32a Undo the two outer screws (arrowed)...

7.32b... and withdraw the number plate light panel from the tailgate

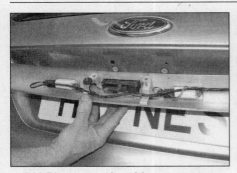

7.33 Disconnect the wiring connectors at the number plate lights, and tailgate release and lock switches

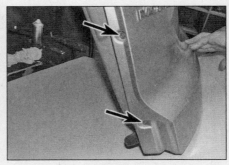

7.34a Undo the two screws at each end (arrowed)…

7.34b… and the two screws (arrowed) above the number plate securing the lower outer moulding to the tailgate

33 Disconnect the wiring connectors at the number plate lights, and tailgate release and lock switches **(see illustration)**. Release the wiring from the cable-ties and clips and remove the number plate light panel.
34 Undo the two screws at each end, and the two screws above the number plate securing the lower outer moulding to the tailgate **(see illustrations)**.
35 Pull the moulding to the rear on each side to disengage the clips at the base of the light unit **(see illustration)**.
36 Pull the moulding down to disengage the clips along the lower edge, securing the moulding to the tailgate. Remove the moulding from the car **(see illustrations)**.
37 Squeeze together the two tabs on the

bulbholder and withdraw the bulbholder from the light unit.
38 From inside the tailgate, undo the two nuts securing the light unit to the tailgate **(see illustration)**.
39 Withdraw the light unit, disengage the outer locating tabs and remove the unit from the car **(see illustration)**.
40 Refitting is a reversal of removal.

Number plate light

41 The procedure is described as part of the bulb renewal procedure in Section 5.

High-level brake light

42 The procedure is described as part of the bulb renewal procedure in Section 5.

8 Headlight adjuster components – removal and refitting

Adjuster switch

1 Refer to Section 4, paragraphs 14 to 17.

Adjuster motor

2 The motor is integral with the headlight, and is not available separately. The headlight is removed as described in Section 7.

9 Headlight beam alignment – general information

1 All models are equipped with an electrical vertical beam adjuster unit – this can be used to adjust the headlight beam to compensate for the load which the car is carrying. An adjuster switch is provided on the facia. Refer to the car's handbook for further information.
2 Accurate adjustment of the headlight beam is only possible using optical beam-setting equipment, and this work should therefore be carried out by a Ford dealer or suitably-equipped workshop.
3 For reference, the headlights can be finely adjusted by rotating the adjuster screws fitted to the top of each light unit.

7.35 Pull the moulding to the rear on each side to disengage the clips at the base of the light unit

7.36a Pull the moulding down to disengage the clips along the lower edge…

7.36b… then remove the moulding from the car

7.38 Undo the two nuts (arrowed) securing the light unit to the tailgate

7.39 Withdraw the light unit and disengage the outer locating tabs

Driving on the left or right

Note: *For information on the lighting control module, see Section 22.*

4 On vehicles with adaptive front headlights (the headlight reflectors turn in the direction of the steering) it is possible to adjust the headlight beams for driving on the right-hand or left-hand side of the road. Remove the headlight as described in Section 7.

5 Depress the two tabs and remove the cover from the rear of the headlight unit **(see illustration 5.26)**.

6 Press the lever on the side of the reflector upwards for driving on the right, and down for driving on the left.

---

10 Xenon gas discharge headlight system – component removal, refitting and adjustment

General information

1 Xenon gas discharge headlights are available as an optional extra on all models covered in this manual. The bulbs produce light by means of an electric arc, rather than by heating a metal filament as in conventional halogen bulbs. An electronically-operated shutter is fitted in front of the bulb which angles the light for dipped beam, then re-angles the light for main beam. A conventional halogen bulb is also fitted to augment the main beam light output. The arc is generated by a control circuit which operates at voltages of above 28 000 volts. The intensity of the emitted light means that the headlight beam has to be controlled dynamically to avoid dazzling other road users. An electronic control unit monitors the vehicle's pitch and overall ride height by sensors mounted on the front and rear suspension, and adjusts the beam range using the range control motors built into the headlight units.

⚠ **Warning: The discharge bulb starter circuitry operates at extremely high voltages. To avoid the risk of electric shock, ensure that the battery negative lead is disconnected before working on the headlight units (see Chapter 5A Section 4), then additionally switch the dipped beam on and off to discharge any residual voltage.**

Main beam

2 Proceed as described in Section 5.

Dipped beam

Caution: The dipped beam bulb is under gas pressure of at least 10 bars, therefore it is recommended that protective glasses are worn during this procedure.

3 Remove the headlight (see Section 7).

4 Depress the two tabs and remove the cover from the rear of the headlight unit **(see illustration 5.26)**.

5 Disconnect the wiring plug, then undo

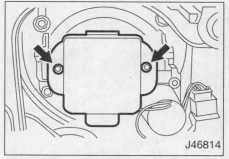

10.5 Undo the bolts (arrowed) and pull the bulb and module rearwards

the two retaining bolts and pull the bulb and module rearwards **(see illustration)**. If the glass is accidentally touched, clean it with methylated spirit.

6 Fit the new bulb using a reversal of the removal procedure.

Sidelight and direction indicator

7 Proceed as described in Section 5.

Lighting control module

Note: *If a new module is to be fitted, it must be configured using Ford dedicated diagnostic equipment. Entrust this task to a Ford dealer or suitably-equipped specialist.*

8 The lighting control module is fitted to vehicles with xenon high-intensity gas discharge lights, or models with adaptive front lighting system. The module is located behind the glovebox on the passenger's side.

9 Remove the glovebox as described in Chapter 11, Section 27.

10 Disconnect the wiring plug, then undo the two bolts and remove the module.

11 Refitting is a reversal of removal.

Front ride height sensor

12 The sensor is attached to the lower control arm of the left-hand wheel. Apply the handbrake, then jack up the front of the vehicle and support it on axle stands (see 'Jacking and vehicle support'). Remove the wheel.

13 Undo the bolt securing the sensor arm bracket to the control arm.

14 Undo the two nuts securing the sensor bracket to the vehicle body.

15 Disconnect the wiring plug as the sensor is withdrawn.

16 Refitting is a reversal of removal. Note that if a new sensor has been fitted, then a calibration procedure must be carried out. This requires access to Ford diagnostic equipment – entrust this task to a Ford dealer or suitably-equipped specialist.

Rear ride height sensor

17 The sensor is secured to the lower control arm and the rear subframe. Chock the front wheels, then jack up the rear of the vehicle and support it on axle stands (see 'Jacking and vehicle support').

11.3 Undo the two lower screws (arrowed) securing the instrument panel to the facia

18 Disconnect the sensor wiring plug, then undo the nuts and remove the sensor, bracket and lever arm assembly.

19 Refitting is a reversal of removal. Note that if a new sensor has been fitted, then a calibration procedure must be carried out. This requires access to Ford diagnostic equipment – entrust this task to a Ford dealer or suitably-equipped specialist.

Driving on the left or right

20 On models equipped with xenon gas discharge headlights, the 'dipping' characteristics of the unit can be set-up for countries who drive on the left or right. Remove the headlight as described in Section 7.

21 Depress the two tabs and remove the cover from the rear of the headlight unit **(see illustration 5.26)**.

22 Press the lever on the side of the reflector upwards for driving on the right, and down for driving on the left.

Beam adjustment

23 The basic alignment procedure of the headlights is the same as normal halogen headlights (see Section 9). However, before the procedure is attempted, the ride height sensors must be calibrated using dedicated Ford test equipment. Therefore this task should be entrusted to a Ford dealer or suitably-equipped specialist.

---

11 Instrument panel – removal and refitting

Note: *If a new instrument panel is to be fitted, the configuration information stored within the unit must be uploaded to Ford diagnostic equipment prior to removal, and downloaded to the new unit once installed. Entrust this task to a Ford dealer or suitably-equipped specialist.*

Removal

1 Disconnect the battery negative lead as described in Chapter 5A Section 4.

2 Remove the steering column upper shroud as described in Chapter 11, Section 27.

3 Undo the two lower screws securing the instrument panel to the facia **(see illustration)**.

11.4a Insert a round-ended steel rule into the upper centre of the instrument panel...

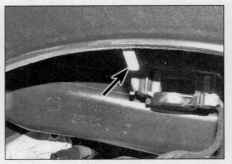

11.4b... to push up the upper retaining tab (arrowed)

11.5 Withdraw the instrument panel and disconnect the wiring connector

4 Using a round-ended steel rule, insert the rule into the upper centre of the instrument panel to push up the upper retaining tab **(see illustrations)**.
5 Withdraw the instrument panel from the facia, disconnect the wiring connector and remove the panel **(see illustration)**.

Refitting

6 Refitting is a reversal of removal.

12 Horns – removal and refitting

Removal

1 The horns are located under the front bumper on the right-hand side.

12.4 Horn mounting bracket retaining bolt (arrowed)

2 Remove the front bumper as described in Chapter 11, Section 6.
3 Disconnect the wiring plugs from the horns.
4 Unscrew the mounting bracket retaining bolt, and remove the horns **(see illustration)**.
5 If necessary, undo the retaining nut(s) and remove the horn(s) from the mounting bracket.

Refitting

6 Refitting is a reversal of removal.

13 Wiper arm – removal and refitting

Removal

1 Operate the wiper motor, then switch it off so that the wiper arm returns to the park position.

13.3a Prise up the wiper arm spindle nut cover...

2 Before removing an arm, mark its parked position on the glass with a strip of adhesive tape.
3 Prise up the wiper arm spindle nut cover, then slacken and remove the spindle nut **(see illustrations)**. Recover the washer.
4 Lift the blade off the glass, and pull the wiper arm off its spindle. Note that on some models, the wiper arms may be very tight on the spindle splines – it should be possible to lever the arm off the spindle, using a flat-bladed screwdriver (take care not to damage the windscreen cowl panel). In extreme cases, it may even be necessary to use a small puller to free the arm **(see illustration)**.

Refitting

5 Ensure that the wiper arm and spindle splines are clean and dry, then refit the arm to the spindle. Align the wiper blade with the tape fitted on removal.
6 Refit the spindle nut, tightening it securely, and clip the nut cover back into position.

14 Windscreen wiper motor and linkage – removal and refitting

Removal

1 Remove the windscreen cowl panel as described in Chapter 11, Section 23.
2 Undo the three bolts securing the wiper motor and linkage assembly to the scuttle **(see illustrations)**.

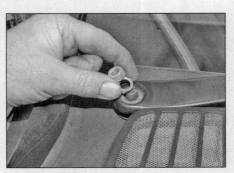

13.3b... then remove the retaining nut and washer

13.4 If necessary, use a small puller to free the wiper arm

14.2a Undo the two right-hand bolts (arrowed)...

14.2b... and left-hand bolt (arrowed) securing the wiper motor and linkage assembly to the scuttle

14.3a Withdraw the motor and linkage assembly from its location...

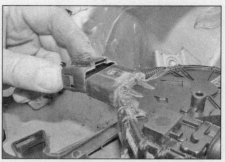

14.3b... and disconnect the motor wiring plug

14.5a Unscrew the crank arm retaining nut...

14.5b... and lift the crank arm off the motor spindle

14.6 Wiper motor retaining screws (arrowed)

3 Withdraw the motor and linkage assembly from its location, and disconnect the motor wiring plug **(see illustrations)**.

4 If the motor is to be removed, move the motor crank arm to a position where all three motor retaining screws will be accessible after removal of the crank arm.

5 Hold the crank arm using an open-ended spanner and unscrew the crank arm retaining nut. Lift the crank arm off the motor spindle **(see illustrations)**.

6 Undo the three retaining screws and remove the motor from the linkage frame **(see illustration)**.

Refitting

7 Prior to refitting the motor, reconnect the wiring plug, then operate the motor using the windscreen wiper switch. Turn the switch off and allow the motor to stop in the park position. Disconnect the wiring plug.

8 Refit the motor to the linkage frame and tighten the retaining screws securely.

9 Bring the crank arm into position over the motor and align it between the two arrows on the linkage frame **(see illustration)**.

10 Fit the crank arm to the motor spindle, then refit the retaining nut and tighten it securely.

11 Reconnect the wiring plug, then refit the motor and linkage assembly to the scuttle and securely tighten the three retaining bolts.

12 Refit the windscreen cowl panel as described in Chapter 11, Section 23.

15 Tailgate wiper motor – removal and refitting

Removal

1 Remove the tailgate trim panel as described in Chapter 11, Section 27.

2 Remove the wiper arm as described in Section 13.

3 Disconnect the wiper motor wiring plug.

4 Remove the three motor mounting bolts, recover the washers, and withdraw the motor from the tailgate **(see illustration)**.

Refitting

5 Refitting is a reversal of removal. Ensure

that the wiper motor spindle grommet stays in place in the tailgate as the spindle is fitted back through.

16 Washer system components – removal and refitting

Washer fluid reservoir

1 The windscreen washer fluid reservoir is located behind the front bumper on the left-hand side.

2 Remove the front bumper as described in Chapter 11, Section 6.

14.9 Align the crank arm between the two arrows on the linkage frame

15.4 Tailgate motor mounting bolts

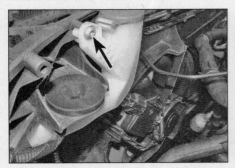

16.3 Undo the retaining bolt (arrowed) and remove the washer reservoir filler neck

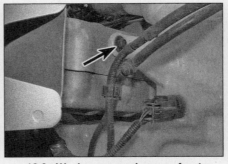

16.6a Washer reservoir upper front retaining bolt (arrowed)…

16.6b… lower front retaining bolt (arrowed)…

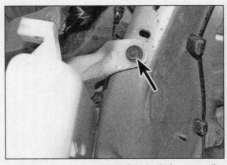

16.6c… and rear retaining bolt (arrowed)

16.11 Disconnect the wiring plug and the washer hoses from the washer pump

3 Undo the retaining bolt and remove the reservoir filler neck **(see illustration)**.

4 Remove the engine management powertrain control module (PCM) as described in Chapter 4A, Section 10, or Chapter 4B, Section 12, as applicable.

5 Disconnect the wiring plugs and the washer hoses from the washer pump(s) and fluid level sensor. Anticipate some spillage of washer fluid (have a suitable container ready).

6 Undo the three reservoir retaining bolts, and remove the reservoir from the car **(see illustrations)**.

7 Refitting is a reversal of removal. Make sure the washer hoses are securely reconnected to their original positions.

Washer fluid pump

8 If possible, siphon the fluid from the reservoir into a suitable container using a long tube inserted through the filler neck.

9 Firmly apply the handbrake, then jack up the front of the vehicle and support it securely on axle stands (see 'Jacking and vehicle support').

10 Undo the fasteners and remove the engine undertray (where fitted), followed by the shield under the radiator.

11 Disconnect the wiring plug and the washer hoses from the washer pump **(see illustration)**. Anticipate some spillage of washer fluid (have a suitable container ready).

12 Prise the pump from the reservoir, and recover the rubber sealing grommet. If all the fluid was not removed, position a container beneath the reservoir.

13 Examine the rubber sealing grommet, and renew if necessary.

14 Refitting is a reversal of removal, but take care not to push the grommet into the reservoir when refitting the pump. Make sure that the pump is securely fitted in its sealing grommet, and make sure that the fluid hose(s) are securely reconnected.

Fluid level sensor

15 If possible, siphon the fluid from the reservoir into a suitable container using a long tube inserted through the filler neck.

16 Firmly apply the handbrake, then jack up the front of the vehicle and support it securely on axle stands (see 'Jacking and vehicle support').

17 Undo the fasteners and remove the engine undertray (where fitted), followed by the shield under the radiator.

18 Disconnect the wiring plug from the fluid level sensor **(see illustration)**. Anticipate

some spillage of washer fluid (have a suitable container ready).

19 Prise the sensor from the reservoir, and recover the rubber sealing grommet. If all the fluid was not removed, position a container beneath the reservoir.

20 Examine the rubber sealing grommet, and renew if necessary.

21 Refitting is a reversal of removal, but take care not to push the grommet into the reservoir when refitting the sensor. Make sure that the sensor is securely fitted in its sealing grommet, and make sure that the wiring plug is securely reconnected.

Windscreen washer jet

22 Open the bonnet, and support it on its stay.

23 Prise out the retainers and remove the sound deadening pad from inside the bonnet **(see illustration)**.

24 Pull the T-piece hose connector off the end of the washer jet **(see illustration)**.

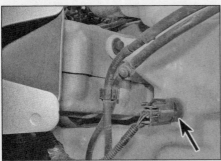

16.18 Washer fluid level sensor (arrowed)

16.23 Prise out the retainers and remove the sound deadening pad from inside the bonnet

16.24 Pull the T-piece hose connector off the end of the washer jet

16.25a Release the wiring connector from the clip on the bonnet...

16.25b... then disconnect the connector

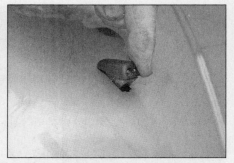

16.26a Push the jet forward and lift it up at the rear...

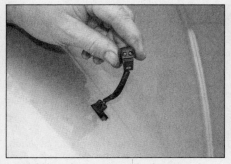

16.26b... then remove the jet from the outside of the bonnet

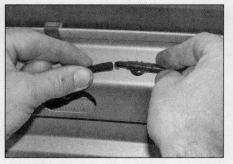

16.29 Disconnect the washer hose at the T-piece connector on the tailgate

16.30a Insert a screwdriver up through the hole in the tailgate...

25 Release the wiring connector from the clip on the bonnet, then disconnect the connector **(see illustrations)**.
26 Push the jet forward, lift it up at the rear and remove the jet from the outside of the bonnet **(see illustrations)**.
27 Refitting is a reversal of removal.

Tailgate washer jet

Hatchback models

28 Remove the tailgate trim panel as described in Chapter 11, Section 27.
29 Disconnect the washer hose at the T-piece connector on the tailgate **(see illustration)**.
30 Insert a screwdriver up through the hole in the tailgate and depress the tab on the underside of the jet, then remove the jet from the outside of the tailgate **(see illustrations)**.

31 Refitting is a reversal of removal.

Estate models

32 Remove of the high-level brake light is described in Section 7.
33 Lift the tabs on the high-level brake light and remove the jet from the light unit **(see illustration)**.
34 Refitting is a reversal of removal.

Headlight washer jet

35 Remove the front bumper as described in Chapter 11, Section 6.
36 Lift the jet cover to extend the jet, then unclip the cover from the jet.
37 Release the tabs securing the jet body to the inside of the bumper and remove the jet from the bumper.
38 Refitting is a reversal of removal.

17 Audio/DVD units –
removal and refitting

Note: *This Section applies only to standard-fit audio equipment.*
Note: *If a Ford 'Keycode' unit is fitted, and the battery is disconnected, the unit will not function again on reconnection until the correct security code is entered.*
Note: *If a new audio unit is to be fitted, it must be configured using Ford diagnostic equipment. Entrust this task to a Ford dealer or suitably-equipped specialist.*

Removal

1 Disconnect the battery negative lead as described in Chapter 5A Section 4.

16.30b... to depress the tab (arrowed) on the underside of the jet...

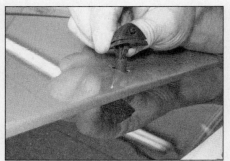

16.30c... then remove the jet from the outside of the tailgate

16.33 Lift the tabs on the high-level brake light and remove the jet from the light unit

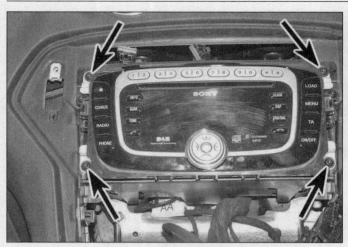

17.3a Undo the bolt in each corner of the audio unit (arrowed)...

17.3b... pull the audio unit from the facia...

Audio unit

2 Remove the facia upper centre switch panel as described in Section 4.

3 Undo the bolt in each corner of the audio unit. Pull the audio unit from the facia, and disconnect the wiring plugs and aerial lead **(see illustrations)**.

Audio unit with DVD navigation system

4 Removal of the audio unit requires the use of Ford special tools No GV3301 **(see illustration)**. Equivalent tools may be available from car audio specialist.

5 Lift out the centre console trim pad located under the ashtray **(see illustration 4.18)**.

6 On manual transmission models, unscrew the gear lever knob then unclip the gear lever gaiter trim surround. Lift the gaiter and the gear lever reverse detent mechanism off the gear lever shaft **(see illustrations 4.19a, 4.19b and 4.19c)**.

7 On automatic transmission models, unclip the selector lever trim surround from the centre console.

8 Starting at the rear, carefully pull up the centre console upper section to release the retaining clips, then disengage the front tabs and remove the upper section **(see illustration 4.21)**. Where applicable, disconnect the switch wiring connectors. On automatic transmission models, feed the selector lever trim surround through the aperture as the console upper section is removed.

9 On models up to 04/2010, carefully prise out the two triangular trim covers at each upper corner of the facia centre panel. Where applicable, disconnect the wiring connector from the power switch **(see illustration 4.22)**. On models from 04/2010, carefully unclip the side trim around and below the facia centre panel. Where applicable, disconnect the wiring connector from the power switch.

10 Undo the six retaining screws securing the centre panel to the facia **(see illustration 4.23a)**.

11 Carefully prise out the blanking plates in the lower corners of the centre panel **(see illustration)**.

12 Insert the four special tools into the slots in each corner of the audio control panel, with the straight edges toward the outside. Note that the tools are marked 'top left', etc. Pull the facia centre panel, complete with the audio unit from the facia.

13 Release the clocking catches and disconnect the wiring plugs as the unit is withdrawn.

CD autochanger

Note: *If a new autochanger is to be fitted, the new unit must be configured using Ford diagnostic equipment (WDS). Entrust this task to a Ford dealer or suitably-equipped specialist.*

14 Where applicable, undo the retaining screws and remove the cover over the autochanger.

15 Undo the two nuts and withdraw the unit from the mounting frame. Disconnect the wiring plug and remove the unit from the car.

Refitting

16 Refitting is a reversal of removal.

18 Loudspeakers – removal and refitting

Removal

Main door speakers

1 Remove the relevant door inner trim panel, as described in Chapter 11 Section 13.

17.3c... and disconnect the wiring plugs and aerial lead

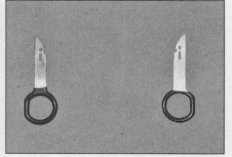

17.4 Ford special tools for audio unit removal

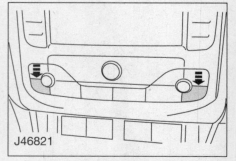

17.11 Prise out the blanking plates (arrowed) in the lower corners of the centre panel

18.2a Disconnect the wiring plug...

18.2b... then undo the three speaker retaining screws (arrowed)

18.3a Carefully prise free the speaker panel at the front of the door...

2 Disconnect the wiring plug, then undo the three screws and remove the speaker from the door **(see illustrations)**.

Front door tweeters

3 Using a plastic spatula or similar, carefully prise free the speaker panel at the front of the door. Disconnect the speaker wiring connector and remove the panel **(see illustrations)**.
4 Depress the tabs around the periphery of the speaker and withdraw the speaker from the panel **(see illustrations)**.

Rear door tweeters

5 Remove the rear door inner trim panel, as described in Chapter 11 Section 13.
6 Depress the tabs around the periphery of the speaker and withdraw the speaker from the panel**(see illustrations)**.

Facia speaker

7 Carefully prise up the grille panel from the upper centre of the facia. Disconnect the wiring connector for the sunlight sensor and remove the panel **(see illustrations)**.
8 Undo the two screws, disconnect the wiring plug and remove the speaker from the facia.

Subwoofer

9 The subwoofer is located in the spare wheel well in the luggage compartment.
10 Remove the loadspace side trim on the left-hand side as described in Chapter 11, Section 27.

18.3b... then disconnect the speaker wiring connector

18.4a Depress the tabs (arrowed) around the periphery of the speaker...

18.4b... and withdraw the front speaker from the panel

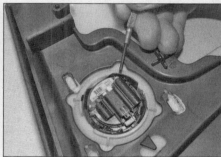

18.6a Depress the tabs around the periphery of the speaker...

18.6b... and withdraw the rear speaker from the panel

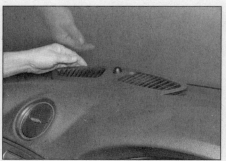

18.7a Carefully prise up the grille panel from the upper centre of the facia...

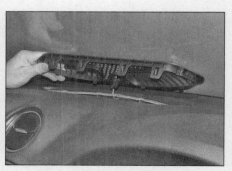

18.7b... and disconnect the wiring connector for the sunlight sensor

11 Trace the speaker wiring back to the connector and disconnect the wiring connector.

12 Undo the eight retaining screws and remove the subwoofer from the car.

Refitting

13 Refitting is a reversal of removal.

19 Radio aerial – removal and refitting

1 Removal and refitting of the aerial requires the headlining to be removed. This is an involved task, requiring patience and dexterity. Consequently, we recommend you entrust this task to a Ford dealer or upholstery specialist.

20 Parking aid components – general information, removal and refitting

General information

1 The parking aid system is available on all models. Four ultrasound sensors located in each bumper measure the distance to the closest object behind or in front the car, and inform the driver using acoustic signals from speakers located in the facia and behind the rear loadspace trim. The nearer the object, the more frequent the acoustic signals.

2 The system includes a control module and self-diagnosis program, and therefore, in the event of a fault, the vehicle should be taken to a Ford dealer or suitably-equipped specialist who will be able to interrogate the system.

Parking aid module (PAM)

Removal

3 The control unit is located behind the right-hand loadspace side trim panel. Remove the loadspace side trim as described in Chapter 11, Section 27.

4 Undo the two retaining bolts, and remove the PAM. As the unit is removed, disconnect the wiring plugs.

Refitting

5 Refitting is a reversal of removal.

Range/distance sensor

Removal

6 Remove the relevant bumper as described in Chapter 11, Section 6.

7 Disconnect the sensor wiring plug, then push the retaining clips apart, and pull the sensor from position **(see illustrations)**.

Refitting

8 Refitting is a reversal of removal. Press the sensor firmly into position until the retaining clips engage.

Front speaker

Removal

9 Remove the instrument panel as described in Section 11.

10 Disconnect the wiring plug, then undo the two screws and remove the speaker from the facia **(see illustration)**.

Refitting

11 Refitting is a reversal of removal.

Rear speaker

Removal

12 On Saloon and Hatchback models, remove the rear door aperture trim panel on the right-hand side as described in Chapter 11, Section 27. Disconnect the wiring plug, undo the two screws and remove the speaker from the C-pillar.

13 On Estate models, remove the parcel shelf support on the right-hand side as described in Chapter 11, Section 27. Disconnect the wiring plug, undo the two screws and remove the speaker.

Refitting

14 Refitting is a reversal of removal.

21 Anti-theft alarm system and engine immobiliser – general information

1 An anti-theft alarm and immobiliser system is fitted as standard equipment. Should the system become faulty, the vehicle should be taken to a Ford dealer or specialist for examination. They will have access to a special diagnostic tester which will quickly trace any fault present in the system.

22 Electronic control modules – removal and refitting

Note: *All of these modules are included in the vehicle's sophisticated self-diagnosis system. Should a fault occur, have the system interrogated using a fault code reader/ Ford test equipment, via the diagnostic socket located under the driver's side of the facia.*

Removal

1 Disconnect the battery negative lead as described in Chapter 5A Section 4.

Generic electronic module (GEM)

2 The GEM is integral with the passenger compartment fuse/relaybox. This module is responsible for the management of the following functions:

● Current distribution.
● Headlights.
● Headlight range adjustment.
● Foglamps.
● Sidelights.
● Reversing lights.
● High-level brake light.
● Interior lights.
● Wipers.
● Heated windscreen.
● Cruise control.
● Central locking.
● Anti-theft system.
● Handbrake switch.
● Brake fluid level monitoring.
● Fuel pump.
● Battery charging.
● Databus communications.

3 Remove the passenger's lower facia trim panel as described in Chapter 11, Section 27.

4 Turn the locking catch through 90° and

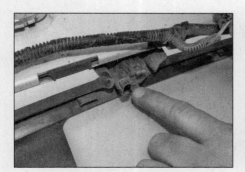

20.7a Push the retaining clips apart...

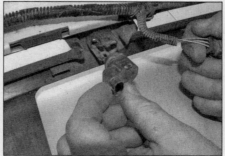

20.7b... and pull the sensor from position

20.10 Parking aid speaker located in the facia

lower the generic electronics module from its location **(see illustrations)**. Lift the module from the two lower pivots, disconnect the wiring plugs and remove the module.

Lighting control module (LCM)

5 This module is only fitted to vehicles equipped with adaptive front lights (AFS) or xenon high-intensity gas discharge headlights (HID). On models with AFS it controls the movement of the reflectors as the steering is operated, and on models with HID, it controls the range control as the suspension compresses or extends.
6 Renewal of the module is described in Section 10.

Keyless vehicle module (KVM)

7 Renewal of the KVM (also known as the keyless entry system module) is described in Chapter 11, Section 19.

Climate control module (CCM)

8 Removal of the CCM (which is integral with the heater/air conditioning system control panel) is described in Chapter 3, Section 10.

Door control module (DCM)

9 Remove the door inner trim panel as described in Chapter 11, Section 13.
10 Disconnect the wiring plugs, then undo the retaining bolts and release the door control module from the door **(see illustration)**.

Powertrain control module (PCM)

11 Renewal of the module is described in Chapter 4A, Section 10, or Chapter 4B, Section 12, as applicable.

Restraint control module (RCM)

12 Renewal of the module is described in Section 24.

Refitting

13 Refitting is a reversal of removal. If a new module has been fitted, software will need to be downloaded from Ford. Entrust this task to a Ford dealer or suitably-equipped specialist.

23 Airbag system – general information, precautions and system de-activation

General information

1 Driver's and front seat passenger's airbags are fitted as standard equipment on all models. The driver's airbag is fitted to the steering wheel centre pad, while the passenger's unit is fitted to the top of the facia.
2 Models equipped with higher specification equipment packages also have side airbags, which fire from modules built into the front seats, side curtain airbags, which are deployed from modules in the headlining and a driver's knee airbag deployed from a module under the facia.
3 The system is armed only when the ignition is switched on, however, a reserve power source maintains a power supply to the

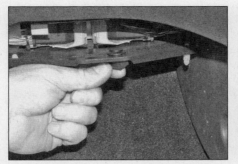

22.4a Turn the locking catch through 90°...

system in the event of a break in the main electrical supply. The system is activated by a 'g' sensor (deceleration sensor), incorporated in the electronic control unit. Note that the electronic control unit also controls the front seat belt tensioners, fitted to all models.
4 The airbags are inflated by gas generators, which force the bags out from their locations. Although these are safety items, their deployment is violently rapid, and this may cause injury if they are triggered unintentionally.

Precautions

⚠️ *Warning: The following precautions must be observed when working on vehicles equipped with an airbag system, to prevent the possibility of personal injury.*

General precautions

5 The following precautions must be observed when carrying out work on a vehicle equipped with an airbag:
a) *Do not disconnect the battery with the engine running.*
b) *Before carrying out any work in the vicinity of the airbag, removal of any of the airbag components, or any welding work on the car, de-activate the system as described in the following sub-Section.*
c) *Do not attempt to test any of the airbag system circuits using test meters or any other test equipment.*
d) *If the airbag warning light comes on, or any fault in the system is suspected, consult a Ford dealer without delay. Do not attempt to carry out fault diagnosis, or any dismantling of the components.*

Precautions when handling an airbag

a) *Transport the airbag by itself, bag upward.*
b) *Do not put your arms around the airbag.*
c) *Carry the airbag close to the body, bag outward.*
d) *Do not drop the airbag or expose it to impacts.*
e) *Do not attempt to dismantle the airbag unit.*
f) *Do not connect any form of electrical equipment to any part of the airbag circuit.*

Precautions when storing an airbag

a) *Store the unit in a cupboard with the airbag upward.*

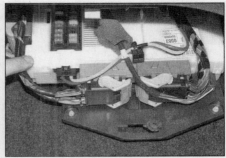

22.4b... and lower the generic electronics module from its location

22.10 Disconnect the wiring plugs from the door control module

b) *Do not expose the airbag to temperatures above 80°C.*
c) *Do not expose the airbag to flames.*
d) *Do not attempt to dispose of the airbag – consult a Ford dealer.*
e) *Never refit an airbag which is known to be faulty or damaged.*

De-activation of airbag system

6 The system must be de-activated as follows, before carrying out any work on the airbag components or surrounding area.
a) *Switch off the ignition.*
b) *Remove the ignition key.*
c) *Switch off all electrical equipment.*
d) *Disconnect the battery negative lead as described in Chapter 5A Section 4.*
e) *Insulate the battery negative lead to prevent any possibility of contact.*
f) *Wait for at least three minutes before carrying out any further work.*

24 Airbag system components – removal and refitting

⚠️ *Warning: Refer to the precautions given in Section 23 before attempting to carry out work on the airbag components.*

Driver's airbag unit
Models up to 13/07/2009

1 De-activate the airbag system as described in Section 23. The airbag unit is an integral part of the steering wheel centre pad.

24.9 Insert a small screwdriver into the access hole in the reverse of the steering wheel

24.10a Move the screwdriver toward the horizontal position…

24.10b… to release the wire spring (arrowed)…

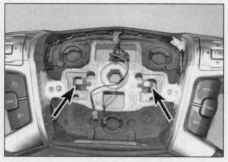

24.10c… from the lugs (arrowed) on the steering wheel

24.12a Withdraw the airbag from the steering wheel…

2 Remove the steering column shrouds as described in Chapter 11, Section 27.

3 Insert a flat-bladed screwdriver into the access hole at the base of the steering wheel and into contact with the airbag retaining wire spring. Push the screwdriver upwards to release the wire spring from the lug on the steering wheel, while at the same time pulling the base of the airbag away from the steering wheel.

4 Locate the two access holes in the reverse of the steering wheel and insert the screwdriver into one of the holes. Lift the screwdriver to release the wire spring from the lug on the

steering wheel, while at the same time pulling that side of the airbag away from the steering wheel. Release the other wire spring in the same way.

5 Once the airbag retaining wire springs have been released, withdraw the airbag from the steering wheel and disconnect the main wiring plug and the two earth leads. Remove the airbag and store it in a safe place, with reference to the precautions in Section 23.

6 Refitting is a reversal of removal, noting the following points:

a) *The battery must still be disconnected when reconnecting the airbag wiring.*

b) *Ensure that the airbag wiring plug is securely reconnected.*

c) *The airbag must be firmly pressed into place to secure the retaining wire spring.*

Models from 13/07/2009

7 De-activate the airbag system as described in Section 23. The airbag unit is an integral part of the steering wheel centre pad.

8 Remove the steering column shrouds as described in Chapter 11, Section 27.

9 Turn the steering wheel 90° to the left so the spokes are uppermost. Insert a small screwdriver into the access hole in the reverse of the steering wheel, with the screwdriver angled at approximately 50° to the horizontal and engaged under the airbag retaining wire spring **(see illustration)**.

10 Move the screwdriver toward the horizontal position to release the wire spring from the lug on the steering wheel, while at the same time pulling the side of the airbag away from the steering wheel **(see illustrations)**.

11 Turn the steering wheel 180° to the right so the spokes are uppermost, then repeat the procedure described in paragraphs 9 and 10.

12 Once the airbag retaining wire springs have been released, withdraw the airbag from the steering wheel and disconnect the main wiring plug and the two earth leads **(see illustrations)**. Remove the airbag and store it in a safe place, with reference to the precautions in Section 23.

24.12b… and disconnect the main wiring plug…

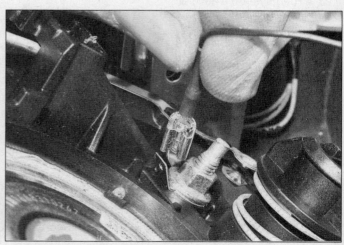

24.12c… and the earth leads

24.16a Disconnect the airbag wiring connector (arrowed)...

24.16b... then undo the two bolts (arrowed) securing the airbag support bracket to the facia crossmember

24.17a Undo the airbag support bracket nuts and upper retaining nuts (arrowed)...

13 Refitting is a reversal of removal, noting the following points:

a) *The battery must still be disconnected when reconnecting the airbag wiring.*
b) *Ensure that the airbag wiring plug is securely reconnected.*
c) *The airbag must be firmly pressed into place to secure the retaining wire spring.*

Passenger's airbag unit

14 De-activate the airbag system as described in Section 23.
15 Remove the glovebox as described in Chapter 11, Section 27.
16 Disconnect the airbag wiring connector, then undo the two bolts securing the airbag support bracket to the facia crossmember **(see illustrations)**.
17 Undo the two airbag support bracket nuts and the six nuts securing the airbag frame to the facia and facia crossmember, then remove the assembly from under the facia **(see illustrations)**.
18 Refitting is a reversal of removal, bearing in mind the following points:

a) *The battery must still be disconnected when reconnecting the airbag wiring.*
b) *Make sure that the wiring connector is securely reconnected.*
c) *Tighten the mounting bolts securely.*

Driver's knee airbag unit

19 De-activate the airbag system as described in Section 23.
20 Remove the driver's lower facia trim panel as described in Chapter 11, Section 27. The knee airbag is an integral part of the lower facia trim panel and cannot be individually removed.

Restraint control module (RCM)

21 De-activate the airbag system as described in Section 23.
22 Remove the centre console as described in Chapter 11, Section 28.
23 Disconnect the module wiring connectors, then undo the three retaining bolts and remove the module from the car**(see illustration)**.
24 Refitting is a reversal of removal.

Airbag clockspring (rotary connector)

25 De-activate the airbag system as described in Section 23.
26 Remove the steering wheel as described in Chapter 10 Section 15.
27 Remove the steering column shrouds as described in Chapter 11, Section 27.
28 Disconnect the wiring connector from the base of the clockspring **(see illustration)**.
29 Undo the three screws and remove the clockspring from the steering column **(see illustrations)**.
30 Refitting is a reversal of removal.

24.17b... followed by the lower retaining nuts (arrowed)

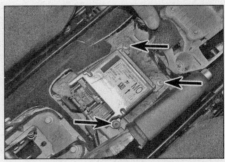

24.23 Restraint control module retaining bolts (arrowed)

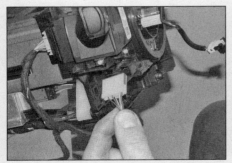

24.28 Disconnect the clockspring wiring connector

24.29a Undo the three screws (arrowed)...

24.29b... and remove the clockspring from the steering column

24.33 Centralise the clockspring so that the yellow indicator is visible in the clockspring window (arrowed)

31 Before refitting the steering wheel, the clockspring unit should be centralised (unless it is known absolutely that the steering wheel was centralised before removal, and that the clockspring has not been turned during or since its removal).

32 The procedure for centralising should be written on the clockspring itself. If this procedure conflicts significantly with what appears below, consult a Ford dealer for the latest information.

33 First, turn the clockspring anti-clockwise gently, until resistance is felt. Now turn the clockspring about two and a half turns clockwise, until the yellow indicator is visible in the clockspring window**(see illustration)**.

34 Refit the steering column shrouds and steering wheel as described in Chapter 11 Section 27 and Chapter 10 Section 15.

Side airbags

35 The side airbags are located internally within the front seat backrest, and no attempt should be made to remove them. Any suspected problems with the side airbag system should be referred to a Ford dealer.

Side curtain airbags

36 The modules for the side curtain airbags are located at the sides of the headlining. It is strongly recommended that any work which requires even just the removal of the headlining, never mind any work on the side curtain airbags, be referred to a Ford dealer.

Ford Mondeo wiring diagrams

Diagram 1

At the time of writing, certain wiring diagram technical information was unavailable. As a result these diagrams are a representative set covering most major electrical systems typically encountered on this model range.

 WARNING: *This vehicle is fitted with a supplemental restraint system (SRS) consisting of a combination of driver (and passenger) airbag(s), side impact protection airbags and seatbelt pre-tensioners. The use of electrical test equipment on any SRS wiring systems may cause the seatbelt pre-tensioners to abruptly retract and airbags to explosively deploy, resulting in potentially severe personal injury. Extreme care should be taken to correctly identify any circuits to be tested to avoid choosing any of the SRS wiring in error.*
For further information see airbag system precautions in body electrical systems chapter.
Note: The SRS wiring harness can normally be identified by yellow and/or orange harness or harness connectors.

Key to symbols

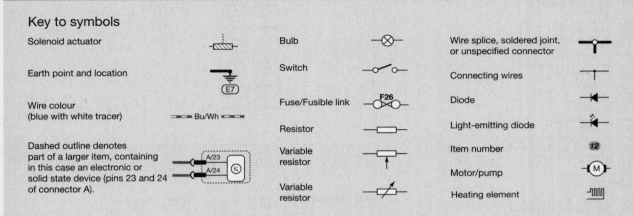

Solenoid actuator	
Earth point and location	E7
Wire colour (blue with white tracer)	Bu/Wh
Dashed outline denotes part of a larger item, containing in this case an electronic or solid state device (pins 23 and 24 of connector A).	A/23 A/24
Bulb	
Switch	
Fuse/Fusible link	F26
Resistor	
Variable resistor	
Variable resistor	
Wire splice, soldered joint, or unspecified connector	
Connecting wires	
Diode	
Light-emitting diode	
Item number	12
Motor/pump	M
Heating element	

Engine fusebox ②

F1	10A	Transmission control unit
F2	5A	Glow plug monitoring
F3	70A	Engine cooling fan
F3	80A	Power steering
F4	60A	Glow plugs
F5	60A	Engine cooling fan
F6	10A	Engine management
F7	5A	Relay coils
F8	10A	Engine management
F9	10A	Engine management
F10	10A	Engine management
F11	10A	Engine management
F12	10A	Engine management
F13	15A	Air conditioning relay
F14	15A	Diesel filter heater
F15	40A	Starter relay
F16	80A	Diesel auxiliary heater
F17	60A	Passenger fusebox supply A
F18	60A	Passenger fusebox supply B
F19	60A	Rear fusebox supply C
F20	60A	Rear fusebox supply D
F21	-	Spare
F22	30A	Windscreen wiper control module
F23	25A	Heated rear window
F24	30A	Headlight washer
F25	30A	ABS valves
F26	40A	ABS pump
F27	30A	Fuel fired heater
F28	40A	Heater blower
F29	-	Spare
F30	-	Spare
F31	15A	Horn
F32	5A	Fuel fired heater remote control
F33	5A	Light switch control unit, engine compartment fusebox coils
F34	40A	LH heated windscreen
F35	40A	RH heated windscreen
F36	5A	ABS
F37	10A	Heated washer jets

F37	10A	Heated washer jets
F38	5A	Adaptive cruise control
F39	15A	Adaptive front lighting system
F40	-	Spare
F41	20A	Instrument cluster
F42	10A	Engine management, transmission control, power steering
F43	5A	Headlight levelling, adaptive front lighting
F44	-	Spare
F45	15A	Rear wiper

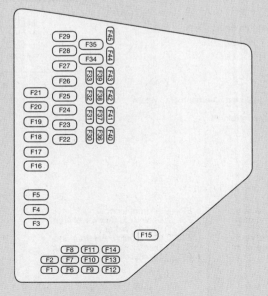

H47342

Ford Mondeo wiring diagrams

Diagram 2

Passenger fusebox 5

F1	5A	Rain sensor
F2	10A	SRS supply
F3	7.5A	ESP yaw rate sensor, accelerator pedal supply
F4	7.5A	Electronic feed, electronic fuse
F5	-	Spare
F6	15A	Audio system
F7	7.5A	Steering wheel control unit
F8	5A	Instrument cluster
F9	15A	Main beam
F10	20A	Electric sunroof
F11	7.5A	Reversing lights
F12	-	Spare
F13	15A	Front foglight
F14	15A	Front washer
F15	10A	Adaptive cruise control
F16	-	Spare
F17	10A	Interior lights
F18	5A	Engine immobiliser
F19	15A	Cigar lighter
F20	-	Spare
F21	5A	Alarm
F22	20A	Fuel pump
F23	-	Spare
F24	5A	Ignition switch
F25	10A	Fuel filler flap
F26	5A	Alarm, diagnostic socket
F27	5A	Steering column unit, climate control unit
F28	5A	Stop light switch

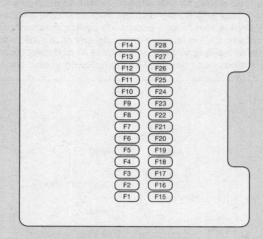

Rear fusebox 6

FA1	25A	LH front door control unit
FA2	25A	RH front door control unit
FA3	25A	LH rear door control unit
FA4	25A	RH rear door control unit
FA5	10A	Rear door locking (without rear door control units)
FA6	15A	Accessory sockets
FA7	5A	Relay coils
FA8	20A	Steering column lock
FA9	-	Spare
FA10	30A	Electric driver's seat
FA11	20A	Accessories, trailer control unit
FA12	-	Spare
FB1	5A	Parking aid control unit
FB2	15A	Suspension control unit
FB3	15A	Heated driver's seat
FB4	15A	Heated front passenger seat
FB5	15A	LH rear heated seat
FB6	-	Spare
FB7	15A	RH rear heated seat
FB8	-	Spare
FB9	30A	Electric passenger's seat
FB10	10A	Alarm horn
FB11	-	Spare
FB12	-	Spare
FC1	-	Spare
FC2	-	Spare
FC3	-	Spare
FC4	-	Spare
FC5	7.5A	CD changer, rear seat entertainment system
FC6	-	Spare
FC7	5A	Seat memory control unit
FC8	20A	Keyless entry
FC9	-	Spare
FC10	-	Spare
FC11	-	Spare
FC12	-	Spare

4 and 5 door models

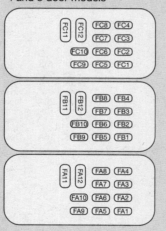

Estate models

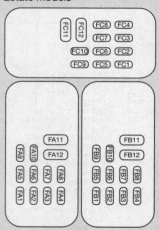

Earth locations

E1	Strut tower next to battery
E2	On sill below LH front door
E3	RH front inner wing
E4	On sill below LH front door
E5	Behind RH rear wheel arch
E6	LH front inner wing
E7	LH front inner wing
E8	Behind LH rear wheel arch
E9	Radio bracket
E10	On sill below RH front door
E11	On sill below LH front door
E12	On sill below RH front door

H47343

Colour codes

Wh	White	**Og**	Orange
Bu	Blue	**Rd**	Red
Gy	Grey	**Pk**	Pink
Ye	Yellow	**Gn**	Green
Bn	Brown	**Vt**	Violet
Bk	Black	**Sr**	Silver
Na	Natural	**Lg**	Light green

Key to items

1 Battery
2 Engine fusebox
  R1 = starter relay
  R9 = horn relay
3 Starter motor
4 Alternator
5 Passenger fusebox
  a = control unit
  b = battery saver relay
6 Rear fusebox
7 Ignition switch
8 Horn
9 Horn switch
10 Steering wheel control unit
11 Cigar lighter 1
12 Cigar lighter 2
13 Luggage compartment accessory socket
14 Engine cooling fan
15 Glow plug control unit
16 Glow plugs

Diagram 3

H47344

Starting & charging (without keyless system)

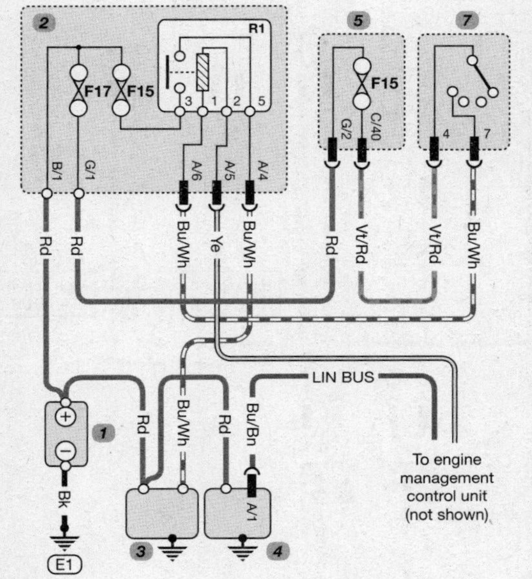

Horn

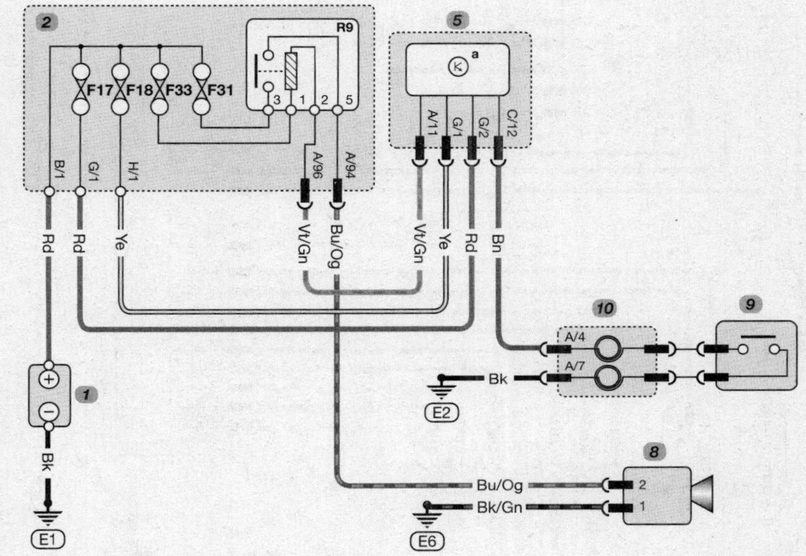

Cigar lighter & accessory sockets

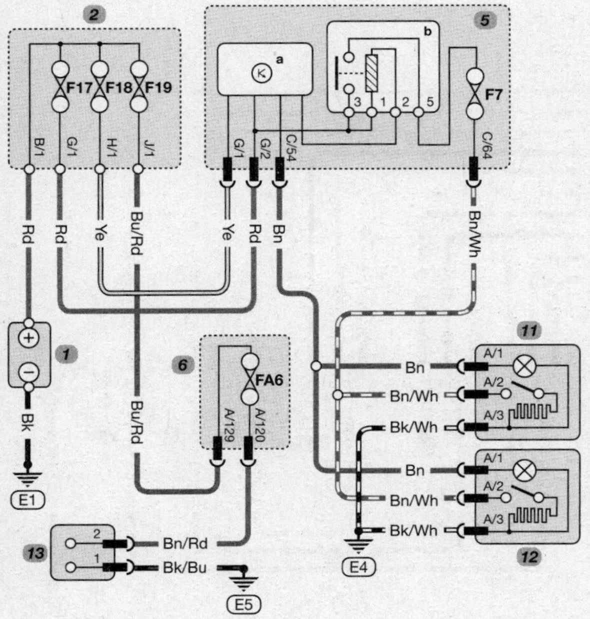

Engine cooling fan

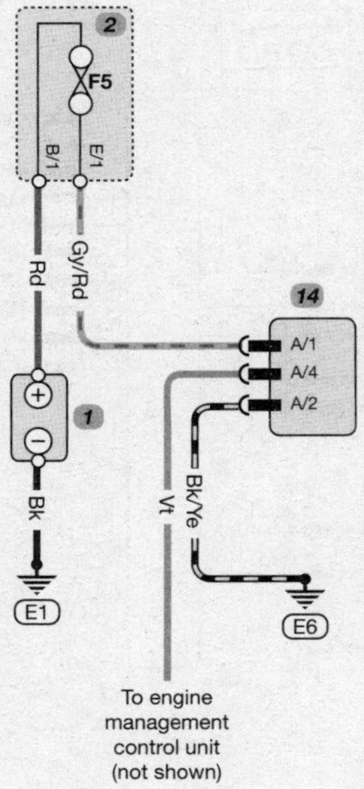

Diesel preheating

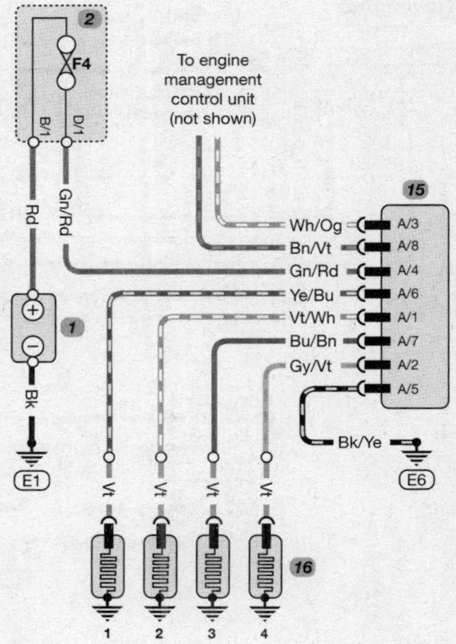

Colour codes

Wh	White	**Og**	Orange
Bu	Blue	**Rd**	Red
Gy	Grey	**Pk**	Pink
Ye	Yellow	**Gn**	Green
Bn	Brown	**Vt**	Violet
Bk	Black	**Sr**	Silver
Na	Natural	**Lg**	Light green

Key to items

1 Battery
2 Engine fusebox
   R7 = ignition relay
5 Passenger fusebox
   a = control unit
10 Steering wheel control unit
20 LH headlight unit
   a = sidelight
   b = main beam
   c = dip beam

d = headlight levelling
21 RH headlight unit
   a = sidelight
   b = main beam
   c = dip beam
   d = headlight levelling
22 Lighting switch control unit
24 Stop light switch
25 LH rear light unit 1
   a = stop/tail light

26 LH rear light unit 2
   a = tail/fog light
   b = reversing light
27 RH rear light unit 1
   a = stop/tail light
28 RH rear light unit 2
   a = tail/fog light
   b = reversing light
29 Reversing light switch
30 High level stop light

31 LH number plate light
32 RH number plate light
33 LH front foglight
34 RH front foglight

Diagram 4

H47345

Headlights

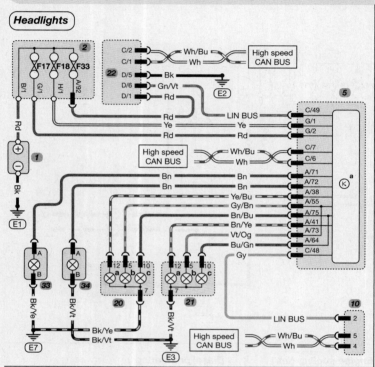

Headlight levelling

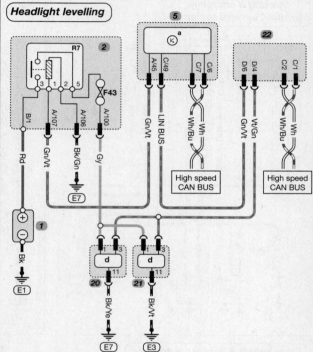

Rear lights

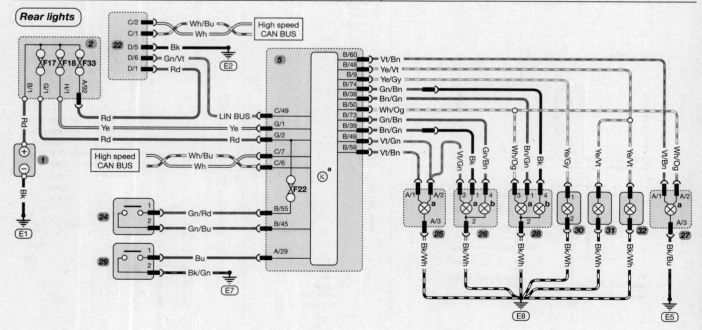

Colour codes

Wh	White	**Og**	Orange
Bu	Blue	**Rd**	Red
Gy	Grey	**Pk**	Pink
Ye	Yellow	**Gn**	Green
Bn	Brown	**Vt**	Violet
Bk	Black	**Sr**	Silver
Na	Natural	**Lg**	Light green

Key to items

1 Battery
2 Engine fusebox
  a = control unit
  R7 = ignition relay
5 Passenger fusebox
  b = battery saver relay
6 Rear fusebox
  a = heated rear window relay
10 Steering wheel control unit
35 Luggage compartment light

36 Luggage compartment lid switch
37 LH footwell light
38 RH footwell light
39 LH vanity mirror light
40 RH vanity mirror light
41 Glovebox light
43 Heated rear window
44 Heated front/rear window switch
45 Audio unit
46 CD changer

47 LH front tweeter
48 LH front speaker
49 RH front tweeter
50 RH front speaker
51 LH rear tweeter
52 LH rear speaker
53 RH rear tweeter
54 RH rear speaker
55 Audio antenna
56 Car phone antenna

Diagram 5

H47346

Interior lighting

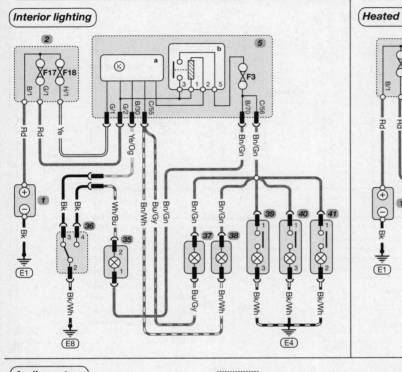

Heated rear window

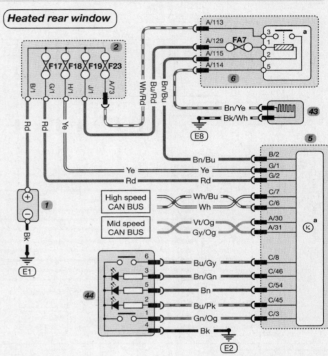

Audio system

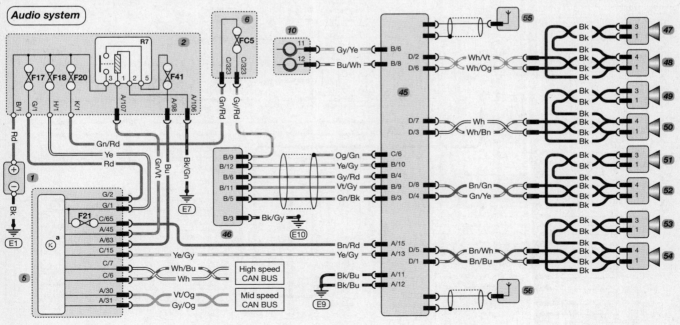

Colour codes

Wh	White	**Og**	Orange
Bu	Blue	**Rd**	Red
Gy	Grey	**Pk**	Pink
Ye	Yellow	**Gn**	Green
Bn	Brown	**Vt**	Violet
Bk	Black	**Sr**	Silver
Na	Natural	**Lg**	Light green

Key to items

1 Battery
2 Engine fusebox
  R3 = compressor clutch relay
  R5 = heater blower relay
  R7 = ignition relay
5 Passenger fusebox
  a = control unit
10 Steering wheel control unit
60 Evaporator temperature sensor
61 Climate control switch/control unit
  a = control unit
  b = heater bloer switch
  c = air conditioning switch
  d = recirculation switch
62 Heater blower motor
63 Heater blower resistors
64 Compressor clutch
65 Recirculation motor
66 Instrument cluster
67 Steering wheel controls
68 Handbrake switch
69 Low washer fluid switch
70 Low brake fluid switch
71 Fuel gauge sender unit

Diagram 6

H47347

Manual climate control

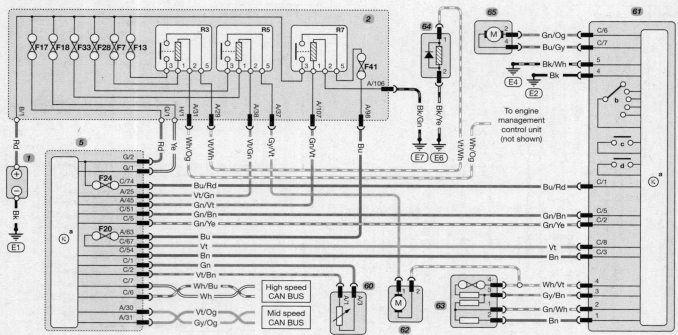

Instrument cluster

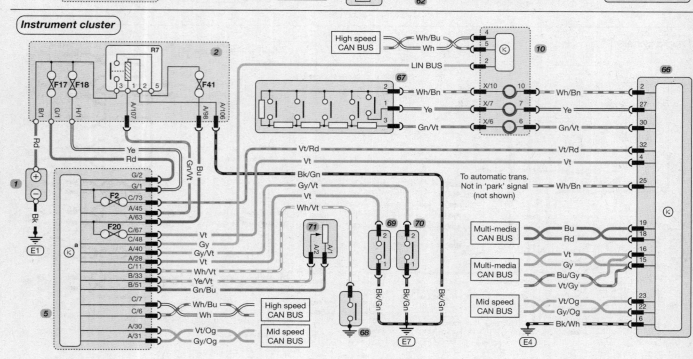

Colour codes

Wh	White	**Og**	Orange
Bu	Blue	**Rd**	Red
Gy	Grey	**Pk**	Pink
Ye	Yellow	**Gn**	Green
Bn	Brown	**Vt**	Violet
Bk	Black	**Sr**	Silver
Na	Natural	**Lg**	Light green

Key to items

1 Battery
2 Engine fusebox
  R7 = ignition relay
  R8 = intermittent wiper relay
  R10 = headlight washer relay
  R11 = front wiper relay
5 Passenger fusebox
  a = control unit
  b = battery saver relay

c = front washer relay
d = rear washer relay
6 Rear fusebox
  b = rear wiper relay
10 Steering wheel control unit
75 Headlight washer pump
76 Front washer pump
77 Rain sensor
78 LH heated washer jet

79 RH heated washer jet
80 Front wiper motor
81 Rear wiper motor

Diagram 7

H47348

Wash/wipe

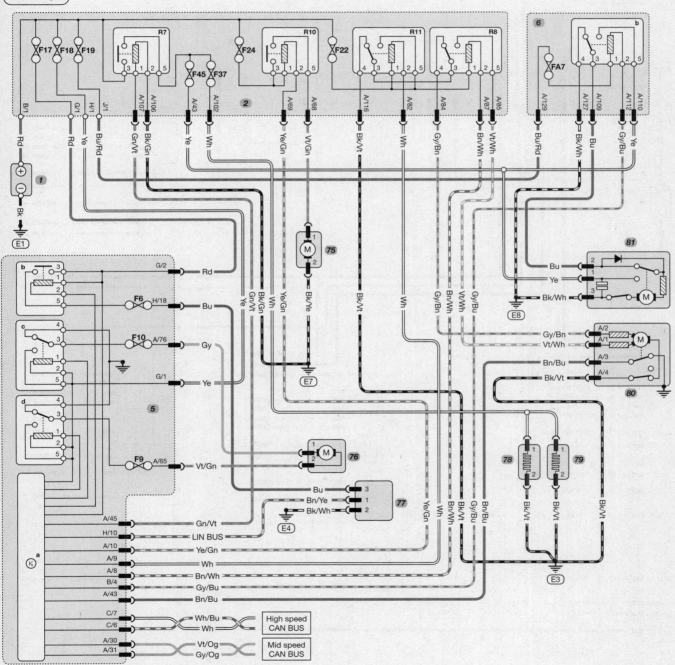

Colour codes

Wh	White	Og	Orange
Bu	Blue	Rd	Red
Gy	Grey	Pk	Pink
Ye	Yellow	Gn	Green
Bn	Brown	Vt	Violet
Bk	Black	Sr	Silver
Na	Natural	Lg	Light green

Key to items

1 Battery
2 Engine fusebox
5 Passenger fusebox
   a = control unit
   b = battery saver relay
6 Rear fusebox
85 Front door lock switch
86 Driver's door control unit
87 Passenger' door control unit
88 LH rear door control unit
89 RH rear door control unit
90 Driver's door window motor
91 Passenger's door window motor
92 LH rear door window motor
93 RH rear door window motor
94 Passenger's door window control switch
95 LH rear door window control switch
96 RH rear door window control switch

Diagram 8

H47349

Electric windows

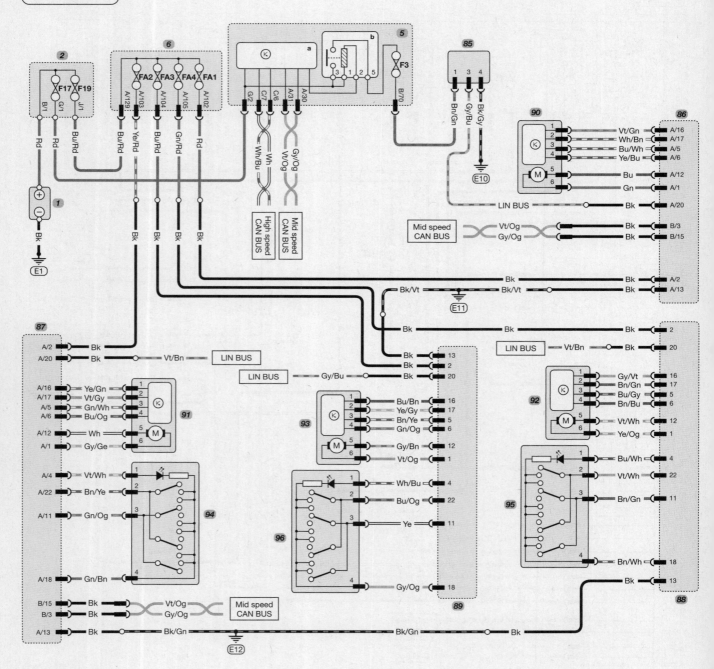

Colour codes

Wh	White	**Og**	Orange
Bu	Blue	**Rd**	Red
Gy	Grey	**Pk**	Pink
Ye	Yellow	**Gn**	Green
Bn	Brown	**Vt**	Violet
Bk	Black	**Sr**	Silver
Na	Natural	**Lg**	Light green

Key to items

1 Battery
2 Engine fusebox
5 Passenger fusebox
  a = control unit
  b = battery saver relay
6 Rear fusebox
7 Ignition switch
85 Front door lock switch
86 Driver's door control unit

87 Passenger's door control unit
97 LH mirror assembly
98 RH mirror assembly
99 Sunroof switch
100 Sunroof motor assembly

Diagram 9

H47350

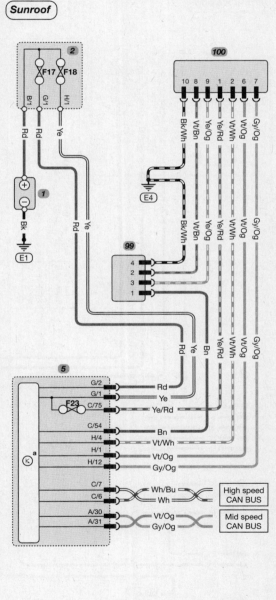

Electric mirrors

Sunroof

Colour codes

Wh	White	**Og**	Orange
Bu	Blue	**Rd**	Red
Gy	Grey	**Pk**	Pink
Ye	Yellow	**Gn**	Green
Bn	Brown	**Vt**	Violet
Bk	Black	**Sr**	Silver
Na	Natural	**Lg**	Light green

Key to items

1 Battery
2 Engine fusebox
5 Passenger fusebox
  a = control unit
  e = tailgate unlock relay
  f = fuel filler flap unlock relay
  g = fuel filler flap lock relay
6 Rear fusebox
86 Driver's door control unit

87 Passenger's door control unit
88 LH rear door control unit
89 RH rear door control unit
105 Tailgate release switch
106 Tailgate lock motor
107 Fuel filler flap motor
108 Driver's door lock assembly
109 Passenger's door lock assembly
110 LH rear door lock assembly

111 RH rear door lock assembly
112 RF receiver

Diagram 10

H47351

Central locking

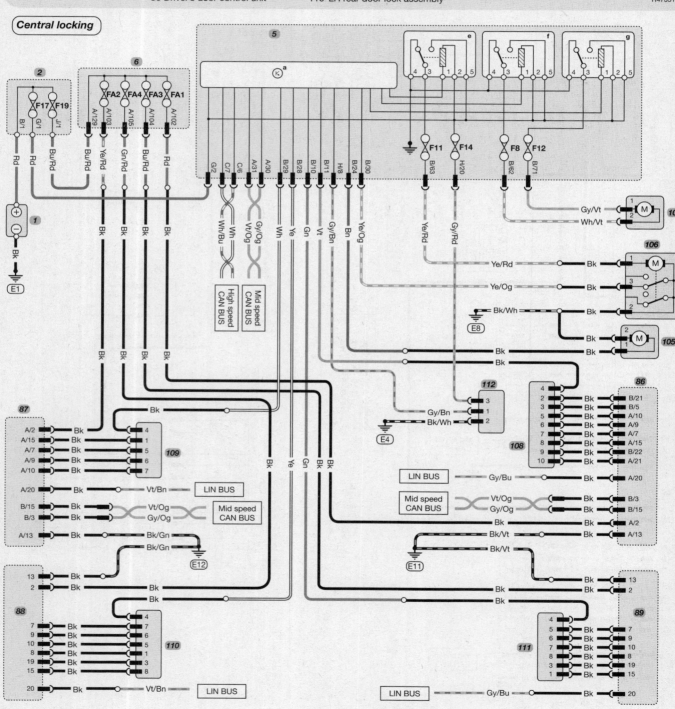

Reference REF•1

Dimensions and weights

Note: *All figures are approximate and may vary according to model. Refer to manufacturer's data for exact figures.*

Dimensions

Overall length:

    Saloon . . . .   4844 mm

    Hatchback . . . .   4802 mm

    Estate . . . .   4856 mm

Overall width (including door mirrors) . . . .   2078 mm

Overall height (unladen):

    Saloon and Hatchback . . . .   1500 mm

    Estate . . . .   1512 mm

Wheelbase . . . .   2850 mm

Front track . . . .   1589 mm

Rear track . . . .   1605 mm

Weights

Kerb weight . . . .   Refer to information contained on the vehicle identification plate

Gross vehicle weight . . . .   Refer to information contained on the vehicle identification plate

Maximum roof load (including weight of rack) . . . .   75 kg

Conversion factors

Length (distance)

Inches (in)	x 25.4	= Millimetres (mm)	x 0.0394	= Inches (in)
Feet (ft)	x 0.305	= Metres (m)	x 3.281	= Feet (ft)
Miles	x 1.609	= Kilometres (km)	x 0.621	= Miles

Volume (capacity)

Cubic inches (cu in; in³)	x 16.387	= Cubic centimetres (cc; cm³)	x 0.061	= Cubic inches (cu in; in³)
Imperial pints (Imp pt)	x 0.568	= Litres (l)	x 1.76	= Imperial pints (Imp pt)
Imperial quarts (Imp qt)	x 1.137	= Litres (l)	x 0.88	= Imperial quarts (Imp qt)
Imperial quarts (Imp qt)	x 1.201	= US quarts (US qt)	x 0.833	= Imperial quarts (Imp qt)
US quarts (US qt)	x 0.946	= Litres (l)	x 1.057	= US quarts (US qt)
Imperial gallons (Imp gal)	x 4.546	= Litres (l)	x 0.22	= Imperial gallons (Imp gal)
Imperial gallons (Imp gal)	x 1.201	= US gallons (US gal)	x 0.833	= Imperial gallons (Imp gal)
US gallons (US gal)	x 3.785	= Litres (l)	x 0.264	= US gallons (US gal)

Mass (weight)

Ounces (oz)	x 28.35	= Grams (g)	x 0.035	= Ounces (oz)
Pounds (lb)	x 0.454	= Kilograms (kg)	x 2.205	= Pounds (lb)

Force

Ounces-force (ozf; oz)	x 0.278	= Newtons (N)	x 3.6	= Ounces-force (ozf; oz)
Pounds-force (lbf; lb)	x 4.448	= Newtons (N)	x 0.225	= Pounds-force (lbf; lb)
Newtons (N)	x 0.1	= Kilograms-force (kgf; kg)	x 9.81	= Newtons (N)

Pressure

Pounds-force per square inch (psi; lbf/in²; lb/in²)	x 0.070	= Kilograms-force per square centimetre (kgf/cm²; kg/cm²)	x 14.223	= Pounds-force per square inch (psi; lbf/in²; lb/in²)
Pounds-force per square inch (psi; lbf/in²; lb/in²)	x 0.068	= Atmospheres (atm)	x 14.696	= Pounds-force per square inch (psi; lbf/in²; lb/in²)
Pounds-force per square inch (psi; lbf/in²; lb/in²)	x 0.069	= Bars	x 14.5	= Pounds-force per square inch (psi; lbf/in²; lb/in²)
Pounds-force per square inch (psi; lbf/in²; lb/in²)	x 6.895	= Kilopascals (kPa)	x 0.145	= Pounds-force per square inch (psi; lbf/in²; lb/in²)
Kilopascals (kPa)	x 0.01	= Kilograms-force per square centimetre (kgf/cm²; kg/cm²)	x 98.1	= Kilopascals (kPa)
Millibar (mbar)	x 100	= Pascals (Pa)	x 0.01	= Millibar (mbar)
Millibar (mbar)	x 0.0145	= Pounds-force per square inch (psi; lbf/in²; lb/in²)	x 68.947	= Millibar (mbar)
Millibar (mbar)	x 0.75	= Millimetres of mercury (mmHg)	x 1.333	= Millibar (mbar)
Millibar (mbar)	x 0.401	= Inches of water (inH₂O)	x 2.491	= Millibar (mbar)
Millimetres of mercury (mmHg)	x 0.535	= Inches of water (inH₂O)	x 1.868	= Millimetres of mercury (mmHg)
Inches of water (inH₂O)	x 0.036	= Pounds-force per square inch (psi; lbf/in²; lb/in²)	x 27.68	= Inches of water (inH₂O)

Torque (moment of force)

Pounds-force inches (lbf in; lb in)	x 1.152	= Kilograms-force centimetre (kgf cm; kg cm)	x 0.868	= Pounds-force inches (lbf in; lb in)
Pounds-force inches (lbf in; lb in)	x 0.113	= Newton metres (Nm)	x 8.85	= Pounds-force inches (lbf in; lb in)
Pounds-force inches (lbf in; lb in)	x 0.083	= Pounds-force feet (lbf ft; lb ft)	x 12	= Pounds-force inches (lbf in; lb in)
Pounds-force feet (lbf ft; lb ft)	x 0.138	= Kilograms-force metres (kgf m; kg m)	x 7.233	= Pounds-force feet (lbf ft; lb ft)
Pounds-force feet (lbf ft; lb ft)	x 1.356	= Newton metres (Nm)	x 0.738	= Pounds-force feet (lbf ft; lb ft)
Newton metres (Nm)	x 0.102	= Kilograms-force metres (kgf m; kg m)	x 9.804	= Newton metres (Nm)

Power

Horsepower (hp)	x 745.7	= Watts (W)	x 0.0013	= Horsepower (hp)

Velocity (speed)

Miles per hour (miles/hr; mph)	x 1.609	= Kilometres per hour (km/hr; kph)	x 0.621	= Miles per hour (miles/hr; mph)

Fuel consumption*

Miles per gallon, Imperial (mpg)	x 0.354	= Kilometres per litre (km/l)	x 2.825	= Miles per gallon, Imperial (mpg)
Miles per gallon, US (mpg)	x 0.425	= Kilometres per litre (km/l)	x 2.352	= Miles per gallon, US (mpg)

Temperature

Degrees Fahrenheit = (°C x 1.8) + 32   Degrees Celsius (Degrees Centigrade; °C) = (°F - 32) x 0.56

It is common practice to convert from miles per gallon (mpg) to litres/100 kilometres (l/100km), where mpg x l/100 km = 282

Spare parts are available from many sources, including maker's appointed garages, accessory shops, and motor factors. To be sure of obtaining the correct parts, it will sometimes be necessary to quote the vehicle identification number. If possible, it can also be useful to take the old parts along for positive identification. Items such as starter motors and alternators may be available under a service exchange scheme – any parts returned should be clean.

Our advice regarding spare parts is as follows.

Officially appointed garages

This is the best source of parts which are peculiar to your car, and which are not otherwise generally available (eg, badges, interior trim, certain body panels, etc). It is also the only place at which you should buy parts if the car is still under warranty.

Accessory shops

These are very good places to buy materials and components needed for the maintenance of your car (oil, air and fuel filters, light bulbs, drivebelts, greases, brake pads, touch-up paint, etc). Components of this nature sold by a reputable shop are usually of the same standard as those used by the car manufacturer.

Besides components, these shops also sell tools and general accessories, usually have convenient opening hours, charge lower prices, and can often be found close to home. Some accessory shops have parts counters where components needed for almost any repair job can be purchased or ordered.

Motor factors

Good factors will stock all the more important components which wear out comparatively quickly, and can sometimes supply individual components needed for the overhaul of a larger assembly (eg, brake seals and hydraulic parts, bearing shells, pistons, valves). They may also handle work such as cylinder block reboring, crankshaft regrinding, etc.

Engine reconditioners

These specialise in engine overhaul and can also supply components. It is recommended that the establishment is a member of the Federation of Engine Re-Manufacturers, or a similar society.

Tyre and exhaust specialists

These outlets may be independent, or members of a local or national chain. They frequently offer competitive prices when compared with a main dealer or local garage, but it will pay to obtain several quotes before making a decision. When researching prices, also ask what extras may be added – for instance fitting a new valve, balancing the wheel and tyre disposal all both commonly charged on top of the price of a new tyre.

Other sources

Beware of parts or materials obtained from market stalls, car boot sales, on-line auctions or similar outlets. Such items are not invariably sub-standard, but there is little chance of compensation if they do prove unsatisfactory. In the case of safety-critical components such as brake pads, there is the risk not only of financial loss, but also of an accident causing injury or death.

Second-hand components or assemblies obtained from a car breaker can be a good buy in some circumstances, but this sort of purchase is best made by the experienced DIY mechanic.

Vehicle identification

Modifications are a continuing and unpublicised process in car manufacture, quite apart from major model changes. Spare parts manuals and lists are compiled upon a numerical basis, the individual vehicle identification numbers being essential to correct identification of the component concerned.

When ordering spare parts, always give as much information as possible. Quote the car model, year of manufacture, body and engine numbers as appropriate.

The vehicle identification plate is located at the base of the driver's door B-pillar, and can be viewed with the door open **(see illustration)**. In addition to many other details, it carries the Vehicle Identification Number (VIN), maximum vehicle weight information, and codes for interior trim and body colours.

The vehicle identification number is also stamped into the driver's-side floor panel beside the front seat, and may also be viewed through the base of the windscreen on the passenger's side **(see illustration)**.

The engine identification codes are situated on the front face of the cylinder block, either on a plate, or stamped directly to the centre or side, of the block face. On some models, the engine type is shown on a sticker affixed to the timing belt cover.

Other identification numbers or codes are stamped on major items such as the gearbox, etc.

Emission level stage identification

On 2.0 litre diesel engines, references are constantly made throughout this manual to engines to emission level Stage III/IV or engines to emission level Stage V. The easiest way to identify these engines is to refer to the underbonnet check point photos on page 0•11, or use the engine codes listed in Chapter 2C Section 1.

VIN plate at the base of the driver's door pillar

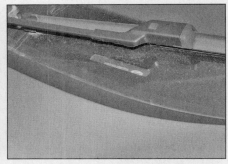

VIN is visible on the passenger side of the windscreen

Whenever servicing, repair or overhaul work is carried out on the car or its components, observe the following procedures and instructions. This will assist in carrying out the operation efficiently and to a professional standard of workmanship.

Joint mating faces and gaskets

When separating components at their mating faces, never insert screwdrivers or similar implements into the joint between the faces in order to prise them apart. This can cause severe damage which results in oil leaks, coolant leaks, etc upon reassembly. Separation is usually achieved by tapping along the joint with a soft-faced hammer in order to break the seal. However, note that this method may not be suitable where dowels are used for component location.

Where a gasket is used between the mating faces of two components, a new one must be fitted on reassembly; fit it dry unless otherwise stated in the repair procedure. Make sure that the mating faces are clean and dry, with all traces of old gasket removed. When cleaning a joint face, use a tool which is unlikely to score or damage the face, and remove any burrs or nicks with an oilstone or fine file.

Make sure that tapped holes are cleaned with a pipe cleaner, and keep them free of jointing compound, if this is being used, unless specifically instructed otherwise.

Ensure that all orifices, channels or pipes are clear, and blow through them, preferably using compressed air.

Oil seals

Oil seals can be removed by levering them out with a wide flat-bladed screwdriver or similar implement. Alternatively, a number of self-tapping screws may be screwed into the seal, and these used as a purchase for pliers or some similar device in order to pull the seal free.

Whenever an oil seal is removed from its working location, either individually or as part of an assembly, it should be renewed.

The very fine sealing lip of the seal is easily damaged, and will not seal if the surface it contacts is not completely clean and free from scratches, nicks or grooves. If the original sealing surface of the component cannot be restored, and the manufacturer has not made provision for slight relocation of the seal relative to the sealing surface, the component should be renewed.

Protect the lips of the seal from any surface which may damage them in the course of fitting. Use tape or a conical sleeve where possible. Where indicated, lubricate the seal lips with oil before fitting and, on dual-lipped seals, fill the space between the lips with grease.

Unless otherwise stated, oil seals must be fitted with their sealing lips toward the lubricant to be sealed.

Use a tubular drift or block of wood of the appropriate size to install the seal and, if the seal housing is shouldered, drive the seal down to the shoulder. If the seal housing is unshouldered, the seal should be fitted with its face flush with the housing top face (unless otherwise instructed).

Screw threads and fastenings

Seized nuts, bolts and screws are quite a common occurrence where corrosion has set in, and the use of penetrating oil or releasing fluid will often overcome this problem if the offending item is soaked for a while before attempting to release it. The use of an impact driver may also provide a means of releasing such stubborn fastening devices, when used in conjunction with the appropriate screwdriver bit or socket. If none of these methods works, it may be necessary to resort to the careful application of heat, or the use of a hacksaw or nut splitter device. Before resorting to extreme methods, check that you are not dealing with a left-hand thread!

Studs are usually removed by locking two nuts together on the threaded part, and then using a spanner on the lower nut to unscrew the stud. Studs or bolts which have broken off below the surface of the component in which they are mounted can sometimes be removed using a stud extractor.

Always ensure that a blind tapped hole is completely free from oil, grease, water or other fluid before installing the bolt or stud. Failure to do this could cause the housing to crack due to the hydraulic action of the bolt or stud as it is screwed in.

For some screw fastenings, notably cylinder head bolts or nuts, torque wrench settings are no longer specified for the latter stages of tightening, "angle-tightening" being called up instead. Typically, a fairly low torque wrench setting will be applied to the bolts/nuts in the correct sequence, followed by one or more stages of tightening through specified angles.

When checking or retightening a nut or bolt to a specified torque setting, slacken the nut or bolt by a quarter of a turn, and then retighten to the specified setting. However, this should not be attempted where angular tightening has been used.

Locknuts, locktabs and washers

Any fastening which will rotate against a component or housing during tightening should always have a washer between it and the relevant component or housing.

Spring or split washers should always be renewed when they are used to lock a critical component such as a big-end bearing retaining bolt or nut. Locktabs which are folded over to retain a nut or bolt should always be renewed.

Self-locking nuts can be re-used in non-critical areas, providing resistance can be felt when the locking portion passes over the bolt or stud thread. However, it should be noted that self-locking stiffnuts tend to lose their effectiveness after long periods of use, and should then be renewed as a matter of course.

Split pins must always be replaced with new ones of the correct size for the hole.

When thread-locking compound is found on the threads of a fastener which is to be re-used, it should be cleaned off with a wire brush and solvent, and fresh compound applied on reassembly.

Special tools

Some repair procedures in this manual entail the use of special tools such as a press, two or three-legged pullers, spring compressors, etc. Wherever possible, suitable readily-available alternatives to the manufacturer's special tools are described, and are shown in use. In some instances, where no alternative is possible, it has been necessary to resort to the use of a manufacturer's tool, and this has been done for reasons of safety as well as the efficient completion of the repair operation. Unless you are highly-skilled and have a thorough understanding of the procedures described, never attempt to bypass the use of any special tool when the procedure described specifies its use. Not only is there a very great risk of personal injury, but expensive damage could be caused to the components involved.

Environmental considerations

When disposing of used engine oil, brake fluid, antifreeze, etc, give due consideration to any detrimental environmental effects. Do not, for instance, pour any of the above liquids down drains into the general sewage system, or onto the ground to soak away. Many local council refuse tips provide a facility for waste oil disposal, as do some garages. You can find your nearest disposal point by calling the Environment Agency on 08708 506 506 or by visiting www.oilbankline.org.uk.

Note: It is illegal and anti-social to dump oil down the drain. To find the location of your local oil recycling bank, call 08708 506 506 or visit www.oilbankline.org.uk.

The jack supplied with the car's tool kit should only be used for changing the roadwheels – see Wheel changing at the front of this book. When carrying out any other kind of work, raise the car using a hydraulic (or 'trolley') jack, and always supplement the jack with axle stands positioned under the jacking/support points (see illustration). If the roadwheels do not have to be removed, consider using wheel ramps – if wished, these can be placed under the wheels once the car has been raised using a hydraulic jack, and then lowered onto the ramps so that it is resting on its wheels.

Only ever jack the car up on a solid, level surface. If there is even a slight slope, take great care that the car cannot move as the wheels are lifted off the ground. Jacking up on an uneven or gravelled surface is not recommended, as the weight of the car will not be evenly distributed, and the jack may slip as the car is raised.

As far as possible, do not leave the car unattended once it has been raised, particularly if children are playing nearby.

Before jacking up the front of the car, ensure that the handbrake is firmly applied. When jacking up the rear of the car, place wooden chocks in front of the front wheels, and engage first gear.

To raise the front and/or rear of the car, use the jacking/support points under the front/rear subframes, or at the front and rear ends of the door sills, which are located at the places marked by a notch in the sill's lower flange (see illustration). Position a block of wood with a groove cut in it on the jack head to prevent the car's weight resting on the sill edge; align the sill edge with the groove in the wood so that the car's weight is spread evenly over the surface of the block. Supplement the jack with axle stands (also with slotted blocks of wood) positioned as close as possible to the jacking points.

When using a hydraulic jack or axle stands, always try to position the jack head or axle stand head under one of the relevant jacking points.

Providing care is taken (and a block of wood is used to spread the load), the centre of the front subframe and centre of the rear axle beam, may be used as support points. It may be safe also to use reinforced areas of the floor pan ('chassis legs'), particularly those in the region of suspension mountings, as support points – consult a Ford dealer for advice before using anything other than the approved jacking points, however.

Do not jack the car under any other part of the sill, sump, floor pan, or directly under any of the steering or suspension components.

Never work under, around, or near a raised vehicle, unless it is adequately supported on stands. Do not rely on a jack alone, as even a hydraulic jack could fail under load.

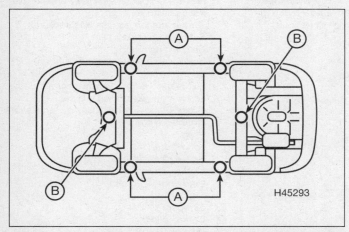

Sill jacking/supporting points (A) and chassis jacking points (B)

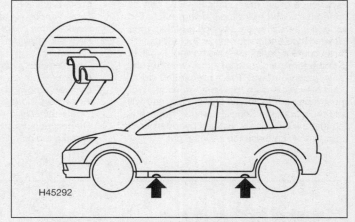

Jacking points on sill flanges are indicated by notches

Introduction

A selection of good tools is a fundamental requirement for anyone contemplating the maintenance and repair of a motor vehicle. For the owner who does not possess any, their purchase will prove a considerable expense, offsetting some of the savings made by doing-it-yourself. However, provided that the tools purchased meet the relevant national safety standards and are of good quality, they will last for many years and prove an extremely worthwhile investment.

To help the average owner to decide which tools are needed to carry out the various tasks detailed in this manual, we have compiled three lists of tools under the following headings: *Maintenance and minor repair, Repair and overhaul,* and *Special.* Newcomers to practical mechanics should start off with the *Maintenance and minor repair* tool kit, and confine themselves to the simpler jobs around the vehicle. Then, as confidence and experience grow, more difficult tasks can be undertaken, with extra tools being purchased as, and when, they are needed. In this way, a *Maintenance and minor repair* tool kit can be built up into a *Repair and overhaul* tool kit over a considerable period of time, without any major cash outlays. The experienced do-it-yourselfer will have a tool kit good enough for most repair and overhaul procedures, and will add tools from the *Special* category when it is felt that the expense is justified by the amount of use to which these tools will be put.

Maintenance and minor repair tool kit

The tools given in this list should be considered as a minimum requirement if routine maintenance, servicing and minor repair operations are to be undertaken. We recommend the purchase of combination spanners (ring one end, open-ended the other); although more expensive than open-ended ones, they do give the advantages of both types of spanner.

☐ *Combination spanners:*
   Metric - 8 to 19 mm inclusive
☐ *Adjustable spanner - 35 mm jaw (approx.)*
☐ *Spark plug spanner (with rubber insert) - petrol models*
☐ *Spark plug gap adjustment tool - petrol models*
☐ *Set of feeler gauges*
☐ *Brake bleed nipple spanner*
☐ *Screwdrivers:*
   Flat blade - 100 mm long x 6 mm dia
   Cross blade - 100 mm long x 6 mm dia
   Torx - various sizes (not all vehicles)
☐ *Combination pliers*
☐ *Hacksaw (junior)*
☐ *Tyre pump*
☐ *Tyre pressure gauge*
☐ *Oil can*
☐ *Oil filter removal tool (if applicable)*
☐ *Fine emery cloth*
☐ *Wire brush (small)*
☐ *Funnel (medium size)*
☐ *Sump drain plug key (not all vehicles)*

Repair and overhaul tool kit

These tools are virtually essential for anyone undertaking any major repairs to a motor vehicle, and are additional to those given in the *Maintenance and minor repair* list. Included in this list is a comprehensive set of sockets. Although these are expensive, they will be found invaluable as they are so versatile - particularly if various drives are included in the set. We recommend the half-inch square-drive type, as this can be used with most proprietary torque wrenches.

The tools in this list will sometimes need to be supplemented by tools from the *Special* list:

☐ *Sockets to cover range in previous list (including Torx sockets)*
☐ *Reversible ratchet drive (for use with sockets)*
☐ *Extension piece, 250 mm (for use with sockets)*
☐ *Universal joint (for use with sockets)*
☐ *Flexible handle or sliding T "breaker bar" (for use with sockets)*
☐ *Torque wrench (for use with sockets)*
☐ *Self-locking grips*
☐ *Ball pein hammer*
☐ *Soft-faced mallet (plastic or rubber)*
☐ *Screwdrivers:*
   Flat blade - long & sturdy, short (chubby), and narrow (electrician's) types
   Cross blade – long & sturdy, and short (chubby) types
☐ *Pliers:*
   Long-nosed
   Side cutters (electrician's)
   Circlip (internal and external)
☐ *Cold chisel - 25 mm*
☐ *Scriber*
☐ *Scraper*
☐ *Centre-punch*
☐ *Pin punch*
☐ *Hacksaw*
☐ *Brake hose clamp*
☐ *Brake/clutch bleeding kit*
☐ *Selection of twist drills*
☐ *Steel rule/straight-edge*
☐ *Allen keys (inc. splined/Torx type)*
☐ *Selection of files*
☐ *Wire brush*
☐ *Axle stands*
☐ *Jack (strong trolley or hydraulic type)*
☐ *Light with extension lead*
☐ *Universal electrical multi-meter*

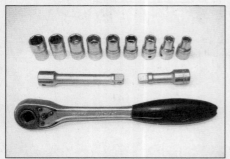

Sockets and reversible ratchet drive

Brake bleeding kit

Torx key, socket and bit

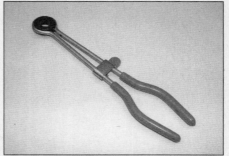

Hose clamp

Angular-tightening gauge

Special tools

The tools in this list are those which are not used regularly, are expensive to buy, or which need to be used in accordance with their manufacturers' instructions. Unless relatively difficult mechanical jobs are undertaken frequently, it will not be economic to buy many of these tools. Where this is the case, you could consider clubbing together with friends (or joining a motorists' club) to make a joint purchase, or borrowing the tools against a deposit from a local garage or tool hire specialist.

The following list contains only those tools and instruments freely available to the public, and not those special tools produced by the vehicle manufacturer specifically for its dealer network. You will find occasional references to these manufacturers' special tools in the text of this manual. Generally, an alternative method of doing the job without the vehicle manufacturers' special tool is given. However, sometimes there is no alternative to using them. Where this is the case and the relevant tool cannot be bought or borrowed, you will have to entrust the work to a dealer.

- [ ] *Angular-tightening gauge*
- [ ] *Valve spring compressor*
- [ ] *Valve grinding tool*
- [ ] *Piston ring compressor*
- [ ] *Piston ring removal/installation tool*
- [ ] *Cylinder bore hone*
- [ ] *Balljoint separator*
- [ ] *Coil spring compressors (where applicable)*
- [ ] *Two/three-legged hub and bearing puller*
- [ ] *Impact screwdriver*
- [ ] *Micrometer and/or vernier calipers*
- [ ] *Dial gauge*
- [ ] *Tachometer*
- [ ] *Fault code reader*
- [ ] *Cylinder compression gauge*
- [ ] *Hand-operated vacuum pump and gauge*
- [ ] *Clutch plate alignment set*
- [ ] *Brake shoe steady spring cup removal tool*
- [ ] *Bush and bearing removal/installation set*
- [ ] *Stud extractors*
- [ ] *Tap and die set*
- [ ] *Lifting tackle*

Buying tools

Reputable motor accessory shops and superstores often offer excellent quality tools at discount prices, so it pays to shop around.

Remember, you don't have to buy the most expensive items on the shelf, but it is always advisable to steer clear of the very cheap tools. Beware of 'bargains' offered on market stalls, on-line or at car boot sales. There are plenty of good tools around at reasonable prices, but always aim to purchase items which meet the relevant national safety standards. If in doubt, ask the proprietor or manager of the shop for advice before making a purchase.

Care and maintenance of tools

Having purchased a reasonable tool kit, it is necessary to keep the tools in a clean and serviceable condition. After use, always wipe off any dirt, grease and metal particles using a clean, dry cloth, before putting the tools away. Never leave them lying around after they have been used. A simple tool rack on the garage or workshop wall for items such as screwdrivers and pliers is a good idea. Store all normal spanners and sockets in a metal box. Any measuring instruments, gauges, meters, etc, must be carefully stored where they cannot be damaged or become rusty.

Take a little care when tools are used. Hammer heads inevitably become marked, and screwdrivers lose the keen edge on their blades from time to time. A little timely attention with emery cloth or a file will soon restore items like this to a good finish.

Working facilities

Not to be forgotten when discussing tools is the workshop itself. If anything more than routine maintenance is to be carried out, a suitable working area becomes essential.

It is appreciated that many an owner-mechanic is forced by circumstances to remove an engine or similar item without the benefit of a garage or workshop. Having done this, any repairs should always be done under the cover of a roof.

Wherever possible, any dismantling should be done on a clean, flat workbench or table at a suitable working height.

Any workbench needs a vice; one with a jaw opening of 100 mm is suitable for most jobs. As mentioned previously, some clean dry storage space is also required for tools, as well as for any lubricants, cleaning fluids, touch-up paints etc, which become necessary.

Another item which may be required, and which has a much more general usage, is an electric drill with a chuck capacity of at least 8 mm. This, together with a good range of twist drills, is virtually essential for fitting accessories.

Last, but not least, always keep a supply of old newspapers and clean, lint-free rags available, and try to keep any working area as clean as possible.

Micrometers

Dial test indicator ("dial gauge")

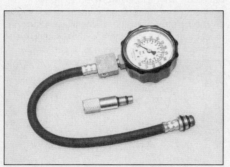

Oil filter removal tool (strap wrench type)

Compression tester

Bearing puller

This is a guide to getting your vehicle through the MOT test. Obviously it will not be possible to examine the vehicle to the same standard as the professional MOT tester. However, working through the following checks will enable you to identify any problem areas before submitting the vehicle for the test.

It has only been possible to summarise the test requirements here, based on the regulations in force at the time of printing. Test standards are becoming increasingly stringent, although there are some exemptions for older vehicles.

An assistant will be needed to help carry out some of these checks.

The checks have been sub-divided into four categories, as follows:

1 Checks carried out **FROM THE VEHICLE INTERIOR**

2 Checks carried out **WITH THE VEHICLE ON THE GROUND**

3 Checks carried out **WITH THE VEHICLE RAISED AND THE WHEELS FREE TO TURN**

4 Checks carried out on **YOUR VEHICLE'S EXHAUST EMISSION SYSTEM**

1 Checks carried out **FROM THE VEHICLE INTERIOR**

Handbrake (parking brake)

☐ Test the operation of the handbrake. Excessive travel (too many clicks) indicates incorrect brake or cable adjustment.

☐ Check that the handbrake cannot be released by tapping the lever sideways. Check the security of the lever mountings.

☐ If the parking brake is foot-operated, check that the pedal is secure and without excessive travel, and that the release mechanism operates correctly.

☐ Where applicable, test the operation of the electronic handbrake. The brake should engage and disengage without excessive delay. If the warning light does not extinguish, or a warning message is displayed when the brake is disengaged, this could indicate a fault which will need further investigation.

Footbrake

☐ Depress the brake pedal and check that it does not creep down to the floor, indicating a master cylinder fault. Release the pedal, wait a few seconds, then depress it again. If the pedal travels nearly to the floor before firm resistance is felt, brake adjustment or repair is necessary. If the pedal feels spongy, there is air in the hydraulic system which must be removed by bleeding.

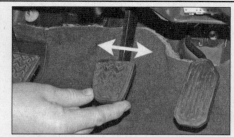

☐ Check that the brake pedal is secure and in good condition. Check also for signs of fluid leaks on the pedal, floor or carpets, which would indicate failed seals in the brake master cylinder.

☐ Check the servo unit (when applicable) by operating the brake pedal several times, then keeping the pedal depressed and starting the engine. As the engine starts, the pedal will move down. If not, the vacuum hose or the servo itself may be faulty.

Steering wheel and column

☐ Examine the steering wheel for fractures or looseness of the hub, spokes or rim.

☐ Move the steering wheel from side to side and then up and down. Check that the steering wheel is not loose on the column, indicating wear or a loose retaining nut. Continue moving the steering wheel as before, but also turn it slightly from left to right.

☐ Check that the steering wheel is not loose on the column, and that there is no abnormal movement of the steering wheel, indicating wear in the column support bearings or couplings.

☐ Check that the ignition lock (where fitted) engages and disengages correctly.

☐ Steering column adjustment mechanisms (where fitted) must be able to lock the column securely in place with no play evident.

Windscreen, mirrors and sunvisor

☐ The windscreen must be free of cracks or other significant damage within the 'swept area' of the windscreen. This is the area swept by the windscreen wipers. A second test area, known as 'Zone A', is the part of the swept area 290 mm wide, centred on the steering wheel centre line. Any damage in Zone A that cannot be contained in a 10 mm diameter circle, or any damage in the remainder of the swept area that cannot be contained in a 40 mm diameter circle, may cause the vehicle to fail the test.

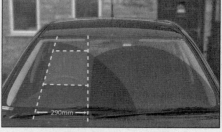

☐ Any items that may obscure the drivers view, such as stickers, sat-navs, anything hanging from the interior mirror, should be removed prior to the test.

☐ Vehicles registered after 1st August 1978 must have a drivers side mirror, and either an interior mirror, or a passenger's side mirror. Cameras (or indirect vision devices) may replace the mirrors, but they must function correctly.

☐ The driver's sunvisor must be capable of being stored in the "up" position.

Seat belts, seats and supplementary restraint systems (SRS)

Note: *The following checks are applicable to all seat belts, front and rear.*

☐ Examine the webbing of all the belts (including rear belts if fitted) for cuts, serious fraying or deterioration. Fasten and unfasten each belt to check the buckles. If applicable, check the retracting mechanism. Check the security of all seat belt mountings accessible from inside the vehicle, ensuring any height adjustable mountings lock securely in place.

☐ Where the seat belt is attached to a seat, the frame and mountings of the seat form part of the belt mountings, and are to be inspected as such.

☐ Any airbag, or SRS warning light must extinguish a few seconds after the ignition is switched on. Failure to do so indicates a fault which must be investigated.

☐ Seat belts with pre-tensioners, once activated, have a "flag" or similar showing on the seat belt stalk. This, in itself, is a reason for test failure.

☐ Check that the original airbag(s) is/are present, and not obviously defective.

☐ The seats themselves must be securely attached and the backrests must lock in the upright position. The driver's seat must also be able to slide forwards/rearwards, and lock in several positions.

Doors

☐ Both front doors must be able to be opened and closed from outside and inside, and must latch securely when closed.

☐ The rear doors must open from the outside.

☐ Examine all door hinges, catches and striker plates for missing, deteriorated, or insecure parts that could effect the opening and closing of the doors.

Speedometer

☐ The vehicle speedometer must be present, and appear operative. The figures on the speedometer must be legible, and illuminated when the lights are switched on.

2 Checks carried out **WITH THE VEHICLE ON THE GROUND**

Vehicle identification

☐ Number plates must be in good condition, secure and legible, with letters and numbers correctly spaced – spacing at (A) should be 33 mm and at (B) 11 mm. At the front, digits must be black on a white background and at the rear

black on a yellow background. Other background designs (such as honeycomb) are not permitted.

☐ The VIN plate and/or homologation plate must be permanently displayed and legible.

Electrical equipment

☐ Switch on the ignition and check the operation of the horn.

☐ Check the windscreen washers and wipers, examining the wiper blades; renew damaged or perished blades. The wiper blades must clear a large enough area of the windscreen to provide an 'adequate' view of the road, and be able to be parked in a position where they will not affect the drivers' view.

☐ On vehicles first used from 1st September 2009, the headlight washers (where fitted) must operate correctly.

☐ Check the operation of the stop-lights. This includes any lights that appear to be connected – Eg. high-level lights.

☐ Check the operation of the sidelights and number plate lights. The lenses and reflectors must be secure, clean and undamaged.

☐ Check the operation and alignment of the headlights. The headlight reflectors must not be tarnished and the lenses must be undamaged. Where plastic lenses are fitted, check they haven't deteriorated to the extent where they affect the light ouput or beam image. It's often possible to restore the plastic lens using a suitable polish or aftermarket treatment.

☐ Where HID or LED headlights are fitted, check the operation of the cleaning and self-levelling functions.

☐ The headlight main beam warning lamp must be functional.

☐ On vehicles first used from 1st March 2018, the daytime running lights (where fitted) must operate correctly.

☐ Switch on the ignition and check the operation of the direction indicators (including the instrument panel tell-tale) and the hazard warning lights. Operation of the sidelights and stop-lights must not affect the indicators – if it does, the cause is usually a bad earth at the rear light cluster. Indicators should flash at a rate of between 60 and 120 times per minute – faster or slower than this could indicate a fault with the flasher unit or a bad earth at one of the light units.

☐ The hazard warning lights must operate with the ignition on and off.

☐ Check the operation of the rear foglight(s), including the warning light on the instrument panel or in the switch. Note that the foglight

must be positioned in the centre or driver's side of the vehicle. If only the passenger's side illuminates, the test will fail.

☐ The warning lights must illuminate in accordance with the manufacturers' design (this includes any warning messages). For most vehicles, the ABS and other warning lights should illuminate when the ignition is switched on, and (if the system is operating properly) extinguish after a few seconds. Refer to the owner's handbook.

☐ On vehicles first used from 1st September 2009, the reversing lights must operate correctly when reverse gear is selected.

☐ Check the vehicle battery for security and leakage.

☐ Check the visible/accessible vehicle wiring is adequately supported, with no evidence of damage or deterioration that could result in a short-circuit.

Footbrake

☐ Examine the master cylinder, brake pipes and servo unit for leaks, loose mountings, corrosion or other damage. If ABS is fitted, this unit should also be examined for signs of leaks or corrosion.

☐ The fluid reservoir must be secure and the fluid level must be between the upper (**A**) and lower (**B**) markings.

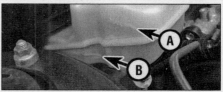

☐ Check the fluid in the reservoir for signs of contamination.

☐ Inspect both front brake flexible hoses for cracks or deterioration of the rubber. Turn the steering from lock to lock, and ensure that the hoses do not contact the wheel, tyre, or any part of the steering or suspension mechanism. With the brake pedal firmly depressed, check the hoses for bulges or leaks under pressure.

Steering and suspension

☐ Have your assistant turn the steering wheel from side to side slightly, up to the point where the steering gear just begins to transmit this movement to the roadwheels. Check for excessive free play between the steering wheel and the steering gear, indicating wear or insecurity of the steering column joints, the column-to-steering gear coupling, or the steering gear itself. With a standard (380 mm diameter) steering wheel, there should be no more than 13 mm of free play for rack-and-pinion systems, and no more than 75 mm for non-rack-and-pinion designs.

☐ Have your assistant turn the steering

wheel more vigorously in each direction, so that the roadwheels just begin to turn. As this is done, examine all the steering joints, linkages, fittings and attachments. Renew any component that shows signs of wear or damage. On vehicles with hydraulic power steering, check the security and condition of the steering pump, drivebelt and hoses.

☐ Note that all movement checks on power steering systems are carried out with the engine running.

☐ Check that the vehicle is standing level, and at approximately the correct ride height.

Exhaust system

☐ Start the engine. With your assistant holding a rag over the tailpipe, check the entire system for leaks. Repair or renew leaking sections.

3 Checks carried out **WITH THE VEHICLE RAISED AND THE WHEELS FREE TO TURN**

Jack up the front and rear of the vehicle, and securely support it on axle stands. Position the stands clear of the suspension assemblies. Ensure that the wheels are clear of the ground and that the steering can be turned from lock to lock.

Steering mechanism

☐ Have your assistant turn the steering from lock to lock. Check that the steering turns smoothly, and that no part of the steering mechanism, including a wheel or tyre, fouls any brake hose or pipe or any part of the body structure.

☐ Examine the steering rack rubber gaiters for damage or insecurity of the retaining clips. If power steering is fitted, check for signs of damage or leakage of the fluid hoses, pipes or connections. Also check for excessive stiffness or binding of the steering, a missing split pin or locking device, or severe corrosion of the body structure within 30 cm of any steering component attachment point.

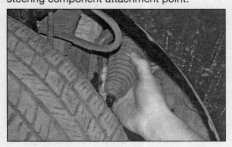

☐ Check the track rod end ball joint dust covers. Any covers that are missing, seriously damaged, deteriorated or insecure, may fail inspection.

Front and rear suspension and wheel bearings

☐ Starting at the front right-hand side, grasp the roadwheel at the 3 o'clock and 9 o'clock positions and rock gently but firmly. Check for free play or insecurity at the wheel bearings, suspension mountings, or suspension mountings, pivots and attachments.

☐ Now grasp the wheel at the 12 o'clock and 6 o'clock positions and repeat the previous inspection. Spin the wheel, and check for roughness or tightness of the front wheel bearing.

☐ If excess free play is suspected at a component pivot point, this can be confirmed by using a large screwdriver or similar tool and levering between the mounting and the component attachment. This will confirm whether the wear is in the pivot bush, its retaining bolt, or in the mounting itself (the bolt holes can often become elongated).

☐ Carry out all the above checks at the other front wheel, and then at both rear wheels.

Springs and shock absorbers

☐ Examine the suspension struts (when applicable) for serious fluid leakage, corrosion, or damage to the casing. Also check the security of the mounting points.

☐ If coil springs are fitted, check that the spring ends locate in their seats, and that the spring is not corroded, cracked or broken.

☐ If leaf springs are fitted, check that all leaves are intact, that the axle is securely attached to each spring, and that there is no deterioration of the spring eye mountings, bushes, and shackles.

☐ The same general checks apply to vehicles fitted with other suspension types, such as torsion bars, hydraulic displacer units, etc. Ensure that all mountings and attachments are secure, that there are no signs of excessive wear, corrosion or damage, and (on hydraulic types) that there are no fluid leaks or damaged pipes.

☐ Check any suspension and anti-roll bar link ball joint dust covers. Any covers that are missing, seriously damaged, deteriorated or insecure, may fail inspection.

☐ Examine each shock absorber for signs of leakage, corrosion of the casing, missing, detached or worn pivots and/or rubber bushes.

Driveshafts (fwd vehicles only)

☐ Rotate each front wheel in turn and inspect the inner and outer joint gaiters for splits or damage. Also check that each driveshaft is straight and undamaged.

Braking system

☐ If possible without dismantling, check brake pad wear and disc condition. Ensure that the friction lining material has not worn excessively, (A) and that the discs are not fractured, pitted, scored or badly worn (B). As a general rule, if the friction material is less than 1.5 mm thick, the inspection will fail.

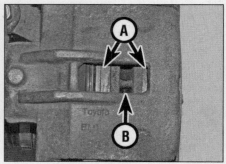

☐ Examine all the rigid brake pipes underneath the vehicle, and the flexible hose(s) at the rear. Look for corrosion, chafing or insecurity of the pipes, and for signs of bulging under pressure, chafing, splits or deterioration of the flexible hoses.

☐ Look for signs of fluid leaks at the brake calipers or on the brake backplates. Repair or renew leaking components.

☐ Slowly spin each wheel, while your assistant depresses and releases the footbrake. Ensure that each brake is operating and does not bind when the pedal is released.

☐ Examine the handbrake mechanism, checking for frayed or broken cables, excessive corrosion, or wear or insecurity of the linkage. Check that the mechanism works on each relevant wheel, and releases fully, without binding.

☐ Check the ABS sensors' wiring for signs of damage, deterioration or insecurity.

☐ It is not possible to test brake efficiency without special equipment, but a road test can be carried out later to check that the vehicle pulls up in a straight line.

Fuel and exhaust systems

☐ Inspect the fuel tank (including the filler cap), fuel pipes, hoses and unions. All components must be secure and free from leaks. Locking fuel caps must lock securely and the key must be provided for the MOT test.

☐ Examine the exhaust system over its entire length, checking for any damaged, broken or missing mountings, security of the retaining clamps and rust or corrosion.

☐ If the vehicle was originally equipped with a catalytic converter or particulate filter, one must be fitted.

Wheels and tyres

☐ Examine the sidewalls and tread area of each tyre in turn. Check for cuts, tears, lumps, bulges, separation of the tread, and exposure of the ply or cord due to wear or damage. Check that the tyre bead is correctly seated on the wheel rim, that the valve is sound and properly seated, and that the wheel is not distorted or damaged.

☐ Check that the tyres are of the correct size for the vehicle, that they are of the same size and type on each axle, and that the pressures are correct. The vehicle will fail the test if the tyres are obviously under-inflated.

☐ Check the tyre tread depth. The legal minimum at the time of writing is 1.6 mm over the central three-quarters of the tread width. Abnormal tread wear may indicate incorrect front wheel alignment or wear in steering or suspension components.

☐ Check that all wheel bolts/nuts are present.

☐ If the spare wheel is fitted externally or in a separate carrier beneath the vehicle, check that mountings are secure and free of excessive corrosion.

Body corrosion

☐ Check the condition of the entire vehicle structure for signs of corrosion in load-bearing areas. (These include chassis box sections, side sills, cross-members, pillars, and all suspension, steering, braking system and seat belt mountings and anchorages.) Any corrosion which has seriously reduced the thickness of a load-bearing area (or is within 30 cm of safety-related components such as steering or suspension) is likely to cause the vehicle to fail. In this case professional repairs are likely to be needed.

☐ Damage or corrosion which causes sharp or otherwise dangerous edges to be exposed will also cause the vehicle to fail.

Towbars

☐ Check the condition of mounting points (both beneath the vehicle and within boot/hatchback areas) for signs of corrosion, ensuring that all fixings are secure and not worn or damaged. There must be no excessive play in detachable tow ball arms or quick-release mechanisms.

☐ Examine the security and condition of the towbar electrics socket. If the later 13-pin socket is fitted, the MOT tester will check its' wiring functions/connections are correct.

General leaks

☐ The vehicle will fail the test if there is a fluid leak of any kind that poses an environmental risk.

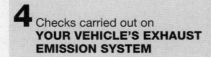

4 Checks carried out on YOUR VEHICLE'S EXHAUST EMISSION SYSTEM

Petrol models

☐ The engine should be warmed up, and running well (ignition system in good order, air filter element clean, etc).

☐ Before testing, run the engine at around 2500 rpm for 20 seconds. Let the engine drop to idle, and watch for smoke from the exhaust. If the idle speed is too high, or if dense blue or black smoke emerges for more than 5 seconds, the vehicle will fail. Typically, blue smoke signifies oil burning (engine wear); black smoke means unburnt fuel (dirty air cleaner element, or other fuel system fault).

☐ An exhaust gas analyser for measuring carbon monoxide (CO) and hydrocarbons (HC) is now needed. If one cannot be hired or borrowed, have a local garage perform the check.

CO emissions (mixture)

☐ The MOT tester has access to the CO limits for all vehicles from 1st August 1992. The CO level is measured at idle speed, and at 'fast idle' (2500 to 3000 rpm). The following limits are given as a general guide:

At idle speed – Less than 0.3% CO
At 'fast idle' – Less than 0.2% CO
Lambda reading – 0.97 to 1.03

☐ If the CO level is too high, this may point to poor maintenance, a fuel injection system problem, faulty lambda (oxygen) sensor or catalytic converter. Try an injector cleaning treatment, and check the vehicle's ECU for fault codes.

HC emissions

☐ The MOT tester has access to HC limits for all vehicles. The HC level is measured at 'fast idle' (2500 to 3000 rpm). The following limits are given as a general guide:

At 'fast idle' – Less than 200 ppm

☐ Excessive HC emissions are typically caused by oil being burnt (worn engine), or by a blocked crankcase ventilation system ('breather'). If the engine oil is old and thin, an oil change may help. If the engine is running badly, check the vehicle's ECU for fault codes.

Diesel models

☐ If the vehicle was fitted with a DPF (Diesel Particulate Filter) when it left the factory, it will fail the test if the MOT tester can see smoke of any colour emitting from the exhaust, or finds evidence that the filter has been tampered with.

☐ The only emission test for diesel engines is measuring exhaust smoke density, using a calibrated smoke meter.

☐ This test involves accelerating the engine to its maximum unloaded speed a minimum of once, and a maximum of 6 times. With the smoke meter connected, the engine is accelerated quickly to its maximum speed. If the smoke level is at or below the limit specified, the vehicle will pass. If the level is more than the specified limit then two further accelerations are carried out, and an average of the readings calculated. If the vehicle is still over the limit, a further three accelerations are carried out, with the average of the last three calculated after each check.

Note: *On engines with a timing belt, it is VITAL that the belt is in good condition before the test is carried out.*

Vehicles registered after 1st July 2008
Smoke level must not exceed 1.5m-1 – Turbo-charged and non-Turbocharged engines

Vehicles registered before 1st July 2008
Smoke level must not exceed 2.5m-1 – Non-turbo vehicles
Smoke level must not exceed 3.0m-1 – Turbocharged vehicles:

☐ If excess smoke is produced, try fitting a new air cleaner element, or using an injector cleaning treatment. If the engine is running badly, where applicable, check the vehicle's ECU for fault codes. Also check the vehicle's EGR system, where applicable. At high mileages, the injectors may require professional attention.

Engine

- [ ] Engine fails to rotate when attempting to start
- [ ] Engine rotates, but will not start
- [ ] Engine difficult to start when cold
- [ ] Engine difficult to start when hot
- [ ] Starter motor noisy or excessively-rough in engagement
- [ ] Engine starts, but stops immediately
- [ ] Engine idles erratically
- [ ] Engine misfires at idle speed
- [ ] Engine misfires throughout the driving speed range
- [ ] Engine hesitates on acceleration
- [ ] Engine stalls
- [ ] Engine lacks power
- [ ] Engine backfires
- [ ] Oil pressure warning light illuminated with engine running
- [ ] Engine runs-on after switching off
- [ ] Engine noises

Cooling system

- [ ] Overheating
- [ ] Overcooling
- [ ] External coolant leakage
- [ ] Internal coolant leakage
- [ ] Corrosion

Fuel and exhaust systems

- [ ] Excessive fuel consumption
- [ ] Fuel leakage and/or fuel odour
- [ ] Excessive noise or fumes from exhaust system

Clutch

- [ ] Pedal travels to floor – no pressure or very little resistance
- [ ] Clutch fails to disengage (unable to select gears)
- [ ] Clutch slips (engine speed increases, with no increase in vehicle speed)
- [ ] Judder as clutch is engaged
- [ ] Noise when depressing or releasing clutch pedal

Manual transmission

- [ ] Noisy in neutral with engine running
- [ ] Noisy in one particular gear
- [ ] Difficulty engaging gears
- [ ] Jumps out of gear
- [ ] Vibration
- [ ] Lubricant leaks

Automatic transmission

- [ ] Fluid leakage
- [ ] General gear selection problems
- [ ] Transmission will not downshift (kickdown) with accelerator pedal fully depressed
- [ ] Engine will not start in any gear, or starts in gears other than Park or Neutral
- [ ] Transmission slips, shifts roughly, is noisy, or has no drive in forward or reverse gears

Driveshafts

- [ ] Vibration when accelerating or decelerating
- [ ] Clicking or knocking noise on turns (at slow speed on full-lock)

Braking system

- [ ] Vehicle pulls to one side under braking
- [ ] Noise (grinding or high-pitched squeal) when brakes applied
- [ ] Excessive brake pedal travel
- [ ] Brake pedal feels spongy when depressed
- [ ] Excessive brake pedal effort required to stop vehicle
- [ ] Judder felt through brake pedal or steering wheel when braking
- [ ] Brakes binding
- [ ] Rear wheels locking under normal braking

Suspension and steering

- [ ] Vehicle pulls to one side
- [ ] Wheel wobble and vibration
- [ ] Excessive pitching and/or rolling around corners, or during braking
- [ ] Wandering or general instability
- [ ] Excessively-stiff steering
- [ ] Excessive play in steering
- [ ] Lack of power assistance
- [ ] Tyre wear excessive

Electrical system

- [ ] Battery will not hold a charge for more than a few days
- [ ] Ignition/no-charge warning light remains illuminated with engine running
- [ ] Ignition/no-charge warning light fails to come on
- [ ] Lights inoperative
- [ ] Instrument readings inaccurate or erratic
- [ ] Horn inoperative, or unsatisfactory in operation
- [ ] Windscreen wipers inoperative, or unsatisfactory in operation
- [ ] Windscreen washers inoperative, or unsatisfactory in operation
- [ ] Electric windows inoperative, or unsatisfactory in operation
- [ ] Window glass fails to move
- [ ] Central locking system inoperative, or unsatisfactory in operation

Introduction

The vehicle owner who does his or her own maintenance according to the recommended service schedules should not have to use this section of the manual very often. Modern component reliability is such that, provided those items subject to wear or deterioration are inspected or renewed at the specified intervals, sudden failure is comparatively rare. Faults do not usually just happen as a result of sudden failure, but develop over a period of time. Major mechanical failures in particular are usually preceded by characteristic symptoms over hundreds or even thousands of miles. Those components which do occasionally fail without warning are often small and easily carried in the vehicle.

With any fault-finding, the first step is to decide where to begin investigations. Sometimes this is obvious, but on other occasions, a little detective work will be necessary. The owner who makes half a dozen haphazard adjustments or replacements may be successful in curing a fault (or its symptoms), but will be none the wiser if the fault recurs, and ultimately may have spent more time and money than was necessary. A calm and logical approach will be found to be more satisfactory in the long run. Always take into account any warning signs or abnormalities that may have been noticed in the period preceding the fault – power loss, high or low gauge readings, unusual smells, etc – and remember that failure of components such as fuses or spark plugs may only be pointers to some underlying fault.

The pages which follow provide an easy-reference guide to the more common problems which may occur during the operation of the vehicle. These problems and their possible causes are grouped under headings denoting various components or systems, such as Engine, Cooling system, etc. The general Chapter which deals with the problem is also shown in brackets; refer to the relevant part of that Chapter for system-specific information. Whatever the fault, certain basic principles apply. These are as follows:

Verify the fault. This is simply a matter of being sure that you know what the symptoms are before starting work. This is particularly important if you are investigating a fault for someone else, who may not have described it very accurately.

Don't overlook the obvious. For example, if the vehicle won't start, is there fuel in the tank? (Don't take anyone else's word on this particular point, and don't trust the fuel gauge either!) If an electrical fault is indicated, look for loose or broken wires before digging out the test gear.

Cure the disease, not the symptom. Substituting a flat battery with a fully-charged one will get you off the hard shoulder, but if the underlying cause is not attended to, the new battery will go the same way. Similarly, changing oil-fouled spark plugs for a new set will get you moving again, but remember that the reason for the fouling (if it wasn't simply an incorrect grade of plug) will have to be established and corrected.

Don't take anything for granted. Particularly, don't forget that a 'new' component may itself be defective (especially if it's been rattling around in the boot for months), and don't leave components out of a fault diagnosis sequence just because they are new or recently-fitted. When you do finally diagnose a difficult fault, you'll probably realise that all the evidence was there from the start.

Consider what work, if any, has recently been carried out. Many faults arise through careless or hurried work. For instance, if any work has been performed under the bonnet, could some of the wiring have been dislodged or incorrectly routed, or a hose trapped? Have all the fasteners been properly tightened? Were new, genuine parts and new gaskets used? There is often a certain amount of detective work to be done in this case, as an apparently-unrelated task can have far-reaching consequences.

Diesel engine fault diagnosis

The majority of starting problems on small diesel engines are electrical in origin. The mechanic who is familiar with petrol engines but less so with diesel may be inclined to view the diesel's injectors and pump in the same light as the spark plugs and distributor, but this is generally a mistake.

When investigating complaints of difficult starting for someone else, make sure that the correct starting procedure is understood and is being followed. Some drivers are unaware of the significance of the preheating warning light – many modern engines are sufficiently forgiving for this not to matter in mild weather, but with the onset of winter, problems begin. Glow plugs in particular are often neglected – just one faulty plug will make cold-weather starting very difficult.

As a rule of thumb, if the engine is difficult to start but runs well when it has finally got going, the problem is electrical (battery, starter motor or preheating system). If poor performance is combined with difficult starting, the problem is likely to be in the fuel system. The low-pressure (supply) side of the fuel system should be checked before suspecting the injectors and high-pressure pump. The most common fuel supply problem is air getting into the system, and any pipe from the fuel tank forwards must be scrutinised if air leakage is suspected.

Engine

Engine fails to rotate when attempting to start

- ☐ Battery terminal connections loose or corroded (see *Weekly checks*)
- ☐ Battery discharged or faulty (Chapter 5A Section 3)
- ☐ Broken, loose or disconnected wiring in the starting circuit (Chapter 5A Section 2)
- ☐ Defective starter solenoid or ignition switch (Chapter 5A Section 9 or Chapter 5B Section 2)
- ☐ Defective starter motor (Chapter 5A Section 8)
- ☐ Starter pinion or flywheel ring gear teeth loose or broken (Chapter 2A Section 15, Chapter 2B Section 17, Chapter 2C Section 15 or Chapter 5A Section 8)
- ☐ Engine earth strap broken or disconnected (Chapter 5A Section 7)
- ☐ Engine suffering 'hydraulic lock' (eg from water drawn into the engine after traversing flooded roads, or from a serious internal coolant leak) – consult a main dealer for advice.

Engine rotates, but will not start

- ☐ Fuel tank emptyBattery discharged (engine rotates slowly) (Chapter 5A Section 3)
- ☐ Battery terminal connections loose or corroded (see *Weekly checks*)
- ☐ Ignition components damp or damaged – petrol models (Chapter 1A Section 19 or Chapter 5B Section 2)
- ☐ Immobiliser fault, or 'uncoded' ignition key being used (Chapter 12 Section 21)
- ☐ Broken, loose or disconnected wiring in the ignition circuit – petrol models (Chapter 1A Section 19 or Chapter 5B Section 2)
- ☐ Worn, faulty or incorrectly-gapped spark plugs – petrol models (Chapter 1A Section 22)
- ☐ Preheating system faulty – diesel models (Chapter 5A Section 11)
- ☐ Fuel injection/engine management system fault (Chapter 4A Section 9, Chapter 4B Section 3 or Chapter 4C)
- ☐ Air in fuel system – diesel models (Chapter 4BSection 4)
- ☐ Major mechanical failure (eg timing belt snapped) (Chapter 2A, Chapter 2B, Chapter 2C or Chapter 2D)

Engine difficult to start when cold

- ☐ Battery discharged (Chapter 5A Section 3)
- ☐ Battery terminal connections loose or corroded (see *Weekly checks*)

- ☐ Worn, faulty or incorrectly-gapped spark plugs – petrol models (Chapter 1A Section 22)
- ☐ Other ignition system fault – petrol models (Chapter 1A Section 19 or Chapter 5B Section 2)
- ☐ Preheating system faulty – diesel models (Chapter 5A Section 10)
- ☐ Fuel injection/engine management system fault (Chapter 4A Section 9, Chapter 4B Section 3 and Chapter 4C)
- ☐ Wrong grade of engine oil used (*Weekly checks*, Chapter 1A Section 7 or Chapter 1B Section 6)
- ☐ Low cylinder compression (Chapter 2A Section 2, Chapter 2B Section 2 or Chapter 2C Section 2)

Engine difficult to start when hot

- ☐ Air filter element dirty or clogged (Chapter 1A Section 23 or Chapter 1B Section 22)
- ☐ Fuel injection/engine management system fault (Chapter 4A Section 9, Chapter 4B Section 3 or Chapter 4C)
- ☐ Low cylinder compression (Chapter 2A Section 2, Chapter 2B Section 2 or Chapter 2C Section 2)

Starter motor noisy or excessively-rough in engagement

- ☐ Starter pinion or flywheel ring gear teeth loose or broken (Chapter 2A Section 15, Chapter 2B Section 17, Chapter 2C Section 15 or Chapter 5A Section 9)
- ☐ Starter motor mounting bolts loose or missing (Chapter 5A Section 8)
- ☐ Starter motor internal components worn or damaged (Chapter 5ASection 9)

Engine starts, but stops immediately

- ☐ Loose or faulty electrical connections in the ignition circuit – petrol models (Chapter 1A Section 19 or Chapter 5B Section 2)
- ☐ Vacuum leak at the throttle housing or inlet manifold – petrol models (Chapter 4A Section 9 or Chapter 4A Section 11)
- ☐ Blocked injectors/fuel injection system fault (Chapter 4A Section 9 or Chapter 4B Section 3)

Engine (continued)

Engine idles erratically

- ☐ Air filter element clogged (Chapter 1A Section 23 or Chapter 1B Section 22)
- ☐ Vacuum leak at the throttle housing, inlet manifold or associated hoses – petrol models (Chapter 4A Section 9 or Chapter 4C)
- ☐ Worn, faulty or incorrectly-gapped spark plugs – petrol models (Chapter 1A Section 22)
- ☐ Uneven or low cylinder compression (Chapter 2A Section 2, Chapter 2B Section 2 or Chapter 2C Section 2)
- ☐ Camshaft lobes worn (Chapter 2A Section 9, Chapter 2B Section 9 or Chapter 2C Section 7)
- ☐ Blocked injectors/fuel injection system fault (Chapter 4A Section 9, or Chapter 4B Section 3)

Engine misfires at idle speed

- ☐ Worn, faulty or incorrectly-gapped spark plugs – petrol models (Chapter 1A Section 22)
- ☐ Vacuum leak at the throttle housing, inlet manifold or associated hoses – petrol models (Chapter 4A or Chapter 4C)
- ☐ Blocked injectors/fuel injection system fault (Chapter 4A Section 9, Chapter 4B Section 3 or Chapter 4C)
- ☐ Faulty injector(s) – diesel models (Chapter 4B Section 11)
- ☐ Uneven or low cylinder compression (Chapter 2A Section 2, Chapter 2B Section 2 or Chapter 2C Section 2)
- ☐ Disconnected, leaking, or perished crankcase ventilation hoses (Chapter 4C)

Engine misfires throughout the driving speed range

- ☐ Fuel pump faulty, or delivery pressure low – petrol models (Chapter 4A Section 8)
- ☐ Fuel tank vent blocked, or fuel pipes restricted (Chapter 4A Section 7 or Chapter 4B Section 7)
- ☐ Vacuum leak at the throttle housing, inlet manifold or associated hoses – petrol models (Chapter 4A Section 9 or Chapter 4C)
- ☐ Worn, faulty or incorrectly-gapped spark plugs – petrol models (Chapter 1A Section 22)
- ☐ Faulty injector(s) – diesel models (Chapter 4B Section 11)
- ☐ Faulty ignition module – petrol models (Chapter 5B Section 2)
- ☐ Uneven or low cylinder compression (Chapter 2A Section 2, Chapter 2B Section 2 or Chapter 2C Section 2)
- ☐ Blocked injector/fuel injection system fault (Chapter 4A Section 9 or Chapter 4B Section 3)
- ☐ Blocked catalytic converter (Chapter 4A Section 11, Chapter 4B Section 17 or Chapter 4C)
- ☐ Engine overheating (Chapter 3)

Engine hesitates on acceleration

- ☐ Worn, faulty or incorrectly-gapped spark plugs – petrol models (Chapter 1A Section 22)
- ☐ Vacuum leak at the throttle housing, inlet manifold or associated hoses – petrol models (Chapter 4A Section 9 or Chapter 4C)
- ☐ Blocked injectors/fuel injection system fault (Chapter 4A Section 9 or Chapter 4B Section 3)
- ☐ Faulty injector(s) – diesel models (Chapter 4B Section 11)

Engine stalls

- ☐ Vacuum leak at the throttle housing, inlet manifold or associated hoses – petrol models (Chapter 4A Section 9 or Chapter 4C)
- ☐ Fuel filter choked (Chapter 1B Section 10)
- ☐ Fuel pump faulty, or delivery pressure low – petrol models (Chapter 4A Section 8)
- ☐ Fuel tank vent blocked, or fuel pipes restricted (Chapter 4A Section 9 or Chapter 4B Section 3)
- ☐ Blocked injectors/fuel injection system fault (Chapter 4A Section 9 or Chapter 4B Section 3)
- ☐ Faulty injector(s) – diesel models (Chapter 4B Section 11)

Engine lacks power

- ☐ Air filter element blocked (Chapter 1A Section 23 or Chapter 1B Section 22)
- ☐ Fuel filter choked (Chapter 1B Section 10)
- ☐ Fuel pipes blocked or restricted (Chapter 4A Section 9 or Chapter 4B Section 3)
- ☐ Worn, faulty or incorrectly-gapped spark plugs – petrol models (Chapter 1A Section 22)
- ☐ Engine overheating (Chapter 3)
- ☐ Fuel tank level low – diesel models (Chapter 4B Section 4)
- ☐ Accelerator pedal position sensor faulty (Chapter 4A Section 6 or Chapter 4B Section 6)
- ☐ Vacuum leak at the throttle housing, inlet manifold or associated hoses – petrol models (Chapters 4A or 4C)
- ☐ Blocked injectors/fuel injection system fault (Chapter 4A or 4B)
- ☐ Faulty injector(s) – diesel models (Chapter 4B Section 11)
- ☐ Fuel pump faulty, or delivery pressure low – petrol models (Chapter 4A Section 8)
- ☐ Uneven or low cylinder compression (Chapter 2A Section 2, Chapter 2B Section 2 or Chapter 2C Section 2)
- ☐ Blocked catalytic converter (Chapter 4A Section 11, Chapter 4B Section 17 or Chapter 4C Section 4)
- ☐ Brakes binding (Chapter 1A Section 13, Chapter 1B Section 12 or Chapter 9)
- ☐ Clutch slipping (Chapter 6)

Engine backfires

- ☐ Vacuum leak at the throttle housing, inlet manifold or associated hoses – petrol models (Chapter 4A)
- ☐ Blocked injectors/fuel injection system fault (Chapter 4A Section 9 or Chapter 4B Section 3)
- ☐ Blocked catalytic converter (Chapter 4A Section 11, Chapter 4B Section 17 or Chapter 4C)
- ☐ Faulty ignition module – petrol models (Chapter 5B Section 2)

Oil pressure warning light illuminated with engine running

- ☐ Low oil level, or incorrect oil grade (see *Weekly checks*)
- ☐ Faulty oil pressure switch, or wiring damaged (Chapter 2A Section 14, Chapter 2B Section 14 or Chapter 2C Section 12)
- ☐ Worn engine bearings and/or oil pump (Chapter 2A Section 13, Chapter 2B Section 13, Chapter 2C Section 11 or Chapter 2D Section 16)
- ☐ High engine operating temperature (Chapter 3)
- ☐ Oil pump pressure relief valve defective (Chapter 2A Section 13, Chapter 2B Section 13 or Chapter 2C Section 11)
- ☐ Oil pump pick-up strainer clogged (Chapter 2A Section 13, Chapter 2B Section 13 or Chapter 2C Section 11)

Engine runs-on after switching off

- ☐ Excessive carbon build-up in engine (Chapter 2A Section 1, Chapter 2B Section 1 or Chapter 2C Section 1)
- ☐ High engine operating temperature (Chapter 3)
- ☐ Fuel injection/engine management system fault (Chapter 4A Section 9, Chapter 4B Section 3 or Chapter 4C)

Engine noises

Pre-ignition (pinking) or knocking during acceleration or under load

- ☐ Ignition timing incorrect/ignition system fault – petrol models (Chapter 5BSection 4 or Chapter 1A Section 22)
- ☐ Incorrect grade of spark plug – petrol models (Chapter 1A)
- ☐ Incorrect grade of fuel (Chapter 4A Section 3 or Chapter 4B Section 3)
- ☐ Knock sensor faulty – petrol models (Chapter 4A Section 10)

Engine (continued)

☐ Vacuum leak at the throttle housing, inlet manifold or associated hoses – petrol models (Chapter 4A)
☐ Excessive carbon build-up in engine (Chapter 2A Section 1, Chapter 2B Section 1 or Chapter 2C Section 1)
☐ Fuel injection/engine management system fault (Chapter 4A Section 9, Chapter 4B Section 3 or Chapter 4C)
☐ Faulty injector(s) – diesel models (Chapter 4B Section 11)

Whistling or wheezing noises

☐ Leaking inlet manifold or throttle housing gasket – petrol models (Chapter 4A)
☐ Leaking exhaust manifold gasket or pipe-to-manifold joint (Chapter 4A Section 11 or Chapter 4B Section 17)
☐ Leaking vacuum hose (Chapter 4A Section 9, Chapter 4B Section 3, Chapter 4C or Chapter 9Section 13)
☐ Blowing cylinder head gasket (Chapter 2A Section 11, Chapter 2B Section 11 or Chapter 2C Section 9)
☐ Partially blocked or leaking crankcase ventilation system (Chapter 4C)

Tapping or rattling noises

☐ Worn valve gear or camshaft (Chapter 2A Section 9, Chapter 2B Section 9 or Chapter 2C Section 7)
☐ Ancillary component fault (coolant pump, alternator, etc) (Chapter 3, 5A, etc)

Knocking or thumping noises

☐ Worn big-end bearings (regular heavy knocking, perhaps less under load) (Chapter 2DSection 16)
☐ Worn main bearings (rumbling and knocking, perhaps worsening under load) (Chapter 2DSection 16)
☐ Piston slap – most noticeable when cold, caused by piston/bore wear (Chapter 2D Section 2)
☐ Ancillary component fault (coolant pump, alternator, etc) (Chapter 3, 5A, etc)
☐ Engine mountings worn or defective (Chapter 2A Section 16, Chapter 2B Section 18 or Chapter 2C Section 16)
☐ Front suspension or steering components worn (Chapter 10)

Cooling system

Overheating

☐ Insufficient coolant in system (see *Weekly checks*)
☐ Thermostat faulty (Chapter 3 Section 3)
☐ Radiator core blocked, or grille restricted (Chapter 3 Section 6)
☐ Cooling fan faulty, or resistor pack fault (Chapter 3 Section 4)
☐ Inaccurate coolant temperature sensor (Chapter 3 Section 5)
☐ Airlock in cooling system (Chapter 1A Section 30, Chapter 1B Section 30 or Chapter 3 Section 1)
☐ Expansion tank pressure cap faulty (Chapter 3 Section 6)
☐ Engine management system fault (Chapter 4A Section 10, Chapter 4B Section 12 or Chapter 4C)

Overcooling

☐ Thermostat faulty (Chapter 3 Section 3)
☐ Inaccurate coolant temperature sensor (Chapter 3 Section 5)
☐ Cooling fan faulty (Chapter 3 Section 4)
☐ Engine management system fault (Chapter 4A Section 9, 10, Chapter 4B Section 12 or Chapter 4C)

External coolant leakage

☐ Deteriorated or damaged hoses or hose clips (Chapter 1A Section 10 or Chapter 1B Section 8)

☐ Radiator core or heater matrix leaking (Chapter 3 Section 2)
☐ Expansion tank pressure cap faulty (Chapter 1A Section 10 or Chapter 1B Section 8)
☐ Coolant pump internal seal leaking (Chapter 3 Section 7)
☐ Coolant pump gasket leaking (Chapter 3 Section 7)
☐ Boiling due to overheating (Chapter 3 Section 1)
☐ Cylinder block core plug leaking (Chapter 2D Section 13)

Internal coolant leakage

☐ Leaking cylinder head gasket (Chapter 2A Section 11, Chapter 2B Section 11 or Chapter 2C Section 9)
☐ Cracked cylinder head or cylinder block (Chapter 2A Section 11, Chapter 2B Section 11, Chapter 2C Section 9 or Chapter 2D Section 7)

Corrosion

☐ Infrequent draining and flushing (Chapter 1A Section 30 or Chapter 1B Section 30)
☐ Incorrect coolant mixture or inappropriate coolant type (see *Weekly checks*)

Fuel and exhaust systems

Excessive fuel consumption

☐ Air filter element dirty or clogged (Chapter 1A Section 23 or Chapter 1B Section 22)
☐ Fuel injection system fault (Chapter 4A Section 9, Chapter 4B Section 3 or Chapter 4C)
☐ Engine management system fault (Chapter 4A Section 10, Chapter 4B Section 12 or Chapter 4C)
☐ Crankcase ventilation system blocked (Chapter 4C)
☐ Tyres under-inflated (see *Weekly checks*)
☐ Brakes binding (Chapter 1A Section 13, Chapter 1B Section 12 or Chapter 9 Section 1)
☐ Fuel leak, causing apparent high consumption (Chapter 1A Section 10, Chapter 1B Section 8, Chapter 4A Section 4 or Chapter 4B Section 3)

Fuel leakage and/or fuel odour

☐ Damaged or corroded fuel tank, pipes or connections (Chapter 4A Section 4, Chapter 4B Section 3 or Chapter 4C)
☐ Evaporative emissions system fault – petrol models (Chapter 4C Section 2)

Excessive noise or fumes from exhaust system

☐ Leaking exhaust system or manifold joints (Chapter 1A Section 16, Chapter 1B Section 15, Chapter 4A Section 11 or Chapter 4B Section 17)
☐ Leaking, corroded or damaged silencers or pipe (Chapter 1A Section 16, Chapter 1B Section 15, Chapter 4A Section 12 or Chapter 4B Section 18)
☐ Broken mountings causing body or suspension contact (Chapter 1A Section 16 or Chapter 1B Section 15)

Clutch

Pedal travels to floor – no pressure or very little resistance

- [ ] Air in hydraulic system/faulty master or slave cylinder (Chapter 6 Section 3)
- [ ] Faulty hydraulic release system (Chapter 6 Section 5)
- [ ] Clutch pedal return spring detached or broken (Chapter 6 Section 2)
- [ ] Broken diaphragm spring in clutch pressure plate (Chapter 6 Section 4, 6)

Clutch fails to disengage (unable to select gears)

- [ ] Air in hydraulic system/faulty master or slave cylinder (Chapter 6 Section 4)
- [ ] Faulty hydraulic release system (Chapter 6 Section 5)
- [ ] Clutch disc sticking on transmission input shaft splines (Chapter 6 Section 6)
- [ ] Clutch disc sticking to flywheel or pressure plate (Chapter 6 Section 6)
- [ ] Faulty pressure plate assembly (Chapter 6 Section 6)
- [ ] Clutch release mechanism worn or incorrectly assembled (Chapter 6 Section 6)

Clutch slips (engine speed increases, with no increase in vehicle speed)

- [ ] Faulty hydraulic release system (Chapter 6 Section 5)

- [ ] Clutch disc linings excessively worn (Chapter 6 Section 6)
- [ ] Clutch disc linings contaminated with oil or grease (Chapter 6 Section 6)
- [ ] Faulty pressure plate or weak diaphragm spring (Chapter 6 Section 6)

Judder as clutch is engaged

- [ ] Clutch disc linings contaminated with oil or grease (Chapter 6 Section 6)
- [ ] Clutch disc linings excessively worn (Chapter 6 Section 6)
- [ ] Faulty or distorted pressure plate or diaphragm spring (Chapter 6).
- [ ] Worn or loose engine or transmission mountings (Chapter 2A Section 16, Chapter 2B Section 18 or Chapter 2C Section 16)
- [ ] Clutch disc hub or transmission input shaft splines worn (Chapter 6 Section 6)

Noise when depressing or releasing clutch pedal

- [ ] Faulty hydraulic release system (Chapter 6 Section 5)
- [ ] Worn or dry clutch pedal bushes (Chapter 6 Section 2)
- [ ] Worn or dry clutch master cylinder piston (Chapter 6 Section 2)
- [ ] Faulty pressure plate assembly (Chapter 6 Section 6)
- [ ] Pressure plate diaphragm spring broken (Chapter 6 Section 6)
- [ ] Broken clutch disc cushioning springs (Chapter 6 Section 6)

Manual transmission

Noisy in neutral with engine running

- [ ] Lack of oil (Chapter 7A Section 6)
- [ ] Input shaft bearings worn (noise apparent with clutch pedal released, but not when depressed)
- [ ] (Chapter 7A Section 8)
- [ ] *Clutch release bearing system (noise apparent with clutch pedal depressed, possibly less when released)
- [ ] (Chapter 6 Section 6)

Noisy in one particular gear

- [ ] Worn, damaged or chipped gear teeth (Chapter 7A Section 8)*

Difficulty engaging gears

- [ ] Clutch fault (Chapter 6 Section 6)
- [ ] Worn, damaged, or poorly-adjusted gearchange (Chapter 7A Section 8)
- [ ] Lack of oil (Chapter 7A Section 6)
- [ ] Worn synchroniser units (Chapter 7A Section 8)*

Jumps out of gear

- [ ] Worn, damaged, or poorly-adjusted gearchange (Chapter 7A Section 8)
- [ ] Worn synchroniser units (Chapter 7A Section 8)*
- [ ] Worn selector forks (Chapter 7A Section 8)*

Vibration

- [ ] Lack of oil (Chapter 7A Section 6)
- [ ] Worn bearings (Chapter 7A Section 8)*

Lubricant leaks

- [ ] Leaking driveshaft or selector shaft oil seal (Chapter 7A Section 4)
- [ ] Leaking housing joint (Chapter 7A Section 8)*
- [ ] Leaking input shaft oil seal (Chapter 7A Section 4)*

* Although the corrective action necessary to remedy the symptoms described is beyond the scope of the home mechanic, the above information should be helpful in isolating the cause of the condition, so that the owner can communicate clearly with a professional mechanic.

Automatic transmission

Fluid leakage

Note: *Due to the complexity of the automatic transmission, it is difficult for the home mechanic to properly diagnose and service this unit. For problems other than the following, the vehicle should be taken to a dealer service department or automatic transmission specialist. Do not be too hasty in removing the transmission if a fault is suspected, as most of the testing is carried out with the unit still fitted.*

- [ ] Automatic transmission fluid is usually dark in colour. Fluid leaks should not be confused with engine oil, which can easily be blown onto the transmission by airflow.
- [ ] To determine the source of a leak, first remove all built-up dirt and grime from the transmission housing and surrounding areas using a degreasing agent, or by steam-cleaning. Drive the vehicle at low

speed, so airflow will not blow the leak far from its source. Raise and support the vehicle, and determine where the leak is coming from.

General gear selection problems

- [ ] Chapter 7B Section 3 deals with checking and adjusting the selector mechanism on automatic transmissions. The following are common problems which may be caused by a poorly-adjusted mechanism:
  - a) Engine starting in gears other than Park or Neutral.
  - b) Indicator panel indicating a gear other than the one actually being used.
  - c) Vehicle moves when in Park or Neutral.
  - d) Poor gear shift quality or erratic gear changes.
- [ ] Refer to Chapter 7B Section 3 for the selector mechanism adjustment procedure.

Automatic transmission (continued)

Transmission will not downshift (kickdown) with accelerator pedal fully depressed

☐ Low transmission fluid level (Chapter 7B Section 2).
☐ Incorrect selector mechanism adjustment (Chapter 7B Section 3).

Engine will not start in any gear, or starts in gears other than Park or Neutral

☐ Incorrect selector mechanism adjustment (Chapter 7B Section 3).

Transmission slips, shifts roughly, is noisy, or has no drive in forward or reverse gears

☐ There are many probable causes for the above problems, but unless there is a very obvious reason (such as a loose or corroded wiring plug connection on or near the transmission), the car should be taken to a franchise dealer or specialist for the fault to be diagnosed. The transmission control unit incorporates a self-diagnosis facility, and any fault codes can quickly be read and interpreted by a dealer with the proper diagnostic equipment.

Driveshafts

Vibration when accelerating or decelerating

☐ Worn inner constant velocity joint (Chapter 8 Section 6)
☐ Bent or distorted driveshaft (Chapter 8 Section 6)
☐ Worn intermediate bearing (Chapter 8Section 5)

Clicking or knocking noise on turns (at slow speed on full-lock)

☐ Worn outer constant velocity joint (Chapter 8 Section 2)
☐ Lack of constant velocity joint lubricant, possibly due to damaged gaiter (Chapter 8 Section 3, 4)

Braking system

Vehicle pulls to one side under braking

Note: *Before assuming that a brake problem exists, make sure that the tyres are in good condition and correctly inflated, that the front wheel alignment is correct, and that the vehicle is not loaded with weight in an unequal manner. Apart from checking the condition of all pipe and hose connections, any faults occurring on the anti-lock braking system should be referred to a Ford dealer for diagnosis.*

☐ Worn, defective, damaged or contaminated brake pads on one side (Chapter 1A Section 13, Chapter 1B Section 12 or Chapter 9 Section 4)
☐ Seized or partially-seized brake caliper or wheel cylinder piston (Chapter 1A Section 13, Chapter 1B Section 12 or Chapter 9)
☐ A mixture of brake pad lining materials fitted between sides (Chapter 1A Section 13, Chapter 1B Section 12 or Chapter 9)
☐ Brake caliper mounting bolts loose (Chapter 9)
☐ Worn or damaged steering or suspension components (Chapter 1A Section 15, Chapter 1B Section 14 or Chapter 10)

Noise (grinding or high-pitched squeal) when brakes applied

☐ Brake pad friction lining material worn down to metal backing (Chapter 1A Section 13, Chapter 1B Section 12 or Chapter 9)
☐ Excessive corrosion of brake disc (may be apparent after the vehicle has been standing for some time (Chapter 1A Section 13, Chapter 1B Section 12 or Chapter 9)
☐ Foreign object (stone chipping, etc) trapped between brake disc and shield (Chapter 1A Section 13, Chapter 1B Section 12 or Chapter 9)

Excessive brake pedal travel

☐ Faulty master cylinder (Chapter 9 Section 10)
☐ Air in hydraulic system (Chapter 9 Section 2)
☐ Faulty vacuum servo unit (Chapter 9 Section 12)

Brake pedal feels spongy when depressed

☐ Air in hydraulic system (Chapter 9 Section 2)
☐ Deteriorated flexible rubber brake hoses (Chapter 1A Section 13, Chapter 1B Section 12 or Chapter 9 Section 3)
☐ Master cylinder mounting nuts loose (Chapter 9 Section 10)
☐ Faulty master cylinder (Chapter 9 Section 10)

Excessive brake pedal effort required to stop vehicle

☐ Faulty vacuum servo unit (Chapter 9 Section 12)
☐ Faulty vacuum pump – diesel models (Chapter 9 Section 21)
☐ Disconnected, damaged or insecure brake servo vacuum hose (Chapter 9 Section 3)
☐ Primary or secondary hydraulic circuit failure (Chapter 9 Section 3)
☐ Seized brake caliper or wheel cylinder piston (Chapter 9)
☐ Brake pads incorrectly fitted (Chapter 9)
☐ Incorrect grade of brake pads fitted (Chapter 9)
☐ Brake pad linings contaminated (Chapter 1A Section 13, Chapter 1B Section 12 or Chapter 9)

Judder felt through brake pedal or steering wheel when braking

Note: *Under heavy braking on models equipped with ABS, vibration may be felt through the brake pedal. This is a normal feature of ABS operation, and does not constitute a fault*

☐ Excessive run-out or distortion of discs (Chapter 9)
☐ Brake pad linings worn (Chapter 1A Section 13, Chapter 1B Section 12 or Chapter 9)
☐ Brake caliper mounting bolts loose (Chapter 9)
☐ Wear in suspension or steering components or mountings (Chapter 1A Section 15, Chapter 1B Section 14 or Chapter 10)
☐ Front wheels out of balance (see *Weekly checks*)

Brakes binding

☐ Seized brake caliper (Chapter 9)
☐ Incorrectly-adjusted handbrake mechanism (Chapter 9 Section 14)
☐ Faulty master cylinder (Chapter 9 Section 10)

Rear wheels locking under normal braking

☐ Rear brake pad linings contaminated or damaged (Chapter 1A Section 13 or Chapter 1B Section 12)
☐ Rear brake discs warped (Chapter 1A Section 13, Chapter 1B Section 12 or Chapter 9 Section 9)

Suspension and steering

Vehicle pulls to one side

Note: *Before diagnosing suspension or steering faults, be sure that the trouble is not due to incorrect tyre pressures, mixtures of tyre types, or binding brakes.*

- ☐ Defective tyre (see *Weekly checks*)
- ☐ Excessive wear in suspension or steering components (Chapter 1A Section 15, Chapter 1B Section 14 or Chapter 10)
- ☐ Incorrect front wheel alignment (Chapter 10 Section 22)
- ☐ Accident damage to steering or suspension components (Chapter 1A Section 15 or Chapter 1B Section 14)

Wheel wobble and vibration

- ☐ Front wheels out of balance (vibration felt mainly through the steering wheel) (see *Weekly checks*)
- ☐ Rear wheels out of balance (vibration felt throughout the vehicle) (see *Weekly checks*)
- ☐ Roadwheels damaged or distorted (see *Weekly checks*)
- ☐ Faulty or damaged tyre (see *Weekly checks*)
- ☐ Worn steering or suspension joints, bushes or components (Chapter 1A Section 15, Chapter 1B Section 14 or Chapter 10)
- ☐ Wheel nuts loose (Chapter 1A Section 17 or Chapter 1B Section 16)

Excessive pitching and/or rolling around corners, or during braking

- ☐ Defective shock absorbers (Chapter 1A Section 15, Chapter 1B Section 14 or Chapter 10)
- ☐ Broken or weak spring and/or suspension component (Chapter 1A Section 15, Chapter 1B Section 14 or Chapter 10)
- ☐ Worn or damaged anti-roll bar or mountings (Chapter 1A Section 15, Chapter 1B Section 14 or Chapter 10)

Wandering or general instability

- ☐ Incorrect front wheel alignment (Chapter 10 Section 22)
- ☐ Worn steering or suspension joints, bushes or components (Chapter 1A Section 15, Chapter 1B Section 14 or Chapter 10)
- ☐ Roadwheels out of balance (see *Weekly checks*)
- ☐ Faulty or damaged tyre (see *Weekly checks*)
- ☐ Wheel nuts loose (Chapter 1A Section 17 or Chapter 1B Section 16)
- ☐ Defective shock absorbers (Chapter 1A Section 15, Chapter 1B Section 14 or Chapter 10)

Excessively-stiff steering

- ☐ Seized steering linkage balljoint or suspension balljoint (Chapter 1A Section 15, Chapter 1B Section 14 or Chapter 10)
- ☐ Incorrect front wheel alignment (Chapter 10 Section 22)
- ☐ Steering rack damaged (Chapter 10 Section 17)
- ☐ Power steering system fault (Chapter 10)

Excessive play in steering

- ☐ Worn steering column/intermediate shaft joints (Chapter 10)
- ☐ Worn track rod end balljoints (Chapter 1A Section 15, Chapter 1B Section 14 or Chapter 10 Section 21)
- ☐ Worn steering rack (Chapter 10 Section 17)
- ☐ Worn steering or suspension joints, bushes or components (Chapter 1A Section 15, Chapter 1B Section 14 or Chapter 10)

Lack of power assistance

- ☐ Power steering system fault (Chapter 10)
- ☐ Faulty steering rack (Chapter 10 Section 17)

Tyre wear excessive

Tyres worn on inside or outside edges

- ☐ Tyres under-inflated (wear on both edges) (see *Weekly checks*)
- ☐ Incorrect camber or castor angles (wear on one edge only) (Chapter 10 Section 22)
- ☐ Worn steering or suspension joints, bushes or components (Chapter 1A Section 15, Chapter 1B Section 14 or Chapter 10)
- ☐ Excessively-hard cornering or brakingAccident damage

Tyre treads exhibit feathered edges

- ☐ Incorrect toe-setting (Chapter 10 Section 22)

Tyres worn in centre of tread

- ☐ Tyres over-inflated (see *Weekly checks*)

Tyres worn on inside and outside edges

- ☐ Tyres under-inflated (see *Weekly checks*)

Tyres worn unevenly

- ☐ Tyres/wheels out of balance (see *Weekly checks*)
- ☐ Excessive wheel or tyre run-out
- ☐ Worn shock absorbers (Chapter 1A Section 15, Chapter 1B Section 14 or Chapter 10)
- ☐ Faulty tyre (see *Weekly checks*)

Electrical system

Battery will not hold a charge for more than a few days

Note: *For problems associated with the starting system, refer to the faults listed under 'Engine' earlier in this Section.*

- ☐ Battery defective internally (Chapter 5A Section 4)
- ☐ Battery terminal connections loose or corroded (see *Weekly checks*)
- ☐ Auxiliary drivebelt worn or incorrectly adjusted (Chapter 1A Section 25 or Chapter 1B Section 24)
- ☐ Alternator not charging at correct output (Chapter 5A Section 6, 6)
- ☐ Alternator or voltage regulator faulty (Chapter 5A Section 6)
- ☐ Short-circuit causing continual battery drain (Chapter 5A Section 2 or Chapter 12 Section 2)

Ignition/no-charge warning light remains illuminated with engine running

- ☐ Auxiliary drivebelt broken, worn, or incorrectly adjusted (Chapter 1A Section 25 or Chapter 1B Section 24)
- ☐ Internal fault in alternator or voltage regulator (Chapter 5A Section 6)
- ☐ Broken, disconnected, or loose wiring in charging circuit (Chapter 5A Section 2 or Chapter 12 Section 2)

Ignition/no-charge warning light fails to come on

- ☐ Broken, disconnected, or loose wiring in warning light circuit (Chapter 5A Section 2 or Chapter 12 Section 2)
- ☐ Alternator faulty (Chapter 5A Section 6)

Electrical system (continued)

Lights inoperative

- [ ] Bulb blown (Chapter 12 Section 5)
- [ ] Corrosion of bulb or bulbholder contacts (Chapter 12 Section 5)
- [ ] Blown fuse (Chapter 12 Section 3)
- [ ] Faulty relay (Chapter 12 Section 3)
- [ ] Broken, loose, or disconnected wiring (Chapter 12 Section 2)
- [ ] Faulty switch (Chapter 12 Section 4)

Instrument readings inaccurate or erratic

Fuel or temperature gauges give no reading

- [ ] Faulty gauge sender unit (Chapter 3 Section 5, Chapter 4A Section 8 or Chapter 4B Section 8)
- [ ] Wiring open-circuit (Chapter 12 Section 2)
- [ ] Faulty gauge (Chapter 12 Section 11)

Fuel or temperature gauges give continuous maximum reading

- [ ] Faulty gauge sender unit (Chapter 3 Section 5, Chapter 4A Section 8 or Chapter 4B Section 8)
- [ ] Wiring short-circuit (Chapter 12 Section 2)
- [ ] Faulty gauge (Chapter 12 Section 11)

Horn inoperative, or unsatisfactory in operation

Horn operates all the time

- [ ] Horn push either earthed or stuck down (Chapter 12 Section 12)
- [ ] Horn cable-to-horn push earthed (Chapter 12 Section 2)

Horn fails to operate

- [ ] Blown fuse (Chapter 12 Section 3)
- [ ] Cable or connections loose, broken or disconnected (Chapter 12 Section 2)
- [ ] Faulty horn (Chapter 12 Section 12)

Horn emits intermittent or unsatisfactory sound

- [ ] Cable connections loose (Chapter 12 Section 2)
- [ ] Horn mountings loose (Chapter 12 Section 12)
- [ ] Faulty horn (Chapter 12 Section 12

Windscreen wipers inoperative, or unsatisfactory in operation

Wipers fail to operate, or operate very slowly

- [ ] Wiper blades stuck to screen, or linkage seized or binding (Chapter 12 Section 14)
- [ ] Blown fuse (Chapter 12 Section 3)
- [ ] Battery discharged (Chapter 5A Section 3)
- [ ] Cable or connections loose, broken or disconnected (Chapter 12 Section 2)
- [ ] Faulty relay (Chapter 12 Section 3)
- [ ] Faulty wiper motor (Chapter 12 Section 14)

Wiper blades sweep over too large or too small an area of the glass

- [ ] Wiper blades incorrectly fitted, or wrong size used (see *Weekly checks*)
- [ ] Wiper arms incorrectly positioned on spindles (Chapter 12 Section 13)
- [ ] Excessive wear of wiper linkage (Chapter 12 Section 14)
- [ ] Wiper motor or linkage mountings loose or insecure (Chapter 12 Section 14)

Wiper blades fail to clean the glass effectively

- [ ] Wiper blade rubbers dirty, worn or perished (see *Weekly checks*)
- [ ] Wiper blades incorrectly fitted, or wrong size used (see *Weekly checks*)
- [ ] Wiper arm tension springs broken, or arm pivots seized (Chapter 12 Section 13)
- [ ] Insufficient windscreen washer additive to adequately remove road film (see *Weekly checks*)

Windscreen washers inoperative, or unsatisfactory in operation

One or more washer jets inoperative

- [ ] Blocked washer jetDisconnected, kinked or restricted fluid hose (Chapter 12 Section 16)
- [ ] Insufficient fluid in washer reservoir (see *Weekly checks*)

Washer pump fails to operate

- [ ] Broken or disconnected wiring or connections (Chapter 12 Section 2)
- [ ] Blown fuse (Chapter 12 Section 3)
- [ ] Faulty washer switch (Chapter 12 Section 4)
- [ ] Faulty washer pump (Chapter 12 Section 16)

Washer pump runs for some time before fluid is emitted from jets

- [ ] Faulty one-way valve in fluid supply hose (Chapter 12 Section 16)

Electric windows inoperative, or unsatisfactory in operation

Window glass will only move in one direction

- [ ] Faulty switch (Chapter 12 Section 4)

Window glass slow to move

- [ ] Battery discharged (Chapter 5A Section 3)
- [ ] Regulator seized or damaged, or in need of lubrication (Chapter 11 Section 15)
- [ ] Door internal components or trim fouling regulator (Chapter 11 Section 13)
- [ ] Faulty motor (Chapter 11 Section 15)

Window glass fails to move

- [ ] Blown fuse (Chapter 12 Section 3)
- [ ] Faulty relay (Chapter 12 Section 3)
- [ ] Broken or disconnected wiring or connections (Chapter 12 Section 2)
- [ ] Faulty motor (Chapter 11 Section 15)

Central locking system inoperative, or unsatisfactory in operation

Complete system failure

- [ ] Remote handset battery discharged, where applicable (Chapter 1A Section 29 or Chapter 1B Section 29)
- [ ] Blown fuse (Chapter 12 Section 3)
- [ ] Faulty relay (Chapter 12 Section 3)
- [ ] Broken or disconnected wiring or connections (Chapter 12 Section 2)
- [ ] Faulty motor (Chapter 11 Section 19)

Latch locks but will not unlock, or unlocks but will not lock

- [ ] Remote handset battery discharged, where applicable (Chapter 1A Section 29 or Chapter 1B Section 29)
- [ ] Faulty master switch (Chapter 12 Section 4)
- [ ] Broken or disconnected latch operating rods or levers (Chapter 11 Section 16)
- [ ] Faulty relay (Chapter 12 Section 3)
- [ ] Faulty motor (Chapter 11 Section 19)

One solenoid/motor fails to operate

- [ ] Broken or disconnected wiring or connections (Chapter 12 Section 2)
- [ ] Faulty operating assembly (Chapter 11 Section 16)
- [ ] Broken, binding or disconnected latch operating rods or levers (Chapter 11 Section 16)
- [ ] Fault in door latch (Chapter 11 Section 16)

A

ABS (Anti-lock brake system) A system, usually electronically controlled, that senses incipient wheel lockup during braking and relieves hydraulic pressure at wheels that are about to skid.

Air bag An inflatable bag hidden in the steering wheel (driver's side) or the dash or glovebox (passenger side). In a head-on collision, the bags inflate, preventing the driver and front passenger from being thrown forward into the steering wheel or windscreen.

Air cleaner A metal or plastic housing, containing a filter element, which removes dust and dirt from the air being drawn into the engine.

Air filter element The actual filter in an air cleaner system, usually manufactured from pleated paper and requiring renewal at regular intervals.

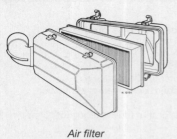

Air filter

Allen key A hexagonal wrench which fits into a recessed hexagonal hole.

Alligator clip A long-nosed spring-loaded metal clip with meshing teeth. Used to make temporary electrical connections.

Alternator A component in the electrical system which converts mechanical energy from a drivebelt into electrical energy to charge the battery and to operate the starting system, ignition system and electrical accessories.

Ampere (amp) A unit of measurement for the flow of electric current. One amp is the amount of current produced by one volt acting through a resistance of one ohm.

Anaerobic sealer A substance used to prevent bolts and screws from loosening. Anaerobic means that it does not require oxygen for activation. The Loctite brand is widely used.

Antifreeze A substance (usually ethylene glycol) mixed with water, and added to a vehicle's cooling system, to prevent freezing of the coolant in winter. Antifreeze also contains chemicals to inhibit corrosion and the formation of rust and other deposits that would tend to clog the radiator and coolant passages and reduce cooling efficiency.

Anti-seize compound A coating that reduces the risk of seizing on fasteners that are subjected to high temperatures, such as exhaust manifold bolts and nuts.

Asbestos A natural fibrous mineral with great heat resistance, commonly used in the composition of brake friction materials. Asbestos is a health hazard and the dust created by brake systems should never be inhaled or ingested.

Axle A shaft on which a wheel revolves, or which revolves with a wheel. Also, a solid beam that connects the two wheels at one end of the vehicle. An axle which also transmits power to the wheels is known as a live axle.

Axleshaft A single rotating shaft, on either side of the differential, which delivers power from the final drive assembly to the drive wheels. Also called a driveshaft or a halfshaft.

B

Ball bearing An anti-friction bearing consisting of a hardened inner and outer race with hardened steel balls between two races.

Bearing The curved surface on a shaft or in a bore, or the part assembled into either, that permits relative motion between them with minimum wear and friction.

Bearing

Big-end bearing The bearing in the end of the connecting rod that's attached to the crankshaft.

Bleed nipple A valve on a brake wheel cylinder, caliper or other hydraulic component that is opened to purge the hydraulic system of air. Also called a bleed screw.

Brake bleeding Procedure for removing air from lines of a hydraulic brake system.

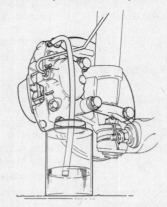

Brake bleeding

Brake disc The component of a disc brake that rotates with the wheels.

Brake drum The component of a drum brake that rotates with the wheels.

Brake linings The friction material which contacts the brake disc or drum to retard the vehicle's speed. The linings are bonded or riveted to the brake pads or shoes.

Brake pads The replaceable friction pads that pinch the brake disc when the brakes are applied. Brake pads consist of a friction material bonded or riveted to a rigid backing plate.

Brake shoe The crescent-shaped carrier to which the brake linings are mounted and which forces the lining against the rotating drum during braking.

Braking systems For more information on braking systems, consult the *Haynes Automotive Brake Manual*.

Breaker bar A long socket wrench handle providing greater leverage.

Bulkhead The insulated partition between the engine and the passenger compartment.

C

Caliper The non-rotating part of a disc-brake assembly that straddles the disc and carries the brake pads. The caliper also contains the hydraulic components that cause the pads to pinch the disc when the brakes are applied. A caliper is also a measuring tool that can be set to measure inside or outside dimensions of an object.

Camshaft A rotating shaft on which a series of cam lobes operate the valve mechanisms. The camshaft may be driven by gears, by sprockets and chain or by sprockets and a belt.

Canister A container in an evaporative emission control system; contains activated charcoal granules to trap vapours from the fuel system.

Canister

Carburettor A device which mixes fuel with air in the proper proportions to provide a desired power output from a spark ignition internal combustion engine.

Castellated Resembling the parapets along the top of a castle wall. For example, a castellated balljoint stud nut.

Castor In wheel alignment, the backward or forward tilt of the steering axis. Castor is positive when the steering axis is inclined rearward at the top.

Catalytic converter A silencer-like device in the exhaust system which converts certain pollutants in the exhaust gases into less harmful substances.

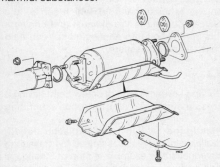

Catalytic converter

Circlip A ring-shaped clip used to prevent endwise movement of cylindrical parts and shafts. An internal circlip is installed in a groove in a housing; an external circlip fits into a groove on the outside of a cylindrical piece such as a shaft.

Clearance The amount of space between two parts. For example, between a piston and a cylinder, between a bearing and a journal, etc.

Coil spring A spiral of elastic steel found in various sizes throughout a vehicle, for example as a springing medium in the suspension and in the valve train.

Compression Reduction in volume, and increase in pressure and temperature, of a gas, caused by squeezing it into a smaller space.

Compression ratio The relationship between cylinder volume when the piston is at top dead centre and cylinder volume when the piston is at bottom dead centre.

Constant velocity (CV) joint A type of universal joint that cancels out vibrations caused by driving power being transmitted through an angle.

Core plug A disc or cup-shaped metal device inserted in a hole in a casting through which core was removed when the casting was formed. Also known as a freeze plug or expansion plug.

Crankcase The lower part of the engine block in which the crankshaft rotates.

Crankshaft The main rotating member, or shaft, running the length of the crankcase, with offset "throws" to which the connecting rods are attached.

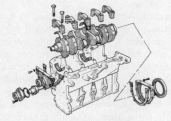

Crankshaft assembly

Crocodile clip See Alligator clip

D

Diagnostic code Code numbers obtained by accessing the diagnostic mode of an engine management computer. This code can be used to determine the area in the system where a malfunction may be located.

Disc brake A brake design incorporating a rotating disc onto which brake pads are squeezed. The resulting friction converts the energy of a moving vehicle into heat.

Double-overhead cam (DOHC) An engine that uses two overhead camshafts, usually one for the intake valves and one for the exhaust valves.

Drivebelt(s) The belt(s) used to drive accessories such as the alternator, water pump, power steering pump, air conditioning compressor, etc. off the crankshaft pulley.

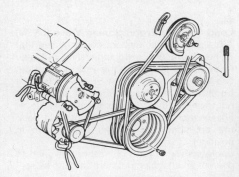

Accessory drivebelts

Driveshaft Any shaft used to transmit motion. Commonly used when referring to the axleshafts on a front wheel drive vehicle.

Drum brake A type of brake using a drum-shaped metal cylinder attached to the inner surface of the wheel. When the brake pedal is pressed, curved brake shoes with friction linings press against the inside of the drum to slow or stop the vehicle.

E

EGR valve A valve used to introduce exhaust gases into the intake air stream.

Electronic control unit (ECU) A computer which controls (for instance) ignition and fuel injection systems, or an anti-lock braking system. For more information refer to the *Haynes Automotive Electrical and Electronic Systems Manual.*

Electronic Fuel Injection (EFI) A computer controlled fuel system that distributes fuel through an injector located in each intake port of the engine.

Emergency brake A braking system, independent of the main hydraulic system, that can be used to slow or stop the vehicle if the primary brakes fail, or to hold the vehicle stationary even though the brake pedal isn't depressed. It usually consists of a hand lever that actuates either front or rear brakes mechanically through a series of cables and linkages. Also known as a handbrake or parking brake.

Endfloat The amount of lengthwise movement between two parts. As applied to a crankshaft, the distance that the crankshaft can move forward and back in the cylinder block.

Engine management system (EMS) A computer controlled system which manages the fuel injection and the ignition systems in an integrated fashion.

Exhaust manifold A part with several passages through which exhaust gases leave the engine combustion chambers and enter the exhaust pipe.

F

Fan clutch A viscous (fluid) drive coupling device which permits variable engine fan speeds in relation to engine speeds.

Feeler blade A thin strip or blade of hardened steel, ground to an exact thickness, used to check or measure clearances between parts.

Feeler blade

Firing order The order in which the engine cylinders fire, or deliver their power strokes, beginning with the number one cylinder.

Flywheel A heavy spinning wheel in which energy is absorbed and stored by means of momentum. On cars, the flywheel is attached to the crankshaft to smooth out firing impulses.

Free play The amount of travel before any action takes place. The "looseness" in a linkage, or an assembly of parts, between the initial application of force and actual movement. For example, the distance the brake pedal moves before the pistons in the master cylinder are actuated.

Fuse An electrical device which protects a circuit against accidental overload. The typical fuse contains a soft piece of metal which is calibrated to melt at a predetermined current flow (expressed as amps) and break the circuit.

Fusible link A circuit protection device consisting of a conductor surrounded by heat-resistant insulation. The conductor is smaller than the wire it protects, so it acts as the weakest link in the circuit. Unlike a blown fuse, a failed fusible link must frequently be cut from the wire for replacement.

G

Gap The distance the spark must travel in jumping from the centre electrode to the side electrode in a spark plug. Also refers to the spacing between the points in a contact breaker assembly in a conventional points-type ignition, or to the distance between the reluctor or rotor and the pickup coil in an electronic ignition.

Adjusting spark plug gap

Gasket Any thin, soft material - usually cork, cardboard, asbestos or soft metal - installed between two metal surfaces to ensure a good seal. For instance, the cylinder head gasket seals the joint between the block and the cylinder head.

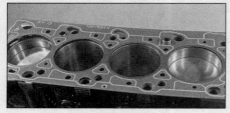

Gasket

Gauge An instrument panel display used to monitor engine conditions. A gauge with a movable pointer on a dial or a fixed scale is an analogue gauge. A gauge with a numerical readout is called a digital gauge.

H

Halfshaft A rotating shaft that transmits power from the final drive unit to a drive wheel, usually when referring to a live rear axle.

Harmonic balancer A device designed to reduce torsion or twisting vibration in the crankshaft. May be incorporated in the crankshaft pulley. Also known as a vibration damper.

Hone An abrasive tool for correcting small irregularities or differences in diameter in an engine cylinder, brake cylinder, etc.

Hydraulic tappet A tappet that utilises hydraulic pressure from the engine's lubrication system to maintain zero clearance (constant contact with both camshaft and valve stem). Automatically adjusts to variation in valve stem length. Hydraulic tappets also reduce valve noise.

I

Ignition timing The moment at which the spark plug fires, usually expressed in the number of crankshaft degrees before the piston reaches the top of its stroke.

Inlet manifold A tube or housing with passages through which flows the air-fuel mixture (carburettor vehicles and vehicles with throttle body injection) or air only (port fuel-injected vehicles) to the port openings in the cylinder head.

J

Jump start Starting the engine of a vehicle with a discharged or weak battery by attaching jump leads from the weak battery to a charged or helper battery.

L

Load Sensing Proportioning Valve (LSPV) A brake hydraulic system control valve that works like a proportioning valve, but also takes into consideration the amount of weight carried by the rear axle.

Locknut A nut used to lock an adjustment nut, or other threaded component, in place. For example, a locknut is employed to keep the adjusting nut on the rocker arm in position.

Lockwasher A form of washer designed to prevent an attaching nut from working loose.

M

MacPherson strut A type of front suspension system devised by Earle MacPherson at Ford of England. In its original form, a simple lateral link with the anti-roll bar creates the lower control arm. A long strut - an integral coil spring and shock absorber - is mounted between the body and the steering knuckle. Many modern so-called MacPherson strut systems use a conventional lower A-arm and don't rely on the anti-roll bar for location.

Multimeter An electrical test instrument with the capability to measure voltage, current and resistance.

N

NOx Oxides of Nitrogen. A common toxic pollutant emitted by petrol and diesel engines at higher temperatures.

O

Ohm The unit of electrical resistance. One volt applied to a resistance of one ohm will produce a current of one amp.

Ohmmeter An instrument for measuring electrical resistance.

O-ring A type of sealing ring made of a special rubber-like material; in use, the O-ring is compressed into a groove to provide the sealing action.

Overhead cam (ohc) engine An engine with the camshaft(s) located on top of the cylinder head(s).

Overhead valve (ohv) engine An engine with the valves located in the cylinder head, but with the camshaft located in the engine block.

Oxygen sensor A device installed in the engine exhaust manifold, which senses the oxygen content in the exhaust and converts this information into an electric current. Also called a Lambda sensor.

P

Phillips screw A type of screw head having a cross instead of a slot for a corresponding type of screwdriver.

Plastigage A thin strip of plastic thread, available in different sizes, used for measuring clearances. For example, a strip of Plastigage is laid across a bearing journal. The parts are assembled and dismantled; the width of the crushed strip indicates the clearance between journal and bearing.

Plastigage

Propeller shaft The long hollow tube with universal joints at both ends that carries power from the transmission to the differential on front-engined rear wheel drive vehicles.

Proportioning valve A hydraulic control valve which limits the amount of pressure to the rear brakes during panic stops to prevent wheel lock-up.

R

Rack-and-pinion steering A steering system with a pinion gear on the end of the steering shaft that mates with a rack (think of a geared wheel opened up and laid flat). When the steering wheel is turned, the pinion turns, moving the rack to the left or right. This movement is transmitted through the track rods to the steering arms at the wheels.

Radiator A liquid-to-air heat transfer device designed to reduce the temperature of the coolant in an internal combustion engine cooling system.

Refrigerant Any substance used as a heat transfer agent in an air-conditioning system. R-12 has been the principle refrigerant for many years; recently, however, manufacturers have begun using R-134a, a non-CFC substance that is considered less harmful to the ozone in the upper atmosphere.

Rocker arm A lever arm that rocks on a shaft or pivots on a stud. In an overhead valve engine, the rocker arm converts the upward movement of the pushrod into a downward movement to open a valve.

Rotor In a distributor, the rotating device inside the cap that connects the centre electrode and the outer terminals as it turns, distributing the high voltage from the coil secondary winding to the proper spark plug. Also, that part of an alternator which rotates inside the stator. Also, the rotating assembly of a turbocharger, including the compressor wheel, shaft and turbine wheel.

Runout The amount of wobble (in-and-out movement) of a gear or wheel as it's rotated. The amount a shaft rotates "out-of-true." The out-of-round condition of a rotating part.

S

Sealant A liquid or paste used to prevent leakage at a joint. Sometimes used in conjunction with a gasket.

Sealed beam lamp An older headlight design which integrates the reflector, lens and filaments into a hermetically-sealed one-piece unit. When a filament burns out or the lens cracks, the entire unit is simply replaced.

Serpentine drivebelt A single, long, wide accessory drivebelt that's used on some newer vehicles to drive all the accessories, instead of a series of smaller, shorter belts. Serpentine drivebelts are usually tensioned by an automatic tensioner.

Serpentine drivebelt

Shim Thin spacer, commonly used to adjust the clearance or relative positions between two parts. For example, shims inserted into or under bucket tappets control valve clearances. Clearance is adjusted by changing the thickness of the shim.

Slide hammer A special puller that screws into or hooks onto a component such as a shaft or bearing; a heavy sliding handle on the shaft bottoms against the end of the shaft to knock the component free.

Sprocket A tooth or projection on the periphery of a wheel, shaped to engage with a chain or drivebelt. Commonly used to refer to the sprocket wheel itself.

Starter inhibitor switch On vehicles with an automatic transmission, a switch that prevents starting if the vehicle is not in Neutral or Park.

Strut See MacPherson strut.

T

Tappet A cylindrical component which transmits motion from the cam to the valve stem, either directly or via a pushrod and rocker arm. Also called a cam follower.

Thermostat A heat-controlled valve that regulates the flow of coolant between the cylinder block and the radiator, so maintaining optimum engine operating temperature. A thermostat is also used in some air cleaners in which the temperature is regulated.

Thrust bearing The bearing in the clutch assembly that is moved in to the release levers by clutch pedal action to disengage the clutch. Also referred to as a release bearing.

Timing belt A toothed belt which drives the camshaft. Serious engine damage may result if it breaks in service.

Timing chain A chain which drives the camshaft.

Toe-in The amount the front wheels are closer together at the front than at the rear. On rear wheel drive vehicles, a slight amount of toe-in is usually specified to keep the front wheels running parallel on the road by offsetting other forces that tend to spread the wheels apart.

Toe-out The amount the front wheels are closer together at the rear than at the front. On front wheel drive vehicles, a slight amount of toe-out is usually specified.

Tools For full information on choosing and using tools, refer to the *Haynes Automotive Tools Manual*.

Tracer A stripe of a second colour applied to a wire insulator to distinguish that wire from another one with the same colour insulator.

Tune-up A process of accurate and careful adjustments and parts replacement to obtain the best possible engine performance.

Turbocharger A centrifugal device, driven by exhaust gases, that pressurises the intake air. Normally used to increase the power output from a given engine displacement, but can also be used primarily to reduce exhaust emissions (as on VW's "Umwelt" Diesel engine).

U

Universal joint or U-joint A double-pivoted connection for transmitting power from a driving to a driven shaft through an angle. A U-joint consists of two Y-shaped yokes and a cross-shaped member called the spider.

V

Valve A device through which the flow of liquid, gas, vacuum, or loose material in bulk may be started, stopped, or regulated by a movable part that opens, shuts, or partially obstructs one or more ports or passageways. A valve is also the movable part of such a device.

Valve clearance The clearance between the valve tip (the end of the valve stem) and the rocker arm or tappet. The valve clearance is measured when the valve is closed.

Vernier caliper A precision measuring instrument that measures inside and outside dimensions. Not quite as accurate as a micrometer, but more convenient.

Viscosity The thickness of a liquid or its resistance to flow.

Volt A unit for expressing electrical "pressure" in a circuit. One volt that will produce a current of one ampere through a resistance of one ohm.

W

Welding Various processes used to join metal items by heating the areas to be joined to a molten state and fusing them together. For more information refer to the *Haynes Automotive Welding Manual*.

Wiring diagram A drawing portraying the components and wires in a vehicle's electrical system, using standardised symbols. For more information refer to the *Haynes Automotive Electrical and Electronic Systems Manual*.

Note: *References throughout this index are in the form* **"Chapter number" • "Page number"**. *So, for example, 2C•15 refers to page 15 of Chapter 2C.*

Note: References throughout this index are in the form "Chapter number" • "Page number". So, for example, 2C•15 refers to page 15 of Chapter 2C.

Preserving Our Motoring Heritage

< The Model J Duesenberg Derham Tourster. Only eight of these magnificent cars were ever built – this is the only example to be found outside the United States of America

Almost every car you've ever loved, loathed or desired is gathered under one roof at the Haynes Motor Museum. Over 300 immaculately presented cars and motorbikes represent every aspect of our motoring heritage, from elegant reminders of bygone days, such as the superb Model J Duesenberg to curiosities like the bug-eyed BMW Isetta. There are also many old friends and flames. Perhaps you remember the 1959 Ford Popular that you did your courting in? The magnificent 'Red Collection' is a spectacle of classic sports cars including AC, Alfa Romeo, Austin Healey, Ferrari, Lamborghini, Maserati, MG, Riley, Porsche and Triumph.

A Perfect Day Out

Each and every vehicle at the Haynes Motor Museum has played its part in the history and culture of Motoring. Today, they make a wonderful spectacle and a great day out for all the family. Bring the kids, bring Mum and Dad, but above all bring your camera to capture those golden memories for ever. You will also find an impressive array of motoring memorabilia, a comfortable 70 seat video cinema and one of the most extensive transport book shops in Britain. The Pit Stop Cafe serves everything from a cup of tea to wholesome, home-made meals or, if you prefer, you can enjoy the large picnic area nestled in the beautiful rural surroundings of Somerset.

John Haynes O.B.E.,
Founder and
Chairman of the
museum at the wheel
of a Haynes Light 12. >

< Graham Hill's Lola Cosworth Formula 1 car next to a 1934 Riley Sports.

The Museum is situated on the A359 Yeovil to Frome road at Sparkford, just off the A303 in Somerset. It is about 40 miles south of Bristol, and 25 minutes drive from the M5 intersection at Taunton.

Open 9.30am - 5.30pm (10.00am - 4.00pm Winter) 7 days a week, *except Christmas Day, Boxing Day and New Years Day*

Special rates available for schools, coach parties and outings Charitable Trust No. 292048